STUDIES ON SLAVERY,

In Easy Lessons.

COMPILED INTO EIGHT STUDIES, AND SUBDIVIDED INTO SHORT LESSONS FOR THE CONVENIENCE OF READERS.

By JOHN FLETCHER,
OF LOUISIANA.

NATCHEZ:
PUBLISHED BY JACKSON WARNER.
1852.

PRINTED BY SMITH & PETERS,
Franklin Buildings, Sixth Street below Arch, Philadelphia.

PUBLISHER'S PREFACE.

THIS is a legitimate topic of general interest, and it assumes a preponderating importance to the people of the Southern American States, when the fact is taken into consideration that a general league against the institution of African slavery has been entered into and consummated between most of the civilized nations of the earth, and public opinion in many of the sister States of our own National Union has taken the same direction. The result is, to have arraigned the slaveholding States before the mighty bar of public opinion, on the charge of holding, as property, more than ten hundred millions of dollars' worth of what does not belong to them, which is and never can be the property of man; and this charge embraces, within its scope, the crimes of theft, robbery, rapine, and cruelty.

The time has come when the South must enter her plea of defence, not because the accusers are foreign nations, of which it may justly be said, before their charges are entertained, "Physician, heal thyself," but because our accusers are among our own brethren, bound to us by freedom's holiest associations and religion's most sacred ties.

The author of the "Studies on Slavery" has the double advantage of a full comprehension of the subject both in its Northern and Southern aspect. Born and educated in the former, and qualified by a long residence in the latter section of our Union, he is amply qualified to weigh the prejudices, the teachings, and the arguments of the one, against the facts, the justifications, the religious and political sanctions of the other.

Mr. Fletcher has not only marshalled into his line of impregnable defence the mandates and sanctions of the Sacred Writings concerning the slave institutions, but he has drawn powerful auxiliaries from the sources of ancient history. His exegesis of biblical passages, in the original languages in which they were communicated by inspiration to the world, shows his sound scholarship, as well as his reverence of the literal sense and specific meaning of God's holy and unimpeachable standard and rule of life and action.

The author has also analyzed the fountain of Moral Philosophy, and detected the bitter waters of error so industriously infused by the eloquent and magical pens of such writers as Dr. Samuel Johnson, Dr. Paley, Dr. Channing, Dr. Wayland, Mr. Barnes, and others. He has confined himself to the moral and ethical bearings of the question, scarcely touching upon its political aspects,—a course calculated to render the book far more useful to the dispassionate seekers after truth, who may belong to different political sects.

Neither time nor labour has been spared in the authorship of the work; and it is believed that, while it is written with candour and calmness, it will be received by the people of the North as well as of the South as a sincere and enlightened endeavour to seek for truth, and thus allay the tumultuous and disorganizing fanaticism of those who have not had opportunity to study the subject, and are incapable of acting upon it with understanding and true decision.

PROEMIAL.

PHILOSOPHY knows no obligation that binds one man to another without an equivalent. If one man could be subjected to another, who is not bound to render any thing in return, it would be subversive to good morals and political justice. Such a relation cannot exist, only so far as to reach the immediate death of the subjected. But it has been the error of some good men to suppose that slavery presented such a case. It has been their misfortune also to receive the following succedaneums as axioms in the search for truth:—

"All men are born equal."

"The rights of men are inalienable."

"No man has power to alienate a natural right."

"No man can become property."

"No man can own property in another."

"The conscience is a distinct mental faculty."

"The conscience infallibly distinguishes between right and wrong."

"No man is under any obligation to obey any law when his conscience dictates it to be wrong."

"The conscience empowers any man to nullify any law; because the conscience is a part and parcel of the Divine mind."

"Slavery is wholly founded on force."

"Slavery originates in the power of the strong over the weak."

"Slavery disqualifies a man to fulfil the great object of his being."

"The doctrines of the Bible forbid slavery."

"There is no word, either in the Old or the New Testament, which expresses the idea of slave or slavery."

"Slavery places its subjects beyond moral and legal obligation: therefore, it can never be a legal or moral relation."

"Slavery is inconsistent with the moral nature of man."

"To hold in slavery is inconsistent with the present state of morals and religion."

"Slavery is contrary to the will of God."

"No man can hold a slave, and be a Christian."

Averments of this order are quite numerous. Fanatics receive them; and some others do not distinguish them from truths.

At any age, and in any country, where such errors are generally adopted, and become the rules of political action, morals and religion are always in commotion, and in danger of shipwreck: for, although, where man has only approached so far towards civilization that even the enlightened can merely perceive them as rudimental, yet the great principles that influence human life, morality and religion, are, everywhere, and always have been the same.

STUDIES ON SLAVERY.

Study I.

LESSON I.

"*The Elements of Moral Science: By* FRANCIS WAYLAND, D.D., *President of Brown University, and Professor of Moral Philosophy. Fortieth Thousand. Boston*, 1849." Pp. 396.

THIS author informs us that he has been many years preparing the work, with a view to furnish his pupils with a text-book free from the errors of Paley. Like Paley, whom he evidently wishes to supersede, he has devoted a portion of his strength to the abolition of slavery. We propose to look into the book with an eye to that subject alone. President Wayland says:

P. 24. "Moral Law is a form of expression denoting an order of sequence established between the moral quality of actions and their results."

Pp. 25, 26. "An order of sequence established, supposes, of necessity, an Establisher. Hence Moral Philosophy, as well as every other science, proceeds upon the supposition of the existence of a Universal Cause, the Creator of all things, who has made every thing as it is, and who has subjected all things to the relations which they sustain. And hence, as all relations, whether moral or physical, are the result of his enactment, an order of sequence once discovered in morals, is just as inviolable as an order of sequence in physics.

"Such being the fact, it is evident that the moral laws of God can never be varied by the institutions of man, any more than the physical laws. The results which God has connected with actions will inevitably occur, all the created power in the universe to the contrary notwithstanding.

"Yet men have always flattered themselves with the hope that they could violate the moral law and escape the consequences which

God has established. The reason is obvious. In physics, the consequent follows the antecedent, often immediately, and most commonly after a stated and well-known interval. In morals, the result is frequently long delayed; the time of its occurrence is always uncertain:—Hence, 'because the sentence against an evil work is not *speedily* executed, therefore the hearts of the sons of men are fully set in them to do evil.' But time, whether long or short, has neither *power* nor *tendency* to change the order of an established sequence. The time required for vegetation, in different orders of plants, may vary; but, yet, wheat will always produce wheat, and an acorn will always produce an oak. That such is the case in morals, a heathen poet has taught us. '*Raro, antecedentum scelestum deseruit pede pœna claudo.*' HOR. lib. iii. car. 2.

"A higher authority has admonished us, 'Be not deceived; God is not mocked; whatsoever a man soweth, that shall he reap.' It is also to be remembered, that, in morals as well as in physics, the harvest is always more abundant than the seed from which it springs."

To this doctrine we yield the highest approval.

The first obvious deduction from the lesson here advanced is, that the laws of God, as once revealed to man, never lose their high moral qualities nor their divine character, at any subsequent age of the world. The law, which God delivered to Moses from Mount Sinai, authorizing his chosen people to buy slaves, and hold them as an inheritance for their children after them, is, therefore, the law of God now. The action of the law may be suspended at a particular time or place, from a change of contingencies,—yet the law stands unaffected.

We hope no one doubts the accuracy of the doctrine thus fairly stated in these "Elements." But we shall see how fatal it is to some portions of the author's positions concerning slavery. And we propose to show how this doctrine, as connected with slavery, has been, and is elucidated in scripture. The twenty-eighth chapter of Deuteronomy shows that the fruits of wickedness are all manner of curses, finally terminating in slavery or death.

Here, slavery, as a threatened punishment, distinctly looks back to a course of wickedness for its antecedent. The same idea is spread through the whole Scriptures: "Whosoever committeth sin, is the *servant* of sin." *John* viii. 34. "I am carnal, sold under sin." *Rom.* vii. 14. "Behold, for your iniquities have ye sold yourselves." *Isa.* l. 1. See, also, *Jer.* xiii. 22.

The biblical scholar will recollect a multitude of instances where this doctrine is clearly advanced, recognising sin as the antecedent of slavery.

Abraham was obedient to the voice of God. His conduct was the antecedent; and the consequent was, God heaped upon him many blessings; and among them, riches in various things,—"*male and female slaves*," some of whom were "*born in his house*," and some "*bought uith his money;*" and God made a covenant with him, granting him, and his seed after him, the land of Canaan for an everlasting possession.

But this gift, as it is the continuance of all other blessings, was accompanied with a condition, which is well explained in *Genesis*, xviii. 19: "For I know him, that he will command his children and *his household* after him, and they shall keep the way of the Lord to do justice and judgment; that the Lord may bring upon Abraham that which he hath spoken of him."

Scholars will concede the fact that "*his household*" is a term by which his slaves are particularly included, over whom his government was extended; and, without its proper maintenance, the covenant so far on his part would be broken.

From the wording of the covenant it is evident that Abraham had slaves before the covenant was made, since it embraced regulations concerning slaves, but, in no instance, hints that the existence of slavery was adverse to the law of God, or that the holding of slaves, as slaves, was contrary to his will. The deduction is, that slavery exists in the world by Divine appointment; and that the act of owning slaves is in conformity with the moral law.

The doctrine, that sin is the antecedent of slavery, is further elucidated and made still more manifest by the recognition of the institution by the biblical writers, where they place sin and slavery in opposition to holiness and freedom:—thus, figuratively, making righteousness the antecedent of freedom. "Stand fast, therefore, in the liberty wherewith Christ has made us free, and be not entangled again with the yoke of bondage." *Gal.* v. 1. "And ye shall know the truth, and the truth shall make you free." *John* iii. 32.

The abuse of slavery, like the abuse of any thing else, is doubtless a great sin. Of the blessings God bestows on man, there is perhaps no one he does not abuse; and while we examine the laws of God, as presenting to the mind the vast field of cause and effect, —of antecedent and consequent,—we may be led to a reflection on the necessity of a conformity thereto, lest a long continuance of such abuses shall become the antecedent to future calamities and woes, either to ourselves or posterity; woes and calamities prefigured by those nations and tribes already under the infliction of slavery, as a just punishment of sin.

Thus far, we thank the Rev. Dr. Wayland for this fair *exposé* of his views of the moral law of God; and if he will apply them now to the institution of slavery,—if he will unfetter his intellect from the manacles imposed on it by a defective education on that subject, and cut himself loose from the prejudices that his associations have gathered around him, we may yet have occasion to rejoice over him as one once an estray from the fold of truth, but now returned, "sitting in his right mind and clothed." And will not Mr. Fuller and Professor Taylor rejoice with us!

LESSON II.

In those "Elements of Moral Science," we find the following, p. 29:

"From what has been said, it may be seen that there exists, in the actions of men, an element which does not exist in the actions of brutes. * * * * * * We can operate upon brutes only by fear of punishment, and hope of reward. We can operate upon man, not only in this manner, but also by an appeal to his consciousness of right and wrong; and by such means as may improve his moral nature. Hence, all modes of punishment, which treat men as we treat brutes, are as unphilosophical as they are thoughtless, cruel, and vindictive. Such are those systems of criminal jurisprudence which have in view nothing more than the infliction of pain upon the offender."

It was unnecessary to inform us that man possesses higher mental endowments than the brute. But the main object of the author in the foregoing paragraph is his deduction; that, because we can operate on man by an appeal to his consciousness of right and wrong, therefore any other mode of governing him is wrong. This *consequent* we fail to perceive. We also fail in the perception that his postulate is universally true: which we think should have been proved before he can claim assent to the deduction. If this our view be correct, we beg the reverend author to reflect how far he may have made himself obnoxious to the charge of sophistry!

If President Wayland intends, by the clause,—"and by such means as may improve his moral nature,"—to include *corporeal punishment*, then his mind was unprepared to grapple with the subject; for, in that case, the whole paragraph is obscure, without object, and senseless. We most readily agree that to govern man by appeals to his consciousness of right and wrong is highly proper where the mind is so well cultivated that no other government is required.

But, however unhappy may be the reflection, too large a proportion of the human family will not fall within that class. How often do we see among men, otherwise having some claim to be classed with the intelligent, those of acknowledged bad habits; habits which directly force the sufferer downward to poverty, disgrace, disease, imbecility, and death,—on whom argument addressed to their "consciousness of right and wrong," "is water spilled on the ground."

Children, whose ancestors have, for ages, ranked among the highly cultivated of the earth,—each generation surpassing its predecessor in knowledge, in science, and religion,—have been found to degenerate, oftener than otherwise, when trained solely by arguments addressed to their reason, and unaccompanied by physical compulsion.

What then are we to expect from man in a savage state, whose ancestors have been degenerating from generation to generation, through untold ages,—him, who has scarcely a feeling in common with civilized man, except such as is common to the mere animal,—him, whom deteriorating causes have reduced to the lowest grade above the brute?

Domberger spent twelve years in passing through the central parts of Africa, from north to south. He found the negroes, in a large district of country, in a state of total brutality. Their habits were those only of the wild brutes. They had no fixed residences. They lay down wherever they might be when disposed to sleep. They were not more gregarious than the wild goats. So far as he could discover, they had not a language even, by which to hold intercourse with each other. They possessed no power by which they were enabled to exhibit moral degradation, any more than the wild beasts.

Hanno, the Carthaginian navigator, in his Periplus, eight hundred years before the birth of Christ, gives a similar account of a race he calls Gætuli.

It is possible that man, in these extreme cases, where there is very little to unlearn, might sooner be regenerated, elevated to civilization, physical and mental power, than in other cases where there may be far more proof of mental capacity, but where the worst of intellectual and physical habits have stained soul and body with, perhaps, a more indelible degradation.

It would be a curious experiment, and add much to our knowledge of the races of man, to ascertain how many generations, under the most favourable treatment, it would require to produce an equal to Moses, or a David, a Newton, or the learned Dr. Wayland himself, (if such be possible,) from these specimens of man presented before us! And we now inquire, what course of treatment will you propose, as the most practical, to elevate such a race to civilization?

It appears to us God has decided that slavery is the most effectual.

"Therefore my people are gone into captivity, because they have no knowledge." *Isa.* v. 13. "And they forsook the Lord, and served Baal and Ashteroth. And the anger of the Lord was hot against Israel, and he delivered them into the hands of the spoilers that spoiled them, and he *sold* them into the hands of their enemies round about." *Judg.* ii. 13, 14. See also, iii. 6–8. "If his children forsake my law and walk not in my judgments: if they break my statutes, and keep not my commandments: then will I visit their transgressions with the rod and their iniquity with stripes." *Ps.* lxxxviii. 30–32. "He that troubleth his own house shall inherit the wind: and the fool shall be the servant (עֶבֶד *ebed, slave*) to the wise of heart." *Prov.* ii. 29. "And her daughters shall go into captivity. Thus will I execute judgments in Egypt: and they shall know that I *am* the Lord." *Ezek.* xxx. 18. *See also the preceding part of the chapter.*

It is highly probable that among savage tribes, punishment and the infliction of pain are often applied with no higher view than to torture the object of displeasure. But to us it seems remarkably unfortunate, in a student of moral and civil jurisprudence, to suggest that legal punishment, among civilized men, is ever awarded or ordered with any such feeling. If our education has given us a correct view of the subject, the man who inflicts pain even on the brute, solely on the account of such a feeling, instantly, so far as it is known, sinks to the grade of a savage; and much more explicitly when the object of revenge is his fellow man. On the contrary, when "the offender" has given unquestionable evidence of a depravity too deeply seated for any hope of regeneration, and the law orders his death, it selects that mode of execution which inflicts the least suffering, and which shall have also the greatest probable influence to deter others who may be downward bound in the road of moral deterioration. There never has been a code of laws among civilized nations, where the object of punishment was to inflict pain on the implicated; only so far as was thought necessary to influence a change of action for the better. The object of punishment invariably has been the improvement of society.

If the Rev. Dr. Wayland had been teaching legislation to savages, or, perhaps, their immediate descendants, his remarks, to which we allude, might have been in place. But may we inquire to what cause are *we* indebted for them?

Permit us to inquire of the Doctor, where now are to be found the "systems of criminal jurisprudence" to which he alludes? Does he imagine that such system has some *likeness* to the government of the civilized man over his slave? Or, in their government, does he propose to abolish corporeal punishment, because he may think that will destroy the institution itself? For "a servant (עֶבֶד *abed, a slave*) will not be corrected by words; for, though he understand, he will not answer." *Prov.* xxix. 19.

We cannot pass over the paragraph we have quoted, without expressing the most bitter regret to learn from Dr. Wayland's own words, that he recognises the fact, without giving it reproval, that "we" punish "brutes" with no other view than to inflict pain. To *us*, such an idea is most repugnant and awful! And we hope—we pray Him who alone hath power to drag up from the deep darkness of degradation, that the minds of such men may be placed under the controlling influence of a rule that will compel to a higher sense of what is proper, and to a more clear perception of what is truth!

LESSON III.

The learned Doctor says:

P. 49. "By conscience, or moral sense, is meant that faculty by which we discern the moral quality of actions, and by which we are capable of certain affections in respect to this quality.

"By *faculty* is meant *any particular part* of our constitution, by which we become affected by the various qualities and relations of beings around us?" * * * "Now, that we do actually observe a moral quality in the actions of men, must, I think, be admitted. Every human being is conscious, that, from childhood, he has observed it." * * * * *

P. 50. "The question would then seem reduced to this: Do we perceive this quality of actions by a single faculty, or by a combination of faculties? I think it must be evident from what has been already stated, that this is, in its nature, simple and ultimate, and *distinct from every other notion.*

"Now, if this be the case, it seems self-evident that we must have a *distinct* and *separate faculty*, to make us acquainted with the existence of this *distinct* and *separate quality.*"

And for proof, he adds: "This is the case in respect to all other distinct qualities: it is, surely, reasonable to suppose, that it would be the case in this."

What! have we a distinct faculty by which we determine one thing to be red, and another distinct faculty by which we discover a thing to be black; another distinct faculty by which we judge a thing to be a cube, and another distinct faculty by which we determine it to be a triangle? Have we one distinct faculty by which we find a melon, and another by which we find a gourd? What! one distinct faculty by which we determine a professor of moral philosophy to be a correct teacher, and another by which we discover him to be a visionary?

This faculty of *moral sense* puts us in mind of Dr. Testy's description of the peculiar and distinct particles upon the tongue, which render a man a liar, a lunatic, or a linguist; a treacher, a tattler, or a teacher, and so on. His theory is that every mental and moral quality of a man has its distinct particle, or little pimple, upon the tongue, whereby the quality is developed; or, by the aid of which the man is enabled to make the quality manifest. Long practice in examining the tongues of sick people enabled him, he says, to make the discovery. We should like to know what acuminated elevation of the cuticle of the tongue represented "conscience or moral sense," as a separate and distinct faculty!

Why does he not at once borrow support from the extravagancies of phrenology, and assert, according to the notions of its teachers, that, since the brain is divided into distinct organs for the exercise of each distinct faculty, therefore there must be a distinct faculty for the conception of each idea? There is surely an evident relation between this theory of the author and the doctrines of Gall; nor will the world fail to associate it with the phantasies of Mesmer.

But we ask the author and his pupils to apply to this theory the truism of Professor Dodd: "It is, at all times, a sufficient refutation of what purports to be a statement of facts, to show that the only kind of evidence by which the facts could possibly be sustained, does not exist."

The theory by which the Doctor arrives at the conclusion that we possess a separate and distinct faculty for the perception of each separate and distinct quality, assimilates to that of a certain quack, who asserted that the human stomach was *mapped* off, like Gall's cranium, into distinct organs of digestion; one solely for beef-steak, one for mutton-chops, and another for plum-pudding!

It is a great point with certain of the higher class of abolition writers to establish the doctrine that man possesses a distinct mental power, which they call *conscience*, or *moral sense*, by which he is enabled to discover, of himself, and without the aid of study, teaching, or even inspiration, what is right and what is wrong.

The practice is, the child is taught by them that slavery is very wicked; that no slaveholder can be a good man; and much of such matter. Books are put into the hands of the schoolboy and the youth, inculcating similar lessons, fraught with lamentation and sympathy for the imaginary woes of the slave, and hatred and disgust towards the master; and when maturer years are his, he is asked if he does not feel that slavery is very wicked; and the professors of moral philosophy then inform him that he feels so because he possesses "a distinct mental faculty"—distinct from the judgment—which teaches those who cultivate it, infallibly, all that is right and wrong; that this conscience, or moral sense, is more to be relied on than the Bible—than the ancient inspirations of God!

Hence, Channing says:

"That same inward principle, which teaches a man what he is bound to do to others, teaches equally, and at the same instant, what others are bound to do to him." * * * "His *conscience*, in revealing the moral law, does not reveal a law for himself only, but speaks as a universal legisator." * * * "There is no deeper principle in human nature than the consciousness of right." Vol. ii. p. 33.

And Barnes, on Slavery, says:

P. 381. "If the Bible could be shown to defend and countenance slavery as a good institution, it would make thousands of infidels; for there are multitudes of minds that will see more clearly that slavery is against all the laws which God has written on the human soul, than they would see, that a book, sanctioning such a system, had evidence of Divine origin."

And this same author makes Dr. Wayland say:

P. 310. "Well may we ask, in the words of Dr. Wayland, (pp. 83, 84,) whether there was ever such a moral superstructure raised on such a foundation? The doctrine of purgatory from a versė of Maccabees; the doctrine of papacy from the saying of Christ to Peter; the establishment of the Inquisition from the obligation to extend the knowledge of religious truth, all seem nothing to it. If the religion of Christ allows such a license from such precepts as these, the New Testament would be the greatest curse that ever was inflicted on our race."

This book, as quoted by Barnes, we have not seen.

Such is the doctrine of these theologians, growing out of the possession, as they imagine, of this *distinct moral faculty*, infallibly teaching them the truth touching the moral quality of the actions of men. And what is its effect upon their scarcely more wicked pupils? One of them, in a late speech in Congress, says:

"Sir, I must express the most energetic dissent from those who would justify modern slavery from the Levitical law. My *reason* and *conscience* revolt from those interpretations which

Torture the hallowed pages of the Bible,
To sanction crime, and robbery, and blood,
And, in oppression's hateful service, libel
'Both man and God!'"

The ignorant fanaticism, so proudly buoyant even in repose upon its ill-digested reason,—here so flippantly uttered,—to us bespeaks a dangerous man, (as far as he may have capacity,) in whatever station he may be found. The most hateful idolatry has never presented to the world a stronger proof of a distorted imagination giving vent to the rankest falsehood. It is to be deeply regretted that such intellects are ever permitted to have any influence upon the minds of the young. We deem it would be a fearful inquiry, to examine how far the strange assassinations, lately so common at the North, have been the direct result of that mental training of which we here see an example. We fear too little is thought of the quick transition from this erroneous theology to the darkened paths of man when enlightened alone by his own depraved heart.

The saying is true, however awful: He who rejects or dispels the plain meaning of the Bible, rejects our God, and is an idolater; and God alone can give bound to his wicked conceptions.

The foregoing extracts show us a specimen of the arguments and conclusions emanating from the doctrine that the conscience is a distinct mental power, and that it infallibly teaches what is right before God. We deem it quite objectionable—quite erroneous!

We present the proposition: The judgment is as singly employed in the decision of what is right and wrong, as it is in the conclusion that all the parts of a thing constitute the whole of it. True, the judgment, when in the exercise of determining what is right and wrong in regard to our own acts, has been named *conscience.* But it remains for that class of philosophers, who argue that man possesses a faculty of *clairvoyance*, to establish that man has also a sister faculty, which they call *conscience*, or *moral sense;* and that it exists as an independent mental power, distinct from judgment.

Most men live without reflection. They think of nothing but the objects of sense, of pressing want, and the means of relief. The wonderful works of nature create no wonder. A mine of sea-shells on the Andes excites no surprise. Of the analogies or dissimilarities between things, or their essential relations, the mind takes no notice. Even their intellectual powers exist almost without their cognisance. Their mental faculties are little improved or cultivated; and, as they are forced to the Gazetteer for the description of some distant locality, so they would be to their logic, before they could speak of their own mental functions.

The teaching of this doctrine, untrue as it is, may, therefore, be very harmful; as ill-informed individuals often form a very erroneous judgment about right and wrong, and, under the influence of its teachings, may come to think and believe that their conclusion concerning right and wrong is the product of their infallible guide, the *conscience*, or *moral sense*, and therefore past all doubt and beyond question; that their minds are under the influence and control of a *new* and *spiritually higher law* than the law of the land, or even the moral law as laid down in the Bible, when not in unison with their feelings. And we venture to prophesy, in case this doctrine shall gain general credence, that such will be the rocks on which multitudes will founder; for simple and ill-informed people may thus be led, and doubtless are, to do very wicked and mischievous acts, under the influence of this belief—a belief of their possessing this power, which no one ever did possess, unless inspired.

"There is a way that seemeth right unto a man, but the end thereof are the ways of death." *Prov.* xvi. 25.

Thus we see there is a class of theologians, who, in hot pursuit of abolitionism, seem ready to sacrifice their Bible and its religion to the establishment of such principles as they deem wholly contradictory to, and incompatible with, the existence of slavery; and it is hence that they attempt to teach that man possesses an intuitive sense of its wrong. But shall we not be forced, with regret, to acknowledge, that there are quacks in divinity as well as in physic?

LESSON IV.

We do not charge Dr. Wayland with being the author of this new doctrine that man possesses an independent and distinct power, faculty, or sense, by the exercise of which he perceives right and wrong, or, in other words, the moral quality of the actions of men, and upon which perception he may rest with safety, as to its accuracy and truthfulness; for the same doctrine has been suggested by greater men than Dr. Wayland, long ago. Lord Shaftesbury, Dr. Hutchinson, and Dr. Reid have laid the foundation; the latter of whom says, (p. 242,) "The testimony of our moral faculty, like that of the external senses, is the testimony of nature, and we have the same reason to rely upon it." Again: "As we rely upon the clear and distinct testimony of our eyes, concerning the figures and colours of bodies about us, we have the same reason, with security, to rely upon the clear and unbiassed testimony of our conscience with regard to what we ought or ought not to do."

Such sentiments may seem to some to be deducible from an indistinct and indefinite reference to our judgment after the understanding has been improved by moral culture, when such judgment, by a mere looseness of language, is sometimes described as if the writers confounded it with the state of mind and moral perfectibility produced by the reception of the Holy Ghost. Thus, Archbishop Secker, in his Fourth Lecture on the Catechism, says:

"How shall all persons know what they are taught to believe is really true?

"*Answer.* The greater part of it, when it is once duly proposed to them, they may perceive to be so by the light of their own reason and conscience."

Now it is evident that the bishop's answer is predicated upon the supposition that the understanding has been cultivated in conformity to the principles of moral truth.

But, from such hasty, perhaps thoughtless, snatches of speculation, occasionally found in some few of the older metaphysical writers, our author and his co-associates in this belief have drawn their materials, remodelled the parts, and reared, even as to heaven, a lofty structure upon a doubtful, tottering base, bringing untold social and political evils upon society, and spiritual death, in its fall, to all who shelter under it. But for the good of the world, in opposition to such a doctrine, truth has erected her column of solid masonry, against which the fanaticism and sophistry of these builders can only, like successive drops of water, carry down the walls some useless portions of the cement.

We repeat, how tottering must be the argument founded upon analogy where there is no relation! We all agree that the senses make truthful representations: all see, smell, and taste alike; vinegar will be sour to the savage, as well as the savant. But is their judgment the same about the moral qualities of actions? What says this moral sense, this conscience, in the savage, who is taught to steal from his friend and torture his enemy? Does the reverend doctor think his moral sense will dictate the same conclusion? What right has he, then, to say, it is the voice of nature—of God? Does he fail to perceive that the moral quality of actions is distinguished by man in conformity to his experience, his training, his education?

We see that men often differ about the moral quality of an action. It might be that no two men would have the same idea about the moral quality of a particular action. Would the conscience, this moral sense, or faculty, in such case, be right in each one? If not, who is to determine which is right and which is wrong? And further, of what use to man can be this distinct, independent, and unchangeably truthful power, which, nevertheless, brings him no certainty? But has the mind of man ever found out that God has overdone, or unnecessarily done, any thing? Will these theorists reflect, that, in case God had seen fit to bestow such a sense on man, inspiration would have been useless, and the Bible not wanted? And the condition of man upon the earth would be wholly stationary instead of progressive. And permit us to inquire, whether this notion of theirs is the reason why some of these theorists speak so rashly, we might say blasphemously, of that sacred volume, upon the condition which they dictate?

The truth is, we have no such infallible guide. The idea of right and wrong, either theologically or physically considered, is always fixed through an exertion of the powers of the understanding. We have no instinctive power reaching the case. Our judgment, our feelings are often unstable, irregular, and sometimes antagonistic. In abstruse cases, very often we cannot even satisfy ourselves what is right; and will it be said that we do not often fail to see the object, design, and law of God touching a case?

On every decision on a question of right or wrong, a train of mental action is called into operation, comparing the ideas already in the mind with the facts of the case under review, and noting the similarity of these facts to our idea of right, or whether the facts conform to our idea of wrong. This decision we call judgment: but when the decision reaches to the question of right or wrong, touching our own conduct only, logicians have agreed to call it conscience; not a distinct action from judgment—much less a distinct faculty; and by no means carrying with it more proof of accuracy and correctness than is our judgment about any other matter, where the ideas and facts are equally manifest and accurately presented.

There is another consideration which to us gives proof that the conscience or moral sense is not an independent faculty of the mind, nor to be relied on at all as infallible. Many of us have noticed the changes that imperceptibly come over our moral feelings, and judgment of right and wrong, conscience or moral sense, through the influences of association and habit. Our affluent neighbour, who manifests to others many virtues and some follies, our mind, by association and habit, regards as a perfect model of human greatness and perfection. Thus a corrupt government soon surveys a corrupt people; and a somewhat licentious, but talented and accomplished clergyman, soon finds his hearers in fashion. Nor is it unfrequent, that which should stigmatize a father is beheld with admiration by the son. Thus wealth, to most, is desirable, but its desirability has been created by association; we recollect the objects it enables us to command, often the objects of our principal pursuit. The quality the mind associates with these gratifications, it eventually associates with that which procures them. Thus, we perceive, the mind is able to form a moral estimate upon considerations wholly artificial, which could never happen in case the moral sense was independent, and a distinct faculty teaching us infallible truth.

But how are we to account for the fact that some of the finest intellects, as well as the most learned men, have fallen into this most dangerous error? It should be a subject of deep thought!

We discover, in some men of the highest order of intellects, the power of arriving, as it were instantaneously, at a conclusion, giving it the appearance of being intuitive, rather than the result of what would be, when analyzed, a long chain of reasoning. Thus, the instant and happy thought often springing to the mind when in some sudden or unforeseen difficulty. The nice and instant perception, often displayed by medical men, of the condition of the patient, is an example; and hence the astonishing accuracy of judgment, sometimes noticed in the military commander, from a mere glance of the eye.

In such cases the mind is often not conscious of any mental action; and others, who observe these facts, are led, sometimes, to confound what, in such cases, is a deductive judgment, with intuitiveness. The judgment, thus formed without any perceptible succession of thought, is merely the result of acquirement from long experience and habits of active ratiocination. Some few instances of this unconscious and rapid thought have been exemplified by mathematicians, when the calculator could give no account how he arrived at the conclusion. Will any one claim that they abstract their answers from the most abstruse propositions intuitively, or by instinct, or by any new and distinct faculty of the mind? This habit of mind is as applicable to morals as to any thing else. But in mathematics the data are everywhere the same; whereas in morals the data are as different among men as are their conditions of life; because our ideas of right and wrong, existing in the mind before the judgment is formed on the case to be considered, were introduced by the aid of the senses, through the medium of experience and education; and it is, therefore, quite obvious that the idea of right in one man may be quite like the idea of wrong in another.

But it remains to show the fallacy of the argument by which Dr. Wayland arrives at his conclusion. Let us examine the paragraph quoted, and sift from verbiage the naked points of the argument:

"We do actually observe a moral quality in the actions of men."

"Do we perceive this quality of actions by a single faculty, or a combination of faculties? This notion" (the perception of the moral quality of an action) "is, in its nature, simple and ultimate, and distinct from every other notion."

"We have a distinct faculty to make us acquainted with the existence of all other distinct qualities." "Therefore, it is self-evident that this is a separate and distinct faculty."

The syllogism is defective because the idea of right or wrong is not simple nor ultimate, but complex, and ever subject to change from the influence of any new light presented to the mind. Nor is it true that we possess a distinct faculty to make us acquainted with each distinct quality; for, if so, the mind would be merely a very large bundle of faculties; and we should neither possess nor stand in need of any reasoning powers whatever, because the naked truth about every thing would always stand revealed before us by these faculties; which, we think, is not the fact.

In syllogistic argument, the first principles must be something that cannot be otherwise—unalterable—an eternal truth; "because these qualities cannot belong to the conclusion unless they belong to the premises, which are its causes."

The syllogism will then stand thus:

It is not true our notion, or idea, of the moral quality of an action "is simple and ultimate, and distinct from any other idea or notion:"

It is not true that we have a distinct faculty to make us acquainted with the existence of all other distinct qualities:

Therefore, it is not true, nor self-evident, that we perceive the moral qualities of an action, or that we have the idea or notion of it, by the aid of a single distinct and separate faculty.

The "notion" advanced by Dr. Wayland, on this subject, appears to us so strange, that it would be difficult to conceive it to have been issued or promulgated by a schoolman, did we not know how often men, led by passion, some by prejudice, argue from false premises to which they take no heed, or, from a want of information, honestly mistake for truths.

LESSON V.

P. 206. "IT" (slavery) "supposes that the Creator intended one human being to govern the physical, intellectual, and moral actions of as many other human beings as, by purchase, he can bring within his physical power, and that one human being may thus acquire a right to sacrifice the happiness of any number of other human beings, for the purpose of promoting his own."

This proposition is almost a total error. Slavery supposes the Creator intended that the interest of the master in the slave who, by becoming his slave, becomes his property, should secure to the slave that protection and government which the slave is too degenerate to supply to himself; and that such protection and government are necessary to the happiness and well-being of the slave, without which he either remains stationary or degenerates in his moral, mental, and physical condition.

P. 207. "It" (slavery) "renders the eternal happiness of the one party subservient to the temporal happiness of the other."

This is equally untrue. Slavery subjects one party to the command of another who is expected to feel it a duty to so "command his household" that "they shall keep the way of the Lord, to do justice and judgment."

This is the voice of God on the subject, as heretofore quoted. The learned Dr. Wayland is evidently wholly unacquainted with the spirit and intention, and, we may add, origin of the institution of slavery; yet he has, doubtless, been studying some of its abuses.

But suppose a man to study nothing of Christianity but its abuses, and from these alone undertake to describe what he conceives to be its results, its character, and suppositions; he doubtless would make what Dr. Wayland would very justly call a distorted representation; and perhaps, he might safely use a harsher phrase. But would such a representation be productive of any good in the world? It might do much mischief by spreading, broadcast, its errors and misrepresentations; a most delicious food for the morbid appetite of the ignorant and fanatic infidel! Yes, infidelity has its fanatics as well as abolitionism!

"Obey them that have rule over you, and submit yourselves: for they watch for your souls as they that must give account, that they may do it with joy and not with grief: for that is unprofitable for you." *Heb.* xiii. 17.

P. 207. "If argument were necessary to show that such a system as this must be at variance with the ordinance of God, it might easily be drawn from the effects which it produces, both upon morals and national wealth."

The author, in this instance, as he has in many others, designs to produce an effect on the mind of his reader from what he does not say, as well as from what he does say. We acknowledge this mode to be quite noncommittal, while, on the minds of some, it may be very skilfully used to produce an impression. But we confess ourselves ignorant of any logical rule by which it is entitled to produce any on us. The mode of speech used is intended to produce the impression that the proposition is someway self-evident, and therefore stands in no need of proof or argument. But how the proposition, that slavery is "at variance with the ordinances of God" is self-evident, and needs no proof nor argument, we have not the "moral sense" or "faculty" to discover. But as Dr. Wayland proposes, nevertheless, to prove its truth by its effects on morals and wealth, let us listen to the evidence.

Idem. "Its effects must be disastrous upon the morals of both parties. By presenting objects on whom passion may be satiated without resistance and without redress, it tends to cultivate in the master, pride, anger, cruelty, selfishness, and licentiousness. By accustoming the slave to subject his moral principles to the will of another, it tends to abolish in him all moral distinctions; and thus fosters in him lying, deceit, hypocrisy, dishonesty, and a willingness to yield himself up to the appetites of his master."

This is his proof that slavery is "at variance with the ordinances of God," as he has drawn it from its effect on morals;—in which we think him singularly unfortunate. He asks us to receive, as proof of the truth of the proposition, a combination of propositions all requiring proof of their truth, but of the truth of which he offers no proof.

This view of the state of the argument, we imagine, would be sufficient to condemn it in all well-schooled minds; but, nevertheless, we propose to show that which he offers as proof is not true; and even if true, is no proof of the truth of the proposition he endeavours to sustain.

In regard to the master, the effect complained of may or may not exist, as may be the fact whether the master is or is not capable of administering the charge and government of slaves wisely for himself and them. But these abuses, when found to exist, are no proof of the moral impropriety of the institution; for, if so, the abuses of a thing are proof that the thing itself is evil. There are many abuses of government: is government, therefore, at variance with the ordinances of God? The same of matrimony; and is it, therefore, to be set aside? Some men make an abusive use of their education, and, in consequence, would have been more valuable members of society in a state of comparative ignorance: are our universities, therefore, to be abolished? Money has been said to be "the root of all evil;" it, to some extent, is the representative of wealth and power; the possession of either of which may, in some individuals, sometimes apparently enable the possessor "to cultivate pride, anger, cruelty, selfishness, and licentiousness." The same may be said of power of any kind. But has not Dr. Wayland learned that there are cases where the effect would be and is entirely the reverse?—where power, wealth, or even the possession of slaves, produces in the possessor a greater degree of humility, placidity or mildness, sympathy or charity for others, and orderly conduct in himself? Does the reverend moral philosopher make so low an estimate of the value of civilization—of the influence of Christianity—as not to admit the capability of enjoying a blessing without abusing it?

If Dr. Wayland's argument be founded on truth, it will be easy to show that any system of things must be at variance with the ordinances of God which permit the possession of either power or wealth: consequently, in such case, we must and should all go back to the savage state. We ask this learned standard author to read the history of Abraham and Isaac, and inform us whether slavery produced the effect on them which he supposes to be an entailment of the institution; for the effect must be proved to be an unchangeable, a universal and unavoidable consequence, before it can receive the character of evidence in the case to which he applies it.

But Dr. Wayland thinks that slavery "tends to abolish all moral distinctions in the slave"—"fosters in him lying, deceit, hypocrisy, dishonesty, and a willingness to yield himself up to minister to the appetites of his master;" and, therefore, "is at variance with the ordinances of God."

If the doctor had seen the native African and slave in the wild, frantic joy of his savage worship, tendered to his chief idol-god, the imbodiment of concupiscence; if he had seen all the power of the Christian master centered to effect the eradication of this heathen belief, and the habits it engendered; had he witnessed the anxiety of the master for the substitution of the precepts of Christianity; if he had seen the untiring efforts of the masters, sometimes for several generations, before this great object could be accomplished, and the absolute necessity of its accomplishment before the labour of the slave could ordinarily become to him an article of full and desirable profit,—he would probably never have written the paragraph we have quoted!

But since, in the honest, we may perhaps say the amiable, simplicity of his mind, he has composed this lesson for his pupil, which, like the early dew in imperceptible showers on the tender blade, becomes the daily nutriment of his juvenile mind and the habitual aliment of its maturity, we deem it necessary to make one further brief remark in proof of its entire inadequacy to the task assigned it in his argument, as a particular and special, and of its total untruthfulness as a general and comprehensive, maxim in morals.

Our experience is, that the crimes here named, when detected in the slave, are punished, and, if necessary, with severity, if for no other reason, because they render the slave less valuable to his master. The master wishes to find in his slave one on whom he can rely with certainty; in whom there is no dissonance of interest from his own, and whose honesty and obedience are past doubt. The qualities which are the exact opposite of the crimes imputed are, therefore, sedulously cultivated in the slave,—and truly, very often, with small success. But we are surprised at the doctrine which proclaims a system of government that ever punishes and looks with displeasure on "lying, deceit, hypocrisy, and dishonesty," to be the very thing to foster and nourish those vices! When such is proved to be the fact, we shall regard it as a new discovery in morals.

As to the last clause of what he has adduced as proof of his proposition, we say that any one who is in the employ, or even the company, of another, either as a friend, wife, child, or hireling, as well as slave, may manifest a growing willingness to minister to the appetites of such person; and such inclination, or willingness, will operate to the benefit or injury of those so influenced, in proportion as such appetite is good or bad, or tends to good or evil: but this influence, whether tending to benefit or injury, is not an exclusive incident of slavery, and, therefore, cannot with any propriety, be quoted either for or against it: for, everywhere, "evil communications corrupt good manners."

LESSON VI.

Dr. Wayland informs us that slavery is at variance with the ordinances of God, because it diminishes the amount of national wealth. If the diminishing of national wealth be proof of the variance from the ordinances of God, then it will follow that whatever will increase such wealth must be in conformity to such ordinances,—a position which we think no one will attempt to maintain. But let us notice the evidence he adduces to prove that slavery diminishes national wealth. His first proof is, that slavery does not "impose on all the necessity of labour;" but that it "restricts the number of labourers—that is, of producers—by rendering labour disgraceful."

Now this is surely a proposition which requires to be proved itself before it can be received as a proof of an antecedent proposition; and President Wayland seems to have perceived that, under the general term, "labourers," it would be incapable of proof; and, therefore, he informs us that by labourers he means producers. The logicians will agree that there is a disjointedness in this proposition (very common in this author) to which exception might be taken; but we suppose Dr. Wayland means that slavery decreases the number of those whose labour is employed in the production of the articles or products of agriculture; for we do not presume he means that the labours of the law, physic, divinity, the mechanic arts, commerce, politics or war, are rendered disgraceful by slavery, but agriculture alone; and that, therefore, it is at variance with the ordinances of God, because it thus diminishes the amount of national wealth. If this is not his meaning, we confess ourselves unable to find any meaning in it.

We know of no surer method to test its truth or falsehood than for the Slave States to compare their number of agricultural producers with those of the Free States, having relation to the entire population. The result will be found wholly adverse to the reverend moralist's position. In fact, so great is the disproportion between the numbers of agricultural labourers in the Slave States, compared to those in the Free, that the articles of their produce often fall down to prices ruinous to the agriculturist, which very seldom, or never, happens in the Free States. Let Dr. Wayland study the statistics touching this point, and he will find himself in error.

But the proposition of President Wayland includes this minor proposition: That the increase of agricultural products, to the greatest possible extent, increases national wealth. We are very far from discovering the truth of this; because the increase of a production, beyond utility and demand, can add nothing to the value of the production, since value depends upon utility and demand. If this position be true, which we think very few at this day will dispute, it is quite obvious that President Wayland, and even Adam Smith, (from whom we suppose the former has received this notion,) are quite mistaken when they predicate the amount of labour to be the sole measure, or, in fact, the amount of wealth; since that position must render the amount of labour and the amount of wealth terms of convertible significance, which, in fact, is seldom the case. Such, then, being the state of the argument, Dr. Wayland's proposition is, in effect: That the production of the articles of agriculture, to an extent beyond any demand or value, is in conformity to the ordinances of God; and, therefore, their production, to any less extent, is at variance with those ordinances, because the first increases and the latter decreases national wealth. We shall leave these contradictions for the consideration of the professor of moral philosophy and his pupils.

The second witness Dr. Wayland introduces to prove the truth of his proposition, that slavery lessens the amount of national wealth, is that slavery takes from the labourer the natural stimulus to labour,—the desire of individual benefit,—and substitutes the fear of punishment: And for the third and last, that slavery removes from both parties the disposition and motive to frugality; by which means national wealth is diminished.

If national wealth be the desideratum, in order not to be at variance with the ordinances of God, it matters not whether the contributors to it did so contribute through the selfish view of personal aggrandizement and a desire of elevation above their fellows, or whether they did so to relieve themselves from some stigma or personal infliction that a refusal might be expected to fasten upon them. The motive in both cases is the same—a desire to benefit themselves. Thus Dr. Wayland, therefore, makes a distinction where, in reality, there is no difference.

But again, if the amount of labour be the criterion of the amount of national wealth, as he seems to suppose, it can make no difference, in a national point of view, whether A and B squander the result of their labours into the possession of C and D, or retain it themselves; because the change of possession in no way destroys the thing possessed. It might be gathered, from this part of Dr. Wayland's argument, that the greatest misers would be the most efficient builders of national wealth, and, therefore, most in accordance with the ordinances of God.

We are somewhat at loss to perceive the precise idea the author affixes to the term "national wealth." Whether this be his or our fault, we leave for others to decide.

Has it ever occurred to the reverend author to estimate the wealth of a nation by the moral, physical, and individual welfare of the population?

But we cannot attempt, or undertake, to expose, nor explain, all the false reasoning, distorted views, and prejudiced conclusions found heaped up, in heterogeneous confusion, by the abolition writers. The dissection of mental putridity is as unwelcome a task as that of the animal carcass in a state of decomposition.

If we cast our eyes over the surface of human life, we notice that wealth and power usually travel hand in hand; but that wealth is distributed unequally, varied from the lofty possessions of royal power down to the most scanty pittance of poverty and want;—yet leaving a vast majority in possession of nothing save life, and their right to the use of the elements of nature. It is with these lower classes we have the most to do. The wants of these, most generally, are physical: indeed, we sometimes find them only on a level with the brute. Thus, the African mountaineer is prone and content to feed on the decaying remains of what he may find, and wanders, like the hyena, upon the trail of what he hopes to find his prey; while the savage islanders of the distant seas are satisfied with what the ocean heaves on shore. We notice that these wants are increased by climate; hence, the native of the extreme north, content with his flitch of blubber, yet robs the bear of his hide for a blanket. These wants we also find enlarged by the least contact with civilization. Hence we see the African, on the western coast of his continent, garnished out with the gewgaws of Europe, and the Indian of our own clime with the trinkets of trade. And thus we may notice that, as civilization and capital increase in any country, new objects of desire, new individual wants increase in proportion. Hence, the farm-house now exhibits its carpet, whereas Queen Elizabeth was content with straw!

All these wants require some action, on the part of those who desire their gratification, to continue their supply, or it must cease; because, as a general rule, the product of individual labour must bound the supply of individual wants, in all cases where the individual possesses no capital which yields an additional revenue.

But a large portion of those in savage life produce nothing; so, also, a portion from civilized society seem ever disposed to break through the rules of civilization, to retrograde as to morals, and subsist by trick or some dishonesty. They produce nothing, and are, therefore, a total drawback on the welfare of others. We find, also, another portion, the product of whose labour is inadequate to the supply of their individual wants, and who are without capital to supply the deficiency. Such must die, or resort to charity; or retrograde, and live by their wits. Good men, in all ages, have striven to obviate these evils. The Levitical law did so by permitting the unfortunate man to sell himself, as a slave, for six years, or for life, as he might choose, under the state of the case; or, in case he did not so choose to sell himself, but became indebted beyond his means, the law forced his sale, and also that of his whole family. Although, to some, this law may look harsh, yet its spirit, intention, and effect were in favour of the general good, of morals, and of life. Yet it was slavery; and we take liberty here to say, although some may not be prepared to receive it, that such ever was, is now, and ever will be the spirit, intention, and effect of slavery, when not disfigured by its abuse.

We have in vain looked through these "Elements" for some proposal of the author to meet such cases as those of savages, and of those degenerating and deteriorating poor, in all countries, known to be so from the fact that they ever strive to live by their wits. And here we may remark that it is evident the system of alms-giving must terminate when the capitalists shall find the amount of alms beyond their surplus revenue; and no one will deny that the whole system has a direct tendency towards a general bankruptcy. We therefore ask Dr. Wayland to make a proposal that shall be a permanent and effectual remedy in the cases under consideration.

Now, very few will say, but that if society can find out some humane plan by which beggars and thieves can be forced, if force be necessary, to yield a product of labour equal to the supply of their necessary wants, the ordinances of God will not sanction the act.

From imperfection, perhaps, in the organization of society, we not only see individuals branching off, and taking a downward road, but also, in all old countries, from the very stimulus of nature, a constant tendency to such an increase of population as lessens the value of labour by overstocking the demand, whereby its product becomes less than is required for the supply of individual wants. The consequences resulting from these facts, so ruinous to individual morals and happiness, often become national evils and the causes of national deterioration. But, under the Levitical law, and in all countries with similar provisions, the effect has been, and ever will be, a division of such population into a separate caste,—not national deterioration.

With a view to remedy the evils to which we have invited the attention of the Rev. Dr. Wayland, Sismondi, book vii. chap. 9, has proposed, that inasmuch, as he says, the low wages of the labouring poor redound wholly to the pecuniary benefit of the capitalists who employ them, those capitalists shall be charged by law with their support, when wages become too low to supply the necessary wants of the labourer; at the same time bestowing power on the capitalists to prevent all marriages when the labourer can give no evidence of a prospect of increased means of subsistence, satisfactory to the capitalist, that he will not be burdened with the support of the offspring. We are, by no means, the advocates of Sismondi's proposed arrangement. But if the labourers, since in some sense they may be considered freemen, give their consent to it, we do not perceive that it would be "at variance with the ordinances of God."

The author of these "Elements" and Sismondi, we believe, differed little, if any, on the subject of the abolition of slavery touching the negro race. Will he say, the proposal of that philosopher to benefit the condition of the labouring poor, if carried into effect as suggested, would be "at variance with the ordinances of God?" Yet, all the world perceive that it is a mere modification of slavery, containing conditions more obnoxious to human nature than appertains to any condition of slavery now known beyond the African shores.

Man has ever been found to advance in moral improvement civilization, and a stable and healthy increase of population, only in proportion as they have been taught to supply their necessary wants by the products of individual labour. This is what first distinguishes civilized from savage life. The savage relies wholly upon the elements, the casualties that bring him advantage, and the spontaneous productions of nature. The idea of supplying his wants through the products of labour never enters the mind. And will it be denied that, even in civilized countries, they who solely rely upon begging, trick, and dishonesty, for their support, are always found to be deteriorating, both in morals and in their physical ability, rapidly receding from all the characteristics of civilization, in the direction towards savage life. Indeed, a tendency to move in the same direction is often perceptible among those who only partially supply the wants of civilized support by the product of individual labour, and rely upon their wits for the remainder, thus, to some extent, becoming the plunderers of society. We would have been happy to have found the causes why these things are so, as well as to have found the remedy, in "The Elements of Moral Science."

But let us contemplate, for a moment, a certain class of freemen, the lazaroni of Italy, who exist, merely, upon one small dish of macaroni, daily issued to them from the Hospital of St. Lazarus. We are all familiar with the condition of these people. Let us compare theirs with what would be the condition of the beggars and thieves of some other countries, were they placed under the control of some salutary power, whereby their necessary wants would be supplied by the product of their individual labour. We need not ask which condition is most "at variance with the ordinances of God!"

Dr. Wayland has retained, for his last witness, the old trite charge that slavery impoverishes the soil; that, therefore, it constantly "migrates from the old to new regions," "where alone the accumulated manure of centuries" can "sustain a system at variance with the laws of nature." "Hence," he says, "slavery in this country is acknowledged to have impoverished many of our most valuable districts."

We are not aware how far Dr. Wayland has founded this statement upon facts drawn from his own observation. Has he done so at all; or has he, carelessly and without reflection, adopted it from the assertions of others notoriously destitute of ability to form an opinion with accuracy, or else too deeply prejudiced to give their opinion any value? Does he wish us to infer that the plough and the hoe, in the hands of a slave, communicate some peculiar poison to the soil; and by reason of which "the ground shall not henceforth yield her strength?" Will he please explain how the effect of which he complains is produced? If he finds it merely in the mode of cultivation, we then inquire whether the same mode would not produce the same effect, even if the plough and hoe were held by freemen? If so, then it is evident that "the impoverishment of many of our most valuable districts" is not the result of slavery, but of a bad mode of cultivation. Or, will the doctor contend that if those valuable districts had been cultivated by free hired men, the evils from negligence in the labourer would be remedied? "He that is a hireling fleeth, because he is a hireling, and careth not for the sheep." *John* x. 13.

Dr. Wayland will not deny that the "heathen round about," of whom the Jews were permitted to buy slaves, were a slave-holding people; but we have no account that their country was impoverished thereby. The Canaanites, whom the Israelites drove out from Palestine, were slaveholders; yet the country was represented as very fertile, even to "overflowing with milk and honey." The Danites found "Laish very good," *Judg.* xviii. 9. And the children of Judah "found fat pasture and good" about Gedar. 1 *Chron.* iv. 40. "*For they of Ham had dwelt there of old!*"

For many centuries, slavery extended over every part of Europe, yet history gives us no account of the ruin of the soil. In Greece and Rome, the numbers of slaves were extended to millions beyond any number these States possess; but their historians failed to discover their destructive influence on the fertility of those countries.

Before the impoverishment of the soil can, with any force, be adduced as proof against slavery, it must be proved to be a necessary consequence; which, we apprehend, will be a difficult labour, since the sluggishness and the idleness of the Canaanites, and of the nations round about, left their country overflowing with milk and honey, abounding in fat pastures and good, notwithstanding their population were, to a large extent, slaves;—since, also, the servile cultivation of the soil in Greece and Rome did not impoverish it; and since slavery, which everywhere abounded in Europe, never produced that effect.

If Dr. Wayland will discover the legitimate cause of this impoverishment of the soil in the Slave States, and teach the planters a better mode of cultivation, we doubt not he will receive their thanks, and deserve well of his country, as a public benefactor.

LESSON VII.

Dr. Wayland says:

P. 209. "The moral precepts of the Bible are diametrically opposed to slavery."

P. 210. "The moral principles of the gospel are directly subversive of the principles of slavery." * * * "If the gospel be diametrically opposed to the *principles* of slavery, it must be opposed to the *practice* of slavery; and, therefore, were the principles of the gospel fully adopted, slavery could not exist."

Dr. Wayland having conceived himself to possess a distinct faculty, which reveals to him, with unerring truthfulness, whatever is right and all that is wrong, may be expected to consider himself fully able to decide, in his own way, what instruction God intended to convey to us, on the subject of slavery, through the books of Divine revelation; yet, we cannot but imagine that St. Paul would be somewhat astonished, if presented with the doctor's decision for his approval, and that he would cry out:

"Who art thou that judgest another man's servant? To his

own master, he standeth, or falleth: yea, he will be holden up; for God is able to make him stand."

But although we cannot boast of possessing this unerring moral guide, which, of late years, seems to be so common a possession among that class who ardently desire us to believe that they have monopolized all the knowledge of God's will on the subject of slavery, yet we may venture a remark on the logical accuracy of Dr. Wayland's argument.

It seems to be a postulate in his mind that the gospel is diametrically opposed to, and subversive of, the principles of slavery. We do not complain of this syllogistic mode; but we do complain, as we have done before, that his postulate is not an axiom, a self-evident truth, or made equal thereto by the open and clear declarations of Christ or his apostles. This defect cannot be remedied by ever so many suppositions, nor by deductions therefrom. Nor will those of a different faith from Dr. Wayland, on the subject of "conscience," or "moral sense," be satisfied to receive the declarations of this his "distinct faculty" as the fixed decrees of eternal truth. His assertions and arguments may be very convincing to those who think they possess this distinct faculty, especially if their education and prejudices tend to the same conclusion.

But if what President Wayland says about slavery be true, then to hold slaves is a most heinous sin; and he who does so, and never repents, can never visit Paul in heaven. He necessarily is placed on a parallel with the thief and robber; and Dr. Channing has been bold enough to say so.

But has Paul ever hinted to us any such thing as that the holding of slaves is a sin? Yet he gives us instruction on the subject and relations of slavery. What excuse had St. Paul for not telling us what the Rev. Dr. Wayland now tells us, if what he has told us be true? And if it be true, what are we to think of Paul's verity, when he asserts that he has "not shunned to declare all the counsel of God?"

Did Jesus Christ ever hint such an idea as Dr. Wayland's? What are we to understand, when he addresses God, the Father, and says, "I have given unto them the words thou gavest me, and they have received them?" What are we to deduce from his remark on a slaveholder, and who notified him of that fact, when he says to his disciples, "Verily I say unto you, I have not found so great faith, no, not in Israel?" What impression was this remark calculated to produce on the minds of the disciples? Does Dr.

Wayland found his assertion on *Luke* xvii. 7–10? or does he agree with Paley that Christ privately condemned slavery to the apostles, and that they kept such condemnation secret to themselves, to prevent opposition to the introduction of Christianity, and left the most wicked sin of slave-holding to be found out by a mere innuendo? Or does Dr. Wayland claim, through the aid of his distinct moral-faculty infallibility teaching him the truth, to have received some new light on the subject of slavery, which the FATHER deemed not prudent to be intrusted to the SON, and, therefore, now more lucid and authoritative than what was revealed to the apostles?

The Archbishop Secker has made a remark which appears to us conclusive, and also exactly to fit the case. In his Fifth Lecture on the Catechism, he says:—

"Supposing the Scripture a true revelation, so far as it goes; how shall we know, if it be a full and complete one too, in all things necessary? I answer: Since our Saviour had the Spirit without measure, and the writers of Scripture had as large a measure of it as their commission to instruct the world required, it is impossible that, in so many discourses concerning the terms of salvation as the New Testament contains, they should all have omitted any *one thing* necessary to the great end which they had in view. And what was not necessary when the Scripture was completed, cannot have become so since. For the faith was, once for all, 'delivered to the saints,' *Jude* 3; and 'other foundation can no man lay,' 1 *Cor.* iii. 11, than what was laid then. The sacred penmen themselves could teach no other doctrine than Christ appointed them; and he hath appointed no one since to make addition to it."

But it may be proper to take some further notice how the author of these "Elements" attempts to prove the truth of the proposition that "the moral precepts of the Bible are diametrically opposed to slavery." He says, "God can make known to us his will, either directly or indirectly."

He may, in express terms, command or forbid a thing; this will be directly;—or he may command certain duties, or impose certain obligations, with which some certain course of conduct is inconsistent; in which case the inconsistent course of conduct will be indirectly forbidden.

We have not followed Dr. Wayland's exact words, because we found them somewhat confused, and rather ambiguous. We prefer to have the case clearly stated, and we then accept the terms, and repeat the question, "Has God imposed obligations on man which are inconsistent with the existence of domestic slavery?"

In proof that he has, Dr. Wayland presents the Christian duty "to preach the gospel to all nations and men, without respect to circumstances or condition." We agree that such is our duty, so far as we may have the power; and it appears to us as strange how that duty can interfere with the existence of slavery, because the practical fact is, slavery brings hundreds of thousands of negroes into a condition whereby the duty may be performed, and many thereby do come to some knowledge of the gospel, who would, otherwise, have none.

Every Christian slaveholder feels it to be his duty. Is it denied that this duty is ever performed?

But if it is incompatible with the institution of slavery for the slave to be taught Christianity, then Christianity and slavery can never co-exist in the same person. Therefore, Dr. Wayland must prove that no slave can be a Christian, before this argument can have weight.

The man who owns a slave has a trust; he who has a child has one also. In both cases the trustee may do as he did who "dug in the earth and hid his lord's money." We cheerfully deliver them up to the lash of Dr. Wayland.

The author of the "Elements of Moral Science" next presents the marriage contract, and seems desirous to have us suppose that its obligations are incompatible with slavery. His words are—

"He has taught us that the conjugal relation is established by himself; that husband and wife are joined together by God; and that man may not put them asunder. The marriage contract is a contract for life, and is dissoluble only for one cause, that of conjugal infidelity. Any system that interferes with this contract, and claims to make it any thing else than what God has made it, is in violation of his law."

This proposition is bad; it is too verbose to be either definite or correct. There are many things that will interfere with the provisions of this proposition, and yet not be in violation of the laws of God. Suppose one of President Wayland's pupils has married a wife, and yet commits a crime. He is arrested, and the president is his judge. When about to pronounce sentence of imprisonment for life, the pupil reads to his judge the foregoing paragraph, and argues that he cannot receive such sentence, because it will interfere with the marriage contract, and, therefore, be in violation of the laws of God.

We trust some will deem this a sufficient refutation of the proposition.

But if we take the proposition as its author has left it, we have yet to learn that any slaveholder will object to it; although it may be he will differ with them on the subject of what constitutes Christian marriage, among pagan negroes or their pagan descendants.

Will the reverend moralist determine that a promiscuous intercourse is the conjugal relation established by God himself; that such is the marriage contract which no man may put asunder? Will he decide that an attempt to regulate the conduct of men, bond or free, who manifest such a state of morals, is in violation of the laws of God? Who are his pupils, when he shall say that an attempt to enforce the laws of God, in practice among men, is a violation of them?

So far as our experience goes, masters universally manifest a desire to have their negroes marry, and to live with their wives and children, in conformity to Christian rules. And one reason, if no other, is very obvious. The master wishes to secure the peace and tranquillity of his household. And we take this occasion to inform Dr. Wayland and his coadjutors, that a very large proportion of the punishments that are awarded slaves are for violations of what, perhaps, he may call the marriage contract, so anxious is the master to inculcate the obligations of marriage among them.

It is true, some slaves of a higher order of physical and moral improvement, influenced by the habits and customs of their masters, habituate themselves to a cohabitation with one companion for life; and, in all such cases, the master invariably gives countenance to their wishes; indeed, in some instances, masters have deemed them worthy of having their wishes sanctioned and solemnized by the ceremonies of the church ritual. And in all such cases, superior consideration and advantages are always bestowed, not only in reward of their merit, but as an encouragement for others.

The African negro has no idea of marriage as a sacred ordinance of God. Many of the tribes worship a *Fetish*, which is a personification of their gross notions of procreation; but it inculcates no idea like that of marriage; and we have known the posterity of that people, four or five generations removed from the African native, as firmly attached to those strange habits as if they had been constitutional. Negroes, who have only arrived to such a state of mental and moral development, would find it somewhat difficult to comprehend what the Christian church implied by the marriage covenant! Therefore, where there was no reason to believe that its duties were understood, or that their habits and conduct would be influenced by it any longer than until they should take some new notion, a ceremony of any high order has been thought to do injury. A rule, often broken, ceases to be venerated. And we feel quite sure that some Christians would deem it quite improper to permit those to join in any sacred ceremony which neither their physical nor mental development would permit them to comprehend or obey, whether freemen or slaves.

In the articles drawn up at Ratisbon by Melancthon, we find, Article 16, *De Sacram. Matrimo.:*

"The sacrament of matrimony belongs only to Christians. It is a holy and constant union of one single man with one single woman, confirmed by the blessing and consecration of Jesus Christ."

And St. Paul says, *Eph.* v. 32, of matrimony: "This is a great mystery: but I speak concerning Christ and the Church."

We know not whether the author of the "Elements" believes, with Melancthon, that matrimony is a Christian sacrament or not. We believe the majority of modern Protestants do not so consider it, although Luther says, *De Matrimonio:*

"Matrimony is called a sacrament, because it is the type of a very noble and very holy thing. Hence the married ought to consider and respect the dignity of this sacrament."

Question:—Would Melancthon, or Luther, or the author of these "Elements," consent to perform the marriage ceremony, joining, in the holy bonds of matrimony, two negroes, who neither understood the Christian duties it imposed, and of whom it was well known that they would not regard the contract as binding any longer than their fancy or passions might dictate. A Christian sacrament is not only a sign of Christian grace, but the seal of its insurance to us, and the instrument of the Holy Ghost, whereby faith is conferred, as a Divine gift, upon the soul. We feel it a Christian duty to "not give that which is holy to dogs," nor "cast pearls before swine." Is Dr. Wayland of the same opinion?

It may be well to advise our author of some facts in proof of what state of connubial feelings exist among African negroes. We quote from Lander, vol. i. p. 312:

"The manners of the Africans are hostile to the interests and advancement of women."

P. 328. "A man is at liberty to return his wife to her parents, at any time, without adducing any reason for his dislike." * * * "The children, if any, the mother is by no means permitted to take along with her; but they are left behind with the father, who delivers them over to the care of other women."

P. 158. "A man thinks as little of taking a wife as of cutting an ear of corn; affection is altogether out of the question."

Vol. ii. p. 208. "Africans, generally speaking, betray the most perfect indifference on losing their liberty, or in being deprived of their relations; while love of country is, seemingly, as great a stranger to their breasts as social tenderness and domestic affection."

We quote from the Christian Observer, vol. xix. p. 890: "Mr. Johnson was appointed to the care of Regent's Town, June, 1816. * * * Natives of twenty-two different nations were there collected together: * * * none of them had learned to live in a state of marriage."

Proofs of this trait in the African character may be accumulated; and a very determined disposition to live in a state of promiscuous intercourse is often noticeable, in their descendants, for many generations, notwithstanding the master endeavours to restrain it by corporeal punishment. But yet, under this state of facts, our laws forbid the separation of children from mothers, under ages stipulated by law.

It is the interest of the master to have his slaves orderly—to possess them of some interest which will have a tendency to that result. Their quiet settlement in families has been thought to be among the most probable and influential inducements to insure the desired effect, and to produce a moral influence on them. Besides this interest of the master, his education on the subject of marriage must be allowed to have a strong influence on his mind to favour and foster in his slaves a connection which his own judgment teaches him must be important to their happiness and his own tranquillity, to say nothing of his duty as a Christian. Indeed, we never heard of a master who did not feel a strong desire, a pride, to see his slaves in good condition, contented and happy; and we venture to assert, that no man, who entertained a proper regard for his own character, would consent to sell a family of slaves, separately, to different individuals, when the slaves themselves manifested good conduct, and a habit, or desire, to live together in conformity to the rules of civilized life. Even a casual cohabitation is often caught at by the master, and sanctioned, as permanent, if he can do so in accordance with the conduct and feelings of the negroes themselves.

That the owners of slaves have sometimes abused the power they possessed, and outraged the feelings of humanity in this behalf, is doubtless a fact. Nor do we wish to excuse such conduct, by saying that proud and wealthy parents sometimes outrage the feelings of common sense and of their own children in a somewhat similar way. These are abuses that can be, and should be corrected; and we are happy to inform Dr. Wayland that we have lived to see many abuses corrected, and hope that many more corrections may follow in their train. But we assure him that the wholesale denunciations of men who, in fact, know but little about the subjects of their distress, may produce great injury to the objects of their sympathies, but no possible benefit. And let us now, with the best feeling, inform Dr. Wayland, and his co-agitators, of one result of his and their actions in this matter. We assert what we know.

Thirty years ago, we occasionally had schools for negro children; nor was it uncommon for masters to send their favourite young slaves to these schools; nor did such acts excite attention or alarm; and, at the same time, any missionary had free access to that class of our population. But when we found, with astonishment, that our country was flooded with abolition prints, deeply laden with the most abusive falsehoods, with the obvious design to excite rebellion among the slaves, and to spread assassination and bloodshed through the land;—when we found these transient missionaries, mentally too insignificant to foresee the result of their conduct, or wholly careless of the consequences, preaching the same doctrines;—these little schools and the mouths of these missionaries were closed. And great was the cry. Dr. Wayland knows whereabout lies the wickedness of these our acts! Let him and his coadjutors well understand that these results, whether for the benefit or injury of the slave, have been brought about by the work of their hands.

If these transient missionaries were the only persons who had power to teach the gospel to the slave, who has deprived the slaves of the gospel?

If these suggestions are true, will not Dr. Wayland look back upon his labours with dissatisfaction? Does he behold their effects with joy? Has he thrown one ray of light into the mental darkness of benighted Africa? Has he removed one pain from the moral disease of her benighted children? If so perfectly adverse have been his toils, will he expect us to countenance his school, sanction his morality, or venerate his theology? A very small portion of poison makes the feast fatal!

Does he complain because some freemen lower themselves down to this promiscuous intercourse with the negro? We are dumb; we deliver them up to his lash! Or does he complain because we do not marry them ourselves? We surely have yet to learn, because we decline such marriages, and a deteriorated posterity, that, therefore, we interfere with the institution of marriage, or make it something which God did not. We had thought that the laws of God all looked towards a state of physical, intellectual, and moral improvement; and that such an amalgamation as would necessarily leave a more deteriorated race in our stead, would be sin, and would be punished, if in no other way, yet still by the very fact of such degradation. Or does Dr. Wayland deny that the negro is an inferior race of man to the white? If the slave and master were of the same race, as they once were in all parts of Europe, intermarriage between them would blot out the institution, as it has done there. In such case, his argument might have some force.

Under the Spanish law, a master might marry his female slave, or he might suffer any freeman to marry her; but the marriage, in either case, was emancipation to her. The wife was no longer a slave; and so by the Levitical law. See *Deut.* xxi. 14.

The laws of the Slave States of our Union forbid amalgamation with the negro race; consequently such a marriage would be a nullity, and the offspring take the condition of the mother.

The object of this law is to prevent the deterioration of the white race.

Thus we have seen that all the practical facts relating to the influence of the slavery of the Africans among us, touching the subject of marriage, as to them, are in opposition to what Dr. Wayland seems to suppose. In short, the slavery of the negroes in these States has a constantly continued tendency to change—to enforce an improvement of the morals of the African—to an approximation of the habits of Christian life.

LESSON VIII.

It is conceded by Dr. Wayland, that the Scriptures do not directly forbid or condemn slavery. In search of a path over this morass of difficulty, he says that the Scripture goes upon the "fair ground of teaching moral principles" "directly subversive of the principles of slavery;" and quotes the golden rule in proof; and thus comes to the conclusion that, "if the gospel be diametrically opposed to the *principle* of slavery, it must be opposed to the *practice* of slavery." In excuse for this mode being pursued by the Author of our religion, he says—

P. 212. "In this manner alone could its object, a universal moral revolution, have been accomplished. For, if it had forbidden the *evil*, instead of subverting the *principle*,—if it had proclaimed the unlawfulness of slavery and taught slaves to *resist* the oppression of their masters,—it would instantly have arrayed the two parties in deadly hostility, through the civilized world; its announcement would have been the signal of servile war; and the very name of the Christian religion would have been forgotten amidst the agitations of universal bloodshed."

We have heretofore attempted to show that this doctrine is extremely gross error;—its very assertion goes to the extinction, the denial of the divinity of Jesus Christ and his religion. And we deeply lament that this was not one of the errors of Paley which Dr. Wayland has seen fit to expunge from his book. (*See his Preface.*)

Paley says, third book, part ii. chap. 3—"Slavery was a part of the civil constitution of most countries, when Christianity first appeared; yet no passage is to be found in the Christian Scriptures by which it is condemned or prohibited. This is true, for Christianity, soliciting admission into all nations of the world, abstained, as behooved it, from intermeddling with the civil institutions of any. But does it follow, from the silence of Scripture concerning them, that all the civil institutions which then prevailed were right? Or that the bad should not be exchanged for better?"

"Besides this, the discharging the slaves from all obligation to obey their masters, which is the consequence of pronouncing slavery to be unlawful, would have had no better effect than to let loose one half of mankind upon the other. Slaves would have been tempted to embrace a religion which asserted their right to freedom; masters would hardly have been persuaded to consent to claims founded on such authority; the most calamitous of all contests, a *bellum servile*, might probably have ensued, to the reproach, if not the extinction, of the Christian name."

In these thoughtless remarks of Paley, abolition writers seem to have found a mine of argument, from which they have dug until they deemed themselves wealthy.

Channing, vol. ii. p. 101, says—

"Slavery, in the age of the apostle, had so penetrated society, was so intimately interwoven with it, and the materials of servile war were so abundant, that a religion preaching freedom to the slave would have shaken the social fabric to its foundation, and would have armed against itself the whole power of the state. Paul did not then assail the institution. He satisfied himself with spreading principles, which, however slowly, could not but work its dissolution."

This author, thus having satisfied himself with a display which the greater portion of his readers deem original, commences, p. 103, and quotes from "The Elements of Moral Science," p. 212:

"This very course, which the gospel takes on this subject, seems to have been the only one that could have been taken in order to effect the universal abolition of slavery. The gospel was designed, not for one race or for one time, but for all races and for all times. It looked, not at the abolition of this form of evil for that age alone, but for its universal abolition. Hence, the important object of its author was to gain it a lodgment in every part of the known world:" and concludes with our quotation from the author.

Dr. Barnes "fights more shy;" he sees "the trap." The Biblical Repertory has unveiled to his view the awful abyss to which this doctrine necessarily leaps. Yet the abyss must be passed; the facts, the doctrine of Paley, and the gulf, must be got over, in some way, or abolition doctrines must be given up. For thirty pages, like a candle-fly, he coquets around the light of this doctrine, until he gathers courage, and finally falls into it under the plea of "expediency." He quotes Wayland's Letters to Fuller, p. 73, which says—

"This form of expediency—the inculcating of a fundamental truth, rather than of the duty which springs immediately out of it, seems to me *innocent.* I go further: in some cases, it may be really demanded," &c.

"And a certain ruler asked him, saying, Good Master, what shall I do to inherit eternal life." *Luke* xviii. 18.

This man was rich—probably had slaves. Was it *inexpedient* for the Son of God to have plainly told him of its wickedness? Was not the occasion quite appropriate, if such had been the Saviour's view?

When the keeper of the prison said to Paul and Silas, "Sirs, what shall I do to be saved?" was it *inexpedient* in them to have mentioned *this sin?*

When the subject of slavery was mentioned in Corinthians, Ephesians, Colossians, in Timothy, Titus, and Peter, was it still *inexpedient?* And in the case of Philemon, "the dearly beloved and fellow-labourer," when Paul was pleading for the runaway slave, in what did the *inexpediency* consist? When the centurion applied to the Son of God, and *boasted that he owned slaves*, can we bring forward this paltry excuse?

This doctrine of Paley has been so commonly quoted, let us be excused for presenting a remark from the "Essays," reprinted from the Princeton Review, second series, p. 283:

"It is not by argument that the abolitionists have produced the present unhappy excitement. Argument has not been the character of their publications. Denunciations of slave-holding as man-stealing, robbery, piracy, and worse than murder; consequently vituperation of slaveholders as knowingly guilty of the worst of crimes; passionate appeals to the feelings of the inhabitants of the Northern States; gross exaggerations of the moral and physical condition of the slaves, have formed the staple of their addresses to the public."

P. 286. "Unmixed good or evil, however, in such a world as ours, is a rare thing. Though the course pursued by the abolitionists has produced a great preponderance of mischief, it may incidentally occasion no little good. It has rendered it incumbent on every man to endeavour to obtain, and, as far as he can, to communicate, definite opinions and correct principles on the whole subject. * * * The subject of slavery is no longer one on which men are allowed to be of no mind at all. * * * The public mind is effectually aroused from a state of indifference; and it is the duty of all to seek the truth, *and to speak in kindness, but with decision.* * * * We recognise no authoritative rule of truth and duty but the word of God. * * * Men are too nearly upon a par as to their powers of reasoning, and ability to discover truth, to make the conclusions of one mind an authoritative rule for others." * * *

The subject for consideration is: If the abolitionists are right in insisting that slave-holding is one of the greatest of all sins,—that it should be immediately and universally abandoned, as a condition of church communion, or of admission into heaven,—how comes it that Christ and his apostles did not pursue this sin *in plain and determined opposition?* How comes it that the teachings of the abolitionists, on the subject of slavery, are so extremely different from those of Jesus Christ and his apostles? The mind is forced to the conclusion that, if the abolitionists are right, Jesus Christ and his apostles are wrong! We agree that, if slave-holding is a sin, it should at once be abandoned. The whole subject is resolved to one single question: *Is slave-holding, in itself, a crime before God?*

The abolitionists say that it is; we assert that it is not; and we look to the conduct of Christ and his apostles to justify our position. Did they shut their eyes to the enormities of a great offence against God and man? Did they temporize with a heinous evil, because it was common and popular? Did they abstain from even exhorting masters to emancipate their slaves, though an imperative duty, from fear of consequences? Was slavery more deeply rooted than idolatry? or more deeply interwoven with the civil institutions? more thoroughly penetrated through every thing human—their prejudices, literature, hopes, and happiness? Was its denunciation, if a sin, attended with consequences more to be dreaded than death by torture, wild beasts, the crucifix, the fagot, and the flame? Did the apostles admit drunkards, liars, fornicators, adulterers, thieves, robbers, murderers, and idolaters to the Christian communion, and call them "dearly beloved and fellow-labourers?" Did the Son of God ever intimate of any such unrepentant man, that he had "not found so great faith, no, not in Israel?"

What are we then to think of the intellect of that man who shall affirm that Jesus Christ and his apostles classed the slave-holder with the worst of these characters? Yea, what can such a man think of himself? Did the apostles counsel thieves and robbers how they should advisedly conduct themselves in the practice of these crimes? Were those who had been *robbed* carefully gathered up and sent back to some known *robber*, to be *robbed* again? And, on such occasion, did any of the apostles address such *robber* in the language of affection, saying, "I thank my God, making mention of thee always in my prayers, hearing of thy love and faith, which thou hast towards the Lord Jesus and toward all saints?"

No one in his senses will deny that the Scriptures condemn injustice, cruelty, oppression, and violence, whether exhibited in the conduct of the master towards his slave or any other person:—crime being the same, whether committed in the relation of master and slave, husband and wife, or the monarch and his subjects. It may so happen that great crimes are committed by persons in these relations. But what is the argument worth which asserts *it is very wicked to be a schoolmaster*, because some schoolmaster whipped his pupil too much, or another not enough, or a third, in an angry, wicked state of mind, has put one to death?

Who has ever asserted that marriage was not a Divine institution, because some in that state live very unhappily together, and others have conspired against the happiness or life of those whom the institution made it their duty to protect?

Dr. Wayland's proposition, when analyzed and freed from verbiage, is this: the teaching of moral principles, subversive of the abuse of a thing, is proof that the teacher is opposed to the thing itself! and, if true, we say, is as applicable to every other institution among men, as to slavery.

LESSON IX.

Dr. Wayland says, p. 213—

"It is important to remember that two grounds of moral obligation are distinctly recognised in the gospel. The first is our duty to man as man, that is, on the ground of the relation which men sustain to each other; the second is our duty to man as a creature of God, that is, on the ground of the relation which we all sustain to God. On this latter ground, many things become our duty which would not be so on the former. It is on this ground that we are commanded to return good for evil, to pray for them that despitefully use us, and, when we are smitten on one cheek, to turn also the other. To act thus is our duty, not because our fellow-man has a right to claim this course of conduct from us, but because such conduct in us will be well-pleasing to God. And when God prescribes the course of conduct which will be well-pleasing to him, he by no means acknowledges the right of abuse in the injurious person, but expressly declares, 'Vengeance is mine and I will repay it, saith the Lord!' Now, it is to be observed, that it is precisely upon this latter ground that the slave is commanded to obey *his* master. It is never urged, like the duty of obedience to parents, *because it is right;* but because the cultivation of meekness and forbearance under injury will be well-pleasing unto God. Thus servants are commanded to be obedient to their own masters, 'in singleness of heart, as unto Christ; doing the will of God from the heart, with good-will doing service, as to the Lord, and not to man.' *Eph.* v. 5–7.

"Servants are commanded to count their masters worthy of all honour, that the name of God and his doctrine be not blasphemed. 1 *Tim.* vi. 1. That they may adorn the doctrine of God our Saviour in all things. *Titus* iii. 9.

"The manner in which the duty of servants or slaves is inculcated, therefore, affords no ground for the assertion that the gospel authorizes one man to hold another in bondage, any more than the command to honour the king, when that king was Nero, authorized the tyranny of the emperor; or the command to turn the other cheek when one was smitten, justifies the infliction of violence by an injurious man."

Added to the foregoing, we find the following note:

"I have retained the above paragraph, though I confess that the remarks of Professor Taylor, of the Union Theological Seminary of Virginia, have led me seriously to doubt whether the distinction, to which it alludes, is sustained by the New Testament."

Why then did he retain it?

In his preface to the fourth edition, which is inserted in the present, after expressing his acknowledgments for the criticisms with which gentlemen have favoured him, he says—

"Where I have been convinced of error, I have altered the text. Where I have only *doubted*, I have suffered it to remain; as it seemed profitless merely to exchange one *doubtful* opinion for another."

We beg to know what *doubtful opinion* would have been introduced by the deletion of this, which he acknowledges to be doubtful? Why did he not go to the Bible, and inquire of Jesus

Christ and the apostles for advice in such a case? "And immediately Jesus stretched forth his hand, and caught him, and said unto him, O thou of little faith, wherefore didst thou doubt?" *Matt.* xiv. 31.

In *Matt.* xxi. 21, we find that the doubting mind is destitute of Christian power; and the same in *Mark* xi. 23. Jesus, speaking to his disciples, says to them, *Luke* xii. 29, "Neither be ye of a doubtful mind." Does any one imagine that Luke would have left any thing in his book that he thought doubtful? But we find in *Rom.* xiv. 1, "Him that is weak in the faith receive ye, but not to doubtful disputations." This surely needs no comment. The poison of doubt is rejected in 1 *Tim.* ii. 8; and the apostle in *Rom.* xiv. 23, says, "And he that doubteth is damned if he eat, because he eateth not of faith, for whatsoever is not of faith is sin." How awful is the condition of him who shall attempt to preach a doctrine, and that an important one too, as the doctrine of the Bible, of which he doubts! A doctrine in which he can have no faith! Who shall say it would not be a palpable attempt to change the meaning and alter the sense of the Scripture from its true interpretation?

"Ye shall not add unto the word which I command you, neither shall ye diminish aught from it, that ye may keep the commandments of the Lord your God, which I command you." *Deut.* iv. 2.

"But there be some that trouble you, and pervert the gospel of Christ. But though we, or an angel from heaven, preach any other gospel unto you than that which we have preached unto you, let him be accursed. As we said before, so say we now again, if any man preach any other gospel unto you than that ye have received, let him be accursed." *Gal.* 1. 7–9.

"I Jesus have sent mine angel to testify unto you these things in the churches. * * * For I testify unto every man that heareth the words of the prophecy of this book, if any man shall add unto those things, God shall add unto him the plagues that are written in this book; and if any man shall take away from the words of the book of this prophecy, God shall take away his part out of the book of life." *Rev.* xxii. 16–19.

"Every word of God is pure. * * * Add not unto his words, lest he reprove thee, and thou be found a liar." *Prov.* xxx. 5–6.

We have not seen the remarks of Professor Taylor; but we can easily imagine that a professor of theology, free from the delirium of abolitionism, would not have found it a difficult labour to prove

4

that the main point of the author's argument was contradicted by Scripture, and that even he himself attempted to sustain it only by assumption. We regret that President Wayland has not given us Professor Taylor's remarks that made him "doubt." We, however, will venture our "remark" that the author's assertion, "the inculcation of the duty of slaves affords no evidence that the Scriptures countenance slavery, more than the command to honour the king authorized the tyranny of Nero," is a comparison where there is no parallel. Dr. Wayland must first make it appear that all kings, or chief magistrates, are, necessarily, wicked tyrants, like Nero; and that the wicked tyranny is a part and parcel of the thing to be honoured, before his parallel between slavery and monarchy can be drawn; and since, then, the deduction will be useless, we suppose he will not make the attempt.

The parallel that might have been sustained is this: The inculcation of the duty of slaves to obey their masters does not authorize masters to abuse their power over their slaves, any more than the command to honour the king authorized the tyranny of Nero;—from which the deductions are, that masters have a right to command their slaves as things in their peculiar relation, and not as things having a different relation. The master has no right to command a slave, as if the slave stood in the relation of a horse; nor even a horse, as if the horse stood in the relation of a piece of timber: so the king has no right to govern his subjects as if they were idiots or brutes, but as enlightened free-men, if such be their condition.

The object of the government is the happiness no more of the governor than of the governed. This principle, so profusely illustrated in Scripture, it would seem the abolitionists run to shipwreck, in every approach they make towards it.

There are a class of abolition writers who never fail to compare St. Paul's instruction, to live in obedience to the civil authority, (making no exception even when the worst of monarchs are in power,) with his instruction to slaves to obey their masters; and then say that no argument is to be drawn from the latter in favour of slavery, any more than there is from the former in favour of the wickedness of the Emperor Nero. To some, this position may look quite imposing; while others will associate it with the false position of a wicked, unprincipled lawyer, who is ambitious only to gain his case, and carés not by what falsehood, or by what means. But it is truly mortifying to see such an argument presented, and attempted to be sustained, by any one who pretends to be an honest man, and a disciple of the Lord Jesus Christ. And we cannot but reflect that such an one must be in one of three predicaments; either in that of the lawyer, or his understanding must be so obtuse he cannot reason, or so crazed by fanaticism as to be equally stultified in intellect. Yet these men present this argument, or position, with an air which displays the utmost confidence of their having obtained a victory, and of their having established for themselves a lofty intellectual character.

Jesus Christ and his apostles everywhere reprimanded and condemned crime, outrage, and oppression, whether to superiors, equals, or inferiors. Yet these qualities of action must take their character from the facts of the case. The parent will feel it his duty to compel, by force, his froward child to do right; yet the same action directed to his neighbour, or equal, may be manifestly wrong, or even sinful. The crimes of monarchs and the crimes of masters are everywhere condemned, as well as the crimes of all other men. Yet to be a monarch or a master is nowhere condemned, *per se*, as a sinful condition of itself.

All history agrees that Nero was a wicked, bad prince; he was wicked and bad because his acts were wicked and bad; not because he was a prince or an emperor. Slaves are ordered to be obedient to their masters. Is there any one so crazy as therefore to suppose that the master has a right to overwork, starve, murder, or otherwise misuse his slave? We are all commanded to be obedient to the civil power. Does this give the chief ruler the right to practise the wickedness of Nero?

Is there any proof that Philemon murdered, or was recklessly cruel to his slaves? What justice is there in comparing his character as only on an equality with that of Nero? Was Nero, with all his sins, admitted into the church of Christ? Where is the parallel between him and the "beloved" of the apostle?

We feel authorized to affirm that St. Paul would have rejected from the church a slaveholder, who murdered, starved, or otherwise maltreated his slaves, because these crimes would have been proof of his want of the Christian character. The same evidence of wicked conduct would have excluded any other man, even the emperor, from the church; yet, since slaveholders, who had not been guilty of such enormities, were admitted to the church, and distinguished as "beloved," this fact becomes proof that slaveholding is no evidence of a sinful character. So monarchs and emperors, who gave proof of the possession of the Christian character, were always admissible to the Christian church. This fact also becomes demonstration, that being a monarch or an emperor gave no proofs of a sinful character.

Will Dr. Wayland undertake to prove that the admission of Constantine to the Christian church gave any license to the wicked murders and hateful hypocrisy of the Emperor Phocas? Or will he venture to extend his argument, and say that the command of marital and filial obedience proves nothing in their favour; since we are commanded to yield a like obedience to the king, although that king be the wicked Phocas? The fact is, the mere character of chief-magistrate, of husband, of parent or slaveholder, is quite distinct from the character which their acts may severally heap upon them. It is, therefore, quite possible for us to reverence and obey the king, yet hold in contempt the person who fills the throne.

Civil government, the relations of parent and child, husband and wife, and slavery itself, are all ordinances of Divine wisdom, instituted for the benefit of man, under the condition of his fallen state. But because these relations are in accordance with the ordinances of God, it by no means follows that the abuses of them are so.

Suppose those who wish to abolish the institution of marriage should present the same argument in their behalf which Dr. Wayland has in this case, it will surely be just as legitimate in the one as the other. But will not Dr. Wayland readily say that there is no parallel between the particular relations compared? We doubt not, he would consider it too stupid to even require refutation.

LESSON X.

OUR author says, as before quoted—

P. 209. "That the precepts of the Bible are diametrically opposed to slavery."

In proof, he offers one precept:

"Thou shalt love thy neighbour as thyself, and All things whatsoever ye would that men should do unto you, do ye even so unto them."

Upon which he says, for argument—

"1. The application of these precepts is universal. Our neighbour is every one whom we may benefit. The obligation respects all things whatsoever. The precept, then, manifestly extends to men as men, or men in every condition; and if to all things whatsoever, certainly to a thing so important as the right of personal liberty.

"2. Again, by this precept it is made our duty to cherish a tender and delicate respect for the right the meanest individual possesses over the means of happiness bestowed on him by God, as we cherish for our own right over our own means of happiness, or as we desire any other individual to cherish for it. Now, were this precept obeyed, it is manifest that slavery could not in fact exist for a single instant. The principle of the precept is absolutely subversive of the principle of slavery. That of the one is the entire equality of right; that of the other, the entire absorption of the rights of one in the rights of the other."

We propose to make no comment upon these arguments. We cannot do battle against phantoms. But we shall take this golden rule, which we most devoutly reverence, and show that it inculcates slavery, upon a statement of facts.

The 28th chapter of Deuteronomy contains the revelations of blessings and curses promised the Jews, and, we may add, all mankind, for obedience to the laws of God, and for disobedience to the same. At the 68th verse, they were told that they should again be sent to Egypt; or that they should be exposed for sale; or that they should expose themselves for sale, as the passage may be read, and that no man should buy them; or that there should not be buyers enough to give them the benefit even of being slaves, whereby they could be assured of protection and sustenance. This was most signally verified at the time Jerusalem was sacked by Titus; and not only in Egypt, but in many other places, thousands of the Hebrew captives were exposed for sale as slaves. But thousands of them, thus exposed, died of starvation, because purchasers could not be found for them. The Romans considered them too stubborn, too degraded, to be worthy of being slaves to them, refusing to buy them. Their numbers, compared to the numbers of their purchasers, were so great that the price became merely nominal; and thousands were suffered to die, because purchasers could not be had at any price. Their death was the consequence.

Now let us apply the truly golden rule or precept, relied upon by Dr. Wayland in support of abolitionism. Would it teach to buy these slaves, or not?

The same incident happened once again to all the Jews, who were freemen in Spain, during the reign of Ferdinand and Isabella, when 800,000 Jews were driven from that kingdom in one day; vast multitudes of whom famished to death because, although anxious to do so, they could not find for themselves even a master! Let us ask, what would the precept teach in this case?

Nor has such a peculiar relation of facts been confined to the Jews alone. In 1376, the Florentines, then a travelling, trading, or commercial people, but in many instances quite forgetful of the rules of Christian honesty, became exceedingly obnoxious to their neighbours, especially to the subjects of the church of Rome. To many of them, murder and robbery became a mere pastime. From individuals the moral poison was communicated to their government. The church was despoiled of her patrimony, her subjects of their homes. The church remonstrated until patience was exhausted, when Gregory XI. issued his papal bull, delivering each individual of that nation, in all parts of the earth, who did not instantly make reparation, up to pillage, slavery, or death.

Let us notice how Walsingham witnessed this matter in England, where a large portion of the traders were of that people, all liable, if freemen, to be put to death by any one who might choose to inflict the punishment; and their effects were legally escheated to whomsoever might seize them. Slavery was their only remedy. The Anglo-Saxon Normans, the natives of the realm, had not yet, as a people, sufficiently emerged from the poverty and darkness of the times to give them protection. This, to us so strange a relation between the church and civil government, in regard to the Florentines, produced an action on the part of the king by which he became their personal master. Thus they became slaves, not of the crown, but of the individual who sat upon the throne. Did he act in conformity to this precept or not?

John and Richard Lander were sent by the "London African Association" to explore some parts of Africa. On the 24th of March, 1830, they were only one half day's travel from the sea-coast, at which point they say, vol. i. p. 58:

"Meantime the rainy season is fast approaching, as is sufficiently announced by repeated showers and occasional tornadoes; and, what makes us still more desirous to leave this abominable place, is the fact, as we have been told, that a sacrifice of no less than three hundred human beings, of both sexes and all ages, is about to take place. We often hear the cries of these poor creatures; and the heart sickens with horror at the bare contemplation of such a scene as awaits us, should we remain here much longer."

It is to be regretted that since the abolition of the slave-trade in Africa, slaves have become of little value in that country. That the Africans in many places have returned to sacrifice and cannibalism, is also true, and a cause of deep sorrow to the philanthropist; but, considering the state and condition of these savages, there is no alternative;—the slave there, if he cannot be sold, is at all times liable to be put to death.

Suppose you buy, and then turn them loose there; they will again and instantly be the subjects of slavery; and even there, slavery is some protection, for, so long as the savage master chooses or is able to keep his slave alive, he is more sure of the usual means of living. But, let us present this state of facts to the Christian, and ask him to apply the golden rule; and, in case the slave-trade with Africa had not now been abolished, what would he deem it his duty to do for the practical and lasting benefit of these poor victims, whom the sympathy of the world has thus consigned to sacrifice and death?

The people of the Slave States have determined not to countenance amalgamation with the slave race; they have determined not to set the slaves free, because they have previously resolved that they will not, cannot live under the government of the negro. In full view of these evils, they have resolved that they will not suffer the presence of that race in their community, on terms of political or social equality. They have, therefore, further resolved, in furtherance of its prevention, to oppose it while life shall last.

Now, Dr. Wayland says—

P. 215. "The slaves were brought here without their own consent; they have been continued in their present state of degradation without their own consent, and they are not responsible for the consequences. If a man have done injustice to his neighbour, and have also placed impediments in the way of remedying that injustice, he is as much under obligations to remove the impediments in the way of justice as he is to do justice."

The ancestors of our slaves were brought from beyond sea by the people of Old England, and by the people of New England, and particularly by the people of Rhode Island, among the descendants of whom the reverend doctor resides. The ancestors of these slaves were sold to our ancestors for money, and guaranteed, by them, to be slaves for life, and their descendants after them, as they said, both by the laws of God and man. Whether this was false, whether they were stolen and cruelly torn from their homes, the reverend doctor has better means of determining than we. We may sell, we will not free them.

Under this statement of facts, let the reverend doctor apply the golden rule and his own argument to himself. Let him then buy, and set them free in Rhode Island; or send them to Africa, if their ancestors "were unlawfully torn from thence."

"Wo unto you, scribes and pharisees, hypocrites! because ye build the tombs of the prophets, and garnish the sepulchres of the righteous, and say, If we had been in the days of our fathers, we should not have been partakers with them in the blood of the prophets. Wherefore, ye be witness unto yourselves, that ye are the children of them that killed the prophets." *Matt.* xxiii. 29, 30, 31.

"For they bind heavy burdens, and grievous to be borne, and lay them on men's shoulders; but they themselves will not move them with one of their fingers." *Idem.* 4.

Within the last year, our sympathies have been excited by an account now published to the world, of an African chieftain and slaveholder, who, during the year previous, finding himself cut off from a market on the Western coast, in consequence of the abolition of the slave-trade with Europe and America,—the trade with Arabia, Egypt, and the Barbary States not being sufficient to drain off the surplus number,—put to death three thousand!

The blood of these massacred negroes now cries from the ground unto Dr. Wayland and his disciples—

"Apply, oh, apply to bleeding Africa the doctrine of the golden rule, and relieve us, poor African slaves, from starvation, massacre, and death. Come, oh, come; buy us, that we may be your slaves, and have some chance to learn that religion under which you prosper. Then 'we shall build up the old wastes'—'raise up the former desolations,' and 'repair the waste cities, the desolations of many generations.' 'And strangers shall stand and feed your flocks, and the sons of the alien shall be your ploughmen, and your vine-dressers.' 'Then ye shall be named the priests of the Lord; men shall call you the ministers of our God.'" *Isa.* lxi. 4, 5, 6.

We shall here close our remarks on the Rev. Dr. Wayland's

book; and however feeble they may be, yet we can conscientiously say, we have no "*doubt*" about the truth of our doctrine.

"Forever, O Lord, thy word is settled in heaven. Thy faithfulness is unto all generations; thou hast established the earth, and it abideth. They continue, this day, according to thine ordinances; for all are thy servants," (עֲבָדֶיךָ *ebedeka, slaves.*) *Ps.* cxix. 89, 90, 91.

LESSON XI.

AMONG those who have advocated views adverse to those of our present study, we are compelled to notice Dr. Paley, as one of the most influential, the most dignified, and the most learned. He defines slavery to be "an obligation to labour for the benefit of the master, without the contract or consent of the servant." He says "that this obligation may arise, consistently with the laws of nature, from three causes: 1st, from crimes; 2d, from captivity; and 3d, from debt." He says that, "in the first case, the continuance of the slavery, as of any other punishment, ought to be proportionate to the crime. In the second and third cases, it ought to cease as soon as the demand of the injured nation or private creditor is satisfied." He was among the first to oppose the African slave-trade. He says, "Because, when the slaves were brought to the African slave-market, no questions were asked as to the origin of the vendors' titles: Because the natives were incited to war for the sake of supplying the market with slaves: Because the slaves were torn away from their parents, wives, children, and friends, homes, companions, country, fields, and flocks, and their accommodation on shipboard not better than that provided for brutes: Because the system of laws by which they are governed is merciless and cruel, and is exercised, especially by their English masters, with rigour and brutality."

But he thinks the American Revolution, which had just then happened, will have a tendency to accelerate the fall of this most abominable tyranny, and indulges in the reflection whether, in the providence of God, the British legislature, which had so long assisted and supported it, was fit to have rule over so extensive an empire as the North American colonies.

Dr. Paley says that slavery was a part of the civil constitution of most countries when Christianity appeared; and that no passage is found in the Christian Scriptures by which it is condemned or prohibited. But he thinks the reason to be, because "Christianity, soliciting admission into all nations of the world, abstained, as behooved it, from intermeddling with the civil institutions of any; but," says he, "does it follow from the silence of Scripture concerning them, that all the civil institutions that then prevailed were right? or, that the bad should not be exchanged for better? Besides," he says, "the discharging the slaves from all obligations to their masters would have had no better effect than to let loose one half of mankind upon the other. Besides," he thinks "it would have produced a servile war, which would have ended in the reproach and extinction of the Christian name."

Dr. Paley thinks that the emancipation of slaves should be carried on very gradually, by provision of law, under the protection of government; and that Christianity should operate as an alterative, in which way, he thinks, it has extinguished the Greek and Roman slavery, and also the feudal tyranny; and he trusts, "as Christianity advances in the world, it will banish what remains of this odious institution."

In some of his other writings, Dr. Paley suggests that Great Britain, by way of atoning for the wrongs she has done Africa, ought to transport from America free negroes, the descendants of slaves, and give them location in various parts of Africa, to serve as models for the civilization of that country.

Dr. Paley's Treatise on Moral and Political Philosophy, from which the foregoing synopsis is taken, was published to the world in 1785; but it had been delivered in lectures, almost *verbatim*, before the University of Cambridge, several years previous; and it is now a class-book in almost every high literary institution where the English language is spoken. It is, therefore, a work of high authority and great influence.

But we think his definition of the term slavery is not correct. Let us repeat it: "An obligation to labour for the benefit of the master, without the contract or consent of the servant."

Many, who purchase slaves to be retained in their own families, first examine and consult with the slave, and tell him—"My business is thus; I feed and clothe thus; are you willing that I should buy you? For I will buy no slave who is not willing."

To this, it is usual for the slave to say, "Yes, master! and I hope you will buy me. I will be a good slave. You shall have no fault to find with me, or my work."

By all the claims of morality, here is a contract and consent, and the statute might make it legal. But who will say that the condition of slavery is altered thereby? But, says one, this supposition does not reach the case, because all the obligations and conditions of slavery previously existed; and, therefore, the "contract" and "consent" here only amounted to a contract and consent to change masters.

Suppose then, from poverty or misfortune, or some peculiar affection of the mind, a freeman should solicit to place himself in the condition of slavery to one in whom he had sufficient confidence, (and we have known such a case,)—a freeman anxiously applying to his more fortunate friend to enter into such an engagement for life; suppose the law had sanctioned such voluntary slavery, and, when entered into, made it obligatory, binding, and final for ever. There would be nothing in such law contrary to the general powers of legislation, however impolitic it might be; and such a law did once exist among the Jews.

"And if a sojourner or a stranger wax rich by thee, and thy brother that dwelleth by him wax poor, and sell himself unto the stranger or sojourner by thee, or to the stock of the stranger's family; after that he is sold, he may be redeemed again; and one of his brethren may redeem him. Either his uncle or his uncle's son may redeem him, or any that is nigh of kin unto his family may redeem him; or, if he be able, he may redeem himself: * * * and if he be not redeemed in one of these years,—then he shall go out in the year of Jubilee, both he and his children with him." *Lev.* xxv. 47–54. "Now these are the judgments which ye shall set before them. If ye buy an Hebrew servant, six years shall he serve, and in the seventh he shall go out free for nothing. If he came in by himself, he shall go out by himself; if he were married, then his wife shall go out with him. If his master have given him a wife, and she have borne him sons or daughters, the wife and her children shall be her master's, and he shall go out by himself; and if the servant shall plainly say, 'I love my master, my wife, and my children; I will not go out free,'—then his master shall bring him unto the judges; he shall bring him unto the door, or unto the door-post, and his master shall bore his ear through with an awl, and he shall serve him for ever." *Ex.* xxi. 1–6.

It is clear, then, that "to contract and consent," or the reverse, is no part of the qualities of slavery. Erase, then, that portion of Dr. Paley's definition as surplusage; it will then read, "an obligation to labour for the benefit of the master."

Now, there can be no obligation to do a thing where there is no possible power to do it; and more especially, if there is no contract. But it does not unfrequently occur, that a slave, from its infancy, old age, idiocy, delirium, disease, or other infirmity, has no power to labour for the benefit of the master; and the want of such ability may be obviously as permanent as life, so as to exclude the idea of any prospective benefit. Yet the law compels the master to supply food, clothes, medicine, pay taxes on, and every way suitably protect such slave, greatly to the disadvantage of the master. Or, a case might be, for it is presumable, that the master, from some obliqueness of understanding, might not wish some slave, even in good health, to labour at all, but who would prefer, at great expense, to maintain such slave in luxury and idleness, clothed in purple and fine linen, and faring sumptuously every day: surely, such slave, would be under no obligation to labour for the benefit of the master, when, to do so, would be acting contrary to his will and command. Yet none of these circumstances make the slave a freeman, or alter at all the essentials of slavery.

The slave, then, may or may not be under obligation to labour for the benefit of the master. Therefore, the "obligation to labour for the benefit of the master" is surplusage also, and may be erased. So the entire definition is erased—not a word left!

The fact is, Dr. Paley took some of the most common incidents accompanying the thing for the thing itself; and he would have been just as logically correct had he said, that "slavery was to be a hearty feeder on fat pork," because slaves feed heartily on that article. In his definition Dr. Paley has embraced none of the essentials of slavery.

We propose to notice the passage—"This obligation may arise, consistently with the laws of nature, from three causes: 1st, from crime; 2d, from captivity; 3d, from debt."

The first consideration is, what he means by "obligation." In its usual acceptation, the term means something that has grown out of a previous condition, as the obligations of marriage did not, nor could they exist until the marriage was had. If he only means that the "obligations" of slavery arise, &c., then he has told us nothing of the arising of slavery itself. But as he has used the word in the singular number, and given it three progenitors, we may suppose, that, by some figure of rhetoric, not usual in works of this kind, he has used the consequent for the cause. In that case, the sentence should read, "Slavery may arise, consistently with the laws of nature, from three causes," &c.; which is what we suppose the doctor really meant.

The next inquiry is, what did Dr. Paley mean by "the laws of nature?" Permit us to suffer him to answer this inquiry himself.

In the twenty-fourth chapter of his "Natural Theology," a work of great merit, he says—

"The wisdom of the Deity, as testified in the works of creation, surpasses all idea we have of wisdom drawn from the highest intellectual operations of the highest class of intelligent beings with whom we are acquainted. * * * The degree of knowledge and power requisite for the formation of created nature cannot, with respect to us, be distinguished from infinite. The Divine omnipresence stands in natural theology upon this foundation. In every part and place of the universe, with which we are acquainted, we perceive the exertion of a power which we believe mediately or immediately to proceed from the Deity. For instance, in what part or point of space, that has ever been explored, do we not discover attraction? In what regions do we not discover light? In what accessible portion of our globe do we not meet with gravitation, magnetism, electricity? together with the properties, also, and powers of organized substances, of vegetable or animated, nature? Nay, further we may ask, what kingdom is there of nature, what corner of space, in which there is any thing that can be examined by us, where we do not fall upon contrivance and design? The only reflection, perhaps, which arises in our minds from this view of the world around us, is that the laws of nature everywhere prevail; that they are uniform and universal. But what do we mean by the laws of nature? or by any law? Effects are produced by power, not by law; a law cannot execute itself; a law refers to an agent."

By the "laws of nature," then, Dr. Paley clearly means the laws of God.

Now be pleased to look at the close of Dr. Paley's remarks on slavery, where he trusts that, "as Christianity advances in the world, it will banish what remains of that odious institution." How happens it that an institution which arises consistently with the laws of God should be odious to him, unless the laws of God and Dr. Paley are at variance on this subject?

LESSON XII.

It will be recollected, that Dr. Paley has presented a number of facts, displaying acts of oppression and cruelty, as arguments against the African slave-trade. These facts are arranged and used in place as arguments against the institution of slavery itself; and the verbose opponents of this institution have always so understood it, and so used this class of facts. It is this circumstance that calls for our present view of these facts, rather than any necessity the facts themselves impose of proving their exaggeration or imaginary existence; and doubtless, in many cases, most heartless enormities were committed. But what do they all prove? Truly, that some men engaged in the traffic were exceedingly wicked men.

Such men would fashion the traffic to suit themselves, and would, doubtless, make their business an exceedingly wicked one. But none of the enormities named, or that could be named, constituted a necessary part of the institution of slavery, or necessarily emanated from it. What enormities have wicked men sometimes committed in the transportation of emigrants from Germany and Ireland? Wicked men, intrusted with power, have, at least sometimes, been found to abuse it. Is it any argument against the institution of marriage, because some women have made their husbands support and educate children not their own? Or, because some men murder, treat with cruelty, or make their wives totally miserable and wretched? None of these things were any part of the institution of marriage, but the reverse of it. Apply this view also to the institution of Christianity, for nothing has been more abused. Already, under its very banners, as it were, have been committed more enormities than would probably attend that of slavery through all time. Yet the institution of Christianity has not been even soiled thereby; but its character and usefulness have become brighter and more visible. In proportion to the importance of a thing is its liability to abuse. A worthless thing is not worth a counterfeit.

We have before us the testimony of travellers in regard to the indifference felt by the Africans on being sold as slaves; of their palpable want of love and affection for their country, their relatives, and even for their wives and children. Nor should we forget that a large portion of this race are born slaves to the chieftains, whose wars with each other are mere excursions of robbery and theft.

Lander, vol. i. p. 107, speaking of Jenna, says—

"It must not be imagined that because the people of this country are almost perpetually engaged in conflicts with their neighbours, the slaughter of human beings is therefore very great. They pursue war, as it is called, partly as an amusement, or to *keep their hands in it;* and partly to benefit themselves by the capture of slaves."

One decrepit old woman was the victim of a hundred engagements, at Cape La Hoo, during a three years' war. Lander describes those who claim to be free, as *the war men of the path,* who are robbers. He says, p. 145, "they subsist solely by pillage and rapine."

Such is the condition of the poor free negro in Africa. The chieftain often, it is true, has goats, sheep, fields of corn and rice; but we mistake when we suppose that the slaves, the surplus of whom were formerly sent to market, were the proprietors of such property. At Katunqua, p. 179, Lander describes the food to be "such as lizards, rats, locusts, and caterpillars, which the natives roast, grill, bake, and boil." No people feed on such vermin who possess fields and flocks.

We can form some notion of their companionship, from p. 110: "It is the custom here, when the governor dies, for two of his favourite wives to quit the world on the same day;" but in this case they ran and hid themselves. Also, p. 182: "This morning a young man visited us, with a countenance so rueful, and spoke in a tone so low and melancholy, that we were desirous to learn what evil had befallen him. The cause of it was soon explained by his informing us that he would be doomed to die, with two companions, as soon as the governor's dissolution should take place."

There is little or no discrepancy among travellers in their descriptions of the Africans. Their state of society must have been well known to Paley; yet Paley gives us a picture of their state of society from imagination, founded upon that state of society with which his pupils were conversant: "Because the slaves were torn away from their parents, wives, children, and friends, homes, companions, country, fields, and flocks."

If the picture drawn by Paley were the lone consideration addressed to our commiseration in the argument against slavery as a Divine institution of mercy, we should, perhaps, be at some loss to determine what amount was due from us to the African slave, who had thus been *torn from the danger of being put to death! —thus torn from his fields of lizards and locusts, and flocks of caterpillars!*

But what shall we think of an argument, founded on relations in England, but applied to Africa, where no such relations exist?

It is a rule to hesitate as to the truthfulness of all that is stated, when the witness is discovered to be under the influence of a prejudice so deeply seated as to mislead the mind, and especially when we discover a portion of the stated facts to be either not true or misapplied.

The reasons assigned by Dr. Paley why the Christian Scriptures did not prohibit and condemn slavery, we deem also quite erroneous:—"For Christianity, soliciting admission into all nations of the world, abstained, as behooved it, from intermeddling with the civil institutions of any;" and then asks, with an air of triumph, "But does it follow from the silence of Scripture concerning them, that all the civil institutions that prevailed were right? or that the bad should not be exchanged for better?"

We wish to call particular attention to this passage, for, even after having examined the books of the Greek philosophers, we are constrained to say we have never seen a more beautiful sophism.

Is it a fact, then, that Jesus Christ and his apostles did compromise and compound with sin, as Dr. Paley thinks it behooved them, and with the design to avoid opposition to the introduction of Christianity?

Say, thou humble follower of the lowly Jesus, art thou ready to lay down thy life for Him who could truckle to sin—to a gross, an abominable sin, which alone would destroy the purity of his character and the divinity of his doctrine? In all love, we pray Him who holds your very breath in his hand, to cause you to tremble, before you shall say that Jesus Christ was a liar, and his apostles perjured!

"I am the true vine; and my Father is the husbandman * * * as the Father hath loved me, so have I loved you; continue ye in my love. Greater love hath no man than this, that a man lay down his life for his friends. Ye are my friends if ye do whatsoever I command you. Henceforth I call you not *servants*, for the *servant* knoweth not what his Lord doeth; but I have called you friends; for ALL THINGS that I have heard of my Father, I have made known unto you." *John* xv. 1, 9, 13, 15.

"And when they were come to him, he said unto them; ye know, from the first day that I came into Asia, after what manner I have been with you, at all seasons, serving the Lord with all humility of mind, and with many tears and temptations, which befell me by the lying in wait of the Jews. And how I kept back nothing that was profitable unto you; but have showed you, and have taught you publicly and from house to house. Wherefore, I take you to record this day, that I am pure from the blood of all men. For I have not shunned to declare unto you ALL THE COUNSEL OF GOD." *Acts* xx.

Had St. Paul foreseen the attack upon his character, made by Dr. Paley, seventeen hundred and eighty-five years after, and that upon his Master and their religion, he need not have altered his language to have repelled the slander.

"Simon Peter, a servant and apostle of Jesus Christ, to them that have obtained like precious faith with us, through the righteousness of God and of our Saviour Jesus Christ: grace and peace be multiplied unto you, through the knowledge of God and of Jesus Christ our Lord, according as his divine power hath given unto us ALL THINGS THAT PERTAIN UNTO LIFE AND GODLINESS, through the knowledge of him that hath called us to glory and virtue." 2 *Pet.* i. 1, 2, 3.

And what says this holy man,—what says this same Peter, touching the subject of Dr. Paley's remarks?

"Servants, be subject to your masters with all fear; not only to the good and gentle, but also to the froward, * * * for hereunto were ye called." 1 *Pet.* ii. 18–21.

Permit us to inquire whether the language of Jesus Christ himself, of St. Paul and St. Peter, does not, in a strong degree, contradict the supposition of Dr. Paley? And let us inquire whether it is probable that a class of men, devoted to the promulgation of a doctrine which ran so counter to many of the civil institutions, customs, habits, and religions then in the world, as to have subjected them to death, would have secretly kept back a part of their creed, when, to have made it known, could not have increased their danger; and, especially, as by the creed itself, such keeping back would have insured to them the eternal punishment hereafter?

"Now we have received, not the spirit of the world, but the spirit which is of God: that we might know the things that are freely given to us of God; which things we also speak, not in the words which man's wisdom teacheth, but which the Holy Ghost teacheth." 1 *Cor.* ii. 12, 13. "And Jesus came and spake unto them, saying; all power is given unto me in heaven and in earth. Go ye, therefore, and teach all nations, baptizing them in the name of the Father, and of the Son, and of the Holy Ghost, teaching them to observe ALL THINGS whatsoever I have commanded you; and lo, I am with you alway, even unto the end of the world." *Matt.* xxviii. 18–20. "And now, O Father, glorify thou me, with thine own self, with the glory which I had with thee before the world was. I have manifested thy name unto the men which thou gavest me out of the world. Now they have known ALL THINGS whatsoever thou hast given me of thee: for I have given unto them the WORDS which thou gavest me, and they have received them, and have known surely that I came out from thee." *John* xvii. 5–8.

It is not possible that we could have had greater evidence that the whole counsel of God, illustrating the Christian duty, was delivered to the apostles, and through them, to the world. Besides, the very presumption of the incompleteness of the instruction undermines the divinity of the doctrine.

There is, perhaps, no one who does not feel pain, sometimes almost unspeakable, when we see a great man leaning upon the staff of error, especially when such error is palpable, gross, and calamitous in its tendency and effects.

But, cheering as the early ray of hope, and welcome as the rest-giving witness of a covenant, will be the proof that human weakness still had power to wade from out the miry labyrinth of error—to stand upon the rock from whence even human eyes might behold some few glimpses of the rising effulgence of truth.

We have some evidence that Dr. Paley did, at a later period of his life, adopt a more consistent view of the Christian Scriptures, touching the subject of this inquiry. In his "Horæ Paulinæ," a work of exceeding great merit, on the subject of Paul's letter to the Corinthian church, he enumerates and classifies the subjects of Paul's instruction, among which slavery is conspicuously mentioned, and then says—"That though they" (the subjects) "be exactly agreeable to the circumstances of the persons to whom the letter was written, nothing, I believe, but the existence and reality of the circumstances" (subjects) "could have suggested them to the writer's thought."

In all Christian love and charity, we are constrained to believe that he had discovered his error; and that, had his life been spared longer, he, with diligence and anxiety, would have expunged from his works charges so reflecting on himself, and contrary to the character of the God of our hope.

LESSON XIII.

SLAVERY existed in Britain when history commenced the records of that island. It was there found in a state and condition predicated upon the same causes by which its existence is now continued and perpetuated in Africa. But as early as the year 692–3 A. D., the Witna-Gemot, convoked by Ina, began to manifest a more elevated condition of the Britons. Without abolishing slavery, they regulated its government, ameliorated the old practice of death or slavery being the universal award of conquest; by submission and baptism the captive was acknowledged to merit some consideration; life, and, in some cases, property were protected against the rapacity of the conqueror; the child was secured against the mere avarice of the savage parent, and heavy punishment was announced against him who should sell his countryman, whether malefactor, slave, or not, to any foreign master.

He who has the curiosity to notice the steps by which the Britons emerged from savage life, in connection with their condition of slavery, may do well to examine the works of William of Malmsbury, Simeon of Durham, Bede, Alcuin, Wilkins, Huntingdon, Hoveden, Lingard, and Wilton. But he will not find the statutes of the monarchies succeeding Ina free from these enactments until he shall come down near the fourteenth century. Thus, generations passed away before these statutes came to be regarded with general respect. National regeneration has ever been thus slow. Thus, savage life has ever put to death the captive; while we find that slavery, among such tribes, has ever been introduced as a merciful provision in its stead, and is surely a proof of one step towards a more elevated state of moral improvement. But in the case of Britain and the whole of Europe, the slave was of the same original stock with the master; he, therefore, presented no physical impediment to amalgamation, by which has been brought about whatever of equality now exists among their descendants.

But in the close of this study, we propose to take some notice of the arguments of another most distinguished writer in favour of the abolition of slavery, as it now affects the African race.

In 1777, the celebrated Dr. Samuel Johnson wrote his argument in favour of the freedom of the negro slave who accompanied his master from Jamaica to Scotland, and who there brought suit in the Court of Sessions for his freedom. This argument has been deemed by so many to be unanswerable, and ever since that time so generally used as a *seed argument* in the propagation of abolition doctrines, that we feel it worthy of notice and examination.

Johnson was a bitter opponent of negro slavery; yet, strange, he ever advocated the justice of reducing the American colonies and the West India Islands to the most abject condition of political slavery to the British crown. This system is fully advocated, and garnished by his sarcasm and ridicule, in his famous work, entitled "Taxation no Tyranny." "How is it," says he, "that we hear the loudest yelps for liberty among the drivers of negroes."

Not long after he wrote *this* argument, on the occasion of a dinner-party at Dilly's, he said, "I am willing to love all mankind, *except an American;*" whereupon, adds his biographer, "he breathed out threatenings and slaughter, calling them rascals, robbers, pirates, and exclaiming, he'd burn and destroy them."

Some knowledge of a man's peculiar notions relevant to a subject will often aid the mind in a proper estimate of the value of his opinion and judgment concerning correlative matters. His biographer says—

"I record Dr. Johnson's argument fairly upon this particular case;" * * * "but I beg leave to enter my most solemn protest against his general doctrine with respect to the slave-trade; for I will most resolutely say that his unfavourable notion of it was owing to prejudice, and imperfect or false information. The wild and dangerous attempt, which has for some time been persisted in, to obtain an act of the legislature to abolish so very important and necessary a branch of commercial interest, must have been crushed at once, had not the insignificance of the zealots who vainly took the lead in it, made the vast body of the planters, merchants, and others, whose immense properties are involved in the trade, reasonably enough suppose that there would be no danger. The encouragement which the attempt has received excites my wonder and indignation; and though some men of superior abilities have supported it, whether from a love of temporary popularity when prosperous, or a love of general mischief when desperate, my opinion is unshaken. To abolish a *status*, which in all ages God has sanctioned and man has continued, would not only be robbery to an innumerable class of fellow-subjects, but it would be extreme cruelty to African savages, a portion of whom it saves from massacre or intolerable bondage in their own country, and introduces into a much happier state of life." *Boswell's Life of Johnson*, vol. ii. pp. 132, 133.

On the same page, the biographer adds—

"His violent prejudices against our West-Indian and American settlers, appeared whenever there was an opportunity." * * * "Upon an occasion, when in company with several very grave men at Oxford, his toast was: 'Here's to the next insurrection of the negroes in the West Indies!' I, with all due deference, thought that he discovered a zeal without knowledge."

This was surely bold in Boswell!

Since the culmination of the great British lexicographer, it has been unusual to hear a whisper in question of his high moral accuracy, of his singularly nice mental training, or the perspicuous and lofty display of these qualities in all his works. Even at this day, such a whisper may be proof of temerity. But truth is of higher import than the fear of individual rebuke, or of our literary faith that any one hero in the walks of erudition heretofore went down to the tomb without one mental or classical imperfection.

Argument in favour of a negro claiming his liberty, referred to in *Boswell's Life of Johnson*, p. 132.

"It must be agreed that in most ages many countries have had part of their inhabitants in a state of slavery; yet it may be doubted whether slavery can ever be supposed the natural condition of man. It is impossible not to conceive that men in their original state were equal; and very difficult to imagine how one would be subjected to another but by violent compulsion. An individual may, indeed, forfeit his liberty by a crime; but he cannot by that crime forfeit the liberty of his children. What is true of a criminal seems true likewise of a captive. A man may accept life from a conquering enemy on condition of perpetual servitude; but it is very doubtful whether he can entail that servitude on his descendants; for no man can stipulate without commission for another. The condition which he himself accepts, his son or grandson would have rejected. If we should admit, what perhaps may with more reason be denied, that there are certain relations between man and man which may make slavery necessary and just, yet it can never be proved that he who is now suing for his freedom ever stood in any of those relations. He is certainly subject by no law, but that of violence, to his present master, who pretends no claim to his obedience but that he bought him from a merchant of slaves, whose right to sell him never was examined. It is said that according to the constitutions of Jamaica he was legally enslaved; these constitutions are merely positive, and apparently injurious to the rights of mankind, because whoever is exposed to sale is condemned to slavery without appeal, by whatever fraud or violence he might have originally been brought into the merchant's power. In our own time, princes have been sold, by wretches to whose care they were intrusted, that they might have an European education; but when once they were brought to a market in the plantations, little would avail either their dignity or their wrongs. The laws of Jamaica afford a negro no redress. His colour is considered as a sufficient testimony against him. It is to be lamented that moral right should ever give way to political convenience. But if temptations of interest are sometimes too strong for human virtue, let us at least retain a virtue where there is no temptation to quit it. In the present case there is apparent right on one side, and no convenience on the other. Inhabitants of this island can neither gain riches nor power by taking away the liberty of any part of the human species. The sum of the argument is this: No man is by nature the property of another. The defendant is, therefore, by nature, free. The rights of nature must be some way forfeited before they can be justly taken away. That the defendant has, by any act, forfeited the rights of nature, we require to be proved; and if no proof of such forfeiture can be given, we doubt not but the justice of the court will declare him free."

The author of this production has artfully surrounded his subject with such a plausibility of concessive proposals, doubtful suggestions, indefinite words and propositions, as will require a sifting of his ideas into a more distinct view. And we fear some will find his argument thus vague and indeterminate; the mind will pass it by, as one of those learned masterpieces of logic, so distant from the eye of our common judgment, that they will sooner yield their assent than endure the labour of examination.

The first suggestion we would offer on the subject of this production is its total inapplicability to the case. The negro was held a slave in Jamaica. The inquiry was not, whether he was so held in obedience to the British law regulating the institution of slavery in Jamaica. The only question was, whether a slave in Jamaica, or elsewhere, who had by any means found his way into Scotland, was or was not free by operation of law. Not a word is directed to that point. And the court of session must have regarded its introduction before them as an argument in the case, as idle and as useless as would have been a page from his Rasselas. The British government established negro slavery by law in all her colonies, but made no provision by which the slave, when once found on the shores of England, could be taken thence again into slavery.

The object, no doubt, was wholly to prevent their introduction there, in favour to her own labouring poor. The British monarchy retained the whole subject of slavery under its own control. The colonies had no voice in the matter. They had no political right to say that the slave, thus imposed on them, should, after he had found his way into any part of the British Isles, be reclaimed, and their right of property in him restored. Their political condition differed widely from the condition of these United States at the formation of this republic.

They, as colonial dependants, had no power to dictate protection to their own rights, or to insist on a compromise of conflicting interests to be established by law.

Dr. Johnson's argument is exclusively directed against the political and moral propriety of the institution of slavery as a state or condition of man anywhere, instead of the true question at issue. The argument, taken as a whole, is, therefore, a sophism, of the order which dialecticians call "*ignoratio elenchi;*" a dodging of the question; a substitution of something for the question which is not; a practice common among the pert pleaders of the day—sometimes, doubtless, without their own perception of the fact. In regard to him who uses this sophism to effect the issue, the conclusion is inevitable,—he is either dishonest or he is ignorant of his subject. And when we come to examine this celebrated production as an argument against the moral propriety of the existence of the institution of slavery in the world, we shall find every pillar presented for its foundation a mere sophism, now quite distinctly, and again more feebly enunciated, as if with a more timid tongue, and left to inquiry, adorned by festoons of doubt and supposition.

We shall requote some portions, with a view to their more particular consideration. And, first, "Yet it may be doubted whether slavery can ever be supposed the natural condition of man." This clause, when put in the crucible, reads, "Yet slavery can never exist in conformity to the law of God." Whoever doubts this to be the sense, we ask him to suppose what the sense is! The author did not choose these few words to express the proposition, because the law of God *could* readily be produced in contradiction: "*Whosoever committeth sin is the servant* (δοῦλος, *doulos*, SLAVE) *of sin.*" Besides, then, he loses the benefit of the sophism,—the substitution of the condition of man in his fallen state, through the ambiguity of the word "natural," for the condition of the first man, fresh from the hand of the Creator. This sophism is one of great art and covertness; so much so, that it takes its character rather from its effect on the mind than from its language; and we therefore desire him who reads, to notice the whole chain of thought passing in the author's mind,—lest he forget how our present state is the subject of contemplation offered as data, when, on the word "natural," as if it were a potter's wheel, our *original condition* is turned to the front, a postulate, from which we are left to compare and conclude.

The doctrine of the Bible is, that slavery is the consequence of sin. If "natural" be taken to mean the quality of a state of perfect holiness and purity, then slavery cannot be the natural condition of man; no *doubts* are required in the case. But if "natural" is used to express the quality of our condition under sin, sinking us under the curse of the law, then the propriety of its use will not be "doubtful," when applied to slavery, because it is a consequent of the quality of the condition. "Cursed is every one that continueth not in all things which are written in the book of the law to do them." The proposition, as thus explained, we think of no value in the argument; but, as left by the author, obscure, its real meaning and intent not obviously perceived nor easily detected, and he may have thought it logical and sound.

"It is impossible not to conceive that men, in their original state, were equal."

Here is another sophism, which the learned call *petitio principii*, introduced without the least disguise,—the assumption of a proposition without proof, which, upon examination, is not true. If the author mean, by "original state," the state of man in paradise, we have no method of examining facts, except by a comparison of Adam with Eve, who was placed in subjection. And if we may be permitted to examine the state of holy beings more elevated than was man,—"For thou hast made him a little lower than the angels,"—then, by analogy, we shall find it possible to conceive that men, in the original state, were not equal, since even the angels, who do the commands of God, are described as those "that excel in strength."

But if Dr. Johnson mean the state of man after the fall, then Cain was told by God himself, that, if he did well, he should have rule over Abel.

"And very difficult to imagine how one would be subjected to another, but by violent compulsion." The object of this singular remark is to enforce the proposition, That slavery is incompatible with the law of God, which is not true.

"And if the servant shall plainly say, 'I love my master * * * I will not go out free:' then his master shall bring him * * * and he shall serve (be a slave to) him for ever."

But if it shall be said the value of the passage quoted resides in the term "violent compulsion;" that "violent compulsion," sufficient to make a man a slave, is incompatible with the law of God, then it will have no weight in the argument, because the "violent compulsion" used may be in conformity to the law of God. "And I will cause thee to serve (be a slave) to thine enemies in the land which thou knowest not."

"An individual may indeed forfeit his liberty by crime; but he cannot forfeit the liberty of his children."

This, as a proposition, presents a sophism of the order *non causa pro causa*, in reverse. We all agree a man may forfeit his liberty by crime; but how are we to deduce from this fact that the liberty of the child cannot be affected by the same crime? The truth is, the crime that deprives a parent of liberty, may, or may not, deprive the child. The framework of this sophism is quite subtle; it implies the sophism, "*a dicto secundum quid, ad dictum simpliciter*," to have full effect on the mind. Because, in truth, the crime that deprives the parent of liberty does not invariably involve the liberty of the child, we are, therefore, asked to assent to the proposition that it never does. But, perhaps, an analysis of the proposition before us may be more plain to some, when we remark, what is true in all such compound sophisms, that the proposition containing it is divisible into two distinct propositions.

In this case, the first one is true,—the second not. If, by crime, a man forfeits his life, he forfeits his liberty. If he is put to death previous to a condition of paternity, its prospect is cut off with him. Those beings who, otherwise, might have been his descendants, will never exist. Hence rude nations, from such analogy, in case of very high crimes, destroyed, with the parent, all his existing descendants. Ancient history is full of such examples. The principle is the same as the more modern attaint, and is founded, if in no higher law, in the common sense of mankind; for, when the statute establishing attaints is repealed, the public mind and the descendant both feel that the attaint essentially exists, even without law to enforce it. Who does not perceive that the descendants of certain traitors are effectually attainted at the present day, even among the most enlightened nations. He who denies that the crime of the parent can affect the liberty of the child, must also deny that the character of the parent can affect him; a fact that almost universally exists, and which every one knows.

"Let his children be continually vagabonds and beg; * * * let his posterity be cut off; * * * let the iniquities of his fathers be remembered with the Lord."

This doctrine was recognised and practised by the church, even in England, in the more early ages. Let one instance suffice. About the year 560, Mauricus, a Christian king of Wales, committed perjury and murdered Cynetus,—whereupon, Odouceus, Bishop of Llandaff, in full synod, pronounced excommunication, and cursed, for ever, him and all his offspring. See Milton's ΕΙΚΟΝΟΚΛΑΣΤΗΣ, cap. 28.

This principle actively exists in the physical world. The parent contracts some loathsome disease—the offspring are physically deteriorated thereby. He whose moral and physical degradation are such that slavery to him is a blessing, with few exceptions, will find his descendants fit only for that condition. The children of parents whose conduct in life fostered some mental peculiarity, are quite likely, with greater or less intensity, to exhibit traces of the same. "The parents have eaten sour grapes, and the children's teeth are set on edge." The law is not repealed by the mantle of love, which, in mercy, the Saviour has spread over the world, any more than forgiveness blots out the fact of a crime. The hope of happiness hereafter alleviates present suffering, but, in no sense, annihilates a cause which has previously existed.

"A man may accept life from a conquering enemy on condition of perpetual servitude; but it is very doubtful whether he can entail that servitude on his descendants; for no man can stipulate, without commission, for another."

All that is presented as argument here, is founded upon the proposition, that no man can stipulate for his descendants, whether unborn or not.

If what we have before said be true, little need be said on the subject of this paragraph. For we have already seen that the conduct of the ancestor, to an indefinite extent, both physically influences and morally binds the condition of the offspring. It is comparatively but a few ages since, over the entire world, the parent had full power, by law, to put his children to death for crime, or to sell them into slavery for causes of which he was the judge. And it may be remarked, that such is the present law among, perhaps, all the tribes who furnish from their own race slaves for the rest of the world. It is not necessary here to show why a people, who find such laws necessary to their welfare, also find slavery a blessing to them.

Civilization has ameliorated these, to us, harsh features of parental authority; yet, to-day, the world can scarcely produce a case where the condition of the child has not been greatly affected by the stipulations, the conduct, the influences of the parent, wholly beyond its control. The relation of parent has ever been found a sufficient commission to bind these results to the condition of the offspring.

"But our fathers dealt proudly, and hardened their necks, and hearkened not to thy commandments, and refused to obey; * * * and in their rebellion appointed a captain to return to their bondage."

"The condition which he (the captive) accepts, his son or grandson would have rejected."

This, at most, is supposititious, and, as an argument, we think, extremely weak; because it implies, either that the acceptance of the parent was not the result of necessity, and the wisest choice between evils, or that the rejection, by the son, was the fruit of extravagant pretension.

"He that is extravagant will quickly become poor, and poverty will enforce dependence and invite corruption." * * * "I have avoided that empyrical morality that cures one vice by the means of another." *Johnson's Rambler.*

"If we should admit, what perhaps with more reason may be denied, that there are certain relations between man and man, which may make slavery necessary and just, yet it can never be proved, that he, who is suing for his freedom, ever stood in any of these relations."

We cannot pretend to know what were the particular facts in relation to the slavery of the individual then in Scotland. It is not, however, pretended that the facts in relation to this slave were not the facts in relation to all others. No suggestion of any illegality as to his slavery in Jamaica is made, other than the broad ground of the illegality of slavery itself. This is quite evident from what follows:

"He is certainly subject, by no law but that of violence, to his present master, who pretends no claim to his obedience, but that he bought him from a merchant of slaves, whose right to sell him was never examined."

In the passage under consideration, we are confined wholly to negro slavery; and had Dr. Johnson been serious in admitting that slavery, under "certain relations," was "necessary and just," he would have yielded his case; because, then, the slave in hand would have been placed in the category of proving that he did not exist under these relations. Johnson well knew that slavery existed in Jamaica by the sanction of the British Parliament, and he manifests his contempt for it, by the assertion that the slave was held only by the law of force. He was, therefore, not reaching for the freedom of that particular slave, but for the subversion of slavery as a condition of man.

The author has heretofore signified a willingness to admit the lawfulness of slavery, when induced by "crime or captivity;" but now denies the validity of such admission, because the relations of "crime and captivity" can never be proved. The apparent object of his admission was merely to rally us, by his liberality, to the admission that these relations could never be proved; and we admit they never can be in the way he provides; and he therefore announces the demonstration of the proposition, that slavery can never be just, because "these relations," which alone make it so, can never be established. But what are the reasons? They are the very causes which render the Africans obnoxious to the condition of slavery—the degraded, deteriorated, and savage state of that people. The negro slave, in his transit from the interior of Africa, is often sold many times, by one master and chieftain to another, before he reaches the western coast, whence he was transferred by the slave factors to the English colonies. No memory of these facts, or of the slave's origin, is preserved or attempted. Under these circumstances, though each individual of these slaves induced the condition by "crime or captivity," such fact could never be established in the English colony. To attempt proof there of any fact touching the case, would be as idle and futile as to attempt such proof in regard to the biography of a baboon. Besides, the truth is, a very large portion of these slaves were born slaves in Africa, inheriting their condition from a slave ancestry of unknown ages, and recognised to be slaves by the laws and customs of the various tribes there, and sent to market as a surplus commodity, in accordance to the laws and usages among them, enforced from time immemorial.

So far as we have knowledge of the various families of man, we believe it to have ever been the practice for one nation to receive the national acts of another as facts fixed, and not subject to further investigation or alteration by a foreign people, especially when none but the people making the decision were affected by it. Johnson surely must have agreed to such a practice, because an opposite course, so far as carried into action, would have involved every nation in universal war and endless bloodshed. Besides, the right to usurp such control would involve the right to enslave, and can only exist when the degeneracy of a nation has become too great a nuisance to be longer tolerated with safety by the people annoyed: self-protection will then warrant the right.

If England makes it lawful for her subjects to buy slaves in Africa and hold them in Jamaica, then her subjects may lawfully hold there such as are decided by the laws of Africa to be slaves. But the author of the argument, with all this before him, having dictated what alone shall make a man a slave, would propose to set up a new tribunal contrary to all international law—contrary to the peace of the world—and, finally, as to the object to which it is to be applied, forever abortive: wherefore his argument in effect is, because "these relations," which he admits would justly make a man a slave, cannot be proved, therefore what he admits to be true is not true; and puts us in mind of the sophism: "If, when a man speaks truth, he says he lies, he lies; but he lies when he speaks the truth; therefore, by speaking the truth, he lies!" which we think about as relevant to the question.

In his conclusion, Dr. Johnson frankly acknowledges the position we have assigned him:—

"The sum of the argument is this: No man is, by nature, the property of another. The defendant, therefore, is free by nature. The rights of nature must be someway forfeited before they can be justly taken away."

There are, in our language, but few words of which we make such loose and indefinite use as we do of the word "nature," and its variously modified forms. It would elucidate what we wish to bring to mind concerning the use of this word, to select some verbose author, of a fanatical habit of thought, or enough so to favour a negligence as to the clearness of the ideas expressed by the terms at his command, and compare the varied meanings which his application of the word will most clearly indicate. We do not accuse Dr. Johnson of any want of astute learning, but we wish to present an excuse for explaining that, by his use of the phrases, "men by nature"—"by nature free"—"the rights of nature," he means, *the rights established by the laws of God.* He uses those phrases as synonyms of the Creator, of his providence influencing the condition of man, or the adaptations bestowed on him. The laws of nature are the laws of God. And we are bold to say, no discreet writer uses the words differently. As a sample of its legitimate use, we quote "Milton to Hortlib on Education:"—

"Not to mention the learned correspondence which you hold in foreign parts, and the extraordinary pains and diligence which you have used in this matter, both here and beyond the seas; either by the definite will of God so ruling, or the peculiar sway of *nature*, which also is God's working," &c.

We all agree that God has made the world, and all things therein, and that he established laws for its government, and also for the government of every thing in it. Now we must all agree that it was an act of great condescension, love, and mercy, if God did come down from his throne in heaven, and, from his own mouth instruct a few of the lost men then in the world, his chosen people, what were some of his laws, such as were necessary for them to know and to be governed by, that they might, to the greatest possible extent, live happily in this world, and enjoy eternal life hereafter. Do you believe he did so? You either believe he did, or you believe the Bible is a fable. If you believe he did, then we refer you to *Ex.* xx. and xxi., and to *Lev.* xxv., for what he did then reveal, as his law, on the subject of slavery; not that other important revelations were not made concerning this subject, which we shall have occasion to notice in the course of these studies.

If we believe the Bible to be a true book, then we must believe that God did make these revelations to Moses. Among them, one law permitted the Israelites to buy, and inherit, and to hold slaves. And Dr. Wayland, the author of "The Elements of Moral Science," agrees that what was the law of God must ever remain to be so.

It will follow then, if the laws of God authorize slavery, that a man *by nature may be the property of another*, because, whatever you may think the laws of nature to be, yet they can have no validity in opposition to the laws of God. If it shall be said that Jesus Christ repealed the law as delivered to Moses, then we answer: He says he came not to destroy, but to fulfil the law; and that he fully completed his mission. He had no commission to repeal the law: therefore he had no power to do so.

This portion of Dr. Johnson's argument is consonant with the notions of the advocates of the "higher law" doctrine, who persist that slavery is a sin, because they think it is.

But if the law permitted slavery, then to hold, cannot be a sin, because God "frameth not mischief by a law." See *Ps.* xciv. 20. "Wo unto them that decree unrighteous decrees." *Isa.* x. 1. If the law authorizing the Jews to hold slaves was unrighteous, then God pronounces the wo upon himself, which is gross contradiction.

But the law is "pure, holy, and just;" therefore a law permitting sin must be against itself—which cannot be; for, in such case, the law recoils against itself, and destroys its own end and character.

But again: "The end of the commandment is charity out of a pure heart, and of a good conscience, and faith unfeigned." 1 *Tim.* i. 5. Now it is not charity to permit that which cannot be done with a pure heart, because then conscience and faith are both deceived.

Again: The law "beareth not the sword in vain, but to be a terror to evil works, for he (the instrument executing the law) is the minister of God, a revenger to execute wrath upon him that doeth evil."

If slavery, or to hold slaves, be sin, then also the law granting the license to do so destroys the very object which it was enacted to sustain. But again: If the law allows sin, then it is in covenant with sin; and the law itself, therefore, must be sin.

In short, the doctrine is pure infidelity. It is destructive to the object of law, and blasphemous to God. What are we to think of him who holds that God descended in the majesty of his power upon *Sinai*, and there, from the bottomless treasures of his wisdom and purity, commanding man to wash his garment of every pollution, opened to him—what? Why, an unclean system of morals, stained by a most unholy impurity; but which he is nevertheless to practise to the damning of his soul! Atheism, thou art indeed a maniac!

In the course of these studies, we shall attempt to show that man is not free in the unlimited sense with which the word is here used. Absolute freedom is incompatible with a state of accountability. Say, if you choose, Adam was free in paradise to eat the apple, to commit sin, yet we find his freedom was bounded by an accountability beyond his power to give satisfactory answer: hence the consequent, a change of state, a circumscribing of what you may call his freedom. This, in common parlance, we call punishment; yet our idea of punishment is inadequate to express the full idea; because God cannot be supposed to delight in punishment, or to be satisfied with punishment, in accordance with our narrow views. Such would be inconsistent with the combination of his attributes —a Being so constituted of all power, that each power is predominant, even love and mercy. Thus the law of God clothes the effect in mercy and positive good, inversely to the virulence of the cause, or in direct proportion to its propriety. Thus, righteousness, as a cause, exalteth a nation; but sin is a reproach to any people. Thus the law of God places the sinner under the government of shame, infamy, contempt, as schoolmasters to lead him back to virtue; and it may be observed that the schoolmaster is more forcing in his government in proportion to the virulence of vice, down to the various grades of subjection and slavery, and until the poison becomes so great that even death is a blessing.

But if the mind cannot perceive that the chastenings of the Lord are blessings, let it regard them as lessons. The parent, from the waywardness of the child, perceives that it will fall from a precipice, and binds it with a cord to circumscribe its walk. True, such are poor figures to outline a higher Providence!

The Being who created, surely had power to appoint the government. Can the thing created remain in the condition in which it is placed, except by obedience to the law established for its government? Disobedience must change the condition of the thing and bring it under new restraints—a lessening of the boundaries of freedom. The whole providence of God to man is upon this plan, and is abundantly illustrated, in the holy books, by precept and example. These restraints follow quick on the footsteps of disobedience, until the law—the Spirit shall no longer strive for reformation, but say, "Cut it down; why cumbereth it the ground?"

Is this a too melancholy view? Let us, then, look at obedience and its consequents, and turn the eye from this downward path of mental and physical degradation, pain, misery, want, slavery, and death, to the bright prospect of a more elevated state of progressive improvement, secured to us as a consequent, a reward of obedience; the physical powers improving, the mental elevating, and all our faculties becoming instruments of greater truthfulness, until our condition shall be so elevated that the Creator shall say, "Come ye and sit at my right hand!"

The assertion, that "no man is by nature the property of another," flatters our vanity and tumefies our pride, but is, nevertheless, untrue. We are all absolutely the property of Him who made, and who sustains his right to dispose of us; and does so in conformity to his law. Thus, qualifiedly, we are the property of the great family of man, and are under obligations of duty to all; more pressingly to the national community of which we compose a part, and so on down to the distinct family of which we are a member. It is upon this principle that Fleta says, (book i, chap. 17,) "He that has a companion has a master." See also the same in Bracton, book i. chap. 16.

If, by the laws of God, other men could have no property in us, the laws of civil government could have no right to control us. But if the civil government, by the laws of God, has the right to govern and control us, so far as is for the benefit of ourselves and the community, then it will follow, that when our benefit will be enhanced, and that of the community, by our subjection to slavery, either temporary or perpetual, the laws of God, in mercy, will authorize such subjection. Or, if the state of our degradation be such that our continuance upon the earth be an evil past all remedy, then the laws of God will authorize the civil law to decree our exit.

The providence of God to man is practical. He never deals in the silly abstractions of foolish philosophers. He spends no time in experimenting by eristic syllogisms. He deals alone in his own power, which nowhere ever ceases to act, although wholly beyond our comprehension. Man may long for a full view of the Almighty, yet we are destined here to perceive but the "hinder parts" of his presence—the effect of his power, not Him! Let us worship; and, for our guidance, be content with the pillar of cloud by day and of fire by night!

In conclusion: Should the author of "The Elements of Moral Science" examine this argument of the great dialectician of the past century, with his acknowledged logical acumen, free from the prejudices of his locality, now so abundantly displayed in that portion of his work to which we object, we would suggest the propriety of his applying the discoveries he may make to emendations in his succeeding thousands.

Study II.

LESSON I.

As far as men are able to comprehend Jehovah, the wisest, in all ages, have deduced the fact, that God acts; yet, as an essential Being, he is beyond being acted upon.

That which is manifested by the character of his acts is called his attributes; that is, the thing or quality which we attribute to him as a portion or quality of his essence.

Thus among his attributes, are said to be power, wisdom, truth, justice, love, and mercy. His action is always found to be in conformity and accordance to these attributes. This state of conformity, this certainty of unison of action, is called truth. "Thy word is truth." *John* xvii. 7.

A system of laws, permanently established for the production of some object, we call an institution.

Law is the history of how things are influenced by one another; yet the mind should never disconnect such influence from the attributes of Jehovah; and hence Burke very properly says, "Law is beneficence acting by rule." "The law of the Lord is perfect." *Ps.* xix. 7. The deduction follows that the laws of God are well adapted, and intended to benefit all those who are suitably related under them.

By relation we mean the connection between things,—what one thing is in regard to the influence of another. And hence it also follows that, in case the relation is in utter want of a conformity to the attributes of Jehovah, the actor in the relation becomes an opponent, and, so far, joins issue with God himself. The laws fitting the case operate, and his position is consumed, as it were, by the breath of the Almighty.

But yet an institution may be a righteous one, may exist in

conformity to the laws of God, and particular cases of a relation, seeming to us to emanate from it, be quite the reverse. For example, the institution of marriage may be righteous, may exist in conformity to the laws of God; yet cases of the relation of husband and wife may be a very wicked relation.

Individuals in a relation to each other under an institution are supposed to bear such comparison to each other as will permit the laws of God, influencing the relation, to be beneficial to them; and when such comparative qualities are not the most suitable, or are more or less unsuitable for the relation, the benefits intended by the relation must be proportionably diminished. If wholly unsuitable, then it is found that the conservative influences of the same laws operate in the direction to cause the relation to cease between them.

If a supposed male and female are each distinctly clothed with qualities wholly unsuited to each other in the relation emanating from the institution of marriage, then, in that case, the relation will be sinful between them; and the repulsion, the necessary consequence of a total unsuitableness, will be in constant action in the direction of sweeping it away.

Will it be new in morals to say that it is consistent with the ordinances of Jehovah to bring things into that relation to each other by which they will be mutually benefited?

As an exemplification of the doctrine, we cite the institution of guardianship—guardian and ward; both words derived from the same Saxon root, *weardian*, which implies one who protects and one who is protected.

The institution itself presupposes power in the one and weakness in the other, a want of equality between the parties. And it may be here remarked, that, the greater the inequality, the greater the prospect of benefit growing out of the relation, especially to the weaker party. But when the weak, ignorant, or wayward youth is the guardian, and the powerful and wise man is the ward, then the relation will be sinful, and the repulsion necessarily emanating from the relation must quickly terminate it. No possible benefit could accrue from such a case—nothing but evil. The conservative influence of God's providence must, therefore, suddenly bring it to a close.

Will the assertion be odious to the ear of truth, that the laws of God present the same class of conservative influences in the moral world that is every day discovered in the physical?—that the thing manifestly useless, from which no benefit can accrue, but from which a constant injury emanates, shall be cut away, nor longer "cumber the ground?" Or, where a less degree of enormity and sin have centered, it may be placed under influences of guidance, and controlled into the path of regeneration and comparative usefulness? Surely, if we detach from Jehovah these high attributes, we lessen his character.

When we enter into the inquiry, whether an institution, or the relation emanating from it in a particular case, be sinful or not, it seems obvious that the inquiry must reach the object of the institution and its tendencies, and take into consideration how far they, and the relations created by it, coincide with the laws of God.

The relation of master and slave, and the institution of slavery itself, in the inquiry whether such relation or institution is right or wrong, just or unjust, righteous or sinful, must be subjected to a like examination,—applying the same rules applicable to any other relation or institution,—before we can determine whether or not it exists in conformity to the laws of God.

But human reason is truly but of small compass; and the mercy of God has vouchsafed to man the aids of faith and inspiration. "All scripture is given by inspiration of God." 2 *Tim.* iii. 16.

These are important aids in the examination of all moral subjects, without which we may be "ever learning and never able to come to the knowledge of the truth." 2 *Tim.* iii. 7.

LESSON II.

If it be true that slavery is of divine origin, that its design is to prevent so great an accumulation of sin as would, of necessity, force its subjects down to destruction and death, and to restore those who are ignorantly, heedlessly, and habitually rushing on their own moral and physical ruin, by the renovating influence of divine power, to such a state of moral rectitude as may be required of the recipients of divine grace;—then we should expect to find, in the history of this institution, of its effects, both moral and physical, upon its subjects, some manifestations of such tendencies; some general evidences that, through this ordinance, God has ever blessed its subjects and their posterity with an ameliorated condition, progressive in the direction of his great and final purpose. Let us examine that fact.

In the government of the world, God has as unchangeably fixed his laws producing moral influences, as he has those which relate to material objects. When we discover some cause, which, under similar circumstances, always produces a similar result, we need not hesitate to consider such discovery as the revelation of his will, his law touching its action and the effects produced; and by comparing the general tendency of the effect produced with the previously revealed laws and will of God in relation to a particular matter, we are permitted to form some conclusion whether the cause producing the effect exists and acts in conformity with his general providence towards the matter or subject in question. If so, we may readily conclude that such cause is of his appointment, and that it exists and acts agreeably to his will.

But one of the previously revealed laws of God is, that he ever wills the happiness, not the misery, of his creatures. "Say unto them, As I live, saith the Lord God, I have no pleasure in the death of the wicked; but that the wicked should turn from his way and live: turn ye, turn ye from your evil ways, for why will you die, O house of Israel!" *Ezek.* xxxiii. 11. And we may form some conclusion of a man, a class of people, or a nation, from their condition produced by the general result of their conduct, whether their conduct has been in general conformity with the laws of God. If the general result of the conduct of the thief, gambler, tippler, and drunkard,—of him who lives by trickery and deception, is an accumulation of weight of character among men, a display of useful industry, independence, and wealth among his associates; if himself and family are thereby made visibly more healthy, happy, and wise,—if by these practices he and his family become patterns of piety and of all noble virtues, he may hope; but if the contrary of all these is the final result, we may safely condemn.

Another of the laws of God is, "Thine own wickedness shall correct thee, and thy backslidings shall reprove thee." *Jer.* ii. 19. When the characters just named become so great a nuisance that the strong arm of the law of the land takes away their liberty, places a master over them, in fact reducing them to slavery; forces and compels them to habits of useful industry, and, in a length of time, makes of them useful and good men,—then this law is exemplified; and also the fact is proved, that slavery, thus induced, is attended with and does produce an ameliorated condition as to the morals, and probably as to the intellectual and physical power, of its subjects. This law was also exemplified in the family of Jacob. God, in the order of his providence, had determined and made a covenant with Abraham, to wit: "In the same day the Lord made a covenant with Abram, saying, Unto thy seed have I given this land, from the land of Egypt unto the great river, the river Euphrates." *Gen.* xv. 18. This was to be brought about through the family of Jacob. "And God Almighty bless thee, and make thee fruitful and multiply thee, that thou mayest be a multitude of people, and give the blessing of Abraham to thee, and to thy seed with thee, that thou mayest inherit the land wherein thou art a stranger, which God gave unto Abraham." *Gen.* xxviii. 3, 4.

There are left us enough traces of the conduct of the family of Jacob, whereby we may know the fact that they, although living in the midst of the promised land, had become incorrigibly wicked and licentious. Judah, who seems to have ranked as the head of the family, notwithstanding the impressive lesson in the case of Esau, took to himself a Canaanitish wife, and his eldest sons became so desperately wicked that, in the language of Scripture, God slew them. Even the salt of slavery could not save them. Of Shelah, we have no further account than that he went into slavery in Egypt. Instead of nurturing up his family with propriety and prudence, Judah seems to have idled away his time with his friend the Adullamite, hunting up the harlots of the country. Reuben committed incest; he went up to his father's bed. Simeon and Levi, instigated by feelings of revenge in the case of the Hivites, pursued such a course of deception, moral fraud, and murder, leading on the rest of their brethren to such acts of theft and robbery, that Jacob was constrained to say, "Ye have troubled me, to make me stink among the inhabitants of the land." *Gen.* xxxiv. 30. Jacob found his children so lost to good morals, so sunken in heathenism and idolatry, that, hoping that a change of abode might also produce a change of conduct, he was impelled to command them, saying, "Put away the strange gods that are among you, and be clean, and change your garments, and let us arise and go to Bethel, and I will make there an altar unto God." *Gen.* xxxv. 2, 3.

And let us take occasion here to notice the long-suffering and loving-kindness of the Lord; for, no sooner had they taken this resolution, than Jehovah, to encourage and make them steadfast in this new attempt in the paths of virtue, again appeared to Jacob:

"And God said unto him, I am God Almighty; a nation, and a company of nations shall be of thee, and kings shall come out of thy loins. And the land which I gave to Abraham and to Isaac, to thee I will give it, and to thy seed after thee will I give the land." *Gen.* xxxv. 11, 12.

"But the sow that was washed has returned to her wallowing in the mire." 2 *Pet.* ii. 22.

And what is the next prominent state of moral standing in which we find this family? The young and unsuspecting Joseph brought unto his father their evil report, and hence their revenge. "And when they saw him afar off, even before he came near unto them, they conspired against him to slay him. * * * And they sold Joseph to the Ishmaelites for twenty pieces of silver." *Gen.* xxxvii. 2, and xviii. 28. And against the deed of fratricide there was but one dissenting voice; and he, whose voice it was, dared not boldly to oppose them. He had not the moral courage to contend. Sometimes, in the conduct of men, there may be a single act that gives stronger proof of deep, condemning depravity, than a whole life otherwise spent in wanton, wilful wickedness and sensual sin. Their betrayal of the confidence of an innocent and confiding brother, who neither had the will nor the power to injure them, whose only wish was their welfare, bespeaks a degradation of guilt, a deep and abiding hypocrisy of soul before God and man, and a general readiness to the commission of crimes of so dark a dye, that, it would seem to moral view, no oblations of the good, nor even the prayers of the just, could wash and wipe away the stain. During the history of all time, has God ever chosen such wretches to become the founders of an empire—his own peculiar, chosen people? On the contrary, has not his will, as expressed by revelation, and by the acts of his providence, for ever been the reverse of such a supposition? The laws of God are unchangeable: at all times and among all people, the premises being the same, their operation has been and will ever be the same.

LESSON III.

"Let favour be showed to the wicked, yet will he not learn righteousness; in the land of uprightness will he deal unjustly, and will not behold the majesty of the Lord." *Isa.* xxvi. 10.

"His own iniquities shall take the wicked himself, and he shall be holden by the cords of his sins." *Prov.* v. 22.

"But it shall come to pass, if thou wilt not hearken unto the voice of the Lord thy God, to observe to do all his commandments, and his statutes, which I command thee this day; that all these curses shall come upon thee, and overtake thee:

"Cursed shalt thou be in the city, and cursed shalt thou be in the field; cursed shalt thou be in thy basket and thy store; cursed shall be the fruit of thy body and the fruit of thy land; the increase of thy loins, and the flocks of thy sheep. Cursed shalt thou be when thou comest in; and cursed shalt thou be when thou goest out. The Lord shall send upon thee cursing, vexation and rebuke in all thou settest thy hand unto for to do, until thou be destroyed, and until thou perish quickly; because of the wickedness of thy doings, whereby thou hast forsaken me. And the Lord shall bring thee into Egypt again with ships, the way whereof I spake unto thee. Thou shalt see it no more again; and there ye shall be sold unto your enemies for bondmen (לַעֲבָדִים *la ebedim, for slaves*) and bondwomen (וְלִשְׁפָחוֹת *ve lisheppahoth, and for female slaves*), and no man shall buy you." (That is, they should be worthless.) *Deut.* xxviii. 15–68.

Such, then, are the unchangeable laws of God touching man's disobedience and non-conformity; and, in this instance of their application, have been seen fulfilled, with wonder and astonishment, by the whole world.

Consistent with the laws of God and the providence of Jehovah, there was no other way to make any thing out of the wicked family of Jacob; no other means to fulfil his promise to Abraham, Isaac, and Jacob, except to prepare them in the school of adversity; to reduce them under the severe hand of a master; to place them in slavery, until, by its compulsive operation tending to their mental, moral, and physical improvement, they would become fitted to enjoy the blessing promised their fathers. "Compel them to come in, that my house may be filled." *Luke* xiv.

"And when the sun was going down a deep sleep fell upon Abraham, and a horror of great darkness fell upon him; and He (the Lord) said unto Abram, Know of a surety that thy seed shall be a stranger in a strange land that is not theirs, and shall *serve* (וַעֲבָדוּם *va ebadum, shall be slaves to*) them; and they shall afflict them four hundred years." *Gen.* xv. 12, 13.

God foresaw what condition the wicked family of Jacob would force themselves into; nor is it a matter of surprise that it filled the mind of Abram with horror.

God never acts contrary to his own laws. The Israelites, in slavery four hundred years under hard and cruel masters, kept closely bound to severe labour, and all the attendants of slavery, had no time to run into deeper sins. The humility of their condition and distinction of race would be some preventive to amalgamation, and a preservative to their purity of blood; and would lead them also to contemplate and worship the God of Abraham. And let it ever be remembered that the worship of God is the very highway to intellectual, moral, and physical improvement, however slow, under the circumstances, was their progress.

Let us take the family of Jacob, at the time of the selling of Joseph, and, from what their conduct had been and then was, form some conjecture of what would have been the providence of God, touching their race, at the close of the then coming four hundred years, had not the Divine Mind seen fit to send them into slavery. Does it require much intellectual labour to set forth their ultimate condition? Would not the result have been their total annihilation by the action of the surrounding tribes; or their equally certain national extinction by their amalgamation with them? If, by the providence of God, as manifested among men through all time, one of these conditions must have attached to them, then will it follow that, to them, slavery was their salvation,—under the circumstances of the case, the only thing that could preserve them from death and extinction on earth.

Under such view of the facts, and the salvatory influence of the institution, slavery will be hailed by the good, pious, and godly-minded, as an emanation from the Divine Mind, portraying a fatherly care, and a watchful mercy to a fallen world, on a parallel with the general benevolence of that Deity who comprehended his own work, and the welfare of his creatures.

The slavery of the Israelites in Egypt for the term of four hundred years was a sentence pronounced against them by Jehovah himself, who had previously promised them great worldly blessings, preceded by the promise of his own spiritual forbearance, of his own holy mercy, as the ultimate design of his providence towards them. And we now ask him, who denies that the design of this term of slavery was to ameliorate and suitably prepare that wicked race for the reception and enjoyment of the promises made, to extricate himself from the difficulties in which such denial will involve the subject. We are aware that there are a class of men so holy in their own sight, that, from what they say, one might judge they felt capable of dictating to Jehovah rules for his conduct, and that they spurn in him all that which their view does not comprehend. Do such forget, when they stretch forth their hand, imagining God to be that which suits them, but which he is not, that they make an idol, and are as much idolaters as they would be had they substituted wood and stone? Such, God will judge. We have no hope our feeble voice will be heard where the mind is thus established upon the presumption of moral purity—we might say divine foresight. But, by a more humble class, we claim to be heard, that, as mortal men, reasoning by the light it hath pleased God to give, we may take counsel together in the review of his providences, as vouchsafed to man, and, by his blessing be enabled to see enough to justify the ways of the Almighty against the slanders of his and our enemy.

The theological student will notice the fact of the holy books abounding with the doctrine that the chastenings of the Lord operate the moral, mental, and physical improvement of the chastised; and that such chastenings are ever administered for that purpose, and upon those whose sins call it down upon them. "My son, despise not the chastenings of the Lord; neither be weary of correction: for those whom the Lord loveth he correcteth; even as a father the son in whom he delighteth." *Prov.* iii. 11, 12. "Thus saith the Lord, where is the bill of thy mother's divorcement, whom I have put away? Or which of my creditors is it to whom I have sold you? Behold, for your iniquities have ye sold yourselves, and for your transgressions is your mother put away." *Isa.* l. 1.

The garden of the sluggard produces weeds and want. We know a man of whom it may be said, he is inoffensive; but he is thriftless, indolent, and therefore miserable. He has never learned those virtues that would make him respectable or happy.

LESSON IV.

"*Barnes on Slavery. An Inquiry into the Scriptural Views of Slavery.*" By ALBERT BARNES. *Philadelphia*, 1846.

IN his fourth chapter, on the slavery of the Israelites in Egypt, Rev. Mr. Barnes says—

"The will of God may often be learned from the events of his providence. From his dealings with an individual, a class of men or a nation, we may ascertain whether the course which has been pursued was agreeable to his will. It is not, indeed, always safe to argue that, because calamities come upon an individual, they are sent as a punishment on account of any peculiarly aggravated sin, or that these calamities prove that he is a greater sinner than others;—but when a certain course of conduct *always* tends to certain results—when there are laws in operation in the moral world as fixed as in the natural world—and when there are, uniformly, either direct or indirect interpositions of Providence in regard to any existing institutions, it is not unsafe to infer from these what is the Divine will. It is not unsafe, for illustration, to argue, from the uniform effects of intemperance, in regard to the will of God. These effects occur in every age of the world, in reference to every class of men. There are no exceptions in favour of kings or philosophers; of the inhabitants of any particular climate or region of country; of either sex, or of any age. The poverty and babbling, and redness of eyes, and disease, engendered by intemperance, may be regarded without danger of error, as expressive of the will of God in reference to that habit. They show that there has been a violation of a great law of our nature, ordained for our good, and that such a violation must always incur the frown of the great Governor of the world. The revelation of the mind of God, in such a case, is not less clear than were the annunciations of his will on Sinai.

"The same is true in regard to cities and nations. We need be in as little danger, in general, in arguing from what occurs to them, as in the case of an individual. There is now no doubt among men why the old world was destroyed by a flood; why Sodom and Gomorrah were consumed; why Tyre, Nineveh, Babylon, and Jerusalem were overthrown. If a certain course of conduct, long pursued and in a great variety of circumstances, leads uniformly to health, happiness, and property, we are in little danger of inferring that it is in accordance with the will of God. If it lead to poverty and tears, we are in as little danger of error in inferring that it is a violation of some great law which God has ordained for the good of man. If an institution among men is always followed by certain results; if we find them in all climes, and under all forms of government, and in every stage of society, it is not unsafe to draw an inference from these facts on the question whether God regards the institution as a good one, and one which he designs shall be perpetuated for the good of society.

"It would be easy to make an application of these undeniable principles to the subject of slavery. The inquiry would be, whether, in certain results, always found to accompany slavery, and now developing themselves in our own country, there are no clear indications of what is the will of God."

We subscribe to the doctrine that God often reveals his will concerning a thing by the acts of his providence affecting it. But we contend that God has extended the field of Christian vision by a more direct revelation, and by the gift of faith; and that the mind which can neither hear the revelation, nor feel the faith, is merely the mind of a philosopher, not of a Christian: he may be a believer in a God, but not in the Saviour of the world.

The direction contained in the foregoing quotation, by which we are to discriminate what are the will and law of God, may be considered, when presented by the mere teacher of abolition, among the most artful, because among the most insidious, specimens of abolition logic. It is artful, because, to the unschooled, it presents all that may seem necessary in the foundation of a sound system of theology; and, further, because every bias of the human heart is predisposed to receive it as an entire platform of doctrine. It is insidious and dangerous, because, although the mind acquiesces in its *truth*, yet it is *false* when proposed as the lone and full foundation of religious belief. On such secret and hidden rocks, infidelity has ever established her *lights*, her *beacons* to the benighted voyager; and, in their surrounding seas, the shallops of hell have for ever been the most successful wreckers, in gathering up multitudes of the lost, to be established as faithful subjects of the kingdom of darkness.

The religious fanatical theorists of this order of abolition writers have further only to establish their doctrine about the "conscience," "inward light," or "moral sense,"—that it is a distinct mental power, infallibly teaching what is right, intuitively spreading all truth before them,—and they will then succeed to qualify man, a being fit to govern the universe, and successfully carry on a war against God!

The man thus prepared, if an abolitionist, reasons: "My conscience or moral sense teaches me infallible truth; therefore, my conscience is above all law, or is a 'higher law' than the law of the land. My conscience, feelings, and sympathies all teach me that slavery is wrong. Thus I have been educated. My conscience or moral sense teaches me what are the laws of God, without *possible mistake;* and according to their teaching, slavery is forbidden."

In short, he thinks so; and, therefore, it is so. He "is wiser in his own conceit than seven men that can render a reason."

But we proceed to notice how the doctrine of the author most distinctly agrees with the precepts of infidelity.

"The deist derives his religion by inference from what he supposes discoverable of the will and attributes of God, from nature, and the course of the Divine government." *Watson's Theo. Inst.* vol. ii. p. 542. This learned theologian differs widely from Mr. Barnes. When treating of slavery, Watson frankly admits that we are indebted to direct revelation for our knowledge on the subject.

In page 556, he says—

"Government in masters, as well as in fathers, is an appointment of God, though differing in circumstances; and it is therefore to be honoured. 'Let as many servants as are under the yoke, count their own masters worthy of all honour;' a direction which enjoins both respectful thoughts and humility and propriety of external demeanour towards them. *Obedience* to their commands in all things lawful is next enforced; which obedience is to be grounded on principle, on 'singleness of heart as unto Christ;' thus serving a master with the same sincerity, the same desire to do the appointed work well, as is required of us by Christ. This service is also to be *cheerful*, and not wrung out merely by a sense of duty; 'not with eye-service as men-pleasers;' not having respect simply to the approbation of the master, but 'as the servant of Christ,' making profession of his religion, 'doing the will of God,' in this branch of duty, 'from the heart,' with alacrity and good feeling. The duties of servants, stated in these brief precepts, might easily be shown to comprehend every particular which can be justly required of persons in this station; and the whole is enforced by a sanction which could have no place but in a revelation from God,—'Knowing that whatsoever good thing any man doeth, the same shall he receive of the Lord, whether he be bond or free.' *Eph.* vi. 5. In other words, even the common duties of servants, when faithfully, cheerfully, and piously performed, are by Christianity made rewardable actions: 'Of the Lord ye shall receive a reward.'

"The duties of servants and masters are, however, strictly reciprocal. Hence, the apostle continues his injunctions as to the right discharge of these relations, by saying, immediately after he had prescribed the conduct of servants, 'And ye masters, do the *same things* unto them; that is, act towards them upon the same equitable, conscientious, and benevolent principles as you exact from them. He then grounds his rules, as to masters, upon the great and influential principle, 'knowing that your Master is in heaven;' that you are under authority, and are accountable to him for your conduct to your servants. Thus masters are put under the eye of God, who not only maintains their authority, when properly exercised, by making their servants accountable for any contempt of it, and for every other failure of duty, but holds the master also himself responsible for its just and mild exercise. A solemn and religious aspect is thus at once given to a relation which by many is considered as one merely of interest."

"All the distinctions of good and evil refer to some principle above ourselves; for, were there no Supreme Governor and Judge to reward and punish, the very notions of good and evil would vanish away." *Ellis on Divine Things.*

The qualities good and evil can only exist in the mind as they are measured by a supreme law. "If we deny the existence of a Divine law obligatory on men, we must deny that the world is under Divine government, for a government without rule or law is a solecism." *Watson's Theo. Inst.* vol. i. p. 8.

Divine laws must be the subject of revelation. The law of a visible power cannot be known without some indications, much less the will of an invisible power, and that, too, of an order of existence so far above our own that even its mode is beyond our comprehension. Very true, the providence of God towards any particular course of conduct may be taken as the revelation of his will thus far, but, by no means, preclude the necessity of a more direct revelation, until man shall be able to boast that he comprehends the entire works of Jehovah.

The difference between the Christian and the mere theist is, while the latter admits that a revelation of the will of God is or has been made by significant actions, he contends *that* is a *sufficient revelation* of the laws of God for the guidance of man. "They who never heard of any external revelation, yet if they knew from the nature of things what is fit for them to do, they know all that God can or will require of them." *Christianity as Old as Creation*, p. 233.

"By employing our reason to collect the will of God from the fund of our nature, physical and moral, we may acquire not only a particular knowledge of those laws, which are deducible from them, but a general knowledge of the manner in which God is pleased to exercise his supreme powers in this system." *Bolingbroke's Works*, vol. v. p. 100.

"But they who believe the holy Scriptures contain a revelation of God's will, do not deny that indications of his will have been made by *actions;* but they contend that they are in themselves imperfect and insufficient, and that they were not designed to supersede a direct revelation. They also hold, that a direct communication of the Divine will was made to the progenitors of the human race, which received additions at subsequent periods, and that the whole was at length embraced in the book called, by way of eminence, the Bible." *Watson's Theo. Inst.* vol. i. p. 10.

Faith "is the substance of things hoped for, the evidence of things not seen." *Heb.* xi. 1.

As an instance of revelation, we present *Lev.* xxv. 1, and 44, 45, 46.

"And the Lord spake unto Moses in Mount Sinai, saying: Both thy bondmen and bondmaids, which thou shalt have, shall be of the heathen that are round about you; of them shall ye buy bondmen and bondmaids."

"Moreover, of the children of the strangers that do sojourn among you, of them shall ye buy, and of their families that are with you, which they begat in your land: and they shall be your possession."

"And ye shall take them as an inheritance for your children after you, to inherit them for a possession, they shall be your bondmen for ever; but over your brethren, the children of Israel, ye shall not rule over one another with rigour."

Here is direct revelation, and faith gives us evidence of the truth of its being of Divine origin.

Mr. Barnes proposes, by human reason, without the aid of revelation and faith, to determine what is the will of God on the subject of slavery; and it suggests the inquiry, How extensive must be the intellectual power of him who can reason with God? "For he is not a man, as I am, that I should answer him, and we should come together in judgment; neither is any daysman betwixt us, that might lay his hand upon us both." *Job* ix. 32, 33.

We frankly acknowledge, that, in the investigation of this subject, we shall consider the Divine authority of those writings, which are received by Christians as a revelation of infallible truth, as so established; and, with all simplicity of mind, examine their contents, and collect from them the information they profess to contain, and concerning which information it had become necessary that the world should be experimentally instructed.

But the passage quoted from Mr. Barnes gives us a stronger suspicion of his want of orthodoxy and Christian principle from its connection with what he says, page 310:

"If the religion of Christ allows such a license" (to hold slaves) "from such precepts as these, the New Testament would be the greatest curse ever inflicted on our race."

The fact is, little can be known of God or his law except by faith and revelation. Beings whose mental powers are not infinite can never arrive at a knowledge of all things, nor can we know any thing fully, only in proportion as we comprehend the laws influencing it. In conformity to the present limited state of our knowledge, we can only say, that we arrive at some little, by three distinct means: the senses open the door to a superficial perception of things; the mental powers to their further examination; while faith gives us a view of the superintending control of One Almighty God.

In the proportion our senses are defective, our mental powers deficient, and our faith inactive or awry,—our knowledge will be scanty. The result of all knowledge is the perception of truth. Under the head of the mental powers, philosophers tell us our knowledge is acquired by three methods: intuition, demonstration, and analogy. By intuition they mean when the mind perceives a *certainty* in a proposition where the relation is obvious, as it is obvious that the whole is greater than a part; and such propositions they call axioms.

When the relation of things is not thus obvious, that is, when the proposition involves the *determination* of the relation between two or more things whose relations are not intuitively perceived, the mind may sometimes come to a certainty, concerning the relation, by the interposition of a chain of axioms; that is, of propositions where the relations are intuitively perceived. This is called demonstration.

In all such cases, the mind would perceive the relation, and come to a certainty intuitively, if adequately cultivated and enlarged; or, in other words, all propositions that now, to us, require demonstration, would, to such a cultivation, become mere axioms: consequently, now, where one man sees a mere axiom, another requires demonstration.

But the great mass of our ideas are too imperfect or too complicated to admit of intuitive conclusions; consequently, as to them, we can never arrive at demonstration. Here we substitute facts; and reason, that, as heretofore one certain fact has accompanied another certain fact, so it will be hereafter. This is what the philosophers call analogy. Analogy is thus founded on experience, and is, therefore, far less perfect than intuition or demonstration. That gravitation will always continue is analogical; we do not know it intuitively; nor can we demonstrate it. Analogical propositions are, therefore, to us mere probabilities.

But our knowledge has cognizance of ideas only. These ideas we substitute for the things they represent, in which there is a liability to err. Thus a compound idea is an assemblage of the properties of a thing, and may be incomplete and inadequate; wholly different from any quality in the thing itself. What is our idea of spirit, colour, joy? Yet we may conceive an intelligence so extended as to admit that even analogical problems should become intuitive: with God every thing is intuitively known. But even intuitive propositions sometimes reach beyond our comprehension. Example—a line of infinite length can have no end; therefore, the half of an infinite line would be a line also of infinite length. But all lines of infinite length are of equal length; therefore, the half of an infinite line is equal to the whole. Such fallacies prove that human reason is quite limited and liable to err; and hence the importance of faith in God, in the steadfastness of his laws, and the certainty of their operations. "And Jesus answering said unto them, have faith in God." *Mark* xi. 22. "And when they were come, and had gathered the church together, they rehearsed all that God had done with them, and how he had opened the door of faith unto the Gentiles." *Acts* xiv. 27. "So, then, faith cometh by hearing, and hearing by the word of God." *Romans* x. 17. That is, by revelation. "Now faith is the substance of things hoped for, the evidence of things not seen." *Heb.* xi. 1. "But without faith it is impossible to please God; for he that cometh to God must believe that he is, and that he is the rewarder of them that diligently seek him." *Heb.* xi. 6. "Even so faith, if it hath not works, is dead." *James* ii. 17. "And he said, I will hide my face from them, I will see what their end *shall be;* for they *are* a very froward generation, children in whom there is no faith." *Deut.* xxxii. 20. To which add *Romans* xii. 3.

These passages seem to imply an unchangeable reliance on faith and revelation for all knowledge of God, his laws, and our peace hereafter; and we do feel the most heartfelt regret to see those who claim to be religious teachers, laying the foundation for the most gross infidelity.

LESSON V.

On page 6, Mr. Barnes says—

"The work" (his own) "which is now submitted to the public, is limited to an examination of the Scripture argument on the subject of slavery."

Now, if it shall appear that his exertion has universally been to gloss over the Scripture, or strain it into some meaning favourable to abolition, and adverse to its rational and obvious interpretation, the mind will be forced to the conclusion, that his real object has been to hide the "Scripture argument," and to limit his researches by what he may deem to be sound reason and philosophy; and let it be remembered that such has been the constant practice of every infidel writer, who has ever attempted to reconcile his own peculiar theories to the teachings of the holy books.

"And Abram took Sarài his wife, and Lot his brother's son, and all their substance that they had gathered, and the souls that they had gotten in Haran; and they went forth to go into the land of Canaan; and into the land of Canaan they came." *Gen.* xii. 5.

"And he entreated Abram well for her sake: and he had sheep, and he-asses, and men-servants (וַעֲבָדִים *va abadim, male slaves*), and maid-servants (וּשְׁפָחֹת *vu shephahoth, female slaves*), and she asses and camels." xii. 16. "But Abram said unto Sarai, Behold thy maid (שִׁפְחָתֵךְ *shiphhathek, female slave*) is in thy hand; do unto her as it pleaseth thee. And when Sarai dealt hardly by her, she fled from her face. And the angel of the Lord found her by a fountain of water in the wilderness, by the fountain in the way to Shur. And he said, Hagar, Sarai's maid (שִׁפְחַת *shiphhath, female slave*), whence camest thou and whither wilt thou go? And she said, I flee from the face of my mistress Sarai; and the angel of the Lord said unto her, Return to thy mistress and submit thyself unto her hands." *Gen.* xvi. 6–9.

"And God said unto Abraham, Thou shalt keep my covenant." * * * "This is my covenant." * * * "And he that is eight days old shall be circumcised among you, every man-child in your generations, he that is born in the house, or *bought with money* of any stranger which is not of thy seed. He that is born in thy house, and he that is *bought with thy money* must needs be circumcised; and my covenant shall be in your flesh for an everlasting covenant." *Gen.* xvii. 9, 10, 12, 13. "And all the men of his house, born in the house, and *bought with money* of the stranger, were circumcised with him." *Ver.* 27.

"And Abimelech took sheep and oxen, and men-servants (וַעֲבָדִים *va abadim, male slaves*), and women-servants (וּשְׁפָחֹת *vu shephhahoth, female slaves*), and gave them unto Abraham." *Gen.* xx. 14.

"Wherefore she said unto Abraham, Cast out the bond-woman, and her son. For the son of this bond-woman shall not be heir with my son, even with Isaac. And God said unto Abraham, let it not be grievous in thy sight, because of the lad, and because of thy bond-woman." * * * "And also of the son of the bond-woman I will make a nation, because he is of thy seed." *Gen.* xxi. 10, 12, 13.

"For it is written that Abraham had two sons, the one by a bond-maid, the other by a free-woman. But he who was of the bond-woman was after the flesh, but he of the free-woman was by promise; nevertheless, what saith the scripture? Cast out the bond-woman and her son, for the son of the bond-woman shall not be heir with the son of the free-woman." *Gal.* iv. 22, 23, 30.

"And he said, I am Abraham's servant (עֶבֶד *ebed, male slave*), and the Lord hath blessed my master greatly, and he is become great; and he hath given him flocks and herds, and silver and gold, and man-servants (וַעֲבָדִים *va abadim, and male slaves*), and

maid-servants (וּשְׁפָחֹת *vu shephahoth, and female slaves*), and camels and asses." *Gen.* xxiv. 34, 35.

"And the man waxed great, and went forward, and grew until he became very great. For he had possession of flocks, and possession of herds, and great store of servants (וַעֲבֻדָּה *va abudda, of slaves*), and the Philistines envied him." *Gen.* xxvi. 13, 14.

"And the man (Jacob) increased exceedingly, and he had much cattle, and maid-servants (וּשְׁפָחוֹת *vu shephahoth, and female slaves,*) and men-servants (וַעֲבָדִים *va abadim, and male slaves*), and camels and asses." *Gen.* xxx. 43.

"And I have oxen and asses, flocks, and men-servants (וְעֶבֶד *ve ebed, and male slaves*), and women-servants (וְשִׁפְחָה *ve shiphha. and female slaves*). And I have sent to tell my lord that I may find grace in thy sight." *Gen.* xxxii. 5.

Let us now notice how Mr. Barnes treats the records here quoted. He says, page 70—

"Some of the servants held by the patriarchs were 'bought with money.' Much reliance is laid on this by the advocates of slavery, in justifying the purchase, and consequently, as they seem to reason, the *sale* of slaves now; and it is, therefore, of importance, to inquire, how far the fact stated is a justification of slavery as it exists at present. But one instance occurs, in the case of the patriarchs, where it is said that servants were 'bought with money.' This is the case of Abraham, *Gen.* xvii. 12, 13. 'And he that is eight days old shall be circumcised among you, every man-child in your generations; he that is born in the house, or *bought with money of any stranger*, which is not of thy seed; he that is born in thy house, and *he that is bought with thy money*, must needs be circumcised.' Compare verses 23, 27. This is the only instance in which there is mention of the fact that any one of the patriarchs had persons in their employment who were bought with money. The only other case which occurs at that period of the world is that of the sale of Joseph, first to the Ishmaelites, and then to the Egyptians—a case which, it is believed, has too close a resemblance to slavery as it exists in our own country, ever to be referred to with much satisfaction by the advocates of the system. In the case, moreover, of Abraham, it should be remembered that it is the record of a mere *fact*. There is no command to buy servants or to sell them, or to hold them as property—any more than there was a command to the brethren of Joseph to enter into a negotiation for the sale of their brother. Nor is there any approbation expressed of the fact that they were bought; unless the command given to Abraham to affix to them the seal of the covenant, and to recognise them as brethren in the faith which he held, should be construed as such evidence of approval.

"The inquiry then presents itself, whether *the fact that they were bought* determines any thing with certainty in regard to the nature of the servitude, or to the propriety of slavery as practised now. The Hebrew, in the passages referred to in Genesis, is 'the born in thy house, and *the purchase of silver*,' מִקְנַת־כֶּסֶף—*mi knath keseph*—not incorrectly rendered, 'those bought with money.' The verb קָנָה *kânâ*, from which the noun here is derived, and which is commonly used in the Scriptures when the purchase of slaves is referred to, means *to set upright* or *erect*, to *found* or *create*. *Gen.* xiv. 19, 22. *Deut.* xxxii. 6; *to get for oneself*, *to gain* or *acquire*. *Prov.* iv. 7, xv. 32; to *obtain*, *Gen.* iv. 1; and *to buy*, or *purchase*, *Gen.* xxv. 10; xlvii. 22. In this latter sense it is often used, and with the same latitude of signification as the word *buy* or *purchase* is with us. It is most commonly rendered by the words *buy* and *purchase* in the Scriptures. See *Gen.* xxv. 10; xlvii. 22; xlix. 30; l. 13; *Josh.* xxiv. 32; 2 *Sam.* xii. 3; *Ps.* lxxviii. 54; *Deut.* xxxii. 6; *Lev.* xxvii. 24, and very often elsewhere. It is applied to the purchase of fields, of cattle, of men, and of every thing which was or could be regarded as property. As there is express mention of *silver* or *money* in the passage before us respecting the servants of Abraham, there is no doubt that the expression means that he paid a price for a part of his servants. A part of them 'were born in his house;' a part had been 'bought with money' from 'strangers,' or were foreigners.

"But still, this use of the word in itself determines nothing in regard to the tenure by which they were held, or the nature of the servitude to which they were subjected. It does not prove that they were regarded as *property* in the sense in which a slave is now regarded as a chattel; nor does it demonstrate that the one who was bought ceased to be regarded altogether *as a man*; or that it was regarded as right to sell him again. The fact that he was to be circumcised as one of the family of Abraham, certainly does not look as if he ceased to be regarded *as a man*.

"The word rendered *buy* or *purchase* in the Scriptures, is applied to so many kinds of purchases, that no safe argument can be founded on its use in regard to the kind of servitude which existed in the time of Abraham. A reference to a few cases where this word is used, will show that nothing is determined by it respecting the tenure by which the thing purchased was held. (1.) It is used in the common sense of the word *purchase* as applied to inanimate things, where the property would be absolute. *Gen.* xlii. 2, 7; xliii. 20; xlvii. 19; xxx. 19. (2.) It is applied to the purchase of *cattle*, where the property may be supposed to be *as* absolute. See *Gen.* xlvi. 22, 24; iv. 20; *Job* xxxvi. 33; *Deut.* iii. 19; *and often*, (3.) God is represented as having *bought* his people; that is, as having ransomed them with a price, or purchased them to himself. *Deut.* xxxii. 6: 'Is he not thy Father that hath *bought* thee?' קֹנֶךָ—*kânēkhâ*, thy purchaser. *Exod.* xv. 16: 'By the greatness of thine arm they shall be still as a stone, till thy people pass over; till the people pass over which thou hast *purchased*,' קָנִיתָ, *kânithâ*. See *Ps.* lxxiv. 2. Compare *Isa.* xliii. 3: 'I gave Egypt for thy ransom, Ethiopia and Seba for thee.' But though the word *purchase* is used in relation to the redemption of the people of God, the very word which is used respecting the servants of Abraham, no one will maintain that they were held as *slaves*, or regarded as *property*. Who can tell but what Abraham *purchased* his servants in some such way, by redeeming them from galling captivity? May they not have been prisoners in war, to whom he did an inestimable service in rescuing them from a condition of grievous and hopeless bondage? May they not have been *slaves* in the strict and proper sense, and may not his act of purchasing them have been, in fact, a species of emancipation in a way similar to that in which God emancipates his people from the galling servitude of sin? The mere act of paying *a price* for them no more implies that he continued to hold them as slaves, than it does now when a man purchases his wife or child who have been held as slaves, or than the fact that God has redeemed his people by a price, implies that he regards them as slaves. (4.) Among the Hebrews a man might sell himself, and this transaction on the part of him to whom he sold himself would be represented by the word *bought*. Thus, in *Lev.* xxv. 47, 48: 'And if a sojourner or a stranger wax rich by thee, and thy brother that dwelleth by him wax poor, and *sell himself* unto the stranger or sojourner by thee, or to the stock of the stranger's family, after that he is sold, he may be redeemed again.' This transaction is represented as a *purchase*. Ver. 50: 'And he shall reckon with him that *bought* him, (Heb. *his purchaser*, קֹנֵהוּ *konaihū*), from the year that he was sold unto the year of jubilee,' &c. This was a mere purchase of *time* or *service*.

It gave no right to sell the man again, or to retain him in any event beyond a certain period, or to retain him *at all*, if his friends chose to interpose and redeem him. It gave no right of property in the *man*, any more than the purchase of the unexpired time of an apprentice, or the 'purchase' of the poor in the State of Connecticut does. In no proper sense of the word could this be called *slavery*. (5.) The word *buy* or *purchase* was sometimes applied to the manner in which a *wife* was procured. Thus Boaz is represented as saying that he had *bought* Ruth. 'Moreover, Ruth the Moabitess, the wife of Mahlon, have I *purchased* (קָנִיתִי *kânithi*) to be my wife.' Here the word applied to the manner in which Abraham became possessed of his servants, is applied to the manner in which a wife was procured. So Hosea says, (ch. iii. 2,) 'So I *bought* her to me (another word, however, being used in the Hebrew, כָּרָה *kârâ*) for fifteen pieces of silver, and for an homer of barley, and an half homer of barley.' Jacob purchased his wives, Leah and Rachel, not indeed by the payment of money, but by labour. *Gen.* xxix. 15–23. That the practice of *purchasing* a wife, or paying a *dowry* for her, was common, is apparent from *Exod.* xxii. 17; 1 *Sam.* xviii. 25. Compare *Judg.* i. 12, 13. Yet it will not be maintained that the wife among the Hebrews, was in any proper sense a *slave*, or that she was regarded as subject to the laws which regulate property, or that the husband had a right to sell her again. In a large sense, indeed, she was regarded, as the conductors of the Princeton Repertory (1836, p. 293) allege, as the wife is now, as the *property* of her husband; that is, she was *his* to the exclusion of the claim of any other man; but she was his as his *wife*, not as his *slave*. (6.) The word '*bought*' occurs in a transaction between Joseph and the people of Egypt in such a way as farther to explain its meaning. When, during the famine, the money of the Egyptians had failed, and Joseph had purchased all the land, the people proposed to become his servants. When the contract was closed, Joseph said to them, 'Behold, I have *bought* you—קָנִיתִי *kânithi*—this day, and your land for Pharaoh.' *Gen.* xlvii. 23. The nature of this contract is immediately specified. They were to be regarded as labouring for Pharaoh. The land belonged to him, and Joseph furnished the people seed, or 'stocked the land,' and they were to cultivate it on shares for Pharaoh. The fifth part was to be his, and the other four parts were to be theirs. There was a claim on them for *labour*, but it does not appear that the claim extended farther. No farmers who now work land on shares would be willing to have their condition described as one of *slavery*.

"The conclusion which we reach from this examination of the words *buy* and *bought* as applied to the case of Abraham is, that the use of the word determines nothing in regard to the tenure by which his servants were held. They may have been purchased from those who had taken them as captives in war, and the purchase may have been regarded by themselves as a species of redemption, or a most desirable rescue from the fate which usually attends such captives—perchance from death. The property which it was understood that he had in them may have been merely property in their *time*, and not in their persons; or the purchase may have amounted in fact to every thing that is desirable in emancipation; and, from any thing implied in the *word*, their subsequent service in the family of Abraham may have been entirely voluntary. It is a very material circumstance, also, that *there is not the slightest evidence that either Abraham, Isaac, or Jacob ever sold a slave, or offered one for sale, or regarded them as liable to be sold.* There is no evidence that their servants even descended as a part of an inheritance from father to son. So far, indeed, as the accounts in the Scriptures go, it would be impossible to *prove* that they would not have been at liberty at any time to leave their masters, if they had chosen to do so. The passage, therefore, which says that Abraham had 'servants *bought* with money,' cannot be adduced to justify slavery as it exists now—even if this were all that we know about it. But (4.) servitude in the days of Abraham must have existed in a very mild form, and have had features which slavery by no means has now. Almost the only transaction which is mentioned in regard to the servants of Abraham, is one which could never occur in the slave-holding parts of our country. A marauding expedition of petty kings came from the north and east, and laid waste the country around the vale of Siddim, near to which Abraham lived, and, among other spoils of battle, they carried away Lot and his possessions. Abraham, it is said, then 'armed his trained servants, born in his own house, three hundred and eighteen, and pursued them unto Dan,' and rescued the family of Lot and his goods. *Gen.* xiv. This narrative is one that must for ever show that servitude, as it existed in the family of Abraham, was a very different thing from what it is in the United States. The number was large, and it does not appear that any persons but his servants accompanied Abraham.

They all were armed. They were led off on a distant expedition, where there could have been no power in Abraham to preserve his life, if they had chosen to rise up against him, and no power to recover them, if they had chosen to set themselves free. Yet he felt himself entirely safe when accompanied with this band of armed men, and when far away from his family and his home. What must have been the nature of servitude, where the master was willing to arm such a company, to put himself entirely at their disposal, and lead them off to a distant land?

"Compare this with the condition of things in the United States. Here, it is regarded as essential to the security of the life of the master that slaves shall never be intrusted with arms. 'A slave is not allowed to keep or carry a weapon.'* 'He cannot go from the tenement of his master, or other person with whom he lives, without a pass, or something to show that he is proceeding by authority from his master, employer, or overseer.'† 'For keeping or carrying a gun, or powder, or *shot*, or *club*, or *other weapon whatsoever*, offensive or defensive, a slave incurs, for each offence, thirty-nine lashes, by order of a justice of the peace;'‡ and in North Carolina and Tennessee, twenty lashes, by the nearest constable, *without* a conviction by the justice.§ Here, there is every precaution from laws, and from the dread of the most fearful kind of punishment, against the escape of slaves. Here, there is a constant apprehension that they may rise against their masters, and every security is taken against their organization and combination. Here, there is probably not a single master who would, if he owned three hundred slaves, *dare* to put arms in their hands, and lead them off on an expedition against a foe. If the uniform precautions and care at the South against arming the slaves, or allowing them to become acquainted with their own strength, be any expression of the nature of the system, slavery in the United States is a very different thing from servitude in the time of Abraham; and it does not prove that in the species of servitude existing here it is right to refer to the case of Abraham, and to say that it is '*a good patriarchal system.*' Let the cases be made parallel before the names of the patriarchs are called in to justify the system. But—

* Rev. Cod. Virg. vol. i. p. 453, sections 83, 84.

† Ibid. vol. i. p. 422, section 6. See Paulding on Slavery, p. 146.

‡ 2 Litt. and Smi. 1150; 2 Missouri Laws, 741, section 4.

§ Haywood's Manual, 521; Stroud on the Laws relating to Slavery, p. 102.

"(5.) What *real* support would it furnish to the system, even if it were true that the cases were wholly parallel? How far would it go to demonstrate that *God* regards it as a good system, and one that is to be perpetuated, in order that society may reach its highest possible elevation? Who would undertake to vindicate all the conduct of the patriarchs, or to maintain that all which they practised was in accordance with the will of God? They practised concubinage and polygamy. Is it therefore certain that this was the highest and purest state of society, and that it was a state which God designed should be perpetuated? Abraham and Isaac were guilty of falsehood and deception, (*Gen.* xx. 2, *seq.;* xxvi. 7;) Jacob secured the birthright by a collusive fraud between him and his mother, (*Gen.* xxvii.) and obtained no small part of his property by cunning, (*Gen.* xxx. 36–43,) and Noah was drunk with wine, (*Gen.* ix. 21;) and these things are recorded merely *as facts*, without any decided expression of disapprobation; but is it therefore to be inferred that they had the approbation of God, and that they are to be practised still, in order to secure the highest condition of society?

"Take the single case of polygamy. Admitting that the patriarchs held slaves, the argument in favour of polygamy, from their conduct, would be, in all its main features, the same as that which I suggested, in the commencement of this chapter, as employed in favour of slavery. The argument would be this:—That they were good men, the 'friends of God,' and that what such men practised freely cannot be wrong; that God permitted this; that he nowhere forbade it; that he did not record his disapprobation of the practice; and that whatever God permitted in such circumstances, without expressing his disapprobation, must be regarded as in itself a good thing, and as desirable to be perpetuated, in order that society may reach the highest point of elevation. It is perfectly clear that, so far as the conduct of the patriarchs goes, it would be just as easy to construct an argument in favour of polygamy as in favour of slavery—even on the supposition that slavery existed then essentially as it does now. But it is not probable that polygamy would be defended now as a good institution, and as one that has the approbation of God, even by those who defend the 'domestic institutions of the South.' The truth is, that the patriarchs were good men in their generation, and, considering their circumstances, were men eminent for piety. But they were imperfect men; they lived in the infancy of the world; they had comparatively little light on the subjects of morals and religion; and it is a very feeble argument which maintains that a thing is *right, because any one or all of the patriarchs practised it.*

"But after all, what *real* sanction did God ever give either to polygamy or to servitude, as it was practised in the time of the patriarchs? Did he command either? Did he ever express approbation of either? Is there an instance in which either is mentioned with a sentiment of approval? The mere *record* of actual occurrences, even if there is no declared disapprobation of them, proves nothing as to the Divine estimate of what is recorded. There is a *record* of the '*sale*' of Joseph into servitude, first to the Ishmaelites, and then to Potiphar. There is no expression of disapprobation. There is no exclamation of surprise or astonishment, as if a deed of enormous wickedness were done, when brothers sold their own brother into hopeless captivity. *This* was done also by those who were subsequently reckoned among the 'patriarchs,' and some of whom at the time were probably pious men. Will it be inferred that God approved this transaction; that he meant to smile on the act, when brothers sell their own brothers into hopeless bondage? Will this record be adduced to justify kidnapping, or the acts of parents in barbarous lands, who, forgetful of all the laws of their nature, sell their own children? Will the record that the Ishmaelites took the youthful Joseph into a distant land, and sold him there as a slave, be referred to as furnishing evidence that God approves the conduct of those who kidnap the unoffending inhabitants of Africa, or *buy* them there, and carry them across the deep, to be sold into hopeless bondage! Why then should the fact that there is a *record* that the patriarchs held servants, or bought them, without any expressed disapprobation of the deed, be adduced as evidence that God regards slavery as a good institution, and intends that it shall be perpetuated under the influence of his religion, as conducing to the highest good of society? The truth is, that the mere record of a *fact*, even without any sentiment of approbation or disapprobation, is no evidence of the views of him who makes it. Are we to infer that Herodotus approved of all that he saw or heard of in his travels, and of which he made a record? Are we to suppose that Tacitus and Livy approved of all the deeds the memory of which they have transmitted for the instruction of future ages? Are we to maintain that Gibbon and Hume believed that all which they have recorded was adapted to promote the good of mankind? Shall the biographer of Nero, and Caligula, and Richard III., and Alexander VI., and Cæsar Borgia be held responsible for approving of all that these men did, or of commending their example to the imitation of mankind? Sad would be the office of an historian were he to be thus judged. Why then shall we infer that *God* approved of all that the patriarchs did, even when there is no formal approbation expressed; or infer, because such transactions have been *recorded*, that *therefore* they are right in his sight?"

Does the mind hesitate as to the design of this laboured and lengthy argument? That its object is to do away, to destroy the scriptural force of the facts stated in these records? Does not this argument substantially deny that Abraham had slaves bought with money? And even if he did have them, then that it was just as wicked at that time as he thinks it to be now? Or, if he shall thus far fail, then to bring down the characters of Abraham, Isaac, and Jacob to a level with Nero, Caligula, Richard III., and Cæsar Borgia? And the holy books themselves to the standard of Herodotus, Tacitus, and Livy; and inure our mind to compare them with the writings of Hume and Gibbon?

The writer who lessens our veneration for the characters of the ancient worshippers of Jehovah; who, as by a system of special pleading, attempts to overspread the simple announcements of the holy books with doubt and uncertainty, however conscientious he may be in these labours of his hand, while he assumes a most awful responsibility to God, must ever call down upon himself the universal and determined opposition of the intelligent and good among men.

The more secret, the more adroit the application of the poison, the more intensely wicked is the hand that presents it.

LESSON VI.

MR. BARNES has devoted twenty-four pages of his book to the slavery of the Hebrews in Egypt, wherein we find no instance that his *test* is applied with either fairness of deduction or logical accuracy. Indeed, so far as our limited capacity can trace his application to the *test*, he has made but two points:

I. After repeated judgments upon the Egyptians, for hesitating to set the Hebrews free, God, in his providence, effected their deliverance from slavery. Therefore, we are to infer the indignation of God against the institution of slavery. What were the facts of the case? On account of their sins rendering them unfit for the blessings promised their fathers, God imposed on them slavery four hundred years,—at the expiration of which time he delivered them from it. When a free negro becomes a public nuisance, the court will give judgment that he shall be sold to be a slave five years. The term having expired, if the purchaser holds on, and refuses to let him go, the same court will interfere, set him free, and impose heavy penalties on the master. Does the case show that the court feels indignation against the institution of slavery? We think it proves exactly the opposite!

If the four hundred years of slavery operated to fit the Hebrews for the reception of the blessing; if the five years of slavery re-fitted the negro for the rational enjoyment of liberty, we think the providence of God places the institution of slavery in a valuable point of light.

II. In this review of the slavery of the Israelites in Egypt, Mr. Barnes has noticed the fact of their rapid increase, to the extent of their becoming dangerous to the Egyptian government; and he has compared it with the more rapid increase of the slaves over the whites in the Slave States; and suggests a similar danger to the government of the United States,—adding, that such increase "can be arrested by nothing but emancipation." Now all this may be true; but in what light does it show for the institution of slavery? Does Mr. Barnes really mean to say, what is the fact, that the condition of slavery is so well adapted to the negro race, that, by it, their comforts, peace of mind, and general happiness are made so certain and well-secured to them, that they increase rapidly? And that, as they are a race of people whom we do not desire to bear rule over us, or become more numerous than they now are, it would be good policy, and he desires, to set them free, in order that they may be deprived of their present comforts, peace of mind, and happiness, with the view to lessen their increase, and waste them away? If such really be his view, we may regard it as an extraordinary instance of his Christian counsel, and form some idea of what he would be as a slave-holder. But the same increase of the slaves happened in Egypt in a different age, and in reference to a different class of men; nor could any exertion correct it. We may apply the *test*, and safely infer, THAT GOD SMILES ON THE INSTITUTION OF SLAVERY.

There is, in this chapter on the slavery of the Hebrews, an allusion made to the States of Ohio and Kentucky, (see page 102;) the one represented as "adorned with smiling villages, and cottages, and churches, and the aspect of neatness, thrift, and order;" and that the other wears "the aspect of ignorance, irreligion, neglect, and desolation;" and that the reason of the difference is, because "God smiles upon the free State, and frowns upon the one where slavery exists."

We do not deem it necessary to question or even examine the correctness of the view of Kentucky, as presented to us by Mr. Barnes: so far as the argument is concerned, we will take it as established. If the institution of slavery is of Divine origin, or if we are to form a notion of the will of God respecting it from his providences affecting the institution, we must keep our eye upon the subject of slavery, not upon those otherwise conditioned. We must look to the slave in Kentucky, and compare his conditions there with his conditions in a state of freedom; and Mr. Barnes has furnished us with data, proving that in Kentucky the slaves are in a rapid state of propagation and increase.

Page 95, he says—"The whites were to the slaves—

	In 1790.	In 1840.
North Carolina,	2.80 to 1	1.97 to 1
South Carolina,	1.31 " 1	79 " 1
Georgia,	1.76 " 1	1.44 " 1
Tennessee,	13.35 " 1	3.49 " 1
Kentucky,	5.16 " 1	3.23 " 1

"From this it is apparent that, in spite of all the oppressions and cruelties of slavery, of all the sales that are effected, of all the removals to Liberia, and of all the removals by the escape of the slaves, there is a regular gain of the slave population over the free in the slave-holding States. No oppression prevents it here more than it did in Egypt, and there can be no doubt whatever that, unless slavery shall be arrested in some way, the increase is so certain that the period is not far distant when, in all the Slave States, the free whites will be far in the minority. At the first census, taken in 1790, in every Slave State there was a very large majority of whites. At the last census, in 1840, the slaves outnumbered the whites in South Carolina, Mississippi, and Louisiana. The tendency of this, from causes which it would be easy to state, can be arrested by nothing but emancipation."

But Mr. Barnes does not state what those causes are; and will he acknowledge that they really are what we have before stated? So far as these facts teach any thing, it is that God smiles on the institution of slavery. Let it be true, as Mr. Barnes says it is, that Ohio exhibits a state of prosperity, and Kentucky a state of "*desolation*,"—the legitimate deduction is, that those, having the direction and government of affairs in Ohio are wiser and more intelligent than those of the same class in Kentucky. We shall leave all further view of the matter to Mr. Barnes and the people of Kentucky.

The four hundred years of slavery in Egypt were not a sentence on the Hebrews for the especial benefit of the Egyptians, but for that of the Hebrews themselves. The court did not sentence the free negro, who had become a nuisance, to five years of slavery, for the especial benefit of the purchaser, but for the prospect of amelioration in the negro himself. The races of Ham were not made subject to slavery for the especial benefit of Shem and Japheth; but because, in such slavery, their condition would be more elevated, and better, than in a state of freedom. The slave-owner may be very wicked, and God may destroy him for his wickedness, and yet his merciful designs, by the institution of slavery, not be affected thereby. An eastern monarch, determined to destroy his minister, sent him a present of a thousand slaves and a hundred elephants. The minister dared not refuse the present; but not being able profitably to employ them, was ruined. But the condition of the slave and the elephant was not injured. The poor-house was not made for the especial benefit of its keeper, but for its subjects.

LESSON VII.

The benefit of the slave-owner depends on a different principle, upon the wisdom, propriety, and prudence with which he governs and manages his slaves. If he neglect their morals, suffering them to become idle, runaways, dissolute, thieves, robbers, and committers of crime, he is made, to some extent, responsible; or if he neglect to supply suitable clothing, food, and medicine, attention in sickness, and all other necessary protection, he is liable to great loss; his profit may be greatly diminished; or, if he abuse his slave with untoward cruelty, he may render him less fit for labour,—may destroy him altogether; or the law may set in, and compel the slave to be sold to a less cruel master. *The interest of the master has become protection to the slave;* and this principle holds good in all countries, in all ages, and among all men. But it is yet said, that there are men who most outrageously abuse, and sometimes kill their slaves. Very true and because some men do the same to their wives, is it any argument against marriage? It proves that there are men who are not fit to be slave-owners. And what is the providence of God, as generally manifested, in these cases? That such husband does not enjoy the full blessing designed by the institution of marriage; or such marriage is, in some way, shortly set aside. That such slave-owner does not enjoy the full benefit a different course would insure to him; or, in some way, he is made to cease being a slave-owner. Such instances are most direct and powerful manifestations against the abuses,—not of the institution itself.

But God has not left his displeasure of the abuses of slavery to be found out by our poor, dim, mortal eyes; by our weak view of his manifestations. He made direct laws on the subject.

"But the seventh day is the sabbath of the Lord thy God; *in it* thou shalt not do any work, thou, nor thy son, nor thy daughter, thy *man-servant* (עַבְדְּךָ *abeddeka, male slave,*) nor thy *maid-servant* (וַאֲמָתְךָ *va amatheka, nor thy female slave*), nor thy cattle, nor thy stranger that is within thy gates." *Gen.* xx. 10.

"But the seventh day is the sabbath of the Lord thy God; in it thou shalt not do any work, thou, nor thy son, nor thy daughter, nor thy man-servant (וְעַבְדְּךָ *ve abeddeka, male slave*), nor thy maid-servant (וַאֲמָתְךָ *va amatheka, female slave*), nor thine ox, nor thine ass, nor any of thy cattle, nor thy stranger that is within thy gates; that thy man-servant (עַבְדְּךָ *abeddeka, male slave*) and thy maid-servant (וַאֲמָתְךָ *va amatheka, female slave*) may rest as well as thou." *Deut.* v. 14.

But we find laws correcting abuses of quite a different nature; abuses that grow out of the perverse nature of man towards his fellow-man of equal grade, touching their mutual rights in property:

"Thou shalt not covet thy neighbour's house, thou shalt not covet thy neighbour's wife, nor his *man-servant* (וְעַבְדּוֹ *ve abeddo, male slave*), nor his *maid-servant* (וַאֲמָתוֹ *va amatho, female slave*), nor his ox, nor his ass, nor any thing that is thy neighbour's." *Exod.* xx. 17.

"Neither shalt thou desire thy neighbour's wife, neither shalt thou covet thy neighbour's house, his field, or his *man-servant* (וְעַבְדּוֹ *ve abeddo, male slave*), or his *maid-servant* (וַאֲמָתוֹ *va amatho, female slave*), his ox, or his ass, or any thing that is thy neighbour's." *Deut.* v. 21—the 18th of the Hebrew text.

It does appear to us that these statutes speak volumes—portraying the providences of God, and his design in regard to the institutions of slavery. The word covet, as here used, as well as its original, implies that action of the mind which reaches to the possession of the thing ourselves, and to the depriving of our neighbour, without a glimpse at the idea of payment, reciprocity, or compromise; consequently, it is the exact action of mind, which, when cultivated into physical display, makes a man a thief. The command forbids that the mind shall be thus exercised, for the command only reaches to the exercise of the mind; an exercise, which, from the very nature of it, must for ever draw us deeper into crime. It is a command that well comes to us from Jehovah direct, because it is a command that man could never enforce: the individual, and Jehovah alone, can only and surely tell when it is broken. But it may be broken in various ways; it may be broken by writing books persuading others that it is no crime, that it is even praiseworthy, by any other course of conduct, to weaken the tenure of the proprietor in the property named.

"But fools do sometimes fearless tread,
Where angels dare not even look!"

We hold the doctrine good that, whenever we find that the providence of God frowns upon the abuse of a thing, such abuse is contrary to his law. So, also, the doctrine is indisputably true that all laws, all providences against the abuse of a thing, necessarily become laws and providences for the protection of the thing itself; consequently, it always follows that they contemplate protection.

Mr. Barnes compares the slavery of the Hebrews in Egypt to the condition of slavery in the United States, and complains of the harsh treatment of the slaves in the latter country. See p. 92:

"Preventing the slaves from being taught to read and write; prohibiting, as far as possible, all knowledge among themselves of their own numbers and strength; forbidding all assemblages, even for worship, where there might be danger of their becoming acquainted with their own strength, and of forming plans for freedom; enacting laws of excessive severity against those who run away from their masters; appointing severe and disgraceful punishments, either with or without the process of law, for those who are suspected of a design to inform the slaves that they are men and that they have the rights of human beings; and solemnly prohibiting the use of arms among the slaves, designed to prevent their rising upon their masters, or 'joining themselves to an enemy to fight against their masters,' and 'getting up out of the land.'"

We did suppose from this passage that Mr. Barnes might desire us to lie down, and *let the slaves kill or make slaves of us.* But he has presented us with his cure for all these wrongs on pages 383, 384. He says—

"Now here, I am persuaded, is a wise model for all other denominations of Christian men, and the true idea of all successful efforts for the removal of this great evil from the land. Let all the evangelical denominations but follow the simple example of the Quakers in this country, and slavery would soon come to an end. There is not power of numbers and influence out of the church to sustain it. Let every denomination in the land *detach itself* from all connection with slavery, without saying a word against others; let the time come when, in all the mighty denominations of Christians, it can be assured that the evil has ceased *with them* FOR EVER; and let the voice, from each denomination, be lifted up in kind, but firm and solemn, testimony against the system; with no 'mealy' words; with no attempt at apology; with no wish to blink it; with no effort to throw the sacred shield of religion over so great an evil; and the work is done. There is no public sentiment in this land, there could be none created, that would resist the power of such testimony. There is no power *out* of the church that could sustain slavery an hour, if it were not sustained in it. Not a blow need be struck. Not an unkind word need be uttered. No man's motive need be impugned. No man's proper rights invaded. All that is needful is for each Christian man, and every Christian church, to stand up in the sacred majesty of such a solemn testimony; to free themselves from all connection with the evil, and utter a calm and deliberate voice to the world; and THE WORK WILL BE DONE!"

This looks very much like converting the church into an instrument of political power. We might indulge in severe remarks. We might quote some very cogent and rebuking passages of Scripture; but, since we believe that where the spirit of Christ is, he will be there also, we do not deem it necessary.

From the very considerable labour evidently bestowed in the preparation of the *test*, apparently to be applied in his reasoning on this subject, a feeling of disappointment rests upon the mind when we discover how little use Mr. Barnes has made of it.

We have given a view of Mr. Barnes's peroration; his complaints; the wrongs that excite his sympathy; and his final conclusion of the whole matter. We have attempted to reason by the same rule he has adopted, and, so far as he has chosen to apply it, leave it to others to judge whether it is not most fatal to the cause he advocates.

LESSON VIII.

WE are told that book-making, among some, has become a trade. That some men write books to order, to suit the market; that there is no knowing what may be an author's principles, or whether he has any at all, by what may be in his book.

The principal object of such a writer must be his money—his pay: if in great haste to get it in possession, he may be expected sometimes to be careless; and unless very talented and experienced in the subject on which he writes, to record contradictions.

Page 83, Mr. Barnes says—"The Hebrews were not essentially distinguished from the Egyptians, as the Africans are from their masters in this land, by colour." But he continues, pages 86 and 87—"They (the Hebrews) were a *foreign* race, as the African race is with us. They were not Egyptians, any more than the nations of Congo are Americans. They were not of the children of Ham. They were of another family; they differed from the Egyptians, by whom they were held in bondage, as certainly as the African does from the Caucasian or the Malay divisions of the great family of man."

In page 228, on another subject, he says—"If, therefore, it be true that slavery did not prevail in Judea; that there is no evidence that the Hebrews engaged in the traffic, and that the prophets felt themselves at liberty to denounce the system as contrary to the spirit of the Mosaic institutions, these FACTS will furnish an important explanation of some things in regard to the subject in the New Testament, and will prepare us to enter on the inquiry how it was regarded by the Saviour; for if slavery did not exist in

Palestine in his time: if he never came in contact with it, it will not be fair to infer that he was not opposed to it, because he did not often refer to it, and expressly denounce it."

This is in strict conformity with the following:

Page 242. "There is no conclusive evidence that he ever came in contact with slavery at all. * * * There is no proof which I have seen referred to from any contemporary writer, that it existed in Judea in his time at all; and there is no evidence from the New Testament that he ever came in contact with it."

Also, page 244. "There is not the slightest proof that the Saviour ever came in contact with slavery at all, either in public or in private life."

Also, page 249. "We have seen above, that there is no evidence that when the Saviour appeared, slavery in any form existed in Judea, and consequently there is no proof that he ever encountered it."

Permit us to compare these statements with *Matt.* viii. 5–14:

"And when Jesus was entered into Capernaum, there came unto him a centurion, beseeching him, (verse 6,) and saying, Lord, my *servant*, &c. (Verse 9,) For I am a man of authority, having soldiers under me; and I say to this man go, and he goeth; and to another, Come, and he cometh, and to my SERVANT (δούλῳ, *slave*), Do this, and he doeth it," &c.

Also, *Luke* vii. 2–10. "And a certain centurion's *servant* (δοῦλος, *slave*) was sick," &c. * * * "beseeching him that he would come and heal his *servant* (δοῦλον, *slave.*) (Verse 10,) "And they that were sent, returning to the house, found the *servant* (δοῦλον, *slave*) whole that had been sick."

So also, *Luke* xix. 12–16. (Verse 13,) "And he called his ten *servants* (δούλους, *slaves*), &c. Also *John* viii. 33–36: "And they answered him, we be Abraham's seed, and were never *in bondage* (δεδουλεύκαμεν, *in slavery*) to any man; how sayest thou, Ye shall be made free? (Verse 34,) "Jesus answered them, Verily, verily, I say unto you, whoever committeth sin is the servant (δοῦλος, *slave*) of sin." (Verse 35,) "And the servant (δοῦλος, *slave*) abideth not in the house for ever, but the Son abideth ever. If the Son therefore make you free, you shall be free indeed."

Permit us also to compare them with the following, Mr. Barnes's *own statements*. See page 250: "All that the argument does require, whatever conclusion we may reach as to the manner in which the apostles treated the subject, is, the admission of the *fact*, that slavery *everywhere* abounded; that it existed in forms of great severity and cruelty; that it involved all the essential claims that are now made by masters to the services or persons of slaves; that it was protected by civil laws; that the master had the right of transferring his slaves by sale, donation, or testament; that in general he had every right which was supposed to be necessary to perpetuate the system; and that it was impossible that the early preachers of Christianity should not encounter this system, and be constrained to adopt principles in regard to the proper treatment of it."

And, again, page 251: "It is fair that the advocates of the system should have all the advantage which can be derived from the fact, that the apostles found it in its most odious forms, and in such circumstances as to make it proper that they should regard, and treat it as an evil, if Christianity regards it as such at all."

And, again, pages 259, 260: "I am persuaded that nothing can be gained to the cause of anti-slavery by attempting to deny that the apostles found slavery in existence in the regions where they founded churches, and that those sustaining the relation of master and slave were admitted to the churches, if they gave real evidence of regeneration, and were regarded by the apostles as entitled to the common participation of the privileges of Christianity."

But there are other errors in this "Scriptural View of Slavery," page 245:

"He (the Saviour) never uttered a word *in favour* of slavery, * * * not even a *hint* can be found, in all he said, on which a man * * * who meant to keep one already in his possession, could rely to sustain his course."

We ask that this assertion of Mr. Barnes shall be compared with *Luke* xvii. 7–11:

"But which of you having a servant (*δοῦλον, slave*) ploughing, or feeding cattle, will say unto him, by and by, when he has come from the field, Go, sit down to meat? And will not rather say unto him, Make ready wherewith I may sup, and gird thyself and serve me, till I have eaten and drunken, and afterward thou shalt eat and drink? Doth he thank that servant (*δούλῳ, slave*) because he did the things that were commanded him? I trow not." "So likewise ye, when ye shall have done all those things which are commanded you, say, We are unprofitable servants; we have done that which was our duty to do."

And, again, Mr. Barnes says: "The nations of Palestine were devoted to destruction, not to servitude." See page 118.

Compare this with the following, from page 156: "There were particular reasons operating for subjecting the nations around Palestine to servitude, which do not exist now. They were *doomed* to servitude for *sins*."

LESSON IX.

Deut. xxiii. 9. "When the host goeth forth against thine enemies, then keep thee from every wicked thing"—directions what to do, or what not to do, in time of war, being continued, the 15th and 16th verses read thus:

"Thou shalt not deliver up to his master the servant (*slave*) which is escaped unto thee." * * * "He shall dwell with thee, *even* among you in that place which he shall choose in one of thy gates where it liketh him best; thou shalt not oppress him."

This passage is quoted by Mr. Barnes, upon which he says, page 140—

"I am willing to admit that the command *probably* relates only to the slaves which escaped to the country of the Hebrews from surrounding nations; and that in form it did not contemplate the runaway slaves of the Hebrews in their own land."

Pray, then, for what purpose does he speak as follows?

"A seventh essential and fundamental feature of the Hebrew slavery was, that the runaway slave was not to be restored to his master; on this point the law was absolute."

And to sustain this assertion, he quotes this same passage from Deuteronomy, and, commenting thereon, says, pages 140, 141—"This solemn and fundamental enactment would involve the following results or effects. (1.) No laws could ever be enacted in the Hebrew commomwealth by which a runaway slave could be restored to his master. No revolution of the government, and no change of policy, could ever modify this principle of the constitution. (2.) No magistrate could on any pretence deliver up a runaway slave."

Then, again, page 190:

"Slaves of the United States are to be restored to their masters, if they endeavour to escape. We find among the fundamental principles of the Mosaic laws a provision that the slave was *never* to be restored, if he attempted to do thus. He was to find in the land of Judea an asylum. The power and authority of the commonwealth were pledged for his protection."

And yet, again, page 226:

"As one of the results of this inquiry, it is apparent that the Hebrews were not a nation of slaveholders."

We present these passages to shows Mr. Barnes's mode of argument. But let us examine, for a moment, the indications of the holy books on the subject of runaway slaves. When David had protected the flocks of Nabal, upon the mountains of Carmel, on a holiday, he sent his young men, to ask a present, as some compensation for the same.

"And Nabal answered David's servants, and said, Who is David? and who is the son of Jesse? There be many servants (עֲבָדִים *abadim, slaves*) nowadays that break away every man from his master. Shall I then take my bread, and my water, and my flesh that I have killed for my shearers, and give *it* unto men, whom I know not whence they be?" 1 *Sam.* xxv. 10, 11.

We think the indications are that for slaves to run away was a common occurrence, and that it was immoral to give them countenance or protection; and Nabal, pretending that David might be one of that class, excused himself from bestowing the present on that account.

"And it came to pass at the end of three years, that two of the servants (עֲבָדִים *abadim, slaves*) of Shemei ran away unto Achish, son of Maachah king of Gath; and they told Shemei, saying, Behold thy servants (עֲבָדֶיךָ *abadeka, slaves*) *be* in Gath. And Shemei arose and saddled his ass, and went to Gath to Achish to seek his servants (עֲבָדָיו *abadav, slaves*); and Shemei went and brought his servants (עבדיו *abadav, slaves*) from Gath." 1 *Kings*, ii. 39, 40.

If it can be said that Jehovah has views and wishes, then it may be said, that the views and wishes of Jehovah on the subject of runaway slaves must, at all times, be the same. "In him there is no variableness, nor shadow of turning."

"And she had a *hand-maid* (שִׁפְחָה *shiphehah, female slave*), an Egyptian (מִצְרִית *mitserith, Egyptian, a descendant of Misraim, the second son of Ham*), whose name was Hagar." *Gen.* xvi. 1.

Upon a feud between her and her mistress, her mistress dealt hardly by her, and she ran away: "And the angel of the Lord found her by a fountain of water in the wilderness, by the fountain in the way to Shur." (8th verse,) "And he said, Hagar, Sarai's maid, whence comest thou? and whither wilt thou go? And she said, I flee from the face of my mistress Sarai." (The angel did not say to her, "Here is a shilling; get into Canada as soon as possible!") "And the angel of the Lord said unto her, Return to thy mistress and submit thyself under her hands." *Gen.* xvi. 7–9.

On page 117, Mr. Barnes says—

"In the laws of Moses, there is but one way mentioned by which a foreigner could be made a slave; that is, by purchase. *Lev.* xxv. 44. And it is remarkable that the Hebrews were not permitted to make slaves of the captives taken in war."

Let us compare this assertion, made by Mr. Barnes, with the 31st of Numbers:

"And the Lord spake unto Moses saying, Avenge the children of Israel of the Midianites. * * * (Verse 9,) And the children of Israel took all the women of Midian captives, and their little ones. * * * (Verse 11,) And they took all the spoils and all the prey, both of men and of beasts. (Verse 12,) And they brought the captives and the prey unto Moses and Eleazar the priest. * * * (Verse 25,) And the Lord spake unto Moses, saying, Take the sum of the prey that was taken, both of man and beast. * * * (Verse 27,) And divide the prey into two parts, between them that took the war upon them, who went out to battle, and between all the congregation. * * * (Verse 28,) And levy a tribute unto the Lord of the men of war which went out to battle, one soul of five hundred, both of the persons and of the beeves. * * * (Verse 30,) And of the children of Israel's half, thou shalt take one portion of fifty of the persons, &c. * * * (Verse 32,) And the booty, being the rest of the prey, which the men of war had, was * * * sheep. (Verse 35,) And thirty-two thousand persons in all. * * * (Verse 36,) And the half which was the portion of them that went out to war, was, &c. * * * sheep, &c. (Verse 40,) "And the persons were sixteen thousand, of which the Lord's tribute was thirty and two persons. (Verse 42) And the children of Israel's half which Moses divided from the men that warred * * * was, &c. * * * sheep, &c. * * * (Verse 46,) and sixteen thousand persons. (Verse 47,) Even of the children of Israel's half, Moses took one portion of fifty, both of man and of beast, and gave them unto the Levites which kept the charge of the tabernacle of the Lord, as the Lord commanded Moses."

LESSON X.

In ancient times, all persons conquered in battle were liable to be put to death by the national laws then existing. If the conqueror suffered the captive to escape death, imposing on him only the cutting off his thumbs, hands, or ears; or, without these personal deformations, subjecting him to slavery, as was often the case, especially when the captive was of low grade,—it was ever regarded as an act of mercy in the conqueror.

In the 17th verse of the thirty-first chapter of Numbers, Moses commanded that "every male among the little ones, and every woman who had known a man," should be killed, even after they had been taken to the Israelitish camp; and that none should be reserved for slaves, except female children, of whom, it appears, there were thirty-two thousand. The booty taken in this war, was distributed by Moses, in comformity to the especial direction of God himself, as follows:—(Verse 25,) "And the Lord spake unto Moses, saying, (verse 26,) Take the sum of the prey that was taken, *both* of man and of beast, thou, and Eleazar the priest, and the chief fathers of the congregation, (verse 28,) and levy a tribute unto the Lord of the men of war which went out to battle: one soul of five hundred, *both* of the PERSONS, and of the beeves, and of the asses, and of the sheep: (verse 29,) Take it of their half, and give it unto Eleazar the priest, *for* a heave-offering of the Lord. (Verse 30,) And of the children of Israel's half, thou shalt take one portion of fifty of the PERSONS, of the beeves, of the asses, and of the flocks, of all manner of beasts, and give them to the Levites which keep the charge of the tabernacle of the Lord. (Verse 31,) And Moses and Eleazar did as the Lord commanded Moses."

Houbigant, in his commentary upon this chapter, has given us the following

Table of the distribution of the booty of this war:

Sheep.....675,000	To the Soldiers....337,500......	To the Lord......	675
	" People......337,500......	" Levites...	6,750
Beeves.... 72,000	" Soldiers.... 36,000......	" Lord......	72
	" People...... 36,000......	" Levites...	720
Asses..... 61,000	" Soldiers.... 30,500......	" Lord......	61
	" People...... 30,500......	" Levites...	610
Persons.. 32,000	" Soldiers.... 16,000......	" Lord......	32
	" People...... 16,000......	" Levites...	320

This table has been adopted by Dr. Adam Clark in his Commentary, to which he adds—

"In this table the booty is equally divided between the people and the soldiers; a five-hundredth part being given to the Lord, and a fiftieth part to the Levites." And this learned divine, in his commentary on the 28th verse, says—"And levy a tribute unto the Lord, one soul of five hundred, &c. * * * The *persons* to be employed in the Lord's service, under the Levites: the *cattle* either for sacrifice or for the use of the Levites. (Verse 30.) Some monsters have supposed that *one* out of every *five hundred* of the captives was offered in sacrifice to the Lord! But this is abominable. When God chose to have the life of a man, he took it in the way of *justice*, as in the case of the Midianites above; but never in the way of *sacrifice*."

In the 29th verse, we learn that the Lord's portion was to be given to Eleazar the priest, "for a heave-offering of the Lord." The word *heave-offering* is rendered from the word תְּרוּמַת *terūmath*, from the root רוּם *rūm*, which means a lifting up, exalting, elevation of rank, while the form here used means a gift, a contribution, associated with the idea of being lifted up, exalted, elevated to a higher condition. Hence, when the priest presented a heave-offering, he moved his censer upwards, in a perpendicular line, with the view to intimate the elevating tendency resulting from the relation of the person offering, the thing offered, and the one to whom it is offered; whereas, in a wave-offering, he moved his censer in a horizontal line, intimating a relation of steadfastness and unchangeability. Because the cross is represented by perpendicular and horizontal lines, some early commentators have imagined that the heave and wave-offerings were typical of the cross of Christ. The word "heave," as here used, is purely Saxon; *heafan*, to lift, to raise, to move upward. We may well say *to heave up;* but it is bad Saxon to say *heave down.* From this same

Saxon word comes our word *heaven*, on account of the notion of its lofty location, and the elevating influence of the acts of him who shall reach it; each act which makes us nearer heaven may not inappropriately be considered a heave-offering to the Lord. The corollary is, that if God had regarded the making these children slaves a sin,—since sin always deteriorates and degrades, the reverse of elevation or lifting up,—he never could have ordered any of them to be given to him as a *heave-offering*.

We trust to establish the point that the enslavement of such people as we find the African hordes now to be, to those who have a more correct knowledge of God and his laws,—of those most wicked Midianites, to those to whom God had most especially revealed himself,—must, so long as the laws of God operate, have an elevating influence upon those so enslaved. Thus we shall perceive that the Hebrew word, translated into our old Saxon *heave-offering* was the most appropriate, and significant of the facts of the case, that could be expressed by language.

Our received version of this chapter, which is a good translation of the original, contains no word by which we directly express the idea of slavery: so is it in the original. But we trust the readers of either will not be found so awry as not to perceive that the idea and facts are as fully and substantially developed as though those terms were used in each.

In the most of languages, an idea, and facts in relation to it, may be and are often expressed without the use of the name of the idea, and sometimes of the facts. The Greek is well deemed a most particular and definite language. In Thucydides, liber vii. caput 87, this sentence occurs: ἔπειτα πλὴν Ἀθηναίων, καὶ εἴτινες Σικελιωτῶν ἢ Ἰταλιωτῶν ξυνεστράτευσαν, τοὺς ἄλλους ἀπέδοντο. Here, there is no word expressing the idea of slavery. Literally, it is: "Then, except the Athenians, and some of the Sicilians or Italians, who had engaged in the war, all others were sold." Yet Dr. Smith, the rector of Holy Trinity Church, in Chester, England, who lived at an age beyond the reach of prejudice or argument on the subject of slavery, (he was born in 1711,) has correctly translated the passage thus: "But, after this term, all but the Athenians, and such of the Sicilians and Italians as had joined with them in the invasion, were sold out for slaves." *Smith's Thucyd.* p. 285.

And permit us further to inquire how the assertion of Mr. Barnes, page 117, that, "in the laws of Moses there is but *one* way mentioned by which a foreigner could be made a slave; that is, by purchase, *Lev.* xxv. 44; and it is remarkable that the Hebrews were not permitted to make slaves of the captives taken in the war"—will compare with *Deut.* xx. 10–16:

"And when thou comest nigh unto a city to fight against it, then proclaim peace unto it." * * * "And it shall be, if it make answer of peace, and open unto thee, then it shall be, *that* all the people *that* is found therein, shall be tributaries unto thee, and *shall serve thee*" (וַעֲבָדוּךָ *va abaduka, shall be slaves to thee*). "And if it will make no peace with thee, but will make war against thee, then thou shalt besiege it." And when the hand of thy God hath delivered it into thy hands, thou shalt smite every male thereof with the edge of the sword." "But the women, and the little ones, and the cattle, and all that is within the city, *even* all the spoil thereof, shalt thou take unto thyself; and thou shalt eat the spoil of thine enemies, which the Lord thy God hath given thee." "Thus shalt thou do unto all the cities *which are* very far off from thee, which *are* not of the cities of those nations."

It is evident that the captives here allowed to be made were to be slaves, from what follows on the same subject, in the same book, xxi. 10–15: When thou goest forth to war against thine enemies, and the Lord thy God hath delivered them into thy hands, and thou hast taken them captive, and seest among the captives a beautiful woman, and hast a desire unto her, that thou wouldst have her to thy wife: then thou shalt bring her home to thy house, and she shall shave her head and pare her nails: and she shall put the raiment of her captivity from off her, and shall remain in thy house, and bewail her father and her mother a full month: and after that, thou shalt go in unto her, and be her husband, and she shall be thy wife. And it shall be, if thou have no delight in her, then thou shalt let her go whither she will; but thou shalt not sell her at all for money: thou shalt not make merchandise of her, because thou hast humbled her."

Thus the fact is proved, that if he had not thus made her his wife, she would have been his slave and an article of merchandise.

LESSON XI.

In the introductory part of Mr. Barnes's book, he makes some remarks in the nature of an apology for his undertaking to examine the subject of slavery. Page 20, he says—

"Belonging to the same *race* with those who are held in bondage. We have a right, *nay*, we are bound to express the sympathies of brotherhood, and 'to remember those who are in bonds as bound with them.'"

We were not aware of any fact relating to Mr. Barnes's descent; nor did we before know from what race he was descended.

We were truly much surprised at this avowal, and endeavoured to imagine that he had used the word in some general and indefinite sense, as some do when they say animal *race*, and human *race*. But on examining his use of the word, page 20: "How is a foreign *race*, with so different a complexion, and in reference to which, so deep-seated prejudices and aversions exist, in every part of the land, to be disposed of if they become free?"—and page 27: "And the struggles which gave liberty to millions of the Anglo-saxon *race* did not loosen one rivet from the fetter of an African;" page 83: "The Hebrews were not essentially distinguished from the Egyptians, as the Africans are from their masters in this land, by colour;" and page 86: "They were a foreign *race*, as the African *race* is with us;" and page 96: "There are in the United States now, according to the census of 1840, 2,486,465 of a foreign *race* held in bondage;" and page 97: "It would have been as just for the Egyptians to retain the Hebrews in bondage as it is for white Americans to retain the African race;"—we were forced to conclude that the author understood his language and its meaning.

Such, then, being the fact, we cannot find it in our heart to blame him for "expressing the sympathies of brotherhood." But we feel disposed with kindness to relieve his mind from the burthen of such portion of sympathy for those of his *race* who are in slavery, as he may conceive to be a duty imposed by the injunction, "Remember those who are in bond, as bound with them." We will quote the passage, *Heb.* xiii. 3: "Remember them that are in bonds, as bound with them." It is translated from the Greek—

Μιμνήσκεσθε τῶν δεσμίων ὡς συνδεδεμένοι, *Mimnēskěsthe tōn děsmiōn hōs sunděděměnoi.* The words translated "bonds," "bound with," &c. are derived from the root δέω, *deo*, and signifies to bind, to bring together, to chain, to fetter, to hinder, to restrain, &c., which meaning falls into all its derivations. When one was accused of some offence, and was, on that account, restrained, so that he might be surely had at a trial for the same, such restraint would be expressed, as the case required, by some of its derivations. Hence we have δέσις, *děsis*, the act of binding; δέσμα, *desma*, a bond, a chain; δέσμιος, *desmios*, chained, fettered, imprisoned, &c.; δεσμός, *desmos*, a bond, chain, knots, cords, cables; δεσμόω, *desmŏō*, to enchain, to imprison; δεσμοφύλαξ, *desmophulax*, a jailer, &c.

The word is used, differently varied, in *Matt.* xvi. 19; xviii. 18; *Acts* viii. 23; xx. 23; xxiii. 21; xxvi. 29; *Rom.* vii. 2; 1 *Cor.* vii. 39; *Eph.* iv. 3; *Philip.* i. 16; *Col.* iv. 18; 2 *Tim.* ii. 9; *Philem.* 10; *Heb.* x. 34; xi. 36; and never used, in any sense whatever, to express any condition of slavery. St. Paul was under the *restraint* of the law upon a charge of heresy. All the Christians of his day were very liable to like danger. His only meaning was that all such should be remembered, as though they themselves were suffering a like misfortune. Suppose he had expressed the idea more diffusely and said, "Remember all Christians who, for teaching Christ crucified, are persecuted on the charge of teaching a false religion, as though you yourselves were persecuted with them."

Such was the fact. Surely no one, by any course of rational deduction, could construe it into an injunction to remember or do any thing else, in regard to slavery or its subjects, unless upon the condition that the slave was, by some means, under restraint upon a similar charge. St. Paul was never married; cannot be said to have looked with very ardent eyes upon the institution of marriage; by many is thought to have been unfavourably disposed towards it. We have among us, to this day, some who pretend that they think it a great evil, are its bitter enemies, and give evidence that, if in their power, they would totally abolish it. Suppose such a man should say that, because he belonged to the same *race* with those who were bound in the bonds of wedlock, it was his privilege to express the sympathies of brotherhood, and expostulate against that evil institution; nay, that he was enjoined by St. Paul to do so, in this passage, "Remember those who are in bonds, as bound with them,"—what would be the value of this appeal to St. Paul? But the very word he uses, in the passage quoted, is also used, almost invariably, in the gospels, to express the restraint imposed by matrimony; yet it is never used to express any condition, or quality, or station, in regard to slavery.

The naked, unadorned proposition presented by Dr. Barnes is, that, because St. Paul enjoined the Hebrew Christians to sympathize with, to remember all those who were labouring under persecution on the account of their faith in Christ, they were also bound to remember, to sympathize with the slaves, on the account of their being in slavery, as though they were slaves themselves. We feel that such argument must ever be abortive.

From the delicacy of Dr. Barnes's situation, as "belonging to the same *race* with those held in bondage," we feel it a duty to treat the position with great forbearance. Had it come from one of the more favoured race of Shem, or the still more lofty *race* of Japheth, we should have felt it an equal duty to have animadverted with some severity.

It would have appeared like a design to impose on those ignorant of the original; and might have put us in mind of the cunning huckster, with his basket of addled eggs,—although unexpectedly broken in the act of their delivery to the hungry traveller; yet the incident was remembered by the recorder of propriety.

LESSON XII.

Antioch is said to have been the birthplace of St. Margaret,—of which there are many legends, to one of which we allude. It brings to mind some early views of Christianity; besides, at her time, a large portion of the population of Antioch were slaves, and are alluded to in the legend.

She was the daughter of the priest of Apollo, and was herself a priestess to the same god. She is said to have lived in the time and under the authority of the Præfect Olybius, who became devoted to her mental and personal accomplishments and very great beauty. He is said to have sought her in marriage, and, after great labour and exertion, to have brought about such a state of affairs as to insure her approval and consent. But, although thus the affianced bride of Olybius, by some means she had held intercommunion with the private teachers of Christianity, and was converted to its faith; a fact known only to her and them.

Upon such a state of things, arrives from Probus, Rome's imperial lord, Vopiscus, charged to admonish the præfect how fame bore tidings of the frequent apostasy from the true religion of the gods, and the increase of the unholy faith of the Galileans at Antioch; and that the laws were made to be executed upon the godless, whose wicked and incestuous rites offend the thousand deities of Rome.

Olybius well knows that the least faltering on his part would probably be followed by his being shown the mandate for Vopiscus to supersede him in the government; for which he determines to not give him the least pretence: hence he orders the immediate arrest of all suspected; convenes his council in the halls of justice, and announces thus his views:

"Hear me, ye priests on earth, ye gods in heaven!
By Vesta, and her virgin-guarded fires;
By Mars, the sire and guardian god of Rome;
By Antioch's bright Apollo; by the throne
Of him whose thunder shakes the vaulted skies;
And that dread oath I add, that binds the immortals,
The unblessed waters of Tartarean Styx;
Last, by the avenger of despised vows,
The inevitable, serpent-haired Eumenides,
Olybius swears, thus mounting on the throne
Of justice, to exhaust heaven's wrath on all
That have cast off their fathers' gods for rites
New and unholy. From my heart, I blot
Partial affection and the love of kindred;
Even if my father's blood flowed in their veins,
I would obey the emperor and the gods!"

MILLMAN.

* * * The prisoners are ushered in, heard, and ordered to death; among whom a female veiled, as if Phœbus-chosen!

"What! dare they rend our dedicated maids,
Even from our altars? Haste! withdraw the veil,
In which her guilty face is shrouded close.
Ha! their magic mocks my sight! I seem to see
What cannot be——Margarita!
Answer, if thou art she!"

His mind was agonized at the thoughts of her position: silently, to himself, he says—

> "——————This pale and false Vopiscus
> Hath from great Probus wrung his easy mandate;
> Him Asia owns her præfect, if Olybius
> Obey not this fell edict." * * *

Much art and great argument were privately used to produce her recantation; to which she calmly answers—

> ——————"Who disown their Lord
> On earth, will He disown in heaven!"

* * * Sent to the arena; the torture and execution of the prisoners proceed, according to the order of their arraignment. The populace become enraged, and loudly demand the blood of the apostate priestess; while the præfect, in his palace, digests a plan to *surely* save her life. The high-priest of Apollo, her father, in his robes of office and with his official attendants, must boldly enter the arena, and offer pardon, in the name of his god, to any one who utters the cabalistic word signifying "I RECANT;" must hastily apply to each in person; at Margarita, one instructed must imitate her voice; instantly the priest is to throw the mantle of the god upon her; and the attendants, by force, to carry her to the palace of Olybius, where, instead of her execution, her marriage with Olybius is to take place.

The procession of priests (of whom none but her father, and her sister in disguise as a proxy for the act of recantation, knew the secret) are urged instantly to action: "For, says Olybius, "my very soul is famished in every moment of delay!"

The procession moves in all pomp and splendour, with a view to produce an alterative effect on the mind of the maddened populace. Its approach to the arena is proclaimed by a sentinel there; on hearing which, Margarita falls at the feet of the *headsman*, and successfully implores instant death, that her father may be spared the misery of witnessing it. She breathes a prayer in forgiveness of Olybius, and receives the stroke of death as the procession enters. The father rages, demands torture to make the Christians say how they enthralled her: a Christian teacher explains, as with "a still, small voice;" the priests of Apollo listen!

Rage and excitement had reached the utmost bound. There was a pause, as the recess between two raging storms. The stillness reached even the palace, and reason did feel as if

"There was darkness over all the land. Olybius, then:—
What means this deathlike stillness? Not a sound
Or murmur, from yon countless multitudes;
A pale, contagious horror seems to creep
Even to our palace. Men gaze mutely round,
As in their neighbour's face to read a secret
They dare not speak themselves:
Even thus, along his vast domains of silence,
Dark Pluto gazes, when the sullen spirits
Speak only with fixed look and voiceless motion.
'Tis misery! Speak; Olybius orders; speak to me,
Nor let mine own voice, like an evil omen,
Load this hot air unanswered."

A messenger announces the death of Margarita; Olybius rushes to kill him; but, recovering self-command—

—————————"Oh, I'm sick
Of this accursed pomp: I will not use
Its privilege of revenge. Fatal trappings
Of proud authority! That * * * * *
* * * shine and burn into the very entrails!
Supremacy!! the great prerogative
Of being blasted by superior misery!"

A second messenger announces that

"The enchantress Margarita, by her death,
Hath wrought upon the changeful populace,
That they cry loudly on the Christian's God:
Emboldened multiutudes, from every quarter,
Throng forth, and in the face of day proclaim
Their lawless faith. They have taken up the body,
And hither, as in proud ovation, bear it,
With clamour and with song. All Antioch crowds
Applauding round them."

We are favoured only with the song of the slaves, who, upon that holiday, intermingled in the throng about the palace of Olybius, to which the body of Margarita has been borne; by which we may perceive how Christianity has elevated them above thoughts of their condition:

SONG OF THE SLAVES.

Sing to the Lord! Oh, let us shout his praise!
More lofty pæans let our masters raise.
Midst clouds of golden light, a pathway clear,
With soaring soul, these martyred saints have trod
To Him, the only true Almighty God!
Earth's tumults wild and pagan darkness drear,
To bonds of peace and songs of joy give way:
Behold! we bring you light—one everlasting day!

Sing to the Lord! No more shall frantic Sibyl's yell,
Watchful Augurs, or those of magic spell,
No, not Isis, nor yet Apollo's throne,
No, nor even Death, with Lethean bands,
Shall longer bind the soul; before us stands
Him of the Cross of Calvary:—His groan
Of death burst forth from its eternal womb,
While angel spirits shout, and open wide the tomb!

Sing to the Lord! The Temple's veil is rent!
From Moab's plains, the Slave, an outcast, sent
From this cold world shall, soaring, fly to heaven,
From depths of Darkness, Night, and Orcus dread.
Each spirit woke at the Eternal's tread
On the head of Death! a promise given
To all Earth's houseless, homeless, and forlorn,
Before the Ages were—or His Eldest Son was born!

Sing to the Lord! Lo! while God's rebels rave,
He plunges down, and renovates the slave—
Vengeance and love at once bestowed on man.
See! crushed is Baal's, proud Moloch's temple falls;
Shout to the Lord! No more shall blood-stained walls,
Nor mountain grove, nor all the gods of Ham,
Dispel a Saviour's love! Correction's rod
Hath won the world,—for Heaven and Thee, O God!

It is one of the providences of Jehovah, that the very wretched forget their wrath, and the broken in spirit their violence. And it may be well for those who examine moral conduct by the evidences of the providences of God, to notice how wrath conduces to wretchedness, and violence to a breaking down of the spirit.

Olybius was by no means prepared to adopt the humiliating doctrines of the new faith; but he perceived it to be well adapted to the condition of those in the extremely low walks of life. By it the slave was taught to become "the freeman of the Lord," and the wretched, destitute, and miserable, to become "heirs of God, and joint-heirs with Christ." These doctrines, and the whole system, being founded upon the pillars of Humility, Faith, Hope, and Charity, were an arrangement to make the most humble as happy as the most exalted; as to happiness and hopes of heaven, it made all men equal; nor is it surprising that the low classes more readily become its converts.

Olybius may have seen some beautiful features in this system; but his philosophy forbid his faith. He calmly decided that it was a superstition too low to combat—worthy only of contempt. But he perceived that the blood of a hundred made a thousand Christians, and was convinced the only remedy was to improve and elevate the mind,—to imbue it with deep religious feeling and principle, a reverence and veneration for the gods.

He deeply felt the wound inflicted by the presence of Vopiscus, and would gladly have proved to the emperor that change of government, either as to ruler or its general system, could not affect the condition of this new doctrine. But he had no knowledge of the Christian's God, nor of his attributes as a distinct Being; and hence, although he may be regarded as a most deadly enemy, yet, since the providences of Jehovah, through the mild light of the gospel, begin to develop themselves to the human understanding, we may deem his report to the emperor, on the Christian superstition, to be ONE OF ITS MOST UNDYING PANEGYRICS; as an extract from which, we may well imagine, he wrote thus:—

Olybius to the Emperor Probus.

* * * "Great reforms on moral subjects do not occur, except under the influence of religious principle. Political revolutions and changes of policy and administration do indeed occur from other causes, and secure the ends which are desired. But, on subjects pertaining to right and wrong; on those questions where the rights of an inferior and down-trodden class are concerned, we can look for little advance, except from the operation of religious principle.

"Unless the inferior classes have power to assert their rights by arms, those rights will be conceded only by the operations of conscience and the principles of religion. There is no great wrong in any community which we can hope to rectify by new considerations of policy, or by a mere revolution. The relations of *Christianity* are not reached by political revolutions, or by changes of policy or administration.

"Political revolutions occur in a higher region, and the condition of the *Christian* is no more affected by a mere change of government, than that of the vapours of a low, marshy vale is affected by the tempest and storm in the higher regions of the air. The storm sweeps along the Apennines, the lightnings play, and the thunders utter their voice, but the malaria of the Campagna is unaffected, and the pestilence breathes desolation there still. So it is with Christianity. Political revolutions occur in higher places, but the malaria of *Christianity* remains settled down on the low plains of life, and not even the surface of the pestilential vapour is agitated by all the storms and tempests of political changes; it remains the same deadly, pervading pestilence still. Under all the forms of despotism; in the government of aristocracy, or an oligarchy; under the administration of a pure democracy, or the forms of a republican government; and in all the changes from one to the other, *Christianity* remains still the same. Whether the *prince* is hurled from the throne, or rides into power on the tempest of revolution, the down-trodden Christian is the same still:—and it makes no difference to him whether the *prince* wears a crown, or appears in a plain, republican garb,—'whether Cæsar is on the throne, or slain in the senate-house.'"

In these imputed sentiments of Olybius, the indications of the will of Jehovah, in establishing and protecting the *institutions* of *Christianity*, by his providences towards it, is vividly portrayed to the Christian eye. Jehovah would not suffer "the gates of hell to prevail against it." Of the very materials intended by its enemies for its destruction, he made them build its throne.

The scene, by which we have introduced this imaginary report of Olybius to the emperor, has been merely to remove from the mind any bias tending to a partial conception of the indications of the will of God, as evinced by his providences therein described, that we may more readily discover the fact, that, instead of showing Christianity to be worthy only of contempt, Olybius did pronounce its eulogium.

Change the words *Christian* and *Christianity* into *slave* and *slavery; prince* into *master*, and it then is what Mr. Barnes did say, and has said, (pages 25, 26, 27,) word for word, about the institution of slavery; and, as if desirous to portray the providences of God towards it down to the present time, continuously says. See pages 27 and 28—

"Slavery among the Romans remained substantially the same under the Tarquins, the consuls, and the Cæsars; when the tribunes gained the ascendency, and when the patricians crushed them to the earth. It lived in Europe when the northern hordes poured down on the Roman Empire; and when the caliphs set up the standard of Islam in the Peninsula. It lived in all the revolutions of the Middle Ages,—alike, when spiritual despotism swayed its sceptre over the nations, and when they began to emerge into freedom. In the British realms, it has lived in the time of the Stuarts, under the Protectorate, and for a long time under the administration of the house of Hanover. With some temporary interruptions, it lived in the provinces of France through the revolution. It lived through our own glorious Revolution; and the struggles which gave liberty to millions of the Anglo-Saxon race did not loosen one rivet from the fetters of an African, nor was there a slave who was any nearer to the enjoyment of freedom after the surrender of Yorktown, than when Patrick Henry taught the notes of liberty to echo along the hills and vales of Virginia. So in all changes of political administration in our own land, the condition of the slave remains unaffected. Alike whether the Federalists or Republicans have the rule; whether the star of the Whig or the Democrat is in the ascendant; the condition of the slave is still the same. The pæans of victory, when the hero of New Orleans was raised to the presidential chair, or when the hero of Tippecanoe was inaugurated, conveyed no * * * intimation of a change to the slave; nor had he any more hope, nor was his condition any more affected, when the one gave place to his successor, or the other was borne to the grave. And so it is now. In all the fierce contests for rule in the land; in the questions about changes in the administration, there are nearly three millions of our fellow-beings, who have no interest in these contests and questions, and whose condition will be affected no more, whatever the result may be, than the vapour that lies in the valley is by the changes from sunshine to storm on the summits of the Alps or the Andes."

This may be all true, but what is the indication of God's will, as taught by these, his providences towards it? "And now I say unto you refrain from these men, and let them alone; for if this counsel or this work be of men, it will come to nought; but if it be of God, ye cannot overthrow it; lest haply ye be found even to fight against God." *Acts* v. 38, 39.

LESSON XIII.

Thus, it has pleased God, at an early age of the world, to reveal to the mind of man this mode of learning his will by the indications of Providence.

But Mr. Barnes has given us further data, whereby we may be enabled to examine more deeply into the indications of God's will touching the institution of slavery, by reference to his providences concerning it, growing out of the universality and ancientness of the institution. Thus, page 112, he says—"That slavery had an existence when Moses undertook the task of legislating for the Hebrews, there can be no doubt. We have seen that servitude of some kind prevailed among the patriarchs; that the traffic in slaves was carried on between the Midianites and the Egyptians, * * * and that it existed among the Egyptians. It was undoubtedly practised by all the surrounding nations, for history does not point us to a time when slavery did not exist. * * * There is even evidence that slavery was practised by the Hebrews themselves, when in a state of bondage; and that though they were as a nation 'bondmen to Pharaoh,' yet they had servants in their families who had been 'bought with money.' * * * At the very time that the law was given respecting the observance of the passover, and before the exode from Egypt, this statute appears among others: 'This is the ordinance of the passover: there shall no stranger eat thereof: but every man-servant, *that is bought for money*, when thou hast circumcised him, then shall he eat thereof.' It is clear, from this, that the institution was always in existence, and that Moses did not originate it." Again, page 117: "A Hebrew might be sold to his brethren if he had been detected in the act of theft, and had no means of making restitution according to the provisions of the law. *Exod.* xxii. 3. 'He shall make full restitution; if he have nothing, then he shall be sold for his theft.'" "This is in accordance with the common legal maxim, *Luat in corpore, qui non habet in aere.* The same law prevailed among the Egyptians, and among the Greeks also till the time of Solon. * * * By the laws of the twelve tables, the same thing was enacted at Rome. A native-born Hebrew might be a servant in a single case in virtue of his birth. If the master had given to a Hebrew, whom he had purchased, a wife, and she had borne him children; the children were to remain in servitude." See *Exod.* xxi. 4. Again, page 250: "It is unnecessary to enter into proof that slavery abounded in the Roman Empire, or that the conditions of servitude were very severe and oppressive. This is conceded on all hands." And page 251: "Slavery existed generally throughout the Roman Empire was very great." * * * Page 252: "Of course, according to this, the number of slaves could not have been less than sixty millions in the Roman Empire, at about the time when the apostles went forth to preach the gospel." And again, page 253: "The slave-trade in Africa is as old as history reaches back. Among the ruling nations of the north coast, the Egyptians, Cyrenians, and Carthaginians, slavery was not only established, but they imported whole armies of slaves, partly for home use, and partly, at least by the Carthaginians, to be shipped for foreign markets."

"They were chiefly drawn from the interior, where kidnapping was just as much carried on then as now. Black male and female slaves were even an article of luxury, not only among the above-named nations, but in Greece and Italy."

Mr. Barnes has quoted and adopted the foregoing, and many other passages, from the Biblical Repository. (See Bib. Rep. pp. 413, 414.) And again, page 259 of Barnes: * * * "And it is a rare thing, perhaps a thing that never has occurred, that slavery did not prevail in a country which furnished slaves for another country."

Many of the foregoing statements are facts as well established as *any* part of history. But these truths, honestly admitted by Mr. Barnes, are pregnant with important considerations touching the institution of slavery and the providence of God towards it.

LESSON XIV.

Mr. Barnes says, page 381—

"If slavery is to be defended, it is not to be by arguments drawn from the Bible, but by arguments drawn from its happy influences on agriculture, commerce, and the arts; * * * on its elevating the black man, and making him more intelligent and happy than he would be in his own land; on its whole benevolent bearing on the welfare of the slave, in this world and the world to come."

It must give every good man the deepest grief to discover this growing disposition among religious teachers to thrust aside the teachings of the Bible, and to place in its stead the worldly advantages and personal considerations of individual benefit. What shall we think of the religious feeling and orthodoxy of him who places "agriculture, commerce, and the arts" in higher authority than the books of Divine revelation. Thus, this teacher says, "If the Bible teaches slavery, then the Bible is the greatest curse that could happen to *our race;*" yet allows, that if slavery shall have a beneficial and happy influence on "agriculture, commerce, and the arts," it may be sustained and defended. Such is the obvious deduction from the proposition! Mistaken man! But, since we say that slavery is most triumphantly sustained and defended by the Bible, let us take a view of it agreeably to Mr. Barnes's direction. So far as we have means, it may be well to examine the negro in his native ranges.

About thirty years ago, we had a knowledge of an African slave, the property of Mr. Bookter, of St. Helena Parish, La. Sedgjo was apparently about sixty years of age—was esteemed to be unusually intelligent for an African. We propose to give the substance of his narrative, without regard to his language or manner. For a length of time we made it an object to draw out his knowledge and notions; and on the subject of the Deity, his idea was that the power which made him was *procreation;* and that, as far as regarded his existence, he needed not to care for any other god. This deity was to be worshipped by whatever act would represent him as *procreator.* It need not be remarked that this worship was the extreme of indecency; but the more the act of worship was wounding to the feelings or sense of delicacy, the more acceptable it was to the god. The displays of this worship could not well be described.

Sedgjo's account put us in mind of Maachah, the mother of Asa. In this worship, it was not uncommon to kill, roast, and eat young children, with the view to propitiate the god, and make its parents prolific. So also the first-born of a mother was sometimes killed and eaten, in thankfulness to the god for making them the instruments of its *procreation*. The king was the owner and master of the whole tribe. He might kill and do what else he pleased with them. The whole tribe was essentially his slaves. But he usually made use of them as a sort of soldiers. Those who were put to death at feasts and sacrifices were generally persons captured from other tribes. Persons captured were also slaves, might be killed and eaten on days of sacrifice, or sold and carried away to unknown countries. If one was killed in battle, and fell into the hands of those who slew him, they feasted on him at night. If they captured one alive who had done the tribe great injury, a day was set apart for all the tribe to revenge themselves and feast on him. The feet and palms of the hands were the most delicious parts. When the king or master died, some of his favourite wives and other slaves were put to death, so that he yet should have their company and services. The king and the men of the tribe seldom cultivated the land; but the women and captured slaves are the cultivators. They never whip a slave, but strike him with a club; sometimes break his bones or kill him: if they kill him, they eat him.

Sedgjo belonged to the king's family; sometimes commanded as head man; consequently, had he not been sold, would have been killed and eaten. The idea of being killed and eaten was not very dreadful to him; he had rather be eaten by men than to have the flies eat him.

He once thought white men bought slaves to eat, as they did goats. When he first saw the white man, he was afraid of his red lips; he thought they were raw flesh and sore. It was more frightful to be eaten by red than by black lips.

On shipboard, many try to starve, or jump into the sea, to keep themselves from being eaten by the red-lips. Did they but know what was wanted of them, the most would be glad to come. He cannot tell how long he was on the way to the ships, nor did he know where he was going; thinks he was sold many times before he got there; never saw the white man till he was near the sea; all the latter part of his journey to the coast the people did not kill or eat their slaves, but sold them. Their clothing is a small cloth about the loins. The king and some others have a large cloth about the shoulders. Many are entirely naked all their lives. Sedgjo has no wish to go back; has better clothing here than the kings have there; if he does more work, he has more meat. If he is whipped here, he is struck with a club there. There, always afraid of being killed; jumped like a deer, if, out of the village, he saw or met a stranger; is very glad he came here; here he is afraid of nobody.

Such is the substance of what came from the negro's own lips. It was impossible to learn from him his distinct nation or tribe. Mr. Bookter thought him an Eboe, which was probably a mistake.

The Periplus, or voyage of Hanno, was made 570 years before the Christian era. Its account was written in Punic, and deposited in the temple of Moloch, at Carthage. It was afterwards translated into Greek; and thence into English, by Dr. Faulkner, a sketch of which may be found in the "Phœnix of Rare Fragments," from which we quote, pp. 208–210:

"Beyond the Lixitiæ dwell the inhospitable Ethiopians, who pasture a wild country, intersected by large mountains, from which they say the river Lixus flows. In the neighbourhood of the mountains lived the 'Troglodytæ,' (people who burrowed in the earth,) men of various appearance, whom the Lixitiæ described as swifter in running than horses. * * * Thence we proceeded towards the east the course of a day, * * * from which proceeding a day's sail, we came to the extremity of the lake, that was overhung by large mountains, inhabited by savage men clothed in skins of wild beasts, who drove us away by throwing stones, and hindered us from landing. * * * Thence we sailed towards the south twelve days, * * * the whole of which is inhabited by Ethiopians, who would not wait our approach, but fled from us. Their language was not intelligible, even to the Lixitiæ who were with us. * * * When we had landed, we could discover nothing in the daytime except trees; in the night we saw many fires burning, and heard the sound of pipes, cymbals, drums, and confused shouts. We were then afraid, and our diviners ordered us to abandon the island; * * * at the bottom of which lay an island like the other, having a lake, and in this lake another island, full of savage people, the greater part of whom were women, whose bodies were hairy, and whom our interpreters called *Gorillæ*. Though we pursued the men, we could not seize any of them; all fled from us, escaping over the precipices, and defending themselves with stones. Three women were however taken; but they attacked their conductors with their teeth and hands, and could not be prevailed on to accompany us. Having killed them, we flayed them, and brought their skins with us to Carthage."

See also King Humpsal's History of African Settlements, translated from the Punic books, by Sallust and into English by H. Stewart, page 221:

"The Gætuli and the Libyans, as it appears, were the first nations that peopled Africa; a rude and savage race, subsisting partly on the flesh of wild beasts, and partly, like cattle, on the herbs of the field. Among these tribes social intercourse was unknown; and they were utter strangers to laws, or to civil government; wandering during the day from place to place, as inclination prompted; at night, wherever chance conducted them they took up their transient habitation." See page 224, same book: "At the back of Numidia, the Gætuli are reported to inhabit, a savage tribe, of which a part only made use of huts; while the rest, less civilized, lead a roving life, without restraint or fixed habitation. Beyond the Gætuli is the country of the Ethiopians."

In *Judg*. iii. 7, 8, we have as follows: "And the children of Israel did evil in the sight of the Lord, and forgot the Lord their God. * * * Therefore the anger of the Lord was hot against Israel, and he sold them into the hand of *Chusan Rishathaim*, (כּוּשַׁן רִשְׁעָתַיִם) which means the "*wicked Ethiopians*." Let us notice its similarity of sentiment with a record in hieroglyphics, in the temple of Karnac, where *Cush* is used as the general term to mean the negro tribes: thus, "*Kush, barbarian, perverse race;*" and there inscribed over the figures of negro captives, two thousand years before our Christian era. See Gliddon's Lectures, page 42.

We quote from Horne's "Introduction to the Study of the Scriptures," thus: "It is a notorious fact that these latter" (the Canaanites) "were an abominably wicked people."

"It is needless to enter into any proof of the depraved state of their morals; they were a wicked people in the time of Abraham; and even then were devoted to destruction by God. But their iniquity was not yet full. In the time of Moses, they were idolaters; sacrificers of their own crying and smiling infants; devourers of human flesh; addicted to unnatural lusts; immersed in the filthiness of all manner of vice." See *Christian Observer* of 1819, p. 732.

But let us look at the negro tribes in more modern days. We quote from Lander, p. 58: "What makes us more desirous to leave this abominable place, is the fact (as we have been told) that a sacrifice of no less than *three hundred* human beings, of both sexes and all ages, is shortly to take place. We often hear the cries of many of these poor wretches; and the heart sickens with horror at the bare contemplation of such a scene as awaits us should we remain here much longer."

And page 74: "We have longed to discover a solitary virtue lingering among the natives of this place, (Badagry,) but as yet our search has been ineffectual."

And page 77: "We have met with nothing but selfishness and rapacity, from the chief to the meanest of his people. The religion of Badagry is Mohammedanism, and the worst species of paganism; that which sanctions and enjoins the sacrifice of human beings, and other abominable practices, and the worship of imaginary demons and fiends."

Page 110: "It is the custom here, when a governor dies, for two of his favourite wives to quit the world on the same day, in order that he may have a little pleasant, social company in a future state."

Page 111: "The reason of our not meeting with a better reception at Loatoo, when we slept there, was the want of a chief to that town, the last having followed the old governor to the eternal shades, for he was his slave. Widows are burned in India, just as they are poisoned or *clubbed* here; but in the former country, I believe no male victims are destroyed on such occasions."

"At Paoya, (page 124,) several chiefs in the road have asked us the reason why the Portuguese do not purchase as many slaves as formerly; and make very sad complaints of the stagnation in this branch of traffic."

Page 158: "At Leograda, a man thinks as little of taking a wife as cutting an ear of corn. Affection is altogether out of the question."

Page 160: "At Eitcho, it will scarcely be believed, that not less than one hundred and sixty governors of towns and villages between this place and the seacoast, all belonging to Yariba, have died from natural causes, or have been slain in war, since I was last here; and that of the inhabited places through which we have passed, not more than a half-dozen chiefs are alive at this moment, who received and entertained me on my return to Badagry, three years ago."

Page 176: "They seem to have no social tenderness; very few of those amiable private virtues which would win our affection, and none of those public qualities that claim respect or command admiration. Their love of country is not strong enough in their bosoms to incite them to defend it against the irregular incursions of a despicable foe. * * * Regardless of the past as reckless of the future; the present alone influences their actions. In this respect they approach nearer to the brute creation than perhaps any other people on the face of the globe."

Page 181: "In so large a place as this, where two-thirds of the population are slaves." * * *

Page 192: "The cause of it was soon explained by his informing us that he would be doomed to die with two companions, (slaves,) as soon as their governor's dissolution should take place."

Page 227: "In the forenoon we passed near a spot where our guides informed us a party of Falatahs, a short time ago, murdered twenty of their slaves, because they had not food sufficient," &c.

Page 232: "At Coobly, he would rather have given us a boy (slave) instead of the horse."

Page 233: "Monday, June 14th.—The governor's old wife returned from Boossa this morning, whither she had gone in quest of three female slaves who had fled from her about a fortnight since. She has brought her fugitives back with her, and they are now confined in irons."

Page 272: "Both these days the men have been entering the city; and they have brought with them only between forty and fifty slaves."

Page 278: "The chief benefits resulting to Bello from the success of the rebels, were a half-yearly tribute, which the magia agreed to pay him in slaves."

Page 282: "At Yaooris.—And many thousands of his men, fearing no law, and having no ostensible employment, are scattered over the face of the whole country. They commit all sorts of crimes; they plunder, they burn, they destroy, and even murder, and are not accountable to any earthly tribunal for their actions."

Page 312: "At Boossa.—The manners of the Africans too, are

hostile to the interest and advancement of woman, and she is very rarely placed on an equality with her husband."

Page 228: "A man is at liberty to return his wife to her parents at any time, and without adducing any reason."

Page 345: "The Sheikh of Bornou has recently issued a proclamation, that no slaves from the interior countries are to be sent for sale farther west than Wowow,—so that none will be sent in future from thence to the seaside. The greatest and most profitable market for slaves is said to be at Timbuctoo, whither their owners at present transport them to sell to the Arabs, who take them over the deserts of Tahara and Libya to sell in the Barbary States. An Arab has informed us that many of his countrymen trade as far as Turkey, in Europe, with their slaves, where they dispose of them for two hundred and fifty dollars each. * * * Perhaps it would be speaking within compass to say that four-fifths of the whole population of this country, (the Eboe,) likewise every other hereabouts, are slaves."

Vol. ii. page 208: "It may appear strange that I should dwell so long on this subject, for it seems quite natural that every one, even the most thoughtless barbarian, would feel at least some slight emotion on being exiled from his native land and enslaved; but so far is this from being the case, that Africans, generally speaking, betray the most perfect indifference on losing their liberty and being deprived of their relatives; while love of country is seemingly as great a stranger to their breasts as social tenderness and domestic affection. We have seen many thousands of slaves; some of them more intelligent than others; but the poor little fat woman whom I have mentioned,—the associate of beasts and wallowing in filth,—whose countenance would seem to indicate only listnessness, stupidity, and perhaps idiotism, without the smallest symptom of intelligence—she alone has shown any thing like regret on gazing on her native land for the last time."

Page 218: "It has been told us by many that the Eboe people are confirmned Anthropophagi; and this opinion is more prevalent among the tribes bordering on that kingdom than with the nations of more remote districts."

We shall close our extracts from Lander's work, by the following, showing that the Africans made slaves of the two Landers themselves.

Page 225: "The king then said, with a serious countenance, that there was no necessity for further discussion respecting the white men, (the two brothers Lander,) his mind was already made up on the subject; and for the first time, he briefly explained himself, to this effect: That circumstances having thrown us in the way of his subjects, by the laws and usages of the country he was not only entitled to our own persons, but had equal rights to those of our attendants. That he should take no further advantage of his good fortune than by exchanging us for as much English goods as would amount in value to twenty slaves."

The following we transcribe from Stedman's Narrative, vol. ii. page 267: "I should not forget to mention that the Gingo negroes are supposed to be Anthropophagi, or cannibals, like the Caribbee Indians, instigated by habitual and implacable revenge. Among the rebels of this tribe, after the taking of Boucore, some pots were found on the fire, with human flesh, which one of the officers had the curiosity to taste; and declared that it was not inferior to some kinds of beef or pork. I have since been informed, by a Mr. Vaugils, an American, who, having travelled a great number of miles inland in Africa, at last came to a place where human arms, legs, and thighs hung upon wooden shambles, and were exposed to sale like butcher's meat. And Captain John Keen, formerly of the Dolphin, but late of the Vianbana schooner, in the Sierra Leone Company's service, positively assured me that, a few years since, when he was on the coast of Africa, in the brig Fame, from Bristol, Mr. Samuel Briggs, owner, trading for wool, ivory, and gold-dust, a Captain Dunningen, with the whole crew belonging to the Nassau schooner, were cut in pieces, salted, and eaten by the negroes of Great Drewin."

But this is nothing to what is related, on good authority, respecting the Giagas, a race of cannibals who are said to have overrun a great part of Africa. These monsters, it is said, are descended from the Agows and Galia, who dwell in the southern extremity of Abyssinia, near the sources of the Nile. Impelled by necessity or the love of plunder, they left their original settlements, and extended their ravages through the heart of Africa, till they were stopped by the Western Ocean. They seized on the kingdom of Benguela, laying to the south of Angola; and in this situation they were found by the Romish missionaries, and by our countryman, Andrew Battel, whose adventures may be found in Purchas's Pilgrim. Both he, and the Capuchin Cavozzi, who resided long among them and converted several of them to Christianity, gave such an account of their manners as is enough to chill the blood with horror. We shall spare our readers the horrid detail, only observing that human flesh is one of their delicacies, and that they devour it, not from a spirit of revenge, or from any want of other food, but as the most agreeable dainty. Some of their commanders, when they went on an expedition, carried numbers of young women along with them, some of whom were slain almost every day, to gratify this unnatural appetite." See Modern Universal History, vol. xvi. p. 321; also Anzito; also Edin. Encyc. vol. ii. p. 185.

In continuation of this subject, permit us to take a view of these tribes, at a time just before the slave-trade commenced among them with Christian nations. The Portuguese were first to attempt to colonize portions of Africa, with the double view of extending commerce and of spreading the Christian faith. They commenced a settlement of that kind in the regions of Congo, as early as 1578; shortly after which, the Angolas, an adjoining nation, being at war with each other, one party applied to Congo and the Portuguese for aid, which was lent them. Soon a battle took place, in which 120,000 of the Angolas and Giagas were slain. See Lopez's Hist. of Congo.

About the same time, we find in *Dappus de l'Afrique*, the following data:

"The natives of Angola are tall and strong; but, like the rest of the Ethiopians, they are so very lazy and indolent, that although their soil is admirably adapted to the raising of cattle and the production of grain, they allow both to be destroyed by the wild beasts with which the country abounds. The advantages which they enjoy from climate and soil are thus neglected. * * * We are told that the people in some of the idolatrous provinces still feed on human flesh, and prefer it to all other; so that a dead slave gives a higher price in market than a living one. The cannibals are in all probability descended from the barbarous race of the Giagas, by whom the greater part of the eastern and south-eastern provinces were peopled. One most inhuman custom still prevails in this part of the kingdom, and that is, the sacrificing of a number of human victims at the burial of their dead, in testimony of the respect in which their memory is held. The number of these unhappy victims is therefore always in proportion to the rank and wealth of the deceased; and their bodies are afterwards piled up in a heap upon their tombs. * * * This prince (Angola Chilvagni) became a great warrior, enlarged the Angolic dominions, and died much regretted; and was succeeded by his son, Dambi Angola. Unlike his father, he is described as a monster of cruelty, and, happily for his subjects, his reign was of short duration. Nevertheless, he was buried with great magnificence; and, according to the barbarous custom of the country, a mound was erected over his grave, filled with the bones of human victims, who had been sacrificed to his manes."

"He was succeeded by Ngola Chilvagni, a warlike and cruel prince, who carried his victorious arms within a few leagues of Loando. * * * Intoxicated with success, he fancied himself a God, and claimed divine honours. * * * Ngingha was elected his successor, a prince of so cruel a disposition that all his subjects wished his death; which, happily for them, soon arrived. Nevertheless, he was buried with the usual pomp, with the usual number of sacrifices. His son and successor, Bandi Angola, discovered a disposition still more cruel than his father's. * * * To counteract these and other idolatrous rites, and to soften that barbarity of manners which so generally prevailed, the Portuguese, when they established themselves in the country, (1578,) were at great pains to introduce the invaluable blessings of Christianity. * * * so that from the year 1580 to 1590, we are informed, no less a number than 20,000 were converted and publicly professed Christianity." * *

"Her remains were no sooner deposited beside her sisters, in the church which she had built, than Mona Zingha declared his abhorrence to Christianity, and revived the horrid Giagan rites. Five women, of the first rank, were by his orders buried in the queen's grave, and upwards of forty persons of distinction were next sacrificed. * * * He wrote the viceroy at Loando, that he had abjured the Christian religion, which he said he had formerly embraced merely out of respect * * * to his queen, and that he now returned to the ancient sect of the Giagas. That there might remain no doubt of his sincerity in that declaration, he followed it with the sacrifice of a great number of victims, in honour of their bloody and idolatrous rites, with the destruction of all Christian churches and chapels, and with the persecution of the Christians in all parts of his kingdom."

And we may here remark that even the nations of the coast could never be persuaded to abolish human sacrifice, nor to the introduction of Christianity, to any extent, until after the introduction of the slave-trade with christian nations. See also Osborn's

Collection of Travels, vol. ii. p. 537 ; Mod. Universal Hist. vol. 43; and Edin. Encyc. vol. ii. pp. 107, 109, 110, 113.

Over two hundred years ago, and during the reign of Charles I. of England, Sir Thomas Herbert, (not Lord Edward Herbert, who wrote a deistical book, entitled, "Truth,") a gentleman of most elevated connection, and a scholar devoted to science and general literature, with a mind adorned by poetry and influenced by the strongest impulses of human sympathy; and one, of whom Lord Fairfax said,

> "He travelled, not with lucre sotted,
> But went for knowledge—and he got it!"

This author, in his Tour in Africa, writes thus: "The inhabitants here along the Golden coast of Guinea, and Benin, bounded with Tombotu, (Timbuctoo,) Gualata, and Mellis, and watered by the great river Niger, but, especially in the Mediterranean (inland) parts, know no God, nor are at all willing to be instructed by nature—"Scire nihil jucundissimum." Howbeit the Divel, who will not want his ceremonie, has infused prodigious idolatry into their hearts, enough to relish his pallet, and aggrandize their tortures, where he gets power to fry their souls, as the raging sun has scorched their cole-black carcasses. * * * Those countries are full of black-skinned wretches, rich in earth, as abounding with the best minerals and with elephants, but miserable in Demonomy. * * * Let one character serve for all. For colour they resemble chimney-sweepers; unlike them in this, they are of no profession, except rapine and villany make one; for here, *Demonis omnia plena.* * * * But in Loango and the Anziqui the people are little other than divels incarnate; not satisfied with nature's treasures, as gold, precious stones, flesh in variety, and the like; the destruction of men and women neighbouring them, whose dead carcasses they devour with a vulture relish and appetite; whom if they miss, they serve their friends such scurvy sauce, butchering them, and thinking they excuse all in a compliment that they know no better way to express love than in making two bodies in one, by an inseparable union; yea, some, as some report, proffering themselves to the shambles, accordingly are disjointed and set to sale upon the stalls. * * * The natives of Africa being propagated from Cham, both in their visages and natures, seem to inherit his malediction. * * * They are very brutes. A dog was of that value here that twenty salvages (slaves) have been exchanged for one of them; but of late years the exchange here made for negroes, to transport into the Cariba isles and continent of America, is become a considerable trade."

It will be remembered how great have been the exertions of the British Government to abolish totally the slave-trade in Africa. A great number of slave ships were captured, and the negroes found on board sent to Sierra Leone. Strong hopes were entertained that "*poor, suffering Africa*" was about to be civilized.

We quote from the Hibernian Auxiliary Missionary Report, Christian Observer; 1820, pages 888 and 889:

"The slave-trade, which like the (fabled) upas, blasts all that is wholesome in its vicinity, has, in one important instance, been here overruled for good. It has been made the means of assembling on one spot, and that on a Christian soil, individuals from almost every nation of the western coast of Africa. It has been made the means of introducing to civilization and religion many hundreds from the interior of that vast continent, who had never seen the face of a white man, nor heard the name of Jesus. And it will be made the means under God of sending to the nations beyond the Niger and the Zaire, native missionaries who will preach the Redeemer in the utmost parts of the country, and enable their countrymen to hear in their own tongue the wonderful works of God. European avarice and native profligacy leave no part of Africa unexplored for victims; and these slaves, rescued by our cruisers, and landed on the shores of our colony, are received by our missionaries and placed in their schools."

The sympathies of the world were excited on this subject, and every civilized heart cried *amen*, in union with the impulsive feelings of this Hibernian Report.

But let us remember to inquire a little into the facts, and examine whether these hopes were well or ill founded. We quote from vol. xix. of the Christian Observer, page 890:

"Mr. Johnson was appointed to the care of Regent's Town, in the month of June, 1816. On looking narrowly into the actual condition of the people intrusted to his care, he felt great discouragement. Natives of twenty-two different nations were there collected together. A considerable number of them had been but recently liberated from the holds of slave-vessels. They were greatly prejudiced against one another, and in a state of continual hostility, with no common medium of intercourse but a little broken English. When clothing was given to them, they would sell it, or throw it away: it was difficult to induce them to put it on; and it was not found practicable to introduce it among them, until led to it by the example of Mr. Johnson's servant-girl. None of them, on their first arrival, seemed to live in a state of marriage; some of them were soon afterwards married by the late Mr. Butscher; but all the blessings of the marriage state and of female purity appeared to be quite unknown. * * * Superstition, in various forms, tyrannized over their minds; many devil's houses sprang up, and all placed their security in wearing gregrees. Scarcely any desire of improvement was discernable. * * * Some, who wished to cultivate the soil, were deterred from doing so by the fear of being plundered of the produce. Some would live in the woods, apart from society; and others subsisted by thieving and plunder: they would steal poultry and pigs from any who possessed them, and would eat them raw; and not a few of them, particularly of the Eboe nation, the most savage of them all, would prefer any kind of refuse meat to the rations which they received from Government."

Doubtless Mr. Johnson and his successors have done all that good men could do, even under the protection of the British Government; but have they, in the least, affected the slave-trade of Africa, otherwise than to divert its direction, or have they diminished it to any observable extent? True, its course has been changed, and its enormities thereby increased tenfold. Instead of its subjects being brought under the regenerating influences of Christianity, they are sacrificed at the shrine of friends at home, or sent among pagans or Mohammedans! Let the Christian philosopher think of these things.

While we recollect the proclamation of the Emperor of Bourno, let us look at the slave-trade as now carried on with the Barbary States, the Arab tribes, and Egypt and Asia, as well as Turkey in Europe. We quote from "Burckhart's Travels in Nubia," as reported in the Christian Observer, vol. xix. p. 459:

"The author had a most favourable opportunity of collecting intelligence and making observations on this subject, (slavery,) as connected with the northeastern parts of Africa by travelling with companies of slaves and slave-merchants through the deserts of Nubia. * * * The chief mart in the Nubian mountains, for the Egyptian and the Arabian slave-trade, is Shendy. * * * To this emporium, slaves are brought from various parts of the interior, and particularly from the idolatrous * * * tribes in the vicinity of Darfour, Bozgho, and Dar Saley."

Our traveller calculated the number sold annually in the market of Shendy at five thousand. "Far the larger part of these slaves are under the age of fifteen."

See page 460: "Few slaves are imported into Egypt without changing masters several times. * * * A slave, for example, purchased at Fertit, is transferred at least six times before he arrives at Cairo. These rapid changes, as might be expected, are productive of great hardship to the unfortunate individuals, especially in the toilsome journey across the deserts. Burckhart saw on sale at Shendy, many children of four of five years old, *without their parents.* * * * Burckhart has entered into the details of cruelties of another kind, practised on the slaves to raise their pecuniary value. The particulars are not suitable for a work of miscellaneous perusal. * * * The great mart, however, for the supply of European and Asiatic Turkey with the kind of slaves required as guardians for the harem, Mr. Burckhart informs us, is not at Shendy, but at a village near Siout, in Upper Egypt, *inhabited chiefly by Christians.*" (Abyssinians, we suppose.)

The mode of marching slaves is described as follows: "On the journey, they are tied to a long pole, one end of which is tied to a camel's saddle, and the other, which is forked, is passed on each side of the slave's neck, and tied behind with a strong cord, so as to prevent him drawing out his head: in addition to this, his right hand is also fastened to the pole, at a short distance from the head, thus leaving only his legs and left arm at liberty. In this manner he marches the whole day behind the camel: at night he is taken from the pole and put in irons. While on the route to Souakim, I saw several slaves carried along in this way. Their owners were afraid of their escaping, or of becoming themselves the objects of their vengeance; and in this manner they would continue to be confined until sold to a master, who, intending to keep them, would endeavour to attach them to his person. In general, the traders seem greatly to dread the effects of sudden resentment in their slaves; and if a grown-up boy is to be whipped, his master first puts him in irons."

Page 333: "Females with children on their backs follow the caravans on foot; and if a camel breaks down, the owner generally loads his slaves with the packages; and if a boy in the evening can only obtain a little butter with his *dhourra* bread, and some grease every two or three days to smear his body and hair, he is contented, and never complains of fatigue. Another cause which induces the merchants to treat the slaves well (?) is their anxiety to dissipate the horror which the negroes all entertain of Egypt and the white people. It is a common opinion in the black slave countries that the Ouleder Rif, or children of Rif, as the Egyptians are there called, devour the slaves, who are transported thither for that purpose: of course, the traders do every thing in their power to destroy this belief; but, notwithstanding all their endeavours, it is never eradicated from the mind of the slaves."

Page 462: "The manners of the people of Souakim are the same as those I have already described in the interior, and I have reason to believe that they are common to the whole of eastern Africa, including Abyssinia, where the character of the inhabitants, as drawn by Bruce, seems little different from that of these Nubians. I regret that I am compelled to represent all the nations of Africa which I have yet seen, in so bad a light."

We next quote from the Family Magazine, 1836, page 439, as follows: "Many of the Dayaks have a rough, scaly scurf on their skin, like the Jacong of the Malay Peninsula. * * * The female slaves of this race, which are found among the Malays, have no appearance of it. * * * With regard to their funeral ceremonies, the corpse * * * remains in the house till the son, the father, or the next of blood, can procure or purchase a slave, who is beheaded at the time the corpse is burned, in order that he may become the *slave* of the deceased in the next world. * * * Nobody can be permitted to marry till he can present a human head of some other tribe to his proposed bride. * * * The head-hunter proceeds in the most cautious manner to the vicinity of the villages of another tribe, and lies in ambush till he can surprise some heedless, unsuspecting wretch, who is instantly decapitated. * * * When the hunter returns, the whole village is filled with joy, and old and young, men and women, hurry out to meet him, and conduct him, with the sound of brazen cymbals, dancing, in long lines, to the house of the female he admires, whose family likewise come out to greet him with dances, and provide him with a seat, and give him meat and drink. He holds the bloody head still in his hand, and puts part of the food into his mouth, after which the females of the family receive the head from him, which they hang up to the ceiling over the door. If a man's wife die, he is not permitted to make proposals of marriage to another till he has procured another head of a different tribe. The heads they procure in this manner, they preserve with great care, and sometimes consult in divination. The religious opinions connected with this practice are by no means correctly understood: some assert they believe that every person whom a man kills in this world becomes his *slave* in the next. * * * The practice of stealing heads causes frequent wars among the tribes of the Idean. Many persons never can obtain a head; in which case they are. generally despised by the warriors and the women. To such a height is it carried, however, that a person who has obtained eleven heads has been seen, and at the same time he pointed out his son who, a young lad, had procured three."

James Edward Alexander, H. L. S., during the years 1836 and 1837, made an excursion from the Cape of Good Hope into the interior of South Africa and the countries of the Namaquas, Boschmans, and Hill Damaras, under the auspices of Her Majesty's Government and the Royal Geographical Society, which has been published in two volumes; from which we extract, vol. i. page 126: "I was anxious to ascertain the extent of knowledge among the tribe (Damaras) with which I now dwelt; to learn what they knew of themselves, and of men and things in general; but I must say that they positively know nothing beyond tracing game and breaking in jack-oxen. They did not know one year from another; they only knew that at certain times the trees and flowers bloom, and then rain was expected. As to their own age, they knew no more what it was than idiots. Some even had no names. Of numbers, of course, they were nearly or quite ignorant; few could count above five; and he was a clever fellow who could count his ten fingers. Above all they had not the least idea of God or of a future state. They were, literally like the beasts which perish."

Page 163, 164, and 165: "At Chubeeches the people were very poor. * * * Standing in need of a shepherd, I observed here two or three fine little Damara boys, as black as ebony. * * * I said to the old woman to whom Saul belonged, 'You have two boys, and they are starving; you have nothing to give them.' 'This is true,' she replied. 'Will you part with Saul?' said I; 'I want a shepherd, and the boy wants to go with me.' 'You will find him too cunning,' returned the old dame. 'I want a clever fellow,' said I. 'Very well,' she replied; 'give me four cotton handkerchiefs and he is yours.' 'Suppose,' said I, 'you take two handkerchiefs and two strings of glass beads?' 'Yes! that will do;' and so the bargain was closed; and thus a good specimen of

Damara flesh and blood was bought for the value of about four shillings. * * * I told him to go and bring his skins; on which he informed me that he had none, saving what he stood in—and that was his own sable hide, with the addition of the usual strap of leather around his waist, from which hung a piece of jackal's skin in front. Constant exposure to the vicissitudes of the weather, without clothes, hardens the skin of the body like that of the face; and still it is difficult to sleep at nights without proper covering. In cold weather, the poor creatures of Namaqua Land, who may have no karosses, sit cowering over a fire all night, and merely doze with their heads on their knees."

Vol. ii. page 23: "Can any state of society be considered more low and brutal than that in which promiscuous intercourse is viewed with the most perfect indifference; where it is not only practised, but spoken of without any shame or compunction? Some *rave* about the glorious liberty of the savage state, and about the innocence of the children of nature, and say that it is chiefly by the white men that they become corrupt. The Boschmans of Ababres had never seen white men before; they were far removed from the influence of the Europeans."

Vol. i. page 102: "Notwithstanding that some people maintain that there is no nation on earth without religion in some form, however faintly it may be traced in their minds, yet, after much diligent inquiry, I could not discover the slightest feeling of devotion towards a higher and invisible power among the Hill Damaras."

In Mohammedan countries, the most unfavourable portions of the slave's existence, as such, is while in the hands of the geeleb, or slave-merchant, and until he is sold to one who designs to keep him permanently. In the first instance, if negroes, they suffer much in the journey from the place of purchase to that of sale. For instance, it has been known, in the journey from Sennaar and Darfour to the slave-mart at Cairo, or even the intermediate one at Siout, the loss in a slave caravan, of men, women, camels, and horses, amounted to not less than 4000. The circumstances of the mart itself scarcely appear in a more favourable aspect than those of the journey,—whether we regard the miserable beings, as in the market at Cairo, crowded together in enclosures like the sheep-pens in Smithfield market, amid the abominable stench and uncleanness which result from their confinement; whether, as at another great mart at Muscat, we perceive the dealer walking to and fro, with a stick in his hand, between two lots of ill-clothed boys and girls, whom he is offering for sale, proclaiming aloud, as he passes, the price fixed on each; or else leading his string of slaves through the narrow and dirty streets, and calling out their prices as he exhibits them in this ambulatory auction. * * * The slaves, variously exhibited, usually appear quite indifferent to the process, or only show an anxiety to be sold, from knowing that as slaves, finally purchased, their condition will be much ameliorated. * * * How little slavery is dreaded is also shown by the fact that even *Mohammedan parents or relatives* are, in cases of emergency, ready enough to offer their children for sale. During the famine which a few years since drove the people of Mosul to Bengal, one could not pass the streets without being annoyed by the solicitations of parents to purchase their boys and girls for the merest trifle; and even in Koordistan, where no constraining motive appeared to exist, we have been sounded as to our willingness to purchase young members of the family. Europeans in the East are scarcely considered amenable to any general rules, but Christians generally are not allowed to possess any other than negro slaves." *London Penny Mag.* 1834, pp. 243, 244; also, *Sketches of Persia*, and *Johnson's Journey from India.*

LESSON XV.

Quotations from books of authority, portraying the universal state of degradation of the African hordes, may be made to an unlimited extent. Our object has been to present some idea of what the negro is in his own country, when beyond the influence of American slavery. We will now advance some views of him and his race, as they present themselves *in* this American slavery. And here let us premise that the population of the African tribes is estimated at 50,000,000, 40,000,000 of whom are deemed to be slaves; that the wars among them are not so much wars to make freemen slaves, as they are to appropriate the slaves of one owner to the rightful ownership of another, according to their notions of law and their customs of right. Among them, conquest always subjects to slavery. When slaves take a captive, he is the property of their master. Slavery exists there according to their laws and customs; and there is no evidence, nor in fact is it probable, that even the slave-trade with America has ever increased the extent or degree of slavery in Africa.

We quote from a truly able and sympathetic writer, J. Morier's "Second Journey through Persia," as reported in the Christian Observer, vol. xvi. page 808:

"During the time we were at the Brazils, the slave-trade was in full vigour, and a visit to the slave-market impressed us more with the iniquity of this traffic than any other thing that could be said or written on the subject. On each side of the street where the market was held, were large rooms in which the negroes were kept; and during the day, they were seen in melancholy groups, waiting to be delivered from the hands of the trader, whose dreadful economy might be traced in their persons, which at that time were little better than skeletons. If such were their state on shore, with the advantage of air and space, what must have been their condition on board the ship that brought them hither? It is not unfrequent that slaves escape to the woods, where they are almost as frequently retaken. When this is the case, they have an iron collar put about their necks, with a long hooked arm extending from it, to impede their progress through the woods, in case they should abscond a second time. Yet amid all this misery, it was pleasing to observe the many negroes who frequented the churches, and to see them, in form and profession, at least making a part of a Christian congregation."

Mr. Morier's statement may bear testimony to abuses of slavery; but it certainly bears testimony to another thing more important to the slave. "The fear of the Lord is the beginning of wisdom." *Prov.* ix. 10.

And we here beg leave to remark that we shall, in all instances, draw our proofs from the enemies of the institution. We quote from Berbick's Notes on America, page 20, and reported in vol. xvi. of the Christian Observer, published in London, May 10th, page 109:

"I saw two female slaves and their children sold by auction in the street; an incident of common occurrence here, though horrifying to myself and many other strangers. I could hardly bear to see them handled and examined like cattle; and when I heard their sobs and saw the *big tears* rolling down their cheeks at the thought of being separated, I could not refrain from weeping with them."

This may have been very cruel in the white man; but who has

ever heard of a negro in Africa displaying such a strength of tenderness and feeling of sympathy as here manifested? And how are we to account for it in this instance, if not by the regenerating influence of a few generations in American and Christian slavery? However slow the action, the condition of the mental faculties was improved and the moral condition ameliorated. But in the same page, he says—

"A traveller told me that he saw, a few weeks ago, one hundred and twenty sold by auction in the streets of Richmond, and that they filled the air with their lamentations."

The case of the women was not solitary, and doubtless we shall find such proof of an improved state of the affections quite common. But this good man continuously pursues the subject:

"It has also been confidently alleged, that the condition of slaves in Virginia, under the mild treatment they are said to experience, is preferable to that of our English labourers. I know and lament the degrading state of dependent poverty to which the latter have been gradually reduced by the operation of laws originally designed for their comfort and protection. I know also that many slaves pass their lives in comparative ease, and seem to be unconscious of their bonds, and that the *most wretched* of our paupers might even envy the allotment of the *happy* negro."

We will now quote from Lieutenant Francis Hall, of the British Light Dragoons. In his Travels in Canada and the United States, published in London, 1818, pages 357 to 360, he says—

"I took the boat this morning, and crossed the ferry over to Portsmouth, the small town which I told you was opposite to this place, (Norfolk.) It was court-day, and a large crowd of people was gathered about the door of the court-house. I had hardly got upon the steps to look in, when my ears were assailed by the voice of singing, and turning round to observe from what quarter it came, I saw a group of about thirty negroes, of different sizes and ages, following a rough-looking white man, who sat carelessly lolling in his sulkey. They had just turned round the corner, and were coming up the main street, to pass by the spot where I stood, on their way out of town. As they came nearer, I saw some of them loaded with chains to prevent their escape, while others had hold of each other's hands, strongly grasped, as if to support themselves in their affliction. I particularly noticed a poor mother, with an infant, as she walked along, while two small children had hold of her apron on either side, almost running, to keep up with the rest. They came along singing a little wild hymn, of sweet and mournful melody, flying, by Divine instinct of the heart, to the consolations of religion, the last refuge of the unhappy, to support them in their distress."

We have no knowledge of Lieutenant Hall's powers of deduction, nor of what he thought this *story* proved. But it will surely give us new views of Africa, if he will travel there, and find such a scene there, among the many slaves he may *now* see naked, tied to poles, and leaving their country for ever. The world has been flooded with stories of this description, some of which prove the abuses of slavery, but all of them prove some amelioration, both mentally and physically, in the condition of the slave here, when compared with the condition of the African at home, whether bond or free.

Mr. Barnes has admitted one into his book, pages 136, 137, and 138, which adds strength to our position: its length excludes a copy. We quote again from the Christian Observer, vol. xv. p. 541: "Missions of the United Brethren at Surinam."—Mr. Campbell writes: "On the plantations and at Sommelsdyk there was a great desire among the negroes to hear the gospel, which finds entrance into many of their hearts. * * * At Paramaribo, the negro congregation consisted, at the close of 1813, of 550." "On the 30th of August, 1814, the same missionary writes that the word of God among the negroes in Paramaribo continues to increase, and we have great reason to rejoice and take courage when we see marked proofs of the Divine blessing upon our feeble ministry." See page 542. "Antigua."—"A letter from this island, dated, Grace Hill, Jan. 14th, 1814. * * * The congregation of Christian negroes at this place consisted, at the close of 1813, of 2087 persons." Again, page 543: "Some poor negroes, who, although they sigh under the pressure of slavery and various hardships, or ailments of body, seek consolation and refreshment from the meritorious passion of Jesus, are enabled, with tears of joy, to lay hold on these words of Scripture: 'I reckon that the sufferings of this present time are not worthy to be compared with the glory which shall be revealed in us.'" Again, p. 554: "Jamaica."—Mr. Lang, the missionary, writes thus, on the 5th February, 1814: "It pleases the Lord still to bless our labours with success, so as to encourage us to believe that he has thoughts of peace regarding the negroes in Jamaica also, and will visit them yet more generally with his salvation," &c. Page 546: "Danish

Islands.—The number of Christian negroes belonging to the different missions in the Danish Islands, was, at the end of 1813, as follows:

At Friedensthal, St. Croix	5,100
" Friedensberg "	2,396
" New Hernhutt, St. Thomas	949
" Nisky "	1,304
" Bethany, St. Jan	474
" Emmaus "	952
Total	11,175

"*St. Kitts.*—On the 10th August, 1814, the missionaries write that they have lately had several very pleasing instances of negroes departing this life in reliance on the merits of the Saviour, with great joy and the sure and steadfast hope of everlasting life."

Among us it seems to be but little known what have been the providences of God towards the slaves of the West Indies. The following sketch is taken from the Report of the Moravian Missionaries, as found in the Christian Observer, vol. xvi. page 64:

Missions to the Slaves in the

Danish Islands.	When begun.	No. of Settlements.	No. of Missionaries.
St. Thomas	1732	2	32
St. Croix		3	
St. Jan.		2	
British Islands.			
Jamaica	1754	4	10
Antigua	1756	3	16
	1817	1	
St. Kitts	1775	1	4
Barbadoes.	1738	3	11
South America generally.	1765	1	4
		20	77

The Dutch took possession of the Cape of Good Hope in 1650. Slaves from various parts of Africa, Mozambique, and the Malay Islands were introduced; we have no means of knowing to what extent. Somerville found the city of Cape Town to contain 1145 houses, 5500 white and free people of colour, and 10,000 slaves. In all of the years 1736–1792, and 1818, the Moravians established 27 missionaries to the blacks. But they, nor no other people, have ever been able to produce any considerable effect there, or elsewhere, upon the natives, except upon such as were in slavery among a Christian people. The sound of the gospel had no charms for the wild, roving savage.

But, as reported in the Christian Observer, vol. xiv. page 830, Campbell says—"In the colony of the Cape of Good Hope, considerable efforts have been made of late, particularly by Sir John Cradock, aided by the zeal of the colonial chaplain, the Rev. Mr. Jones, to diffuse the blessings of Christian instruction, not only among the slaves, but among all classes. * * * Several of the negroes read the New Testament tolerably well, and repeat questions from Walls's Catechism: on the Lord's day they were well-dressed, and attended church." But, page 829, same vol.: "At Cape Town, Mohammedanism is much on the increase. The free Mohammedans are strenuous in their efforts to make proselytes among the slaves," &c.

We have endeavoured to show that the providences of God towards the African races in slavery to Christian nations, tend to their deliverance from idolatry, and to their restoration to an acceptable worship of the true God. And may we not inquire whether the introduction to this worship was not foretold by the prophets? "Thus saith the Lord, The labour of Egypt, and merchandise of Ethiopia and of the Sabeans, men of stature, shall come over unto thee, and they shall be thine: they shall come after thee; in chains they shall come over, and they shall fall down unto thee, they shall make supplication unto thee, saying, *Surely*, God is in thee; and *there* is none else, there *is* no God" *beside*. *Isa.* xlv. 14.

"From beyond the rivers of Ethiopia, my suppliants, even the daughters of my dispersed, shall bring mine offering."

"I will also leave in the midst of thee an afflicted and poor people, and they shall trust in the name of the Lord." *Zeph.* iii. 10, 12.

The progress of the Christian religion among the slaves of the United States is known to the world, and needs no mention here. No such accounts have ever come from the African tribes at any period of time. These indications of the providence of God seem to show that he smiles upon the institution of African slavery in all Christian lands, and "that its tendencies are to elevate the black man, and make him more intelligent and happy than he would be in his own land, and that it has a benevolent bearing on the welfare of the slave in this world and the world to come."

LESSON XVI.

OUR limits will not permit an extended accumulation of the testimony showing the degenerate condition of the African hordes, nor of those facts showing the ameliorating effect of American slavery upon that race of mankind. A large volume would not contain more than an abstract. This effect is obvious to any one acquainted with the race; while the deep degradation of the races from which they have descended has caused some *philosophers* to adopt the opinion that they are not of a common origin with the white races of the earth. But we present the doctrine that sin—that any want of conformity to the laws of God touching our health and happiness, our physical and mental improvement and condition, has a direct tendency to deteriorate the animal man, and that a general abandonment and disregard of such laws, through a long series of generations, will be sufficient to account for the lowest degradation found to exist. We believe there is truth in the saying, "The fathers have eaten sour grapes, and the children's teeth are set on edge;" that, when the progenitors for a series of ages manifest some particular quality or tendency of action, the same may be found, even in an increased degree, in their descendants; and that this principle holds true to some extent through the whole animal world. Further, that such progressive tendency to some particular mental or physical condition may be obviated, and its action reversed, by a sufficient controlling influence or force.

And if it shall be found that there may be truth in this position, we might submit the inquiry: If God in his wisdom foresaw that the family of Jacob would become so degraded, in one generation, that it would require the counteracting influence of four hundred years of slavery to place them in a condition fit to receive and enjoy the blessings promised their fathers; how long will it require a similar state of control to produce a like renovation among the descendants of Ham, the degraded Africans? But we think, so far as the inquiry can interest us, it has been answered by St. Paul: "Let as many servants (*δοῦλοι, douloi, slaves*) as are under the yoke, count their own masters worthy of all honour, that the name of God and his doctrine be not blasphemed. And they that have believing masters, let them not despise them because they are brethren; but rather do *them* service (δουλευέτωσαν, *be slaves to them,*) because they are faithful and beloved partakers of the benefit. These things teach and exhort. If any man teach otherwise, and consent not to wholesome words, even to the words of our Lord Jesus Christ, and to the doctrine which is according to godliness, he is proud, knowing nothing, but doting about questions and strifes of words, whereof cometh envy, strife, railings, evil surmisings, perverse disputings of men of corrupt minds, and destitute of the truth, supposing that gain is godliness: from such withdraw thyself. But godliness, with contentment, is great gain, for we brought nothing into this world, and it is certain that we can carry nothing out; and having food and raiment, let us be therewith content. But they that will be rich fall into temptation and a snare, and into many foolish and hurtful lusts, which drown men in destruction and perdition. For the love of money is the root of all evil; which while some covet after, they have erred from the faith, and pierced themselves through with many sorrows. But thou, O man of God! flee these things; and follow after righteousness, godliness, faith, love, patience, meekness. Fight the good fight of faith; lay hold on eternal life, whereunto thou art also called, and hast professed a good profession before many witnesses. I give thee charge, in the sight of God who quickeneth all things, and before Jesus Christ, who before Pontius Pilate witnessed a good confession, that thou keep this commandment (ἐντολήν, *an order, a command, a precept, a charge, injunction*) *without spot* (ἄσπιλον, *free from stain, spotless, faultless*), unrebukable (ἀνεπίληπτον, *of whom no hold can be taken, not to be attacked, irreprehensible*), until the appearing of our Lord Jesus Christ." 1 *Tim.* vi. 1–14.

Thus St. Paul has told us how long this doctrine shall be taught; that it shall be taught free from any alteration, change; free from any stain, pure and spotless; and that his manner of teaching it shall be plain, simple, open, and bold; so that there could be no hold taken of him; and the doctrines, instructions, counsels and commands here given were to be so taught, until the coming of our Lord Jesus Christ.

But Mr. Barnes says, page 194—

"If we may draw an inference also from this case, (the Hebrews in Egypt,) in regard to the manner in which God would have such a people (slaves in America) restored to freedom, it would be in favour of immediate emancipation."

God himself sentenced the Hebrews to slavery for four hundred years. "And when the sun was going down, a deep sleep fell upon Abram; and lo, a horror of great darkness fell upon him. And he said unto Abram, Know of a surety that thy seed shall be a stranger in a land that is not theirs, and shall serve (וַעֲבָדוּם *va æbadum, shall be slaves to, or shall slave themselves to*) them, and they shall afflict them four hundred years." *Gen.* xv. 12, 13. At the expiration of which time he delivered them from it. An instance drawn from their case can be legitimately applied only to one where the term of servitude has been determined.

God made no attempt to liberate the Hebrews until the expiration of the term allotted them for servitude. Mr. Barnes evidently applies his inference to the abolition of the institution generally, and thus places himself in opposition to St. Paul. But our mind has come to the decision that the apostle is the higher authority. And the inquiry is also left upon the mind, whether, in the matter of his whole book, Mr. Barnes has not "run before he was sent;" whereby he may have subjected himself to the mortification of again seeing, in his own case, the counsels of Achitophel turned into foolishness.

LESSON XVII.

Mr. Barnes has quoted some few passages of Scripture to which he applies a meaning we deem erroneous; but we attach no blame to him on this account; because our English version itself, of the passages referred to, has a tendency to lead to an inadequate conception of the idea conveyed by the original. The doctor says, page 128—"That even the servant that was *bought* was to have compensation for his labour; and there are some general principles laid down, which, if applied, would lead to that: thus, *Jer.* xxii. 13, 'Wo unto him that buildeth his house by unrighteousness, and his chambers by wrong; that uses his neighbour's *service* without wages, and giveth him not for his work.'" He quotes this same passage for the same purpose, pp. 353 and 360, and seems to regard it as a secure pillar, and on which he founds his doctrines. The words, "*that* useth his neighbour's service without wages, and giveth him not for his work," are translated from

מְשַׁפֵּט בְּרֵעֵהוּ יַעֲבֹד חִנָּם וּפֹעֲלוֹ לֹא יִתֶּן־לוֹ׃

The passage admits of two additional readings, thus: *Who shall judge for a neighbour as to his slave undeservedly no wages, no gifts;* or, *Who shall have adjudged as to his neighbour that he shall slave himself, undeservedly or gratuitously, without wages or reward.* The meaning is: *Who shall corruptly judge that his neighbour shall not receive wages or compensation for the services of his slave;* or, that the neighbour himself shall so slave himself to another without wages or compensation. The word עֶבֶד *a slave* is often used as a verb, to express such action as would be that of a slave.

On page 67, Mr. Barnes says—"And the word, ἀνδραποδίστης, *andrapodistēs*, occurs once, 1 *Tim.* i. 10, with the most marked disapprobation of the thing denoted by it. 'The law is made for murderers of fathers, murderers of mothers, for manslayers, for whoremongers, for *man-stealers*, for liars,' &c."

The truth is, that the word δοῦλος, *doulos*, is the peculiar word to denote slavery, and is so used in the New Testament and everywhere else; but this word also means *slave*, &c., and is never used disconnected from the idea of slavery, but carries with it the idea of some change, as to *place*, *condition*, *possession*, or *ownership*. We shall notice how some men are striving to change the Greek, as to the meaning of the word δοῦλος, *doulos*, because, unless they do so, the New Testament is strongly against them. However, of the word used in 1 *Tim.* i. 10, ἀνδραποδισταῖς, *andrapodistais*, it is true, that it is used "with the most marked disapprobation of the thing denoted by it;" and it is just as true that the thing denoted by it is *the stealing and enticing away other men's slaves!* *Slave-stealers* is its only and legitimate meaning in the place used. Had St. Paul intended to express the idea, *men-stealers*, he would have used the word ἀνθρωποκλεπταῖς, *anthropokleptais;* which would have expressed the very thing wanted by Mr. Barnes. We shall examine these words in another portion of our study. But Mr. Barnes does not appear to be aware why it was that St. Paul instructed Timothy that the law was made for *slave-stealers:* for whose benefit we will explain; and by which explanation he will learn that the abolitionists commenced their labours during the days of the apostles. From some of the relations of Christianity, not

well understood by the Gentile churches, the idea was entertained by some that the operation of Christianity abolished the bonds of matrimony between a believing and an unbelieving party; that it abolished the authority of an unbelieving parent over a believing child; that it abolished slavery in case the slave was converted to the faith, and especially if the master belonged to the household of God. On these subjects and others, the Corinthian church addressed St. Paul for instruction and advice. It is to be regretted that their letter has not come down to us; but, we can gather what it contained, from the answer of St. Paul: "Now concerning the things whereof ye wrote unto me." 1 *Cor.* vii. 1.

Touching the subject before us, see his answer in the 20th to the 25th verse; and the same subject continued in *Eph.* vi. 5–10; also *Col.* iii. 22–25; he found it necessary to instruct Titus on this subject: see *Tit.* ii. 9–15; and, finally, as in the passage before us, and also vi. 1–15. St. Peter also found it necessary to correct the errors of these abolitionists, and to give them instruction on this subject. 1 *Pet.* ii. 18–25.

Had St. Paul regarded slavery as an evil, he certainly had no excuse for not denouncing it. Nor do we know of any of the early fathers of the church that did so. St. Ignatius, in his second epistle to Polycarp, says—"Overlook not the men and maid *servants.* Let them be the more subject to the glory of God, that they may obtain from him a better liberty. Let them not desire to be set *free* at public cost, that they be not slaves to their own lusts." See also, *General Epistle of Barnabas*, xiv. 15: "Thou shalt not be bitter in thy commands towards any of thy servants that trust in God, lest thou chance not to fear him who is over both; because he came not to call any with respect to persons, but whomsoever the Spirit prepared."

Such is the construction of the human mind, and of human language, that whenever a thing is made a subject of remark, or merely brought to mind, it, of necessity, must be so, in one of three positions: either a thing to be commended; to be reprehended; or as a thing of total indifference. A glaring sin and gross evil could not have been a thing of indifference to Jesus Christ and his apostles. They, therefore, cannot be supposed to have acted honestly in not condemning a sin, when by them mentioned, or brought to mind. It is a supposition too gross for refutation!

But it is conceded by Mr. Barnes, page 260, that "the apostles did not openly denounce slavery as an evil, or require that those who were held in bondage should be at once emancipated. * * * These things seem to me to lie on the face of the New Testament; and whatever argument they may furnish to the advocates of slavery in disposing of these facts, it seems plain that the facts themselves cannot be denied."

The facts, then, must stand in commendation and approval. They cannot be got rid of by arguing ever so ingeniously, that Jesus Christ and his apostles were cunning; that they acted with prudence; that they dexterously taught it to be an evil by implication; or that they acted with deep-seated and far-reaching expediency; nor by any other subterfuge by which the enemies of God are striving to mould his essence and character into an idol to suit themselves.

LESSON XVIII.

"If, however, it should be conceded that this passage (*Lev.* xxv. 45, 46) means that the heathen might be subjected to perpetual bondage, and that the intention was not that they should be released in the year of jubilee, still it will not follow that this is a justification of perpetual slavery as it exists in the United States. For, even on that supposition, the concession was one made to *them*, not to any other people." *Barnes*, p. 156.

This is not the first time the abolitionists have presented this proposition, and seem to deem it as insurmountable. Therefore, it may merit a few words of inquiry.

Is it contended that God ever grants or denies, or, in other words, acts, except in conformity with some universal rule or law of his providence and government? For, to suppose otherwise, must involve the consideration of an inferior and capricious being. If God, on any occasion, permitted slavery, then it is deducible from the unchangeableness of God and his laws, that he always permits it, when all the circumstances and conditions shall be found to exist as they were when he did so permit it. The Jews, as a nation, were God's people; his worshippers, his church. "And ye shall be unto me a kingdom of priests, and a holy nation." *Exod.* xix. 6. "For thou art a holy people unto the Lord thy God: The Lord thy God hath chosen thee to be a special people unto himself, above all people that are upon the face of the earth." *Deut.* vii. 6.

But, in the order of God's providence, other people were to be the recipients of the grace of God also: "And it shall come to pass in the last days, that the mountain of the Lord's house shall be established in the top of the mountains, and shall be exalted above the hills: all nations shall flow unto it." *Isa.* ii. 2.

"Sing and rejoice, O daughter of Zion; for lo, I come, and I will dwell in the midst of thee, saith the Lord. And many nations shall be joined to the Lord in that day, and shall be my people." *Zech.* ii. 10, 11.

This is in strict conformity with the promise of Jehovah to Isaac: "And in thy seed shall all the nations of the earth be blessed." *Gen.* xxvi. 4.

The time of this great enlargement of the church of God was the advent of the Saviour. The Christian church succeeded as heirs of all the promises, benefits, and free grace of the ancient church and people of God;—in fact, became heirs of Abraham;—"And the father of circumcision to them, who are not of the circumcision only, but who walk in the steps of that faith of our father Abraham, which he had being yet uncircumcised. For the promise that he should be the heir of the world was not to Abraham, or to his seed through the law, but through the righteousness of faith." * * * "Therefore it is of faith, that it might be by grace; to the end the promise might be sure to all the seed; not to that only which is of the law, but to that also which is of the faith of Abraham, who is the father of us all, (as it is written, I have made thee the father of many nations,) before him whom he believed, even God, who quickeneth the dead, and calleth those things which be not, as though they were." *Romans* iv. 11, 12, 16, 17.

"Therefore remember, that ye being in times past Gentiles in the flesh, who are called uncircumcision by that which is called the circumcision in the flesh made by hands;

"That at that time ye were without Christ, being aliens from the commonwealth of Israel, and strangers from the covenant of promise, having no hope, and without God in the world.

"But now in Christ Jesus, ye who sometime were afar off, are made nigh by the blood of Christ; for he is our peace, who hath made both one; and hath broken down the middle wall of partition between us." *Eph.* ii. 11, 12, 13, 14.

"Know ye, therefore, that they which are of faith, the same are children of Abraham. And the scripture foreseeing that God would justify the heathen by faith, preached before the gospel to Abraham, saying, In thee shall all nations be blessed." *Gal.* iii. 7, 8.

And wherefore Peter very properly describes the Gentile church of Christ by similar language applied to the Jews, the chosen people of God to whom the promises of the law were made: "But ye are a chosen generation, a royal priesthood, a holy nation, a peculiar people; that ye should show forth the praises of him who hath called you out of darkness into his marvellous light; which in time past were not a people, but are now a people of God; which had not obtained mercy, but have now obtained mercy." 1 *Peter* ii. 9, 10.

The theological student will recollect many more very pertinent proofs of the heirship of the Christian church to the chosen people of God. "Think not I am come to destroy the law, or the prophets; I come not to destroy the law, but to fulfil." *Matt.* v. 17.

So far then as the Gentile nations have become Christianized, have become the followers of Christ, so far they have, through faith, become the peculiar people of God, and heirs and children of Abraham; and, as heirs, succeeded to all things resulting from the providence and grace of God to his peculiar people.

The broad and universal principle concerning slavery is, that a want of knowledge of the true God, a want of conformity to his law, have a constantly deteriorating effect, whereas, on the contrary, a knowledge of Jehovah and a conduct in conformity to his law, (since the fallen state of man renders him unable to comply with the law) the application of God's grace, and free forgiveness through faith and repentance, shall have the redeeming effect of a full compliance with the law. As the one position is deteriorating, forcing as it were downward to destruction and death,—the other is as constantly elevating towards all perfection and life eternal.

Thus the mercy of God is manifested to the degraded and heathen nations, by substantially placing them under a protection and guidance, which, however slow may be the progress, must of necessity have an elevating influence on thousands, in proportion as they, with heart-felt willingness, yield themselves to it. "Oh, that men would praise the Lord for his goodness, and for his wonderful works to the children of men! For he satisfieth the longing soul, and filleth the hungry soul with goodness. Such as sit in darkness and the shadow of death, being bound in affliction and iron; because they rebelled against the words of God, and contemned the counsels of the Most High: therefore, he brought down their heart with labour; they fell down, there was none to help. Then they cried unto the Lord in their trouble, and he raised them out of their distresses. He brought them out of darkness and the shadow of death, and brake their bands in sunder. Oh, that men would praise the Lord for his goodness, and for his wonderful works to the children of men." *Psa.* cvii. 8–15.

In conclusion, we may remark, that under this view of the law, the announcements of holy writ, so far as they regard the subject under consideration, are as applicable to the Christian people of the present day as they at any time were to the Hebrews themselves.

"Thus saith the Lord, The labour of Egypt, and merchandise of Ethiopia, and of the Sabeans, men of stature, shall come over unto thee, and they shall be thine: they shall come after thee; in chains they shall come over, and they shall fall down unto thee, they shall make supplication unto thee, *saying*, Surely God is in thee; and there is none else, *there* is no God" *beside*. *Isa.* xlv. 14.

LESSON XIX.

Mr. Barnes has referred to Vatalbus, Rabbi Solomon, Abenezra Joh. Casp. Miégius, Constitutiones Servi Hebræi, Ugolin, Maimonides, Michaelis, John's Archæology, Selden de Uxore Hebraica, and some other books which are not at hand, in support of his doctrine, and the points on which he predicates it. We did not doubt the accuracy of these references and quotations; but, page 149, we find the following in his book: "It would appear from Josephus, that on the year of jubilee *all* slaves were set at liberty;" and he refers to "Antiquities," vol. ii. chap. xii. sec. 3, which, so far as it refers to slavery, reads thus: "Accordingly I enjoin thee to make no more delays, but to make haste to Egypt, and to travel night and day, and not to draw out the time, and to make the slavery of the Hebrews and their sufferings to last the longer."

We do not see how the passage warrants the assertion of Mr. Barnes, and apprehended some mistake, such as a young lawyer, willing to appear very learned, might make, by affixing to his brief a long list of authorities, merely from an examination of his index.

But the sentence here quoted from Mr. Barnes, containing the proposition that Josephus said, in his Antiquities, vol. ii. chap. xii. sec. 3, that all slaves were set at liberty in the year of jubilee, is consecutively followed in his book, thus: "The fiftieth year is called by the Hebrews the *jubilee*, wherein debtors are freed from their debts, and slaves are set at liberty." And this sentence is marked as quoted from Josephus, and as though it was the exact passage to be found in the place just before referred to. The fact is, this sentence is *nearly* a *part* of what may be found in book iii. chap. xii. sec. 3 of Antiquities, thus: "And that fiftieth year is called by the Hebrews the jubilee wherein debtors are freed from their debts, and slaves are set at liberty; which slaves became such, though they were of the same stock, by transgressing some of those laws whose punishment was not capital, but they were punished by this method of slavery."

Suppose the mistake to be in the number of the book, still, does the passage, as fully quoted, give any authority for the assertion of Mr. Barnes? Thus the mind is led to inquire what credit is to be given to these references?

But we hasten to give a few extracts illustrative of Mr. Barnes's thought and argument. He says, p. 126—

"Considering the universal prevalence of slavery when the gospel was preached, it is not probable that any considerable number would be found, who were masters and servants in the sense of a voluntary servitude on the part of the latter." He says—

Page 273: "The permanency of the institution (slavery) can derive no support from what they (the apostles) said on the subject, and in no manner depends on it."

Page 300: "It is only the antagonistic fanaticism of a fragment of the South, which maintains the doctrine that slavery is, in itself, a good thing, and ought to be perpetuated. It cannot by possibility be perpetuated."

Page 301: "*The South, therefore, has to choose between emancipation, by the silent and holy influence of the gospel, securing the elevation of the slaves to the stature and character of freemen*, or to abide the issue of a long continued conflict against the laws of God."

Page 306: "And if a Christian master at the present time * * * should be troubled in his conscience in regard to his right to hold slaves, there is no part of the apostolic writings to which he could turn to allay his feelings or calm his scruples."

Page 311: "Now this undeniable fact, that the right of the master over the person and services of the slave, is never recognised at all in the New Testament."

Page 312: "Whatever distinction of complexion there may be, it is the doctrine of the Bible that all belong to one and the same great family, and that, in the most important matters pertaining to their existence, they are on a level."

Page 315: "Up to the time when its truths (the gospel's) were made known, the great mass of mankind had no scruples about its propriety; they regarded one portion of the race as inferior to the other, and as born to be slaves. Christianity disclosed the great truth that all men were on a level; that all were equal."

Page 317: "If a man should in fact render to his slaves 'that which is just and equal;' would he not restore them to freedom? Would any thing short of this be *all* that is just and equal?"

Page 322: "No man has a right to *assume* that when the word δοῦλος, *doulos*, occurs in the New Testament, it means a *slave*."

Page 331: "No argument in favour of slavery can be derived from the injunctions addressed by the apostles to the slaves themselves."

Page 340: "From the arguments thus far presented in regard to the relations of Christianity to slavery, it seems fair to draw the conclusion, that the Christian religion lends no *sanction* to slavery."

Page 341: "The Saviour and his apostles inculcated such views of man as *amount* to a prohibition of slavery." Page 345: "He (Jesus Christ) was not a Jew, except by the accident of his birth, but he was a *man;* in his human form there was as distinct a relation to the African * * * as there was to the Caucasian."

We have understood that one popular clergyman at the North (an abolitionist) has gone so far as to say that Jesus Christ was a *negro!* To what folly and extravagance will not wickedness subject its slaves!

Mr. Barnes says, page 375—"These considerations seem to me to be conclusive proof that Christianity was *not* designed to extend and perpetuate slavery; but that the spirit of the Christian religion would remove it from the world, *because it is an evil, and displeasing to God.*"

To all of which, worthy of answer, it may be well to apply the sentiment which he attributes to Dr. Fuller, that the New Testament is not silent on the subject of slavery; that it recognises the relation; that it commands slaves to obey their masters, and gives reasons why they should do so. And it may be steadily affirmed, if slavery be a sin, that such commands and counsels are not only a *suppressio veri*, but a *suggestio falsi;* not only a suppression of the truth, but a suggestion of what is false!

If it shall be said that God merely sanctioned or permitted slavery in the time of the patriarchs, who will say that he did not enjoin it in the time of Moses? A repeal of this injunction demanded a countervailing revelation of no equivocal character, clear and decided, without the admission of a doubt.

"And God spake unto Moses in Mount Sinai, saying, * * * But thy bond-men and bond-maids which thou shalt have, shall be of the heathen that are round about you; of them shall ye buy bond-men and bond-maids. Moreover, of the children of the strangers that do sojourn among you, of them shall ye buy and of their families, which they beget in your land; and they shall be your possession. And ye shall take them as an inheritance, for your children after you, to inherit them for a possession: they shall be your bond-men for ever." *Lev.* xxv. 1, 44, 45, 46.

Mr. Barnes has adduced no proof that this law was ever repealed; nor do the holy books contain any evidence of such repeal; yet he has denied the existence of slavery in Judea, at the time of the advent of the Saviour. See pp. 228, 242, 244, and 249, before quoted, and, we trust, sufficiently refuted. But we now add, that at the time Jesus Christ and his apostles were on the earth, Judea was a province of Rome. Now, since it was clear that slavery was inculcated by the Hebrew laws, unless it was forbidden by the Roman, we could not come to the conclusion that slavery did not exist in Judea at their time, even if Jesus Christ and his apostles had never alluded to it.

But,—see *Matt.* xxvi. 51: "Behold, one of them which were with Jesus stretched out his hand and drew his sword and struck the servant (δοῦλον, *doulon*, *slave*) of the high-priest," then some suitable but different word would have been used, as in the following: "And the servants (δοῦλοι, *douloi*, *slaves*) and officers (ὑπηρέται, *hupēretai*, *attendants*, *persons who aid*, *assistants*) stood there," *John* xviii. 18; proving the fact that both slaves and other attendants were present, and that the *slave* was named distinctly from such other attendants. There can be no doubt about these facts; and in proof that slavery was not forbidden by the Roman laws, we quote from Mr. Barnes, page 251: "In Italy, it was computed that there were three slaves to one freeman; and in this part of the empire alone, their numbers amounted to more than twenty millions."

Page 252: * * * "The number of slaves could not have been less than sixty millions in the Roman Empire, at about the time the apostles went forth to preach the gospel."

Page 254: * * * "The following places are mentioned, either as *emporia* for slaves or countries from which they were procured: Delos, Phrygia, and Cappadocia, Panticapæum, Diascurias, and Phanagoria on the Euxine or Black Sea; Alexandria and Cadiz; Corsica, Sardinia, and Britain; Africa and Thrace."

And does it astonish us that in these dark ages of human degradation, Britain helped to supply Rome with slaves? It should be remembered that conquest gave the right in ancient days to enslave all barbarous and deeply degraded nations; and it might be inquired whether such principle was not alluded to by the prophet: "Shall the prey be taken from the mighty, or the lawful captive delivered." *Isa.* xlix. 24. History will inform us that all these nations were of the lowest order. St. Jerome, in his writings against Jovinian, informs us what were the morals of Britain. He says—"Why should I refer to other nations, when I myself, when a youth in Gaul, have seen the Atticotti, a British tribe, eating human flesh? Should they find shepherds tending their herds of swine or cattle, and flocks of sheep in the woods, they are wont to cut off the fleshy parts of the men, and the breasts of the women, which are esteemed the most delicious food."

Who then is to say that Britain is not now indebted for her high state of intellectual improvement to the pike, bludgeon, and sword of the Roman, Dane, Saxon, and Norman? And can we say that the hand of God was not in this? The same providences and principles that have ever applied to degraded Africa apply to all degraded nations, and even to individual men. "Whosoever committeth sin is the servant (δοῦλος, *doulos, slave*) of sin."

And it may be said that nations and individuals thus enslave themselves. "Behold, for your iniquities ye have sold yourselves." *Isa.* l. 1. These principles may be seen every day operating among the most degraded of even the most enlightened nations. The history of the present day informs us of the deep degradation of the African tribes; and that even in their own country the great mass are slaves. Consistently with the laws of God, they could not be otherwise; and even slavery among themselves, subject to sacrifice and death as we have seen it, is yet better for them than a state of freedom. We have seen how the free hordes roam like the brutes, making that place home where night overtook them. Suppose such to be cannibals, of which we have proof, it might so happen, that, in one day, one half of their number would be destroyed by themselves. Therefore, as distressing as slavery must be among them, yet it is far preferable to their dejected condition of freedom.

We know of no one who pretends to believe that the masses of the African tribes have increased in number since the commencement of our era; whereas, a few scattering individuals, brought into slavery, within the last few generations, in these States, have increased to near four millions; nearly one-twelfth of the number of the entire population of Africa. However wicked may be the Christian master, how much more is slavery to be desired by the negro than any condition among these pagan hordes! We, therefore, do not deem it presumptuous to say, that so degraded is the condition of the African in his own land, that it has been elevated in proportion as it has been affected by the slave-trade, and more especially with Christian nations. The first tendencies towards civilization, and whatever dawning of mental development there may be now noticed among the African tribes, are traceable alone to that source. And the Christian philosopher might well inquire whether, in the providence of God, its existence, from the time of Noah to the present, has not been the saving principle which has alone preserved the tribes of Ham from the condition of Sodom and Gomorrah, and other nations long since wasted away.

LESSON XX.

Mr. Barnes has quoted and adopted the following passage from President Wayland, page 310: "If the religion of Christ allows such a license (to hold slaves) from such precepts as these, the New Testament would be the greatest curse that ever was inflicted on *our race*." On the account of the avowal of Dr. Barnes as to *his race*, heretofore noticed, we feel a degree of gladness that the above passage is not original with him: we should expect to find in him a sympathy on this subject, unpleasant to encounter, because legitimately acting on his mind. A man may be a philosopher or a Christian, yet the ties of nature, the sympathies of kindred are not abated.

We are informed that heretofore, written arguments in favour of abolitionism by Dr. Wayland and against it by Dr. Fuller, have been published. We have not seen the work; but are told that the abolitionists claim victory for Dr. Wayland, and that the opponents also claim it for Dr. Fuller; and from the foregoing passage as quoted, we conclude that Dr. Wayland found himself, at least, in *straits* on the subject. If such be the fact, it may account why the abolitionists thought Dr. Barnes's present work necessary. But, however these things may be, the passage from Dr. Wayland is a volume of deep instruction, announcing the feelings and theological consistency, we might say fanaticism, of, we hope, but a few extraordinary men, now appearing in our land; men, we doubt not, conscientious in their opinion that God designs the government of the world to be in strict conformity with human reason, and who cannot, therefore, pray in the spirit of the Son: "Father, if thou be willing, remove this cup from me: nevertheless, not my will, but thine, be done." *Luke* xxii. 42. "If any man have not the spirit of Christ, he is none of his." *Rom.* viii. 9.

In the book before us, the author falls into one error, common to every writer on his side of the question: That slavery is the cause of the degradation of the Africans and the slaves generally. We maintain that the converse is the true state of the case. Another error is the substitution of what may be abuses of slavery for the institution itself. This author, like most of the abolition writers of whom we have any knowledge, evinces an inability to enter into an impartial consideration of the subject, from his deep and overshadowing prejudices against it. Indeed, the whole work, from page to page, carries proof of a previous determination to condemn, not less obvious than in the instance of the judge who, in summing up a case, said—"It is true, in this case, the accused has proved himself innocent; but, since a guilty man might prove himself so, and since I myself have always been of the opinion that he was guilty, it will be the safest to condemn."

The style of the work before us is always diffuse and declamatory, sometimes elevated, but often cumbrous; still his language bears the impress of classical learning and a cultivated mind; but there is in the work a want of conciseness; it abounds in contradictory positions and a frequent inconclusiveness of deduction, which make it obnoxious to a charge of carelessness. But may we not account for these defects by the urgent solicitude of his readers?

The morbid appetite of the Northern abolitionists was probably hungry for the work. Having no wish to *oppose* his pecuniary views, we refrain from further extracts, lest we should infringe his copyright. Nor did we at all contemplate a classical review of the work. The book contains about 400 pages. If it could be condensed, like a pot of new-brewed and foaming, into potable beer, to a fourth of that size, it might well claim such attention; and from the specimens of ability displayed, if it were proved that the doctor has suffered his zeal to run ahead of the truth in regard to his *race*, we should judge him fully competent to the task of such improvement.

Study III.

LESSON I.

"*The Works of William Ellery Channing, D. D., in six volumes. Tenth Edition. Boston,* 1849.

THESE volumes include essays, sermons, and lectures on various subjects. The style is easy, flowing, and persuasive; the language is generally clear, often elevated, sometimes sublime. Few can read the book and not feel the evidence, whatever may be the error of his doctrine, that the author added to his literary eminence a purity of intention. Such a work must always make a deep impression on the reader. It is this fact that prompts the present essay. It may be said of Channing what Channing said of Fenelon:

"He needs to be read with caution, as do all who write from their own deeply excited minds. He needs to be received with deductions and explanations. * * * We fear that the very excellencies of Fenelon may shield his errors. Admiration prepares the mind for belief; and the moral and religious sensibility of the reader may lay him open to impressions which, while they leave his purity unstained, may engender causeless solicitude." Vol. i. p. 185.

Dr. Channing's sympathies for every appearance of human suffering, for every grade of human imperfection, gave a peculiar phasis, perhaps most amiable to his intellect, religion, and writings. He sought perfection for himself—he was ardent to behold it universal. Heaven must for ever be the home of such a spirit. But the scenes of earth gave agitation and grief. Limited, in his earthly associations, to the habits of the North, the very purity of his heart led him to attack what he deemed the most wicked sin of the South. His politics were formed upon the model of his mind.

Religion spread before him her golden wing, and science aided in the elevation of his view.

But, O thou Being, God Eternal! why not this earth made heaven? Why thy most perfect work imperfection? Why thy child, clothed with holiness or shod with the gospel, run truant to thy law, thy providence and government?

But, lo, we are not of thy council. We were not called when the foundations of eternity were laid. We are, truly, all very small beings. Our virtues, even purity, may lead in error. May not our best intentions lead down to wo?

"It is a fact worthy of serious thought, and full of solemn instruction, that many of the worst errors have grown out of the religious tendencies of the mind. So necessary is it to keep watch over our whole nature, to subject the highest sentiments to the calm, conscientious reason. Men, starting from the idea of God, have been so dazzled by it, as to forget or misinterpret the universe." *Channing*, vol. i. p. 14.

LESSON II.

VOLUME ii. page 14, Dr. Channing says—

"1. I shall show that man cannot be justly held and used as property.

"2. I shall show that man has sacred rights, the gifts of God, and inseparable from human nature, of which slavery is the infraction.

"3. I shall offer some explanations to prevent misapplication of these principles.

"4. I shall unfold the evils of slavery.

"5. I shall consider the argument which the Scriptures are thought to furnish in favour of slavery.

"6. I shall offer some remarks on the means of removing it.

"7. I shall offer some remarks on abolitionism.

"8. I shall conclude with a few reflections on the duties belonging to the times."

In support of the first proposition, to wit, "I will show that man cannot be justly held and used as property," the doctor has advanced seven arguments. He says, page 18—"It is plain, that, if one man may be held as property, then every other man may be so held." * * * "Now let every reader ask himself this plain question: Could I, can I, be rightfully seized, and made an article of property," &c. Page 19: "And if this impression be delusion, on what single moral conviction can we rely? * * * The consciousness of indestructible rights is a part of our moral being. The consciousness of our humanity involves the persuasion that we cannot be owned as a tree or brute. As men, we cannot justly be made slaves. Then no man can be rightfully enslaved."

The first idea we find, touching property, is in *Gen.* i. 26: "And let them have dominion over the fish of the sea, and over the fowl of the air, and over the cattle, and over all the earth, and over every creeping thing that creepeth upon the earth." Verse 28th: "And God blessed them, and God said unto them, Be fruitful, and multiply, and replenish the earth and subdue it: and have dominion over the fish of the sea, and over the fowl of the air, and over every living thing that moveth upon the earth."

In *Lev.* xxv. 44: "Both thy bond-men and bond-maids which thou shalt have shall be of the heathen, that are round about you: of them shall ye buy bond-men and bond-maids." Verse 45: "Moreover of the children of the strangers that do sojourn among you, of them shall ye buy, and of their families that are with you which they beget in your land, and they shall be your possession." Verse 46: "And ye shall take them as an inheritance for your children after you, to inherit them for a possession, they shall be your bondmen for ever."

And if we look at the first verse of this chapter, that the foregoing was announced by God himself to Moses from Sinai; and from which it would seem that God and Dr. Channing were of quite a different opinion on this subject.

We know not what notion Dr. Channing may have entertained of "man's indestructible rights." But let us ask, what rights has he that may not be destroyed? The right to breath? Suppose, by his own wantonness, carelessness, or wickedness, he is submerged in water, what becomes of his right to breathe, since he can no longer exercise it? Can you name any right that, under the providence of God, may not be destroyed? Freemen have rights, but subject to alteration, and even extinction; slaves have rights, but subject to the same changes. There is no such thing as an "indestructible right" appertaining to any existence, save to the Great Jehovah! He must be an immortal God who can possess an *indestructible right.* We use the word "right" in Dr. Channing's sense—just claim, legal title, ownership, the legal power of exclusive possession. You ask, has not man an *indestructible right* to worship God? We answer, no! Man has no such right to worship God; such right would make him a partner. The worship of God is a *duty* which man owes; the forbearance of which is forbidden by the moral law, by justice and propriety. Nothing can be forbidden or ordered touching an *indestructible right;* for such command, if to be obeyed, changes the quality of the right; or rather shows that it was not indestructible.

Such arguments may seem to give great aid and beauty to a mere rhetorical climax, but, before the lens of analyzation, evaporates into enthusiastic declamation,—which, in the present case, seems to be addressed to the sympathies, prejudices, and impulses of the human heart.

In his writings on slavery, in fact through all his works, we find a fundamental error, most fatal to truth. He makes the conscience the great *cynosura* of all that is right in morals, and of all that is true in religion.

Hence, in the passage before us,—"The consciousness of *indestructible rights* is a part of our moral being,"—the *consciousness* of such rights is his proof that we possess them; therefore, "the consciousness of our humanity involves the persuasion (proof) that we cannot be owned;" and, therefore, "as men (being men) we cannot justly be made slaves." So, page 25: "Another argument against the right of property in man, may be drawn from a very obvious principle of moral science, the conscience." Page 33. "His conscience, in revealing the moral law, does not reveal a law for himself only, but speaks as a universal legislator. He has an *intuitive conviction* that the obligations of this divine code press on others as truly as on himself. * * * There is no deeper principle in human nature than the consciousness of rights."

Vol. iii. page 18: "By this I mean that a Christian minister should beware of offering interpretations of Scripture which are repugnant to *any clear discoveries* of reason, or dictates of *conscience.*"

Page 93: "We believe that all virtue has its foundation in the moral nature of man; that is, conscience, or his sense of duty."

Page 164: "One of the great excellencies of Christianity is that it does not deal in minute regulations; but, that, having given broad views of duty," &c., * * * "it leaves us to apply these rules, and express their spirit, according to the promptings of the *divine monitor* within us"—the conscience.

Vol. vi. page 308: "We have no higher law than our conviction of duty."

"Conscience is the supreme power within us. Its essence, its grand characteristic, is sovereignty. It speaks with divine authority. Its office is to command, to rebuke, to reward; and happiness and honour depend on the reverence with which we listen to it." Vol. iii. pp. 335, 336.

Such passages plainly expose the view of what Dr. Channing calls *conscience:* in answer to which we say, the conscience may be a poor guide to truth. The African savage feels a clear conscience when he kills and eats his captive. The Hindoo mother is governed by her conscience when she plunges her new-born infant beneath the flood, a sacrifice to her gods. The idolaters of Palestine were subdued by conscience when they thrust their suckling infants into the flames to appease Moloch; yet God did not think it was right, and forbade them to do so.

The truth is, the conscience is merely that part of the judgment which takes notice of what it deems right or wrong; consequently, is as prone to be in error as our judgment about any other matter.

For the accuracy of this definition, we refer to all the standard writers on logic, and those on the human understanding, treating on the subject. And in fact, Dr. Channing is forced to recede from his position when he finds that Abraham, Philemon, and some good men even of the present day, were slave-owners; and in vol. vi. page 55, he says—"It is a solemn truth, not yet understood as it should be, that the worst institutions may be sustained, the worst deeds performed, the most merciless cruelties inflicted by the *conscientious* and the good."

And again, page 57: "The great truth is now insisted on, that evil is evil, no matter at whose door it lies; and that men acting from conscience and religion may do nefarious deeds, needs to be better understood."

Would it not have been more frank for Dr. Channing to have said, that the conscience would be an unerring guide so long as it agreed with his, but when it did not, why, then he would inquire into the matter?

It is to be lamented that, among the unlearned at the present day, a confused idea of something tantamount to the conscience being a divine monitor within us has taken a deep root among the minds of men; having grown out of the fact that such was the doctrine of some of the fanatical teachers of former days.

If we shall be permitted to speak of property, in reference to our and its relation to the Divine Being, then we cannot strictly say that man can *own property*. Jehovah stands in no need. Behold the cattle upon a thousand hills are his; all is the work of his hand; all, all is his property alone! At most, God has only intrusted the possession, the administration of the subjects of his creation, to man for the time being,—to multiply, to replenish and subdue. It is only in reference to our relation to one another that we can advance the idea of property. Man was commanded to have dominion over the whole earth, to replenish and subdue, in proportion to the talent bestowed on him for that purpose. This command presupposes such a state of things as we find, of advancement, progression, and improvement. But in the course of the Divine administration, God has seen fit to bestow on one man ten talents, and on another but one; and who shall stand upon the throne of the Almighty, and decide that he of the ten talents shall have no relation with the progression of him of but one talent?

"Take therefore the talent from him, and give it unto him of ten talents. For unto every one that hath shall be given, and he shall have abundance: but from him that hath not shall be taken away even that which he hath." *Matt.* xxv. 28, 29; see also *Luke* xvii. 24–26.

And what, in the course of Divine providence, is to become of him who buried his talent in the earth, and from whom it was taken away? "Blessed is that servant whom his Lord when he cometh shall find so doing. Of a truth I say unto you, that he will make him ruler over all that he hath." *Luke* xii. 43, 44. "Jesus answered them, Verily I say unto you, whoever committeth sin is the servant (δοῦλος, *doulos, slave*) of sin." *John* viii. 34. "Behold for your iniquities have ye sold yourselves." *Isa.* l. 1. "Cursed be Canaan; a servant of servants shall he be unto his brethren." *Gen.* ix. 25. עֶבֶד עֲבָדִים *ebed, ebedim,* a most abject slave shall he be!

LESSON III.

The second argument in support of his first proposition is, "A man cannot be seized and held as property, because he has rights;" to enforce which, he says—"Now, I say, a being having *rights* cannot justly be made property; for this claim over him virtually annuls all his rights." We see no force of argument in this position. It is also true that all domestic animals, held as property, have rights. "The ox knoweth his owner, and the ass his master's crib." They all have "the right of petition;" and ask, in their way, for food: are they the less property?

But his third argument in support of his first proposition is, that man cannot justly be held as property, on the account of the "essential equality of man." If to be born, to eat, to drink, and die alike, constitutes an essential equality among men, then be it so! What! the African savage, born even a slave amid his native wilds, who entertains no vestige of an idea of God, of a future state of existence, of moral accountability; who has no wish beyond the gratification of his own animal desire; whose parentage, for ages past, has been of the same order; and whose descendants are found to require generations of constant training before they display any permanent moral and intellectual advancement; what, such a one essentially equal to such a man as Dr. Channing?

The truth is, such a man is more essentially equal with the brute creation. We shall consider the subject of the equality in another part of our study, to which we refer. We, therefore, only remark, that the doctrine is a chimera.

His fourth argument in support of the proposition is, "That man cannot justly be held as property, because property is an exclusive right. "Now," he says, "if there be property in any thing, it is that of a man in his own person, mind, and strength." "Property," he repeats, "is an exclusive right."

If a man has an exclusive right to property, he can alienate it; he may sell, give, and bequeath it to others. If a man is the property of himself, suppose he shall choose to sell himself to another, and deliver himself in full possession to the purchaser, as he had before been in the full possession of himself—whose property will he be then? See a case in point in *Deut.* xv. 12–17; see also *Exod.* xxi. 1–7.

His fifth argument is that, "if a human being cannot without infinite injustice be seized as property, then he cannot, without equal wrong, be held and used as such." If a human being shall be found a nuisance to himself and others in a state of freedom, then there will be no injustice in his being subjugated, by law, to such control as his qualities prove him to require in reference to the general good; even if the subject shall not choose such control as a personal benefit to himself.

The sixth argument is, that a human being cannot be held as property, because, if so held, "the latter is under obligation to give himself up as a chattel to the former. "Now," he says, "do we not instantly feel, can we help feeling, that this is false?" And that "the absence of obligation proves the want of the right."

We suppose all acknowledge God as the author of the moral law. The moral law forcibly inculcates submission to the civil or political law, even independent of any promise to do so. Now, no one can have a right to act in contradiction to law. The absence of this right, then, proves the existence of the obligation.

For his seventh argument, he says—"I come now to what is, to my mind, the great argument against seizing and using a man as property. He cannot be property in the sight of God and justice, because he is a rational, moral, immortal being; because created in God's image, and therefore in the highest sense his child; because created to unfold godlike faculties, and to govern himself by a Divine law, written on his heart, and republished in God's word."

Dr. Channing adds a page or two in the same impulsive strain, of the same enthusiastic character. We may admire his style, his language, the amiable formation of his mind, but we see nothing like precision or logical deduction in support of his proposition. We see nothing in it but the declamation of a learned, yet an over-ardent, enthusiastic mind. His whole book is but a display of his mental formation. He could love his friends; yea, his enemies. He could have rewarded virtue, but he never could have punished sin. He could have forgiven the greatest outrage, but he never could have yielded a delinquent to the rigid demands of justice. He was a good man, but he never could have been an unbending judge.

The laws of God have been made for the government and benefit of his creatures. God, nor his law, is, like man, changeable.

His law, as expressed or manifested towards one class of objects, is also expressed and manifested towards all objects similarly situated. The law, brought into action by an act of Cain, would also have been brought into action by a similar act of Abel. The law condemnatory of the shedding of blood is still in fearful existence against all who shall have brought themselves within the category of Cain's acts, the most of which have probably not been recorded.

We anticipate from another portion of our studies, that "sin is any want of conformity unto the law of God." Sin is as necessarily followed by ill consequences to the sinner as cause is by effect. A man commits a private murder; think ye, he feels no horrors of mind—no regrets? Is the watchfulness he finds necessary to keep over himself for fear of exposure, through the whole of life, not the effect of the act? Is not his whole conduct, his friendships and associations with men, his very mental peculiarities, his estimate of others, often all influenced and directed in the path of his personal safety, the avoidance of suspicion? And is all this no punishment? Probably, to have been put to death would have been a much less suffering; and who can tell how far this long, fearful, and systematic working of his mind is to affect the mental peculiarities of his offspring? Shall he, who, by wanton thoughtlessness, regardless of propriety, the moral law, and the consequences of its breach, contracts some foul, loathsome, consuming disease, that burns into the bones, and becomes a part of his physical constitution, leave no trace of his sin on his descendants? Deteriorated, feeble, and diseased, they shall not live out half their days!

A long-continued course of sin, confined to an individual, or extended to a family or race of people, deteriorates, degenerates, and destroys. Such deterioration, continued perhaps from untold time, has brought some of the races of men to what we now find them; and the same causes, in similar operation, would leave the same effect on any other race; and Dr. Channing's "child of God" ceases to be so. "Ye are of your father, the devil." *John* viii. 44. "And Dr. Channing's man, created to unfold godlike faculties, and to govern himself by a Divine law written on his heart," ceases to act as he supposes: "And the lusts of your father ye will do: he was a murderer from the beginning, and abode not in the truth; because there is no truth in him." *John* viii. 44. And what saith the Spirit of prophecy to these degenerate sons of earth? "When thou criest, let thy companions deliver thee; but the wind shall carry them away; vanity shall take them; but he that putteth his trust in me shall possess the land, and shall inherit my holy mountain." *Isa.* lvii. 13.

"And if thou shalt say in thy heart, wherefore came these things upon me? For the greatness of thine iniquity are thy skirts discovered, and thy heels made bare. Can the Ethiopian change his skin, or the leopard his spots? Then may ye also do good that are accustomed to do evil. Therefore will I scatter them as stubble that passeth away by the wind of the wilderness. This is thy lot, the portion of thy measures from me, saith the Lord: because thou hast forgotten me, and trusted in falsehood. Therefore, will I discover thy skirts upon thy face, that thy shame may appear." *Jer.* xiii. 22–26.

"And I will sell your sons and your daughters into the hand of the children of Judah, and they shall sell them to the Sabeans, to a people far off: for the Lord hath spoken it." *Joel* iii. 8.

And what saith the same Spirit to those of opposite character?

"The sons also of them that afflicted thee shall come bending unto thee; and they that despised thee shall bow themselves down at the soles of thy feet." *Isa.* lx. 14.

"And strangers shall stand and feed your flocks, and the sons of the alien shall be your ploughmen and your vine-dressers." *Ibid.* lxi. 5.

"They (my people) shall not labour in vain, nor bring forth trouble; they are the seed of the blessed of the Lord, and their offspring with them. And it shall come to pass, before they shall call, I will answer; and while they are yet speaking, I will hear." *Ibid.* lxv. 234.

What are the threatenings announced in prospect of their deterioration and wickedness?

"And thou (Judah) even thyself, shalt discontinue from thy heritage that I gave thee; and I will cause thee *to serve* (עֲבַדְתִּיךָ *be a slave to*) thine enemies in a land which thou knowest not." *Jer.* xvii. 4.

"Are ye not as the children of the Ethiopians unto me, O children of Israel? saith the Lord. * * * Behold the eyes of the Lord God are upon this sinful kingdom, and I will destroy it from off the face of the earth; saving that I will not utterly destroy the house of Jacob, saith the Lord." *Amos* ix. 7, 8.

The consequences of sin are degradation, slavery, and death:

"A righteous man hateth lying; but a wicked man is loathsome and cometh to shame."

"He that troubleth his own house shall inherit the wind; and the fool shall be *servant* (עֶבֶד *ebed, slave*) to the wise of heart."

"As righteousness tendeth to life, so he that pursueth evil, pursueth it to his own death." *Prov.*

Dr. Channing has suffered his idea of property to bring him great mental suffering: he evidently associates, under the term *property*, those qualities and relations only, which are properly associated in an inanimate object of possession, or at most in a brute beast. He has, no doubt, suffered great misery from the reflection that a human being has ever been reduced to such a condition. But his misery has all been produced by his adherence to his own peculiar definition of the word *property*. His definition is not its exact meaning, when applied to a slave. Had the doctor attempted an argument to show that the word *property* could not consistently be applied to a slave, he might, perhaps, have improved our language, by setting up a more definite boundary to the meaning of this term, and saved himself much useless labour.

Mankind apply the term *property* to slaves: they have always done so; and since Dr. Channing has not given us an essay upon the impropriety of this use of the word, perhaps the accustomed usage will be continued. But we imagine that no one but the doctor and his disciples will contend that it expresses the same complex idea when applied to slaves, which is expressed by it when applied to inanimate objects, or to brute beasts. It will be a new idea to the slaveholder to be told that the word *property*, as applied to his slaves, converts them at once into brute beasts, no longer human beings; that it deprives them of all legal protection; and that he, the master, in consequence of the use of this word, stands in the same relation to his slave that he does to his horse; and we apprehend he will find it quite as difficult to comprehend how this metamorphosis is brought about, as it is for the doctor and his disciples, how the slave is property.

We may say a man has property in his wife, his children, his hireling, his slave, his horse, and a piece of timber,—by which we mean that he has the right to use them, in conformity to the relations existing between himself and these several objects. Because his horse is his property, who ever dreamed that he had therefore the right to use him as a piece of timber?

No man has a right to use any item of property in a different manner than his relations with it indicate; or, in other words, as shall be in conformity with the laws of God. Our property is little else than the right of possession and control, under the guidance of the laws by which we are in possession for the time being.

The organization of society is the result of the conception of the general good. By it one man, under a certain chain of circumstances, inherits a throne; another, a farm; one, the protection of a bondman, or whatever may accrue to these conditions from other operating causes; and another, nothing. If Dr. Channing and his disciples can find out some new principles by which to organize society, producing different and better results, they will then do what has not been done.

LESSON IV.

The doctrine that slavery, disease, and death are the necessary effects of sin, we humbly claim to perceive spread on every page of the holy books. This doctrine is forcibly illustrated in the warning voice of Jehovah to the Israelites. They were emphatically called his children—peculiar people—his chosen ones. He made covenants with them to bless them; yet all these were founded upon their adherence to the Divine law. These promises repealed no ordinance of Divine necessity in their behalf. He expressed, revealed the law, so far as it was important for them at the time, and then says, *Deut.* xxviii. 14–68:—

"15. But it shall come to pass, if thou wilt not hearken unto the voice of the Lord thy God, to observe to do all his commandments and his statutes which I command thee this day, that all these curses shall come upon thee and overtake thee:

"16. Cursed *shalt* thou *be* in the city, and cursed *shalt* thou *be* in the field.

"17. Cursed *shall be* thy basket and thy store.

"18. Cursed *shall be* the fruit of thy body, and the fruit of thy land, the increase of thy kine, and the flocks of thy sheep.

"19. Cursed *shalt* thou *be* when thou comest in, and cursed *shalt* thou *be* when thou goest out.

"20. The Lord shall send upon thee cursing, vexation, and rebuke, in all that thou settest thy hand unto for to do, until thou be destroyed, and until thou perish quickly: because of the wickedness of thy doings whereby thou hast forsaken me.

"21. The Lord shall make the pestilence cleave unto thee, until he have consumed thee from off the land, whither thou goest to possess it.

"22. The Lord shall smite thee with a consumption, and with a fever, and with an inflammation, and with an extreme burning, and with the sword, and with blasting, and with mildew: and they shall pursue thee until thou perish.

"23. And thy heaven that is over thy head shall be brass, and the earth that *is* under thee *shall be* iron.

"24. The Lord shall make the rain of thy land powder and dust: from heaven shall it come down upon thee, until thou be destroyed.

"25. The Lord shall cause thee to be smitten before thine enemies: thou shalt go out one way against them, and flee seven ways before them; and shalt be removed into all the kingdoms of the earth.

"26. And thy carcass shall be meat unto all fowls of the air, and unto beasts of the earth, and no man shall fray *them* away.

"27. The Lord will smite thee with the botch of Egypt, and with the emerods, and with the scab, and with the itch, whereof thou canst not be healed.

"28. The Lord shall smite thee with madness, and blindness, and astonishment of heart:

"29. And thou shalt grope at noonday, as the blind gropeth in darkness, and thou shalt not prosper in thy ways; and thou shalt be only oppressed and spoiled evermore, and no man shall save *thee*.

"30. Thou shalt betroth a wife, and another man shall lie with her: thou shalt build a house, and thou shalt not dwell therein: thou shalt plant a vineyard, and shalt not gather the grapes thereof.

"31. Thine ox *shall be* slain before thine eyes, and thou shalt not eat thereof: thy ass *shall be* violently taken away from before thy face, and shall not be restored to thee: thy sheep *shall be* given unto thine enemies, and thou shalt have none to rescue *them*.

"32. Thy sons and thy daughters *shall* be given unto another people, and thy eyes shall look, and fail *with longing* for them all the day long: and there *shall be* no might in thy hand.

" 33. The fruit of thy land and all thy labours shall a nation which thou knowest not eat up: and thou shalt be only oppressed and crushed always:

" 34. So that thou shalt be mad for the sight of thy eyes which thou shalt see.

" 35. The Lord shall smite thee in the knees, and in the legs, with a sore botch that cannot be healed, from the sole of thy foot unto the top of thy head.

" 36. The Lord shall bring thee, and thy king which thou shalt set over thee, unto a nation which neither thou nor thy fathers have known, and there shalt thou *serve* (וְעָבַדְתָּ *ve abadta, and shall slave yourselves to*) other gods, wood and stone:

" 37. And thou shalt become an astonishment, a proverb, and a by-word, among all nations whither the Lord shall lead thee.

" 38. Thou shalt carry much seed out unto the field, and shalt gather *but* little in: for the locust shall consume it.

" 39. Thou shalt plant vineyards and dress *them*, but shalt neither drink of the wine, nor gather *the grapes:* for the worms shall eat them.

" 40. Thou shalt have olive-trees throughout, but thou shalt not anoint *thyself* with the oil: for thine olive shall cast *his fruit.*

" 41. Thou shalt beget sons and daughters, but thou shalt not enjoy them, for they shall go *into captivity.*"

(*Into captivity* is translated from בַּשֶּׁבִי *bashshebi;* the prefix preposition *in*, *into*, &c. here makes *bash.* The root is *shebi.* The translation is correct, but the idea extends to such a possession of the captive as includes the idea of a right of property. The same word is used when dumb beasts are taken as spoil in war; thus, *Amos* iv. 10, שְׁבִי סוּסֵיכֶם *shebi susekem, I have taken your horses, i. e.* I have *captured* your horses,—the right of property in the horses is changed. The idea in the text is, *they shall go into slavery.*)

"42. All thy trees and fruit of thy land shall the locust consume.

" 43. The stranger that *is* within thee shall get up above thee very high; and thou shalt come down very low.

"44. He shall lend to thee, and thou shalt not lend to him: he shall be the head, and thou shalt be the tail.

" 45. Moreover, all these curses shall come upon thee, and shall pursue thee, and overtake thee, till thou be destroyed: because thou hearkenedst not unto the voice of the Lord thy God, to keep his commandments and his statutes which he commanded thee.

"46. And they shall be upon thee for a *sign*, and for a wonder, and upon thy seed for ever."

(*For a sign* אוֹת *oth, a mark, sign, &c.* It may be noted that this word is used in *Gen.* iv. 15 : "And the Lord set a *mark* upon Cain," אוֹת *oth, mark, sign, &c.*)

"47. Because thou servedst not the Lord thy God with joyfulness and with gladness of heart for the abundance of all *things.*

"48. Therefore shalt thou *serve* (עָבַדְתָּ *be a slave to*) thine enemies which the Lord shall send against thee, in hunger, and in thirst, and in nakedness, and in want of all *things:* and he shall put a yoke of iron upon thy neck, until he have destroyed thee.

"49. The Lord shall bring a nation against thee from far, from the end of the earth, *as swift* as the eagle flieth, a nation whose tongue thou shalt not understand;

"50. A nation of fierce countenance, which shall not regard the person of the old, nor show favour to the young:

"51. And he shall eat the fruit of thy cattle, and the fruit of thy land, until thou be destroyed: which *also* shall not leave thee *either* corn, wine, or oil, *or* the increase of thy kine, or flocks of thy sheep, until he have destroyed thee.

"52. And he shall besiege thee in all thy gates, until thy high and fenced walls come down, wherein thou trustedst, throughout all thy land: and he shall besiege thee in all thy gates throughout all thy land which the Lord thy God hath given thee.

"53. And thou shalt eat the fruit of thine own body, the flesh of thy sons and of thy daughters which the Lord thy God hath given thee, in the siege and in the straitness wherewith thine enemies shall distress thee:

"54. So *that* the man *that* is tender among you, and very delicate, his eye shall be evil toward his brother, and toward the wife of his bosom, and toward the remnant of his children which he shall leave.

"55. So that he will not give to any of them of the flesh of his children whom he shall eat: because he hath nothing left him in the siege, and in the straitness wherewith thine enemies shall distress thee in all thy gates.

"56. The tender and delicate woman among you, which would not adventure to set the sole of her foot upon the ground for delicateness and tenderness, her eye shall be evil toward the husband of her bosom, and toward her son, and toward her daughter,

"57. And toward her young one that cometh out from between

her feet, and toward her children which she shall bear: for she shall eat them for want of all *things* secretly in the siege and straitness wherewith thine enemy shall distress thee in thy gates.

"58. If thou wilt not observe to do all the words of this law that are written in this book, that thou mayest fear this glorious and fearful name THE LORD THY GOD.

"59. Then the Lord will make thy plagues wonderful, and the plagues of thy seed, *even* great plagues, and of long continuance, and sore sicknesses and of long continuance.

"60. Moreover, he will bring upon thee all the diseases of Egypt, which thou wast afraid of, and they shall cleave unto thee.

"61. Also every sickness, and every plague which is not written in the book of this law, them will the Lord bring upon thee, until thou be destroyed.

"62. And ye shall be left few in number, whereas ye were as the stars of heaven for multitude; because thou wouldest not obey the voice of the Lord thy God.

"63. And it shall come to pass, *that* as the Lord rejoiced over you to do you good, and to multiply you; so the Lord will rejoice over you to destroy you and to bring you to nought; and ye shall be plucked from off the land whither thou goest to possess it.

"64. And the Lord shall scatter thee among all people from the one end of the earth even to the other, and thou shalt *serve* (עָבַדְתָּ, *be slave to*) other gods which neither thou nor thy fathers have known, *even* wood and stone.

"65. And among these nations shalt thou find no ease, neither shall the sole of thy foot have rest: but the Lord shall give thee there a trembling heart, and failing of eyes, and sorrow of mind.

"66. And thy life shall hang in doubt before thee; and thou shalt fear day and night, and shalt have none assurance of thy life:

"67. In the morning thou shalt say, Would God it were even! and at even shalt thou say, Would God it were morning! for the fear of thy heart wherewith thou shalt fear, and for the sight of thine eyes which thou shalt see.

"68. And the Lord shall bring thee into Egypt again with ships, by the way whereof I spake unto thee. Thou shalt see it no more again: and there ye shall be sold unto your enemies for bond-men and bond-women, and no man shall buy *you*."

Ye shall be sold, *i. e.* be exposed to sale, or expose yourselves to sale, as the word הִתְמַכַּרְתֶּם *hith maccartem* may be rendered;

they were vagrants, and wished to become slaves that they might be provided with the necessaries of life." *Clarke's Commentary.*

The markets were overstocked with them, says Josephus: * * * "They were sold with their wives and children at the lowest price, there being many to be sold, and few purchasers."

Hegesippus also says—"There were many captives offered for sale, but few buyers, because the Romans disdained to take the Jews for slaves, and there were not Jews remaining to redeem their countrymen."

"When Jerusalem was taken by Titus, of the captives who were sent into Egypt, those under seventeen were sold; but so little care was taken of them, that 11,000 of them perished for want." *Bishop Newton.*

St. Jerome says—"After their last overthrow by Adrian, many thousands of them were sold, and those who could not be sold were transported into Egypt, and perished by shipwreck and famine, or were massacred by the inhabitants."

A similar condition happened to the Jews in Spain, when, under the reign of Ferdinand and Isabella, they were driven out of that kingdom, concerning which, Abarbinel, a Jewish writer says—"Three hundred thousand, young and old, women and children, (of whom he was one,) not knowing where to go, left on foot in one day: some became a prey, some perished by famine, some by pestilence,—some committed themselves to the sea, but were sold for slaves when they came to any coast; many were drowned and burned in the ships which were set on fire. In short, all suffered the punishment of God the Avenger."

Benson, in his Commentary, says—"How these instances may affect others, I know not, but for myself I must acknowledge, they not only convince, but astonish me beyond expression. They are truly, as Moses foretold they would be, *a sign and a wonder for ever.*"

Scott says—"Numbers of captives were sent by sea into Egypt, (as well as into other countries,) and sold for slaves at a vile price, and for the meanest offices; and many thousands were left to perish from want; for the multitude was so great that purchasers could not be found for them all at any price. * * * To such wretchedness is every one exposed, who lives in disobedience to God's commands. * * * None will suffer any misery above his deserts: but, indeed, we are all exposed to this woful curse, for breaking the law of God."

Henry says—"I have heard of a wicked man, who, on reading these threatenings, was so enraged that he tore the leaf out of his Bible."

Upon a review of all this evidence, to what conclusion is the mind inclined? Are there no circumstances under which man may become a slave—"property, in the sight of God and justice?"

Dr. Channing says, vol. ii. page 28—"Such a being (man) was plainly made to obey a law within himself. This is the essence of a moral being. He possesses, as part of his nature, and the most essential part, a cause of duty, which he is to reverence and follow."

This is in accordance with his idea of conscience—"the Divine monitor within us." But we are forced to differ from Dr. Channing. To obey the law of God, not some creature of man's, or our own judgment, is the creed we inculcate; and we further teach that "such a being was plainly made" "to reverence and follow" the law of God, not his own opinion or the feelings of his own heart.

If this doctrine is not true in theology, can it be so in regard to slavery, or any thing else?

Page 29, he says—"Every thing else may be owned in the universe; but a moral, rational being cannot be property. Suns and stars may be owned, but not the lowest spirit. Touch any thing but this. Lay not your hand upon God's rational offspring. The whole spiritual world cries out, FORBEAR!"

We do not quote this as an argument. If his postulate be true concerning the "law within himself," he needs no argument; his opinion is enough: his feeling, his "sense of duty" governs the matter. But, while his disciples "reverence and follow" their "sense of duty," by obeying a law within themselves, and, according to their conscience, "own the sun and stars," may not those who believe the Bible to be the word of God, who "reverence and follow" it, as their "sense of duty," and obey it as a law within themselves, according to their conscience, own slaves?

But Dr. Channing continues—"The highest intelligences recognise their own nature, their own rights, in the humblest human being. By that priceless, immortal spirit which dwells in him, by that likeness of God which he wears, tread him not in the dust, confound him not with the brute." And he then gravely adds—"We have thus seen that a human being cannot rightfully be held and used as property. No legislation, not that of all countries or worlds, could make him so. Let this be laid down as a first, fundamental truth."

Such were his opinions. We view them, if not the ravings, at least the impressions, of fanaticism. When counsellor Quibble saw his client Stultus going to the stocks, he cried out, "It is contrary to my sense of justice; to the laws of God and man; no power can make it right!" *Yet Stultus is in the stocks!*

But what shall we say of him who makes the sanction of his own feelings the foundation of his creed, of his standard of right? What of him, who, in his search for truth, scarcely or never alludes to the Bible as the voice of God, as the Divine basis of his reasons, as the pillar on which argument may find rest? Has some new revelation inspired him? Has he heard a voice louder and more clear than the thunder, the trumpet from the mount of God? Has he beheld truth by a light more lucid than the flaming garments of Jehovah? Or has he only seen a cloud, not from the top of Sinai, but from the dismal pit of human frailty?

LESSON V.

Dr. Channing's second proposition is: "Man has sacred rights, the gifts of God, and inseparable from human nature, of which slavery is the infraction;" in proof of which he says, vol. ii. p. 23—"Man's rights belong to him as a moral being, as capable of perceiving moral distinctions, a subject of moral obligation. As soon as he becomes *conscious* of a duty, a kindred *consciousness* springs up, that he has a *right* to do what the sense of duty enjoins, and that no foreign will or power can obstruct his moral action without crime."

Suppose man has rights described; suppose he feels *conscious*, as he says; does that give him a right to do wrong, because his sense of duty enjoins him to do so? And may he not be prevented from so doing? Was it indeed a crime in God to turn the counsels of Ahithophel into foolishness?

Page 33. "That some inward principle which teaches a man what he is bound to do to others, teaches equally, and at the same instant, what others are bound to do to him!" Suppose a few Africans, on an excursion to capture slaves, find that this "inward principle" teaches them that they are bound to make a slave of Dr. Channing, if they can; does he mean that, therefore, he is bound to make slaves of them?

Idem, p. 33. "The sense of duty is the fountain of human rights. In other words, the same inward principle which teaches the former, bears witness to the latter."

If the African's sense of duty gives the right to make Dr. Channing a slave, we do not see why he should complain; since, by his own rule, the African's sense of duty proves him to possess the right which his sense of duty covets.

Page 34. "Having shown the foundation of human rights in human nature, it may be asked, what they are. * * * They may all be comprised in the right, which belongs to every rational being, to exercise his powers for the promotion of his own and others' happiness and virtue. * * * His ability for this work is a sacred trust from God, the greatest of all trusts. He must answer for the waste or abuse of it. He consequently suffers an unspeakable wrong when stripped of it by others, or forbidden to employ it for the ends for which it is given."

We regret to say that we feel an objection to Channing's argument and mode of reasoning, for its want of definiteness and precision. If what he says on the subject of slavery were merely intended as eloquent declamations, addressed to the sympathies and impulses of his party, we should not have been disposed to have named such an objection. But his works are urged on the world as sound logic, and of sufficient force to open the eyes of every slaveholder to the wickedness of the act, and to force him, through the medium of his "moral sense," to set the slaves instantly free.

A moral action must not only be the voluntary offspring of the actor, but must also be performed, to be judged by laws which shall determine it to be good or bad. These laws, man being the moral agent, we say, are the laws of God; by them man is to measure his conduct.

Locke says, "Moral good and evil are the conformity or disagreement of our voluntary actions to some law, whereby good or evil is drawn upon us from the will or power of the lawmaker."

But the doctrine of Dr. Channing seems to be that this law is each man's *conscience*, *moral sense*, *sense of duty*, or the *inward principle.* If the proposition of Mr. Locke be sound logic, what becomes of these harangues of Dr. Channing?

We say, that the law, rule, or power that decides good or evil, must be from a source far above ourselves; for, if otherwise, the contradictory and confused notions of men must necessarily banish all idea of good and evil from the earth. In fact, the denial of the elevated, the Divine source of such law, is also a denial that God governs; for government without law is a contradiction.

If the conscience, as Dr. Channing thinks, is the guide between right and wrong according to the law of God; then the law of God must be quite changeable, because the minds of men differ. Each makes his own deduction; therefore, in that case, the law of God must be what each one may severally think it to be; which is only other language to say there is no law at all. "Every way of a man is right in his own eyes." *Prov.* xxi. 2. But, "The statutes of the Lord are right." *Ps.* xix. 8. The laws of God touching the subject of slavery are spread through every part of the Scriptures. Human reason may do battle, but the only result will be the manifestation of its weakness. The institution of slavery must, of necessity, continue in some form, so long as sin shall have a tendency to lead to death; so long as Jehovah shall rule, and exercise the attributes of mercy to fallen, degraded man.

But let us for a moment view the facts accompanying the slavery of the African race, and compare them with the assertion, p. 35, that every slave "suffers a grievous wrong;" and, p. 49, that every slave-owner is a "robber," however unconscious he may be of the fact.

So far as history gives us any knowledge of the African tribes, for the last 4000 years, their condition has been stationary; at least they have given no evidence of advancement in morals or civilization beyond what has been the immediate effect of the exchange of their slaves for the commodities of other parts of the world. So far as this trade had influence, it effected almost a total abolition of cannibalism among them. That the cessation of cannibalism was the result of an exchange of their slaves as property for the merchandise of the Christian nations, is proved by the fact that they have returned to their former habits in that respect upon those nations discontinuing the slave-trade with them. Which is the greatest wrong to a slave, to be continued in servitude, or to be butchered for food, because his labour is not wanted by his owner?

No very accurate statistics can be given of African affairs; but their population has been estimated at 50,000,000, and to have been about the same for many centuries; of which population, even including the wildest tribes, far over four-fifths have ever been slaves among themselves. The earliest and the most recent travellers among them agree as to the facts, that they are cannibals; that they are idolaters, or that they have no trace of religion whatever; that marriage with them is but promiscuous intercourse; that there is but little or no affection between husband and wife, parent and children, old or young; that in mental or moral capacity, they are but a grade above the brute creation; that the slaves and women alone do any labour, and they often not enough to keep them from want; that their highest views are to take slaves, or to kill a neighbouring tribe; that they evince no desire for improvement, or to ameliorate their condition. In short, that they are, and ever have been, from the earliest knowledge of them, savages of the most debased character. We have, in a previous study, quoted authority in proof of these facts, to which we refer.

Will any one hesitate to acknowledge, that, to them, slavery, regulated by law, among civilized nations is a state of moral, mental, and physical elevation? A proof of this is found in the fact that the descendants of such slaves are found to be, in all things, their superiors. If their descendants were found to deteriorate from the condition of the parents, we should hesitate to say that slavery was to them a blessing. Which would man consider the most like an act of mercy in Jehovah, to continue them in their state of slavery to their African master, brother, and owner, or to order them into that condition of slavery in which we find them in these States? Which state of slavery would a man prefer, to a savage, or to a civilized master?

The Hebrews, Medes, Persians, Chaldeans, Syrians, Greeks, and Romans have, on the borders of Africa, to some extent, amalgamated with them, from time immemorial. But such amalgamation has never been known to attain to the position, either physically, mentally, or morally, of their foreign progenitors; perhaps superior to the interior tribes, yet often they scarcely exhibit a mental or moral trace of their foreign extraction. The thoughtless, those of slovenly morals, or those of none at all, from among the descendants of Japheth, have commingled with them in the new world; but the amalgamation never exhibits a corresponding elevation in the direction of the white progenitor. The connection may degrade the parent, but never elevate the offspring. The great mass look upon the connection with abhorrence and loathing;

and pity or contempt always attends the footsteps of the aggressor. These feelings are not confined to any particular country or age of the world. Are not these things proof that the descendants of Ham are a deteriorated race? Will the declarations of a few distempered minds, as to their religion, feeling, and taste, weigh in contradiction? What was the judgment of Isaac and Rebecca on this subject? See *Gen.* xxvi. 35; xxvii. 46; also xxviii. 1.

Since the days of Noah, where are their monuments of art, religion, science, and civilization? Is it not a fact that the highest moral and intellectual attainment which the descendants of Ham ever displayed is now, at this time, manifested among those in servile pupilage? The very fact of their being property gives them protection. What, he their "robber," who watches over their welfare with more effect and integrity than all their ancestry together since the days of Noah! By the contrivance of making them *property*, has God alone given them the protection which 4000 years of sinking degradation demand, in an upward movement towards their physical, mental, and moral improvement, their rational happiness on earth, and their hopes of heaven. What, God's agent in this matter a *robber* of them!

Let us assure the disciples of Dr. Channing that there are thousands of slaves too acute observers of truth to come to such a conclusion; who, although from human frailty they may sometimes seem to suffer an occasional or grievous wrong, can yet give good reason in proof that slavery is their only safety. Let us cast the mind back to a period of five hundred years ago. A Christian ship, intent on new discoveries, lands on the African coast. The petty chieftain there, is and about to sacrifice a number of his slaves, either to appease the manes of his ancestor, to propitiate his gods, or to gratify his appetite by feasting. Presents have been made to the natives; it is thought their friendship is secured; the Christians are invited to the *fête*, the participants are collected, the victims brought forward, and the club uplifted for the blow. The Christians, struck with surprise, or excited by horror, remonstrate with the chief; to which he sullenly replies: "Yonder *my* goats, *my* village, all around *my* domain*; these are my slaves!*" meaning that, by the morals and laws that have from time immemorial prevailed there, his rights are absolute; that he feels it as harmless to kill a slave as a goat, or dwell in his village. But the clothing of the Christian is presented, the viands of art are offered, the food of civilization is tasted, the cupidity of the savage is tempted, and the *fête* celebrated through a novel and more valuable offering. What, these Christians, who have bought these slaves, *robbers!*

Let us look back to the days of the house of Saul, when, perhaps, David, hiding himself from his face amid the villages of Ammon, chanced upon the ancestors of Naomah, the mother of Rehoboam, a later king of Israel. Finding them about to sacrifice a child upon the altar of Moloch, "Stay thy hand!" says the son of Jesse; "I have a message to thee from the God of Israel; deliver me the child for these thirty pieces of silver!" And, according to the law of the God of his fathers, it becomes his "bond-man for ever." What, was David a robber in all this? Suppose the child to have been sold, resold, and sold again, is the character of the owner changed thereby?

But it is concerning the *rights* of the descendants of these slaves that we have now to inquire. See *Luke* xvii. 7–10:

"7. But which of you having a servant (δοῦλος, *slave*) ploughing or feeding cattle, will say unto him by and by, when he has come from the field, Go, and sit down to meat?

"8. And will not rather say unto him, Make ready wherewith I may sup, and gird thyself, and serve me, till I have eaten and drunken; and afterwards thou shalt eat and drink?

"9. Doth he thank that servant (δουλον, *slave*) because he did the things that were commanded him? I trow not.

"10. So likewise ye, when ye have done all those things which are commanded you, say, We are unprofitable servants: we have done that which was our duty to do."

Suppose a proprietor, in any country or at any age, receives into his employment an individual, who thereafter resides and has a family upon his estate: upon the death of the individual, will his heirs accrue to any of the rights of the proprietor, other than those granted, or those consequent to their own or their ancestor's condition, or those that may accrue by operation of law? Where is the political enactment, the moral precept, the Divine command, teaching an adverse doctrine?

Before we close our view of Dr. Channing's second proposition, we design to notice his use of the word "nature." He says, that man has rights, gifts of God, inseparable from human "nature." We confess that we are somewhat at a loss to determine the precise idea the doctor affixes to this term. The phrase "human nature" is in most frequent use through these volumes. But in vol.

i. page 74, he says—"Great powers, even in their perversion, attest a *glorious nature.*" Page 77: "The infinite materials of illustration which *nature* and life afford." Page 82: "To regard despotism as a law of *nature.*" Page 84: "His superiority to *nature*, as well as to human opposition." Page 95: "We will inquire into the nature and fitness of the measures." Page 98: "The first object in education *naturally* was to fit him for the field." Page 110: "From the principles of our *nature.*" Page 111: "*Nature* and the human will were to bend to his power." *Idem:* "He wanted the sentiment of a common *nature* with his fellow-beings." Page 112: "With powers which might have made him a glorious representative and minister of the beneficent Divinity, and with *natural* sensibilities." Page 119: "Traces out the general and all-comprehending laws of *nature.*" Page 143: "A power which robs men of the free use of their *nature*," &c. Page 146: "Its efficiency resembles that of darkness and cold in the *natural* world." Page 184: "Whose writings seem to be *natural* breathings of the soul." Page 189: "Language like this has led men to very injurious modes of regarding themselves, and their own *nature.*" *Idem:* "A man when told perpetually to crucify *himself*, is apt to include under this word his whole *nature.*" *Idem:* "Men err in nothing more than in disparaging and wronging their own *nature.*" *Idem:* "If we first regard man's highest *nature.*" Page 190: "We believe that the human mind is akin to that intellectual energy, which gave birth to *nature.*" *Idem:* "Taking human *nature* as consisting of a body as well as mind, as including animal desire," &c. *Idem:* "We believe that he in whom the physical *nature* is unfolded." Page 191: "But excess is not essential to self-regard, and this principle of our *nature* is the last which could be spared." Page 192: "Is is the great appointed trial of our moral *nature.*" Page 193: "Our *nature* has other elements or constituents, and vastly higher ones." *Idem:* "For truth, which is its object, is of a universal, impartial *nature.*" Page 196: "Is the most signal proof of a higher *nature* which can be given." *Idem:* "It is a sovereignty worth more than that over outward *nature.*" *Idem:* "Its great end is to give liberty and energy to our *nature.*" Page 198: "Our moral, intellectual, immortal *nature* we cannot remember too much." Page 200: "The moral *nature* of religion." Page 202: "We even think that our love of *nature.*" *Idem:* "For the harmonies of *nature* are only his wisdom made visible."

Page 203: "That progress in truth is the path of *nature*." Page 211: "It has the liberality and munificence of *nature*, which not only produces the necessary root and grain, but pours forth fruits and flowers. It has the variety and bold contrasts of *nature*." *Idem:* "The beautiful and the superficial seem to be *naturally* conjoined." Page 212: "And by a law of his *nature*." Page 213: "These gloomy and appalling features of our *nature*." Page 215: "These conflicts between the passions and the moral *nature*."

We regret that so eminent and accurate a scholar, and so influential a man, should have fallen into such an indefinite and confused use of any portion of our language. If we mistake not, it will require more than usual reflection for the mind to determine what idea is presented by its use in the most of these instances. We know that some use this word so vaguely, that if required to explain the idea they wished to convey by it, they would be unable to do so. But there are those from whom we expect a better use of language. Many English readers pass over such sentences without stopping to think what are the distinct ideas of the writer. There are, in our language, a few words used in our conversational dialect, as if especially intended for the speaker's aid when he only had a confused idea, or perhaps none at all, of what he designed to say; and we extremely regret that words, to us of so important meaning, as *nature* and *conscience*, should be found among that class. The teacher of theology and morals should surely be careful not to lead his pupils into error. Might not the unskilled inquirer infer that *nature* was a substantive existence, taking rank somewhere between man and the Deity? And what would be his notion, derived from such use of the term, of its offices, of its influence on, and man's relation with it? What is our notion as to the definite idea these passages convey?

"*Man has rights, gifts of God, inseparable from human nature, of which slavery is the infraction.*" By "human nature," as here used, we understand *the condition or state of being a man* in a general sense. Our inference is, then, that God has given man rights, that is, all men the same rights, which are inseparable from his state of being a man; consequently, if by any means these rights are taken from him, then his state of being a man is changed, or ceases to exist; and since slavery breaks these rights, therefore a slave is not a man.

But the fact we find to be that the slave is, nevertheless, a man; and hence it follows that these *rights* were not inseparable from his state of being a man, or that he had not the *rights*.

If slavery is sinful because it infringes the rights of man, then any other thing is also sinful which infringes them. Will the disciples of Dr. Channing deny that these rights are infringed by the constitution of the civil government? The law gives parents the right to govern, command, and restrain minor children; to inflict punishment for their disobedience. Is parental authority a sin? Government, in every form, is found to deprive females of a large proportion of the rights which men possess. When married, their rights are wholly absorbed in the rights of the husband. This must be very sinful!

Idiots have no rights. In reality, the very idea of rights vanishes away with the power to exercise them. But in a state of civil government, it is a mere question of expediency how personal rights shall be adjusted; which is very manifest, if we look at the different constitutions of government now in the world. In one, men who follow certain occupations have certain rights as a consequence. Men who are found guilty of certain breaches of the law lose a portion or all their rights. The president of our senate loses the right to vote, except under condition; and we agree that a mere majority shall rule. Thus forty-nine of the hundred cease to find their rights available. They must submit. Man, as a member of civil society, is only a small fraction of an unit, and has no right to exercise a right unconformably to the expression of the sense of the general good. Man has no right to live independent of his fellow-man, like a plant or a tree; consequently, his rights must be determined and bounded by the general welfare. Dr. Channing ceases to be enlightened by moral science when he announces that, because a man is "conscious of duty," therefore, what he may think his right cannot be affected by others "without crime." So reverse may be the fact, that it may be a crime in him to claim the right his conscious duty may suggest.

Man cannot be said to be in possession of all things that he, or such theorists, may deem his rights only in a monocratic state. But how will he retain them? For then, so far as he shall have intercourse with others, every thing will come to be decided by the law of *might;* so that, instead of gaining, he will lose all rights. But suppose him to live without intercourse; what is a naked, abstract right, that yields him nothing above the brute? God never made a man for such a state of life; because it at once includes rebellion to his government; and, therefore, its every movement will be to retrograde.

Will the disciples of Dr. Channing be surprised to find that the only medicine God has prepared for such a loathsome moral disease as will then be developed, is slavery to a higher order of men?

LESSON VI.

Dr. Channing's third position is to offer explanations to prevent misapplication of the principles presented in his first two propositions.

Vol. ii. page 51, he says—"Sympathy with the slave has often degenerated into injustice towards the master." We fully agree with him; and we also admit "that the consciences of men are often darkened by education." This short chapter is evidently written in a spirit of conciliation, and contains many truths eloquently told; yet, he finally grasps his doctrines, and repeats his elucidations.

His fourth position is, "To unfold the evils of slavery." He says the first great evil is the debasement of the slave. Page 60: "This word, (slave,) borrowed from his condition, expresses the ruin wrought by slavery within him. * * * To be an instrument of the physical, material good of another, whose will is his highest law, he is taught to regard as the great purpose of his being. Here lies the evil of slavery. Its whips, imprisonment, and even the horrors of the middle passage from Africa to America, these are not to be named in comparison with this extinction of the proper consciousness of a human being, with the degradation of a man into a brute."

If it be a fact that the debasement of the negro race has been brought about by their having been made slaves in America; then it will be a very strong argument, we are willing to acknowledge, an insurmountable one, against the institution. That Dr. Channing thinks such to be the fact, we have no doubt; for we cannot a moment admit that he would assert what he did not believe was true. But "the consciences of men are often darkened by education." We hold that the assertion is capable of proof, that the debasement of the race was the moral, the necessary effect of a long course of sin; and that, instead of slavery producing the debasement, the fact is, the debasement produced the slavery; or, in other words, slavery is the moral, the necessary effect of the debasement.

The leading object, through all our studies, is the elucidation of the fact, that sin has a poisonous effect upon the moral, mental, and physical man, that is in constant action in the direction of deterioration, debasement, ruin, death. Such we teach to be the doctrine of the holy books, spread through the whole volume, elucidated upon every page; that slavery, like a saviour, steps in upon this descending road, arresting the downward progress, the rapid fall to final, to unalterable ruin and death.

"If his children forsake my law, and walk not in my judgments; if they break my statutes, and keep not my commandments,—then will I visit their transgressions with the rod, and their iniquity with stripes." *Ps.* lxxxix. 30–32. "A righteous man hateth lying: but a wicked man is loathsome, and cometh to shame." *Prov.* xiii. 5. "Thou turnest man to destruction; and sayest, return, ye children of men." *Ps.* xc. 3. "I have therefore delivered unto the mighty one of the heathen; he shall surely deal with him: I have driven him out for his wickedness." *Ezek.* xxxi. 11. "And I will sell your sons and your daughters into the hands of the children of Judah, and they shall sell them to the Sabeans, to a people far off; for the Lord hath spoken it." *Joel* iii. 8. "Nevertheless they shall be his *servants* (לַעֲבָדִים *slaves*), that they may know my *service* (עֲבוֹדָתִי, *slavery*), and the *service* (וַעֲבוֹדַת, *slavery*) of the kingdoms of the countries." 2 *Chron.* xii. 8. "The show of their countenance doth witness against them; and they declare their sin as Sodom, they hide it not. Wo unto their soul! for they have rewarded evil unto themselves." *Isa.* iii. 9. "Therefore my people are gone into captivity, because they have no knowledge; and their honourable men are famished, and their multitude dried up with thirst." "And the mean man shall be brought down, and the mighty man shall be humbled, and the eyes of the lofty shall be humbled: but the Lord of hosts shall be exalted in judgment, and God that is holy shall be sanctified in righteousness." *Isa.* v. 13, 15, 16.

Dr. Channing's book before us goes on to specify this debasement as to the intellect; its influence on the domestic relations; how it "produces and gives license to cruelty." The fact that debasement reaches all these points, we agree to; nay, further, that it reaches to every act and thought. But we refer all these displays of debasement to the result of the degradation, of which slavery is only the moral, the natural consequence. If we find a man debased as to one thing, it is in conformity with the common sense of mankind to expect to find him debased as to another.

Channing, pp. 78, 79. "I proceed to another view of the evils of slavery. I refer to its influence on the master. * * * I pass over many views. * * * I will confine myself to two considerations. The first is, that slavery, above all other influences, nourishes the passion for power and its kindred vices. There is no passion which needs a stronger curb. Men's worst crimes have sprung from the desire of being masters, of bending others to their yoke."

It is to be lamented that man is so prone to sin; that he is not more undeviating in the paths of virtue, of goodness, of perfection. The charge made by Dr. Channing in the passage quoted, we are sorry to acknowledge, is too true. But so far as we have any knowledge of the history of man, even in the absence of slavery, the time has never been when the passion for power and its kindred vices did not find sufficient food for their nourishment. The evil passions alluded to are not so particular as to their food but that, if they do not find a choice thing to nourish themselves on, they will feed and nourish themselves on another.

It, perhaps, would not be difficult to show that the love of power and its kindred vices first operated to bring on us "all our wo;" stimulated Cain to kill Abel; in fact, has been in most powerful action among those causes that have introduced slavery to the world. Slavery gave no birth to these passions. They drove Nebuchadnezzar from his throne down to the degradation of the brute. "Is not this great Babylon that I have built for the house of the kingdom, by the might of my power, and for the honour of my majesty?" *Dan.* iv. 12.

He had great power, great wealth, and, it is true, he had great possessions in slaves. The prophet understood his case, and spoke plainly. If his owning thousands of slaves merely had nursed in him a forgetfulness of God, the seer would not have hesitated so to inform him. Great prosperity in the affairs of the world in his case, as in some others of a somewhat later day, so puffed him up that he forgot who he was. The owning of slaves may puff up a silly intellect—doubtless, often does; but the same intellect would be more likely to be puffed up by a command of a more elevated grade, as officers of government, or, even in private life, by the control of superior amounts of wealth; or even by the conceit of possessing a great superiority of intellect.

Doubtless, the disciples of Dr. Channing will agree that abundant instances of such tumidity might be found in any country, even among those who never owned a slave.

It may be a fact, that, to some, the having control over and owning a slave have a greater tendency to produce the effect of *puffing up* the owner than would his value in money or other property; because it may be a fact that a given amount in one kind of property may possess such tendency to a greater extent than another. But the truth probably is, that one man would be the most puffed up by one thing, and another man by another. We agree that being thus *puffed up* is a sin; that it leads to consequences extremely ruinous, and often fatal. Very small men are also liable to the disease, and they sometimes take it from very slight causes. It is true, "there is no passion that needs a stronger curb." What we contend is, that it is not a necessary consequence of owning slaves, any more than it is of owning any other property, or of possessing any other command of men; and that so far as it is an argument against owning slaves, it is also an argument against owning any other property, or of having any other control, or of possessing any other command among men.

LESSON VII.

Dr. Channing continues his view of the evils of slavery, and says, p. 80, 81—

"I approach a more delicate subject, and one on which I shall not enlarge. To own the persons of others, to hold females in slavery, is necessarily fatal to the purity of a people: that unprotected females, stripped by their degraded condition of woman's self-respect, should be used to minister to other passions in man than the love of gain, is next to inevitable. Accordingly, in such a community, the reins are given to youthful licentiousness. Youth, everywhere in peril, is, in these circumstances, urged to vice with a terrible power. And the evil cannot stop at youth. Early licentiousness is fruitful of crime in mature life. How far the obligation to conjugal fidelity, the sacredness of domestic ties, will be revered amid such habits, such temptations, such facilities to vice as are involved in slavery, needs no exposition. So sure and terrible is retribution even in this life! Domestic happiness is not blighted in the slave's hut alone. The master's infidelity sheds a blight over his own domestic affections and joys. Home, without purity and constancy, is spoiled of its holiest charm and most blessed influences. I need not say, after the preceding explanations, that this corruption is far from being universal. Still, a slave-country reeks with licentiousness. It is tainted with a deadlier pestilence than the plague.

"But the worst is not told. As a consequence of criminal connections, many a master has children born into slavery. Of these, most, I presume, receive protection, perhaps indulgence, during the life of the fathers; but at their death, not a few are left to the chances of a cruel bondage. These cases must have increased since the difficulties of emancipation have been multiplied. Still more, it is to be feared that there are cases in which the master puts his own children under the whip of the overseer, or sells them to undergo the miseries of a bondage among strangers.

"I should rejoice to learn that my impressions on this point are false. If they be true, then our own country, calling itself enlightened and Christian, is defiled with one of the greatest enormities on earth. We send missionaries to heathen lands. Among the pollutions of heathenism, I know nothing worse than this. The heathen who feasts on his country's foe, may hold up his head by the side of the Christian who sells his child for gain, sells him to be a slave. God forbid that I should charge this crime to a people! But, however rarely it may occur, it is a fruit of slavery, an exercise of power belonging to slavery, and no laws restrain or punish it. Such are the evils which spring naturally from the licentiousness generated by slavery."

The owner of slaves who acts in conformity to the foregoing picture, to our mind displays proofs of very great debasement, and his offspring, stained with the blood of Ham, we should deem most likely to be quite fit subjects of slavery: we cannot therefore regret that the laws do not punish nor restrain him from selling them as slaves; we should rather regret that the laws did not compel him to go with them.

That there are instances in the Slave States where the owner of female slaves cohabits with them, and has offspring by them, is true. There may be instances where such parent has sold them into slavery,—they, in law, being his slaves; yet we aver we have never known an instance in which it has been done. That such offspring have been sold as slaves, by the operation of law, must certainly be acknowledged; and that such instances have been more frequent since the action of the abolitionists has aroused the Slave States to a sense of their danger, and thereby caused the laws to be more stringent on the subject of emancipation, is also true. And are you, ye agitators of the slave question, willing to acknowledge this fact? And that your conduct—even you yourselves—are even now the cause, under God, of the present condition of slavery, which many such persons now endure? Is not he who places the obstruction on the highway, whereby the traveller is plunged in death, the guilty one? In what light, think ye, must this class of slaves view you and your conduct? But we wish not to upbraid you. If you are ignorant, words are useless. If you are honest men and know the truth, we prefer to leave you in the hands of God and your own conscience.

We hold that cohabitation with the blacks, on the part of the whites, is a great sin, and is proof of a great moral debasement; nor will we say but that the conservative influences of God's providence may have moved the abolitionists to the action of for ever placing a bar to the emancipation of this class of slaves, such coloured offspring, in order that the enormity of the sin of such cohabitation may be brought home, in a more lively sense, to the minds of their debased parents.

"I saw the Lord sitting upon his throne, and the host of heaven standing on his right hand and on his left.

"And the Lord said, Who will entice Ahab, king of Israel, that he may go up and fall at Ramoth Gilead? And one spake after this manner, and another saying after that manner.

"Then there came out a spirit, and stood before the Lord, and said, I will entice him; and the Lord said unto him, Wherewith?

"And he said, I will go out and be a lying spirit in the mouth of all his prophets. And the Lord said, Thou shalt entice him." 2 *Chron.* xviii. 18–21; 1 *Kings*, xxii. 19.

We wish to state a fact which may not be generally known to the disciples of Dr. Channing: we speak of Louisiana, where we live. Here is a floating population, emigrants from all parts of the world, especially from free countries and states, nearly or quite equal in number to the native-born citizens who have been raised up and grown to maturity amid slaves or as the owners of slaves. If the cohabitation complained of is at all indicated by the mixed-blooded offspring, then the proof of this cohabitation will be far overbalancing on the side of this floating population.

But again, there are instances where an individual from this class, who thus cohabits with some master's slave, and has offspring, and, succeeding in some business, buys her, probably with the intention of emancipation; but, as he becomes a proprietor and fixed citizen, procrastination steals upon him, and he finds himself enthralled by a coloured family for life.

Let the number of these instances be compared with those where the delinquents have been habituated, from the earliest youth, to the incidents of slavery, and the former class is found to be entitled to the same pre-eminence. From this class also there are instances where the white man, so cohabiting with the slave whom he has purchased for the purpose of emancipation, sends her and his offspring to some free State, often to Cincinnati, the Moab of the South! "Let mine outcasts dwell with thee, Moab." *Isa.* xvi. 4.

Let such instances as this last named be contrasted with like instances emanating from among the native-born, or those raised among slaves, and the former class are still far in the majority. In short, the fact is found to be, that those who have been born, raised, and educated among them, and as the owners of slaves, are found more seldom to fall into this cohabitation than those who are by chance among slaves, but had not been educated from youth among them.

Far be it from us to recriminate. Our object alone, in presenting these facts, is to show, to give proof, that slavery is not the cause of the debasement which urges the white man on to cohabitation with the negro.

We will ask no questions as to the frequency of such intercourse in some of the large Northern cities, in which blacks are numerous as well as free, between them and the debased of the whites. What if we should be told, in answer, if the charge were established, that such whites acted from *conscience*, under a sense of the essential equality of the negro with the white man, and under the religious teaching of the advocates of amalgamation!

He who writes on and describes moral influences, must be expected to view them as he has been in the habit of seeing them manifested. We therefore regret exceedingly to see that Dr. Channing has made the assertion that, "to own the persons of others, to hold females in slavery, is necessarily fatal to the purity of a people; that unprotected females, stripped by their degraded condition of woman's self-respect, should be used to minister to other passions in men than the love of gain, is next to inevitable."

If this assertion is warranted by the moral condition of society as displayed before him, may we not find in it a solution of the fact, that those who have been reared up under all the influences of slavery on the master, are far less frequently found to fall into the odious cohabitation with the negro than are those who have not.

However, we have among us some very wicked and debased men, who own slaves, and who have been born and educated in the midst of the influences of the institution of slavery, and who yet cohabit with their female negroes. But the moral sense of the community, from day to day and from year to year, more and more distinctly gives reproof, more and more emphatically points to such the finger of contempt and scorn, and continues to increase in energy, expressing its loathing and abhorrence; and all this is taking place under the influences of slavery on the master. Do all these things give proof that slavery is the progenitor of this debasement, or the reverse?

Dr. Channing was mistaken; his mind was in error: he substituted the consequent for the cause.

We deem it useless to spend time or argument with those who will pertinaciously deny and refuse to listen to facts, unless they shall be in support of their previously conceived views or prejudices. We are aware that the numerical proportion which we have ascribed to what we call "a floating population" may seem incredible to those in other countries, where the facts are quite different. Yet we are sure that such estimate is within the truth.

Here, as everywhere else, the government, the legislative power of the country, is in the hands of the permanent and more elevated and wealthy classes; in the hands of slave-owners. Would such a class consent to laws throwing difficulties in the way of emancipation, if the effect of such laws were to be expended on their own offspring? To the more elevated and cultivated class of community in any country (and here such are all slave-owners) is to be ascribed the tone of moral feeling. Does any man covet for himself the loathing and scorn of community?

The family of the slave-owner is taught to regard the negro as a race of man radically inferior, in moral capacity, in mental power, and even in physical ability, to the white man; that, although he is susceptible of improvement in all these things, and even does improve in the state of slavery to the white man, yet that it would require untold generations to elevate him and his race to the present standing of the white races.

The child, the mere youth, and those of more experience, see proofs of these facts in every comparison. The master feels them to be true, and is taught, that, while he governs with compassion, forbearance, and mercy, and as having regard to their improvement, any familiarity on terms of equality, beyond that of command on his side, and obedience on theirs, is, and must be, disgrace to him. He is taught to consider the negro race, from some cause, to have deteriorated to such extent that his safety and happiness demand the control of a superior; he regards him as a man, entitled to receive the protection of such control; and that he, like every other man, will be called to account unto God, according to the talents God has given him. He is taught, by every hour's experience, to know that slavery to the negro is a blessing. He is taught to feel it a duty to teach, as he would an inferior, the negro his moral duty, his obligations to God, the religion of the Bible, the gospel of Christ.

But the man born and educated in the Free States is taught that "he who cannot see a *brother*, a child of God, a man possessing all the rights of humanity, under a skin darker than his own, wants the vision of a Christian." *Channing*, vol. ii. p. 14. "To recognise as brethren those who want all outward distinctions, is the chief way in which we are to manifest the spirit of him who came to raise the fallen and save the lost." *Ibidem.*

Vol. ii. pp. 20, 21, 22, he says—"Another argument against property (in slaves) is to be found in the essential equality of men." * * * "Nature indeed pays no heed to birth or condition in bestowing her favours. The noblest spirits sometimes grow up in the obscurest spheres. Thus equal are men;—and among these equals, who can substantiate his claim to make others his property, his tools, the mere instruments of his private interest and gratification?" * * * "Is it sure that the slave, or the slave's child, may not surpass his master in intellectual energy, or in moral worth? Has nature conferred distinctions, which tell us plainly who shall be owners and who shall be owned? Who of us can unblushingly lift up his head and say that God has written 'master' there? Or who can show the word 'slave' engraven on his brother's brow? The equality of nature makes slavery a wrong."

May we aid the disciples of Dr. Channing by referring them to *Prov.* xvii. 2, "A wise *servant* (עֶבֶד *ebed, slave*) shall have rule over a son that causeth shame, and shall have part of the inheritance among the brethren?" And will the doctor and his disciples believe the proverb any the more true, when we inform them that it is a matter of frequent occurrence in slave-holding communities. Vol. v. p. 89, 90, he says—"But we have not yet touched the great cause of the conflagration of the Hall of Freedom. Something worse than fanaticism or separation of the Union was the impulse to this violence. We are told that white people and black sat together on the benches of the hall, and were even seen walking together in the streets! This was the unheard-of atrocity which the virtues of the people of Philadelphia could not endure. They might have borne the dissolution of the national tie; but this junction of black and white was too much for human patience to sustain. And has it indeed come to this? For such a cause are mobs and fires to be let loose on our persons and most costly buildings? What! Has not an American citizen a right to sit and walk with whom he will? Is this common privilege denied us? Is society authorized to choose our associates? Must our neighbour's tastes as to friendship and companionship control our own? Have the feudal times come back to us, when to break the law of caste was a greater crime than to violate the laws of God? What must Europe have thought, when the news crossed the ocean of the burning of the Hall of Freedom, because white and coloured people walked together in the streets?

"Europe might well open its eyes in wonder. On that continent, with all its aristocracy, the coloured man mixes freely with his fellow-creatures. He sometimes receives the countenance of the rich, and has even found his way into the palaces of the great. In Europe, the doctrine would be thought to be too absurd for refutation, that a coloured man of pure morals and piety, of cultivated intellect and refined manners, was not a fit companion for the best in the land. What must Europe have said, when brought to understand that, in a republic, founded on the principles of human rights and equality, people are placed beyond the laws for treating the African as a man. This Philadelphia doctrine deserves no mercy. What an insult is thrown on human nature, in making it a heinous crime to sit or walk with a human being, whoever it may be? It just occurs to me, that I have forgotten the circumstance which filled to overflowing the cup of abolitionist wickedness in Philadelphia. The great offence was this, that certain young women of anti-slavery faith were seen to walk the streets with coloured young men!"

Such are the lessons taught the youth as well as the aged of the Free States, even by Dr. Channing himself. We now ask, under the teachings of which school will the pupils be the best prepared for this cohabitation with the negro?

The burning of the Hall of Freedom was, no doubt, a very great outrage, well meriting severe condemnation. Yet we cannot but notice, that Dr. Channing has nowhere, in all his works, said one word about the burning of the Convent on Mount Benedict, by his own townsmen, the good people of Boston.

We care not with what severity he punishes such outrages. But it is the influence of his lesson in palliating the familiarity, and mitigating the evil consequences of a coalition of the white man with the negro, that we present to view. It is with grief that we find him infusing into his disciples this nauseating, disgusting, moral poison; preparing their minds to feel little or no shame in a cohabitation with the negro, so degrading to the white man, and so disgraceful in all Slave States. Yea further, what are we to think of the judgment, of the taste,—may we not add, habits, of a man who could unblushingly publish to the world his partiality to the negro of Jamaica, after his visit there, as follows:

"I saw too, on the plantation where I resided, a gracefulness and dignity of form and motion, rare in my own native New England." Vol. vi. p. 51.

Again, page 52. "The African countenance seldom shows that coarse, brutal sensuality which is so common in the face of the white man."

May we be pardoned for feeling a strong desire,—rather, a curiosity,—to be made acquainted with the faces of the white men with whom he was the most familiar!

LESSON VIII.

In vol. ii. page 82, Dr. Channing says—

"I cannot leave the subject of the evils of slavery, without saying a word of its political influence."

He considers that "slave labour is less productive than free." This is doubtless true; and if so, it proves that the master of the slave does not require of him so much labour as is required of a hired labourer. Are the friends of abolition angry, because, in their sympathy for the slave, they have found something to be pleased with?

He considers that "by degrading the labouring population to a state which takes from them motives to toil, and renders them objects of suspicion or dread," impairs "the ability of a community to unfold its resources in peace, and to defend itself in war."

This proposition includes the idea that the Slave States have degraded a portion of their citizens to a state of slavery. This is not true. Our ancestors, contrary to their will, were forced to receive a degraded race among them, not as citizens, but slaves;—and does it follow now, that we must again be forced to make this degraded race our political equals? Even the British Government, with all its claim to sovereign rule, never dreamed of imposing on us a demand so destructive to our political rights; so blighting to social happiness; so annihilating to our freedom as men; so extinguishing to our very race. Do the friends of abolition deem us so stupid as not to see, if, even when the negro is in slavery, cases of amalgamation happen, that, when he shall be elevated to political freedom, the country would, by their aid, be overspread by it? Do they think that we do not see that such a state of things is degeneracy, degradation, ruin, worse than death to the white men? And will they chide, if, in its prevention, we drench our fields in our own blood in preference? The British Government urged the race here as an article of property, of commerce and profit, as they did their *tea*. They stipulated, they guaranteed them to be *slaves*, they and their posterity for ever—not *citizens!* On such terms alone could they have been received. The South then, as now, to a man would have met death on the battle-field, sooner than have suffered their presence on other conditions.

The British governmental councils, our colonial assemblies, our primitive inquiring conventions never viewed them in any other light. It was not on their account we sought for freedom. It was not in their behalf we fought for liberty. It was not for them our blood ran like water. It was not to establish for them political rights we broke the British yoke, or founded here this great government. Our national synods recognised them only as property; our constitutional charter, only as slaves; our congressional statutes, only as the subjects of their masters.

There is falsity in the very language that frames the proposition which inculcates that these slaves are a portion of population that ever can be justly entitled to equal political rights, or that they are, or ever were, degraded by the community among whom they are now found.

So degraded, both mentally and physically, is the African in his own native wilds, that, however humiliating to a freeman slavery may seem, to him it is an elevated school; and however dull and stupid may be his scholarship, yet a few generations distinctly mark some little improvement. We cannot doubt, some few individuals of this race have been so far elevated in their constitutional propensities that they might be well expected to make provident citizens; and the fact is, such generally become free, without the aid of fanaticism. But what is the value of a *general assertion* predicated alone upon a few exceptions? Some few of our own race give ample proof that they are not fit to take care of themselves: shall we, therefore, subject our whole race to pupilage?

That such a population, such a race of men, is as conducive to national grandeur, either as to resources or defence, as the same number of intellectual, high-minded yeomanry of our own race might be well expected to be, perhaps few contend; and we pray you not to force us to try the experiment. But if such weakness attend the position in which we feel God has placed us, why distress us by its distortion? Why torment our wound with your inexperienced, and therefore unskilful hand? Why strive ye to enrage our passions, by constantly *twitting* us with what is not our fault? Do you indeed wish to destroy, because you have no power to amend? Why, then, your inexperience as to facts, aided by misrepresentation and sophistry in the digestion of language and sentiment,—and we exceedingly regret that we can correctly say, open falsehood,—as found on pages 86, 87?—

"Slavery is a strange element to mix up with free institutions. It cannot but endanger them. It is a pattern for every kind of wrong. The slave brings insecurity on the free. Whoever holds one human being in bondage, invites others to plant the foot on his own neck. Thanks to God, not one human being can be wronged with impunity. The liberties of a people ought to tremble, until every man is free. Tremble they will. Their true foundation is sapped by the legalized degradation of a single innocent man to slavery. That foundation is impartial justice, is respect for human nature, is respect for the rights of every human being. I have endeavoured in these remarks to show the hostility between slavery and 'free institutions.' If, however, I err; if these institutions cannot stand without slavery for their foundation, then I say, let them fall. Then they ought to be buried in perpetual ruins. Then the name of republicanism ought to become a by-word and reproach among the nations. Then monarchy, limited as it is in England, is incomparably better and happier than our more popular forms. Then, despotism, as it exists in Prussia, where equal laws are in the main administered with impartiality, ought to be preferred. A republican government, bought by the sacrifice of half, or more than half of a people, stripping them of their most sacred rights, by degrading them to a brutal condition, would cost too much. A freedom so tainted with wrong ought to be our abhorrence."

Let not the looseness of the doctor's regard for the Union surprise. With him a dissolution of the Union had become a fixed idea. On pages 237 and 238, he says—

"To me it seems not only the right, but the duty of the Free States, in case of the annexation of Texas, to say to the Slaveholding States, 'We regard this act as the dissolution of the Union.' * * * A pacific division in the first instance seems to me to threaten less contention than a lingering, feverish dissolution of the Union, such as must be expected under this fatal innovation. For one, then, I say, that, earnestly as I deprecate the separation of these States, and though this event would disappoint most cherished hopes for my country, still I could submit to it more readily than to the reception of Texas into the confederacy." "I do not desire to share the responsibility or to live under the laws of a government adopting such a policy." * * * "If the South is bent on incorporating Texas with itself, as a new prop to slavery, it would do well to insist on a division of the States. It would, in so doing, consult best its own safety. It should studiously keep itself from communion with the free part of the country. It should suffer no railroad from that section to cross its borders. It should block up intercourse with us by sea and land." Vol. ii. p. 239.

We do not quote these passages for the sake of refuting them. "*In Europe, the doctrine would be thought too absurd for refutation.*" "*What must Europe have thought when*" *these sentiments* "*crossed the ocean.*" * * * "*What must Europe have said, when brought to understand that, in a republic founded on the principles of human rights and equality,*"—and this writer acknowledges the doctrine that "the constitution was a compromise among independent States, and it is well known that geographical relations and the local interest were among the essential conditions on which the compromise was made;" and concerning which, he adds, "Was not the constitution founded on conditions or considerations which are even more authoritative than its particular provisions?" (see vol. ii. p. 237,)—"*What must Europe have said,*" when informed that these sentiments were expressed against the right of the South to hold slaves? Slaves, whom she, herself, in our childhood, had sold us? Why, she must have thought that we were on the eve of a civil war, and that Dr. Channing was about to take command of an army of abolitionists to compel the South to submit to his terms! "*Europe might well open its eyes in wonder*" at such extravagance.

"Such," says our author, are "the chief evils of slavery;" and we are willing to leave it to "Europe" to decide whether he has not furnished us with declamation instead of argument.

Under the head, "Evils of Slavery," he examines those considerations that have been urged in its favour, or in mitigation, which we deem unnecessary to notice further than to note a few passages in which there is between us some unity of sentiment.

Page 89. "Freedom undoubtedly has its perils. It offers nothing to the slothful and dissolute. Among a people left to seek their own good in their own way, some of all classes fail from vice, some from incapacity, some from misfortune."

Page 92. "Were we to visit a slave-country, undoubtedly the most miserable human beings would be found among the free; for among them the passions have a wider sweep, and the power they possess may be used to their own ruin. Liberty is not a necessity of happiness. It is only a means of good. It is a trust that may be abused."

Page 93. "Of all races of men, the African is the mildest and most susceptible of attachment. He loves where the European would hate. He watches the life of a master, whom the North American Indian, in like circumstances, would stab to the heart."

The African may exhibit mildness and attachment in slavery when others would exhibit a reverse feeling; but it is not true that he exhibits these qualities as a fixed moral principle, resulting from intellectual conclusion.

Page 95. "No institution, be it what it may, can make the life of a human being wholly evil, or cut off every means of improvement." *Idem.* "The African is so affectionate, imitative, and docile, that, in favourable circumstances, he catches much that is good; and accordingly the influence of a wise and kind master will be seen in the very countenance and bearing of his slaves." Or, rather, we find traces of these qualities developed among their descendants. But the truth is far below this description.

We had expected to have received light and pleasure from the examination of Dr. Channing's view of slavery in a political attitude. We confess we are disappointed. His political view of it is, at least, jejune. To us, it suggests the superior adaptation of his genius and education to the rhapsody of a prayer-meeting than to the labours of a legislative hall. We doubt much whether he had ever arrived to any very clear and general view of the organization of society. Finding, under this head, very little in his volumes that a politician can descend to encounter, we shall close our present Lesson with a very few remarks.

Capital and labour can exist in but two relations; congenerous or antagonistic. They are never congenerous only when it is true that labour constitutes capital, which can only happen through slavery. The deduction is then clear, that capital for ever governs labour; and the deduction is also as clear, that, out of slavery, capital and labour must be for ever antagonistic. But, again, capital governs labour, because, while capital *now exists*, labour can possess it only by its own consumption. But when the two are congenerous, labour, as a tool, is not urged to its injury, because the tool itself is capital; but when antagonistic, the tool is urged to its utmost power, because its injury, its ruin touches not the capital. Hence, we often hear slave-labour is the less productive. The proposition is not affected by facts attending him who is said to be *free*, but who only labours for his individual support; because while he adds nothing to the general stock of capital, he yet falls within the catalogue of being a slave *to himself:* "The Lord sent him forth *to till* the ground," (לַעֲבֹד *la evod, to slave the ground;*) to do slave-labour for his own support; *to slave himself* for his own subsistence.

Such is the first degree of slavery to which sin has subjected all mankind. Therefore, in such case, labour is capital. But the very moment a lower degradation forces him to sell his labour, capital is the only purchaser, and they at once become antagonistic. On the one hand, labour is seeking for all; on the other, capital is seeking for all. But the capital governs, and always obtains the mastery, and reduces labour down to the smallest pittance. Thus antagonistic are capital and labour, that the former is for ever trying to lessen the value of the other by art, by machinery; thus converting the tool of labour into capital itself. The political difference between the influence of these two relations, capital and labour, is very great. We feel surprised that the sympathies of the abolitionists are not changed, from the miseries where capital and labour are decidedly congenerous, to a consideration of that morass of misery into which the worn-out, broken tools of labour are thrown, with cruel heartlessness, where capital and labour are antagonistic.

Under the one system, beggars and distress from want are unknown, because such things cannot exist under such an organization of society. But, under the other, pauperism becomes a leading element. The history of that class of community, in all free countries, is a monument and record of *free labour.*

We ask the politician to consider these facts, while he searches the history of man for light in the inquiry of what is the most tranquil, and, in all its parts, the most happy organization of society.

Under the head of "The Political Influence of Slavery," Dr. Channing has taken occasion to inform us of his feelings as to the stability of this Union; that he prefers its dissolution to the perpetuation of slavery; and that he proposes a "pacific division." And what is his "pacific division?" Why, he says, (if we must repeat it,) "*the South must studiously keep itself from communion with the Free States; to suffer no railroad from the Free States to cross its border; and to block up all intercourse by sea and land!*" Why, it is "death in the pot!"

O most unhappy man! the most unfortunate of all, to have

left such a record of intellectual weakness and folly behind! But we will forbear.

We think Dr. Channing's declarations and proposals wholly uncalled for. We regret the existence of such feelings at the North. We say *feelings*, because we are bold to say, such sentiments are alone the offspring of the most ignorant, wicked, and black-hearted feelings of the human soul. Their very existence shows a preparedness to commit *treason*, perjury, and the murders of civil war! The disciples of Dr. Channing, on the subject of abolitionism, may be too stupid to perceive it; for "Evil men understand not judgment." *Prov.* xxviii. 5.

We regret this feeling at the North the more deeply on the account of the extraordinary generant quality of sin. For it propagates, not only its peculiar kind, but every monster, in every shape, by the mere echo of its voice! Will they remember, "He that diggeth a pit shall fall into it; and whoso breaketh a hedge, a serpent shall bite him." Or, that, "It is an honour to cease from strife; but every fool will be meddling." *Prov.* But since such feelings do exist, we feel thankful to God that the sin of the initiative in the dissolution of this Union is not with the Slave States. We know there are many good men in the North. Much depends on what they may do. We believe the union of these States need not—will not be disrupted.

But if the laws of Congress can neither be executed nor continued, nor oaths to be true to the constitution longer bind these maniacs, the issue will finally be left in the hand of the God of battles! It becomes the South to act wisely, to be calm, and to hope as long as there can be hope. And to the North, let them say now, before it be too late, "We pray you to forbear. We entreat you to be true to your oaths, and not force us, in hostile array, to bathe our hands in blood."

But, if the term of our great national destiny is to be closed, and war, the most cruel of all wars, is to spread far beyond the reach of human foresight,—the South, like Abraham in olden time, will "arm their trained servants," and go out to the war, SHOUTING UNDER THE BANNER OF THE ALMIGHTY!

LESSON IX.

As a fifth proposition, Dr. Channing says—"*I shall consider the argument which the Scriptures are thought to furnish in favour of slavery.*"

In the course of these studies, we have often had occasion to refer to the Scripture in our support. We have shown that even the Decalogue gave rules in regulation of the treatment of slaves; that commands from the mouth of God himself were delivered to Abraham concerning his slaves; that the Almighty from Sinai delivered to Moses laws, directing him whom they might have as slaves,—slaves forever, and to be inherited by their children after them; rules directing the government and treatment of slaves, who had become such under different circumstances. We have adverted to the spirit of prophecy on the subject of the providence of God touching the matter, to the illustrations of our Saviour, and the lessons of the apostles. Others have done the same before us. But Dr. Channing says, page 99—"In this age of the world, and amid the light which has been thrown on the true interpretation of the Scriptures, such reasoning hardly deserves notice."

Had Tom Paine been an abolitionist, he could scarcely have said more! He continues—"A few words only will be offered in reply. This reasoning proves too much. If usages sanctioned in the Old Testament, and not forbidden in the New, are right, then our moral code will undergo a sad deterioration. Polygamy was allowed to the Israelites, was the practice of the holiest men, and was common and licensed in the age of the apostles. * * * Why may not Scripture be used to stock our houses with wives as well as slaves."

We know not what new light has come to this age of the world, enabling it to interpret the Scriptures more accurately than is afforded by the language of the Scriptures themselves. Whatever it may be, we shall not deprive Dr. Channing nor his disciples of its entire benefit, by the appropriation of its use to ourselves; and therefore we shall proceed to examine his position, by interpreting the Scriptures in the old-fashioned way—understanding them to mean what they say.

The first instance the idea is brought to view which we express by the term *wife*, is found in *Gen.* ii. 20: "There was not found a *help meet* for him." The original is לֹא־מָצָא עֵזֶר כְּנֶגְדּוֹ *not found, discovered, help, aid, or assistance, flowing, proceeding, at, to,* or *for him.* Let it be noticed that the idea is in the singular. The word *ishsha,* used to mean *one woman,* or *wife,* is so distinctly singular, that it sometimes demands to be translated by the word *one,* as we shall hereafter find.

Same chapter, verse 22: "Made he a *woman,*" אִשָּׁה, *ishsha, woman, wife.*

Ver. 23: "Shall be called *woman,*" אִשָּׁה *ishsha, woman, wife.*

Ver. 24: "Therefore shall a man leave his father and his mother, and cleave unto his wife," אִשְׁתּוֹ *ishto, his wife, his woman,* "and they shall be one flesh."

Ver. 25: "The man and his wife," אִשְׁתּוֹ *ishto, wife, woman.*

These terms are all in the singular number. We propose for consideration, how far these passages are to be understood as a law and rule of action among men.

Gen. vii. 7: "And Noah went in, and his sons, and his wife, and his sons' wives with him, into the ark."

Ver. 9: "There went in two and two unto Noah into the ark, the male and female, as God had commanded Noah."

We propose also for consideration, how far these passages are an indication of the law of God, and his providence, as bearing on polygamy.

Exod. xx. 17 (18th ver. of the Hebrew text): "Thou shalt not covet thy neighbour's *wife,*" אֵשֶׁת *esheth,* in the construct state, showing that she was appropriated to the neighbour in the singular number. If the passage had read, Thou shalt not covet thy neighbour's *wives,* or any of them, the interpretation must have been quite different.

So also *Deut.* v. 21: "Neither shalt thou desire thy neighbour's *wife,*" אֵשֶׁת *esheth.*

The twenty-second chapter of Deuteronomy relates the law concerning a portion of the relations incident to a married state; but we find the idea always advanced in the singular number. There was no direction concerning his *wives.* Had the decalogue announced, "Thou shalt have but one wife," the language of these explanations and directions, to be in unison therewith, need not have been changed.

The subject is continued through the first five verses of the twenty-fourth chapter, but we find the idea *wife* still expressed in the same careful language, conveying the idea, as appropriated to one man, in the person of one female only. The term "new wife," here used, does not imply that she is an addition to others in like condition, but that her condition of being a wife is *new*, as is most clearly shown by the word חֲדָשָׁה *hadasha*, from which it is translated. The sentiment or condition explained in this passage is illustrated by our Saviour in *Luke* xiv. 20: "I have married a wife, and therefore I cannot come,"—that is, until the expiration of the year,—having reference to this very passage in Deuteronomy for authority. But this passage is made very plain by a direct command of God: see *Deut.* xx. 7: "And what man is there that hath betrothed a wife, and hath not taken her? Let him go and return unto his house, lest he die in the battle, and another man take her."

But the institution of marriage was established, before the fall of man, by the appropriation of one woman to one man. Now, that this fact, this example, stands as a command, is clear from the words of Jesus Christ, in *Matt.* xix. 4, 5: "And he answered and said, Have ye not read, that he which made them at the beginning, made them male and female, and said, For this cause shall a man leave father and mother and shall cleave unto his wife; and they twain shall be one flesh? Wherefore, they are no more twain, but one flesh."

We trust, "at this age of the world," there is a sufficiency of light, among even the most unlearned of us, whereby we shall be enabled to interpret these scriptures, not to license polygamy, but to discountenance and forbid it, by showing that they teach a contrary doctrine. But, perhaps, the explanation is more decided in *Mark* x. 8–11: "And they twain shall be one flesh: so then they are no more twain, but one flesh." "And he saith unto them, whoever shall put away his wife, and marry another, committeth adultery against her."

Surely, if a man commit adultery by marrying the second when he has turned off the previous, it may be a stronger case of adultery to marry a second wife *without turning off the first one!*

We think St. Paul interprets the Scriptures in the old-fashioned way, *Eph.* v. 31: "For this cause shall a man leave his father and mother, and shall be joined unto his wife, and they *two* shall be *one flesh.*"

See 1 *Cor.* vi. 16–18: "What! know ye not that he which is joined to a harlot is one body? For two, saith he, shall be one flesh. Flee fornication." And further, the deductions that St. Paul made from these teachings are plainly drawn out in his lessons to Timothy: "If a man desire the office of bishop, he desireth a good work. A bishop then must be blameless, the husband of one wife." "Let the deacons be the husbands of one wife." 1 *Tim.* iii. 1, 2, 12.

"These things command and teach. Let no man despise thy youth; but be thou an example of the believers in word, in conversation, in charity, in faith, in purity." 1 *Tim.* iv. 11, 12.

And we now beg to inquire whether this lesson to Timothy is not founded upon the law as delivered to Moses? "And the Lord said unto Moses, Speak unto the priests the sons of Aaron, and say unto them:" * * * "They shall be holy unto their God, and not profane the name of their God." * * * "They shall not take a wife that is a whore, or profane; neither shall they take a woman put away from her husband." * * * "And *he that is* the high priest among his brethren * * * shall take a wife in her virginity." "A widow, or a divorced woman, or profane, or a harlot, these he shall not take; but he shall take a virgin of his own people to wife." "Neither shall he profane his seed among his people: for I the Lord do sanctify him." *Lev.* xxi. 1, 6, 7, 10, 13, 14, 15.

We doubt not it will be conceded that the teachings of the Bible are, that polygamy includes the crime of adultery and fornication, both of which have a tendency towards a general promiscuous intercourse. In addition to the express commands as to the views thus involved, to our mind there are specifications on the subject equally decisive. "If any man take a wife * * * and give occasion of speech against her, * * * then shall the father of the damsel and her mother take and bring forth the tokens; * * * and the damsel's father shall say, * * * and, lo, he hath given occasion of speech against her. * * * And the elders of the city shall take that man and chastise him; and they shall amerce him in a hundred shekels of silver, * * * and she shall be his wife; he may not put her away all his days." "But if this thing is true, and the tokens of her virginity be not found for the damsel; then they shall bring out the damsel to the door of her father's house, and the men of the city shall stone her with stones that she die." * * * "If a man be found lying with a woman married to a husband, then they shall both of them die." * * * "If a damsel *that is* a virgin be betrothed unto a husband, and a man find her in the city and lie with her; then ye shall bring them both out unto the gate of that city, and ye shall stone them with stones that they die." * * * "But if a man find a betrothed damsel in the field, and the man force her and lie with her; then the man only that lay with her shall die." * * * "If a man find a damsel that is a virgin, which is not betrothed, and lay hold on her, and lie with her, and they be found, then the man that lay with her shall give unto the damsel's father fifty *shekels* of silver, and she shall be his wife: * * * he may not put her away all his days." *Deut.* xxii. 13–25, 28, 29.

"A bastard shall not enter into the congregation of the Lord; even unto his tenth generation." *Idem*, xxiii. 2.

"These are the statutes which the Lord commanded Moses between a man and his wife, between the father and his daughter, *being yet* in her youth in her father's house." *Num.* xxx. 16.

"When thou art come into the land which the Lord thy God giveth thee, * * * and shalt say, I will set a king over me," &c. * * * "But he shall not," &c. * * * "Neither shall he multiply wives to himself, that his heart turn not away." *Deut.* xvii. 14–17.

The inferences to be drawn from a review of these statutes, in opposition to polygamy, we deem of easy deduction. We leave them for the consideration of those who shall examine the subject.

We deem it extraordinary that, "at this age of the world," we should find men who seem to think that because Moses had a statute which, under certain circumstances, authorized husbands to divorce their wives, that thereby he permitted polygamy.

"When a man hath taken a wife, and married her, and it come to pass that she find no favour in his eyes, because he hath found some *uncleanness* in her," (it is the same word elsewhere translated *nakedness*,) "then let him write her a bill of divorcement, and give it in her hand, and send her out of his house. And when she is departed out of his house, she may go and be another man's wife. And if the latter husband hate her, and write her a bill of divorcement, and giveth it in her hand, and sendeth her out of his house; or if the latter husband die, which took her to be his wife; her former husband which sent her away may not take her again to be his wife, after that she is defiled; for this is abomination before the Lord." *Deut.* xxiv. 1–4.

Is there any thing here that favours polygamy? Such was the law. But in the original, there is a term used which became the subject of discussion among the Jews, perhaps shortly after its promulgation. This term, in our translation "uncleanness," some understand to mean such moral or physical defects as rendered her marriage highly improper or a nullity; others understand it to mean, or rather to extend to and embrace, all dislike on the part of the husband whereby he became desirous to be separated from her.

This interpretation seemed most conducive to the power of the husband, and, therefore, probably had the most advocates; and it is said that the Jewish rulers so suffered it to be understood, and that even Moses, as a man, suffered it; noticing that where the wife became greatly *hated* by the husband, she was extremely liable to abuse, unless this law was so explained as to permit a divorce. The Jews kept up the dispute about this matter down to the days of our Saviour; when the Pharisees, with the view to place before him a difficult question, and one that might entangle him, if answered adverse to the popular idea, presented it to him, as related in *Matt.* xix. He promptly decides the question, whereupon they say—

"Why did Moses then command to give a writing of divorcement, and to put her away? He saith unto them, Moses, because of the hardness of your hearts, suffered you to put away your wives: but from the beginning it was not so. And I say unto you, Whoever shall put away his wife, except it be for fornication, and shall marry another, committeth adultery; and whoever marrieth her that is put away, doth commit adultery." *Matt.* xix. 7, 8, 9.

Mark describes this interview thus: "And the Pharisees came to him, and asked him, saying, Is it lawful for a man to put away his wife, tempting him? And he answered and said unto them, What did Moses command you? And they said, Moses suffered to write a bill of divorcement, and to put her away. Jesus answered and said unto them, For the hardness of your heart he wrote you this precept: but from the beginning of the creation, God made them male and female." *Mark* x. 2–6.

But do these answers, either way, favour polygamy? Is it not clear that the law was in opposition to it?

It is true, the Jews, corrupted by the neighbouring nations who fell into it, practised the habit to a great extent; and so they did idolatry and many other sins. But was *idolatry allowed to the Israelites?*

What truth can there be in the assertion that they were *allowed* a thing, in the practice of which they had to trample their laws under foot? And, under the statement of the facts, what truth is there in the assertion that "polygamy was licensed in the age of the apostles?"

If such was "the practice of the holiest men," it proves nothing except that the holiest men were in the practice of breaking the law.

It is true that a looseness of adjudication on the subject of divorce grew up, perhaps even from the time of Moses, among the Jews, on account of the dispute about the interpretation of the law. But upon the supposition that the law was correctly interpreted by those who advocated the greatest laxity, which Jesus Christ sufficiently condemned, yet there is found nothing favouring polygamy in it; for even the loosest interpretation supposed a divorce necessary. The dispute was not about polygamy; but about what predicates rendered a divorce legal.

In the books of the Old Testament we find the accounts of many crimes that were committed in those olden days; but can any one be so stupid as to suppose the law permitted those crimes, because the history of them has reached us through these books?

If the polygamy of Jacob, rehearsed in these books, teaches the doctrine that these books permitted polygamy,—then, because these books relate the history of the murder of Abel, it must be said that these books permit murder? And because, in these books, we have the account of the disobedience of Adam and Eve, that therefore disobedience to the command of God is legalized also!

Before we can say that polygamy is countenanced by the Old Testament as well as slavery, we must find some special law to that effect. And some of the advocates of abolition, striving to make a parallel between slavery and polygamy, pretend they have done so in *Lev.* xviii. 18: "Neither shalt thou take a wife to her sister to vex *her*, to uncover her nakedness, besides the other in her life-time."

These advocates interpret this law to permit a man to marry two wives or more, so that no two of them are sisters; and because few take the trouble to contradict them, they seem to think their interpretation to be true, and urge it as such.

It was clear the law permitted no additional wife, so as to allow two or more wives, unless, by the example of Jacob, the law was ameliorated. His example was the taking of sisters; and if the original be correctly translated, his example is condemned by the law cited. We surely fail to see how forbidding polygamy as to sisters, permits it as to others. Louisiana by law forbids any free white person being joined in marriage to a person of colour. If that State, in addition, forbids free white persons being married to slaves, does it repeal the law as to persons of colour?

But to the Hebrew scholar we propose a small error in the translation of this passage. The preceding twelve verses treat on the subject of whom it is forbidden to marry on the account of consanguinity, the last of which names the grand-daughter of a previous wife, declaring such act to be wicked, and closes the list of objections on account of consanguinity, unless such list be extended by the passage under review; for the succeeding sentence is a prohibition of all females who may be unclean; consanguinity is no more mentioned; yet these prohibitions continue to the 23d verse; and it is to be noticed that each prohibition succeeding the wife's grand-daughter commences with a וְ (*vav with sheva*), whereas not one on the ground of consanguinity is thus introduced; illustrating the fact that each prohibition, succeeding the wife's grand-daughter, is founded upon new and distinct causes.

The widow of a deceased husband who had left no issue was permitted to marry his brother; it was even made a duty. Therefore, by parity of reason, there could be no objection, on the account of consanguinity, for the husband of a deceased wife to marry her sister.

It is clear then that the person whom this clause of the law forbids to marry, is some person other than a deceased wife's sister.

We propose for consideration, as nearly literal as may be, to express the idea conveyed—*Thou shalt not take one wife to another, to be enemies*, or *to be exiles, the shame of thy bed-chamber through life.*

The doctrine it inculcates is, if a man has two wives, he must either live in the midst of their rivalry and enmity, or exile one or both; either of which is disgrace. The reading may be varied; but let the Hebrew scholar compare the three first words of the original with *Exod.* xxvi. 3, where they twice occur, and also with the 6th and 17th verses of the same chapter, in each of which they are also found. Let him notice that, in the passage before us, in the word translated *sister*, the *vav*, under *holem*, is omitted; whereas such is not the case in the preceding instances, where the word is correctly translated to express a term of consanguinity; and we think he will abandon the idea that אֲחֹתָהּ *ahotha*, in the passage before us, means *sister;* and if not, the sentence stands a clear, indisputable, and general condemnation of polygamy.

Can Dr. Channing's disciples point out to us a law *allowing* polygamy in as direct terms as the following would have done, substituting the word *wives* for *slaves?*

"Thy *wives* which thou shalt have, shall be of the heathen that are round about you: of them shall ye buy *wives*." "Moreover, of the children of the strangers that sojourn among you, of them shall ye buy *wives*"—"and of their families that are with you, which they beget in your land, and they shall be your *wives*." "And ye shall take them as *wives* for your children after you, and they shall have them for *wives*"—"they shall be your *wives* for ever." Compare *Lev.* xxv. 44, 46.

Until they can do so, until they shall do so, we shall urge their not doing it as one reason why the Scripture "cannot be used to stock our houses with *wives* as well as with slaves."

LESSON X.

Dr. Channing says, page 101, vol. ii.—

"Slavery, at the age of the apostle, had so penetrated society, was so intimately interwoven with it, and the materials of servile war were so abundant, that a religion, preaching freedom to the slave, would have shaken the social fabric to its foundation, and would have armed against itself the whole power of the state. Paul did not then assail the institution. He satisfied himself with spreading principles which, however slowly, could not but work its destruction. * * * And how, in his circumstances, he could have done more for the subversion of slavery, I do not see."

May we request the disciples of Dr. Channing to read the chapter on "Slavery," in Paley's Moral and Political Philosophy, and decide whether the above is borrowed in substance therefrom. And we beg further to inquire, whether it does not place Paul, considering "his circumstances," in an odious position? What, Paul satisfying himself to not do his duty! What, Paul shrink from assailing an institution because deeply rooted in power and sin!

What, Paul, the apostle of God, fearing, hesitating, failing to denounce a great sin, because it was penetrating through and intimately interwoven with society!

Why did he not manifest the same consideration in behalf of other great sins? Would it not be an easier and more rational way to account for his not assailing slavery, by supposing him to have known that it was the providence of God, in mercy, presenting some protection to those too degraded and low to protect themselves? If such supposition describes the true character of the institution of slavery, then the conduct of Paul in regard to it would have been just what it was. Paul lived all his life in the midst of slavery; as a man among men, he had a much better opportunity to know what was truth in the case than Dr. Channing. But as an apostle, Paul was taught of God. Will the disciples of Dr. Channing transfer these considerations from St. Paul to the Almighty, and say that he was afraid to announce his truth, his law, then to the world, lest it should stir up a little war in the Roman Empire? In what position does Dr. Channing place Him, who came to reveal truth, holding death and judgment in his hand!

"Now they have known that all things whatsoever thou hast given me are of thee: For I have given unto them the words which thou gavest me; and they have received them." *John* xvii. 7, 8.

"I take you to record this day, that I am pure from the blood of all *men*, for I have not shunned to declare unto you all the counsel of God." *Acts* xx. 26, 27.

"God forbid: yea, let God be true, but every man a liar." *Rom.* iii. 4.

But we propose to the disciples of Dr. Channing an inquiry: If he could not see how St. Paul in his circumstances could have done more for the subversion of slavery, why did he not take St. Paul for his example, and suffer the matter to rest where St. Paul left it? For he says, vol. iii. page 152—"It becomes the preacher to remember that there is a silent, indirect influence, more sure and powerful than direct assaults on false opinions." Or was he less careless than St. Paul about stirring up a servile war, and of shaking our social fabric to its foundation? Or did the doctor's *circumstances* place him on higher ground than St. Paul? Had "this age of the world" presented him with new light on the true interpretation of the Scriptures? Had the afflatus of the Holy Spirit commissioned him to supersede Paul as an apostle? Are we to expect, through him, a new and improved edition of the gospel? And is this the reason why an argument drawn from the Old Edition now "hardly deserves notice?"

Dr. Channing says, vol. ii. p. 104—"The very name of the Christian religion would have been forgotten amidst the agitations of universal bloodshed." Is then the Christian religion a fabrication of men? Was Christ himself an impostor? And could Dr. Channing loan himself to such a consideration?

"Upon this rock I will build my church: and the gates of hell shall not prevail against it." *Matt.* xvi. 18.

LESSON XI.

The sixth position in the treatise under consideration is, "I shall offer some remarks on the means of removing it." His plan is, page 108—"In the first place, the great principle that man cannot rightfully be held as property, should be admitted by the slaveholder."

Dr. Channing seems to suppose that his previous arguments are sufficient to produce the proposed admission.

Page 109. "It would be cruelty to strike the fetters from a man, whose first steps would infallibly lead him to a precipice. The slave should not leave an owner, but he should have a guardian."

We take this as an admission that the slave is not a fit subject for freedom. But he says—

Page 110. "But there is but one weighty argument against im mediate emancipation; namely, that the slave would not support himself and his children by honest industry."

Dr. Channing's plan in short is, that the names, master and slave, shall be exchanged for guardian and ward; but he awards no compensation to the guardian;—that the negro shall be told he is free; yet he should be compelled to work for his own and his family's support;—that none should be whipped who will toil "from rational and honourable motives."

Page 112. "In case of being injured by his master in this or in any respect, he should be either set free, or, if unprepared for liberty, should be transmitted to another guardian."

Dr. Channing proposes "bounties," "rewards," "new privileges," "increased indulgences," "prizes for good conduct," &c.,

as substitutes for the *lash*. He supposes that the slave may be "elevated and his energies called forth by placing his domestic relations on new ground." "This is essential; we wish him to labour for his family. Then he must have a family to labour for. Then his wife and children must be truly his own. Then his home must be inviolate. Then the responsibilities of a husband and father must be laid on him. It is argued that he will be fit for freedom as soon as the support of his family shall become his habit and his happiness."

Page 114. "To carry this and other means of improvement into effect, it is essential that the slave should no longer be bought and sold."

Page 115. "Legislatures should meet to free the slave. The church should rest not, day nor night, till this stain be wiped away."

We do not choose to make any remark on his plan of emancipation; we shall merely quote one passage from page 106:

"How slavery shall be removed is a question for the slaveholder, and one which he alone can answer fully. He alone has an intimate knowledge of the character and habits of the slaves."

In this we fully concur; and we now ask our readers, what does Dr. Channing's confession of this fact suggest to their minds?

Dr. Channing's seventh proposition is, "To offer some remarks on abolitionism." The considerations of this chapter are evidently addressed to the abolitionists, with which we have no wish to interfere. There are, however, in it, some fine sentiments expressed in his usual eloquent style.

The eighth and concluding subject is, "A few reflections on the duties of the times." These reflections, we are exceedingly sorry to find highly inflammatory; they are addressed alone to the Free States. We shall present a few specimens. They need no comment: there are those to whom pity is more applicable than reproof.

Page 138. "A few words remain to be spoken in relation to the duties of the Free States. These need to feel the responsibilities and dangers of their present position. The country is approaching a crisis on the greatest question which can be proposed to it; a question, not of profit or loss, of tariffs or banks, or any temporary interests; but a question involving the first principles of freedom, morals, and religion."

Page 139. "There are, however, other duties of the Free States, to which they may prove false, and which they are too willing to forget. They are bound, not in their public, but in their individual capacities, to use every virtuous influence for the abolition of slavery."

Page 140. "At this moment an immense pressure is driving the North from its true ground. God save it from imbecility, from treachery to freedom and virtue! I have certainly no feelings but those of good-will towards the South; but I speak the universal sentiments of this part of the country, when I say that the tone which the South has often assumed towards the North has been that of a superior, a tone unconsciously borrowed from the habit of command to which it is unhappily accustomed by the form of its society. I must add, that this high bearing of the South has not always been met by a just consciousness of equality, a just self-respect at the North. * * * Here lies the danger. *The North will undoubtedly be just to the South.* It must also be just to itself. This is not the time for sycophancy, for servility, for compromise of principle, for forgetfulness of our rights. It is the time to manifest the spirit of MEN, a spirit which prizes, more than life, the principles of liberty, of justice, of humanity, of pure morals, of pure religion."

Page 142. "Let us show that we have principles, compared with which the wealth of the world is as light as air. * * * The Free States, it is to be feared, must pass through a struggle. May they sustain it as becomes their freedom! The present excitement at the South can hardly be expected to pass away without attempts to wrest from them unworthy concessions. The tone in regard to slavery in that part of the country is changed. It is not only more vehement, but more false than formerly: once slavery was acknowledged as an evil; now, it is proclaimed to be a good."

Page 143. "Certainly, no assertion of the wildest abolitionist could give such a shock to the slaveholder, as this new doctrine is fitted to give to the people of the North. * * * There is a great dread in this part of the country that the Union of the States may be dissolved by conflict about slavery. * * * No one prizes the Union more than myself."

Page 144. "Still, if the Union can be purchased only by the imposition of chains on the tongue and the press, by prohibition of discussion on the subject involving the most sacred rights and dearest interests of humanity, then union would be bought at too dear a price."

In his concluding note, he says, page 153—"I feel too much about the great subject on which I have written, to be very solicitous about what is said of myself. I feel that I am nothing, that my reputation is nothing, in comparison with the fearful wrong and evil which I have laboured to expose; and I should count myself unworthy the name of a man or a Christian, if the calumnies of the bad, or even the disapprobation of the good, could fasten my thoughts on myself, and turn me aside from a cause which, as I believe, truth, humanity, and God call me to sustain."

LESSON XII.

THE abolition writers and speakers are properly divided into two classes: those who agitate and advocate the subject as a successful means of advancing their own personal and ambitious hopes; sometimes with

> "One eye turned to God, condemning moral evil;
> The other downward, winking at the devil!"

Thus, one seeks office, another distinction or fame. Small considerations often stimulate the conduct of such men.

But we have evidence that another class zealously labour to abolish slavery from the world, because they think its existence a stain on the human character, and that the laws of God make it the duty of every man to "cry aloud and spare not," until it shall cease.

Our author had no secondary views alluring him on to toil; no new purpose; no new summit to gain. What he thought darkness he hated, because he loved the light; what he thought wicked, to his soul was awful and abhorred, because, even in life, he was ever peering into the confines of heaven. Ardour was cultivated into zeal, and zeal into enthusiasm.

In its eagerness to accomplish its object in behalf of liberty, the mind is often prepared to subvert without reflection—to destroy without care. Hence, even the religious may sometimes "record that they have a zeal of God, but not according to knowledge." "For they being ignorant of God's righteousness, and going about to establish their own righteousness, have not submitted themselves unto the righteousness of God." *Rom.* x.

They are convinced that they alone are right. But, "Can a man be profitable unto God, as he that is wise may be profitable unto himself? *Is it* any pleasure to the Almighty, that thou art righteous? or *is it* gain, that thou makest thy ways perfect." *Job* xxii. 2, 3.

"Knowest thou the ordinances of heaven? Canst thou set the dominion thereof in the earth?" Answer thou, Why "leaveth the ostrich her eggs in the earth, and warmeth them in the dust? Why forgetteth she that the foot may crush them, or that the wild beast may break them?"

"Why is she hardened against her young ones, as though they were not hers?" "Why is her labour in vain without fear?"

"Why feedeth the fish upon its fellow, which forgetteth and devoureth its young?"

"Who looketh on the proud and bringeth him low? and treadeth down the wicked in their place? hiding them in the dust, and binding their faces in secret?"

Who hardeneth the heart of Pharaoh? and multiplies signs and wonders before the children of men? Who is he who "hath mercy on whom he will?" Why was Esau hated or Jacob loved before they were born?

Wilt thou say, "Why doth he find fault? for who hath resisted his will." See *Rom.* ix. 19.

Or wilt thou rather say, "Behold I am vile; what shall I answer thee? I will lay my hand upon my mouth. Once have I spoken; but I will not answer thee: yea, twice; but I will proceed no further." *Job* xl. 4.

There are in these volumes several other essays, under different titles, on the same subject; but in most instances, although the language is varied, the same arguments exert their power on the mind of the writer. Aided by the common sympathy of the people among whom he lived, and the conscientious operations of his own mind, his judgment on the decision of the question of right and wrong became unchangeably fixed; while the evidence forced upon him by the only class of facts in relation to the subject which his education and associations in society enabled him to comprehend, became daily more imposing, more exciting in their review, more lucid in their exposing an image of deformity, the most wicked of the offspring of evil. Filled with horror, yet as if allured by an evil charm, his mind seems to have had no power to banish from its sight its horrid vision. Nor is it singular that it should, to some extent, become the *one idea*—his leading chain of thought. To him, the proofs of his doctrine became a blaze of light, so piercingly brilliant that nothing of a contrary bearing was worthy of belief or consideration.

The following extracts will perhaps sufficiently develop the state to which his mind had arrived on this subject of his study. Vol. vi. p. 38, he says—"My maxim is, Any thing but slavery!"

Page 50. "The history of West India emancipation teaches us that we are holding in bondage one of the best races of the human family. The negro is among the mildest and gentlest of men. He is singularly susceptible of improvement from abroad. His children, it is said, receive more rapidly than ours the elements of knowledge."

Page 51. "A short residence among the negroes in the West Indies impressed me with their capacity for improvement; on all sides, I heard of their religious tendencies, the noblest of human nature. I saw, too, on the plantation where I resided, a gracefulness and dignity of form and motion rare in my own native New England. And that is the race which has been selected to be trodden down and confounded with the brute."

If slavery in the West Indies has thus elevated the African tribes above the majority of the people of New England, we will not ask the question, whether the doctor's disciples propose the experiment on their countrymen. But there is, nevertheless, abundant proof that slavery to the white races does necessarily, and from philosophical causes, have the most direct tendency to elevate the moral, mental, and physical ability of the African; in fact, of any other race of men sunk equally low in degradation and ruin.

If the negro slaves of the West Indies exhibit moral, mental, and physical merit in advance of most of Dr. Channing's countrymen, who were never in slavery, we beg to know how it is accounted for; what are the causes that have operated to produce it? For we believe no sane man, who knows any thing of the African savage in his native state, whether bond or free, will so much as give a hint that they are as elevated in any respect as are *his* countrymen, the people of New England. Will the fact then be acknowledged, that slavery, however bad, does yet constitutionally amend and elevate the African savage!

At the moment the foregoing paragraphs were placed on paper, there happened to be present a Northern gentleman, who very justly entertained the most elevated regard for the personal character of Dr. Channing, to whom they were read. His views seemed to be that the extracts from Channing were *garbled*, and the deductions consequent thereon unjustly severe.

We war not with Dr. Channing, nor his character. He no longer liveth. But his works live, and new editions crowd upon the public attention, as if his disciples were anxious to saturate the whole world with his errors, as well as to make known his many virtues. We do not design to garble; and therefore requote the extract more fully, from vol. vi. pp. 50, 51:

"The history of the West India emancipation teaches us that we are holding in bondage one of the best races of the human family. The negro is among the mildest, gentlest of men. He is singularly susceptible of improvement from abroad. His children, it is said, receive more rapidly than ours the elements of knowledge. How far he can originate improvements, time only can teach. His nature is affectionate, easily touched; and hence he is more open to religious impression than the white man. The European race have manifested more courage, enterprise, invention; but in the dispositions which Christianity particularly honours, how inferior are they to the African! When I cast my eyes over our Southern region, the land of bowie-knives, Lynch-law, and duels, of 'chivalry, honour,' and revenge; and when I consider that Christianity is declared to be a spirit of charity, 'which seeketh not its own, is not easily provoked, thinketh no evil, and endureth all things,' and is declared to be 'the wisdom from above, which is first pure, then peaceable, gentle, easy to be entreated, full of mercy and good fruits,'—can I hesitate in deciding to which of the races in that land Christianity is most adapted, in which its noblest disciples are most likely to be reared."

Pp. 52, 53. "Could the withering influence of slavery be withdrawn, the Southern character, though less consistent, less based on principle, might be more attractive and lofty than that of the North. The South is proud of calling itself Anglo-Saxon. Judging from character, I should say that this name belongs much more to the North, the country of steady, persevering, unconquerable energy. Our Southern brethren remind me more of the Normans. They seem to have in their veins the burning blood of that pirate race."

"Who is he that hideth counsel without knowledge? Therefore

have I uttered that I understood not; things too wonderful for me, which I knew not." *Job* xlii. 3.

Will the disciples of Dr. Channing account for the curious facts developed by the census of 1850, as follows?—

"A writer in the New York Observer calls attention to some curious facts derived from the census of the United States. These facts show that there is a remarkable prevalence of idiocy and insanity among the free blacks over the whites, and especially over the slaves. In the State of Maine, every fourteenth coloured person is an idiot or a lunatic. And though there is a gradual improvement in the condition of the coloured race as we proceed West and South, yet it is evident that the Free States are the principal abodes of idiocy and lunacy among them.

"In Ohio, there are just ten coloured persons, who are idiots or lunatics, where there is one in Kentucky. And in Louisiana, where a large majority of the population is coloured, and four-fifths of them are slaves, there is but one of these unfortunates to 4309 who are sane. The proportions in other States, according to the census of 1850, are as follow:—In Massachusetts, 1 in 43; Connecticut, 1 in 185; New York, 1 in 257; Pennsylvania, 1 in 256; Maryland, 1 in 1074; Virginia, 1 in 1309; North Carolina, 1 in 1215; South Carolina, 1 in 2440; Ohio, 1 in 105; Kentucky, 1 in 1053. This is certainly a curious calculation, and indicates that diseases of the brain are far more rare among the slaves than among the free *of the coloured race*."

LESSON XIII.

SYMPATHY probably operates more or less in the mind of each individual of the human family. Traces of it are discovered even in some of the brute creation; but yet we are far from saying that it is merely an animal feeling. But we do say that sympathy often gives a direction to our chains of thought; and that, in some minds, such direction is scarcely to be changed by any subsequent reflection, or even evidence. Some minds seem incapable of appreciating any evidence which does not make more open whatever way sympathy may lead; consequently a full history of its exercise would prove that it has been frequently expended on mistaken facts, imaginary conditions, or fictitious suffering. In such cases, it may produce much evil, and real suffering. It therefore may be of some importance to the sympathizer and to community, that this feeling be under the government of a correct judgment founded on truth.

Among the rude tribes of men, and in the early ages of the world, its action seems to have taken the place of what, in a higher civilization and cultivation of the mind, should be the result of moral principle founded on truth.

But even now, if we look abroad upon the families of men, even to the most intellectual, shall we not find the greater number rather under the government of the former than the latter? One inference surely is, that man, as yet, has not, by far, arrived at the fullest extent of intellectual improvement.

But suppose we say that God punishes sin; or, by the laws of God, sin brings upon itself punishment;—we propose the question, how far, under our relation to our Creator, is it consistent in us to sympathize with such punishment? It may be answered, we are instructed to "remember" to sympathize with those who are under persecution for their faith in Christ; so also, impliedly, with our brethren, neighbours, or those who have done us or our ancestors favours, or those who have given or can give some proof of goodness, when such have fallen, or shall fall into bondage; and, perhaps, with any one giving proof of such amendment as may merit a higher condition. But in all these cases, does not the injunction, "remember," look to an action resulting from principle, emanating from truth, or the conformity of the person or thing to be "remembered" with the law of God?

In the holy books, the word nearest to a synonyme of our word *sympathy*, will be found in *Deut.* vii. 16: "Thou shalt consume all the people which the Lord thy God shall deliver thee; thine eye shall have no *pity* (תָּחוֹס *thehhos*) upon them," (*no sympathy for.*)

So, xix. 13: "Thine eye shall not *pity* (תָחֹוס *thahhos*) him." So xiii. 8 (the 9th of the Hebrew text): "Neither shall thine eye *pity* him," (תָחֹוס *thahhos.*)

This word, when used in relation to punishment, is usually associated with the word implying the "eye," as if the feeling expressed thereby partook more of an animal than a moral sensation. In *Gen.* xlv. 20, our translators finding our idea of sympathy inapplicable to inanimate objects, expressed it by the word "*regard*," meaning *care*, or *concern*. Now, since the command forbids this gush of feeling (whether merely animal or not) in the cases cited, is it not evident that the feeling inculcated as proper must be the produce of moral principle, cultivated and sustained by a truthful perception of the laws of God?

The feeling of sympathy, commiseration, or mercy, is inculcated in the latter clause of *Lev.* xlvi. 26. The circumstances were these: —The descendants of Ham occupied the whole of Palestine, and the most of the adjoining districts. Those of Palestine had become so sunken in idolatry, and the most grievous practices, counteracting any improvement of their race, that God, in his providence, gave them up to be extirpated from the earth, and forbid the Israelites to have any "pity," any sympathy for them; but to slay them without hesitation. While those of the adjacent tribes, who had, since the days of Noah, been denounced as fit subjects of slavery, on the account of their degradation, brought upon them by similar causes, were again specified to Moses as those whom they were at liberty in peace to purchase, or in war to reduce to perpetual bondage.

But such is the deteriorating effect of sin, even individuals of the Israelites themselves were often falling into that condition. But God made a distinction between the condition of these heathen, and the Israelites that might thus fall into slavery. The slavery of the heathen was perpetual, while that of these improvident Jews was limited to six years, unless such slave preferred to continue in his state of slavery; his kin at all times having the right to redeem him, which right of redemption was also extended to the Jewish slave himself. But no such right was ever extended to the heathen slave, or him of heathen extraction. Under this state of facts, the Jewish master is forbidden to use "rigour" towards his Jewish slave: "But over your brethren the children of Israel, ye shall not rule over one another with rigour." This evidently inculcates a feeling of commiseration for such of their countrymen as may have fallen into slavery; and in conformity with such pre cepts, all nations, at all times, who were advanced in civilization, seem to have ever felt disposed to extend relief when practical. Hence Abraham extended relief to the family of Lot: hence the prophet Obed succeeded to deliver from slavery two hundred thousand of the children of Judah from the hand of the king of Israel, during the days of Ahaz. But in no instance have such acts of mercy been manifested by a people sunk as low in degradation as the African races.

For several centuries, Britain supplied slaves for other parts of the world; but, during the time she did so, she took no steps for the redemption of any; and such has invariably been the case at all times of the world. All races of men, sunk in the lowest depths of degradation, have never failed to be in slavery to one another, and to supply other nations with their own countrymen for slaves; and, perhaps, this may be adduced as an evidence of their having descended to that degree of degradation that makes slavery a mercy to them. Sympathy for them could do them no good; because a relief from slavery could not elevate them,—could do them no good, but an injury. Hence such sympathy is forbidden.

The degradation of the children of Jacob became almost extreme; yet they went not into slavery until it was accompanied by a fact of like nature. Who shall say that slavery and the slave-trade in Britain was not one of the steps, under Divine providence, whereby God brought about the elevated condition of the race of man there? Who will say that the slavery of the Israelites in Egypt was not to them a mercy, and did not bring to them an ameliorated, an elevated condition, necessary to them before the Divine law could fulfil its promise to Abraham? But this was a mere temporary slavery; whereas the slavery pronounced on the races of Ham was through all time, perpetual. During the dark ages of the world, the races of men generally became deteriorated to an extraordinary extent. If our doctrine be true, slavery was a necessary consequence, and continued, until by its amendatory influence on the enslaved, in accordance with the law of God, they became elevated above the level of its useful operation.

But, during these periods, the slave in Africa, little sought after by other races, became of small value to the African master, and was the prey, frequently an article of food, even to the slaves themselves, as well as to his own master; and this state of facts existed until the other races of man had mostly emerged from slavery; when the African slave became an article of commerce, and cannibalism, in consequence, became almost forgotten. Was this no blessing? Was this not a mercy—an improved condition?

But, as if God really intended, contrary to the apparent wishes of some men, to fulfil his word, and establish their condition of never-ending bondage, he has suffered the slave-trade with Africa to be abolished among the Christian nations. The great surplus of slaves in Africa has rendered them of little value there; and these anthropophagi have again returned to their ancient habits, giving proof that their condition of slavery, so far as mortal eye can see, is now for ever past hope. The theological philosopher did once hope that the only commerce which could bring them generally in contact with Christian nations would have a permanent influence on the character of these people. But God, in his providence, has seen proper to order it otherwise. The slave-trade that has been carried on between them and Western Asia, for more than four thousand years, now the only external influence on them as a people, may doubtless extend the standard of Islam, and spread some few corruptions of its religious systems. But neither the religion nor the trade carries to the home of these savages a sufficiency of interest to excite new passions or stimulate into existence new habits or chains of thought.

"The rod and reproof give wisdom."

"A *servant* (עֶבֶד *abed, a slave*) will not be corrected by words; for though he understand, he will not answer." *Prov.* xxix. 15, 19.

In close, may we inquire what benefit has resulted to the slave in the South,—what benefit to poor, bleeding Africa, from the sympathy of the world on the subject of their slavery? What, none! If none—has it done them no evil? And will ye continue to do evil? In your weakness, will ye think to contend against God?

LESSON XIV.

The abolitionist will probably consent to the truth of the proposition that God governs the universe. It may be that they will also agree that he is abundantly able to do so. But, whatever may be their decision, it is one of the revealed laws of God, that—

"Thou shalt not make unto thee any graven image, or any likeness *of any thing* that *is* in heaven above, or that *is* in the earth beneath, or that *is* in the water under the earth: thou shalt not bow thyself to them, nor serve them; for I, the Lord thy God, *am* a jealous God, visiting the iniquity of the fathers upon the children unto the third and fourth *generation* of them that hate me."

It is not to be supposed that man can comprehend God as it may be said he comprehends things within the compass of his own understanding. If so, there would have been no need of revelation. Revelation has given us all the knowledge of God necessary to our welfare and happiness. We have not yet learned that man has become able to go beyond revelation in his knowledge of God.

But suppose some one should take it into his fancy to say and believe that the Sabbath was not a Divine institution, or that "Thou shalt not kill," "Thou shalt not commit adultery," "Thou shalt not steal," were mere human contrivances, and contrary to the will and laws of their God; now, if the God who has revealed these laws to us is the genuine God, would not the god who should teach these forbidden acts to be lawful be a different god? And although he would exist only in the imagination of those who believed in such a being, yet would it be any the less idolatry to worship him than it would be if a block were set up to represent him? Is it any sufficient excuse, because such worshipper acts from ignorance, or under the influence of a sincere *conscience?* Is it to be presumed that those who sacrificed their children, and even themselves, to a false god, were not sincere? Did not Paul act with a sincere *conscience* when he persecuted the Christians?

But can we suppose that the real Jehovah would, in a revelation to man of his will, his law, recognise a thing as property among men, when, at the same time, it was contrary to his will and his law that such thing should be property among men?

"Neither shalt thou desire thy neighbour's wife; neither shalt thou covet thy neighbour's house, his field, or his *man-servant* (וְעַבְדּוֹ *his male slave*), or his maid-servant (וַאֲמָתוֹ *his female slave*), his ox, or his ass, or any *thing* that *is* thy neighbour's." *Deut.* v. 21, the 18th of the Hebrew text.

Would it not have been just as easy for God to have said, if such was his will, "*Thou shalt not have slaves*," as to have said this, as follows? "And also of the heathen shall ye buy slaves, and your children shall inherit them after you, and they shall be your slaves for ever!"

But Dr. Channing, speaking of the various exertions now making in behalf of the abolition of slavery, gives us to understand that the Christian philanthropy and the enlightened goodness, (and, he means, sympathy alone,) now pouring forth in prayers and persuasions from the press, the pulpit, from the lips and hearts of devoted men, cannot fail. "This," he says, "must triumph." "It is leagued with God's omnipotence." "It is God himself acting in the hearts of his children." Vol. ii. p. 12. Does Dr. Channing mean the God who revealed the law to Moses? If so, has he changed his mind since that time?

We know that some say that slavery is contrary to their moral sense, contrary to their conscience, that under no circumstances can it be right. But if God has ordained the institution of slavery, not only as a punishment of sin, but as a restraint of some effect against a lower degradation, had not such men better cultivate and improve their "moral sense" and "conscience" into a conformity with the law of God on this subject? They cannot think that, on the account of their much talking, God will change his government to suit their own peculiar views. In our judgment, their views must bring great darkness to the mind, and, we think, distress; for is it not a great distress itself, to be under the government of one we think unjust? We know not but that we owe them, as fellow travellers through this momentary existence, the duty of trying to remove from their minds the cause of such darkness and distress. Shall we counsel together? Will you, indeed, stop for a moment in company with a brother? Will you hear the Bible? Will you, though a child, listen to the voice of God?

All agree that slavery has existed in the world from a very remote age. Wicked men and wicked nations have passed away, but slavery still exists among their descendants. Good men and enlightened nations have gone the way of all that is and has been, but slavery still abides on the earth. Upon the introduction of Christianity, men, who little understood its spirit, suddenly rose up to abolish slavery in cases where the slave became converted to its faith; also to cut loose the believing child from all obligations of obedience to the unbelieving parent, and also the husband or wife from his or her unbelieving spouse. Yet this new doctrine only met the condemnation of Peter and Paul. And even at the present day, we find men ready to give up the religion of Christ, and the gospel itself, rather than their own notions concerning slavery.

"If the religion of Christ allows such a licence" (to hold slaves) "from such precepts as these, the New Testament would be the greatest curse that was ever inflicted on our race." *Barnes on*

Slavery, p. 310. (He quotes the passage from Dr. Wayland's Letters, pp. 83, 84, which work we have not seen.)

Such writers may be *conscientious*, but their writings have only bound the slave in stronger chains. God makes his very enemies build up his throne. Thus the exertions of man are ever feeble when in contradiction to the providence of God. The great adversary has ever been at work to dethrone the Almighty from the minds of men. Abolition doctrines are no new thing in the world. We concede them the age of slavery itself, which we shall doubtless find as old as sin.

Stay thy haste, then, thou who feelest able to teach wisdom to thy Creator: come, listen to the voice of a child; the lessons of a worm; for God is surely able to vindicate his ways before thee!

When Adam was driven out of paradise, he was told—

"Cursed is the ground for thy sake; in sorrow shalt thou eat of it all the days of thy life." "Thorns and thistles shall it bring forth to thee; and thou shalt eat the herb of the field. In the sweat of thy face shalt thou eat bread, till thou return unto the ground."

The expression, "Thou shalt eat the *herb* of the field," we think has a very peculiar significance; for God made "every *herb* of the field before it grew;" and one of the reasons assigned why the "herb was made before it grew," we find to be, that "there was not a man to till the ground." Now, the word *to till* is translated from the word לַעֲבֹד *la ebod*, and means *to slave;* but in English we use the term not so directly. We use more words to express the same idea; we say *to do slave-labour on the ground*, instead of *to slave the ground*, as the expression stands in Hebrew.

The doctrine is, that the herb, on which the fallen sinner is destined to subsist, was not of spontaneous growth; it could only be produced by sweat and toil, even unto sorrow. Sin had made man a slave to his own necessities; he had *to slave the ground* for his subsistence; and such was the view of David, who, after describing how the brute creation is spontaneously provided for, says—

"He causeth the grass to grow for the cattle, and *herb* for the *service* (לַעֲבֹדַת *la ebodath, the slavery*) of man: that he may bring forth food out of the earth." *Ps.* civ. 14.

This state of being compelled to labour with sweat and toil for subsistence, is the degree of slavery to which sin reduced the whole human family. If we mistake not, the holy books include the idea that sin affects the character of man as a moral poison, producing aberrations of mind in the constant direction of greater sins and an increased departure from a desire to be in obedience to the laws of God. If we mistake not, the doctrine also is prominent that idleness is not only a sin itself, but exceedingly prolific of still greater sins. This mild state of slavery, thus imposed on Adam, was a constant restraint against a lower descent into sin, and can be regarded in no other light than a merciful provision of God in protection of his child, the creation of his hand. If it then be a fact that a given intensity of sin draws upon itself a corresponding condition of slavery, as an operating protection against the final effect of transgression, it will follow that an increased intensity of sin will demand an increased severity of the condition of slavery. Thus, when Cain murdered Abel, God said to him—

"Now art thou cursed from the earth, which hath opened her mouth to receive thy brother's blood from thy hand. When thou *tillest* (תַּעֲבֹד *tha ebod, thou slavest*) the ground, it shall not henceforth yield unto thee her strength: a fugitive and a vagabond shalt thou be in the earth." * * * "And the Lord set a mark upon Cain, lest any finding him should kill him."

"Shall not yield unto thee her strength;" either the earth should be less fruitful, or from his own waywardness, it should be less skilfully cultivated by him, or that a profit from his labour should be enjoyed by another; or, perhaps, from the joint operation of them all. Thus an aggravated degree of sin is always attended by an aggravated degree of slavery.

The next final step we discover in the history of slavery appears in Ham, the son of Noah; and he said, "Cursed be Canaan; a servant of servants shall he be unto his brethren." "*Servant of servants*," עֶבֶד עֲבָדִים *ebed ebadim, slave of slaves.* This mode of expression in Hebrew is one of the modes by which they expressed the superlative degree. The meaning is, the *most abject slave* shall he be to his brethren.

Heretofore slavery has been of less intensity; here we find the ordination of the master, and it is not a little remarkable that he is distinctly blessed!

"And he said, I am Abraham's servant. And the Lord hath blessed my master greatly, and he is become great: and he hath given him flocks, and herds, and silver and gold, and *men-ser-*

vants(וַעֲבָדִים *va ebadim, and male slaves*), and *maid-servants* (וּשְׁפָחֹת *va shephahoth, and female slaves*), and camels and asses." "And Sarah, my master's wife, bare a son to my master when she was old: and unto him hath he given all that he hath."

And of Isaac it is said—

"Then Isaac sowed in that land, and received in the same year a hundred fold: and the Lord blessed him, and the man waxed great, and went forward and grew until he became very great: for he had possessions of flocks, and possessions of herds, and great store of servants (וַעֲבֻדָּה *va ebuddah, and a large family of slaves*): *and the Philistines envied him.*" We pray that no one in these days will imitate those wicked Philistines!

And of Jacob it is said—

"And the man increased exceedingly, and had much cattle, and *maid-servants* (וּשְׁפָחוֹת *vu shephahoth*), *and female slaves* and *men-servants* (וַעֲבָדִים *va ebadim, and male slaves*), and camels, and asses." "And the Lord said unto Jacob, Return unto the land of thy fathers, and to thy kindred; and I will be with thee."

"*He that is* despised, and hath a *servant* (עֶבֶד *ebed, a slave*), is better than he that honoureth himself, and lacketh bread." *Prov.* xii. 9.

"I know that whatsoever God doeth, it shall be for ever; nothing can be put to it, nor any thing taken from it: and God doeth it that men should fear before him. That which hath been is now; and that which is to be, hath already been; and God requireth that which is past." *Eccl.* iii. 14.

LESSON XV.

We shall, in the course of these studies, with some particularity examine what evidence there may be that Ham took a wife from the race of Cain; and we propose a glance at that subject now. Theological students generally agree that, in *Genesis* vi. 2, "sons of God" mean those of the race of Seth; and that the "daughters of men" imply the females of the race of Cain. The word "fair," in our version, applied to these females, does not justly teach us that they were white women, or that they were of a light complexion. It is translated from the Hebrew טֹבֹת *tovoth*, being in the feminine plural form, טוֹב *tov*, and merely expresses the idea of what may seem *good* and *excellent* to him who speaks or takes notice: it expresses no quality of complexion nor of beauty beyond what may exist in the mind of the beholder; it is usually translated good or excellent. Immediately upon the announcement that these two races thus intermarry, God declares that his spirit shall not always strive with man, and determines to destroy man from the earth. Is it not a plain inference that such intermarriages were displeasing to him? And is it not also a plain inference, these intermarriages were proofs that the "wickedness of man had become great in the earth?" Cain had been driven out a degraded, deteriorated vagabond. Is there any proof that his race had improved?

The fact is well known that all races of animals are capable of being improved or deteriorated. A commixture of a better with a worse sample deteriorates the offspring of the former. Man is no exception to this rule. Our position is, that sin, as a moral poison, operating in one continued strain in the degradation and deterioration of the race of Cain, had at length forced them down to become exceedingly obnoxious to God. Intermarriage with them was the sure ruin of the race of Seth: it subjected them at once to the curses cleaving to the race of Cain. Even after the flood, witness the repugnance to intermarry with the race of Ham often manifested by the descendants of Shem; and that the Israelites were forbidden to do so.

Now, for a moment, let us suppose that Ham did marry and take into the ark a daughter of the race of Cain. If the general intermixture of the Sethites with the Cainites had so deteriorated the Sethites, and reduced them to the moral degradation of the Cainites, that God did not deem them worthy of longer encumbering the earth before the flood, would it be an extraordinary manifestation of his displeasure at the supposed marriage of Ham with one of the cursed race of Cain, to subject the issue of such marriage to a degraded and perpetual bondage?

But again, in case this supposed marriage of Ham with the race of Cain be true, then Ham would be the progenitor of all the race of Cain who should exist after the flood; and such fact would be among the most prominent features of his history. It would, in such case, be in strict conformity with the usages of these early times for his father to have called him by a name indicative of such fact: instead of calling him Ham, he would announce to him a term implying his relationship with the house of Cain. If such relation did not exist, why did he call him *Canaan?*

Some suppose that this question would be answered by saying that the term was applied to the youngest son of Ham; but all the sons of Ham were born after the flood; yet the planting of the vineyard and the drinking of the wine are the first acts of Noah which are mentioned after that deluge; and further, Canaan, the son of Ham, was most certainly not the individual whose ill-behaviour was simultaneous with and followed by the curse of slavery. Have we any proof, or any reason to believe, that Canaan, the son of Ham, was then even born? But in the catalogue of Noah's sons, even before the planting of the vineyard is mentioned, Ham is called the father of Canaan, even before we are told that he had any sons. Why was he then so called the father of Canaan, unless upon the fact that by his marriage he necessarily was to become the progenitor of the race of Cain in his own then unborn descendants?

Under all the facts that have come down to us, we are not to suppose that there was any Cainite blood in Noah, or in Noah's wife. Why then did Ham choose to commemorate the race of Cain, by naming his fourth son Cain, a term synonymous with Cainite, or Canaanite? And why did the race of Ham do the same thing through many centuries, using terms differently varied, sometimes interchanging the consonant and vowel sounds, as was common in the language they used? These variations, it is true, when descending into a language so remote as ours, might not be noticed, yet the linguist surely will trace them all back to their root, the original of "Cain."

God never sanctions a curse without an adequate cause; a cause under the approbation of his law, sufficient to produce the effect the curse announces. The conduct of Ham to his father proved him to possess a degraded, a very debased mind; but that alone could not produce so vital, so interminable a change in the moral and physical condition of his offspring. And where are we to look for such a cause, unless in marriage? And with whom could such an intermarriage be had, except with the cursed race of Cain? The ill-manners of Ham no doubt accelerated the time of the announcement of the curse, but was not the sole cause. The cause must have previously existed; and the effect would necessarily have been produced, even if it had never been announced.

But again, the condition of slavery imposed on the descendants of Ham, subjected them to be bought and sold; they became objects of purchase as property, for this quality is inseparable from the condition of the most abject slavery. Now the very name *Cain* signifies "*one purchased.*" "I have *gotten* a man from the Lord." The word "gotten," in the original, is the word his mother Eve gave her son for his name, "Cain." *I have purchased*, &c., evidently shadowing forth the fact that his race were to be subjects of purchase.

The history of man since the flood is accompanied with a sufficiency of facts by which we are enabled to determine that the descendants of Ham were black, and that the black man of Africa is of that descent.

"And the Lord set a mark upon Cain, lest any finding him would kill him."

The word "*mark*" is translated from אות *oth;* its signification is, *a mark by which to distinguish; a memorial or warning; miraculous sign or wonder, consisting either in word or deed, whereby the certainty of any thing future is foretold or known;* and hence it partook of the nature of a prophecy. In the present case it was the mark of sin and degradation; it was the token of his condition of slavery, of his being a vagabond on the earth. It distinguished his rank of inferiority and wickedness, proclaiming him to be the man whose greatest punishment was to live and bear his burthens, *below all rivalship.*

Hence its protective influence. Now, by the common consent of all men, at all times, what has been the mark of sin and degradation? Were we even now, among ourselves, about to describe one of exceedingly wicked and degraded character, should we say that he looked very white? Or should we say that his character was black? And so has been the use of the term since language has been able to send down to distant times the ideas and associations of men.

"Their visage is blacker than a coal.'

"Our skin was black."

"I am black: astonishment hath taken hold on me."

"For though thou wash thee with nitre, and take thee much soap, yet thine iniquity is marked before me, saith the Lord God."

And who shall say that the wicked, disgusting mode of life, the practices deteriorating the physical and mental powers imputed to the Cainites, do not constitute what some may call a philosophical cause of the physical development of the mark of sin? Does not our own observation teach us that a single lifetime, spent in the practice of some degrading sins, leaves upon the person the evidence, the mark, the proof of such practice? We are under no compulsion of evidence or belief to suppose that the mark set upon Cain was the product of a moment; but the gradual result of his wicked practices, as a physical and moral cause.

But allow the fact to have been that, in the case of Cain, the physical change was instantaneous, God had the power to institute in a moment what should thereafter be produced only by progression or inheritance. God created man; but, thereafter, man was born and became mature through the instrumentality only of physical causes.

"The shew of their countenance doth witness against them; and they declare their sin as Sodom, they hide it not." *Isa.* iii. 9. In fact, "The faces of them all gather blackness." *Nahum* ii. 10.

But we know that the descendants of Ham were black; nor is it stated that any personal mark was placed upon him, although the name applied to his first-born son, "Cush," signifies that he was black, giving proof that the colour was inherited; but from whom? Not from his father!

"Can the *Ethiopian* (כּוּשִׁי *Cushi, the Cushite, the black man*) change his skin?"

The evidence forced on the mind leads to the conclusion that the descendants of Ham were black, not by the progressive operation of the laws of God on the course of sin which they doubtless practised, but that they were so at birth,—consequently an inheritance from parentage. And a further conclusion also is, that the wife of Ham must have been black, of the race of Cain, inheriting his *mark*, and that *that mark* was black.

A further proof that Ham took to wife a daughter of the race of Cain is found in the traces of evidence indicating her person, who she was. Lamech, of the race of Cain, had a daughter, Naamah; her name is given as the last in the genealogy of Cain. Why did the inspired penman think it necessary to send her name down to us? Why was the genealogy of Cain given us, unless to announce some fact important for us to know? If this whole race were to be cut off by the flood, we see nothing in the genealogy teaching any lesson to the descendants of Noah. Why was the particular line from Cain to Naamah selected, unless she was the particular object designed to be pointed out? Hundreds of other genealogies, commencing in Cain and terminating in some one just at the coming of the flood, existed; but not written down nor transmitted, for the obvious reason that such list could be of no benefit to posterity. Are we not, then, led to believe that there was some design in the preservation of the one terminating in Naamah? But this genealogy could only be preserved through the family of Noah; through whom we also have a genealogy of the line from Seth, terminating in Noah's youngest son. These two stand in a parallel position, at the foot of each separate list. But it is so extremely unusual for ancient genealogies to give the name of a female, who had brothers, that it becomes strong evidence, when such catalogue terminates in the name of such a female, that she personally was the individual on whose account the catalogue was formed. Is not this consideration, and the fact that it could only be preserved by the family of Noah, evidence that they attached sufficient importance to it to make its preservation by them a desirable object?

Inasmuch as Naamah belonged to a race distinct from that of Seth, could the family of Noah have any desire to preserve her lineage from any other cause than that of her having become a member of that family?—in which case the cause of its preservation is obvious, and a thing to have been expected. On any other state of facts, would they have carefully handed down the genealogy, so far as we are informed, of a mere uninteresting woman of the cursed race of Cain, and neglected to have given us the *name* and *genealogy of Noah's wife*, of the more holy race of Seth?

The presumption then being that she did become the wife of one of Noah's sons, the first inquiry is, to which was she attached? A sufficient answer to this question, for the present moment, will be found in the fact that Ham was doomed to perpetual and bitter slavery, while his brothers were blessed and ordained to be his masters. Now since an amalgamation of the races of Seth and Cain was deemed a most grievous sin before the flood, if Japheth or Shem had either of them taken Naamah to wife, it would be past understanding to find them both highly blessed and made the masters of Ham.

But a more direct evidence that Ham did take to wife Naamah, of the race of Cain, is found in the fact that the descendants of Ham commemorated her name by giving it to persons of their race, as descendants might be expected to do, who wished to keep it in remembrance. The name of her mother also is found in similar use.

These names are varied, often, from the original form, as are a great number of proper names found in use among the ancient nations. These words we shall have hereafter occasion particularly to examine. We shall merely add, that in the marriage of Ham and Naamah we may find a reasonable explanation for the otherwise inexplicable speech of Lamech to his two wives,—since such marriage would have produced, what we find was produced, the ruin and degradation of Ham,—we might say, his moral death, his extinguishment, from the race of Seth. Some commentators deduce the name Naamah from the root "*nam*," and consequently make it signify *beautiful*. We give it quite a different origin, which we shall explain at large elsewhere. It is to be expected that men will differ in opinion as to the historical facts of these early days. Some have made Naamah a pure saint; some, the wife of Noah; some, of her brother, Tubal-Cain; some make her the heathen goddess Venus; others, the mother of evil spirits.

Thus diversified have been the speculations of men. We present our view, because we believe it better sustained by Scripture and known facts than any we have examined: but we deem it no way important in the justification of the ways of God to man; for, whatever the truth may be, this we know, that the curse of slavery was, if Scripture be true, unalterably uttered against the race of Ham,—in which condition, as a people, they ever have been and still are found: a condition so well adapted to their physical and mental organization, the result of ages spent in bad, degenerating habits, that when held in such relation by the races of Japheth or Shem, the race of Ham is found gradually to emerge from its native brutality into a state of comparative elevation and usefulness in the world; a condition without which they, as a race, have never been found progressing, but ever exhibiting the desire of wandering backward, in search of the life of the vagabond, in the midst of the wilderness of sin;—unless in this author, Dr. Channing, we find an exception; for he more than intimates that he found the negro women of Jamaica rather to excel the white ones of New England. We believe, according to his own taste and judgment, what he said was true; but we also believe his taste was very depraved, and his judgment of no value on this subject; yet we feel less astonishment at the degenerate sons of Seth before the flood, on the account of their admiration of the black daughters of the race of Cain; and we should feel it a subject of curious solicitude, if Dr. Channing's taste and judgment on this subject were to become the standard among his disciples, whether they will, by their practice, illustrate the habit of these antediluvians!

Study IV.

LESSON I.

In the course of the present study, we propose to notice the doctrine and action of the church as connected with the subject of slavery; and to examine what were the tenets and conduct of those men who claimed to be governed by the immediate teachings of Christ and his apostles.

In this investigation, we must apply to the records of the Catholic Church, although we are aware that, in the minds of some, strong and bitter prejudice may exist against these records; that some will say the canker of corruption had destroyed the very kernel of Christianity in that church.

Bower, a Protestant author, in the preface to his "History of the Popes," 7 vols. quarto, says—

"We must own the popes to have been, generally speaking, men of extraordinary talents, the ablest politicians we read of in history; statesmen fit to govern the world, and equal to the vast dominion they grasped at; a dominion over the minds as well as the bodies and estates of mankind; a dominion, of all that ever were formed, the most wide and extensive, as knowing no other bounds but those of the earth." Page 10, vol. i. 3d edition, London, 1750.

Mr. Bower was a very learned man, had been educated a Catholic, was professor of rhetoric, history, and philosophy in the universities of Rome, Fermo, and Macerata, and counsellor of the Inquisition at Rome. He commenced a work to prove the pope's infallibility and supremacy. But he proved to himself the adverse doctrine. He resigned his professorships and places, removed to London, abjured the Catholic religion, and wrote the work quoted. It is a work of great labour and merit, and well worth the attention of the curious in these matters. But it is proper here to remark, that Mr. Sale, in his preface to his translation of the Koran, has made a severe, yet an unexplained attack, on the character of this writer; but whatever may have been the provocation, we have to view him through his book. It is not always possible for a just degree of merit to be awarded those who lived in former times. We cannot always learn the circumstances influencing them, nor do we often throw our minds back into their peculiar position, by which alone can we be able to give a just value to those influences.

History has handed us a few of the acts of him who lived a thousand years ago; by them we judge, as though he lived to-day, acts which prejudice may have distorted, or favour presented to the lens of time. We must look to the condition of things at the time of the act; to the probable effect under such condition, and to the real effect as developed by time.

Pope Benedict IX. ascended the throne in A. D. 1033. He is very unfavourably known to history. During his time there was a very powerful faction raging against him at Rome, by which, at one time, he was driven into exile. He is said to have sold the popedom, because his debaucheries made him an object of contempt, and he wished to be free from restraint; but in 1041, four years before he abandoned the papal chair, he established, at a council in Aquitaine, the *Treuga Dei*, whence it has been said that, during three days in the week, he permitted any man to commit all sorts of crimes, even murder, free from church censure, &c. By the *Treuga Dei*, for any wrong done him, no person was permitted to revenge himself, from Wednesday evening to Monday morning: construed, as above, by some, that he might do so during the remaining portion of the week.

The facts were, all Europe was still groping in the ignorance of the darkest ages; yet Christianity had been firmly established as a system of faith. The church had always forbidden a revengeful redress of individual wrongs; and, for such acts, her priests ever threatened excommunication. But these charges had little or no effect during these still semi-idolatrous and barbarous ages.

The kings were but heads of tribes, too weak to restrain their nobles, as the nobles were their vassals: under such a state of things, each one strove to redress his own wrongs. This led to constant murders, and every kind of crime. Each state was constantly agitated by civil commotions and bloodshed. Great moral changes are advanced by short steps. The church took this evil in hand, and hence the *Treuga Dei*, a word used in the Latin of that day, a corruption from the Gothic *triggua*, and now found in the Spanish and Italian "*tregua*," and from whence our word *truce*. The curse of God was pronounced against all offenders, and death followed a discovery of the crime. It was thought to be a Divine suggestion, and hence the name. All consented to yield to it as such, and it was found to have a powerful effect. In 1095, it was warmly sustained in the Council of Clermont, under Urban II., and extended to all the holy-days, and perpetually to clerks, monks, pilgrims, merchants, husbandmen, and women, and to the persons and property of all who would engage in crusades, and against all devastations by fire. It was re-established in 1102, by Paschal II.; in 1139, by Innocent II.; in 1180, by Alexander III.; nor would it be difficult to show that the *Treuga Dei*, the *Truce of God*, of Benedict IX., was one of the most important, during the primary steps towards the civilization of Europe; such was the state of society in that age of the world. But we acknowledge that individuals of the Roman church, some of whom obtruded themselves into the priesthood, have been very corrupt men. But have not similar obtrusions happened in every other Christian, Protestant, or worthy association of men? Have we not seen, among the apostles, a Judas, betraying the Saviour of the world? Ananias and Sapphira, attempting to swindle even God himself? Of confidence betrayed among men, need we point to the tragical death of Servetus, which has for ever placed the bloody mark of murder on the face of Calvin?

And may we not find sometimes, among ourselves, lamentable instances of corruption, which, in the blackness of their character, defy the powers of the pen? Instances, where, recreant to every honest, noble, and holy feeling, individuals, hidden, as they think, beneath the robes of righteousness, have carried poverty and distress to the house of the widow, trampling on the rights—may be, the life—of the orphan, and even using the confidence of a brother to betray and rob him?

Nor is it a matter of any exultation to the broken, the wounded mind, that, in all such instances, unless the stink of insignificance shall totally exclude such criminal from the page of history, whatever may be the cloak he may wear, truth will eventually for ever convert it into the burning shirt of Nessus.

But, if you call a dog a thief, he feels no shame. Generations of enforced improvement and the grace of God alone can wipe out the stains of an evil heart. Nor can man alter this his destiny. Therefore, in all ages, and among all men, the tares and the wheat have been found in the same field. What presumption, then, if not blasphemy, in opposition to the word of Jehovah, to say, that the looming light of truth never dawned upon this night of time until the advent of Luther or Knox!

In presenting the action and records of the church and early fathers, we have freely adopted the sentiments and facts digested by Bishop England, to whom, we take occasion here to say, we feel as much indebted, as though we had merely changed a particle or deleted what was irrelevant to our subject. Nor do we know of higher honour we can do this great and good man than to lend our feeble mite to extend the knowledge of his research, his purity, and great learning; and if, in the continuation of this his unfinished study, amid the pagan superstitions and bigoted thousands of Islam in benighted Asia, the conflicts of the Cross and the Wand of Woden, during the dark ages of continental Europe, we may be suffered to feel the elevating influence of his life-giving mantle, we shall also surely feel elevated hopes of a high immortality.

But, it may be well here to remark, that we have no sectarian church to sustain; that we belong to no religious order; nor have, as yet, subscribed to any faith formed by man. And while we advocate the cause of religion and truth, yielding ourselves in all humility to the influence of Divine power, we feel as certain of his final notice, as though we had marched through under a thousand banners at the head of the world. We have all confidence in the word of him who hath said that even the sparrow falleth not without his notice.

But, it is said, when disease infuses bile into the organs of sight, the objects of vision have a peculiar tinge: to blend previous, sometimes numerous, impressions into one perception, is a common action of the mind. Thus the present idea is often modified by those that have preceded; and hence we may conclude how often the mind is under the insensible influence of prejudice. Upon these facts she has enthroned her power.

But he who has schooled his mind in the doctrines of a tranquil devotion, who habituates himself to view all things past, present, and to come, through the medium of cause and effect, as the mere links of one vast chain, reaching from Omnipotence to the present action, may well rise superior to the tumult of passion or the empire of prejudice. And to the utilitarian permit us to say, that prejudice is peculiarly unsuited to the age of moral and physical improvement in which we live. Let no one say, the spirit of improvement has a deep root, and its lofty hopes cannot be subverted; that the most penetrating philosophy cannot prescribe its limits, the most ardent imagination reach its bounds: rather let him reflect that all improvement must for ever follow the footsteps of truth; and that the peculiar province of prejudice is to set us aside from its path.

With such views, let us for a moment consider the circumstances attending the early ages of the Roman church; and let us note that, although her priests were but men, whether her records are not as reliable as if some of her peculiarities had been different, or she had been called by a different name. But we shall not quote or pursue these records down to so late a day as the Protestant Reformation. We hope, therefore, that the Protestant will say that the records we quote are, most decidedly, the records of the church.

LESSON II.

THE moral condition of man was peculiar. To a great extent the religious systems of the Old World had been analyzed by the intelligent; they no longer gave confidence to the mind. The sanctity of the temples was dissipated by the mere speculations of philosophy, and the gods of idolatry tottered on their pedestals.

The nations of the earth were brought in subjection, in slavery, to the feet of imperial Rome; and their gods, being presented face to face, lost their divinity by the rivalship of men.

Such was the condition of the moral world when Christianity was introduced to mankind.

The old religions pretended to give safety by bargain of sacrifice, by penance, and payment, but the religion of Jesus Christ taught that salvation and safety were the free gift of God.

The history of man proves the fact that he has ever been disposed to purchase happiness on earth and felicity in heaven by his own acts, or by the merit of his condition; and hence, we always find that a corrupted Christianity for ever borders on the confines of idolatry. Nor is it difficult to show how this easily runs into all the wild extravagancies of human reason, or, rather, human ignorance; while the simplicity of truth tends to a calm submission, and a desire of obedience to the will and laws of the only true God. The one was the religion of the government of men, of show, of political power, and expediency; the other is of heaven, of truth. "My kingdom is not of this world."

The barbarians of northern Europe and western Asia, while yet only illumined by some faint rays of the Christian light, feeling from habit the want of the external pomp and the governing control of a religious power, in a half-savage, half-heathen state of mind, were disposed to prostrate themselves at the feet of the chief priest of Rome.

In the year 312, under the pontificate of Melchiades, (by the Greeks called Miltiades,) the Emperor Constantine established the Christian church by law. Thus sustained, it became at once the pool in which ambition and crime sought to cleanse their robes. Yet, beneath its waters were priceless pearls. Torn by schism, sometimes by temporal misrule, the church languished,—but lived. For several centuries the future became a mere variation of the past. The ways of God are indeed inscrutable. A flaming meteor in the east now agitated the mind. Like the insects of twilight, thousands marshalled under the crescent light of the prophet. The disciples of Mohammed swept from the earth the churches at Antioch and Alexandria, suddenly made inroads on Europe, conquered Spain, and were in step to overleap the Pyrenees and Alps. Let us step aside, and reconnoitre their host!

The object of the Arabian, Saracen, and Moorish warriors was the propagation of their creed. The alternative was proposed to all,—its embrace, or tribute; if rejected, the chance of war. Persia and Syria were quickly subdued. Egypt and Cyprus gave way, A. D. 645. The slave of Jews or Christians seldom rejected freedom in favour of the cross; if so, he was reduced to the level of the vilest brute. The free were either put to death, or, as a great favour, permitted to be slaves. Thus the Christian master and slave were often in a reversed condition under Mohammedan rule. Sicily and the whole northern Africa substituted the crescent for the Cross; and in quick succession Spain was invaded and the throne of Roderick overturned. Toledo yielded to Mousa; and Fleury, lib. xli. part 25, says—"He put the chief men to death, and subjugated all Spain, as far as Saragossa, which he found open. He burned the towns, he had the most powerful citizens crucified, he cut the throats of children and infants, and spread terror on every side."

Italy was in consternation; the church trembled, and Constantinople was threatened. Crossing the Pyrenees, A. D. 719, they poured down upon France, met Charles, the father of Pepin, and Eude of Aquitaine, who slew Zama, and compelled his troops to raise the siege of Toulouse; but, recovering confidence, their incursions were frequent and bloody; and the historians of that day announce that, upon one occasion alone, they lost 370,000 men upon the fields of France. But these reverses were the bow of hope to the Peninsula. Alphonsus struck a blow, and in one day retook many towns and released from bondage ten thousand Christian slaves. These exertions were continued with intermitted success; and, like the retiring thunder of the retreating storm, the rage of battle became less terrific and at more distant periods; but the standard of Islam still continued to affrighten the world, alternately flaming its red glare over the Peninsula to the mountains of France and the plains of Italy, and until embattled Europe, excited to Croisade, dispelled its power on the banks of the Jordan.

But, let us return. Aistulphus appears amid this flame of war. His Lombards threaten extermination, and brandish the sword at the very gates of Rome. Pepin had now usurped the throne of the Franks. He demanded the confirmation of the church; and, in return, promised protection to the "Republic of God." Rome saw the prospect of her ruin, with searching eyes looked for aid, and confirmed Pepin in his secular power; who, in gratitude, drove for a time the Lombards from Italy, and deposited the keys of the conquered cities on the altar of Saint Peter.

The Roman emperors had now long since removed their court to Constantinople. Their power over western Europe vacillated with the strife of the times. Charlemagne now appears kissing the steps of the throne of the church. Again he appears, master of all the nations composing the Western Empire, and of Rome; and, on Christmas-day, in the year 800, Leo III. placed the crown of the Roman emperors on the head of the son of Pepin. But, as yet, the act of crowning by the pope was a mere form.

Fifty years had scarcely sunk in the past, when the Emperor Basilius expelled Photius from the patriarchal see of his capital. He was charged with having been the tool of the Emperor Michael.. He claimed supremacy over the pope of Rome. Hadrian had now ascended the papal chair, 867. Jealous of the bold spirit of Photius, his excommunication was recorded, and Ignatius installed in his see.

But the Greeks and Bulgarians, jealous for their native priesthood, demanded by what authority the see of Rome claimed jurisdiction over the Old and New Epirus, Thessaly, and Dardania, the country now called Bulgaria. For more than four centuries there had been occasional jealousies between these two churches; certain articles of faith continued subjects of difference; and the questions of temporal and spiritual precedence made them ever watchful. History records that, as early as 606, Phocas, having ascended the imperial throne, treading upon the dead bodies of the Emperor Mauritius, his children and friends,—Cyriacus, the patriarch, exposed to his view the enormity of his crimes, and most zealously exhorted to repentance. The supremacy of order and dignity was instantly granted to the patriarch of Rome, in the person of Boniface III. But his successors, their historians say, wisely refused, disclaimed the favour of Phocas, but claimed it as a Divine right derived from St. Peter. Thus commenced and was made final the severance of the Greek and Roman churches.

But the loss of spiritual rule in the east was accompanied by an enlargement of temporal power in the west. Upon the death of Hadrian, John, the son of Gundo, succeeded to the papal chair; and, upon the demise of Lewis II., (876,) his uncles, Lewis, king of Germany, and Charles the Bald, king of France, were rivals for the vacant throne. Charles and Hadrian were ever at variance. But, seizing upon the moment, because he was more ready at hand, or more yielding to his wishes, John invoked him instantly at Rome, received him with loudest acclamations, and crowned him emperor, just seventy-five years to a day from the elevation of Charlemagne to the Western Empire.

Upon this occasion, Pope John announced that he had elected him emperor in conformity to the revealed will of God; that his act of crowning him made him such; and that the sceptre, under God, was his free gift. This new doctrine was assented to by Charles, and ever after claimed as one of the powers of the pope of Rome. Thus the church of Rome became wholly separated from the Eastern Empire,—"freely losing its hold on a decayed tree, to graft itself upon a wild and vigorous sapling." *D'Aubigne.*

Eutropius, the Lombard, informs us of the rich presents made to

St. Peter for these favours of the pope, and that the emperor ceded to him the dukedoms, Benevento and Spoleti, together with the sovereignty of Rome itself.

Thus we have seen why and how the brawny shoulders of the idolatrous children of the north elevated to the throne, thus how the Franks established the temporal power, of the popes of Rome; yet, perhaps, little was foreseen how this state of things was destined, in the course of events, to elevate the church of Rome, and the power of its pontiffs, to a supremacy of all temporal government. It could not have been foreseen how the genius of Hildebrand (Pope Gregory VII.) should, two hundred years after, carry into full accomplishment, by mere words of peace, "what Marius and Cæsar could not by torrents of blood."

But corruption, to a greater or less extent, necessarily followed such a connection of church and state. It matters not to whom, nor in what age,—give churches temporal power, and they are *liable* to be corrupt.

But the church was still a fountain from which the living waters were dispensed to mankind. Instances of personal wickedness may have been more or less common; yet the spirit of truth found it a focal residence, and diffused its light to the world.

The Christian church is not of the contrivance of man, whose works pass away, but of God, who upholds what he creates, and who has given his promise for its duration. Its object is to satisfy the religious wants of human nature, in whatever degree that nature may be developed; and its efficacy is no greater for the learned than for the unlearned; for the exalted of the earth, than for the slave.

LESSON III.

It is said all nature swarms with life. But every animal, in some way, preys upon his fellow. Even we cannot move our foot without becoming the means of destruction to petty animals capable of palpitating for hours, may be days, in the agonies of death. There is no day upon this earth, in which men, and millions of other animals, are not tortured in some way, to the fullest extent of life.

Let us look at man alone; poor and oppressed; tormented by injustice, and stupified to lethargy; writhing under disease, or tortured by his brethren! Recollect his mental pains! The loss of friends, and the poison of ingratitude; the rage of tyranny, and the slow progress of justice; the brave, the high-minded, the honest, consigned to the fate of guilt!

Dive into the dungeon, or the more obscure prison-house of penury. See the aged long for his end, and the young languish in despair; talents and virtue in eternal oblivion: see malice, vengeance, and cruelty at their work, while they propagate every hour; for severity begets its kind, and hate begets hate.

Look where you will, the heart is torn with anguish; the soul is saddened by sorrow. All things seem at war; all one vast abortion. Such is the rugged surface; and the eye sees no golden sands, no precious gems gleaming from beneath the blackened waters of human suffering. These things are so; creation has grown up; and human life can never effect one tremble of the leaf on which it has found its residence.

But the Christian philosopher views these evidences of a great moral catastrophe without madness. He perceives that sin has sunk man into degradation, slavery, and death. He comprehends his own weakness, and trusts in God.

But there is a man, with all these facts before him, who rages. He makes war on the providence, and determines, as if to renovate the work, of the Almighty. Is he a man of a single idea? If not, let him make a better world; and, while he is thus employed, let us resume our subject.

Slavery, either voluntary or involuntary, whether the immediate result of crime or of mental and physical degradation, is equally the consequent of sin. Let us consider how far its existence is sustained by the laws of justice, of religion, and of God.

Our word, God, is pure Saxon, signifying "perfectly good;" "God is good." "And God saw every thing that he had made, and, behold, *it was* very good."

Suppose the laws of Japan permit voluntary slavery, as did those of Moses. (See *Exod.* xxi. 5; also *Lev.* xxv. 47.) Suppose an African negro, of the lowest grade, destitute and naked, voluntarily finds himself in that island, where the poor, free inhabitants scarcely sustain life by the most constant toil. The negro finds no employment. He can neither buy, beg, nor steal; starvation is at hand. He applies to sell himself, under the law of the country, a slave for life. Is not slavery, in this case, a good, because life is a greater good than liberty? Liberty is worth nothing in opposition to life. Liberty is worth nothing without available possessions to sustain it. The preservation of life is the highest law. The law of God, therefore, would be contradictory, if it forbid a man to sell himself to sustain his life; and the justice and propriety of such law must be universal and eternal, so far as it can have relation with the condition of man upon this earth.

But, "What is life without liberty?" said a beggar-woman! He, who thinks life without liberty worth nothing, must die if he have no means to sustain his liberty. Esther entertained no such notion: "For we are sold, I and my people, to be destroyed and slain, and to perish. But if we had been sold for bond-men, and bond-women, I had held my tongue." *Esth.* vii. 4.

Nor has such ever been the notion of the church. Bergier says, Dict. Theo., Art. *Esclava*—

"That civil liberty became a benefit, only after the establishment of civil society, when man had the protection of law, and the multiplied facilities for subsistence; that, previous to this, absolute freedom would be an injury to a person destitute of flocks, herds, lands, and servants."

"The common possession of all things is said to be of the natural law; because the distinction of possessions and slavery were not introduced by nature, but by reason of man, for the benefit of human life; and thus the law of nature is not changed by their introduction, but an addition is made thereto." *St. Thomas Aquinas*, 1, 2, *q.* 94 *a* 95 *ad* 2.

And the same father says again, 2, 2 *q.* 57 *a* 3 *ad* 2—"This man is a slave, absolutely speaking, rather a son, not by any natural cause, but by reason of the benefits which are produced; for it is more beneficial to this one to be governed by one who has more wisdom, and the other to be helped by the labour of the former. Hence the state of slavery belongs principally to the law of nations, and to the natural law, only in the second degree, not in the first."

But a man having the natural right to *sell* himself proves that he has the same right to *buy* others. The one follows the other. But, suppose the laws of Japan do not permit voluntary slavery for life, or, rather that they have no law on the subject; but that they have a law, that whosoever proves himself to be so degraded that he cannot, or will not sustain himself, but is found loitering, begging, or stealing, shall be forcibly sold a slave for life,—is not the same good effected as in the other case, although the individual may be too debased to perceive it himself? And is it difficult to perceive, that the same deteriorating causes have produced both cases? The doctrine of the church is that "death, sickness, and a large train of what is called natural evils, are considered to be the consequences of sin. Slavery is an evil, and is also a consequence of sin." *Bishop England*, p. 23.

And St. Augustine preached the same doctrine, as long ago as the year 425. See his book, "*Of the City of God,*" liber xix. cap. 15. He says—"The condition of slavery is justly regarded as imposed on the sinner. Hence, we never read *slave* (as one having a master) in Scripture before the just Noe, by this word, punished the sin of his son. Sin, not nature, thus introduced the word."

And St. Ambrose, bishop of Milan, A. D. 390, in his book on "*Elias and Fasting*" c. 5, says—"There would be no slavery today had there not been drunkenness."

And so, St. John Chrysostom, bishop of Constantinople, A. D. 400, Hom. 29, in Gen.: "Behold brethren born of the same mother! Sin makes one of them a servant, and, taking away his liberty, lays him under subjection."

The very expression, "Cursed be Canaan, a servant of servants shall he be to his brethren," most distinctly shows the "sentence to have been the consequent of sin, and especially so when compared with the blessing bestowed upon the two brothers, in which they are promised the *services* of him accursed.

Pope Gelesius I., A. D. 491, in his letter to the bishops of the Picene territory, states, "slavery to have been the consequence of sin, and to have been established by human law."

St. Augustine, lib. xix. cap. 16, "On the City of God," argues at length to show "that the peace and good order of society, as well as religious duty, demand that the wholesome laws of the state regulating the conduct of slaves should be conscientiously observed."

"Slavery is regarded by the church * * * not to be incompatible with the natural law, to be the result of sin by Divine dispensation, to have been established by human legislation; and, when the dominion of the slave is justly acquired by the master, to be lawful, not in the sight of the human tribunal only, but also in the eye of Heaven." *Bishop England*, page 24.

But again, in the works already quoted, "De Civitate Dei," St. Augustine says, liber xix. caput 15, that, "although slavery is the consequence of sin, yet that the slavery may not always light upon the sinful individual, any more than sickness, war, famine, or any other chastisement of this sinful world, whereby it may often happen that the less sinful are afflicted, that they may be turned more to the worship of God, and brought into his enjoyment," and refers to the case of Daniel and his companions, who were slaves in Babylon, and by which captivity Israel was brought to repentance.

In cap. 16, "he presents to view the distinction of bodily employment and labour between the son and the slave; but that each are equally under the master's care; and as it regards the soul, each deserved a like protection, and that therefore the masters were called *patres familias*, or *fathers of households;* and shows that they should consult for the eternal welfare of their slaves as a father for his children; and insists upon the weight and obligation of the master to restrain his slaves from vice, and to preserve discipline with strict firmness, but yet with affection; not by verbal correction alone, but, if requisite, corporeal chastisement, not merely for the punishment of delinquency, but for a salutary monition to others."

And he proceeds to show "that these things become a public duty, since the peace of the vicinage depends upon the good order of its families, and that the safety of the state depends upon the peace and discipline of all the vicinage."

This author also shows, from the etymology of the word "*servus*," that, according to the law of nations at the time, the conqueror had at his disposal the lives of the captives. If from some cause he forbore to put some of them to death, then such one was *servati*, or *servi*, that is, kept from destruction or death, and their lives spared, upon the condition of obedience, and of doing the labours and drudgery of the master."

And we may again inquire whether, when prisoners taken in war, under circumstances attending their capture by which the captor feels himself entitled to put them to death,—it is not a great good to the captured to have their lives spared them, and they permitted to be slaves? The answer will again turn upon the question, whether life is worth any thing upon these terms? And whatever an individual may say, the world will answer like Esther. Thus far slavery is an institution of mercy and in favour of life.

We close this lesson by presenting the condition of slavery among the Chinese, and their laws and customs touching the subject.

M. De Guignes, who traversed China throughout its whole extent, observing with minuteness and philosophical research every thing in relation to its singular race, does not believe slavery existed there until its population had become overloaded, when, as a partial relief from its miseries, they systematically made slaves of portions of their own race.

He says, that in ancient times, "it is not believed that there were slaves in China, except those who were taken prisoners in war, or condemned to servitude by the laws. Afterwards, in times of famine, parents were frequently reduced to the necessity of selling their children. This practice, originated in the pressure of necessity, has continued to exist, and even become common. * * * A person may also sell himself as a slave when he has no other means of succouring his father; a young woman, who finds herself destitute, may in like manner be purchased with her own consent.

"The prisoners of war are the slaves of the emperor, and generally sent to labour on his land in Tartary. The judges have the power to pass the sentence of slavery on culprits such as are sold at public auction; slaves also who belong to persons whose property is confiscated, are sold to the highest bidder by public outcry." See work as quoted by Edin. Encyc., Article, "*China.*"

LESSON IV.

The titles which divines and canonists have considered to be good and valid for the possession of slaves, are purchase, inheritance, gift, birth, slaves made in war, and sentenced for crime; but, in all cases, the title is vitiated when not sustained by the civil law. Yet the civil law may be repealed, or ameliorated, so that prisoners taken in war or crime may not be subject to death or servitude, in which case the validity of the title follows in the footsteps of the civil law; but these conditions primarily exist, as perpetual as the condition of man. The civil law, by its intervention, merely diverts the action during its rule.

But, in all cases of a secondary title, the validity follows the character of the previous holding, as no man can sell, give, or leave by inheritance a better title than that which he has. The question thus runs to the origin of what gives a good title, to wit, the condition that enforces one to be sold, or to sell himself, a slave, in favour of life. True, Blackstone, Montesquieu, and others of less note, contend that no man has a right *to sacrifice his liberty;* and what is their argument? They make an assumption, where there is no parallel, "that liberty is of equal worth to life;" but before their argument is good, they must show that liberty is of more value than life: for surely a man may barter an equal for an equal. They cry, "God gave all men liberty." Even that is a fiction. The truth is, God gave no man liberty, only upon conditions.

But to show that life is of more value than liberty, we need only observe that even with the loss of liberty there is hope—hope of change, of liberty, and of the means of sustaining it; and such hopes have often been realized. There is no truth in the proposition that liberty is of equal value (or rather superior) to life. The doctrine therefore is, that man, in his natural state, is the master of his own liberty, and may dispose of it as he sees proper in favour of life; that he may be deprived of it by force, in consequence of crime, or from his not being able to sustain it; and in all cases where liberty has become of less value than life, and both cannot be sustained, the one may be properly exchanged for the safety of the other. And upon this principle, in those countries where the parent had the right, by their law, to put to death his own children, he also had the right to sell them into slavery; and further, by natural law, where the parent cannot sustain the life of his child, where civil law gives him no power over its life, he yet, in favour of life, may sell him into slavery.

Natural law recognises the principle that the child, of right, is subject to the condition of the parent; and in these enfeebled conditions of man, for sake of more certainty, the civil law usually acknowledges the maternal line. It acknowledges the paternal line only when the elevated condition forms a presumption of equal certainty.

The Divine law recognises a good title to hold slaves among all people. The Divine grant to hold slaves was not an "especial permit to the Hebrews." Abimelech gave slaves to Abraham: had his title been bad, Abraham could not have received them.

Bethuel and Laban gave slaves to their daughters. None of these were Hebrews, yet they held slaves by a good title; for the very act of acceptance, in all these cases, is proof that the title was good.

Besides, the Divine law itself instructed the Israelites to buy slaves of the surrounding nations. See *Lev.* xxv. 44. Can there be a stronger proof of the purity of a title, than this gives of the title by which the "nations round about" held slaves? The same law which permitted the Israelites to buy slaves of the "heathen round about," also permitted the "heathen round about" to hold slaves, because it acknowledges their title to be good.

By an inquiry into the history of these "heathen round about," their religion, civil condition, their manners and customs, as well as the final state to which they arrived, we may form some idea how a good title to hold slaves and to sell them arose among them; and since the laws of God are everlasting, and always applicable to every case where all the circumstances are similar, we may reasonably conclude that the same race, or any other race, then, or at any other period of time, to whom the same descriptions will apply, will also be found attended with the same facts in regard to slavery.

The conclusion therefore is, that from such a people, who have a good right to hold and sell slaves, other people, whose civil laws permit them to do so, may purchase slaves by a good title.

It may not then be wholly an idle labour to compare the history and race of these "heathen round about," with the history, race, and present condition of those African heathen who have from time immemorial held and sold slaves.

But it being shown that the Divine sanction to hold slaves, did, at one time, exist, it devolves on them, who deny its religious legality, now to prove that the sanction had been withdrawn.

LESSON V.

We proceed to prove, by a variety of documents, that the Church of Christ did, at all times during its early ages, consider the existence of slavery and the holding of slaves compatible with a religious profession and the practice of Christian duties.

It is first in order to present the sermons of St. Paul and St. Peter direct upon this subject. Having heretofore quoted them, we now merely repeat the references, and ask for their perusal: See 1 *Cor.* vii. 20–24; *Eph.* vi. 5–9; *Col.* iii. 22 to iv. 1; 1 *Tim.* vi. 1–14; *Tit.* ii. 9–15; *Philemon* entire, and 1 *Pet.* ii. 18–25. These scriptures distinctly teach the doctrine of the Christian church. But it remains to see what was the practice that grew up under it.

Upon the crucifixion of Jesus Christ, the mind cannot well conceive how the apostles could have avoided, from time to time, meeting together for the purposes of consultation and agreement among themselves as to the particulars of their future course; and that such was the fact, we have in evidence, *Acts* i. 15–26, where they did thus meet, and elected Matthias to fill the vacancy in their number. Also, *Acts* ix. 26–31, where Paul was received by them and sent forth as an apostle; but the book in question only gives us the outlines of what they did. Now, there is found among the ancient records of the church what is called "The Canons of the Apostles," which, if not actually written by them, is still known to be in conformity with their doctrine, as developed in their own writings and the earliest usages of the church.

Among these, the canon lxxxi. is the following:

Servos in clerum provehi sine voluntate dominorum, non permittimus, ad eorum qui possident molestiam, domorum enim eversionem talia efficiunt. Siquando autem, etiam dignus servus visus sit, qui ad gradum eligatur, qualis noster quoque Onesimus visus est, et domini concesserint ac liberaverint, et œdibus emiserint, fiat.

We do not permit slaves to be raised to clerical rank without the will of their masters, to the injury of their owners. For such conduct produces the upturning of houses. But if, at any time, even a slave may be seen worthy to be raised to that degree, as even our Onesimus was, and the masters shall have granted and given freedom, and have sent them forth from their houses, let it be done.

This is the first of a series of similar enactments, and it should be observed that it recognises the principle of the perfect dominion of the master, the injury to his property, and requires the very legal formality by which the slave was liberated and fully emancipated.

The slave had the title, without his owner's consent, to the common rights of religion and the necessary sacraments. In using these, no injury was done to the property of his owner; but he had no claim to those privileges which would diminish his value to the owner, or would degrade the dignity conferred, and which could not be performed without occupying that time upon which his owner had a claim.

There are eight other books of a remote antiquity, known as "The Constitutions ascribed to the Apostles," said to be compiled by Pope Clement I., who was a companion of the apostles. It is generally believed that, though Clement might have commenced such a compilation, he did not leave it in the form which it now holds, but, like the Canons of the Apostles, the exhibition of discipline is that of the earliest days.

In book iv. ch. 5, enumerating those whose offerings were to be refused by the bishops as unworthy, we have, among thieves and other sinners,

(Qui) famulos suos dure accipiunt et tractant; id est, verberibus, aut fame afficiunt, aut crudeli servitute premunt.

They who receive and treat their slaves harshly; that is, who whip or famish them, or oppress them with heavy drudgery.

There is no crime in having the slave, but cruelty and oppression are criminal.

In the same book, ch. 11 regards slaves and masters.

De famulis quid amplius dicamus, quam quod servus habeat benevolentiam erga dominum cum timore Dei, quamvis sit impius, quamvis sit improbus, non tamen cum eo religione consentiat. Item dominus servum diligat, et quamvis præstet ei, judicet tamen esse æqualitatem, vel quatenus homo est. Qui autem habet dominum Christianum, salvo dominatu, diligat eum, tum ut dominum, tum ut fidei consortem et ut patrem, non sicut servus ad oculum serviens sed sicut dominum amans, ut qui sciat mercedem famulatûs sui a Deo sibi solvendam esse. Similiter dominus, qui Christianum famulum habet, salvo famulatu, diligat eum tanquam filium, et tanquam fratrem propter fidei communionem.

What further, then, can we say of slaves, than that the servant should have benevolence towards his master, with the fear of God, though he should be impious, though wicked; though he should not even agree with him in religion. In like manner, let the master love his slave, and though he is above him, let him judge him to be his equal at least as a human being. But let him who has a Christian master, having regard to his dominion, love him both as a master, as a companion in the faith, and as a father, not as an eye-servant, but loving his master as one who knows that he will receive the reward of his service to be paid by God. So let the master who has a Christian slave, saving the service, love him as a son and as a brother, on account of the communion of faith.

Ne amaro animo jubeas famulo tuo aut ancillæ eidem Deo confidentibus: ne aliquando gemant adversus te, et irascatur tibi Deus. Et vos servi dominis vestris tanquam Deum repræsentantibus subditi estote cum sedulitate et metu, *tanquam Domino, et non tanquam hominibus.*

Do not command your man-servant nor your woman-servant having confidence in the same God, in the bitterness of your soul; lest they at any time lament against you, and God be angry with you. And you servants be subject to your masters, the representatives of God, with care and fear, as to the Lord, and not to men.

In the eighth book, ch. 33, is a constitution of SS. Peter and Paul, respecting the days that slaves were to be employed in labour, and those on which they were to rest and to attend to religious duties.

Stephen I., who was the pontiff in 253, endeavoured to preserve discipline, and set forth regulations to remedy evils.

Accusatores vero et accusationes, quas sæculi leges non recipiunt, et antecessores nostri prohibuerunt, et nos submovemus.

We also reject these accusers and charges which the secular laws do not receive, and which our predecessors have prohibited.

Soon after he specifies:

Accusator autem vestrorum nullus sit servus aut libertus.

Let not your accuser be a slave or a freed person.

Thus, in the ancient discipline of the church, as in the secular tribunals, the testimony of slaves was inadmissible.

In the year 305, a provincial council was held at Elvira, in the southern part of Spain. The fifth canon of which is—

Si qua domina furore zeli accensa flagris verberaverit ancillam suam, ita ut in tertium diem animam cum cruciatu effundat: eo quod incertum sit, voluntate, an casu occiderit, si voluntate post septem annos; si casu, post quinquennii tempora; acta legitima pænitentia, ad communionem placuit admitti. Quod si infra tempora constituta fuerit infirmata, accipiat communionem.

If any mistress, carried away by great anger, shall have whipped her maid-servant so that she shall within three days die in torture, as it is uncertain whether it may happen by reason of her will or by accident, it is decreed that she may be admitted to communion, having done lawful penance, after seven years, if it happened by her will; if by accident, after five years. But should she get sick within the time prescribed, she may get communion.

Spanish ladies, at that period, had not yet so far yielded to the benign influence of the gospel, and so far restrained their violence of temper, as to show due mercy to their female slaves.

It may be well to observe a beneficial change, not only in public opinion, but even in the court, by reason of the influence of the spirit of Christianity; so that the pagan more than once reproved, by his mercy, the professor of a better faith.

Theodoret (l. 9, de Græc. cur. aff.) informs us that Plato established the moral and legal innocence of the master who slew his slave. Ulpian, the Roman jurist (l. 2, de his quæ sunt sui vel alieni jur.) testifies the power which—in imitation of the Greeks—the Roman masters had over the lives of their slaves. The well-known sentence of Pollio upon the unfortunate slave that broke a crystal vase at supper,—that he should be cast as food to fish,—and the interference of Augustus, who was a guest at that supper, give a strong exemplification of the tyranny then in many instances indulged.

Antoninus Pius issued a constitution about the year 150, restraining this power, and forbidding a master to put his own slave to death, except in those cases where he would be permitted to slay the slave of another. The cruelty of the Spaniards to their slaves, in the province of Bœtica, gave occasion to the constitution; and we have a rescript of Antoninus to Ælius Martianus, the proconsul of Bœtica, in the case of the slave of Julius Sabinus, a Spaniard. In this the right of the masters to their slaves is recognised, but the officer is directed to hear their complaints of cruelty, starvation, and oppressive labour; to protect them, and, if the complaints be founded in truth, not to allow their return to the master; and to insist on the observance of the constitution.

Caius (in l. 2, ad Cornel. de sicar.) states that the cause should be proved in presence of judges before the master could pronounce his sentence. Spartianus, the biographer, informs us that the Emperor Adrian, the immediate predecessor of Antoninus, enacted a law forbidding masters to kill their slaves, unless legally convicted. And Ulpian relates that Adrian placed, during five years, in confinement (relegatio) Umbricia, a lady of noble rank, because, for very slight causes, she treated her female slaves most cruelly. But Constantine the Great, about the year 320, enacted that no master should, under penalty due to homicide, put his slave to death, and gave the jurisdiction to the judges; but if the slave died casually, after necessary chastisement, the master was not accountable to any legal tribunal. (Const. in l. i.; C. Theod. de emendat. servorum.)

As Christianity made progress, the unnatural severity with which this class of human beings was treated became relaxed, and as the civil law ameliorated their condition, the canon law, by its spiritual efficacy, came in with the aid of religion, to secure that, the followers of the Saviour should give full force to the merciful provisions that were introduced.

The principle which St. Augustine laid down was that observed. The state was to enact the laws regulating this species of property; the church was to plead for morality and to exhort to practise mercy.

About the same time, St. Peter, archbishop of Alexandria, drew up a number of penitential canons, pointing out the manner of receiving, treating, and reconciling the "lapsed," or those who, through fear of persecution, fell from the profession of the faith. Those canons were held in high repute, and were generally adopted by the eastern bishops.

The sixth of those canons exhibits to us a device of weak Christians, who desired to escape the trials of martyrdom, without being guilty of actual apostasy. A person of this sort procured that one of his slaves should personate him, and in his name should apostatize. The canon prescribes for such a slave, who necessarily was a Christian and a slave of a Christian, but one-third of the time required of a free person, in a mitigated penance, taking into account the influence of fear of the master, which, though it did not excuse, yet it diminished the guilt of the apostasy.

The general council of Nice, in Bythinia, was held in the year 325, when Constantine was emperor. In the first canon of this council, according to the usual Greek and Latin copies, there is a provision for admitting slaves, as well as free persons who have been injured by others, to holy orders. In the Arabic copy, the condition is specially expressed, which is not found in the Greek or Latin, but which had been previously well known and universally established, "*that this should not take place unless the slave had been manumitted by his master.*"

About this period, also, several of the *Gnostic* and *Manichean* errors prevailed extensively in Asia Minor. The *fanatics* denied the lawfulness of *marriage;* they forbid *meat to be eaten;* they condemned the *use of wine;* they praised extravagantly the monastic institutions, and proclaimed the *obligation on all* to enter into religious societies; they decried the *lawfulness of slavery;* they denounced the *slaveholders* as violating equally the laws of *nature and of religion;* they offered to *aid slaves* to *desert their owners;* gave them *exhortations*, *invitations*, *asylum*, and *protection;* and in all things assumed to be more *holy*, more *perfect*, and more *spiritual* than other men.!!!

Osius, bishop of Cordova, whom Pope Sylvester sent as his legate into the east, and who presided in the council of Nice, was present when several bishops assembled in the city of Gangræ, Paphlagonia, to correct those errors. Pope Symmachus declared, in a council held in Rome, about the year 500, that Osius confirmed, by the authority of the pope, the acts of this council. The decrees have been admitted into the body of canon law, and have always been regarded as a rule of conduct in the Catholic church. The third canon:

Si quis docet servum, pietatis prætextu, dominum contemnere, et a ministerio recedere, et non cum benevolentia et omni honore domino suo inservire. Anathema sit.

If any one, under the pretence of piety, teaches a slave to despise his master, and to withdraw from his service, and not to serve his master with good-will and all respect. Let him be anathema.

Let him be anathema is never appended to any decree which does not contain the expression of unchangeable doctrine respecting belief or morality, and indicates that the doctrine has been revealed by God. It is precisely what St. Paul says in *Gal.* i. 8: "But though we, or an angel from heaven, preach a gospel to you beside that which we have preached to you, let him be anathema." 9: "As we said before to you, so I say now again: If any man preach to you a gospel besides that which you have received; let him be anathema." It is therefore manifest, that although this council of Gangræ was a particular one, yet the universal reception of this third canon, with its *anathema*, and its recognition in the Roman council by Pope Symmachus, gives it the greatest authority; and in Labbe it is further entitled as approved by Leo IV., about the year 850, *dist.* 20, *C. de libell.*

Several councils were held in Africa in the third and fourth centuries, in Carthage, in Milevi, and in Hippo. About the year 422, the first of Pope Celestine I., one was held under Aurelius, archbishop of Carthage, and in which St. Augustine sat as bishop of Hippo and legate of Numidia. A compilation was made of the canons of this and the preceding ones, which was styled the "African Council." The canon cxvi. of this collection, taken into the body of the canon law, decrees that slaves shall not be admitted as prosecutors, nor shall certain freedmen be so admitted, except to complain for themselves; and for this, as well as for the incapacity of several others there described, the public law is cited, as well as the 7th and 8th councils of Carthage.

The great St. Basil was born in 329, and died in 379. His works, called "Canonical," contain a great number of those which were the rules of discipline, not only for Asia Minor, but for the vast regions in its vicinity. The fortieth canon regards the marriages of female slaves. In this he mentions a discipline which was not general, but was peculiar to the north-eastern provinces of the church, requiring the consent of the master to the validity of the marriage-contract of a female slave: this was not required in other places, as is abundantly testified by several documents.

The forty-second canon treats in like manner of the marriages of children without their parents' consent, and generally of those of all slaves without the consent of the owner.

LESSON VI.

It may not be improper now to take a more particular view of the civil world, its condition, and of those wars at the instance of which it had been, and then was, flooded with slaves. As an example, we select the middle of the fifth century:

Attila, to whom the Romans gave the sobriquet, "*Flagellum Dei*," *Scourge of God*, was driven by Ætius out of Gaul in the year 451; and the following year, pouring his wild hordes down upon Italy, conquered Aquillia, Pavia, Milan, and a great number of small cities, and was in the attitude of marching on Rome. The Emperor Valentinian III., who was a weak prince, panic-struck, shut himself up in Ravenna; and his general, Ætius, who had been so victorious in Gaul, partook of the general fear when invaded at home. The destruction of Rome and its imperial power, the slaughter and slavery of the Roman people, and the extinction of the church appeared probable. Under such a state of things, the emperor and his council prevailed on Leo the pontiff himself, supported by Albienus and Tragelius, men of great experience and talent, to undertake an embassy to the enemy's camp, then on the banks of the Minzo. This embassy was accompanied by a most grand and numerous retinue—a small army—armed, not with the weapons of war, but with the crosier and crook. Nor did Attila attempt to hide his joy for their arrival. The most profound attention, the most convincing demonstrations of his kindness to them, were studiously displayed by him.

The terms proposed were readily accepted, and Attila and his army, a tornado fraught with moral and physical ruin to Rome, the church, and the civilized world, silently sank away far behind the Danube.

Nor is it strange that the great success of this embassy should have been attributed to some intervention of miraculous power during the dark ages that followed;—and hence we find that, four hundred years after, in one of Gruter's copies of "The Historica Miscella," it is stated that St. Peter and St. Paul stood, visible alone to Attila, on either side of Leo, brandishing a sword, commanding him to accept whatever Leo should offer; and this is quoted as credible history by Barronius, *ad ann.* 452, *no.* 47–59, and has been painted by Raffaele, at a much later period. The idea was perhaps poetical, and this piece alone would have immortalized the artist. But it is truly singular that this appearance of Peter and Paul should have gained a place in the Roman Breviary, especially as it is nowhere alluded to by Leo, nor by his secretary, Prosper, who was present at that treaty, nor by any contemporary whatever. The facts attached to Attila, in connection with this treaty, were:—His army was extremely destitute, and a contagious and very mortal disease was raging in his camp; in addition to which, Marcian had gathered a large army, then under march for Italy, to join the imperial forces under Ætius, while, at the same moment, another army, sent by Marcian long before, were then ravaging the country of the Huns themselves: of these facts Attila was well advised. These were the agencies that operated on his mind in favour of peace with Valentinian. To us the idea seems puerile to suppose Jehovah sending Peter and Paul, sword in hand, to frighten his Hunnish majesty from making slaves of the Roman people.

Would it not be more consonant with the general acts of his providence to point Attila to his diseased army; to their consequent want of supplies, and to the threatening danger of his being totally cut off by the two armies of Marcian, saying nothing of the possibility of a restored confidence among the then panic-struck Romans? Besides, it has been well ascertained that, at the time of Leo's arrival, he had been hesitating whether to march on Rome—or recross the Alps. See *Bower*, vol. ii. p. 202; also, *Jornandez Rer. Goth.* c. 41, 49.

But, we acknowledge the intervening influences of the Divine will, in this case, as forcibly as it could be urged, even if attended with all the particulars and extravagancies of the poetic painter's fancy. We have alluded to this particle of the history of that day, as it stands upon the records, in order that, while we quote, we may not be misunderstood as to our view of the providences of God.

But to return to our subject:—Upon a review of these times, we may notice the distractions of the church by means of the various heresies which imbittered against each other the different professions of the Christian faith. How the followers of Arius, for more than half a century, spread confusion and violence over the entire Christian world:—How, crushed and driven out by Theodosius, thousands took shelter among the pagans, whose movements they stimulated, and whom we now perceive in progress of the gradual overthrow of the Roman Empire:—How, upon the partial or more general successes of these hordes, their Arian confederates, with a fresh memory of their late oppressions and the cruelties inflicted on them, retaliated with unsparing severity and bloodshed upon their Nicene opponents; while, among all these savage invaders, the Arian creed supplanted and succeeded the pagan worship:—How this wild Attila swept the banks of the Danube and the Rhine, carrying death or desolation to the followers of Pharamond, and to the Goths, who had then already established themselves in the strongholds of ancient Gaul and of the more modern Romans. True, his career was checked on the banks of the Rhone, but, like a hunted lion, he rushed towards the Mediterranean, and, recruiting his force in Pannonia, directed his march to Italy; and to-day, after fourteen centuries, it is said that Aquillia still stands the monument of his barbarity. We have this moment noticed the extraordinary manner in which, it is said, by the monition of Leo, his path of ruin was suddenly directed to the ice-bound fortresses of the north. But the captives made on both sides, in these desolating wars, greatly increased the number of slaves of the white race, which otherwise, from operating causes, would have been diminished.

Up to this time in these regions, and, as we shall see, to a much later time, slavery was the result of that mercy in the victor, whereby he spared the life of the conquered enemy. Its condition did not depend on any previous condition of degradation, of freedom or slavery, nor upon the race or colour of the captive;—and the wars, for ages, which had been and were so productive of slavery, were almost exclusively among those who, in common, claimed a Caucasian origin. Instances of African slavery were rare. The Romans derived some few from their African wars, valued mostly by pride, because they were the most rare.

Thus we read in the Life of Nero, by Tacitus:—"Nero never travelled with less than a thousand baggage-wagons; the mules all shod with silver, and the drivers dressed in scarlet; his African slaves adorned with bracelets on their arms, and the horses decorated with the richest trappings." But these times had passed away. Yet we find in the Life of Alphonso el Casto, that, upon his conquest of Lisbon, 798, he sent seven Moorish slaves as a present to Charlemagne. And also, in Bower's "Lives of the Popes," that in 849, "A company of Moors, from Africa, rendezvoused at Tozar, in Sardinia, and thence made an incursion, by the Tiber, on Rome. But they were mostly lost in a storm before landing. Of those who got on shore, some were killed in battle, some were hanged, and a large number were brought to Rome and reduced to slavery."

Yet the great mass of slaves were of the same race and colour of their masters; and at this age, a most important fact with the Christian, if they were pagans, was their conversion to Christianity.

For the first three hundred years, we may notice how Christianity had threaded her way amidst the troublous and barbarous paganisms of that age. But, at the time to which we have arrived, Christianity had ruled the civilized world for more than a century. And had Providence seen fit to have attended her future path with peace, human sympathy might have fondly hoped that the mild spirit of her religion would have been poured in ameliorating, purifying streams upon the condition and soul of the slave, and like a dissolving oil on the chains that bound him.

LESSON VII.

We present a series of records and documents which elucidate the practice and doctrine of the church in regard to slavery, as we find it in that age.

These records are mostly extracts from Bishop England's Letters, and collated by him with accuracy. Some few, from Bower, Bede, Lingard, and others, will be noticed in their place.

It should be remembered that, in all cases where the contrary is not explicitly announced, the slave is of the same colour and race as the master. At this era of the world, slaves were too common, and their value too little, to warrant the expense of a distant importation. The negro slave, from his exhibiting an extreme variety of the human species, was regarded more as an article of curiosity and pride than usefulness; and therefore was seldom or never found in Europe, except near the royal palaces, or in the trains of emperors.

As early as the days of Polycarp and St. Ignatius, who were disciples of the apostles, Christians had, from motives of mercy, charity, and affection, manumitted many of their slaves in presence of the bishops, and this was more or less extensively practised through the succeeding period. In several churches, it was agreed that if a slave became a Christian, he should be manumitted on receiving baptism. In Rome, the slave was frequently manumitted by the form called *vindicta*, with the prætor's rod. Constantine, in the year 317, Sozomen relates, lib. i. c. 9, transferred this authority to the bishops, who were empowered to use the rod in the church, and have the manumission testified in the presence of the congregation. A rescript of that emperor to this effect is found in the Theodosian code, l. i. c. *De his qui in eccl. manumitt.* The master, who consented to manumit the slave, presented him to the bishop, in presence of the congregation, and the bishop pronounced him free, and became the guardian of his freedom. The rescript was directed to Protogenas, bishop of Sardica, and was in the consulship of Sabinus and Ruffinus.

In book ii. of the same code, is a rescript to Osius, bishop of Cordova, in which the emperor empowers the bishops to grant the privilege of Roman citizenship to such freedmen as they may judge worthy.

In the consulship of Crispus and Constantine, a grant was given to the clergy of manumitting their own slaves when they pleased, by any form they should think proper. About a century later, St. Augustine, bishop of Hippo, informs us (*Sermo. de diversis*, 50) that this form was established in Africa. "The deacon of Hippo is a poor man: he has nothing to give to any person: but, before he was a clergyman, he, by the fruit of his labour and industry, bought some little servants, and is to-day, by the episcopal act, about to manumit them in your sight."

This same bishop writes, (*Enarrat in Ps.* cxxiv.,) "Christ does not wish to make you proud while you walk in this journey, that is, while you are in this life. Has it happened that you have been made a Christian, and you have a man as your master: you have not been made a Christian that you may scorn to serve. When, therefore, by the command of Christ you are the servant of a man, your service is not to him, but to the one that gave you the command to serve. And he says, Hear your masters, according to the flesh, with fear and trembling, and in the simplicity of your hearts, not as eye-servants, as if pleasing men, but, as the servants of Christ, doing the will of God, from your hearts, with a good will. Behold, he did not liberate you from being servants, but he made those who were bad servants to be good servants. Oh, how much do the rich owe to Christ who has thus set order in their houses! So, if there be in his family a faithless slave, and Christ convert him, he does not say to him, Leave your master, because you have now known him who is the true Master! Perhaps this master of yours is impious and unjust, and that you are faithful and just; it is unbecoming that the just and faithful should serve the unjust and the infidel: this is not what he said; but, let him rather serve." This great doctor of the church continues at considerable length to show how Christ, by his own example, exhorts the servants to fidelity and obedience to their masters in every thing, save what is contrary to God's service. Subsequently, he passes to the end of time, and the opening of eternity, and shows many good, obedient, and afflicted servants mingled with good masters among the elect, and bad, faithless, and stubborn servants, with cruel masters, cast among the reprobates.

In his *book* i., *on the Sermon of Christ on the Mount*, he dwells upon the duty of Christian masters to their slaves. They are not to regard them as mere property, but to treat them as human beings having immortal souls, for which Christ died.

Thus we perceive that, though from the encouragement of manumission and the spirit of Christianity, the number of slaves had been greatly reduced and their situation greatly improved, still the principles were recognised of the moral and religious legality of holding slave property, and of requiring that they should perform a reasonable service.

The instances of voluntary slavery, such as that of St. Paulinus, were not rare. It is related, that having bestowed all that he could raise, to ransom prisoners taken by the barbarians who overran the country; upon the application of a poor widow whose son was held in captivity, he sold himself, to procure the means of her son's release. His good conduct procured the affection of his master, and subsequently his emancipation. Thus slavery lost some of its degrading character. This, together with the confusion arising from the turbulence accompanying the invasions, caused a relaxation of discipline: to remedy some of the abuses, Pope Leo issued several letters. The following is an extract from the first of them: it has been taken into the body of the canon law. *Dist.* 5, *Admittuntur*:—

"Admittuntur passim ad ordinem sacrum, quibus nulla natalium, nulla morum dignitas suffragatur: et qui a dominis suis libertatem consequi minime potuerunt, ad fastigium sacerdotii, tanquam servilis vilitas hunc honorem jure capiat, provehuntur, et probari Deo se posse creditur, qui domino suo necdum probare se potuit. Duplex itaque in hac parte reatus est, quod et sacrum mysterium (ministerium) talis consortii vilitate polluitur, et dominorum, quantum ad illicitæ usurpationis temeritatem pertinet, jura solvuntur. Ab his itaque, fratres carissimi, omnes provinciæ vestræ abstineant sacerdotes: et non tantum ab his, sed ab illis etiam, qui aut originali aut alicui conditioni obligati sunt, volumus temperari: nisi forte eorum petitio aut voluntas accesserit, qui aliquid sibi in eos vindicant potestatis. Debet enim esse immunis ab aliis, qui divinæ militiæ fuerit aggregandus; ut a castris Dominicis, quibus nomen ejus adscribitur, nullis necessitatis vinculis abstrahatur."

Persons who have not the qualifications of birth or conduct, are everywhere admitted to holy orders; and they who could not procure freedom from their masters are elevated to the rank of the priesthood; as if the lowliness of slavery could rightfully claim this honour: and, as if he who could not procure the approbation of even his master, could procure that of God. There is, therefore, in this a double criminality: for the holy ministry is polluted by the meanness of this fellowship, and so far as regards the rashness of this unlawful usurpation, the rights of the masters are infringed. Wherefore, dearest brethren, let all the priests of your province keep aloof from these: and not only from these, but also, we desire they should abstain from those who are under bond, by origin or any condition, except perchance upon the petition or consent of the persons who have them in their power in any way. For he who is to be aggregated to the divine warfare, ought to be exempt from other obligations: so that he may not by any bond of necessity be drawn away from that camp of the Lord for which his name has been enrolled.

Prosper, lib. 2 *de vitâ contemplat.* c. 3, and many other writers of this century, treat of the relative duties of the Christian master and his Christian slave. The zeal and charity of several holy men led them to make extraordinary sacrifices during this period, to redeem the captives from the barbarians: besides the remarkable instance of Paulinus, we have the ardent and persevering charity of Exuperius, bishop of Toulouse, who sold the plate belonging to the church, and used glass for the chalice, that he might be able by every species of economy to procure liberty for the enslaved.

Nor was this a solitary instance. About the year 513, Pope Symmachus called a national council, by which, among other enactments, he established the rule that under no circumstances, could the church property be alienated. See Bower, vol. ii. p. 277.

About the year 535, Cæsarius, primate of Arles, applied to Pope Agapetus for means to relieve the poor Christians in Gaul. But, at that time, the church being quite destitute of money, the pope excused himself, and quoted the decree of Symmachus. The Arians, and some others, hence inculcated the doctrine that the alienation of church property, under any circumstances, was sacrilege. The laws of the empire also forbid such alienation, but with the proviso, "except there was no other means by which the poor could be relieved in time of famine, nor the captives be redeemed from slavery." Such was the practice among the most pious of the age.

St. Ambrose did not scruple to melt down the communion-plate of the church of Milan to redeem some captives, who otherwise must have continued in slavery. The Arians charged him with sacrilege: in answer to which he wrote his Apology, which has reached this late day, as the rules and reasons of the church in such cases. He says—"Is it not better that the plate should be melted by the bishop to maintain the poor, when they can be maintained by no other means, than that it should become the spoil and plunder of a sacrilegious enemy? Will not the Lord thus expostulate with us, Why did you suffer so many helpless persons to die with hunger, when you had gold to relieve and support them? Why were so many captives carried away and sold without ransom? Why were so many suffered to be slain by the enemy? It would have been better to have preserved the vessels of living men than lifeless metals. To this, what answer can be returned? Should one say, I was afraid that the temple of God should want its ornaments: Christ would answer, My sacraments require no gold, nor do they please me more for being ministered in gold, as they are not to be bought with gold. The ornament of my sacrament is the redemption of captives; and those alone are precious vessels that redeem souls from death."

The saint concludes that though it would be highly criminal for a man to convert the sacred vessels to his own private use, yet it is so far from being a crime, that he looks upon it as an obligation incumbent on him and his brethren to prefer the living temples of God to the unnecessary ornaments of the material edifices. See Ambrose de Offic. lib. ii. cap. 28; and such was the doctrine of St. Austin, see Possid. Vit. Aug. caput 24; of Acacius of Amida, see Socrat. lib. vii. c. 24; of Deigratias of Carthage, see Vict. de Persec. Vandal, lib. i.; of Cyril of Jerusalem, see Theodoret, lib. ii. c. 27; yea all, who have touched on the subject, have subscribed to the doctrine of St. Ambrose. Even the Emperor Justinian, in his law against sacrilege, forbids the church plate, vestments, or any other gifts, to be sold, or pawned; but adds, "except in case of captivity or famine, the lives and souls of men being preferable to any vessels or vestments whatever." See Codex Just. lib. i. tit. 2. de Sacr. Eccles. leg. 21; also see Bower's Life of Agapetus, p. 354.

It will be readily conceived that the barbarians, in the earlier ages of the Christian church, treated their slaves with cruelty, inconsistent with the spirit of the new religion; and, upon their adoption of the Christian creed, they sometimes ran into an opposite extreme, contrary to the rules of the church. In both cases the church used her authority, and, says Bishop England, upon their embrace of Christianity, "slavery began to assume a variety of mitigated forms among them," which will, in some degree, be developed as we proceed with the history of canonical legislation on that subject.

The rules of the Christian church are evidently founded upon the laws of God, as delivered to Moses: "And if a man smite his servant, or his maid, with a rod, and he die under his hand, he shall be surely punished. Notwithstanding, if he continue a day or two, he shall not be punished: for he is his money."

"If a man smite the eye of his servant, or the eye of his maid, that it perish, he shall let him go free for his eye's sake. And if he smite his man-servant's tooth, or his maid-servant's tooth, he shall let him go for his tooth's sake." *Exod.* xxi. 20, 21, 26, 27. And if a man took his female slave to wife, and became displeased with her * * * she should be free. See *Deut.* xxi. 10–15. But fornication in a female slave was not punished by death, but by stripes. See *Lev.* xix. 20–23.

Neither the laws of Moses, nor indeed of any civilized people, have ever permitted unusual or cruel punishments to be inflicted on the slave. Civilization, as well as Judaism, seems to have inculcated, "Be not excessive toward any; and without discretion do nothing. If thou have a servant, let him be unto thee as thyself, because thou hast bought him with a price." *Eccl.* xxxiii. 29.

Among heathen nations, their laws were to the effect, that when the slave, sick or wounded, was neglected, or abandoned to his fate by his master; yet, if he recovered, the master should lose his property in such slave, and the slave should be free; and such neglect was often otherwise made punishable. The Roman law sanctioned this doctrine: "Si verberatus fuerit *servus* non mortifere, negligentia autem perierit, de vulnerato actio erit, non de occiso." See Lex Aquillia. And so in ancient France, see Fœdere, vol. iii. p. 290: *If negligence or bad treatment towards the slave was proved in the master, the slave was declared free.*

At this day, in all civilized countries, the civil law forbids unusual and cruel punishment of slaves, and also a wanton and careless negligence of them, either in sickness or health. Thus the law punishes the master for his neglect to govern his slaves, by making him responsible for their bad conduct, and the damage their want of proper government may occasion others.

In the year 494, Pope Gelesius admonished the bishops, at their ordinations, that—

"Ne unquam ordinationes præsumat illicitas; ne * * * curæ

aut cuilibet conditioni obnoxium notatumque ad sacros ordines permittat accedere."

*That he should never presume to hold unlawful ordinations; that he should not allow to holy orders * * * any person bound to the service of the court, or liable to bond for his condition* (slavery) *or marked thereto.*

In the year 506, a council was held at Agdle, the sixty-second canon of which is—

"Si quis servum proprium sine conscientiâ judicis occiderit, excommunicatione vel pœnitentia biennii reatum sanguinis emendabit."

If any one shall put his own servant to death, without the knowledge of the judge, let him make compensation for the guilt of blood by excommunication or two years' penance.

Another council was held eleven years later. Many of the canons of this synod are transcripts of those of Agdle. The thirty-fourth is:

"Si quis servum proprium sine consciéntiâ judicis occiderit, excommunicatione biennii effusionem sanguinis expiabit."

If any one shall slay his own servant without the knowledge of the judge, let him expiate the shedding of blood by an excommunication of two years.

This was nearly two hundred years after the law of Constantine forbidding this exercise of power by the master.

The third council of Orleans was held in the year 538.

The thirteenth canon regulates, that if Christian slaves shall be possessed by Jews, and these latter require them to do any thing forbidden by the Christian religion, or if the Jews shall seize upon any of their servants to whip or punish them for those things that have been declared to be excusable or forgiven, and those slaves fly to the church for protection, they are not to be given up, unless there be given and received a just and sufficient sum to warrant their protection.

The canon xxvi. gives a specimen of the early feudalism nearly similar to the subsequent villain service.

"Ut nullus servilibus colonariisque conditionibus obligatus, juxta statuta sedis apostolicæ, ad honores ecclesiasticos admittatur; nisi prius aut testamento, aut per tabulas legitime constiterit absolutum. Quod si quis episcoporum, ejus qui ordinatur conditionem sciens, transgredi per ordinationem inhibitam fortasse voluerit, anni spatio missas facere non præsumat."

Let no one held under servile or colonizing conditions be admitted to church honours, in violation of the statutes of the Apostolic see; unless it be evident that he has been previously absolved therefrom by will or by deed. And if any bishop, being aware of such condition of the person so ordained, shall wilfully transgress by making such unlawful ordination, let him not presume to celebrate mass for the space of a year.

The colonial condition was in its origin different from the mere servile. The *mancipium* or *manu captum* was the *servus* or slave made in war: the *colonus*, or husbandman, though, at the period at which we are arrived, he frequently was in as abject a condition, yet was so by a different process. St. Augustine, in cap. i. lib. x. *De Civitate Dei*, tells us, "Coloni *dicuntur*, qui conditionem debebant genitali solo propter agriculturam sub dominio possessorum." They are called *colonists who owe their condition to their native land, under the dominion of its possessors.*

The following history of various modes by which they became servants, is taken from the work *De Gubernat. Dei*, lib. v., by the good and erudite Salvianus, a priest, who died at Marseilles, about the year 484.

Nonnulli eorum de quibus loquimur, * * * cum domicilia atque agellos suos pervasionibus perdunt, aut fatigati ab exactoribus deserunt, quia tenere non possunt, fundos majorum expetunt, et coloni divitum fiunt. Aut sicut solent hi qui hostium terrore compulsi, ad castella se conferunt, aut qui perdito ingenuæ incolumitatis statu ad asylum aliquod desperatione confugiunt: ita et isti qui habere amplius vel sedem vel dignitatem suorum natalium non queunt, jugo se inquilinæ abjectionis addicunt: in hanc necessitatem redacti, ut exactores non facultatis tantum, set etiam conditionis suæ, atque exultantes non a rebus tantum suis, sed etiam a seipsis, ac perdentes secum omnia sua, et rerum proprietate careant, et jus libertatis amittant. * * * Illud gravius et acerbius, quod additur huic malo servilius malum. Nam suscipiuntur advenæ, fiunt præjudicio habitationis indigenæ, et quos suscipiunt ut extraneos et alienos, incipiunt habere quasi proprios: quos esse constat ingenuos, vertunt in servos.

Some of those, when they lose their dwellings and their little fields by invasion, or leave them, being worried by exactions, as they can no longer hold them, seek the grounds of the larger proprietors, and become the colonists of the wealthy. Or, as is usual with those who are driven off by the fear of enemies, and take refuge in the castles, *or who, having lost their state of safe freedom, fly to some asylum in despair: so they who can no longer have the place or the dignity derived from their birth, subject themselves to the abject yoke of the sojourner's lot; reduced to such necessity, that they are stripped not only of their property, but also of their rank; going into exile not only from what belongs to them but from their very selves, and with themselves losing all that they had, they are bereft of any property in things and lose the very right of liberty.* * * * *A more degrading injury is added to this evil. For they are received as strangers, they become inhabitants bereft of the rights of inhabitants; they who receive them as foreigners and aliens begin to treat them as property, and change into slaves those who, evidently, were free.*

In this picture of the colonist, we may find the outline of the villain of a later age; and in the several enactments and regulations of succeeding legislators and councils, we shall discover the changes which servitude underwent previous to its total extinction in Europe.

Flodoardin, c. 28, History of the church of Rheims, gives us the will of St. Remi, its bishop, who baptized Clovis, upon his conversion in 496, and who was still living in the year 550. This document grants freedom to some of the colonists belonging to that church and retains others in service.

Du Cange says (Art. *Colonus*) that though in several instances the condition of the colonists was as abject as that of slaves, yet generally they were in a better position. *Erant igitur coloni mediæ conditionis inter ingenuos seu liberos et servos.*

LESSON VIII.

From the fact that the slaves of this era were of the same colour and other physical qualities of their masters; from their great number, and consequently little value, their condition became attended with extremely diverse circumstances; so various were, therefore, the relations between them and the master, that it would now be impossible, perhaps, to give an accurate history of their various castes. These facts should be kept in mind, lest we mistake, and find confusion, where distinction was sufficiently clear and obvious.

Muratori, treating of the Roman slaves and freedmen, acknowledges that he is unable accurately to state the conditions on which they manumitted their slaves. In his treatise, "*Sopra i Servi e Liberti Antichi*," he has a passage thus:

Noi non sappiamo se con patti, e con quai patti una vulta si manomettessero que' Servi, che poi continuavano come Liberti a servire in Casa de' loro Padroni, con essere alzati a piu onorati impieghi. Sappiamo bensi dal Tit. *ne Operis Libertorum*, e dall' altro *de bonis Libertorum* ne' Digesti, che moltissimi acquistavano la Liberta con obbligarsi di fare ai Padroni de' Regaii, o delle Fatture, se erano Artefici, *Operas, vel Donum.* Questo si praticava verisimilmente dai soli Mercatanti, ed altri Signori dati all' interarse, ma non gia dalle Nobili Case. Per conto di questo, le antiche Iscrizioni ci fanno vedere, che moltissimi furono coloro, che anche dopo la conseguita Liberta seguitavano a convivere, e servire in quelle medesime Case, non piu come Servi, ma come Liberti, perche probabilmente tornava il conto agli uni e agli altri. I Padroni si servivano di Persone loro confidenti, e gia innestate nella propria Famiglia; ei Liberti cresciuti di onore, e di guadagno poteano cumulare roba per se e per li Figli. Non ho io potuto scoprire se i Romani tenessero Servi Mercenarj come oggidi. O di veri Servi, o di Liberti allora si servivano. Cio posto, maraviglia e, che il Pignoria, in trattando degli Ufizj de' Servi antichi, imbrogliasse tanto le carte, senza distinguere i Servi dai Liberti, e con attribuir molti impieghi ai primi, che pure erano riserbati agli ultimi. E piu da stupire e, citarsi da lui Marmi, che parlano di Liberti, e pure sono presi da esso, come se parlassero di Servi.

We know not whether they manumitted upon condition, or, if so, upon what conditions they manumitted formerly those servants who continued thenceforth as freed persons, but elevated to more honourable employments, to serve in the houses of their masters. We do indeed know in the Tit. de Operis Libertorum, *and in another* de bonis Libertorum *of the Digests, that very many acquired their liberty with the obligation of giving to their masters presents, or doing work if they were artists,* Operas vel donum. *This was in all likelihood practised only by merchants or other masters given to making profit, but not by noble houses. As to these the ancient inscriptions exhibit to us that very many who obtained their freedom, yet continued to live and to do service in those same houses, no longer as slaves, but as freed persons, because probably each party found it beneficial. The patrons kept about them persons in whom they had confidence, and who had already been engrafted on their families; the freed persons, grown to honour and making profit could create property for themselves and for their children. I cannot discover whether the Romans had hireling servants, as is now the case. They had then true slaves and sometimes freed persons. This being the case, it is matter of surprise that Pignoria, in treating of the employment of the ancient slaves, should have been so perplexed as not to be able clearly to distinguish slaves from freed persons, and should have attributed to the former many employments which were specially reserved for the latter: and it is more to be wondered at, that marbles which speak of freed persons are referred to by him and explained as treating of slaves.*

It is clear that even in the days of the Emperor Claudius, to whose reign, A. D. 45, the marble of which he treats refers, and probably long before that period, many of the freedmen of the Roman empire were bound to do certain services for the patrons who had been their masters, and that this obligation descended to their progeny. Hence this would still be a species of servitude.

The barbarians who overran the empire came chiefly from Scythia and Germany, as that vast region was then called which stretches from the Alps to the Northern Ocean. When they settled in the conquered provinces of Gaul and in Italy, they introduced many of their customs as well of government as of policy. Most of their slaves were what the writers of the second, third, and fourth centuries describe as *coloni* and *conditionibus obligati.* As Tacitus describes, in xxv. *De Moribus Germanorum :*

"The slaves in general are not arranged at their several employments in the household affairs, as is the practice at Rome. Each has his separate habitation, and his own establishment to manage. The master considers him as an agrarian dependant, who is obliged to furnish a certain quantity of grain, cattle, or wearing-apparel. The slave obeys, and the state of servitude extends no further. All domestic affairs are managed by the master's wife and children. To punish a slave with stripes, to load him with chains, or condemn him to hard labour, is unusual. It is true that slaves are sometimes put to death, not under colour of justice, or of any authority vested in the master; but in a transport of passion, in a fit of rage, as is often the case in a sudden affray; but it is also true that this species of homicide passes with impunity. The freedmen are nôt of much higher consideration than the actual slaves; they obtain no rank in their master's family, and, if we except the parts of Germany where monarchy is established, they never figure on the stage of public business. In despotic governments they often rise above the men of ingenuous birth, and even eclipse the whole body of the nobles. In other states the subordination of the freedmen is a proof of public liberty."

At all ages, slaves who belonged to the absolute monarch, sometimes became elevated above the native nobility: witness the case of Joseph in Egypt; of Ebed Melech, who was black, in Judea; of Haman, also a black, an Amalekite; of Mordecai, his successor; of Esther the queen; of Daniel the prophet, and Felix, governor of Judea, a Greek slave to the Roman emperor. But such things can never occur in a republic. To a political misfortune of this kind the prophet alludes—"Servants (slaves) have ruled over us"—than which nothing can be more expressive of the loss of liberty.

In the appendix to the Theodosian code, Const. 5, we read—

Inverecundâ arte defendetur, si hi ad conditionem vel originem reposcuntur, quibus tempore famis, cum in mortem penuria cogerentur, opitulari non potuit dominus aut patronus.

It is forbidden as a shameless trick, that an effort should be made to regain to their condition or original state, those whom the master, or patron could not aid, when, in a period of famine, they were pressed nearly to death by want.

This exhibits the obligation on the patron of the person *under condition*, and on the master of the slave, to support them, and the destruction of their title by the neglect of their duty.

Muratori observes, that in process of time, the special agreements and particular enactments regarding the *conditions*, gave such a variety as baffled all attempts at classification and precision.

At a much earlier period, slaves had become a drug in the Italian market. When, about the year 405, Rhadagasius, the Goth, was leading upwards of three hundred thousand of his barbarians into Italy, the Emperor Honorius ordered the slaves to be armed for the defence of the country, by which arming they generally obtained their freedom; Stilichon, the consul, slew nearly one hundred and fifty thousand of the invaders in the vicinity of Florence, and made prisoners of the remainder, who were sold as slaves at the low price of one piece of gold for each.

Jacobs estimates the *aureus* at eleven shillings. It is supposed to have contained about 70 grains of gold, which will make the price of a slave, at that time, about $2.60. But Wilkins (Leges Saxon.) informs us that, in England, about the year 1000, the price of a slave was £2 16*s*. 3*d*. sterling, not quite the value of two horses. But, of these slaves of Stilichon, numbers died within the year, so that Baronius relates (Annals, A. D. 406) that the purchasers had to pay more for their burial than for their bodies; according to the remarks of Orosius, in this state of the market, it was easy for the slave to procure that he should be held *at a condition*, and thenceforth the number under condition greatly increased, and in process of time became more numerous than those in absolute slavery.

In the year 541, the fourth council of Orleans was celebrated, in the thirtieth year of King Childebert. The ninth canon:—Ut episcopus, qui de facultate propria ecclesiæ nihil relinquit, de ecclesiæ facultate si quid aliter quam canones eloquuntur obligaverit, vendiderit aut distraxerit, ad ecclesiam revocetur, (ab ecclesia, *in other editions.*) Sane si de servis ecclesiæ libertos fecit numero competenti, in ingenuitate permaneant, ita ut ab officio ecclesiæ non recedant.

Be it enacted, *That a bishop who has left none of his private property to the church shall not dispose of any of the church property, otherwise than as the canons point out. Should he bind or sell or separate any thing otherwise, let it be recalled for the church. But if, indeed, he has made freemen of slaves of the church to a reasonable number, let them continue in their freedom, but with the obligation of not departing from the duty of the church.*

The canon xxii. of the same council is—

Ut servis ecclesiæ, vel sacerdotum, prædas et captivitates exercere non liceat; qui iniquum est, ut quorum domini redemptionis præstare solent suffragium, per servorum excessum disciplina ecclesiastica maculetur.

That it be not lawful for the slaves of the church, or of the priests, to go on predatory excursions or to make captives, for it is unjust that when the masters are accustomed to aid in redeeming, the discipline of the church should be disgraced by the misconduct of the slaves.

In Judaism, God had established a limited sanctuary for slaves and for certain malefactors, not to encourage crime, but to protect against the fury of passion, and to give some sort of aid to the feeble. Paganism adopted the principle, and the Christian temple and its precincts became, not only by common consent, but by legal enactment, the sanctuary instead of the former. Like every useful institution, this too was occasionally abused.

The xxixth canon was—

Quæcumque mancipia sub specie conjugii ad ecclesiæ septa confugerint, ut per hoc credant posse fieri conjugium, minime eis licentia tribuatur, nec talis conjunctio a clericis defensetur: quia probatum est, ut sine legitimâ traditione conjuncti, pro religionis ordine, statuto tempore ab Ecclesiæ communione súspendantur, ne in sacris locis turpi concubitu misceantur. De quâ re decernimus, ut parentibus aut propriis dominis, prout ratio poscit personarum, acceptâ fide excusati sub separationis promissione reddantur: postmodum tamen parentibus atque dominis libertate concessâ, si eos voluerint propriâ voluntate conjungere.

Let not those slaves who, under pretext of marriage, take refuge within the precincts of the church, imagining that by this they would make a marriage, be allowed to do so, nor let such union be countenanced by the clergy: for it has been regulated that they who form an union, without lawful delivery, should be, for the good order of religion, separated for a fixed period from the communion of the church, so that this vile connection may be prevented in holy places. Wherefore we decree, that such persons, being declared free from the bond of any plighted faith and made to promise a separation, should be restored to their parents or owners, as the case may require; to be, however, subsequently, if the parents or owners should grant leave, married with their own free consent.

As we have seen in some parts of the East at an earlier period, now in this portion of the West, the slaves were made incapable of entering into the marriage-contract without the owner's consent.

In this same council, canon xxx., provision is made for affording to the Christians, who are held as slaves by the Jews, not only sanctuary of the church, but in the house of any Christian, until a fair price shall be stipulated for and paid to the Jewish owner, if the Christian be unwilling to return to his service. *This is a clear recognition of the right of property in slaves.*

Canon xxxi. of this council provides, that "*if any Jew shall bring a slave to be a proselyte to his religion, or make a Jew of a Christian slave, or take as his companion a Christian female slave, or induce a slave born of Christian parents to become a Jew under the influence of a promise of emancipation, he shall lose the title to every such slave. And further, that if any Christian slave shall become a Jew for the sake of being manumitted with condition, and shall continue to be a Jew, the liberty shall be lost and the condition shall not avail him.*"

Canon xxxii. provides, that the "*descendants of a slave, wherever they may be, even after a long lapse of time, though there should be neglect, if found upon the land or possession upon which their parents were placed, shall be held to the original conditions established by the deceased proprietor for the deceased parents, and the priest of the place shall aid in enforcing the fulfilment, and any persons who shall through avarice interpose obstacles, shall be placed under church censures.*"

The doctrine and discipline of the church of the Franks were like that of other churches in the several regions of Christendom at this period.

A fifth council was held at Orleans, in the year 549, the thirty-eighth of King Childebert. The sixth canon of this council relates to the improper ordination of slaves, and also exhibits distinctly the freedmen *under condition*, classing them in the same category with slaves.

Canon vi. Ut servum, qui libertatem a dominis propriis non acceperit, aut etiam jam libertum, nullus episcoporum absque ejus tantum voluntate, cujus aut servus est, aut eum absolvisse dignoscitur, clericum audeat ordinare. Quod si quisquam fecerit, si qui ordinatus est a domino revocetur, et ille qui est collator ordinis, si sciens fecisse probatur, sex mensibus missas tantum facere non præsumat. Si vero sæcularium servus esse convincitur, ei qui ordinatus est benedictione servatâ, honestum ordini domino suo impendat obsequium. Quod si sæcularis dominus amplius eum voluerit inclinare, ut sacro ordini inferre videatur injuriam, duos servos sicut antiqui canones habent, episcopus qui eum ordinavit domino sæculari restituat; et episcopus eum quem ordinavit ad ecclesiam suam revocandi habeat potestatem.

That no bishop shall dare to ordain as a clergyman, the slave who shall not have received licence from his proper owners, or a person already freed, without the permission of either the person whose servant he is, or of the person who is known to have freed him. And if any one shall do so, let him who is ordained be recalled by his master, and let him who conferred the order, if it be proved that he did so knowing the state of the person, not presume to celebrate mass for six months only. But if it be proved that he is the servant of lay persons, let the person ordained be kept in his rank and do service for his owner in a way becoming his order; but if his lay owner debases him under that grade, so as to do any dishonour to his holy order; let the bishop who ordained him give, as the ancient canons enact, two slaves to his master, and be empowered to take him whom he ordained to his church.

The canon regards manumission, and the protection of those properly liberated from slavery, against the injustice of persons who disregarded the legal absolution from service.

Canon xii. Et quia plurimorum suggestione comperimus, eos qui in ecclesiis juxta patrioticam consuetudinem a servitio fuerint absoluti, pro libito quorumcumque iterum ad servitium revocari, impium esse tractavimus, ut quod in ecclesia Dei consideratione a vinculo servitutis absolvitur, irritum habeatur. Ideo pietatis causâ communi consilio placuit observandum, ut quæcumque mancipia ab ingenuis dominis servitute laxantur, in eâ libertate maneant, quam tunc a dominis perceperunt. Hujusmodi quoque libertas si a quocumque pulsata fuerit, cum justitiâ ab ecclesiis defendatur, præter eas culpas pro quibus leges collatas servis revocare jusserunt libertates.

And since we have discovered by information from several, that they who, according to the custom of the country, were absolved from slavery in the churches, were again, at the will of some persons, reduced to slavery; we have regarded it to be an impiety; that what has by a judicial decree been absolved from servitude in the church of God, should be set at nought. Wherefore, through motives of piety, it is decreed by common counsel to be henceforth observed, that whatever slaves are freed from servitude by free masters are to remain in that freedom which they then received from the masters; and should this liberty of theirs be assailed by any person, it shall be defended within the limits of justice by the churches, saving where there are crimes for which the laws have enacted that the liberty granted to servants shall be recalled.

It is quite evident, from Exodus xii. 44, that the Israelites, who were themselves slaves in Egypt, also themselves possessed slaves. Also from Nehemiah vii. 67, that the Jews who were slaves in Babylon, yet, upon their liberation, were found to own 7337 slaves; and from the foregoing it appears that the persons then called *liberti* or freedmen, or the *conditionati* or persons under condition, and probably, in some instances, *coloni* or colonists, had slaves, but were not permitted to liberate them, at least without the consent of their own masters, for the canon speaks of only the servants of the *ingenui*, or those who enjoyed perfect freedom. We see, also, what is evident from many other sources, that persons who had obtained their freedom were for some crimes reduced to servitude, and we shall see, in future times, even freemen are enslaved for various offences.

Again, in the canon xxii. of this council, we find provision which exhibits the caution which was used in regulating the right of sanctuary for slaves. This right was, in Christianity, a concession of the civil power, humanely interposing, in times of imperfect security and violent passion, the protecting arm of the church, to arrest the violence of one party, so as to secure merciful justice for the other, and to make the compositions of peace and equity be substituted for the vengeance or the exactions of power. It was, so far from being an encouragement to crime, one of the best helps towards civilizing the barbarian.

Canon xxii. De servis vero, qui pro qualibet culpâ ad ecclesiæ septa confugerint, id statuimus observandum, ut, sicut in antiquis constitutionibus tenetur scriptum, pro concessâ culpâ datis a domino sacramentis, quisquis ille fuerit, egrediatur de veniâ jam securus. Enimvero si immemor fidei dominus transcendisse convincitur quod juravit, ut is qui veniam acceperat, probetur postmodum pro eâ cum qualicumque supplicio cruciatus, dominus ille, qui immemor fuit datæ fidei, sit ab omnium communione suspensus. Iterum si servus de promissione veniæ datis sacramentis a domino jam securus exire noluerit, ne sub tali contumaciâ requirens locum fugæ domino fortasse disperiat, egredi nolentem a domino eum liceat occupari, ut nullam, quasi pro retentatione servi, quibuslibet modis molestiam aut calumniam patiatur ecclesia: fidem tamen dominus, quam pro concessâ veniâ dedit, nullâ temeritate transcendat. Quod si aut gentilis dominus fuerit, aut alterius sectæ, qui a conventu ecclesiæ probatur extraneus, is qui servum repetit personas requirat bonæ fidei Christianas, ut ipsi in personâ domini servo præbeant sacramenta: quia ipsi possunt servare quod sacrum est, qui pro transgressione ecclesiasticam metuunt disciplinam.

We enact this to be observed respecting slaves, who may for any fault fly to the precincts of the church, that, as is found written in ancient constitutions, when the master shall pledge his oath to grant pardon to the culprit, whosoever he may be, he shall go out secure of pardon. But, if the master, unmindful of his oath, shall be convicted of having gone beyond what he had sworn, so that it shall be proved that the servant who had received pardon was afterwards tortured with any punishment for that fault, let that master who was forgetful of his oath be separated from the communion of all. Again, should the servant secured from punishment by the master's oath, be unwilling to go forth, it shall be lawful for the master, that he should not lose the service of a slave seeking sanctuary by such contumacy, to seize upon such a one unwilling to go out, so that the church should not suffer either trouble or calumny by any means on account of retaining such servant: but let not the master in any way rashly violate the oath that he swore for granting pardon. But, if the master be a gentile, or of any other sect proved without the church, let the person who claims the slave procure Christian persons of good account who shall swear for the servant's security in the master's name: because they who dread ecclesiastical discipline for transgression can keep that which is sacred.

LESSON IX.

Bishop England has, in his eighth letter, alluded to the state of society in England and Ireland at this early day, for the purpose of elucidating the fact that the doctrines of the church concerning slavery and the civil condition of those regions were materially without difference from the other parts of Europe. Some portions of his letter, although, perhaps, too distant from our subject, are, nevertheless, too interesting to omit.

About the year 462, Niell Naoigiallach, or Neill of the Nine Hostages, ravaged the coast of Britain and Gaul. In this expedition a large number of captives were made. One youth, sixteen years of age, by the name of Cothraige, was sold to Milcho, and was employed by him in tending sheep, in a place called Dalradia —within the present county of Antrim. This Cothraige was St. Patrick, subsequently the apostle of Ireland.

St. Patrick, in his Confessions, states that many of his unfortunate countrymen were carried off and made captives, and dispersed among many nations.

The Romans had possession of Britain, and even had not

slavery existed there previously, they would have introduced it; but, the Britons needed not this lesson; they had been conversant with it before: we shall see evidence of the long continuance of its practice.

About the year 450, a party of them, among whom were several that professed the Christian religion, made a piratical incursion upon the Irish coast, under the command of Corotic, or Caractacus, or Coroticus.

Lanigan compiles the following account of this incursion from the *Eccles. History of Ireland*, vol. i. c. iv.

"This prince, Coroticus, though apparently a Christian, was a tyrant, a pirate, and a persecutor. He landed, with a party of his armed followers, many of whom were Christians, at a season of solemn baptism, and set about plundering a district in which St. Patrick had just baptized and confirmed a great number of converts, and on the very day after the holy chrism was seen shining in the foreheads of the white-robed neophytes. Having murdered several persons, these marauders carried off a considerable number of people, whom they went about selling or giving up as slaves to the Scots and the apostate Picts. St. Patrick wrote a letter, which he sent by a holy priest whom he had instructed from his younger days, to those pirates, requesting of them to restore the baptized captives and some part of the booty. The priest and the other ecclesiastics that accompanied him being received by them with scorn and mockery, and the letter not attended to, the saint found himself under the necessity of issuing a circular epistle or declaration against them and their chief Coroticus, in which, announcing himself a bishop and established in Ireland, he proclaims to all those who fear God, that said murderers and robbers are excommunicated and estranged from Christ, and that it is not lawful to show them civility, nor to eat or drink with them, nor to receive their offerings, until, sincerely repenting, they make atonement to God and liberate his servants and the handmaids of Christ. He begs of the faithful, into whose hands the epistle may come, to get it read before the people everywhere, and before Coroticus himself, and to communicate it to his soldiers, in the hope that they and their master may return to God, &c. Among other very affecting expostulations, he observes that the Roman and Gallic Christians are wont to send proper persons with great sums of money to the Franks and other pagans, for the purpose of redeeming Christian captives; while, on the contrary, that monster,

Coroticus, made a trade of selling the members of Christ to nations ignorant of God."

The Britons were frequently invaded by the Scots, upon the abandonment of their country by the Romans; and at the period here alluded to, it is supposed by many that the captives taken from Ireland were in several instances given by their possessors to the plundering and victorious Northmen, by the Britons, in exchange for their own captured relatives, whom they desired to release.

About the year 555, Pope Pelagius held, under the protection of King Childebert, the third council of Paris, in which we find a canon, entitled, "De Servis Degeneribus," concerning "bastard slaves," as follows: (See Du Cange.)

Canon ix. De degeneribus servis, qui pro sepulchris defunctorum pro qualitate ipsius ministerii deputantur, hoc placuit observari, ut sub quâ ab auctoribus fuerint conditione dimissi, sive heredibus, sive ecclesiis pro defensione fuerint deputati, voluntas defuncti circa eos in omnibus debeat observari. Quod si ecclesia eos de fisci functionibus in omni parte defenderit ecclesiæ tam illi, quam posteri eorum, defensione in omnibus potiantur, et occursum impendant.

It is enacted concerning bastard slaves who are placed to keep the sepulchres, because of the rank of that office, that whether they be placed under the protection of the heirs or of the church for their defence, upon the condition upon which they were discharged by their owners, the will of the deceased should be observed in all things in their regard. But, if the church shall keep them entirely exempt from the services and payments of the fisc, let them and their descendants enjoy the protection of the church for defence, and pay to it their tribute.

The *auctores*, or authors, in the original sense, were *owners* or *masters;* and subsequently, especially in Gaul, it was often taken to mean *parents*, which probably, from the context, is here its meaning; and, we find a new title and a new class, where the master having committed a crime with his servant, the offspring was his slave; yet, his natural affection caused the parent to grant him a conditioned freedom, to protect which this canon specified the guardian to be either the heir or the church.

Martin, archbishop of Braga, who presided at the third council of that city, in the year 572, collected, from the councils of the east and the west, the greater portion of the canon law then in force, and made a compendium thereof, which he distributed into eighty-four heads, which formed as many short canons, and thenceforth they were the basis of the discipline in Spain.

The forty-sixth of these canons is—

Si quis obligatus tributo servili, vel aliqua conditione, vel patrocinio cujuslibet domûs, non est ordinandus clericus, nisi probandæ vitæ fuerit et patroni concessus accesserit.

If any one is bound to servile tribute, or by any condition, or by the patronage of any house, he is not to be ordained a clergyman, unless he be of approved life, and the consent of the patron be also given.

This canon is taken into the body of the canon law. *Dist.* 53.

Canon xlvii. Si quis servum alienum causâ religionis doceat contemnere dominum suum et recedere à servitio ejus, durissimè ab omnibus arguatur.

If any person will teach the servant of another, under pretext of religion, to despise his master and to withdraw from his service, let him be most sharply rebuked by all.

This too is taken into the body of the canon law. (17, q. 4, *Si quis.*)

In the year 589, the third council of Toledo, in Spain, was celebrated, in the pontificate of Pope Pelagius II. All the bishops of Spain assembled upon the invitation of King Reccared.

The articles of faith form twenty-three heads of various length; after which follow twenty-three *capitula*, or little chapters or heads of discipline.

The sixth of these is in the following words:

De libertis autem id Dei præcipiunt sacerdotes, ut si qui ab episcopis facti sunt secundum modum quo canones antiqui dant licentiam, sint liberi; et tamen a patrocinio ecclesiæ tam ipsi, quam ab eis progeniti non recedant. Ab aliis quoque libertati traditi, et ecclesiis commendati, patrocinio episcopali regantur: à principe hoc episcopus postulet.

The priests of God decree concerning freedmen, that if any are made by the bishops in the way the ancient canons permit, they shall be considered free; yet so that neither they nor their descendants shall retire from the patronage of the church. Let those freed by others and placed under the protection of the church, be placed under the bishop's protection. Let the bishop ask this of his prince.

This too is taken into the body of the canon law. (12, q. 2, *De libertis.*)

A custom had already gained considerable prevalence, which we shall find greatly extended in subsequent ages, of granting to the churches slaves for its service and support. The administrators of the church property were called *familia fisci.* The church property was in ecclesiastical documents styled the *fisc.* The *fisca regis*, or royal fisc, was a different fund or treasury. It sometimes happened that the clergy who were the administrators sought to obtain from the "conditioned slaves" more than they were bound to give, and also, sometimes, others sought to have their service taken from the church. The capitulary viii. of this third council of Toledo was enacted to remedy this latter grievance.

Innuente (other copies, jubente) atque consentiente domino piissimo Reccaredo rege, id præcipit sacerdotale consilium, ut clericorum (others, clericos) ex familiâ fisci nullus audeat a principe donatos expetere; sed reddito capitis sui tributo ecclesiæ Dei, cui sunt alligati, usque dum vivent, regulariter administrent.

By the suggestion (or by the command) and with the consent of the most pious lord King Reccared, the council of priests directs that no one shall dare to reclaim from the administrators of the church those clergy given by the prince; but having paid their tribute to the church of God, to which they are bound, let them, as long as they live, administer regularly.

In the same council, the canon xv. is the following:

Si qui ex servis fiscalibus ecclesias forte construxerint easque de suâ paupertate ditaverint, hoc procuret episcopus prece suâ auctoritate regiâ confirmari.

If any of the king's special servants shall have built churches, and have enriched them by the contributions from their poverty, let the bishop obtain that it be confirmed by the royal authority.

The *servi fiscales* were the private or patrimonial property of the king.

This also exhibits the principle that the slave was not permitted to contribute, without the consent of his owner, to religious establishments.

A canon of the assembly held in Constantinople, 692:

Canon lxxxv. In duobus vel tribus testibus confirmari omne verbum ex Scriptura accepimus. Servos ergo qui a dominis suis manumittuntur, sub tribus testibus eo frui honore decernimus, qui præsentes libertati vires et firmitatem afferent, et ut iis quæ ipsis testibus facta sunt fides habeatur efficient.

We have learned from the Scripture that every word is con-

firmed in two or three witnesses. We therefore declare that slaves who are manumitted by their masters shall be admitted to enjoy that honour under three witnesses, who may be able to afford security by their presence to the freedom, and who may be able to secure credit for the acts done in their view.

LESSON X.

As late as the year 577, Britain furnished other nations with slaves, which is sufficiently proved by the following extract from Bede:

Nec silentio prætereunda opinio quæ de beato Gregorio, traditione majorum, ad nos usque perlata est: quâ videlicet ex causâ admonitus, tam sedulam erga salutem nostræ gentis curam gesserit. Dicunt, quia die quâdam cum advenientibus nuper mercatoribus multa venalia in forum fuissent conlata, multique ad emendum confluxissent, et ipsum Gregorium inter alios advenisse, ac vidisse inter alia pueros venales positos, candidi corporis ac venusti vultûs, capillorum quoque formâ egregiâ. Quos cum aspiceret, interrogavit, ut ajunt, de quâ regione vel terrâ essent adlati. Dictumque est quod de Brittaniâ insulâ, cujus incolæ talis essent aspectûs. Rursus interrogavit, utrum iidem insulani, Christiani, an paganis adhuc erroribus essent implicati? Dictumque est, quod essent pagani. At ille intimo ex corde longa trahens suspiria: "Heu, proh dolor!" inquit, "quod tam lucidi vultûs homines tenebrarum auctor possidet, tantaque gratia frontispicii mentem ab internâ gratiâ vacuam gestat!" Rursus ergo interrogavit, quod esset vocabulum gentis illius? Responsum est quod Angli vocarentur. At ille, "Benè," inquit, "nam et angelicam habent faciem, et tales angelorum in cœlis decet esse coheredes. Quod habet nomen ipsa provincia de quâ isti sunt adlati?" Responsum est quod Deiri vocarentur iidem provinciales. At ille: "Benè," inquit, "Deiri, de irâ eruti, et ad misericordiam Christi vocati. Rex provinciæ illius, quomodo appellatur?" Responsum est quod *Aella* diceretur. At ille adludens ad nomen ait: "*Alleluia*, laudem Dei creatoris illis in partibus oportet cantari." Accedensque ad Pontificem Romanæ et Apostolicæ sedis, nondum enim erat ipse Pontifex factus, rogavit, ut genti Angliorum in Britanniam aliquos verbi ministros, per quos ad Christum converterentur, mitteret: seipsum paratum esse in hoc opus Domino co-operante perficiendum, si tamen Apostolico Papæ hoc ut fieret placeret. Quod dum perficere non posset; quia etsi pontifex concedere illi quod petierat voluit, non tamen cives Romani ut tam longe ab urbe recederet potuere permittere; mox ut ipse pontificatûs officio functus est, perficit opus diu desideratum: alios quidem prædicatores mittens, sed ipse prædicationem ut fructificaret suis exhortationibus et precibus adjuvans.

Nor is that notice of the blessed Gregory which has come down to us by the tradition of our ancestors to be silently passed over: for, by reason of the admonition that he then received, he became so industrious for the salvation of our nation. For they say, that on a certain day when merchants had newly arrived, many things were brought into the market, and several persons had come to purchase; Gregory himself came among them, and saw exposed for sale, youths of a fair body and handsome countenance, whose hair was also beautiful. Looking at them, they say, he asked from what part of the world they were brought; he was told from the island of Britain, whose inhabitants were of that complexion. Again he asked whether these islanders were Christians or were immersed in the errors of paganism. It was said, that they were pagans. And he, sighing deeply, said, "Alas! what a pity that the author of darkness should possess men of so bright a countenance, and that so graceful an aspect should have a mind void of grace within!" Again he inquired what was the name of their nation. He was told that they were called Angles. He said, "It is well, for they have angelic faces, and it is fit that such should be the coheirs with Angels in Heaven." From what province were they brought, was his next inquiry. To which it was answered, The people of their province are called Deiri. *"Good again," said he,* "Deiri, *(de irâ eruti,) rescued from anger and called to the mercy of Christ." What is the name of the king of that province? He was told,* Aella. *And, playing upon the word, he responded, "Alleluia. The praises of God our Creator ought to be chanted in those regions." And going to the pontiff of the Roman Apostolic See, for he was not yet made pope himself, he besought him to send to Britain, for the nation of the Angles, some ministers of the word, through whom they may be converted to Christ; and stated that he was himself ready, the Lord being his aid, to undertake this work, if the pope should so please. This he was not able to do, for though the pon-*

tiff desired to grant his petition, the citizens of Rome would not consent that he should go to so great distance therefrom. As soon, however, as he was placed in the office of pope, he performed his long desired work: he sent other preachers, but he aided by his prayers and exhortations, that he might make their preaching fruitful.

Gregory became pope in 590. Soon after his elevation to the pontifical dignity, he sought to purchase some of the British youths, in order to have them trained up to be missionaries to their countrymen.

The holy see had already a considerable patrimony in Gaul, bestowed by the piety of the faithful: we shall see from the following epistle of the pope to the priest Candidus, whom he sent as its administrator, the use which was made of its income.

Lib. v. Epist. x.—Gregorius Candido Presbytero eunti ad patrimonium Galliæ.

Pergens auxiliante Domino Deo nostro Jesu Christo ad patrimonium, quod est in Galliis gubernandum, volumus ut dilectio tua ex solidis quos acceperit, vestimenta pauperum, vel pueros Anglos, qui sunt ab annis decem et septem, vel decem et octo, ut in monasteriis dati Deo proficiant, comparet; quatenus solidi Galliarum, qui in terrâ nostrâ expendi non possunt, apud locum proprium utiliter expendantur. Si quid vero de pecuniis redituum, quæ dicuntur ablatæ, recipere potueris, ex his quoque vestimenta pauperum comparare te volumus; vel, sicut præfati sumus, pueros qui in omnipotentis Dei servitio proficiant. Sed quia pagani sunt, qui illic inveniri possunt, volo, ut cum eis presbyter transmittatur, ne quid ægritudinis contingat in viâ, ut quos morituros conspexerit debeat baptizare. Ita igitur tua dilectio faciat, ut hæc diligenter implere festinet.

Gregory *to the Priest Candidus, going to the patrimony of Gaul.*

As you are going, with aid of the Lord Jesus Christ, our God, to govern the patrimony which is in Gaul; we desire that out of the shillings you may receive, you, our beloved, should purchase clothing for the poor, or English youths about the age of seventeen or eighteen, that, being placed in monasteries, they may be useful for the service of God; so that the money of Gaul, which ought not to be expended in our land, may be laid out in its own place beneficially. If you can also get any of the money of that income called tolls, (ablatæ,) *we also desire that you should therewith buy clothing for the poor, or, as we have before said, youths who may become proficients in the service of God. But as they who dwell in that place are pagans, it is our desire that a priest be sent with them lest they should get sick on the journey, and he ought to baptize those whom he may see in a dying state. So let you, our beloved, do, and be alert in fulfilling what we have desired.*

The commission of Pope Gregory to purchase those youths was executed. But, as Lingard observes, (Ant. Anglo-Saxon Chu. c. i.,) "their progress was slow, and his zeal impatient." The result was that St. Augustine and his companions were sent by the pope, and effected the conversion of the island.

In the same chapter, Lingard describes the Saxons who had settled in England, previous to their conversion, and refers to Will. of Malmesbury (*de reg.* l. i., c. 3.)

"The savages of Africa may traffic with the Europeans for the negroes whom they have seized by treachery, or captured in open war; but the most savage conquerors of the Britons sold without scruple, to the merchants of the continent, their countrymen, and even their own children."

"But their ferocity soon yielded to the exertions of the missionaries, and the harsher features of their origin were insensibly softened under the mild influence of the gospel. In the rage of victory, they learned to respect the rights of humanity. Death or slavery was no longer the fate of the conquered Britons; by their submission, they were incorporated with the victors; and their lives and property were protected by the equity of their Christian conquerors. * * * The humane idea, that by baptism all men become brethren, contributed to meliorate the condition of slavery, and scattered the seeds of that liberality which gradually undermined, and at length abolished, so odious an institution. By the provision of the legislature, the freedom of the child was secured from the avarice of an unnatural parent; and the heaviest punishment was denounced against the man who presumed to sell to a foreign master one of his countrymen, though he were a slave or a malefactor."

Lingard here refers to the statutes of Ina, quoted in a previous study. But it may be remarked that here is the earliest notice of the African slave-trade, as a branch of European commerce, compared with the ancient slave-trade carried on with Britain.

In his book, "Pastoralis Curæ," *Of the Pastoral Care*, part 3, c. i. Admonit. vi., Pope Gregory VII. says—

ADMONITIO VI.—Aliter admonendi sunt servi, atque aliter domini. Servi scilicet, ut in se semper humilitatem conditionis aspiciant: domini vero, ut naturæ suæ quâ æqualiter sunt cum servis conditi, memoriam non amittant. Servi admonendi sunt ne dominos despiciant, ne Deum offendant si ordinationi illius superbiendo contradicunt: domini quoque admonendi sunt, quia contra Deum de munere ejus superbiunt, si eos quos per conditionem tenent subditos, æquales sibi per naturæ consortiüm non agnoscunt. Isti admonendi sunt ut sciant se servos esse dominorum: illi admonendi sunt ut cognoscant se conservos esse servorum. Istis namque dicitur: *Servi, obedite dominis carnalibus.* Et rursum: *Quicumque sunt sub jugo servi, dominos suos omni honore dignos arbitrentur:* illis autem dicitur: *et vos, domini, eadem facite illis, remittentes minas, scientes quod et illorum et vester dominus est in cœlis.*

ADMONITION VI.—*Servants are to be admonished in one way, masters in another way: servants indeed, that they should always regard in themselves the lowliness of their condition: masters however, that they lose not the recollection of their nature, by which they are created upon a level with their slaves. Slaves are to be admonished not to despise their masters, lest they offend God, if growing proud they contradict his ordinance: masters too are to be admonished; because they grow proud against God by reason of his gift, if they do not acknowledge as their equals, by the fellowship of nature, those whom by condition they hold as subjects. These are to be admonished that they be mindful that they are the slaves of their masters; those that they recollect that they are the fellow-servants of servants. To these it is said:* Servants, obey your masters in the flesh: *and again,* Whosoever are servants under the yoke, let them consider their masters worthy of all honour: *but to those it is said:* And you, masters, do in like manner to them, laying aside threats, knowing that your and their Master is in heaven.

In his book ii. of Epistles, ep. xxxix., writing to Peter, a subdeacon of Campania, he directs him how to act in the case of a female slave, belonging to a proctor or manager of church property, (*defensor,*) who was anxious to be allowed to become a sister in a monastery, which was not lawful without the consent of her owner. The pope neither orders the master to manumit her nor to permit her profession, for, though he was employed by the church, the religion to which he belonged did not require of him to give away his property, nor had the head of that church power to deprive him thereof; hence he writes—

Preterea quia Felix defensor puellam nomine Catillam habere dicitur, quæ cum magnis lacrymis, et vehementi desiderio habitum conversionis appetit, sed eam præfatus dominus suus converti minime permittit: proinde volumus, ut experientia tua præfatum Felicem adeat, atque puellæ ejusdem animum sollicite requirat; et si ita esse cognoverit, pretium ejusdem puellæ suæ domino præbeat, et huc eam in monasterio dandam cum personis gravibus, Domino auxiliante, transmittat. Ita vero hæc age, ut non per lentam actionem tuam præfatæ puellæ anima detrimentum aliquod in desiderio suo sustineat.

Moreover, because the proctor Felix is said to have a servant named Catilla, who with many tears and vehement desire wishes to obtain the habit of religion; but her aforesaid master will not by any means permit her making profession: it is then our desire that your experience would call upon the said Felix, and carefully examine the disposition of that young woman, and if you should find it such as is stated, pay to the master her price, and send her hither with discreet persons, to be placed, with God's help, in a monastery. But do this, so that the soul of the young woman may not suffer any inconvenience in her desire, through your tardiness.

The following is a deed of gift which the same Pope made, to assure the possession of a slave to the bishop of Porto, one of the suburban sees near Rome. It is curious, not merely as exhibiting the fact that the pope and the See of Rome held and transferred slaves at this period, but also as giving a specimen of a legal document of that date and tenor:—

Lib. X. Ep. LII.—Gregorius, Felici Episcopo Portuensi.

Charitatis vestræ gratiâ provocati, ne infructuosi vobis videamur existere, præcipuè cum et minus vos habere servitia noverimus; ideo Joannem juris ecclesiastici famulum, natione Sabinum, ex massâ Flavianâ, annorum plus minus decem et octo, quem nostra voluntate jam diu possidetis, fraternitati vestræ jure directo donamus atque concedimus; ita ut cum habeatis, possideatis, atque juri proprietatique vestra vindicetis atque defendatis, et quidquid de eo facere volueritis, quippe ut dominus, ex hujus donationis jure libero potiamini arbitrio. Contra quam munificentiæ nostræ chartulam nunquam nos successoresque nostros noveris esse venturos. Hanc autem donationem a notario nostro perscriptam legimus, atque subscripsimus, tribuentes etiam non expectatâ professione vestrâ quo volueritis tempore alligandi licentiam legitimâ stipulatione et sponsione interpositâ. Actum Romæ.

Excited by our regard for your charitable person, that we may not appear to be useless to you, especially as we know you are short of servants: we therefore give and grant to you our brother, by our direct right, John, a servant of the church domain, by birth a Sabine, of the Flavian property, now aged about eighteen years, whom by our will you have a good while had in your possession. So that you may have and possess him, and preserve and maintain your right to him and defend him as your property. And that you may, by the free gift of this donation, enjoy the exercise of your will, to do what you may think proper in his regard, as his lord.

Against which paper of our munificence, you may know that neither we nor our successors are ever to come. And we have read this deed of gift, written out by our notary, and we have subscribed the same, not even awaiting your profession, respecting the time you would desire license to register it in the public acts by interposing the lawful process of signature and covenant. Done at Rome, &c.

The *massa* was generally a portion of land of about twelve acres: and the servants belonging specially thereto are in the documents of this and a later period generally called either *servi de* (or *ex*) *massa*, and when they subsequently became *conditioned*, or freed to a certain extent, they were called *homines de masnada*, or other names equivalent thereto.

Lib. V. Ep. XXXIV.—Gregorius, Athemio Subdiacono.

Quantus dolor, quantaque sit nostro cordi afflictio de his, quæ in partibus Campaniæ contigerunt, dicere non possumus: sed ex calamitatis magnitudine potes ipse cognoscere. Eâ de re, pro remedio captivorum qui tenti sunt, solidos experientiæ tuæ per horum portitorem Stephanum virum magnificum transmisimus, admonentes ut omnino debeas esse sollicitus, ac strenuè peragas, et liberos homines, quos ad redemptionem suam sufficere non posse cognoscis, tu eos festines redimere. Qui vero servi fuerint, et dominos eorum ita pauperes esse compereris, ut eos redimere non assurgant, et hos quoque comparare non desinas. Pariter etiam et servos ecclesiæ qui tuâ negligentiâ perierunt, curabis redimere. Quo cumque autem redemeris, subtiliter notitiam, quæ nomina eorum, vel quis ubi maneat, sive quid agat, seu unde sit, contineat, facere modis omnibus studebis, quam tecum possis afferre cum veneris. Ita autem in hâc re te studiose exhibere festina, ut ii qui redimendi sunt, nullum te negligente periculum possint incurrere, et tu apud nos postea vehementer incipias esse culpabilis, sed et hoc quam maxime age, ut si fieri potest, captivos ipsos minori possis pretio comparare. Substantiam verò sub omni puritate atque subtilitate describe, et ipsam nobis descriptionem cum celeritate transmitte.

GREGORY, *to the Subdeacon Anthemius:*

We cannot express how great is our grief and the affliction of our heart, by reason of what has occurred in a part of Campania; but you may yourself estimate it from the extent of the calamity. Wherefore, we send to your experience, by Stephen, a worthy man, the bearer hereof, money for the aid of those captives who are detained; admonishing you that you ought to be very industrious and exert yourself to discover what freemen are unable to procure their own release, and that you should quickly redeem them. But respecting the slaves, when you shall discover that their masters are so poor as not to have it in their power to release them, you will also not omit to buy them. In like manner you will be careful to redeem the servants of the church who have been lost through your neglect.

You will also be very careful by all means to make a neat brief, which you can bring when you come, containing their names, as also where any one remains, how he is employed, or whence he is. You will be diligent, and so industrious in this transaction, as to give no cause of danger by your neglect, for those who are to be released, nor run the risk of being exceedingly culpable in our view. You will be most particular, above all things, to procure the release of the captives at the lowest possible rate. You will make out the accounts as accurately and as clearly as possible, and send them to us with speed.

The calamity which he bewails was an incursion of the Lombards, who, coming originally from Scandinavia, settled for a while in Pomerania, and about this period ravaged Italy.

LESSON XI.

At this age of the world, there still existed a feeling of rivalship between the Jew, the pagan, and the Christian; and, in truth, between some of the different sects of the latter, as to which system of religion should prevail. This state of facts often rendered the condition of the slave peculiar.

The Jew and the Christian were in opposition from the very origin of Christianity. The first persecutors of the Christians were the relatives of the first Christians; the death of the Saviour and the martyrdom of Stephen, the imprisonment of Peter, the mission of Saul to Damascus, and a variety of other similar facts, exhibit in strong relief the spirit of hatred which caused not merely separation, but enmity. The destruction of Jerusalem, the captivity of the people who preserved the early records of revelation, and the increase of the Christian religion, even under the swords and the gibbets of its persecutors, only increased and perpetuated this feeling.

The pride of the Gentile ridiculed what he denominated superstition: while he smote the believer whom he mocked, he bowed before the idol of paganism. The early heresies of those who professed the Christian name, but separated from Christian unity, sprang generally from the efforts to destroy the mysterious nature of the doctrine of the apostles, and to explain it by the system of some Gentile philosopher, or to modify it by superinducing some Judaic rite or principle. The Jew, the Gentile, and the heretic equally felt elevated by his imagined superiority over the faithful follower of the doctrine of the Galilean. Thus the sword of the persecutor, the scoff of ridicule, and the quibbling of a false philosophy, were all employed against the members of the church; and among those who were by their situation the most exposed to suffering, were the Christian slaves of the enemies of the cross. Even they who belonged to the faithful had peculiar trials, because, frequently, in times of persecution, masters, desirous of obtaining protection, without actually sacrificing to idols, compelled their servants to personate them in perpetrating the crime. They were frequently circumcised, even against their will, by the Jewish owners.

They were frequently mutilated by the infidel master. They were also exposed to the continued hardships and enticements of owners who desired to make them proselytes.

It was, therefore, at an early period after the conversion of Constantine, enacted that no one who was not a Christian should hold a Christian slave, upon that principle contained in *Lev.* xxv. 47, 48. We find in the civil code, lib. i. tit. 10, "Judæus servum Christianum nec comparare debebit, nec largitatis aut alio quocumque titulo consequetur." *A Jew shall not purchase a Christian slave, nor shall he obtain one by title of gift, nor by any other title.*

In a subsequent part of the title the penalty is recited, "non solum mancipii damno mulctetur, verùm etiam capitali sententia punietur." *Not only shall he be mulcted by the loss of the slave, but he shall be punished by a capital sentence.*

By a decree of Valentinian III., found after the Theodosian code, and entitled, "De diversis ecclesiasticis capitibus," bearing date 425, Aquileia, vii. of the ides of July, Jews and pagans were prohibited from holding Christian slaves.

Thus by the laws of the empire at this period, no Jew or Gentile could have any property in a Christian slave. This principle was not adopted until a much later period by the Franks and other nations, and this will account for the diversity of legislation and of judgment which the books of the same period exhibit in various regions.

Another clause of the code was more comprehensive: "Græcus, seu paganus, et Judæus, et Samaritanus, et alius hæreticus, id est, non existens orthodoxus, non potest Christianum mancipium habere." *A Greek or pagan, a Jew, a Samaritan, and any heretic, that is, one not orthodox, cannot hold a Christian slave.*

The authority of Gregory over Sicily was not merely spiritual. He had a temporal supervision, if not a full sovereignty, over the island.—The document is ep. xxxvii. lib. ii. indict. xi.

Gregorius Libertino, Præfecto Siciliæ.

De præsumptione Nasæ Judæi, qui altare nomine B. Heliæ construxerat, et de mancipiis Christianis comparatis.

Ab ipso administrationis exordio, Deus vos in causæ suæ voluit vindicta procedere, et hanc vobis mercedem propitius cum laude servavit. Fertur siquidem quòd Nasas quidam sceleratissimus Judæorum, sub nomine beati Heliæ altare puniendâ temeritate construxerit, multosque illic Christianorum ad adorandum sacrilegâ seductione decepit. Sed et Christiana, ut dicitur, mancipia comparavit, et suis ea obsequiis ac utilitatibus deputavit. Dum igitur severissimè in eum pro tantis facinoribus debuisset ulcisci, gloriosus Justinus medicamento avaritiæ, ut nobis scriptum est, Dei distulit injuriam vindicare. Gloria autem vestra hæc omnia districtâ examinatione perquirat: et si hujusmodi manifestum esse repererit, ita districtissime ac corporaliter in eundem sceleratum festinet vindicare Judæum; quatenus hâc ex causâ et gratiam sibi Dei nomine conciliet, et his se posteris pro suâ mercede imitandum monstret exemplis. Mancipia autem Christiana, quæcumque eum comparasse patuerit, ad libertatem, juxta legum præcepta, sine omni ambiguitate perducite, ne, quod absit, Christiana religio Judais subdita polluatur. Ita ergo omnia districtissimè sub omni festinatione corrigite, ut non solum pro hâc vobis disciplinâ gratias referamus, sed et testimonium de bonitate vestrâ ubi necesse fuerit, præbeamus.

Gregory to Libertinus, Prefect of Sicily:

Concerning the presumption of Nasas, a Jew, who had erected an altar in the name of the blessed Elias; and concerning the procuring of Christian slaves.

God has willed that from the very beginning of your administration you should proceed to the avenging of his cause; and he has mercifully kept this reward for you with praise. It is indeed said that one Nasas, a very wicked man, of the Jewish people, has, with a rashness deserving punishment, constructed an altar under the name of the blessed Elias, and deceitfully and sacrilegeously seduced many Christians thither for adoration. It is also said that he has procured Christian slaves, and put them to his service and profit. It has also been written to us that the most glorious Justin, when he ought to have most severely punished him for such crimes, has, through the soothing of his avarice, put off the avenging of this injury to God.

Do you, glorious sir, most closely examine into all the premises; and if you shall find the allegations evidently sustained, hasten to proceed most strictly to have bodily justice done upon this wicked Jew, so as to procure for yourself the favour of God in this case, and to exhibit for your reward, to those who will come after us, an example for imitation. But, further, do you carry through, according to the prescriptions of the laws, to their liberty, without any cavilling, every and any Christian slaves that it may be evident he procured, lest, which God forbid, the Christian religion should be degraded by subjection to the Jews.

Therefore do all this correction most exactly and quickly, that you may not only have our thanks for preserving discipline, but that we may, when opportunity offers, give you proof of our recognition for your goodness.

Canon xxx. of the fourth council of Orleans:

Cùm prioribus canonibus jam fuerit definitum, ut de mancipiis Christianis, quæ apud Judæos sunt, si ad ecclesiam confugerint, et redimi se postulaverint, etiam ad quoscumque Christianos refugerint, et servire Judæis noluerint, taxato et oblato a fidelibus justo pretio, ab eorum dominio liberentur; ideo statuimus, ut tam justa constitutio ab omnibus Catholicis conservetur.

Whereas it has been decreed by former canons, respecting the Christian slaves that are under the Jews, that if they should fly to the church, or even to any Christians, and demand their redemption, and be unwilling to serve the Jews, they should be freed from their owners upon a fair price being assessed by the faithful and tendered for them: we therefore enact that this so just a regulation shall be observed by all Catholics.

At this period, 541, in this province and kingdom, the Jew had a good title to his Christian slave, and could not be deprived of him except by law, or for value tendered.

The first council of Macon was assembled at the request of King Guntram, or Goutran, one of the sons of Clotaire I., to whom the division of Orleans was left upon the death of his father in 561. This assembly was held in 581. The sixteenth canon is—

Et licet quid de Christianis, qui aut captivitatis incursu, aut quibuscumque fraudibus, Judæorum servitio implicantur, debeat observari, non solum canonicis statutis, sed et legum beneficio pridem fuerit constitutum: tamen quia nunc ita quorundam querela exorta est, quosdam Judæos, per civitates aut municipia consistentes, in tantam insolentiam et proterviam prorupisse ut nec reclamantes Christianos liceat vel precio de eorum servitute absolvi. Idcirco præsenti concilio, Deo auctore, sancimus, ut nullus Christianus Judæo deinceps debeat servire; sed datis pro quolibet bono mancipio xii. solidis, ipsum mancipium quicumque Christianus seu ad ingenuitatem, seu ad servitium, licentiam habeat redimendi: quia nefas est, ut quos Christus Dominus sanguinis effusione redemit persecutorum vinculis maneant irretiti. Quod si acquiescere his quæ statuimus quicumque Judæus noluerit, quamdiu ad pecuniam constitutam venire distulerit, liceat mancipio ipsi cum Christianis ubicumque voluerit habitare. Illud etiam specialiter sancientes, quod si qui Judæus Christianum mancipium ad errorem Judaicum convictus fuerit persuasisse, ut ipso mancipio careat, et legandi damnatione plectetur.

And although the mode of acting in regard to Christians who have been entangled in the service of the Jews by the invasions for making captives, or by other frauds, has been regulated heretofore not only by canonical enactments, but also by favour of the civil laws; yet because now the complaint of some persons has arisen, that some Jews dwelling in the cities and towns have grown so insolent and bold, that they will not permit the Christians demanding it to be freed even upon the ransom of their service; wherefore, by the authority of God, we enact by this present act of council, that no Christian shall henceforth lawfully continue enslaved to a Jew; but that any Christian shall have the power of redeeming that slave either to freedom or to servitude, upon giving for each good slave the sum of twelve shillings (solidum): because it is improper that they whom Christ redeemed by the shedding of his blood, should continue bound in the chains of persecutors. But if any Jew shall be unwilling to acquiesce in these enacted provisions, it shall be lawful for the slave himself to dwell where he will, with Christians, as long as the Jew shall keep from taking the stipulated money. This also is specially enacted, that if any Jew shall be convicted of having persuaded his Christian slave to the adoption of Jewish error, he shall be deprived of the slave and amerced to make a gift.

It was only at this period that we find any of the laws of the Franks introducing the right of a Christian to refuse service to a Jew. This, however, was not the case in all the territory, for that over which Guntram ruled was but a fourth part of the empire.

The following is ep. xxi. lib. iii. indic. xii.

GREGORIUS Venantio, Episcopo Lunensi:

Quod Judæi non possunt Christiana habere mancipia: sed coloni et originarii pensiones illis præbere debent.

Multorum ad nos relatione pervenit, a Judæis in Lunensi civitate degentibus in servitio Christiana detineri mancipia: quæ res nobis tanto visa est asperior, quanto ea fraternitati tuæ patientia operabatur. Oportebat quippe te respectu loci tui, atque Christianæ religionis intuitu, nullam relinquere occasionem, ut superstitioni Judaicæ simplices animæ non, tam suasionibus quam potestatis jure, quodammodo deservirent. Quamobrem hortamur fraternitatem tuam, ut secundum piissimarum legum tramitem, nulli Judæo liceat Christianum mancipium in suo retinere dominio. Sed si qui penes eos inveniuntur, libertas eis tuitionis auxilio ex legum sanctione servetur. Hi vero qui in possessionibus eorum sunt, licet et ipsi ex legum distinctione sint liberi; tamen quia colendis eorum terris diutius adhæserunt, utpote conditionem loci debentes, ad colenda quæ consueverant rura permaneant, pensionesque prædictis viris præbeant: et cuncta quæ de colonis vel originariis jura præcipiunt, peragant, extra quod nihil eis oneris amplius indicatur. Quodsi quisquam de his vel ad alium migrare locum, vel in obsequio suo retinere voluerit, ipse sibi reputet, qui jus colonarium temeritate suâ, jus vero juris dominii sui severitate damnavit. In his ergo omnibus ita te volumus solerter impendi, ut nec direpti gregis pastor reus existas, nec apud nos minor æmulatio fraternitatem tuam reprehensibilem reddat.

GREGORY *to Venantius, Bishop of Luna:*

That Jews should not have Christian slaves, but that colonists and those born on their lands should pay them pensions.

We have learned by the report of many persons that Christian slaves are kept in servitude by the Jews dwelling in the city of Luna, which is the more grievous to us as it has been caused by the remissness of you our brother. For it was becoming you, as well by reason of the place you hold, as from your regard for the Christian religion, not to allow the existence of any occasion by which simple souls may be subjected to the Jewish superstition, not only by the force of persuasion, but by a sort of right arising from power. Wherefore we exhort you, our brother, that, according to the regulation of the most pious laws, it should not be permitted to any Jew to keep a Christian slave under his dominion, and that if any such be found under them, the liberty of such should be secured by the process of law and the aid of protection.

And as regards those who are on their lands, though by strict construction of law they may be free, yet, because they have remained a long time in the cultivation of the soil, as bound to the condition of the place, let them remain to till the lands as they have used to do, and pay their pension to the aforesaid men; and let them do all that the laws require of colonists or persons of origin. Let no additional burthen however be laid on them.

But should any one of these desire to migrate to another place; or should he prefer remaining in his obedience, let the consequences be attributed to him who rashly violated the colonial rights, or who injured himself by the severity of his conduct towards his subject.

It is our wish that you be careful so to give your attention to all these letters as not to be the guilty pastor of a plundered flock, nor that your want of zeal should compel us to reprehend our brother.

The law of the empire in force through Italy and Sicily:

1. Slaves who were Christians could not be held by those who were not Christians.

2. It being unlawful for others than Christians to hold them, these others could have no property in them: the persons so held were entitled to their freedom.

3. The church was the guardian of their right to freedom, and the church acted through the bishop.

4. Consequently it was the duty, as it was the right, of the bishop to vindicate that freedom for those so unjustly detained.

5. The right and duty of the pope was to see that each bishop was careful in his charge, and this part of his charge came as much as any other did under the supervision of his superior and immediate inspector, and it was the duty of that superior to reprehend him for any neglect.

6. The law of each country was to regulate the duty of the master and slave, and if that law made, as in Italy and its environs, the church the proper tribunal for looking to the performance of those duties, any neglect of the church in its discharge would be criminal.

7. Through the greater part of Italy and Sicily, at this period, the pope was the sovereign, and it was only by his paramount influence that the half-civilized Gothic and Lombard chiefs were kept in any order, and their despotism partially restrained.

They were times of anarchy, between which and the present no analogy exists. The Jews and separatists from the church were very numerous, and on their side, as well as on that of their opposers, passion frequently assumed the garb of religion, and the unfortunate slave was played upon by each. The position of the pope was exceedingly difficult, for while he had to restrain the enemies of the church on one side, he had to correct the excesses of its partisans upon the other.

LESSON XII.

THE laws of the empire having declared it unlawful for Jews or pagans to hold Christian slaves, the church took a further step, which, in effect, forbade pagan slaves being sold to Jews, and which, to a considerable extent, suppressed their introduction, by the difficulties with which the following order surrounded the traffic. It is found in lib. v. indic. xiv. epist. xxxi.

GREGORIUS, Fortunato Episcopo Neopolitano:

Ne mancipia quæ Christianam fidem suscipere volunt, Judæis venundentur: sed pretium à Christiano emptore percipiant.

Fraternitati vestræ ante hoc tempus scripsimus, ut hos qui de Judaica superstitione ad Christianam fidem Deo aspirante venire desiderant, dominis eorum nulla esset licentia venundandi: sed ex eo quo voluntatis suæ desiderium prodidissent, defendi in libertatem per omnia debuissent. Sed quia quantum cognovimus, nec voluntatem nostram, nec legum statuta subtili scientes discretione pensare, in paganis servis hâc se non arbitrantur conditione constringi: fraternitatem vestram oportet de his esse solicitam, et si de Judæorum servitio non solum Judæos, sed etiam quisquam paganorum fieri voluerit Christianus, postquam voluntas ejus fuerit patefacta, nec hunc sub quolibet ingenio vel argumento cuipiam Judæorum venundandi facultas sit: sed is qui ad Christianam converti fidem desideret, defensione vestrâ in libertatem modis omnibus vindicetur. Hi vero quos hujusmodi oportet servos amittere, ne forsitan utilitates suas irrationabiliter æstiment impediri, sollicitâ vos hæc convenit consideratione servare: ut si paganos, quos mercimonii causâ de externis finibus emerint, intra tres menses, dum emptor cui vendi debeant non invenitur, fugere ad ecclesiam forte contigerit, et velle se fieri dixerint Christianos, vel etiam extra ecclesiam hanc talem voluntatem prodederint, pretium ibi à Christiano scilicet emptore percipiant. Si autem post præfinitos tres menses quisquam hujusmodi servorum velle suum edixerit, et fieri voluerit Christianus, nec aliquis eum postmodum emere, nec dominus quâlibet occasionis specie audeat venundare, sed ad libertatis proculdubio præmia perducatur: quia hunc non ad vendendum, sed ad serviendum sibi intelligitur comparasse. Hæc igitur omnia fraternitas vestra ita vigilanter observet, quatenus ei nec supplicatio quorumdam valeat, nec persona surripere.

"GREGORY to Fortunatus, Bishop of Naples:

"That slaves who wish to embrace the Christian faith must not be sold to Jews, but (the owners) may receive a price from a Christian purchaser.

"We have before now written to you, our brother, that their masters should not have leave to sell those who, by the inspiration of God, desire to come from the Jewish superstition to the Christian faith; but that from the moment they shall have manifested this determination they should be, by all means, protected to seek their liberty. But, as we have been led to know some persons, not exactly and accurately giving heed to our will, nor to the enactments of the laws, think that, as regards pagan slaves, this law does not apply, it is fit that you, our brother, should be careful on this head; and if among the slaves of the Jews, not only a Jew, but any of the pagans, should desire to become a Christian, to see that no Jew should have power to sell him under any pretext, or by any ingenious device, after this his intention shall have been made known; but let him who desires to become of the Christian faith have the aid of your defence, by all means, for his liberty.

"And respecting those who are to lose such servants, lest they should consider themselves unreasonably hindered, it is fit that you should carefully follow this rule: that, if it should happen that pagans, whom they bought from foreign places for the purpose of traffic, should within three months, not having been purchased, fly to the church and say that they desire to be Christians, or even make known this intention without the church, let the owners be capable of receiving their price from a Christian purchaser. But if, after the lapse of three months, any one of those servants of this description should speak his will and wish to become a Christian, no one shall thereafter dare to purchase him, nor shall his master under any pretext sell him; but he shall unquestionably be brought to the reward of liberty, because it is sufficiently intelligible that this slave was procured for the purpose of service, and not for that of traffic. Do you, my brother, diligently and closely observe all these things, so that you be not led away by any supplication, nor affected by personal regard."

The grounds of the law above given may be partially gathered from the following, which is a letter to the bishop of Catania in Sicily. Lib. v. ind. xiv. epist. xxxii.

GREGORIUS, Leoni Episcopo Catanensi:

De Samarœis qui pagana mancipia emerunt et circumciderunt.

Res ad nos detestabilis, et omnino legibus inimica pervenit, quæ, si vera est, fraternitatem vestram vehementer accusat, eamque de minori solicitudine probat esse culpabilem.

Comperimus autem quod Samaræi degentes Catinæ pagana mancipia emerint, atque ea circumcidere ausu temerario præsumpserint. Atque idcirco necesse est, ut omnimodo zelum in hâc causâ sacerdotalem exercens, cum omni hoc vivacitate ac solicitudine studeas perscrutari: et si ita repereris, mancipia ipsa sine morâ in libertatem modis omnibus vindica, et ecclesiasticam in eis tuitionem impende, nec quidquam dominos eorum de pretio quolibet modo recipere patiaris: qui non solum hoc damno mulctandi, sed etiam aliâ erant pœnâ de legibus feriendi.

"GREGORY to Leo, Bishop of Catania:

"Concerning Samaritans (or Jews) who purchased pagan slaves and circumcised them.

"Accounts have been brought to us of a transaction very detestable and altogether opposed to the laws, and which, if true, shows exceedingly great neglect on the part of you, our brother, and proves you to have been very culpable.

"We have found that some Jews dwelling at Catania have bought pagan slaves, and with rash presumption dared to circumcise them. Wherefore it is necessary that you should exert all your priestly zeal in this case, and give your mind to examine closely into it with energy and care; and, should you find the allegation to be true, that you should by all means, and without delay, secure the liberty of the slaves themselves, and give them the protection of the church; nor should you suffer their masters, on any account, to receive any of the price given for them, for they not only should be fined in this amount, but they are liable also to suffer such other punishment as the laws inflict."

LESSON XIII.

In Judea, the creditor could take the children of the debtor, and keep them as his slaves, to labour until the debt was paid; and among the Gentiles this right was not only in existence, but in most cases the child could be subjected to perpetual slavery, and in many instances the debtor himself could thus be reduced to bondage. Improvement had been made in this respect, as will be seen by the following document, found in lib. iii. indic. xii. epist. xliii.

Gregorius, Fantino Defensori:

De Cosma Syro multis debitis obligato.

Lator præsentium, Cosmas Syrus, in negotio quod agebat, debitum se contraxisse perhibuit, quod, et multis aliis et lacrymis ejus attestantibus, verum esse credidimus. Et quia 150 solidos debebat, volui ut creditores illius cum eo aliquid paciscerentur: quoniam et lex habet, ut homo liber pro debito nullatenus teneatur, si res defuerint, quæ possunt eidem debito addici, creditores ergo suos, ut asserit, ad 80 solidos consentire possibile est. Sed quia multum est ut a nil habente homine 80 solidos petant, 60 solidos per notarium tuum tibi transmisimus; ut cum eisdem creditoribus subtiliter loquaris, rationem reddas, quia filium ejus quem tenere dicuntur, secundum leges tenere non possunt. Et si potest fieri, ad aliquod minus quam nos dedimus, condescendant. Et quidquid de eisdem 60 solidis remanserit, ipsi trade, ut cum filio suo exinde vivere valeat. Si autem nil remanet, ad eamdem summam debitum ejus incidere stude, ut possit sibi libere postmodum laborare. Hoc tamen solerter age, ut acceptis solidis ei plenariam munitionem scripto faciant.

"Gregory, to the Proctor Fantinus:

"*Of Cosmas, the Syrian, deeply in debt.*

"The bearer hereof, Cosmas the Syrian, has informed us that he contracted many debts in the business in which he was engaged. We believe it to be true; he has testified it with many tears and witnesses. And, as he owes 150 shillings, I wish his creditors would make some composition with him. And as the law regulates that no freeman shall be held for a debt, if there be no goods which can be attached for that debt, he says that his creditors may be induced to accept 80 shillings; but it is extravagant on their part to ask 80 shillings from a man who has nothing. We have sent you 60 shillings by your notary, that you may have a discrete conference with his creditors, and explain matters to them, because they cannot legally hold his son, whom they are said to keep. And if they will come down to any thing less, by your efforts, than the sum that we send, should any thing remain of the 60 shillings, give it to him to help to support himself and his son; should nothing be left, exert yourself to have his debt cancelled by that amount sent, so that henceforth he may be free to exert himself for his own benefit. But be careful, in doing this, to get for him a full receipt and discharge in writing for this money that they get."

The law to which the pope refers, and by which the persons of the unfortunate debtor and his family were protected, is found in Novell. 134, c. vii., and was enacted by Justinian I. in 541.

Ne quis creditor filium debitoris pro debito retinere præsumat.

Quia verò et hujuscemodi iniquitatem in diversis locis nostræ reipublicæ cognovimus admitti, quia creditores filios debitorum præsumunt retinere aut in pignus, aut in servile ministerium, aut in conductionem: hoc modis omnibus prohibemus: et jubemus ut si quis hujusmodi aliquid deliquerit, non solum debito cadat, sed tantam aliam quantitatem adjiciat dandam ei qui retentus est ab eo, aut parentibus ejus, et post hoc etiam corporalibus pœnis ipsum subdi a loci judice; quia personam liberam pro debito præsumpserit retinere aut locare aut pignorare.

"That no creditor should presume to retain for debt the son of the debtor.

"And because we have known that this sort of injustice has been allowed in several places of our commonwealth,—that creditors presume to keep the children of their debtors, either in pledge or in slavish employment, or to hire them out. We by all means forbid all this: and we order that, if any person shall be guilty of any of these things, not only shall he lose the debt, but he shall in addition give an equal sum, to be paid to the person that was held by him, or to the parents of such person; and, beyond this, he shall be subjected to corporal punishment by the local judge, because he presumed to restrain or to hire out, or keep in pledge, a free person."

The following document will exhibit in some degree the origin of the principle of escheats to be found in slavery. The slave being freed upon certain conditions, if they were not fulfilled the master of course re-entered upon his rights. The manumitted slave was sometimes allowed, not only freedom, but a certain gift, and often with the condition that, if he had not lawful issue, the gift, and its increase by his industry, should revert to the master or his heir. So, in after times, the lord of the soil, or the monarch, gave portions of land to his vassals upon condition of service, and, upon failure of service or of heirs, his land escheated, or went back to the lord of the soil.

The document is found in lib. v. indic. xiv. epist. xii.

GREGORIUS, Montanæ et Thomæ:

Libertatem dat, et eos cives Romanos efficit.

Cum Redemptor noster totius conditor creaturæ ad hoc propitiatus humanam voluerit carnem assumere, ut divinitatis suæ gratia, dirupto quo tenebamur captivi vinculo servitutis, pristinæ nos restitueret libertati: salubriter agitur, si homines quos ab initio natura liberos protulit, et jus gentium jugo substituit servitutis, in eâ naturâ in quâ nati fuerant, manumittentis beneficio, libertati reddantur. Atque ideo pietatis intuitu, et hujus rei consideratione permoti, vos Montanam atque Thomam famulos sanctæ Romanæ ecclesiæ, cui, Deo adjutore, deservimus, liberos ex hac die, civesque Romanos efficimus, omneque vestrum vobis relaxamus servitutis peculium. Et quia tu, Montana, animum te ad conversionem fateris appulisse monachicam: idcirco duas uncias, quas tibi quondam Gaudiosus presbyter per supremæ suæ voluntatis arbitrium institutionis modo noscitur reliquisse, hac die tibi donamus, atque concedimus omnia scilicet monasterio Sancti Laurentii cui Constantina abbatissa præest, in quo converti Deo miserante festinas, modis omnibus profutura. Si quid vero de rebus suprascripti Gaudiosi te aliquomodo celasse constituerit, id totum ecclesiæ nostræ juri sine dubio mancipetur. Tibi autem, suprascripto Thomæ, quem pro libertatis tuæ cumulo etiam inter notarios volumus militare, quinque uncias, quas præfatus Gaudiosus presbyter per ultimam voluntatem hereditario tibi nomine dereliquit, simul et sponsalia quæ matri tuæ conscripserat, similiter hac die per hujus manumissionis paginam donamus, atque concedimus, eâ sane lege, atque conditione subnexâ, ut si sine filiis legitimis, hoc est, de legitimo susceptis conjugio, te obire contigerit, omnia quæ tibi concessimus, ad jus sanctæ Romanæ ecclesiæ sine diminutione aliquâ revertantur. Si autem filios de conjugio, sicut diximus, cognitos lege susceperis, eosque superstites reliqueris, earumdem te rerum dominum sine quadam statuimus conditione persistere, et testamentum de his faciendi liberam tibi tribuimus potestatem. Hæc igitur, quæ per hujus manumissionis chartulam statuimus, atque concessimus, nos successoresque nostros, sine aliquâ scitote refragatione servare. Nam justitiæ ac rationis ordo suadet, ut qui sua a successoribus desiderat mandata servari, decessoris sui proculdubio voluntatem et statuta custodiat. Hanc autem manumissionis paginam Paterio notario scribendam dictavimus, et propriâ manu unâ cum tribus presbyteris prioribus et tribus diaconis pro plenissimâ firmitate subscripsimus, vobisque tradidimus. Actum in urbe Româ.

"GREGORY to Montana and Thomas:

"He emancipates them, and makes them Roman citizens.

"Since our Redeemer, the Maker of every creature, mercifully vouchsafed to take human flesh, that, breaking the chain by which we were held captive, he may, by the grace of his divinity, restore us to our first liberty, it is then salutary that they whom he at first made free by nature, and whom the law of nations subjected to the yoke of slavery, should in the nature in which they were born be restored to liberty by that kindness of their emancipator. And therefore, moved by this consideration, and in respect to piety, we make you, Montana and Thomas, slaves of the holy Roman church, in whose service we are by God's help engaged, from this day forward free and Roman citizens. And we release to you all your allowance of slavery.

"And because you, Montana, have declared that it was your wish to enter into the monastic state, we give and grant to you this day two ounces, which it is well known were formerly left as a legacy to you for inheritance by the priest Gaudiosus, to be by all means available to the monastery of St. Lawrence, over which Constantina is superioress, and into which you desire anxiously by God's mercy to be admitted. But should it appear that you have concealed any of the effects of the said Gaudiosus, the entire thereof doubtless is by right for the service of our church.

"But to you, the said Thomas, whom, in addition to the bestowal of freedom, we desire to be enrolled in service among our notaries, we likewise this day give and grant, by this charter of manumission, five ounces which the same Gaudiosus the priest left to you by name in his last will, and the portion which he assigned for your mother, but upon this ground and condition well attached, that, should you die without issue by lawful marriage, all those goods which we have granted to you shall come back, without any diminution, under the dominion of the holy Roman church; but should you leave behind you children lawfully recognised from your marriage, we give to you full power to hold the same effects as their owner, and without any condition, and to make free disposition of the same by will.

"Know you, therefore, that what we have thus, by this charter of manumission, enacted and granted to you, bind, without any gainsay, ourselves and our successors for its observance. For the order of justice and of reason requires that he who desires his own commands to be observed by his successors, should also doubtless observe the will and the statutes of his predecessor.

"We have dictated this writing of manumission to be copied by our notary Paterius, and have for its most perfect stability subscribed it with our hand, and with those of three of the more dignified priests and three deacons, and delivered them to you.

"Done in the city of Rome, &c."

One of the subjects which at all times caused slavery to be surrounded with great difficulties was the result of marriage. The liability to separation of those married was a more galling affliction in the Christian law, where the Saviour made marriage indissoluble, and it often happened that an avaricious or capricious owner cared as little for the marriage bond as he did for the natural tie of affection. Hence, as Christianity became the religion of the state, or of the great body of the people, it was imperatively demanded that some restraint should be placed upon that absolute power which the owners sometimes abused, of wantonly making these separations. On the other hand, the association of the sexes made marriage desirable: it was ordained by God to be the general state of the bulk of mankind, and even the self-interest or the avarice of the master calculated upon its results. Then again the slave dreaded separation, not only because of the violence committed on the most sacred affections, but also because, though the husband and wife should be separated by impassable barriers, yet the bond of their union subsisted, and could be severed by death alone.

This was a strong temptation to both master and slave to prefer concubinage to wedlock.

Another difficulty arose, in cases of the colonist, by reason of the claims of the several owners where colonists of distinct estates and different owners intermarried. In the case of perfect slaves, the child generally followed the mother, both as regarded condition and property. This was not, however, universally the case. But the owners of colonized lands set up different claims. At length the dispute was settled in the Roman Empire by a law of Justinian, in 539, Novell. clxii. cap. iii., and confirmed by a decision in a case brought up by the church-wardens of Apamea, in Phrygia, in 541, on the kalends of March, by dividing equally the progeny between the estates to which the parents belonged, giving the preference, in all cases of uneven number, to that estate to which the mother was attached. Nov. clvii. tit. xxxix.

The following law concerning marriages and the separation of married persons from each other, and of children from their parents, is of the same date.

NOVELL. CLVII. *De Rusticis qui in alienis prœdiis nuptias contrahunt.* Tit. xl.

Imp. Justin. August. Lazaro Comiti Orientis.

Præfatio. Ex his quæ diverso modo ad nos relata sunt, didicimus in Mesopotamiâ et Osdroenâ provinciis quidquam delinqui, nostris plane temporibus indignum: consuetudinem etiam apud ipsos esse, ut qui ex diversis originem trahant prædiis, nuptias inter se contrahant. Inde sane conari dominos, de facto jam contractas nuptias dissolvere, aut procreatos filios a parentibus abstrahere, exindeque totum illum locum misere affligi, dum et rusticani viri et mulieres ex unâ parte distrahantur, et proles his adimitur, qui in lucem produxerunt, et solâ nostrâ opus esse providentiâ.

Cap. I. Sancimus igitur, ut prædiorum domini de cætero rusticos suos, prout voluerint, conservent: neque quisquam eos qui jam conjuncti sunt possit secundum consuetudinem prius obtinentem divellere, aut compellere ut terram ad ipsos pertinentem colant, abstrahereve a parentibus filios prætextu conditionis colonariæ. Sed et si quid hujusmodi forte jam factum est, corrigi hoc simul, et restitui efficies, sive filios abstrahi contigerit, sive etiam mulieres, nempe vel a parentibus, vel contubernii consortibus: eo, qui reliquo deinceps tempore hujusmodi aliquid facere præsumpserit, etiam de ipso prædio in periculum vocando. Quare libera sunto contubernia metu, qui dudum ipsis immittitur, et parentes habento ex hac jussione filios suos: nequeuntibus prædiorum dominis subtilibus contendere rationibus, et vel nuptias contrahentes vel filios abstrahere. Qui enim tale quid facere præsumpserit, etiam de ipso prædio in periculum veniet, cui eos vindicare rusticos attentat.

Epilogus. Quæ igitur nobis placuerunt, et per sacram hanc pragmaticam declarantur fornam, eam providentiam habeto magnificentia tua, tibique obtemperans cohors, et qui pro tempore eundem magistratum geret; ut ad effectum deducantur conserventurque, trium librarum auri pœna imminenti ei, qui ullo unquam tempore hæc transgredi attentaverit. Dat. Kal. Maii, Constantinop. D. N. Justin. PP. Aug. Bisil. V. C. Cons.

" *Of country persons who contract marriage on divers estates.*

The Emperor JUSTINIAN AUGUSTUS, to Lazarus the Count of the East.

"Preamble. We have learned by relation in various ways, that a delinquency quite unworthy of our times is allowed in the provinces of Mesopotamia and of Osdroene. They have a custom of having marriage contracted between those born on different estates: whence the masters endeavour to dissolve marriages actually contracted, or to take away from the parents the children who are their issue; upon which account that entire place is miserably afflicted, while country people, husbands and wives, are drawn away from each other, and the children whom they brought into light are taken away from them; and that there needs for the regulation only our provision.

" Chapter I. Wherefore, we enact, that otherwise the masters of the aforesaid keep their colonists as they will; but, it shall not be allowed, by virtue of any custom heretofore introduced and in existence, to put away from each other those who were married, or to force them to cultivate the land belonging to themselves, or to take away children from their parents, under the colour of colonial condition. And you will be careful that if any thing of this sort has haply been already done, the same be corrected and restitution made, whether it be that children were taken away from their parents or women from their consorts of marriage. And for any who shall in future presume to act in this way, it shall be at the hazard of losing the estate itself.

"Wherefore, let marriages of servants be exempt from that fear which has hitherto hung over them: and from the issue of this order, let the parents have their children. It shall not be competent for the lords of the estates to strive by any subtle arguments either to take away those who contract marriage, or their children. For he who shall presume to do any such thing shall incur the risk of losing that estate for which he attempts to claim those colonists.

"Epilogue. That therefore which has been good in our view, and is declared by this sacred pragmatic form, let your magnificence provide to have carried into execution, and the cohort which obeys you, as also he who for the time being shall hold the same magisterial office. To the end, then, that this edict may produce its effect and continue in force, let him who may at any time violate its enactments be liable to a penalty of three pounds of gold.

"Given at Constantinople, on the kalends of May, our most pious lord Justinian being Augustus, and the most renowned Basil being consul."

To rectify this, it became a principle, where an estate was large and the colonists numerous, to confine the choice of the servants within the bounds of the property; and thus marriage had its full sanctity, and families remained without separation.

We have an instance of the exercise of this right, by Pope St. Gregory, in a document found in lib. x. indic. v. epist. 28.

GREGORIUS, Romano Defensori.

De filiis Petri defensoris extra massam in qua nati sunt non jungendis.

Petrus quem defensorem fecimus, quia de massa juris ecclesiæ nostræ, quæ Vitelas dicitur, oriundus sit, experientiæ tuæ bene est cognitum. Et ideo quia circa eum benigni debemus existere, ut tamen ecclesiæ utilitas non lædatur: hac tibi præceptione mandamus, ut eum districte debeas admonere, ne filios suos quolibet ingenio vel excusatione foris alicubi in conjugio sociare præsumat, sed in eâ massâ, cui lege et conditione ligati sunt, socientur. In quâ re etiam et tuam omnino necesse est experientiam esse sollicitam, atque eos terrere, ut qualibet occasione de possessione cui oriundo subjecti sunt exire non debeant. Nam si quis eorum exinde, quod non credimus, exire præsumpserit; certum illi est quia noster consensus nunquam illi aderit, ut foris de massâ in quâ nati sunt, aut habitare aut debeant sociari, sed et superscribi terram eorum. Atque tunc sciatis vos non leve periculum sustinere, si vobis negligentibus quisquam ipsorum quidquam de iis quæ prohibemus facere qualibet sorte tentaverit.

"GREGORY to the Proctor Romanus.

"*Of not marrying the children of Peter the Proctor, without the limits of the estate upon which they were born.*

"You, experienced sir, are well aware that Peter, whom we made a proctor, is a native of the estate of our church territory which is called Vitelas. And as our desire is to act towards him with such favour as is compatible with avoiding any injury to the church, we command you by this precept, that you should strictly warn him not to presume, under any pretext or excuse, to have his children joined in wedlock anywhere but on that estate to which they may be bound by law or by condition. In which matter it is quite necessary that you, experienced sir, be very careful, and instil into them a fear to prevent any of them from going on any account beyond the estate to which they are subject by origin. For if any one of them shall presume, as we believe he will not, to go thence, let him be assured that he shall never have our consent either to dwell or to associate himself without the estate on which he was born, but that the land of any such person shall be more heavily charged (*superscribi*). And know you, that if, by your negligence, any of them shall attempt to do any of those things which we prohibit, you will incur no small danger."

Many of the restrictions on marriage that are found in subsequent ages, under the feudal system, had their origin in this principle, because indeed the vassal, in feudal times, was but a slave under a more loose dominion in a mitigated form.

The following document shows that, in the west, the separation of married persons was very uncommon, (quam sit inauditum atque crudele, *unheard of and cruel.*) It is found in lib. iii. indic. iii. ep. xii.

Gregorius, Maximiano Episcopo Syracusano.

De uxore cujusdam ablatâ et alteri venumdatâ.

Tanta nobis subinde mala, quæ aguntur in istâ provinciâ, nunciantur, ut peccatis facientibus, quod avertat omnipotens Deus, celeriter eam perituram credamus. Præsentium namque portitor veniens lacrymabiliter quæstus est, ante plurimos annos ab homine nescio quo de possessione Messanensis ecclesiæ de fontibus se susceptum, et violenter diversis suasionibus puellæ ipsius junctum, ex quâ juvenculos filios jam habere se asseruit, et quam nunc violenter huic disjunctam abstulisse dicitur, atque cuidam alii venumdedisse. Quod si verum est, quam sit inauditum atque crudele malum, tua bene dilectio perspicit. Ideoque admonemus, ut hoc tantum nefas sub ea vivacite, quam te in causis piis habere certissime scimus, requiras atque discutias. Et si ita, ut supradictus portitor insinuavit, esse cognoveris, non solum quod male factum est, ad statum pristinum revocare curabis; sed et vindictam, quæ Deum possit placare, exhibere modis omnibus festinabis. Episcopum vero, qui homines suos talia agentes corrigere negligit atque emendare, vehementer aggredere, proponens, quia si denuo talis ad nos de quoquam qui ad eum pertinet quærela pervenerit, non in eum qui excesserit, sed in ipsum canonice vindicta procedet.

"GREGORY to Maximian, Bishop of Syracuse.

"*Concerning the wife of some one that was taken away and sold to another.*

"We are told of so many bad things done in that province, that we are led to believe, which may God forbid, the place must soon be destroyed.

"Now, the bearer of these presents complained to us in a pitiable manner, that many years ago, some man whom I know not, belonging to the church of Messina stood as his sponsor at baptism, and prevailed upon him by extreme urgency to marry his servant, by whom, he says, he has now young children, and whom now this man has violently taken away and sold to another. If this be true, you, our beloved, will see plainly how unheard of and how cruel is the evil. We therefore admonish you to look into and to sift so great a crime, with that earnestness which we assuredly know you have in matters of piety: and should you come to know that the fact is as the aforesaid bearer has stated, you will be careful not only to bring back to its former state that which was badly done, but you will quickly, by all means, have that punishment inflicted which may appease God. Give a severe lecture to the bishop that neglected to correct or to amend his people who do such things; setting before him that if a like complaint comes, to us again of any one who belongs to him, canonical process for punishment shall issue, not against the one that shall have done wrong, but against himself."

LESSON XIV.

THE form of a deed of gift found in lib. ii. indic. xi. epist. 18:

GREGORIUS, Theodoro Consiliario.

Acosimum puerum dat per epistolam.

Ecclesiasticis utilitatibus desudantes ecclesiasticâ dignum est remuneratione gaudere, ut qui se voluntariis obsequiorum necessitatibus spontè subjiciunt, dignè nostris provisionibus consolentur.

Quia igitur te Theodorum, virum eloquentissimum, consiliarium nostrum, mancipiorum cognovimus ministerio destitutum, ideo puerum nomine Acosimum, natione Siculum, juri dominioque tuo dari tradique præcipimus. Quem quoniam traditum ex nostrâ voluntate jam possides, hujus te necesse fuit scripti pro futuri temporis testimonio ac robore largitatis auctoritate fulciri: quatenus, Domino protegente, securè eum semper et sine ullius retractionis suspicione, quippe ut dominus, valeas possidere. Neque enim quemquam fore credimus, qui tam parvam largitatem pro tuâ tibi devotione concessam desideret, vel tentet ullo modo revocare: cùm uno eodemque tempore, et verecundum sit a decessoribus benè gesta resolvere, et verecundum sit docere ceteros in suâ quandoque resolutoriam proferre largitate sententiam.

"GREGORY, to Theodore the Counsellor.

"*He, by letter, gives him the boy Acosimus.*

"It is fit that they who labour for the benefit of the church should enjoy a reward from the church, that they who voluntarily and of their own accord have undertaken burthensome duties should be worthily assisted by our provision. Because, therefore, we have known that you, Theodore, our counsellor, a most eloquent man, were not well provided with the service of slaves, we have ordered that a boy, by name Acosimus, of the Sicilian nation, should be given up and delivered to your right and dominion. And as you already have him in your possession by delivery, upon our will, it was necessary to fortify you with the authority of this writing as a testimony to the future and for protection of the gift: so that by God's protection you may have power to possess him as his lord and master, always securely for ever and without any question being raised of his being in any way taken back. Nor indeed do we believe that there is any one who would desire or would attempt in any way to revoke so small a bounty given to you for your devotion, since it would be shameful to undo the good deeds of our predecessors, as it would to teach others that each could from time to time make the revocation of his own gift."

The next document is found in lib. x. indic. v. epist. 40:

GREGORIUS, Bonito Defensori.

De mancipio Fortunati Abbatis.

Filius noster Fortunatus abbas monasterii sancti Severini, quod in hâc urbe Romanâ situm est, latores præsentium, monachos suos, illic pro recolligendis mancipiis juris sui monasterii quæ illic latitare dicuntur dirigens, petiit ut experientiæ tuæ ei debeant adesse solatia. Eâ propter præsenti tibi auctoritate præcipimus, ut eis in omnibus salvâ ratione concurrere ac opitulari festines: quatenus te illic coràm posito, atque in hâc causâ ferente solatia, salubriter hæc citiùs valeant quæ sibi injuncta sunt ad effectum, Deo auctore, perducere.

" GREGORY, to the Proctor Bonitus.

" *Concerning the slave of the Abbot Fortunatus.*

" Our son Fortunatus, the abbot of the monastery of St. Severinus which is in the city of Rome, directing his monks, the bearers of these presents to your neighbourhood, to gather slaves belonging to the rights of his monastery, who are said to be there in concealment, begged that he should have your aid for that object. Wherefore, we command you, by this present order, that you would be alert in giving them all reasonable concurrence and aid; so that you being present there and comforting them in this business, they may, with God's aid, be able in a wholesome manner the sooner to perform the duty which has been laid upon them."

The pope did not consider it unbecoming in the monastery of St. Severinus to hold slaves, nor irreligious for the abbot to send monks to bring back runaways, nor criminal for the monks to go looking for them, nor offensive to God, on his own part, to give letters to his officer and overseers to aid by all reasonable means to discover and to capture them.

The following document enters into details for the recovery of a runaway slave. It is found in lib. vii. ind. ii. epist. 107.

GREGORIUS Sergio Defensori.

De Petro puero fugâ lapso.

Filius noster vir magnificus Occilianus, tribunus Hydruntinæ civitatis, ad nos veniens, puerum unum, Petrum nomine, artis pistoriæ, ex jure germani nostri, ad eum noscitur perduxisse. Quem nunc fugâ lapsum ad partes illas reverti cognovimus. Experientia ergo tua, antequam ad Hydruntinam civitatem valeat is ipse contingere, sub quâ valueris celeritate, vel ad episcopum Hydruntinæ civitatis, vel ad prædictum tribunum, si vel alium quem in loco tuo te habere cognoscis, scripta dirigas, ut uxorem vel filios prædicti mancipii sub omni habere debeant cautelâ atque de ipso sollicitudinem gerere, ut preveniens valeat detineri, et mox, cum rebus suis omnibus quæ ad eum pertinent navi impositis, per fidelem personam huc modis omnibus destinari. Experientia itaque tua cum omni hoc studeat efficaciâ solertiâque perficere, ne de neglectu vel morâ nostros quod non optamus animos offendas.

"GREGORY, to the Proctor Sergius.

"*Concerning Peter, a servant who fled away.*

"Our son Occilianus, a highly respectable man, a tribune of the city of Otranto, brought with him to our cousin, as is known, when he was coming to us, a boy named Peter, a baker, who belonged to that cousin. We have now learned that he has run away, and returned to your country. Let then it be your care, experienced sir, before he shall be able to get back to Otranto, to direct, as quickly as you can, a writing to the bishop of Otranto, or to the foresaid tribune himself, or to any one else whom you know, that you can depute, to have a good care of the wife or children of the said slave, and to be very careful respecting himself, that as soon as he shall arrive he may be detained, and sent with every thing that pertains to him, by all means hither, embarking them on board a ship under care of some faithful person.

"You, experienced sir, will therefore exert yourself to do this with all attention and effect, so as not to displease us by a delay or neglect, which we should not desire."

The following is taken from lib. viii. indic. iii. epist. 4.

GREGORIUS, Fantino Defensori.

De mancipiis Romani spectabilis viri.

Mancipia juris Romani spectabilis memoriæ viri, qui in domo suâ quæ Neapoli sita est monasterium ordinari constituit, habitare in Siciliâ perhibentur. Et quia monasterium ipsum juxta voluntatem ejus, Deo auctore, noscitur ordinatum, experientia tua præsentium portitoribus, qui ad recolligenda mancipia ipsa illuc directi sunt, omni studio solatiari festinet, et recollectis eis, possessiones illi ubi laborare debeant, te solatiante, conducant. Et quidquid eorum labore accesserit, reservato unde ipsi possint subsistere, reliqua ad prædictum monasterium, experientiæ tuæ curâ, annis singulis, auxiliante Domino, transmittantur.

"GREGORY, to the Proctor Fantinus.

"*Concerning the slaves of the honourable man Romanus.*

"The slaves of the man of honourable memory, Romanus, who directed that his house in Naples should be formed into a monastery, are said to dwell in Sicily. And as it is known that, with God's help, the monastery has been established according to the regulations of his will; you, experienced sir, will without delay use your best efforts to aid the bearers of these presents, who are sent thither, to collect those slaves: and when they shall be collected, let them hire lands under your countenance, where they may labour; keeping them out of their produce of labour, whatever may be necessary for their support; let the remainder, under the care of you, experienced sir, be sent, with God's help, every year to the foresaid monastery."

GREGORIUS, Vitali Defensori Sardiniæ.

De Barbaricinis mancipiis comparandis.

Bonifacium præsentium portitorem, notarium scilicet nostrum, nos experientia tua illuc transmisisse cognoscat, ut in utilitatem parochiæ Barbaricina debeat mancipia comparare. Et ideo experientia tua omnino et studio sesolliciteque concurrat, ut bono pretio, et talia debeat comparare, quæ inministerio parochiæ utilia valeant inveniri, atque emptis eis huc Deo protegente is ipse celerius possit remeare. Ita ergo te in hac re exhibere festina, ut te quasi servientium amatorem, quorum usibus emuntur, ostendas, et nobis ipsi te de tuâ valeant sollicitudine commendare.

"GREGORY, to Vitalis, Proctor of Sardinia.

"*Of buying Barbary slaves.*

"Know, experienced sir, that Boniface, our notary, the bearer of these presents, has been sent by us to your place to purchase some Barbary slaves for the use of the hospital. And therefore, you will be careful to concur diligently and attentively with him, that he may buy them at a good rate, and such as would be found useful for the service of the hospital. And that having bought them, he may, under the protection of God, very speedily return hither. Do you then be prompt to show yourself in this business so as to exhibit your affection for those who serve the hospital, and for whose use the purchase is made, and that they may have it in their power to commend you to us for your zeal in their regard."

The word *parochiæ*, which is translated "hospital," is more properly *ptochia* in some of the ancient MSS., which is a sort of Latinized imitation of πτωχία—a house for feeding the poor. Gregory had a large establishment of this description in Rome, attended by pious monks, for whose service those barbarians were purchased. Procopius informs us, lib. ii. de Bello Vandanco, cap. 13, who these Barbary slaves were. "When the Vandals had conquered the Moors of Africa, they were annoyed by the incursions of some of the barbarians of the southern part of Numidia. In order to prevent this, they seized upon them, their wives and children, and transported them to the island of Sardinia: kept prisoners and slaves for some time here, they escaped to the vicinity of Cagliari, and, forming a body of 3000 men, they regained a sort of freedom. Gregory made various efforts to convert them. They who were kept in thraldom were frequently purchased, as in this instance, by the Italians and others."

This is the first instance on record of the purchase of negro slaves by the church, and occurred about the year 600. At that time, white slaves cost less than the expense of importation from Africa.

In his sixth book, ep. 21, Gregory commands the priest Candidus, who was his agent in Gaul, to purchase four of the brothers of one Dominic, who complained to him that they were redeemed from their captors by Jews in Narbonne, and held by them in slavery.

The seventh book, ep. 22, to John, the bishop of Syracuse, is a very curious document. It recites the case of one Felix, who was a slave born of Christian parents, and given in his youth as a present to a Jew by a Christian owner: he served illegally during nineteen years the Jew who, was disqualified from holding a Christian slave; but Maximinian the former bishop of Syracuse, learning the facts, had, as in duty bound, Felix discharged from this service and made free. Five years subsequently, a son of the Jew became, or pretended to become, a Christian, and being thus qualified to hold a Christian slave, claimed Felix as his property. Felix appealed to the pope, and the letter to the bishop of Syracuse is a decision in favour of his freedom, containing also an order to the bishop to protect him and defend his liberty.

LESSON XV.

We have heretofore, in our fifth lesson, noticed the doctrine of the church, that the civil power had the prerogative of making laws in regard to slavery; although, at that time, paganism may be said to have governed the world. And while we travel rapidly through the seventh century, finding the Roman Empire, the mistress of the world, now tottering to decay; the Lombards firmly established in Italy; the Franks in Gaul; the Goths in Spain; the Suevi in Portugal; and all Germany filled by various hordes, governed by their petty chieftains, just now showing some symptoms of civilization, and Christianity in the ascendant; yet we find this doctrine of the church unchanged.

The church may now be considered strong; and although the civil power is regarded as the legitimate legislative authority, yet, in no instance, are the laws found to run counter to the doctrines of the church on this subject.

In the precept of King Clotaire II. for endowing the abbey of Corbey, after the grant of the parcels of land therein recited, he adds, "unà cum terris, domibus, mancipiis, ædificiis, vineis, silvis, pratis, pascuis, farinariis, et cunctis appenditiis," &c.—*Together with the lands, houses, slaves, buildings, vineyards, woods, meadows, pastures, granaries, and all appendages.*

And the abbey not only possessed the slaves as property, but by the same precept had civil jurisdiction over all its territory and all persons and things thereon, to the exclusion of all other judges.

The fourth council of Toledo, in 633, in its fifty-ninth canon, by the authority of King Sisenand and his nobles in Spain, restored to liberty any slaves whom the Jews should circumcise, and in the sixty-sixth canon, by the same authority, Jews were thenceforth rendered incapable of holding Christian slaves. The seventieth and the seventy-first canons regulated the process regarding the freed persons and colonists of the church, and the latter affixed a penalty of reduction to slavery for neglect of formal observances useful to preserve the evidence of title for the colonist. The seventy-second canon places the freed persons, whether wholly manumitted or only conditioned, when settled under patronage of the church, under the protection of the clergy.

The seventy-fourth allows the church to manumit worthy slaves belonging to herself, so that they may be ordained priests or deacons, but still keeps the property they may acquire, as belonging to the church which manumitted them, and restricts them even in their capacity as witnesses in several instances; and should they violate this condition, declares them suspended.

In the year 650, which was the sixth of King Clovis II., a council was held at Chalons. The canon begins with the announcement—

Pietatis est maximæ et religionis intuitus, ut captivitatis vinculum omnino à Christianis redimatur. Unde sancta synodus noscitur censuisse, ut nullus mancipium extra fines vel terminos qui ad regnum domini Clodovei regis pertinent, penitus, debeat venumdare; ne, quod absit, per tale commercium aut captivitatis vinculo, vel, quod pejus est, Judaicâ servitute mancipia Christiana teneantur implicita.

"It is a work of the greatest piety, and the intent of religion, that the bond of captivity should be entirely redeemed from Christians. Whence it is known to be the opinion of the holy synod, that no one ought, at all, to sell a slave beyond the dominions of our lord Clovis the king; lest, which God forbid, Christian slaves should be kept entangled in the chains of captivity, or what is worse, under Jewish bondage."

In the tenth council of Toledo, celebrated in the year 656, in the reign of Receswind, king of the Goths, the seventh chapter is a bitter complaint of the practice, which still prevailed among Christians, of selling Christian slaves to the Jews, to the subversion of their faith or their grievous oppression.

In the year 666, a council was held in Merida, in Spain. The eighteenth canon of which allows that, of the slaves belonging to the church, some may be ordained minor clerks, who shall serve the priests as their masters with due fidelity, receiving only food and raiment.

The twentieth chapter complains of many irregularities in the mode of making freedmen for the service of the church, regulates the mode of making them, and provides for the preservation of the evidence of their obligation and the security of their service.

The twenty-first regulates the extent to which a bishop shall be allowed to grant gifts to his friends, the slaves, the freedmen, or others.

The thirteenth council of Toledo was held in the year 683, in the reign of Ervigius, the successor of Wamba. There was an old law of the Goths, found in lib. v. tit. vii., and repeated in other forms in lib. x. and xi., regulating that no freedman should do an injury or an unkindness to his master, and authorizing the master who had suffered, to bring such offender back again to his state of slavery. And in lib. xvii. the freedman, and his progeny for ever, were prohibited from contracting marriage with the family of their patron or behaving with insolence to them. King Ervigius was reminded by many of his nobles that former kings, in derogation of this law, had given employments about the palace to slaves and to freedmen, and even sustained them in giving offence to their masters, had even sometimes ordered them so to do, and protected them; for this the nobles sought redress. The king called upon the council to unite with him in putting a stop to this indignity. And in the sixth canon we have the detail of the evils set forth, and also the enactment, in concurrence with the king, that thenceforward it shall be unlawful to give any employment whatever about the palace, or in the concerns of the crown, to any slave or freedman.

The third council of Saragossa was celebrated in the year 691, in the reign of Egica, king of the Goths.

In Toledo, it had been enacted, that any freedman of the church, who did not comply with certain regulations, should lose his freedom and be reduced to slavery. One of the conditions was, that any person pretending to have been manumitted, or claiming as the descendant of a freedman, should, upon the death of the bishop, exhibit his papers to the successor of the deceased, within a year, or, upon his neglect, should be declared a slave. The object of this was to discern those who were partially free from the perfect slave, and to cause the former to preserve their muniments.

The fathers of Saragossa, however, discovered that some of the bishops, studying their own gain, had been too rigid in enforcing this law, and thereby reduced several negligent or ignorant persons to bondage; in order then to do justice, they enacted in their fourth chapter, that the year within which the documents should be exhibited should not commence to run until after the new bishop, subsequently to his institution, should have given sufficient notice to those claiming to be put in partial service, to produce their papers.

The sixteenth council of Toledo was held in the year 693. The fifth chapter of the acts, determining when a priest may hold two churches, has the following passage:

Ut ecclesia, quæ usque ad decem habuerit mancipia, super se habeat sacerdotem, quæ vero minus decem mancipia habuerit aliis conjungatur ecclesiis.

"That the church which shall have as many as ten slaves shall have one priest over it, but that one which shall have less than ten slaves shall be united to other churches."

In the tenth chapter of the acts of the same council, not only was excommunication pronounced against all who should be guilty of high treason against Egica, the king of the Gothic nation, but the bishops and clergy united with the nobles (*palatii senioribus*) and the popular representatives in condemning traitors and their progeny to perpetual slavery, (*fisci viribus sub perpetuâ servitute maneant religati.*)

The laws of Ina, king of the West Saxons, about the year 692, were made for the regulation of religion:

Servus, si quid operis patrârit die Dominico ex præcepto domini sui, liber esto, dominus triginta solidos dependito. Verum si id operis injussu domini sui aggressus fuerit, verberibus cæditor, aut saltem virgarum metum precio redimito. Liber, si die hoc operetur injussu domini sui, aut servituti addicitor, aut sexaginta solidos dependito. Sacerdos, si in hanc partem deliquerit, pœna in duplum augeator.

"If a slave shall do any work on the Lord's day, by order of his master, let him become free, and let the master pay thirty shillings, (another copy adds, 'ad witam,' as a fine.) But, if he went to this work without his master's command, let him be cut with whips, (another copy has 'corium perdat,' let him lose his skin,) or at least, let him redeem the fear of the scourge by a price. A freeman, if on this day he shall work without the order of his lord, let him be reduced to slavery, or pay sixty shillings. Should a priest be delinquent in this respect, his penalty shall be increased to double."

In the eighth, the division of the weregild for the killing of a stranger:

Wallus censum pendens annuum, 120 solidorum æstimatur, filius ejus 100. Servus, alias 60, alias 50, solidis valere putatur. Wallus virgarum metum 12 solidis redimito. Wallus quinque terræ hydas possidens 600 solidis æstimandus est.

"A stranger paying a yearly rent is to be rated at 120 shillings, his son at 100. A slave at either 50 or 60, is a fair estimation. Let a stranger redeem his fear of whipping for 12 shillings. A stranger being in possession of five hydes of land is to be valued at 600 shillings."

The seventeenth council of Toledo was celebrated in 694, in the reign of Egica. It was enacted—

Si quis servum proprium sine conscientiâ judicis occiderit, excommunicatione biennii sanguinis se mundabit.

"If any one shall put his own slave to death, without the knowledge of the judge, he shall cleanse himself the blood by an excommunication of two years."

In the council of Berghamstead, near Canterbury, held in 697, under Withred, king of Kent, at which Gebmund, bishop of Rochester, was present, and where a sort of parliament also assembled and gave a civil sanction to the temporal enactments and penalties of the canons, several regulations were made concerning slaves. The Saxon MS. is the adoption of the canons into the common law of Canterbury, and is entitled "*The Judgments of Withred.*"

The ninth canon in this collection is the following:

Si quis servum suum ad altare manumiserit, liber esto, et habilis sit ad gaudendum hereditate et wirigildo, et fas sit ei ubi volet sine limite versari.

"If any person shall manumit his servant at the altar, let him be free, and capable of enjoying inheritance and weregild, and let it be lawful for him to dwell where he pleases without limit."

The tenth canon is:

Si in vesperâ præcedente diem solis postquam sol occubuit, aut in vesperâ præcedente diem lunæ post occasum solis, servus ex mandato domini sui opus aliquod servile egerit, dominus factum octoginta solidis luito.

"If on the evening preceding Sunday, after the sun has set, or on the evening preceding Monday, after the setting of the sun, a slave shall do any servile work by command of his master, let the master compensate the deed by eighty shillings."

The eleventh:

Si servus hisce diebus itineraverit, domino pendat sex solidos, aut flagello cædatur.

"If a servant shall have journeyed on these days, let him pay six shillings to his master, or be cut with a whip."

The thirteenth:

Si paganus uxore nesciâ diabolo quid obtulerit, omnibus fortunis suis plectatur et collistrigio. Sin et ambo pariter itidem fecerint, omnium bonorum suorum amissione ipsa etiam luat et collistrigio.

"If a villain, without the knowledge of his wife, shall have offered any thing to the devil, let him be punished by the loss of all his fortune and by the pillory. And if both did so together, let her also lose all her goods and be punished by the pillory."

The English *villain* was the *colonist* of the European continent, and in the Speculum Saxonicum, lib. i. art. 3, his imperfect liberty is compared with the freeman. Also in Du Cange, Paganus, Pagenses, &c.

The fourteenth:

Si servus diabolo offerat, sex dependat solidos, aut flagro vapulet.

"If a slave offers to the devil, let him pay six shillings, or be whipped."

The fifteenth:

Si quis servo carnem in jejunio dederit comedendam, servus liber exeat.

"If any one shall give his slave flesh-meat to eat on a fast-day, let the slave go out free."

The sixteenth:

Si servus ex sponte suâ eam ederit, aut sex solidis aut flagello.

"If the slave shall eat it of his own motion, let the penalty be either six shillings or a whipping."

After regulating the mode of declaration of swearing and of compurgation, for the king, the bishop, the abbot, the priest, the deacon, the cleric, the stranger, and the king's thane, the twenty-first canon enacts—

Paganus cum quatuor compurgatoribus, capite suo ad altare inclinato, semet eximat.

"Let the villain deliver himself with four compurgators, with his head bowed down to the altar."

The twenty-third:

Si quis Dei mancipium in conventu suo accusaverit, dominus ejus eum simplici suo juramento purgabit, si eucharistiam susceperit. Ad eucharistiam autem si nusquam venerit, habeat in juramento fidejussorem bonum, vel solvat, vel se tradat flagellandum.

"If any person shall accuse a slave of God in his convent, his lord shall purge him with a simple oath, if he shall have received the eucharist. But if he has never côme to the eucharist, let him in his oath have a good surety to answer, or let him pay or give himself up to be whipped."

The slave of God was one belonging to a monastery, of whom there appear to have been a good number in Englánd, at that period, as well as on the continent. The previous canon had legislated for the bishop's dependants as distinguished from the slave of the monastery.

The twenty-fourth canon is:

Si servus viri popularis servum viri ecclesiastici accusaverit, vel servus ecclesiastici servum viri popularis, dominus ejus singulari suo juramento eum expurgabit.

"If the slave of a lay person shall accuse the slave of a clergyman, or if the slave of a clergyman shall accuse the slave of a layman, let his master purge him by his single oath."

The twenty-seventh regulated the punishment of the person who permitted a thievish slave to escape, and, respecting the slave himself, concluded thus:

Si quis eum occiderit, domino ejus dimidium pendito.

"If any one shall slay him, let him pay to his master one-half."

In Germany, however, as yet, in most places paganism prevailed, and human sacrifices were offered. St. Boniface had been sent by the Holy See to endeavour to reclaim to religion and to civilization the nations or tribes that composed this undefined extent of territory. We find in a letter of Pope Gregory III., written in answer to his request for special instructions, about the year 735, the following paragraph:

Hæc quoque inter alia crimina agi in partibus illis dixisti, quod quidam ex fidelibus ad immolandum paganis sua venumdent mancipia. Quod ut magnopere corrigere debeas, frater, commonemus, nec sinas fieri ultra: scelus est enim et impietas. Eis ergo qui hæc perpetraverunt, similem homicidæ indices pœnitentiam.

"You have said that, among other crimes, this was done in those parts, that some of the faithful sold their slaves to pagans to be immolated. Which you should use all your power to correct, nor allow it to be done any more: for it is wickedness and impiety. Impose then upon its perpetrators the same penance as for homicide."

LESSON XVI.

Theodore, archbishop of Canterbury, governed the English church from 670 to 690, when he died. The following extracts are from his canonical regulations:

VII. Græci et Romani dant servis suis vestimenta, et laborant excepto Dominico die. Græcorum monachi servos non habent, Romani habent.

"The Greeks and Romans give clothing to their slaves, and they work except on the Lord's day. The Greek monks have not slaves, the Romans have."

XVII. Ingenuus cum ingenuâ conjungi debet.

"A free man should be married to a free woman."

LXV. Qui per jussionem domini sui occiderit hominem, dies xl. jejunet.

"He who, by the command of his master, shall kill a man, shall fast forty days."

The seventy-first prohibits the intermarriages of those slaves whose owners will prevent their living together.

The seventy-fourth regulates, that if a free pregnant woman be sold into slavery, the child that she bears shall be free; all subsequently born shall be slaves.

LXXIX. Pater filium necessitate coactus in servitium sine voluntate filii tradat.

"A father, compelled by necessity, may deliver his son into slavery without the will of that son."

LXXXIX. Episcopus et abbas hominem sceleratum servum possunt habere, si precium redimendi non habet.

"A bishop or an abbot can hold a criminal in slavery, if he have not the price of his redemption."

CXVII. Servo pecuniam per laborem comparatam nulli licet auferre.

"It is not lawful for any one to take away from a slave the money made by labour."

In the council of Verberie, held in a palace of King Pepin, the sixth canon made regulations in the case of marriage between free persons and slaves. The following are its provisions:

1. If any free person contracted marriage with a slave, being at the time ignorant of the state of bondage of that party, the marriage was invalid.

2. If a person under bond should have a semblance of freedom by reason of condition, and the free person be ignorant of the bondage, and this bond person should be brought into servitude, the marriage was declared originally void.

3. An exception was made where the bond person, by reason of want, should, with the consent of the free party, sell himself or herself into perfect slavery with the consent of the free party; then the marriage was to stand good, because the free party had consented to the enslavement, and profited of its gains.

The seventh canon would seem to show that a slave could hold property in slaves:

Si servus suam ancillam concubinam habuerit, si ita placet, potest illâ dimissâ comparem suam ancillam domini sui accipere: sed melius est suam ancillam tenere.

"If a man-servant shall have his own female slave as a concubine, he shall have power, if he wishes, leaving her, to marry his equal, the female servant of his master: but it is better that he should keep his own servant in wedlock."

The eighth canon provided, in the case of a freedman who, subsequently to his liberation, committed sin with the female slave of his former master, that the master should have power, whether the freedman would or not, to compel him to marry that female slave; and should this man leave her, and attempt a marriage with another woman, this latter must be separated from him.

The thirteenth declares that when a freeman, knowing that the woman whom he is about to marry is a slave, or, not having known it until after marriage, voluntarily upon the discovery consents to the marriage, it is thenceforth indissoluble.

The nineteenth declares that the separation of married parties, by the sale of one who is a slave, does not affect the marriage. They must be admonished, if they cannot be reunited, to remain continent.

The twentieth provides for the case of a male slave freed by letter, (*chartellarius*,) who, having for his wife taken a slave with the lawful consent of her master, and leaving her, takes another as his wife. The latter contract is void, and the parties must separate.

Another assembly was held by King Pepin, in Compeigne, forty-eight miles north-east of Paris, where he had a country-seat. At this assembly also the prelates held a council in 757, and made eighteen canons. The fourth makes provision for the case of a man's giving his free step-daughter in wedlock to a freeman or to a slave. The fifth declares void the marriage between a free person and a slave, where the former was ignorant of the condition of the latter. The sixth regards a case of a complicated description, where a freeman got a civil benefice from his lord, and takes his own vassal with him, and dies upon the benefice, leaving after him the vassal. Another freeman becomes invested with the benefice, and, anxious to induce the vassal to remain, gives him a female serf attached to the soil as his wife. Having lived with her for a time, the vassal leaves her, and returns to the lord's family, to which he owed his services, and there he contracts a marriage with one of the same allegiance. His first contract was invalid, the second was the marriage.

In the year 772, a council was held in Bavaria, at a place called

Dingolvinga, the present city of Ingolstadt, in the reign of Tassilo, duke of Bavaria. The tenth canon of this council decides that a noble woman, who had contracted marriage with a slave, not being aware of his condition, is at liberty to leave him, the contract being void, and she is to be considered free and not to be reduced to slavery. By *noble* we are here to understand *free*, as distinguished from *ignoble*, that is, a slave.

We have then sixteen amendments of the national law.

The first regulates, by the authority of the prince and consent of the whole assembly, that henceforth no slave, whether fugitive or other, should be sold beyond the limits of the territory, under penalty of the payment of his weregild.

In the second, among other things, it is enacted that if a slave should be killed in the commission of house-breaking, his owner is to receive no compensation; and should the felon who is killed in man-stealing, when he could not be taken, whether it be a freeman or a slave that he is carrying off, no weregild shall be paid by the slayer, but he shall be bound to prove his case before a court.

The seventh regards the trial by ordeal of slaves freed by the duke's hand.

The eighth establishes and guards the freedom, not only of themselves, but of their posterity, of those freed in the church, unless when they may be reduced to slavery from inability to pay for damages which they had committed.

The ninth contains, among other enactments, those which explain the tenth canon of the council. After specifying different weregilds for freed persons, it says—

Si ancilla libera dimissa fuerit per chartam aut in ecclesiâ, et post hæc servo nupserit, ecclesiæ ancilla permanebit.

"Should a female slave be emancipated by deed or in the church, and afterwards marry a slave, she shall be a slave to the church."

It then continues, respecting a woman originally free, and the *nobilis* of canon x.:

Si autem libera Bajoaria servo ecclesiæ nupserit, et servile opus ancilla contradixerit, abscedat.

"But if a free Bavarian female shall have married a servant of the church, and the maid will not submit to servile work, she may depart."

Si autem ibi filios et filias generaverit, ipsi servi et ancillæ permaneant, potestatem exinde (exeundi) non habeant.

"But if she shall have there borne sons and daughters, they shall continue slaves, and not have power of going forth."

Her freedom was not, however, immediately destroyed, for the law proceeds—

Illa autem mater eorum, quando exire voluerit, ante annos iii, liberam habeat potestatem.

"But she, their mother, when she may desire to go forth before three years, shall have free power therefor."

In this case the marriage subsisted, but the free woman could separate, without however the marriage-bond being rent. If she remained beyond the time of three years, she lost her freedom; and it shows us that, probably, previous to this amendment, any free woman who married a slave, thereby lost her own freedom; and that the tenth canon, showing the marriage of which it treated to be invalid, showed that the woman should not lose her liberty. The concluding provision of the ninth law is as follows:

Si autem iii annos induraverit opus ancillæ, et parentes ejus non exadomaverunt eam ut libera fuisset, nec ante comitem, ducem, nec ante regem, nec in publico mallo, transactis tribus kalendis Martis, (Martu,) post hæc ancilla permaneat in perpetuum, et quicumque ex ea nati fuerint servi et ancillæ sunt.

"But if she shall have continued three years doing the work of a slave, and her relations have not brought her out so that she should be free, either before the count, or the duke, or the king, or in the public high court, (mall,) when the kalends of March shall have thrice passed, after this she shall remain perpetually a slave, and they who shall be born of her, male and female, shall be slaves."

In 774, Pope Adrian I. delivered to Charlemagne a digest of canon law, then in force, in which we find—

"The third of Gangræ, condemning as guilty of heresy those who taught that religion sanctioned the slave in despising his master; the thirtieth in the African collection, which showed that the power of manumission in the church was derived from the civil authority; the one hundred and second of the same, which declared slaves and freed persons disqualified to prosecute, except in certain cases and for injuries done to themselves."

In a capitulary of Charlemagne, published in such a synod and general assembly in 779, in the month of March, in the eleventh year of his reign, at Duren, on the Roer, (Villa Duria,) between Cologne and Aix-la-Chapelle, there being assembled episcopis, abbatibus, virisque illustribus, comitibus, unâ cum piissimo domino nostro,—"the bishops, abbots, and the illustrious men, the counts, together with our most pious lord,"—we find the following chapter:

XX. De mancipiis quæ venduntur, ut in præsentiâ episcopi vel comitis sit, aut in præsentiâ archdiaconi, aut centenarii, aut in præsentiâ vicedomini, aut judicis comitis, aut ante bene nota testimonia. Et foras marcham nemo mancipium vendat. Qui fecerit, tantis vicibus bannos solvet, quanta mancipia vendidit. Et si non habet precium vivadio, pro servo semetipsum donet comiti, usquèdum ipsos bannos solvat.

"Concerning slaves that are sold, let it be in presence of the bishop, or of the count, or in presence of the archdeacon, or of the judge of the hundred, or in presence of the lord's deputy, or of the judge of the county, or of well known witnesses. And let no one sell a slave beyond the boundary. Whosoever shall do so shall pay as many fines as he sold slaves. And if he has not the money, let him deliver himself to the count in pledge as a slave until he shall pay the fines."

In a capitulary of Pope Adrian I., containing the summary of the chief part of the canon law then in force, as collected from the ancient councils and other sources, delivered to Ingilram, bishop of Metz, or, as it was then called, Divodurum, or oppidum Mediomatricorum, on the 19th of September, xiii. kalendas Octobris, indic. ix. 785, the sixteenth chapter, describing those who cannot be witnesses against priests, mentions not merely slaves, but quorum vitæ libertas nescitur, those *who are not known to be free;* and in the notes of Anthony Augustus, bishop of Tarragona, on this capitulary, he refers for this and another passage, viles personæ, *persons of vile condition*, which is the appellation of slaves, to decrees of the earliest of popes, viz., Anacletus, A. D. 91, and Clement his immediate successor; Evaristus, who was the next, and died A. D., 109; Pius, who died A. D. 157; Calistus, in 222; Fabian, 250; and several others. In chapter xxi. among incompetent witnesses, are recited, nullus servus, nullus libertus—*no slave, no freedman.* The notes of the same author inform us that this portion of the chapter is the copy of an extract from the first council of Nice, and that it is also substantially found in a passage from Pope Pontianus, who died in 235, as well as in several of the early African and Spanish councils, which he quotes.

One of these assemblies, in which Charlemagne published a capitulary, was held at Aix-la-Chapelle (Aquisgranum) in 789, in which eighty-two chapters were enacted. No. xxiii. is founded upon canon iv. of the council of Chalcedon, and upon an enactment of Leo the Great. It prohibited all attempts to induce a slave to embrace either the clerical or monastical state without the will and license of the master. No. xlv. prohibits, among others, slaves from being competent witnesses, or freedmen against their patrons: founded upon the ninety-sixth canon of the African councils. No. lvii. referring to the third canon of the council of Gangræ, prohibits bishops ordaining slaves without the master's license.

In 794 a council was held at Frankfort on the Maine, at which the bishops of a large portion of Europe assisted; the twenty-third canon of which is the following:

De servis alienis, ut a nemine recipiantur, neque ab episcopis sacrentur sine licentiâ dominorum.

"Of servants belonging to others: they shall be received by no one, nor admitted to orders by bishops, without their masters' license."

In the year 697, at another assembly held at Aix-la-Chapelle, the capitulary for the pacification and government of Saxony was enacted by Charlemagne. The eighth chapter is—

Si quis hominem diabolo sacrificaverit, et hostiam in more paganorum dæmonibus obtulerit, morte moriatur.

"If any person shall sacrifice a man to the devil, and offer him as a victim to devils after the fashion of pagans, he shall be put to death."

An explanation of this will be found where Pope Gregory III. answers St. Boniface, who informed him that unfortunate slaves were bought to be thus immolated.

XI. Si quis filiam domini sui rapuerit, morte moriatur.

"If any one shall do violence to his master's daughter, he shall be put to death."

XII. Si quis dominum suum vel dominam suam interfecerit, simili modo puniatur.

"If any one shall kill his master or his mistress, he shall be punished in like manner."

XIV. De minoribus capitulis consenserunt omnes, ad unamquamque ecclesiam curtem et duas mansas terræ pagenses ad ecclesiam recurrentes condonent: et inter centum viginti homines nobiles et ingenuos, similiter et litos, servum et ancillam eidem ecclesiæ tribuant.

"All agreed concerning the smaller congregations, that the colonists frequenting each church should bestow upon it one dwelling, with proper out-offices, and two manses (24 acres) of land; and that they should give to the same church one male slave and one female slave between one hundred and twenty noble and free men, and counting also the conditioned servants."

In this newly settled ecclesiastical province the provision made for the support of religion consisted of land and slaves.

LESSON XVII.

Upon the ascension of Charlemagne to the imperial throne, the Roman Empire may date its extinction. But, in the reign of the Franks, in their succession to the throne of the western empire, we fail to find any change of doctrine on the subject of slavery. But the Lombards had long disturbed Italy: Charlemagne succeeded in reducing them to better order, and, in the year 801, amended their laws. One chapter assimilated to that of France and of Germany:

VI. *De Aldionibus publicis ad jus publicum pertinentibus.*

Aldiones vel Aldianes eâ lege vivant in Italiâ, in servitute dominorum suorum, quâ fiscalini vel liddi vivunt in Franciâ.

"*Of the public Aldions, belonging to the public estate.*

"The Aldions, or Aldians, shall in Italy exist upon the same principle in the service of their masters that the fiscals and lids do exist in France."

The Aldions were bond-men or bond-women, whose persons were not at the disposal of their masters, nor did they pass with the land as colonists did, but their masters or patrons had certain claims upon stated services from them. They were generally either freed persons or the descendants of those who had been manumitted upon the condition of performing stipulated services; and if they failed to perform these, they were liable to be reduced to slavery. The *lidus* or *liddus* or *litus* of the Saxon was so called from being spared in the conquest, and left on the land, with the obligation of paying the master, who owned it and himself, a certain portion of its produce, and doing him other fixed services. Thus neither of them was an absolute slave whose person and property were at the owner's disposal. The slave was manumitted, but this latter description of servants were generally released by deed or charter: hence, when so freed, they were called *chartulani*, *chartellani*, or "chartered." The transition from slavery to this latter kind of servitude was, at the commencement of the ninth century, greatly on the increase.

VIII. *De servis fugacibus.*

Ubique intra Italiam, sive regius, sive ecclesiasticus, vel cujuslibet alterius hominis servus fugitivus inventus fuerit à domino suo sine ullâ annorum præscriptione vindicetur, eâ tamen ratione, si dominus Francus sive Alemannus, aut alterius cujuslibet nationis sit. Si verò Longobardus aut Romanus fuerit, eâ lege servos suos vel adquirat vel admittat, quæ antiquitùs inter eos constitutus est.

"*Concerning runaway slaves.*

"Wheresoever within the bounds of Italy, either the runaway slave of the king or of the church or of any other man shall be found by his master, he shall be restored without any bar of prescription of years; yet upon the provision that the master be a Frank or a German or of any other nation, (foreign.) But if he be a Lombard or a Roman, he shall acquire or receive his slaves by that law which has been established from ancient times among them."

Here is evidence of the prevalent usage of the church holding property in slaves, just as commonly as did the king or any other person.

In the year 805, Charlemagne published a capitulary at Thionville, in the department of Moselle, France, (Theodonis villa.) In the chap. xi. we read—

De servis propriis vel ancillis.

De propriis servis et ancillis, ut non suprà modum in monasteria sumantur, ne deserentur villæ.

"*Concerning their own male or female slaves.*

"Let not an excessive number of their own male or female slaves be taken into the monasteries, lest the farms be deserted."

This capitulary regards principally the regulation of monasteries.

St. Pachomius, who was born in Upper Egypt, in 292, and who was the first that drew up a regular monastic rule, would never admit a slave into a monastery. *Tillemont*, vii. p. 180.

In the year 813, a council was held at Chalons, the portions of whose enactments in any way affecting property or civil rights were confirmed by Charlemagne and made a portion of the law of the empire.

Many of the churches, especially in the country, were curtailed in their income and reduced to difficulties, because the bishops and abbots had large estates within their parishes, and many servants occupied in their cultivation, and the prelates prevented these servants paying tithes to the parish clergy, claiming for themselves an exemption from the obligation. The canon xix. is the following:

Questi sunt præterea quidam fratres, quod essent quidam episcopi et abbates, qui decimas non sinerent dari ecclesiis ubi illi coloni missas audiunt. Proinde decrevit sacer ille conventus, ut episcopi et abbates de agris et vineis, quæ ad suum vel fratrum stipendium habent, decimas ad ecclesias deferri faciant: familiæ vero ibi dent decimas suas, ubi infantes eorum baptizantur, et ubi per totum anni circulum missas audiunt.

"Moreover some brethren have complained, that there were some bishops and abbots who would not permit tithes to be given to those churches where colonists hear mass. Wherefore that holy assembly decreed, that, for those fields and vineyards which they have for their own support or that of their brethren, the bishops and abbots should cause the tithe to be paid to the churches. And let the servants pay their tithes to the church where their infants are baptized, and where during the year they hear mass."

In this we have additional evidence of the fact that large bodies of land, and numerous servants attached to them, were held by bishops and abbots, not only for themselves, but for their churches and their monasteries. The canon xxx. is the following:

Dictum nobis est quod quidam legitima servorum matrimonia potestivâ quâdam præsumptione dirimant, non attendentes illud evangelicum: *Quod Deus conjunxit, homo non separet.* Unde nobis visum est, ut conjugia servorum non dirimantur, etiam si diversos dominos habeant: sed in uno conjugio permanentes dominis suis serviant. Et hoc in illis observandum est, ubi legalis conjunctio fuit, et per voluntatem dominorum.

"It has been stated to us that some persons, by a sort of magisterial presumption, dissolve the lawful marriages of slaves; not regarding that evangelical maxim, *What God hath put together, let man not separate.* Whence it appears to us, that the wedlock of slaves may not be dissolved, even though they have different masters; but let them serve their masters, remaining in one wedlock. And this is to be observed with regard to those where there has been a lawful union, and with the will of the owners."

In the year 816, a council was held at Aix-la-Chapelle, in which a large portion of the canon law then in force regarding the clergy was imbodied into one hundred and forty-five chapters. After the session of the council, the emperor published a capitulary containing thirty chapters; the sixth of which complains of the continued indiscretion of bishops in ordaining servants, contrary to the canons, and forbids such ordinations except upon the master's giving full liberty to the slave. If a servant shall impose upon a bishop by false witnesses or documents of freedom, and thus procure ordination, he shall be deposed and taken back by his owner. If the descendant of a slave who came from abroad shall have been educated and ordained, where there was no knowledge of his condition, should his owner subsequently discover him and prove his property, if this owner grants him liberty, he may keep his clerical rank; but if the master asserts his right and carries him away, though the slave does not lose his character of order, he loses his rank, and cannot officiate. Should masters give servants freedom that they may be capable of ordination, it shall be in the master's discretion to give or to withhold the property necessary to enable the person to get orders.

The archbishops are to have in each province the emperor's authority in the original, to authorize their ordaining the servants of the church, and the suffragan bishops are to have copies of this original, and when such servant is to be ordained, this authority must be read for the people from the pulpit or at the corner of the altar. The like form was to be observed when any of the laity desired to have any servant of the church promoted to orders, or when the like promotion was petitioned for by the prior of a chapter or of a monastery. Lotharius, the emperor, published a capitulary in Rome, in 842.

In the third chapter of the first part, we find the following expression:

In electione autem Romani pontificis nullus, sive liber sive servus, præsumat aliquod impedimentum facere.

"Let no one, whether freeman or slave, presume to create any impediment in the election of the Roman pontiff."

Which leads us to suspect that some slaves possessed considerable power or influence.

In the second chapter, fines are imposed for creating riots in any church. And the chapter concludes in the following words:

Et qui non habet unde ad ecclesiam persolvat, tradat se in servitio eidem ecclesiæ, usque dum totum debitum persolvat.

"And let him who has not the means of paying the church, give himself in servitude to that same church until he pays the whole debt."

By the tenth chapter he restrained the power of manumission.

Quod per xxx annos servus liber fieri non possit, si pater illius servus, aut mater ancilla fuit. Similiter de Aldionibus præcipimus.

"That a slave whose father or whose mother was a slave cannot become free before thirty years of age. We order that the same shall be the case respecting Aldions."

In the twelfth he states that these are but a continuance of the laws of his grandfather Charles and of his father Louis. And in tit. i. 12 of Ulpian, reference is made to a variety of enactments of the ancient Roman law, that a slave manumitted under the age of thirty could not be a Roman citizen except by a special grant of a court.

The thirteenth declares that free women who unite with their own slaves are in the royal power, and are given up, together with their children, to slavery among the Lombards.

The fourteenth enacts that a free woman who shall unite herself to the male slave of another, and remain so for a year and a day, shall, together with her children, become enslaved to her husband's owner.

The fifteenth regulates that if the free husband of a free woman shall, for crime or debt, bring himself into servitude to another, and she not consent to remain with him, the children are free; but if she die, and another free woman, knowing his condition, marries him, the children of this latter shall be slaves.

A number of chapters are also on these records showing the insufficiency of servile testimony. Others provide against the oppression of poor freemen, so that they shall not be easily compelled to sell themselves into slavery.

About the year 860, Pope Nicholas I. sent to the newly converted Christians of Bulgaria answers to several inquiries which they made for the regulation of their conduct. The ninety-seventh regards slaves who accuse their masters to the prince or to the court: and the pope refers them to the obligation of the master as given in chapter vi. of the epistle of St. Paul to the Ephesians, (not to use threatenings towards their servants,) and then asks, how much more strongly does the spirit of this maxim of kindness and affection bear upon the servant, and teach him to be of an humble and forgiving disposition, such as that chapter enjoins; referring also to the direction of our Saviour, *Luke* vi. 37, and the injunction of the apostle, 1 *Thess.* v. 15, for their direction.

At this period of time, the piratical wars of the Northmen, who were perpetually making inroads on the rest of Europe, kept the whole of Christendom in commotion, and marked perhaps the darkest period of the dark ages.

LESSON XVIII.

UNCONNECTED FACTS.

In 1030, Peter, bishop of Girona, in Spain, came to Rome, and begged leave of the pope (John XIX.) to wear the pall twelve days in the year, promising to redeem thirty slaves then in captivity among the Saracens, provided his holiness granted him this request. It was readily granted. See Bower, vol. v. p. 153.

Shortly after the 30th October, 1051, Pope Leo IX., having visited Vercelli and Augsburg, returned to Rome, and held a council soon after Easter, in which he excommunicated Gregory, bishop of Vercelli, for committing adultery with a widow betrothed to his uncle. The bishop was absent when this sentence was given, but he flew to Rome as soon as he heard of it; and upon his promising to perform the penance that his holiness imposed upon him, he was absolved from the excommunication, and restored to the functions of his office. On that occasion the canons issued by other councils against the incontinence of the clergy were confirmed, and "some new ones were added, and, in order to check more effectually the scandalous irregularity of the *Roman* clergy in particular, it was decreed, at the request of the pope, that all women who should for the future prostitute themselves to the priests within the walls of Rome should be condemned to serve as slaves in the Lateran palace." See Herman, ad an. 1051; also Bower, idem, p. 183.

By one of Constantine's laws, they who ravished virgins or stole them, even with their consent, against the will of their parents, (with the view to make slaves of them or not,) were burned alive. Cod. Theodos. l. ix. tit. 29, leg. 1. The severity of this law was somewhat mitigated by Constantius, but he still made it a capital offence. Ibid. leg. 2. It was upon this law, Pope Hadrian II. applied to the emperor for redress against *Eleutherius*, who had carried off his daughter *Stephania* by force, and married her, although she was betrothed to another. See Bower, idem, p. 11. We have a remarkable letter, written by Gregory VII., in January, 1080, in answer to one he had received from Vratislaus, duke of Bohemia, desiring leave to have Divine service performed in the Sclavonian tongue, that is, in the language of the country. That letter the pope answered in the following words:

"As you desire us to allow Divine service to be performed among you in the Sclavonian tongue, know that by no means can I grant your request, it being manifest to all, who will but reflect, that it has pleased the Almighty that the Scripture should be withheld from some, and not understood by all, lest it should fall into contempt, or lead the unlearned into error. And it must not be alleged that all were allowed, in the *primitive times*, to read the Scriptures, it being well known that in those early times the church *connived* at many things, which the holy fathers disapproved and corrected when the Christian religion was firmly established. He cannot therefore grant, but absolutely forbid, by the authority of Almighty God and his blessed apostle Peter, what you ask, and command you to oppose to the utmost of your power all who require it." Greg. l. vii. ep. ii.; also Bower, idem, p. 279.

On the subject of the above letter, it should be remembered none spoke the Sclavonic at that day except the Sclavonians themselves; that the great mass of that people were slaves, either to some few individuals of their own nation, or to the other European nations, by whom they had been captured, or to whom they had been sold. They were a nation of slaves, and hence the Romans called their language *Servian*, from *servus*, a slave. There is still extant among the ancient German archives some account of the physical and moral appearance of this people, representing them as robust, filthy, faithless, and extremely wicked. They called themselves *sclava* or *sclavas*, &c., which word, in their language, implied an elevated distinction, and was in common use as a *suffix* to individual names, indicating that the person was highly elevated among his countrymen, as in this case, Vrati-Slaus—indicating the fact that *Vrati* was famous, elevated, a man of high and honourable distinction. Such men often held immense numbers of their less elevated countrymen in bondage. From the form and meaning of this *suffix*, some modern scholars have erroneously supposed it to have come from the Latin, *laus*. We may form some idea of the feelings of Pope Gregory VII., upon this application, by imagining what would have been the feelings of a Virginia legislature, fifty years ago, had some free African, then there, petitioned to have the laws published in *Eboe*, for the benefit of the slaves. In the above letter, the meaning of the assertion, "in those early times the church *connived at* many things which the holy fathers disapproved," &c., at this late day is very liable to be misconceived. He does not allude to any thing said or done by Jesus Christ or his apostles, but to the action of his predecessors in the pontificate on this very subject. About the year 860, Pope Nicholas I. granted this very privilege to the Sclavonians in Moravia; and about ten years after, the same was renewed by Hadrian II., upon the request of St. Cyril, the apostle of the Moravians. See the Life of Cyril, (Latin,) page 22. And John VIII., in the year 882, confirmed the same, at the request of *Sfento Pulcher*, prince of Moravia, calling it the *license* granted by Pope Nicholas, "of saying the canonical hours and celebrating mass in their native language."

"*The Sclavonian language we justly commend*," says the pope in his letter to the prince, "*and order the praise and the works of Christ our Lord to be celebrated in that tongue, being directed by Divine authority to praise the Lord, not in three only, but in all languages, agreeably to what we find in holy writ—'Praise ye the Lord, all ye nations, and bless him, all ye people.' The apostles announced the wonderful works of God in all languages*," &c., "*and he who made the three chief languages, the Hebrew, the Greek, and the Latin, created all the rest for his praise and glory*." See Johan. ep. 247.

The same privilege was granted by the *Greek* church to the *Russians*, who speak the *Sclavonian* language; and they perform, to this day, as well as the Moravians, Divine service in their native language. The pope, however, ordered the gospel to be first read in *Latin*, and afterwards, for the sake of those who understood not that language, in the *Sclavonian*. (See Bower, idem, p. 37.) It is not relevant to our subject to inquire what facts presented themselves to the mind of Gregory VII., whereby he apprehended that the Scripture might "*fall into contempt*," or they "*lead the un-*

learned into error." But we have seen, in our own day, a wide deviation from the instruction of St. Paul, in a version of the New Testament in Romaic, or modern Greek, evidently translated from our English version, instead of from the ancient Greek; wherein Paul is made to say, 1 *Tim.* i. 10, *anthropokleptas*, which indicates the stealing of a free man—instead of what Paul did say, *andrapodistais*, which indicates the stealing of a slave. It is true, King James's translators substituted "*men-stealers*," without any further allusion that the *men* who were to be the *things stolen* were slaves. It does not appear to have occurred to them that a *free man* could be *stolen*, since in no sense could he be *property*. In said version are other errors of equal magnitude; and we have it from good authority that the Greek patriarch, after an examination of said version, most strictly forbad his people to read it, and, also, to introduce it among them. If such errors were incident to the *Sclavonic*, Gregory VII. had at least some ground for his apprehensions. But the Sclavonians were of the same colour and physical formation of the northern tribes to whom they were in bondage. There was no physical or moral degradation consequent to an amalgamation with them; and such connection did happen to a very great extent, and at this day has very nearly extinguished all caste between them. But in the days of Gregory VII., and long since, the politer nations of the south of Europe regarded those of the north, whether free or in servitude, as but a mere grade, if at all, above barbarians; and this pope seems to have been disposed to have fed them with "milk," and not with "strong meat." *Heb.* v. 12. We may perceive how the south estimated the north at those early times, by an incident related by D'Aubigne, vol. i. p. 96. Reuchlin, a native of Pforzheim, had made himself a distinguished scholar for any age. In 1498, he found his way to Rome, when Argyropylos, a celebrated Greek professor, was lecturing on the elevated standing in literature to which the Greeks had formerly arrived, &c. Reuchlin, highly delighted with the lecture, visited the professor, and addressed him in Greek. Argyropylos, perceiving him to be a German, says, "Whence come you, and do you understand Greek?" Reuchlin replies, "I am a German, and am not quite ignorant of your language." He took up Thucydides and read; when Argyropylos said, in grief, tears, and astonishment, "Alas, alas, Greece cast out and fugitive, is gone to hide herself beyond the Alps!" But the funeral fire of Greece and Rome illumed the extreme north, and by its light the savage freeman and his more savage slave were taught their religion, civilization, and science. "It was this," says D'Aubigne, "that the sons of barbarous Germany and those of ancient Greece met together in the palaces of Rome; thus it was that the east and the west gave each other the right hand of fellowship in this rendezvous of the world, and that the former poured into the hands of the latter those intellectual treasures which it had carried off in its escape from the barbarism of the Turks. God, when his plans require it, brings together in an instant, by some unlooked-for catastrophe, those who seemed for ever removed from each other." This improved condition of the northern nations was foreseen, perhaps already felt, by Innocent IV., in 1254, when he permitted Divine service to be performed in the Sclavonic language, which is noticed by Bower, vol. vi. p. 254. At the close of his remarks on Pope Innocent IV., he says—"We have a great number of letters written by this pope on different occasions, and a decree allowing the *Sclavonians* to perform Divine service in their mother tongue, contrary to a decree of Gregory VII." We beg to notice Pope Gregory IX.; for, "by this pope was confirmed the religious order of *St. Mary de Mercede*, as it is called, an order instituted to make gatherings all over the Christian world for the redemption of Christians taken and kept in *slavery* by the infidels." Bower, idem, p. 236. This order was instituted by James, king of Arragon, about the year 1223, and was confirmed by Gregory on the 17th of January, 1230. The general of this order resides constantly at Barcelona, where it was instituted by the king of Arragon, under the direction of *Raimund de Pennefort*, then canon of that city. See *Oldoinus in notis ad Ciacon. Bullarium in Greg. IX. constit.* 9. About the year 1312, charges of the most wicked and gross nature were had against the *Knights Templars.* Their chief persecutor was King Philip, who suspected them to have encouraged an insurrection during his war in Flanders. Through his influence the whole order were arrested, not only in France, but in all Christendom. Pope Clement V. took charge of their prosecution. But it appearing that thousands of them had and were ready to defend the Christian religion at the expense of their lives, and that many of their order were then in *slavery* among the Saracens, from which they might redeem themselves by repudiating Jesus Christ and his religion, yet they preferred rather to live and die in chains than to purchase freedom at so high a price, their judges considered these facts to overbalance the evidence against them. But through Philip's influence the order was suppressed. See Bower, vol. vi. p. 39. By the laws of Moses, when the Hebrews found it necessary to make war and subdue their enemies in battle, they were directed to put all the men to death, and to make slaves of the women and children. See *Deuteronomy* xx. 13, 14. The milder treatment of the women and children was in mercy, predicated on the presumption of their being more tractable and less unalterably sunk in sin. We perceive the same state of facts when the Lord commanded the Hebrews to put the Canaanites to death. "Thou shalt smite them, and utterly destroy them; thou shalt make no covenant with them, nor show mercy to them: neither shalt thou make marriages with them," &c. *Deut.* vii. 2, 3. Whereas the adjoining and kindred tribes were only devoted to slavery. "Both thy bond-men and thy bond-maids which thou shalt have, shall be of the heathen that are round about you: of them shall ye buy bond-men and bond-maids." *Lev.* xxv. 44. It is, and ever has been, the universal rule to destroy from the earth, whenever sin has sunk its votary so low in the depths of crime that there is no longer even hope of reform. Whereas, for a less degree of depravity, mercy intercedes for the reformation of the victim, by placing him someway in surveillance, either for life or for a term of years. On the same principle is founded the distinction of punishment between homicide attended with premeditated malice, and that which is not so attended.

"Behold, these three years I come seeking fruit on this fig-tree, and find none: cut it down; why cumbereth it the ground? And he answering, said unto him, Lord, let it alone this year also, till I may dig about it, and dung it: and if it bear fruit, well; and if not, then after that thou shalt cut it down." *Luke* xiii. 7.

LESSON XIX.

Our English word *war* is of Saxon origin, (Sax. *waer*,) and from whence has also been derived many of the corresponding terms in the present European languages. Its primary sense implies the action of a competent power in accomplishing something. But, like many other words, its use has degenerated into various shades of meaning. The corresponding Greek term, *palemos*, from *pallo*, or its cognate, *ballo*, seems originally to have been illustrative of offensive and coercive action, and hence implies all the agitative and repulsive movement illustrated by our present word *battle:* whereas the Hebrew term, *laham*, cognate with *Ham*, on whose descendants the curse of slavery was pronounced by Noah, involves the idea of *destruction*, as a thing *burned*, *consumed*, *devoured*, and *destroyed;* hence the Hebrews would say, the sword devoured, that is, eats up, &c.; yet their term *gerav*, or *kerab*, boldly implied offensive and opposing force; hence, to advance upon, or, to approach unto, in which sense it was often used, as well as to imply conflict and war. We wish to illustrate the fact that, when the mind of a Hebrew was in exercise with the complex idea which we express by the term *war*, the conception embraced a larger portion of the simple elements which enter into the complex ideas of destruction, annihilation, and death, than is now found associated in the mind of the more highly cultivated descendants of the Caucasian races. In the idea *war*, with him, the leading sentiment was the extinction of those against whom the *war* was waged. Their *doctrine*, that God governed the world; that the Hebrews were his chosen people; that no war was justifiable unless authorized by Jehovah; that the object of war was to destroy from the earth those who were too wicked to live, or to place in subjection and servitude, those who manifested a less degree of stubbornness, but whose sins made them a nauseant, a nuisance, in the world; that God always governed a war in such a manner as rendered it a punishment for sins. Hence the law of *Deut.* xx. 13, 14, before quoted. Hence the wars of the Israelites are named as "the wars of the Lord," *Numb.* xxi. 14. Hence, we find in *Ex.* xvii. 16, "The Lord hath sworn that the Lord *will have* war with Amalek from generation to generation," and in the preceding verse, that "Moses built an altar and called it *Jehovah-nissi.*" The word *nissi* means the flag, standard, or banner of an army, indicating the centre of command, or the location and movement of the commander, and is sometimes used in the sense of *example*, or model of action, and by figure is also used to mean the commander or leader himself. And Joshua said unto them, "Fear not nor be dismayed, be strong and of good courage: for thus shall the Lord do to all your enemies whom ye fight." *Josh.* x. 25. "He teacheth my hands to war, so that a bow of steel is broken by mine arms." 2 *Sam.* xxii. 35. Also the same, *Ps.* xviii. 34. "With good advice make war." *Prov.* xxiv. 6. *Ps.* xviii. 37: "I have pursued mine enemies and overtaken them; neither did I turn again until they were consumed." 38. "I have wounded them that they were not able to rise. They are fallen under my feet." 39. "For thou hast girded me with strength unto the battle. Thou hast subdued under me those that rose up against me." 40. "Thou hast also given me the necks of mine enemies; that I might destroy them that hate me." 41. "They cried, but there was none to save them: even unto the Lord, but he answered them not." 42. "Then did I beat them small as the dust before the wind: I did cast them out as the dirt in the streets." 43. "Thou hast delivered me from the strivings of the people: and thou hast made me the head of the heathen: a people whom I have not known *shall serve me*," (*abedini, shall be slaves to me.*) 44. "As soon as they shall hear of me, they shall obey me: the strangers shall submit themselves unto me."

"O God the Lord, the strength of my salvation, thou hast covered my head in the day of battle." cxiv. 7.

"Blessed be the Lord God of my strength, which teacheth my hands to war *and* my fingers to fight." cxliv. 1.

So the prophets: "A noise shall come even to the ends of the earth, for the Lord hath a controversy with the nations; he will plead with all flesh: he will give them that are wicked to the sword." *Jer.* xxv. 31.

"And I will smite thy bow out of thy left hand, and will cause thy arrows to fall out of thy right hand.

"Thou shalt fall upon the mountains of Israel, thou, and all thy bands, and the people that is with thee: I will give thee unto the ravenous birds of every sort, and unto the beasts of the field, to be devoured. Thou shalt fall upon the open field: for I have spoken it, saith the Lord God." *Ezek.* xxxix. 3–5.

"At the same time spake the Lord by Isaiah the son of Amos, saying, Go, and loose the sackcloth from off thy loins, and put off thy shoe from thy foot: and he did so, walking naked and barefoot.

"And the Lord said, Like as my servant Isaiah hath walked naked and barefoot three years for a sign and wonder upon Egypt and upon Ethiopia;

"So shall the king of Assyria lead away the Egyptians prisoners, and the Ethiopians captives, young and old, naked and barefoot, even with their buttocks uncovered, to the shame of Egypt." *Isa.* xx. 2, 3, 4.

And again, "The word of the Lord came again unto me, saying, Son of man, prophesy and say, Thus saith the Lord God; Howl ye, Wo worth the day!

"For the day is near, even the day of the Lord is near, a cloudy day: it shall be the time of the heathen.

"And the sword shall come upon Egypt, and great pain shall be in Ethiopia, when the slain shall fall in Egypt, and they shall take away her multitude, and her foundations shall be broken down.

"Ethiopia (*Cush*) and Libya (*Put*) and Lydia (*Ludim*) and all the mingled (*ereb*, *mixed-blooded*) people, and *Chub*, (the Arabians read *Nub*, Nubia,) and the men of the land that is in league, shall fall with them by the sword.

"Thus saith the Lord: They also that behold Egypt (*Mitsraim*) shall fall; and the pride of her power shall come down: from the tower of Syene shall they fall in it by the sword, saith the Lord God.

"And they shall be desolate in the midst of the countries *that are* desolate, and her cities shall be in the midst of the cities *that are* wasted.

"And they shall know that I am the Lord, when I have set a fire in Egypt, (*Mitsraim*,) and when all her helpers shall be destroyed.

"In that day shall messengers go forth from me in ships to make the careless (*betahh*, *confident of one's own security*, *thoughtless*, *unconcerned*, *trusting in themselves*) Ethiopians afraid, and great pain shall come upon them: as in the day of Egypt, (*Mitsraim*:) for lo it cometh!

"Thus saith the Lord God, I will make the multitude of Egypt to cease by the hand of Nebuchadnezzar king of Babylon.

"He and his people with him, the terrible of the nations, shall be brought to destroy the land: and they shall draw their swords against Egypt, and fill the land with the slain.

"And I will make the rivers dry, and sell the land into the hand of the wicked: and I will make the land waste, and all that is therein, by the hand of strangers. I the Lord have spoken it.

"Thus saith the Lord God: I will also destroy the idols, and I will cause their images to cease out of Noph: and there shall be no more a prince of the land of Egypt: and I will put a fear in the land of Egypt.

"And I will make Pathros (a Coptic word signifying *south land, &c.*) desolate, and will set a fire in Zoan, (both *Isoan* and *Isaan; it* means *a wanderer*, &c. and was the name of a city at the mouth of the Nile,) and will execute judgments in *No*.

"And I will pour my fury on Sin, the strength of Egypt; and I will cut off the multitude of No.

"And I will set fire in Egypt: Sin shall have great pain, and No shall be rent asunder, and Noph shall have distresses daily.

"The young men of Aven and Pi-beseth shall fall by the sword: and these cities shall go into captivity.

"At Tehaphnehes also the day shall be darkened, when I shall break there the yokes of Egypt: and the pomp of her strength *shall cease in her:* a cloud shall cover her, and her daughters shall go into captivity. Thus will I execute judgments in Egypt, (*Mithraim*, the same as *Misraim, the son of Ham:*) and they shall know that I am the Lord." *Ezek.* xxx. 1–19.

And so *Zeph.* ii. 12: "Ye Ethiopians also, ye shall be slain by my sword." We shall take occasion to notice this passage elsewhere. And *Joel* iii. 8: "And I will sell your sons and your daughters into the hand of the children of Judah, and they shall sell them to the Sabeans, to a people far off: for the Lord hath spoken it." *Zephaniah* iii. 8–10 may be said to develop the ultimate providence of God touching this matter:

"Therefore, wait ye upon me, saith the Lord, until the day that I rise up to the prey: for my determination is to gather the nations, that I may assemble the kingdoms, to pour upon them mine indignation, *even* all my fierce anger: for all the earth shall be devoured with the fire of my jealousy.

"For then I will turn to the people a pure language, that they may all call upon the name of the Lord, to serve him with one consent.

"From beyond the rivers of Ethiopia, my suppliants, *even* the daughter of my *dispersed* (*Putsi, the daughters of Put;* the word means *dispersed*, because they were scattered and lost as to name) shall bring mine offering." They were evidently the most deteriorated of all the descendants of Ham.

When a people or nation give evidence that they are insensible to all rules of right, either divine or human, it necessarily follows that their hand will be found against every man, and every man's hand against them. The subjugation of such a people, so regardless of all law, can only end in their being put to death, or, in the more merciful provision of the divine law, by reducing them to a state of absolute slavery.

The experience of mankind proves that such heathen, so reduced to a state of bondage, have always given evidence that their moral and even physical condition has been ameliorated by it, and in proportion to the scrupulous particularity by which they to whom they were enslaved successfully compelled and forced them to walk in the paths of rectitude.

Ever since the world has been peopled by nations, none have ever hesitated to make war a protection to themselves against those who thus had become a nuisance in it. To such men, either individually or collectively, reason, justice, law are without effect or influence: nothing short of absolute compulsive force can avail them beneficially. And, indeed, it is upon this principle that civilized communities do essentially, in their prisons and by other mode of restraint, enslave, for life or a term of years, those who have proved themselves too reckless to be otherwise continued among them.

In the year 1437, the Christian right or duty of declaring, or rather of making war against infidels, was proposed to the church for the pope's decision and counsel. Duarte, king of Portugal, was importuned by his brother Ferdinand, to make war on the Moors with a view to the conquest of Tangier. Duarte entertained scruples about his moral and Christian right to do so; and therefore proposed the subject to the theologians and to the pope. Eugenius IV., who then filled the papal chair, decided that there were but two cases in which an offensive war could be justifiably undertaken against unbelievers, &c.: 1st. "When they were in possession of territory which had belonged to Christians, and which the latter sought to recover. 2d. When, by piracy or war, or any other means, they injured or insulted the true believers." In all other cases, proceeded his holiness, hostilities are unjust.

The elements, earth, air, fire, and water, were created for all; and to deprive any creature, without just cause, of these necessary things, was a violation of natural right. See *Lardner*, Hist. Portugal, vol. iii. p. 204. We proceed to instances wherein the records show the church to have declared offensive war.

In 1375, "the Florentines, entering into an alliance with the Visconti of Milan, broke unexpectedly into the territory of the Church, made themselves masters of several cities, demolished the strongholds, drove everywhere out the officers of the pope, and setting up a standard, with the word 'Libertas' in capital letters, encouraged the people to shake off the yoke and resume their liberty: at their instigation, Bologna, Perugia, and most of the chief cities in the pope's dominions openly revolted, and, joining the Florentines, either imprisoned, or barbarously murdered those whom the pope had set over them. Gregory (XI.) was no sooner informed of that general revolt, and the unheard of barbarities committed by the Florentines, and those who had joined them, than he wrote to the people and magistrates of Florence, exhorting them to withdraw their troops forthwith out of the dominions of the Church, to forbear all further hostilities, to satisfy those whom they had injured, and revoke the many decrees they had issued absolutely inconsistent with the ecclesiastical immunity as established by the canons. As they paid no regard to the pope's exhortations, he summoned the magistrates to appear in person, and the people by their representatives, at the tribunal of the apostolic see, by the last day of March, 1376, to answer for their conduct. The Florentines, far from complying with that summons, insulted the pope's messengers in the grossest manner, and, continuing their hostilities, laid waste the greater part of the patrimony, destroying all before them with fire and sword.

"Gregory, therefore, provoked beyond all measure, issued the most terrible bull against them that had ever yet been issued by any pope. For, by that bull, the magistrates were all excommunicated; the whole people and every place and person under their jurisdiction were laid under an interdict. All traffic, commerce, and intercourse with any of that state, in any place whatever, were forbidden on pain of excommunication. Their subjects were absolved from their allegiance; all their rights, privileges, and immunities were declared forfeited; their estates, real and personal, in what part soever of the world, were given away, and declared to be the property of the first who should seize them, *prima occu-*

pantis; all were allowed, and even exhorted and encouraged, to seize their persons, wherever found, as well as their estates, and reduce them to slavery. Their magistrates were declared intestable, and their sons and grandsons incapable of succeeding to their paternal estates, or to any inheritance whatever; their descendants, to the third generation, were excluded from all honours, dignities, and preferments, both civil and ecclesiastic. All princes, prelates, governors of cities, and magistrates were forbidden, on pain of excommunication, to harbour any Florentine, or suffer any in the places under their jurisdiction in any other state or condition than that of a slave." This bull is dated in the palace of Avignon, in some copies the 30th of March, and in some the 20th of April, in the sixth year of Gregory's pontificate, that is, in 1376, (*apud Raynald. ad hunc ann. num.* i. *et seq.*, *et Bzovium, num.* xv.) Walsingham writes, that upon the publication of this bull the Florentine traders who had settled in England, delivered up all their effects to the king, and themselves with them, for his slaves. One of the authors of Gregory's life (*auctor primæ vit. Gregor.*) tells us, that in all other countries, especially at Avignon, they abandoned their effects, and returned, being no where else safe, to their own country. (See Bower, vol. vii. p. 23.)

Again, in 1508 was concluded the famous treaty or league of Cambray, against the republic of Venice: that state had been long aspiring at the government of all Italy. The contracting parties were the pope, the emperor, the king of France, and the king of Spain; and it was agreed that they should enter the state of Venice on all sides; that each of them should recover what that republic had taken from them; that they should therein assist one another: and that it should not be lawful for any of the confederates to enter into an agreement with the republic but by common consent. The duke of Ferrara, the marquis of Mantua, and whoever else had any claims upon the Venetians, were to be admitted into this treaty. The Venetians had some suspicion of what was contriving against them at Cambray, but they had no certain knowledge of it, till the pope informed them of the whole. For Julius II., (then pope,) no less apprehensive of the emperor's power in Italy than the French king's, acquainted the Venetian ambassador at Rome, before he signed the treaty, with all the articles it contained, represented to him the danger that his republic was threatened with, and offered not to confirm the league, but to start difficulties and raise obstacles against it, provided they only restored to him the cities of *Rimini* and *Faenza*. This demand appeared to be very reasonable to the pope, but it was rejected by a great majority of the senate, when communicated to them by their ambassador; and the pope thereupon confirmed the league by a bull, dated at Rome, the 22d of March, 1508. The Venetians, hearing of the mighty preparations that were carrying on all over Christendom against them, began to repent their not having complied with the pope's request and by that means broken the confederacy. They therefore renewed their negotiations with his holiness, and offered to restore to him the city of *Faenza*. But Julius, instead of accepting their offer, published, by way of monitory, a thundering bull against the republic, summoning them to restore, in the term of twenty-four days, all the places they had usurped, belonging to the apostolic see, as well as the profits they had reaped from them since the time they first usurped them. If they obeyed not this summons, within the limited time, not only the city of *Venice*, but all places within their dominions, were, *ipso facto*, to incur a general interdict; nay, all places that should receive or harbour a Venetian. They were, besides, declared guilty of high treason, worthy to be treated as enemies to the Christian name, and all were empowered "to seize on their effects, wherever found, and to enslave their persons." (See *Guicand, et Onuphrius in vita Julii II., et Raymund ad ann.* 1509, *and Bower*, vol. vii. p. 379.)

In 1538 was published the bull of excommunication against Henry VIII. It had been drawn up in 1535, on the occasion of the execution of Cardinal Fisher, bishop of Rochester; had been submitted to the judgment of the cardinals, and approved by most of them in a full consistory. However, the pope, flattering himself that an accommodation with England might still be brought about, delayed the publication of it till then, when, finding an agreement with the king quite desperate, he published it with the usual solemnity, and caused it to be set up on the doors of all the chief churches of Rome. By that bull the king was deprived of his kingdom, his subjects were not only absolved from their oaths of allegiance, but commanded to take arms against him and drive him from the throne; the whole kingdom was laid under interdict; all treaties of friendship or commerce with him and his subjects were declared null, his kingdom was granted to any who should invade it, and all were allowed "to seize the effects of such of his subjects as adhered to him, and enslave their persons." See

Burnet's Hist. of the Reform. l. 3. *Pallavicino*, l. 4. *Saudeos de Schis.* b. i., and *Bower*, vol. vii. p. 447.

We ask permission to introduce a case on the North American soil, of somewhat later date. We allude to an act, or law, passed by the "United English Colonies, at New Haven," in the year 1646, and approved and adopted by a general court or convention of the inhabitants of Windsor, Hartford, and Wethersfield, in the year 1650. We copy from the "Code of 1650," as published by Andrus, and with him retain the orthography of that day:

"This courte having duly weighed the joint determination and agreement of the commissioners of the United English Colonyes, at New Haven, of anno 1646, in reference to the indians, and judging it to bee both according to rules of prudence and righteousness, doe fully assent thereunto, and order that it bee recorded amongst the acts of this courte, and attended in future practice, as occasions present and require; the said conclusion is as follows:

"The commissioners seriously considering the many willful wrongs and hostile practices of the indians against the English, together with their interteining, protecting, and rescuing of offenders, as late our experience sheweth, which if suffered, the peace of the colonyes cannot bee secured: It is therefore concluded, that in such case the magistrates of any of the jurisdictions, may, at the charge of the plaintiff, send some convenient strength, and according to the nature and value of the offence and damage, seize and bring away any of that plantation of indians that shall intertein, protect, or rescue the offender, though hee should bee in another jurisdiction, when through distance of place, commission or direction cannott be had, after notice and due warning given them, as actors, or at least accessary to the injurye and damage done to the English: onely women and children to be sparingly seized, unless known to bee someway guilty: and because it will bee chargeable keeping indians in prison, and if they should escape, they are like to prove more insolent and dangerous after, it was thought fitt, that uppon such seizure, the delinquent, or satisfaction bee again demanded of the sagamore, or plantation of indians guilty or accessary, as before; and if it bee denyed, that then the magistrate of this jurisdiction, deliver up the indian seized by the partye or partyes indammaged, either to serve or to bee shipped out and exchanged for neagers, as the case will justly beare; and though the commissioners foresee that said severe, though just proceeding may provoke the indians to an unjust seizing of some of ours, yet they could not at present find no better means to preserve the peace of the colonyes; all the aforementioned outrages and insolensies tending to an open warr; onely they thought fitt, that before any such seizure bee made in any plantation of indians, the ensuing declaration bee published, and a copye given to the particular sagamores."

LESSON XX.

UNDER the term *war*, mankind have from time immemorial included those acts which the more enlightened nations of modern days have designated by the name of *piracy*, a word derived from the Greek *peirao*. The primary sense is *to dare, to attempt*, &c., as, *to rush* and *drive forward*, &c.; used in a bad sense, as to attempt a thing contrary to good morals and contrary to law, and now mostly applied to acts of violence on the high seas, &c.; the same acts on land being called *robbery*, &c. These acts of violence have generally been founded on the desire of plunder, and in all ages have been recognised as good cause of war against those nations or tribes who upheld and practised them. Such piratical war has ever been considered contrary to the laws of God and repugnant to civilized life; and it may be with the strictest truth asserted that those nations and tribes of people whom God devoted to destruction, and also those of whom he permitted the Jews to make slaves, were distinguished for such predatory excursions. The first account we have of any such predatory war is found in Genesis. True, it is said, they had been subject to Chedorlaomer twelve years, and rebelled, but the manner in which he and his allies carried on the war leaves sufficient evidence of its character, even if they had not disturbed Lot and his household; and it may be well here remarked, that the original parties to this war were of the black races; in fact, progenitors of the very people who were denominated by Moses as the *heathen round about*.

The second instance of this kind of warfare we find carried on by the sons of Jacob against the Hivites. True, they professed to be actuated by a spirit of revenge for the dishonour of Dinah. They put all the adult males to death, made slaves of the women and children, and possessed themselves of all the wealth of Shechem, for which they were reprimanded by Jacob. Their conduct upon this occasion was in conformity to the usages of the heathen tribes who knew not God, and, if persisted in, must have ultimately just as necessarily been fraught with their own destruction and extinction from the earth. And this was no doubt one of the many crimes that gave proof of their deep degradation, and which finally sunk them in slavery. The heathen tribes in all ages have ever been characterized by this kind of warfare, however truly and often the more civilized portions of the world may have been obnoxious to similar charges. The doctrine is, that where such predatory war essentially exists against a people, they, finding no other efficient remedy, are authorized by the laws of God to make war a remedy, to repel force by force, to destroy and kill until they overcome, and, as the case may be, to subjugate and govern or reduce to slavery. And the laws of modern civilized nations regulating the conduct of belligerants are merely an amelioration; but give evidence that such belligerants are already elevated above those grades of human life which look to subjugation and slavery as the only termination of war. But the condition of man, in this higher state of mental and religious improvement, is none the less governed by the laws of Divine power, influencing and adapted to his improved state. *Corollary:* When the time shall come, that all men shall live in strict conformity to the laws of God, war shall cease from the earth, and slavery be no more known; and at that time the Lord will "turn to the people a pure language, that they may all call upon the name of the Lord," to serve him with one consent. "Then from beyond the rivers of Ethiopia, my suppliants, even the daughter of my dispersed, (*phut*) shall bring mine offering." *Zeph.* iii. 9, 10.

We have heretofore alluded to the idolatrous barbarians of the north of Europe and to their inroads upon the more civilized regions of the south. It may be well to take some further notice of these people, to mark the influence of their predatory wars on the morals of those times, and of the influences of the church in counteracting and ameliorating their effect on the character and condition of the Christian world. Their religion was cast upon the model of their savage appetite: easily excited by the love of conquest and plunder, their minds were still further inflamed by their bards, who promised them, after death, daily combats of immortal fury, with glittering weapons and fiery steeds, in the immediate presence of their supreme god, Oden. The wounds of these conflicts were to be daily washed away by the waters of life. Congregated in the great hall of their deity, seated upon the skulls of those they had slain in battle, they spent each night in celebrating in song the victories they had won, refreshing themselves with strong drink out of the skulls on which they rested, while they feasted on the choicest morsels of the victims they had sacrificed to their gods. Constantine, having succeeded to the throne of the Roman Empire, transferred his court to Constantinople. This, a notable step in the downfall of Rome, was followed by his dividing his dominions between three sons and two nephews. The imperial power thus partitioned away, the northern nations, who had been subjected to her rule, no longer regarded Rome as a sovereign power over them: at once the German tribes, among whom were the Franks, overran Gaul: the Picts and Saxons broke into Britain, and the Sarmatians into Hungary. The spirit of war was let loose. As early as the time of the Christian era, scattered from the Caucasus to the north-eastern Pacific, were numerous tribes whom the all-conquering arm of Rome had never reached. Cradled amidst precipitous mountains, savage and wild scenery, howling tempests or eternal snows, the form of their minds and the character of their religion associated with the region of their birth.

Europe has given some of them the appellation, Vandals, Sueves, Alans, Sclavas, Goths, Huns, Tartars, and Veneti. Restless as the elements of their native clime, their leaders ever showed themselves striving for dominion and thirsty for power. Pushing westward, one upon the other, they became somewhat amalgamated in the north of Europe, under the general term of Scandinavians, yet receiving new cognomens or retaining their old as fancy or knowledge of them suggested; yet, in the middle and south of Europe, they were as commonly known by the appellation of Northmen. The most of these people were emphatically warlike and savage. The world possessed no one power sufficiently strong to restrain them. Italy was overrun and Rome itself was captured by the Goths, under Alaric—then by the Herulians, under Odoacer. They in turn were subdued by Theodoric the Ostrogoth—then by the Lombards from Brandenburg, who established a more permanent government. But they, in turn, yielded to the power of the Franks, under Charlemagne, who entered Rome in triumph, and was crowned Emperor of the West, as elsewhere noted by us.

Up to the time of Charlemagne, the Northmen were excited to war, not alone by their love of liberty and a desire to extend their possessions, but also by their hatred to the Christians and their religion; and in the countries further north, this prejudice existed until a much later day. But we have only time to give an example of the character of their inroads on the peace and prosperity of Europe. Scotland had been early engaged in these conflicts. In June, 793, the Northumbrians were alarmed by a large armament on their coast. These barbarians were permitted to land without opposition. The plunder of the churches exceeded their expectations, and their route was marked by the mangled carcasses of the nuns, the monks, and the priests, whom they had massacred. Historians have scarcely condescended to notice the misfortunes of other churches than that of Lindesferne, which became a prey to these barbarians: their impiety polluted the altars; their rapacity was rewarded by its gold and silver ornaments. The monks endeavoured, by concealment, to elude their cruelty; the greater number were discovered and slaughtered. If the lives of the children were spared, they were sold into slavery. (See Lingard.) In 800, these Northmen made an irruption on the German coast, and carried off plunder and captives. They shortly visited France: a large party entered the Loire, and fixed permanent quarters in the island of Hero, and made their incursions thence. The French writers describe them as now pushing in upon their northern coasts, carrying off captives into slavery and loading their vessels with booty. In 841 they entered the Seine, sacked and burned the monastery of St. Ouen, of Jumieges, spared Fontenelle for a ransom, where the monks of St. Denys paid them twenty-six pounds of silver for sixty-eight captives. For nineteen days they ravaged both banks of the river. In 843, they again entered the Loire, took Nantes, when the city was filled by the inhabitants of the neighbouring country, celebrating the festival of St. John, who retired with the bishop and clergy to the cathedral. The gates were soon burst open, and a general slaughter ensued: loaded with booty and captives, they retired to their ships. In 844, they sailed up the Garonne, pillaged Toulouse, made an attempt on Gallicia in Spain, but were repelled by the Saracens. In 845, Ragner Lodbroy, one of their sea-kings, entered the Seine with twenty-six ships, and spread consternation through the land, leaving, in their rear, Christians hanging on trees, stakes, and even in their houses. They entered Paris, when Charles the Bald, by the advice of his lords, paid them seven thousand pounds of silver, and they swore by their gods to never re-enter his kingdom except by his invitation. They ravaged the seacoast on their return homeward, and were wrecked on the shores of Northumbria, where Ragner and the survivors recommenced to plunder. They were attacked by Aella, and Ragner slain. But a formidable fleet, under the command of Ragner's sons, was soon on the coast of the East Angles, and marked their advances to Northumbria in lines of blood and ruin. Aella fell into their hands, and was put to death with untold torture. This incursion of Ragner is noticed by Voltaire, who says that Charles the Bald paid him fourteen thousand marks in gold to retire from France, and adds, in his "General History of Europe," such payments to the Northmen only induced them to continue these piratical incursions. That these wars were most strictly piratical, not undertaken for the good of mankind, but for plunder alone, we beg here to introduce some proof from the early writers.

Adam of Bremen, who, about the year 1080, wrote his work entitled, "De Situ Danae et Reliquarum, Septentrionalium," says of the city of "Lunden," in the island Schönen—"It is a city in which there is much gold, which is procured by those incursions on the barbarous nations on the shores of the Baltic Sea, which are tolerated and encouraged by the king of Denmark on account of the tribute he draws from them." In proof that Voltaire's estimate of the influence of such payments to these northern pirates was just, we advert to their inroads on Ethelred. Soon after he ascended the throne, he was invaded by Sweyn, by some called Sitric, and Olave, and paid them sixteen thousand pounds. Ten years after, he was forced to pay these Northmen thirty thousand pounds, and then, at the expiration of only four years, forty thousand pounds more; each time the Northmen swearing by their gods to never trouble the country again. Yet, twelve years after the last payment, the crown and throne were transferred to Canute. We have an anonymous Latin author, a contemporary of Canute, who informs us to what use these pirate lords applied the vast sums thus procured. The book is entitled, "Emmæ Anglorum Reginæ Encomium,"—The Encomium of Emma, the Queen of England. She was the wife of Canute. Page 166, the author, describing the Danish ships, says—"On the stern of the ships, lions of molten gold were to be seen: on the mast-heads were either birds, whose turning showed the change of the wind, or dragons of various forms, which threatened to breathe out fire. There were to be seen human figures looking like life, glittering with gold and silver; dolphins of precious metals, and centaurs that brought to mind the ancient fables. But how shall I describe the sides of the ships, which swelled out with gold and silver ornaments! But the royal ship exceeded all the rest as far as the king in appearance exceeded the common soldiers or people." This author, in the second book, describing the landing of the Danes, repeats and says—"The ships were so splendid that they seemed a flame of fire, and blinded the eyes of the beholders; the gold flamed on the sides, and silver-work was mingled with it. Who could look upon the lions of gold? Who on the human figures of electrum, (a mixture of gold and silver,) their faces of pure gold? Who on the dragons, gleaming with brilliant gold? Who could look on the carved oxen, that threatened death with their golden horns? Who could look on all these things and not fear a king possessed of so great power?" Jacobs's "Inquiry into the Precious Metals" attributes the accumulation of gold and silver, of which we have seen a specimen among these northern barbarians, to the piracies of these people. Helmodus, in his Sclavonic Chronicles, (*Chronican Sclavicum,*) lib. iii., says the people of Denmark abounded in all riches, the wealthy being clothed in all sorts of scarlet, in purple and fine linen, (nunc non salum scarlatica vario grisio, sed purpurea et bysso induntur;) and he further adds, "that this wealth is drawn from the herring-fishery at the island of Schönen, whither traders of all nations resorting, bring with them gold, silver, and other commodities, for purchasing fish." The fact was, that island became a place of great resort by these pirates for supplies. But we return to sketch these piracies:—In about the year 846, an immense body of Scandinavians ascended the Elbe with six hundred vessels under their king Roric. Hamburg was burned; they then poured down upon Saxony; but, having met with a defeat, and just then learning the fate of Ragner, sent messengers to Louis, king of Germany, sued for peace, and were permitted to retire from the country upon their giving up their plunder and releasing their captives. After leaving the Elbe, Roric went to the Rhine and the Scheldt, destroyed all the monasteries as far as Ghent, and the Emperor Lothaire, unable to subdue him, received him as his vassal and gave him a large territory. In 850, Godfrey, another chieftain, repulsed in an attack on England, sailed up the Seine, and, after some successes, obtained from King Charles a permanent location and territory about Beauvais. In 856, nearly all the coast of France, and to the interior as far as Orleans, was overrun. The churches were plundered, and captives carried away and enslaved. In Flanders, all the chief men and prelates were either slain or in slavery. These pirates circumnavigated Spain, amalgamated with the Moors of Africa; some entered the Gulf of Lyons, and committed depredations in Provence and Italy. All notions of peace, of justice, were wasting away, and the laws of the monarchs and the canons of the councils began to exhibit the ruins of morality. In 861, the Seine is again infested, and Paris terrified. In 883, they poured themselves on both sides of the Rhine, as high as Coblentz, where the Emperor Charles made a treaty with Godfrey and gave him the duchy of Friesland. France was so much overrun by the pagans, that thousands of Christians, to escape death or bondage, publicly renounced their religion and embraced the pagan rites; and not long after, Rollo, the grandfather of William the Conqueror, at the head of his Scandinavian bands, took possession and held the dukedom of Normandy, and forced Charles the Simple to bestow him Gisla his daughter in marriage. In England, Alfred, placing himself at the head of his faithful followers, subdued the Danes, who had overrun his kingdom; and many of them, embracing the Christian religion, were adopted as subjects of the realm. In 893, a fleet of three hundred and thirty sail rendezvoused at Boulogne, under the command of Hastings, for the avowed purpose of conquering for himself a kingdom in Britain. Three years he contended against Alfred, who eventually subdued him, but restored to him all the captives upon his promise to leave the island for ever.

Nor did Ireland escape the ravages of the Northmen. In 783, they landed in the extreme north of the island, and burned the town and abbey of *Dere Columb-kill*, the Londonderry of more modern times. Here the *Hydaher-teagh*, the *chiefs of the oak habitations*, (the *O'Dougherty's* of a latter day,) secured the record of their name in the "*Book of Howth.*" But here the *Tuatha De Danaan*, the Darnii of Ptolemy, washed out even the history of their race in the blood of battle.

In 790, the Danes made a general assault upon this devoted island: in 797, wasted the island of Ragulin, devastated Holm Patrick, and carried away captives, among whom was the sister of

St. Findan, and, shortly after, the saint himself. In 802, they burned the monastery of Hy: in 807, destroyed Roscommon, ravaged the country, and made captives and slaves. In 812, they again burned Londonderry and its abbey; massacred the students and the clergy; nor did they relax their attacks upon the north of the island until, twenty years after, they were driven from the place by Neil Calne, with most incredible slaughter. But yet the whole island was infested by these northern marauders.

In 812, the Irish made a more determined resistance, and the Northmen, after three defeats, escaped from the island. But, in 817, Turgesius, with a large force, overran a large portion of the island, and a large portion of the clergy, monks, and nuns were massacred, and many of the inhabitants taken into captivity.

In 837, two large additional fleets arrived; one entered the Boyne, and the other the Liffy. The masses which they poured upon the country spread in all directions, committing every kind of excess.

In 848, Olchobair McKinde, king of Munster, uniting his troops with those of Dorcan, king of Leinster, was encouraged by a succession of victories over the pagans; yet the archbishop of Armagh and seven hundred of his countrymen were made captive, and sent by Turgesius to Limerick as slaves. But Melseachlin, king of Ireland, defeated Turgesius and put him to death. The Irish now arose on every side and drove the barbarians from the country. But yet, in 850, Dublin was invaded by a band of Northmen, whom the Irish denominated *Fin-gal*, or white strangers, and by another body, called *Dubh-gal*, or black strangers, who took possession of Leinster and Ulster, and ravaged the country. In 853, a sea-king, named Amlave, *Auliffe*, or *Olave*, from Norway, with two brothers, Sitric and Ivor, with large additional forces, arrived, and was acknowledged chief of all the Northmen in the islands. He took possession of Dublin, Limerick, and Waterford, which he enlarged and improved, as if their possession was to be perpetual. But war not only raged between them and the Irish, but the Irish and Danes were in perpetual conflict, different parties of Danes with one another, and discord and strife were constant among the Irish themselves. Carnage and bloodshed, captivity and slavery everywhere covered the island.

In 860, Melseachlin, the king, defeated Auliffe with great slaughter; but, recovering strength, he plundered and burned Armagh, and took a large number of captives, who were sent away for slaves. In 884, Kildare was plundered, and more than 300 sent away for slaves. In 892, Armagh was again captured, and 800 captives sent to the ships. But, in quick succession, Carrol, with Leinster forces, and Aloal Finia, with the men of Bregh, defeated the Danes and retook Dublin, while in other parts of the island the Northmen suffered great reverses; but in 914 we find them again returned and in possession of Dublin and Waterford, but quickly put to the sword by the Irish. Another division succeeded to plunder Cork, Lismore, and Aghadoe; and, in 916, were again in Dublin, ravaged Leinster, and killed Olioll, the king. In 919, they were attacked near Dublin by Niell Glunndubh, king of Ireland. Their resistance was desperate, under the command of the chiefs Ivor and Sitric: here fell the Irish monarch, the choice nobility, and the flower of the army. Donough revenged the death of the king, his father, and the barbarians were again signally defeated; but we find them, in 921, under the command of Godfrey, their king, in possession of Dublin, marching to and plundering Armagh, and, for the first time, sparing the churches and the officiating clergy. A predatory war, without decisive encounters, was continued for more than twenty years, when they suffered two severe defeats from Cougall II., in which their king, Blacar, and the most of his army were slain. In——but the mind sickens, tires at these recitals; a whole army is swept away, and, as if the ocean poured twice its numbers on shore, whole centuries gave no relief. In short, we have a continuation of these scenes of piratical war, until the power and spirit of this restless race of the Northmen were broken at Clontarf, near Dublin, on the 23d of April, 1014, where they suffered an irrecoverable defeat from the Irish, under the command of Brian Boroimhe.

Ireland did well to rejoice in the perfect overthrow of these ruthless invaders; but here fell Brian, whom ninety winters had only nerved for the conflict. Here fell his son Morogh, and his grandson Turlogh, personifications of the rage of battle; here fell a numerous, almost the entire, nobility; here fell Ireland's valiant warriors in unnumbered heaps. The voice of Ireland is yet sometimes heard, but it is the voice of a broken heart; of complaint, of weakness, of weeping, and sadness. In a review of these times and those that followed, the providence of God may be traced by its final development. Where no mercy was, it is infused by hope of gain; and the savage and the captured slave are led to an equal elevation in the service of the altar of the God Jehovah.

The sacrifice of the Lamb is substituted for the victim of war in the woods of Woden; while the proud flashes of the crescent of Islam became dim before the continued ray of the Star of Bethlehem.

LESSON XXI.

THE condition of the slave, throughout the whole of Europe, was attended with some circumstances of great similarity.

The slaves were generally of the same nation, tribe, and people, who formed a constituent portion of the free population of the country where they were, and always of the same colour and race. Even the Sclavonians, on the continent, formed no exception in the more northern parts of Europe. In short, slavery, as it existed in Europe, was only in a very few instances in the south marked by any radical distinction of race: consequently, the condition of the slave could never be as permanent and fixed as it ever must be where strong distinctions of race mark the boundaries between bondage and freedom—although often far more cruel.

The disgrace of the *free*, from an amalgamation with the *slaves*, did not proceed from any consideration as to *race*, but merely from the condition of the slave—more pointed, but somewhat analogous to the disgrace among the more elevated and wealthy, arising from an intermarriage with the ignorant, degraded, or poor. Influenced by such a state of facts, the particulars of his condition were liable to constant change, as affected by accident, the good or ill conduct of the individual slave, the sense of justice, partiality, fancy, or the wants and condition of the master; nor needed it the talent of deep prophecy to have foretold that such a state of slavery must ultimately eventuate in freedom from bondage.

A description of the slaves of Britain will give a general view of those of the continent, for which we refer to Dr. Lingard.

The classes whose manners have been heretofore described constituted the Anglo-Saxon nation. They alone were possessed of liberty, or power, or property. But they formed but a small part of the population, of which not less than two-thirds existed in a state of slavery.

All the first adventurers were freemen; but in the course of their conquests, made a great number of slaves. The posterity of these men inherited the lot of their fathers, and their number was continually increased by freeborn Saxons, who had been reduced to the same condition by debt, or made captives in war, or deprived of liberty in punishment of their crimes, or had voluntarily surrendered it to escape the horrors of want.

The ceremony of the degradation and enslavement of a freeman was performed before a competent number of witnesses. "The unhappy man laid on the ground his sword and his lance, the symbols of the free, took up the bill and the goad, the implements of slavery, and falling on his knees, placed his head, in token of submission, under the hands of his master."

All slaves were not, however, numbered in the same class. In the more ancient laws we find the *esne* distinguished from the *theow;* and read of female slaves of the first, the second, and third rank. In later enactments we meet with *borders*, *cocksets*, *parddings*, and other barbarous denominations, of which, were it easy, it would be useless to investigate the meaning. The most numerous class consisted of those who lived on the land of their lord, near to his mansion, called in Saxon his *tune*—in Latin, his *villa.* From the latter word they were by the Normans denominated *villeins*, while the collection of cottages in which they dwelt acquired the name of *village.* Their respective services were originally allotted to them according to the pleasure of their proprietor. Some tilled his lands, others exercised for him the trades to which they had been educated. In return, they received certain portions of land, with other perquisites, for the support of themselves and their families.

But all were alike deprived of the privileges of freemen. They were forbidden to carry arms. Their persons, families, and goods of every description were the property of their lord. He could dispose of them as he pleased, either by gift or sale: he could annex them to the soil, or remove them from it: he could transfer them with it to a new proprietor, or leave them by will to his heirs.

Out of the hundreds of instances preserved by our ancient writers, one may be sufficient. In the charter by which Harold of Buckenhole gives his manor of Spaulding to the abbey of Croyland, he enumerates among its appendages Colgrin, his bailiff, Harding, his smith, Lefstan, his carpenter, Elstan, his fisherman, Osmund, his miller, and nine others, who probably were his husbandmen; and these with their wives and children. Wherever slaves have been numerous, and of the same race as the master, this variety in their condition has always followed. See the statement of Muratori concerning the Roman slaves; also the laws of Charlemagne concerning those of the Lombards and Goths. These records are proof that slavery, accompanied with such facts, is always in the act of wearing out.

LESSON XXII.

All historians agree that the Sclavonians, who at an early age made their appearance on the north-eastern borders of Europe, came, a countless multitude, pouring down upon those countries from the middle regions of Asia.

The precise place from which they originated, the causes of such emigration, and the successive impulses that pushed them westward, have now, for centuries, been buried beneath the rubbish of the emigrants themselves and the general ignorance that overspread the events of that age.

But there are some facts that assign to them a place among the Hindoo tribes. Brezowski, speaking the Sclavonic of his day, in his travels eastward, was enabled to understand the language of the country as far east as Cochin-China; and scholars of the present day find numerous Indian roots in this language. A similarity of religious rites is to be noticed between the ancient Sclavonians and the Hindoos. They burned their dead, and wives ascended the funeral piles of their husbands. Their principal gods were Bog, and Seva, his wife. They worshipped good spirits called Belbog, and bad spirits called Czarnebog.

These hordes overspread the countries from the Black Sea to the Icy Ocean; and, in their turn, were forced westward by similar hordes of Wends, Veneti, Antes, Goths, and Huns. Thus attacked and pushed in the rear, they poured themselves upon the inhabitants of the more western regions, who, more warlike, and with superior arms, put them to death by thousands, until the earth was covered with the slain. Thus fleeing from death, they met it in front, until the nations then occupying the north and east of Europe, satiated and sickened by their slaughter, seized upon their persons as slaves, and converted them into beasts of burden.

Their numbers exceeding every possible use, the captors exported them to adjoining countries as an article of traffic; and the Venetians, being then a commercial people, enriched themselves by this traffic for many years. All continental Europe was thus filled by this race, from the Adriatic to the Northern Ocean. Thus their national appellation became through Europe the significant term for a man in bondage; and although in their own language their name signified *fame* and *distinction*, yet in all the world besides, it has superseded the Hebrew, the Greek, and Roman terms, to signify the condition of man in servitude. Thus the Dutch and Belgians say *slaaf;* Germans, *sclave;* Danes, *slave* and *sclave;* Swedes, *slaf;* French, *esclave;* the Celtic French, &c., *sclaff;* Italians, *schiavo;* Spanish, *esclavo;* Portuguese, *escravo;* Gaelic, *slabhadh;* and the English, *slave.*

Nor was this signification inappropriate to their native condition. For these countless hordes were the absolute property of their leaders or kings, who were hereditary among them,—as was, also, their condition of bondage.

The Romans called their language *Servian*, from the Roman word *servus*, a bond-man; and from the same cause, also, a district of country low down on the Danube, *Servia*, which name it retains to this day. This country belongs to Turkey, from whence they took the name *serf.* This term has been borrowed from thence, by the Sclavonic Russians, to signify a man in bondage. The whole number of their descendants is now estimated at 100,000,000; and notwithstanding their amalgamation has identified them with the nations with whom they were thus intermingled, yet a thousand years have not ended their condition of bondage in Russia, and 40,000,000 are accounted only as an approximation to the number that still remain in servitude in the north of Europe and Asia.

"The unquestionable evidence of language," says the author of the Decline and Fall, "attests the descent of the Bulgarians from the original stock of the Sclavonian, or more properly Slavonian, race; and the kindred bands of Servians, Bosnians, Rascians, Croatians, Walachians, followed either the standard or example of the leading tribes, from the Euxine to the Adriatic, in the state of captives, or subjects, or allies, or enemies; in the Greek empire, they overspread the land: and the national appellation of the SLAVES has been degraded by chance or malice from the signification of *glory* to that of *servitude.* Chalcocondyles, á competent judge, affirms the identity of the language of the Dalmatians,

Bosnians, Servians, Bulgarians, Poles, (*De Rebus Turcitis*, l. x. p. 283,) and elsewhere of the Bohemians, (l. ii. p. 38.) The same author has marked the separate idiom of the Hungarians.

See the work of John Christopher de Jordan, *De Originibus Sclavicis, Vindobonæ*, 1745, in four parts. Jordan subscribes to the well-known and probable derivation from *slava, laus, gloria*, a word of familiar use in the different dialects and parts of speech, and which forms the termination of the most illustrious names. *De Originibus Sclavicis*, part i. p. 40, part iv. p. 101, 102.

This conversion of a national into an appellative name appears to have arisen in the eighth century, in the oriental France, where the princes and bishops were rich in Sclavonian captives, not of the Bohemian (exclaims Jordan) but of Sorabian race. From thence the word was extended to general use, to the modern languages, and even to the style of the last Byzantines. (See the Greek and Latin Glossaries of Ducange; also Gibbon's Decline and Fall of the Roman Empire, vol. iv. p. 38.)

The Moors, with whom the early Christians in the south of Europe had so many and frequent contentions, at this day differ from all the other African races, in their physical and mental development;—in person, black, with the straight hair of the Arab, whom they exceed in stature and intellect.

The Arabs are admitted to be an amalgamation of the descendants of Shem, of Canaan, and Misrain. Into the particulars of their admixture, it will be as useless to inquire as it would be into the paternity of the goats on their mountains.

The Moors, according to King Hiempsal's History of Africa, as related by Sallust, are descended from an admixture of Medes, Persians, and Armenians with the Libyans and Gætulians, the original occupants of the country. His statement is, that Hercules led a large army of the people to conquer new and unknown countries; that after his death in Spain, it became a heterogeneous mass, made up of a great number of nations, among whom were many ambitious chiefs, each one aspiring to rule; that a portion of this mass, mostly of Japhanese descent, passed over to Africa and seized on the shores of the Mediterranean; that their ships, being hauled ashore, were used for shelter; that the Persians among them passed on to the interior, and mingled with the Gætulians, and in after times were known as Numidians,—whereas those who remained upon the coast intermarried with Libyans, and in course of time, by a corruption of their language, Medi, in the barbarous dialect of Libya, became *Mauri*—now Moor.

To the foregoing, digested from Hiempsal, as given by Sallust, we may add:—To this amalgamation was also adjoined, from time to time, large parties of adventurers from the Hebrews, Greeks, Romans, and from almost every part of Europe, which were all absorbed by the native masses; and between the years 850 and 860, large masses of the Scandinavian hordes were also absorbed into this general amalgam of the races of man.

The instances of slavery, and the laws and customs of the church regulating it, as presented in this study, with few exceptions, have pointed to the case where the white races have been enslaved or have enslaved one another; where no strongly marked physical impediment has branded amalgamation with deterioration and moral disgust; nor is it thought necessary to present an argument to prove that, under such a state of facts, the condition of Europe at the present moment is in strict conformity with the result produced by the unchangeable laws of God touching the subject.

God always smiles upon the strong desire of moral and physical improvement. Had Europe remained under deteriorating influences which determined her moral and physical condition two thousand years ago, her condition as to slavery could not have changed. Nor is it seen that she is yet in so highly favoured a condition as to call upon her the providence of God, charging her with the pupilage of the backslidden nations of the earth.

LESSON XXIII.

It has been heretofore remarked that the great mass of the African tribes are slaves in their own country,—that slavery there subjects them to death at the will of the master, to sacrifice in the worship of their gods, and to all the evils of cannibalism; and yet it has been seen that even such slavery is a more protected state than would be a state of freedom with their religion, and other moral and physical qualities. History points not to the time when their present condition did not exist, nor to the time when their removal, in a state of slavery, to the pagan nations of Asia commenced. Upon the adoption of Mohammedanism there, we find the black tribes of Africa succeeding to them in a state of slavery; and we also find, and history will support the assertion, that in some proportion as the slavery of these tribes was adopted by Christian nations, it was diminished among the Mohammedans; and also, that as the slave-trade with Africa was abolished by the Christians, it was increased there; and also, that in the proportion it has been extended among both or either of these creeds of religion abroad, it has been invariably ameliorated at home. The causes of this state of facts seem to have been these:—The African slave-owner found his bargain with the Christian trader more profitable than with the Mohammedan. He received more value, and in materials more desired by him: the labour of the slave was of more value in America than Asia; and the transportation to the place of destination was attended with less cruelty and hardship by sea than by land. The slave of the African owner was increased in value beyond any native use to which he could be applied, by reason of both or either trade: hence the slave in his native land became of greater interest and concern. The native owner ceased to kill for food the slave whose exportation would produce him a much greater quantity. His passions were curbed by the loss their indulgence occasioned. The sacrifice was stayed by a less expensive, but, in his estimation, a more valuable offering.

The object of our present inquiry is, whether the slavery of the African tribes to the followers of Mohammed is at all recognised or alluded to by the inspired writers. The fact exists, nor can it be contested, although the condition of the African slave is far more degraded among the Asiatics and Arabians than among the Christians, but that even there it is far more elevated than in his native land. "Blessed be the Lord God of Shem, and Canaan shall be his servant." *Gen.* ix. 26. The prophet Daniel was a captive the greater portion of his life, in the very region of country, and among the ancestors of the Mohammedans of the present day, and, of all the prophets, the most to have been expected to have been endowed with prophetic gifts in relation to that country and its future condition. It is proper also to remark that although there is in many instances among the Mohammedans of the present day a mixture of Japhanese descent, yet their main stock is well known to be Shemitic. It should also be noticed that the Shemites have at all times more frequently amalgamated with the descendants of Ham than those of Japhet, consequently more liable to moral and physical deterioration; and here, indeed, we find a reason why it was announced that Japhet should possess the tents of Shem.

Dan. viii. 9: "And out of one of them came forth a little horn, which waxed exceeding great towards the south, and towards the east, and towards the pleasant land. 10. And it waxed great, even to the host of heaven, and it cast down some of the host of the stars to the ground, and stamped upon them. 11. Yea, he magnified himself even to the prince of the host, and by him the daily sacrifice was taken away, and the place of his sanctuary was cast down. 12. And an host was given him against the daily sacrifice by reason of transgression, and it cast down the truth to the ground, and it practised and prospered. 23. And in the latter time of their kingdom, when the transgressors are come to the full, a king of fierce countenance, and understanding dark sentences, shall stand up. 24. And his power shall be mighty, but not by his own power: and he shall destroy wonderfully, and shall prosper, and practise, and shall destroy the mighty and holy people. 25. And through his policy also he shall cause craft to prosper in his hand, and he shall magnify himself in his heart, and by peace shall destroy many: he shall also stand up against the Prince of princes; but he shall be broken without hand."

Dan. xi. 40: "And at the time of the end shall the king of the south push at him, and the king of the north shall come against him like a whirlwind, with chariots, and with horsemen, and with many ships, and he shall enter into the countries, and shall overflow and pass over. 41. He shall enter also into the glorious land, and many countries shall be overthrown; but these shall escape out of his hand, even Edom and Moab, and the chief of the children of Ammon. 42. He shall stretch forth his hand also upon the countries: and the land of Egypt shall not escape. 43. But he shall have power over the treasures of gold and of silver, and over all the precious things of Egypt, and the Libyans and the Ethiopians shall be at his steps."

Of the language used by this prophet, it is proper to remark that there are many variations from the more ancient Hebrew, both as to form of expression and the particular words used, among which Arabicisms and Aramacisms are quite common. Faber supposes that this remarkable vision relates to the history of Mohammedanism: no previous theory has been satisfactory to the Christian world, and it is now generally believed that he has suggested a correct interpretation. We may therefore be allowed to follow him in considering it as descriptive ot the rise and progress of that religion.

Mohammed was born at Mecca. His education was contracted, and his younger days devoted to commercial and warlike pursuits. By his marriage with the widow of an opulent merchant, he rose to distinction in his native city. For several years he frequently retired into the cave of Hera and cherished his enthusiastic sentiments, till, at the age of forty, he stated that he had held communication with the angel Gabriel, and was appointed a prophet and apostle of God. In 612, he publicly announced to his relations and friends that he had ascended through seven heavens to the very throne of Deity, under the guidance of Gabriel, and had received the salutations of patriarchs, prophets, and angels. This monstrous statement, however, did not succeed, except with a very few; and on the death of his uncle Abn Taleb, who had been his powerful protector, he was compelled, in 622, to seek security by flight to Medina. This henceforth became the epoch of Mohammedan chronology; his power was more consolidated, and his influence extended by a large accession of deluded, but determined followers. He very soon professed to have received instructions from the angel Gabriel to propagate his religion by the sword; and power made him a persecutor. In seven years he became the sovereign of Mecca, and this led to the subjugation of all Arabia, which was followed by that of Syria. In less than a century from the period of its rise in the barren wilds of Arabia, the Mohammedan religion extended over the greater part of Asia and Africa, and threatened to seat itself in the heart of Europe.

The unity of God was the leading article of Mohammed's creed. When addressing the Jews, he professed highly to honour Abraham, Moses, and the prophets, and admitted, for the sake of conciliating Christians, that Jesus was the Messiah of the Jews, and will be the judge of all. This compromising policy is seen in the Koran.

Mohammedan morals enforce many principles of justice and benevolence, and inculcate a degree of self-denial, but, at the same time, permit the indulgence of some of the strongest passions of our nature. The representations given of paradise are adapted to gratify the sensuality of men,—and of hell, to awaken their fears of disobeying the Koran or the prophet. "Eastern Christendom," says Mr. Foster, "at once the parent and the prey of hydra-headed heresy, demanded and deserved precisely the inflictions which the rod of a conquering heresiarch could bestow. The king of fierce countenance, and understanding dark sentences, well expresses the character of Mohammed and his religion." "Mohammed," says Gibbon, "with the sword in one hand, and the Koran in the other, erected his throne on the ruins of Christianity and of Rome. The genius of the Arabian prophet, the manners of his nation, and the spirit of his religion involve the causes of the decline and fall of the Eastern empire, and our eyes are curiously intent on one of the most memorable revolutions which impressed a new and lasting character on the nations of the globe."

His first efforts were directed against the Jews, who refused to receive Mohammed's effusions as the revelations of heaven, and, in consequence, suffered the loss of their possessions and lives.

"When Christian churches," says Scott, "were converted into mosques, the 'daily sacrifice' might be said to be taken away," (viii. 11, 12,) and the numbers of nominal Christians who were thus led to apostatize, and of real Christians and ministers who perished by the sword of this warlike, persecuting power, fulfilled the prediction that he cast down some of the host and of the stars to the ground, and stamped on them. It is said that "a host was given him against the daily sacrifice," (or worship of the Christian church, corresponding with the Jewish sanctuary,) "by reason of transgression." A rival priesthood subverted the priesthood of a degenerate church. The imams of Mohammed assumed the place of the apostate teachers of Christianity. The event here predicted was to occur in the latter host of the Grecian empire, (ver. 23,) "when the transgressors are come to the full."

History relates that the remains of the Eastern empire and the power of the Greek church were overthrown by Mohammedans. Their chief endeavoured to diffuse his doctrine, but found that it could not prevail by "its own power," or the inherent moral strength of the system: it was requisite to support his pretensions by "craft" and "policy." Mohammed sanctioned as much of the inspired Scriptures as he thought might tend to obviate the prejudices of the Jews, and incorporated as much of his own system with the errors of the Eastern church as might tend to conciliate Greek Christians.

"Although Mohammedism did not first spring up in the Macedonian empire, yet it now spread from Arabia to Syria, and occupied locally, as well as authoritatively, the ancient dominion of the he-goat." (*Scott.*) It has been remarked, however, by Mr. Foster, (Mohammedism Unveiled,) that the part of Arabia which

included the native country of Mohammed, composed an integral province both of the empire of Alexander and of the Ptolemean kingdom of Egypt. Ptolemy had Egypt, Syria, Arabia, Cælo-syria, and Palestine. The sovereignties of Egypt and Syria, before called the king of the south and the king of the north, disappeared when they were absorbed in the Roman empire, and the new power, or the Saracen and Turkish empires, that succeeded, are now brought to view. But let it be observed, that the Saracens became masters of Egypt, the original territory of the king of the south, and the Turks possessed Syria, or the kingdom of the north, and still retain it. "The king of the south shall push at him." The power of Rome was overthrown in the east by the Saracens. This was the first wo of the revelation, which was to pass away after three hundred years. The Turks then came, a whirlwind of northern barbarians, and achieved a lasting conquest, in a day, of the Asiatic provinces of the Roman empire. The line of march was along the north of Palestine, and the Turkish monarch entered only to pass through and overflow: "he entered into the glorious land;" for, as Gibbon has stated it, the most interesting conquest of the Seljukian Turks was that of Jerusalem, which soon became the theatre of nations. "But Edom and Moab, and the chief of the children of Ammon escaped out of his hand." Even when all the regions round owned the Turkish sway, these retained their detached and separate character, and even received tribute from the pilgrims as they passed to the shrines of Mecca and Medina. Thus they have escaped and maintained their independence of the Porte. A race of monarchs arose to stretch out their hand upon the countries. Othman, Amurath, Bajazet, and Mohammed conquered nation after nation, and finally fixed the seat of their empire at Constantinople. The land of Egypt "did not escape;" it was indeed the last to yield; but, though its forces had vanquished both Christians and Turks, it was at length subdued by Selim I. in 1517, and came into possession of the Ottomans. (*Cox, on Daniel.*) And it may be here remarked, as a fact of well-known history, that the countries known as Libya and Ethiopia have, at all ages of the world, supplied this country with slaves, whoever may have borne rule, and still continue to do the same. Thousands from the interior of Africa are yearly transplanted from the slavery of their native land into those countries now under Mohammedan rule. And it may be well here for the Christian philanthropist to notice, that so far as the slave-trade with Africa has ceased with

Christian nations, to the same extent it has substantially increased with Mohammedan countries.

"And the Libyans and the Ethiopians shall be at his steps,"—a form of speech as clearly indicating the condition of slavery as though ever so broadly asserted. The Hebrew word here translated "at his steps," בְּמִצְעָדָיו *in his footsteps*, &c., i. e. attached or subjected to his interests as slaves, is cognate with the Arabic word مِصْفَاد *metsuad*, and means the chains by which the feet of captive slaves are bound, and in Hebrew form this word is used in *Isa.* iii. 20, צְעָדוֹת *tseadoth*. The whole passage is strictly an Arabicism, and is to be construed, with reference to that language, *chain for the legs*. Of this passage, Adam Clark says, "*Unconquered Arabs* all sought their friendship, and many of them are tributary to the present time." Some commentators seem to understand this passage to mean only that Libyans and Ethiopians would be in courteous attendance, &c. If so, the Hebrew would have read, in *Judg.* iv. 10, רֶגֶל *regel*. "And he went up with ten thousand men *at his feet*." This passage, foretelling the slavery of the Ethiopians to the Mohammedans, may well be compared with *Isa.* xlv. 14, announcing the slavery of the same people to those of the true religion. "Thus saith the Lord, the labour of Egypt and the merchandise of Ethiopia and of the Sabeans, men of stature, shall come over unto thee, and they shall be thine; they shall come after thee, in chains they shall come over, and they shall fall down unto thee; they shall make supplication unto thee, saying, Surely God is in thee, and there is none else, there is no God" *beside*.

LESSON XXIV.

In reflection upon the leading ideas that present themselves in the review of the subjects of this study, we may notice that slavery has been introduced to the world as a mercy in favour of life. That, in its operation, its general tendency is to place the weak, deteriorated, and degraded under the control and government of a wisdom superior to their own; from whence the intellectual, moral, and physical improvement of the enslaved, to some extent, is a consequence as certain as that cause produces its effect.

The world never has, nor will it ever witness a case where the moral, intellectual, and physical superior has been in slavery, as a fixed state, to an inferior race or grade of human life. The law giving superior rule and government to the moral, intellectual, and physical superior is as unchangeable as the law of gravitation. No seeming exception can be imagined which does not lend proof of the existence of such law. The human intellect can make no distinction between the establisher of such law and the author and establisher of all other laws which we perceive to be established and in operation, and which we attribute to God. No one has ever yet denied that obedience to the laws of God effects and produces mental and physical benefits to the obedient, or that their disregard and contempt are necessarily followed by a deterioration of the condition of the disobedient; nor can any one deny that the neglect of obedience to the laws of God, which, in its product, yields to the disobedient mental and physical deterioration, or any one of them, is sin,—and in proportion to its magnitude, so will be its consequent degradation. To be degraded is sin, because the law is improve. No one will pretend that the relation of master and slave is not often attended with sin on the part of the master, on the account of his disobedience to the law of God in his government of his slave; or on the part of the slave, on the account of his disobedience to the same law in his conduct towards his master. Therefore, such master is not as much benefited, not the slave as much improved by the relation, as would otherwise be the case. It is therefore incumbent on the master to search out and exclude all such abuses from the intercourse and reciprocal duties between him and his slave. Placed upon him is the responsible charge of governing both himself and his slave. The responsibility of the master in this respect is of the same order as that of a guardian and that of a parent.

The want of a less affectionate regard in the master towards the slave is supplied and secured to the safety of the slave by the increased watchfulness of the master over the slave from the consideration that the slave is his property. For where affection cannot be supposed sufficiently strong to stimulate a calm and wise action, interest steps in to produce the effect.

That every mind will see and comprehend these truths, where prejudice and education are in contradiction, is not to be expected. The influences of a false philosophy on the mind, like stains of crime on the character, are often of difficult removal. Some forbearance towards those who honestly entertain opposing ideas on this subject, can never disgrace the Christian character,—and we think it particularly the duty of the men of the South, towards the men, women, and children of the Northern States, especially of the unlearned classes. For even among ourselves of the South, we sometimes hear the announcement of doctrines that declare all the most rabid fanatic at the North need claim, on the subject of immediate abolition. We refer to and quote from Walker's Reports of Cases adjudged in the Supreme Court of Mississippi, at the June term, 1818, page 42: "Slavery is condemned by reason and the laws of nature." This false and suicidal assertion, most unnecessarily and irrelevantly introduced, still stands on the records of the Supreme Court of that State, and is an epitaph of the incapacity and stupidity of him who wrote it and engraved it on this monument of Southern heedlessness. We were at first surprised at the silence of the reporter, but, at that day, any criticism by that officer would have been contempt. Yet we may infer that the ingenious and talented gentleman contrived to express his most expunging reprobation, by wholly omitting all allusion to the point in his syllabus of the case.

If in the course of these Studies we shall not have shown that slavery as it exists in the world is commanded by "reason" and the laws of "nature," we shall have laboured in vain; and even now an array of battle is formed, and our enemy has chosen human "reason" for the "bolt of Jove," as wrought from strands of Northern colds, Southern heats, and Eastern winds; in their centre, bound by cloudy fears and avenging fires; for their ægis, "*the laws of nature*" supply Minerva's shield, upon which fanaticism has already inscribed its government over thirty States, far exceeding in purity, they think, that of the God of Israel. And we have come up to the war!—armed neither with the rod of Hermes nor the arrows of Latona's son; but with a word from him of Bethlehem: "Sanctify them through thy truth; thy word is truth."

Study V.

LESSON I.

THE inquirer after truth has two sources by which he can arrive at some knowledge of the will of God:—1st. By faith and revelation; 2d. By the observance of the facts uniformly developed in the material and moral world. The accuracy of his knowledge will be coincident with the accuracy of the mental perceptions and the extent of the research of the inquirer.

In the Bible he will find the declarations of God himself: some of them are express, and some of them implied.

In the second place, he may discover the will of God from the arrangement of his works as manifested in the visible world. Some call this the light of nature; others the laws of nature. But what do they mean other than the light and laws of God? Are not the laws of gravitation as much the laws of God as they would be if set down in the decalogue, although not as important to man in his primary lessons of moral duty?

Let us view the forest as planted by the hand of God: we see some trees made to push their lofty boughs far above the rest; while others, of inferior stem and height, seem to require the partial shade and protection of their more lofty neighbours; others, of still inferior and dwarfish growth, receive and require the full and fostering influence of the whole grove, that their existence may be protected and their organs fully developed for use.

Let us view the tribes of ocean, earth, and air: we behold a regular gradation of power and rule, from man down to the atom.

> Whether with reason or with instinct blest,
> All enjoy that power that suits them best:
> Order is Heaven's first law; and this confess'd,
> Some are, and must be, greater than the rest—

More rich, more wise; but who infers from hence
That such are happier, shocks all common sense.
Heaven to mankind impartial we confess,
If all are equal in their happiness;
But mutual wants this happiness increase.
All nature's difference, keeps all nature's peace:
Condition, circumstance, is not the thing;
Bliss is the same, in subject, or in king!

POPE'S *Essay*.

LESSON II.

THEY who study even only such portion of the works of God as can, seemingly, to some extent be examined by the human mind, never fail to discover a singular affinity between all things, the creation of his hand. This, to us, would be proof, independent of inspiration, that one Creator made the whole world and all things therein.

So great is the affinity between the vegetable and animal kingdoms, that it is to this day a doubt where the one terminates or where the other begins. Naturalists all agree that they both spring from "slightly developed forms, perhaps varied, yet closely connected;" true, "starting away in different directions of life," but ever preserving, it may be an obscure, yet a strict analogy to each other.

These analogies are sufficiently obvious to prove that one power, one and the same general law, has brought them both into existence. Thus the devout worshipper of God may, in some sense, view the vegetable inhabitants of the earth as his brethren.

The animal kingdom may be considered as divisible into five groups. The vertebreta, annulosa, (the articulata of Cuvier,) the radiata, the acrita, (in part the radiata of Cuvier,) and the molusca.

Each one of these groups will be found divisible into five classes. Let us take, for example, the vertebreta, and it is readily divided into the mammalia, reptilia, pisces, amphibia, and aves.

So each one of these classes is divisible into five orders. Let us take, for example, the mammalia; and it is readily divided into the cheirotheria, (animals with more or less perfect hands,) feræ, cetacea, glires, and ungulata.

So each one of these orders is divisible into five genera. Let us take, for example, the cheirotheria, and it is readily divided into the bimana or homo, the quadrumana or simiadæ, the natatorials or vespertilionidæ, the suctorials or lemuridæ, the rasorials or cebidæ.

So each one of these genera is divided in five species. Let us take, for example, the bimana or homo, and it is readily divided into the Caucasian or Indo-European, the Mongolian, the Malayan, the Indian or aboriginal American, and the Negro or African.

Thus we behold man in his relation to the animal world: true, far in advance as to his physical and mental development; yet the natural philosopher finds traces of all his mental powers among the inferior animals, as does the comparative anatomist those of his physical structure.

Does he feel degraded by the fact that God has been pleased to order this relation of brotherhood with the lower orders of creation? Or will he for ever suffer his pride to hedge up the way of progress by the impassable darkness of his own ignorance.

The uniformity of these penta-legal ramifications, which reach down from man through all the orders and groups of the animal world, gives evidence of a preconceived design—of an arrangement by Almighty power—of a God whose thought is law!—while the analogy of animal formation, the traces of affinity in the mental qualities found in all, in proportion as those qualities are more or less developed, and the apparent adaptation of each one to the condition in which it is found, demonstrate the unity of the law which governs their physical being.

These analogies, found to exist between all the individuals of the animal world, and particularly striking and more and more obvious as we proceed from a particular group to its genera and species, have led some philosophers to suppose that the more perfectly developed species have been progressively produced by some instance of an improved development, as an offshoot from the genera, and so on back to its original form of animal life, in obedience to the laws of the great First Cause. But we wish to disturb no man's philosophy. We deem it of little importance to us what method God pursued in the creation of our species; whether we were spoken instantly into life, as was the light, or whether ages were spent in reproducing improved developments from the earlier forms of animal life.

In either case we see nothing contradictory to the inspired writings of Moses. Man is as much the creation of God through one means as another. The wisdom and power required are the same; for his existence alone demonstrates him to be the work of a God. The fact of the existence of these analogies is alone what we propose to notice. And we offer them merely as indications of a course of study that may lead to some important results in elucidation of the mental and physical relations between the different varieties of man.

In further illustration, let us for a moment look at the bovine species, from the genus ruminantia, from the order ungulata, and we find the ox, the bison, the buffalo, the elk, and the goat.

Like the five species of homo, we find the bovine species divided into a great number of families or varieties, of which we need take no further notice. Does any one fail to perceive the analogy between these species of the bos? Are they more obscure, more aberrant than are the relations between the species of man? Examine the high physical development of the most intellectual Caucasian; trace down the line to the diminutive and ill-formed cannibal savage of Africa, the habits and mental development of whom would seem rather allied to the lower orders of animals than to the Caucasian! How will it comport with the general laws manifested by the condition of the animal world and of the obvious inferiority and influence of one over another, in proportion to their apparent superiority in physical and mental development, to place the lowest grade of the African in equal power or in control of the Caucasian brother? Is there any manifestation of the Creator of an arrangement like this, even through the eternity of his own work?

On the contrary, through the whole animal race, we find power and control lodged everywhere in proportion as we find an advance towards perfection in the development bestowed.

In conformity to this law, God gave Adam "dominion" over every living thing that moved upon earth.

It is known to most men, that, under certain circumstances, the race of any animal will improve: so also, under adverse, they degenerate. We see these facts daily in the breeds of domestic animals. We see these changes even in the families of all the species of man. Nor is it a matter of the least importance to our inquiry, whether these species of the race have been produced by an upward movement from the lowest, or a downward degenerating movement from the most elevated. It is sufficient that they exist from some cause; for an individual having been, say an equal, but now degenerate, falls under the influence and control of his superior. And in conformity to this law, it was announced to Eve, the helpmate of Adam, that "he shall rule over thee."

But if these particles of inspiration had never been proclaimed, man would have discovered this law from its constant operation, not only on the family of man, but on every branch of the animal world.

We can spend but little time with such infidel principles as lead some men to say, "Down with your Bible that teaches slavery." "If the religion of Jesus Christ allows slavery, the New Testament is the greatest curse that could be inflicted on man." "Down with your God who upholds slavery; he shall be no God of mine." "Jesus Christ was himself a negro!" Our hearts bleed when we see such evidence of a destroyed intellect. The maniac in his ravings excites our extreme sorrow. We feel no harshness. He has sunk far below resentment. Can we administer to such mental deformity any relief? Will it be absurd to ask him to deduce from nature, as it is found to operate, that the various grades of subjection spread through the animal world exist in conformity to the natural law?

But, says the querist, "Your remarks have a tendency towards the conclusion,—upon the supposition that Adam was created with a perfect, or rather with a very high order of physical organization and mental development,—that the facts of the greater or less degeneration of the people of the world, since his fall, now exhibited by the different species of man upon the earth, had their origin in his transgression. Now, by parity of argument, we may conclude, if such high physical elevation was the original condition of Adam, that each genus of the brute creation also was originally created on a proportional scale. If so, their degeneration is quite as visible as that of man. Yet we have no account that they committed sin and 'fell.'"

We do not say that such was the original condition of the first man. We say, the creation of the animal world was upon principles compatible with progressive improvement; and that as far as these principles are not obeyed, but changed or reversed by the practice of the animal world, that the effect is to remain stationary, or to retrograde and deteriorate.

It is a matter of no importance to our argument what was the first condition of Adam. But allow it to be as querist has stated: We answer, the Bible was given to man for his moral government; not to teach him geology, chemistry, or other sciences. Such matters were left for him to attain by progressive improvement. A minute history of the brute creation, or any portion of it, from the earliest dawn of animal life up to the time of revelation, other than the announcement of their creation and subjection to him, was irrelevant. But man was the very head and governor of the whole animal race. Now, who is to say that the degeneration of the ruler will not produce a change of conduct in the ruled? Who is to say that the poisoned moral feeling of him in command, breaking forth in acts of violence on all around, will not produce a corresponding effect on the animate objects under him? Witness the effect, we need not say on children, but on domestic animals, of the rash, cruel, and crazy treatment of a wicked and inconsistent man?

The idea that the brute creation were injured in condition by the fall of man is put forth by St. Paul, in *Rom.* viii. 9–22, where the word "creature" is translated from the Greek term that implies the whole animal or the whole created world. But no answer to querist is necessary. The fact is sufficient that animals, under habits ill-adapted to their organization, do degenerate.

LESSON III.

HOWEVER insensible individuals themselves may be of the fact, some men, and those of quite different character, find it unpleasant to submit themselves to the great Author of animal life. For they, in substance, make a continual inquiry, How is it to be reconciled that a Being so perfectly good should have admitted into the midst of his works, as a constant attendant of all his sentient creations, so large an admixture of what we call evil?

We might continue the inquiry by adding, Why, in a mere drop of water, do we find the animalculæ manifesting all the agonies and repeating the outrages upon one another strikingly visible among the larger animal developments of the great ocean and of the land? Why such an admixture of pain and misery among men? Why the male of all animals making destructive war on their kind? Why exterminating wars among men? And why the numberless, nameless evils everywhere spread through the world?

And do we forget that the great Creator of animal life brought forth his works and sustains each thing by the unchangeable exercise of his laws? Laws which are found to have a direct tendency to progressive improvement? Will rational beings expect God to change their actions to suit their disregard of them? Will fire cease to burn because we may choose to thrust in the hand? And what if, even in all this, we shall discover his wisdom and goodness by making what we may call punishment for the breach of the law, a pulling back from deeper misery, a powerful stimulus for a change of direction from a downward to an upward movement in the path of progressive improvement? Do we find no satisfaction in this view of the constitution of nature, of the wisdom of God?

These men seem desirous that the works of God should have been on a different footing, or that every thing should have been at once perfect to the extent of his power. Would they then desire to be his equal too? But, at least as to man, the mind incapable of error, the body of suffering! It is possible that under such a dispensation, our mental enjoyments would have been on a par with a mathematical axiom, and our bodies have about as much sympathy for the things around them as has a lump of gold. And how do they know that the rocks, minerals, and trees, yea, the starry inhabitants of the firmament, are not the exact manifestations of what would have been creations of that order? We will not stop here to inquire how far the complaints of these men operate to their own mental and physical injury.

It is a great popular error to suppose all of our own species to be born equals. It involves the proposition that each one also possesses the same faculties and powers, and to the same extent. Even every well-informed nursery-maid is furnished with a good refutation. The grades of physical development are proofs of grades of mind.

Through the whole animal world, as with man, mental action takes place, providing for the sustenance and security of life; and the amount of mental power each one possesses is ever in proportion to the development of the nervous system and animal structure. Upon this earth, the highest grade of such development is found among the Caucasian species of man. Physiologists assert that the African exhibits, in maturity, the imperfect brain &c. of a Caucasian fœtus some considerable time before its birth: so the Malay and Indian, the same at a period nearer birth; while the Mongolian, that of the infant lately born. See *Lloyd's Popular Physiology*. The *beard*, among men the attribute of a full maturity, longest in the Caucasian, is scarcely found among the lower grades of the African.

Colour is also found the darkest where the development is the least perfect, and the most distant from the Caucasian; and hence a philosopher of great learning makes the question pertinent, "May not colour then depend on development also? Development being arrested at so immature a stage in the case of the negro, the skin may take on the colour as an unavoidable consequence of its imperfect organization." The different species and all the varieties of man are nothing but a short history of their different grades of organization and development. One fraction, by a long and more or less strict observance of the laws of nature, becomes, after many generations, quite improved in its organization. From an opposite course, another fraction has degenerated and sunk into degradation. It is now a well-known fact that Caucasian parents too nearly related exhibit offspring of the Mongolian type. So, a particular tribe of Arabs, now on the banks of the Jordan, from an *in-and-in* propagation have become scarcely to be distinguished from Negroes. This is only an instance, but is important when we notice the deteriorating influence such intercourse has among domestic animals. In short, every breach of the laws tending to the path of progressive improvement must have a deteriorating effect on the offspring. There was truth in the ancient adage, "The fathers have eaten sour grapes and the children's teeth are set on edge."

Every private habit and circumstance in life that enervates or deranges the physical system, or disturbs the balance of the mind, stamps its impress on the descendant. The moral and physical condition of the progeny, with slight exceptions the result of an elevating and upward movement, or a downward and deteriorating one, (as the case may be,) is the necessary result of the moral and physical condition of the parentage: and this influence is doubtless felt back for many generations.

But does God make man wicked? does he predestine to evil? These queries may seem pertinent to some, because we are in the habit of considering each individual by itself; whereas each individual is only a link in the chain of phenomena, which owe their existence to laws productive of good, and even of progressive improvement, but of necessity, in their breach, admit these evils, because such breach is sin. Our moral faculties are permitted to range in a wide field; but evil is the result of a disruption of the rules of action. It is the flaming sword elevated to guard our good, showing us the awful truth, the mere bad habit in the parent may become a constitutional inherent quality in the offspring.

We do not suppose these influences always very perceptibly immediate. Many generations are doubtless often required in the full development of an upward movement to a higher order of moral perception; and so in the opposite. Yet we cannot forbear to notice how often the immediate descendant is quite apt to prove its parentage.

Will the theologian object—"You contradict the Scripture. You make five species of man. Whereas they are all the descendants of Noah." Have we not shown ample ground and time for their formation from his stock? Besides, we expect hereafter to prove by Scripture that Ham took a wife from the degenerate race of Cain; which, if so, would alone place his descendants in the attitude of inferiority and subjection.

No! but we advertise the theologian that we shall take the Scripture for our platform. We believe it, and hope to even hold him close to it.

But we now ask for the reflection of all, does not the degenerate man, degraded in constitution below the possibility of his emerging from the depth to which he has sunk, by any self-renovating power, still lingering about his reduced condition, require the aid of one of superior nature, of superior organization and mental development, to act as his adviser, protector, and master? Would not such a provision be a merciful one?

And may we not also inquire, whether the superior endowments here required do not also require to be exercised in bearing rule over the wayward energies of those more degenerate, as a necessary element in the school to a higher advance? And shall we not perceive that such a relation must produce a vast amount of improvement and happiness to both?

Children and inferior persons often show themselves, upon the slightest temptation, false and cruel,—often the inheritance of parental imperfection. Absolute command, sustained by physical force, has alone been found sufficient to eradicate these old, and to found new habits of truthfulness and humanity.

True, the Scripture asserts that all men are equal in the sight of God, just as a father feels an equal parental regard for all his children. The philosophic mind cannot well conceive otherwise than that God feels an equal regard for all parts of his creation; for "The glory of the Lord shall endure for ever: the Lord shall rejoice in his work." But this view reaches not the physical fact; for the father hesitates not to place a guardian over his wayward child, or disinherit the utterly worthless. So God "turneth man to destruction; and sayeth, Return, ye children of men." And how gladly would the parent provide the fatted calf for the worthless son upon his return to honour and virtue! So there is more joy in heaven over the return of one sinner than over ninety-nine who have not gone astray.

The mercy of God shines upon the world in floods of celestial light; for Christianity, in its passports to heaven, judges all men by their own acts. Therefore, the most degraded nature, upon a sight of its deformity, may feel an unchangeable regret, and inherit its portion.

Here Christianity itself points the way to progressive improvement, and commands children to obey their parents, wives their husbands, and servants their masters.

The grace of God is as openly manifested in the welfare of the child or slave, when produced through the interposition of the parent or master, as if the interposition had been more immediate.

LESSON IV.

Intellect is not found to exist only in connection with a corresponding physical organization. In the family of man, if that which may appear a good organization is accompanied by an inferior intellect, we may suspect our nice accuracy of discernment, rather than a discrepancy in the operation of the general law; so also where we may seem to perceive a good intellect, but which produces inferior or unworthy results. We do not always notice the small steps of degeneration. Often the first notice we take is of the fact of a changed condition, as proved by the results: "By their fruits ye shall know them."

The idea that intellect and mental development can be independent of physical organization is an absurdity. A suppressed or incomplete organization must arrest a further enlargement of the mental faculties. These faculties may be improved, brought into action, or even their action to some extent suppressed, by government and culture. Such indeed are the guides to progressive improvement. EXPLANATION:—*Man has no organization by which he could build a honey-comb like a bee.* Will any culture applied to him teach him? *Man has no organization by which he can closely examine spiritual existences:* his ideas about them are therefore variant and confused. Who will arrange their study into a science? *Man has no organization by which he can fully comprehend God.* Will he ever do so in his present state?

Are, then, the actions of the child, and of those persons whose mental development has been arrested at a very early stage, (as has been supposed the case with the lower orders of animals, and of those animals themselves,) the result of some faculty or mental power different from mind? The result of instinct? And what is instinct but mind in the early dawn of its development? Are not such actions as the chick breaking its shell, the young-born infant receiving its natural food, the necessary consequents of the state of their infantile organization, which the earliest development of mind could prompt and enable them to put forth; and will it be deemed beyond the reach of reason, to prove that with the difference of maturity in organization and development, the same general connection of mind and organization is found, through the entire of life as well as infancy?

Philosophers have, with indefatigable labour, endeavoured to enlighten the world on the subject of instinct. Can we be pardoned if we suggest that their theories on this subject signally prove they were but men? Des Cartes says—"Brutes are machines without sensation or ideas; that their actions are the result of external force, as the sound of an organ is the result of the air being forced through the pipes." This is his "instinct." If this be true, then it follows that every action in the material world is instinct. Then the thunder utters its voice, the earth quakes, and the telegraph works by "instinct." Yet, his theory has found an advocate in that very classical Latin poem, "Anti Lucretius," by Cardinal Polignac.

Dr. Reid sustains the mechanical nature of brutes, but classifies their actions into those of habit and those of instinct.

Dr. Darwin says that instinct is mental, and that the actions of brutes result from faculties, the same in nature as those of man, but extremely limited. Smellie takes the same view. Yet Darwin asserts that instinct is the reason; and Smellie, that reason is the result of instinct. Cudworth says that instinct is an intermediate power, taking rank between mind and matter, yet often vibrating from one to the other. Buffon contends that brutes possess an *intellectual principle*, by which they distinguish between pleasure and pain, and desire the one and repel the other. This is his *instinct*.

Reimar divides *instinct* into three classes: *mechanical*, such as the pulsation of the heart; *representative*, such as result from an imperfect kind of memory, and, so far as it is memory, in common with mankind; and *spontaneous*, the same as Buffon's. Cuvier says that instinct consists of ideas that do not result from *sensation*, but flow directly from the brain! Dupont says that there is no such distinct faculty as instinct. His views are analogous to Darwin and Smellie.

Pope, Stahl, and others say, "It is the divinity that stirs within us."

> "And reason raise o'er instinct as you can,
> In this 'tis God directs, in that 'tis man."

Cullen, Hoffman, and others say that *instinct* is the "vis medicatrix naturæ." Dr. John Mason Good says that "*instinct is the law of the living principle*," that "*instinctive actions are the actions of the living principle.*" If so, instinct is as applicable to vegetables as to animals.

Dr. Hancock, in his work on the Physical and Moral Relations of Instinct, has evidently enlarged on the doctrine of Pope and Stahl. He says instinct is the "*impulse*," "*the inspiration of the Holy Spirit;*" and, in his own words, "*which we can only regard as an emanation of Divine wisdom.*"

He asserts that the lower we descend in the scale of animal organization and mental development, the more active and all-pervading over the conduct of the animal is instinct! But, nevertheless, holds that "*instinct* is in such animals an *unconscious intelligence.*" We much admire why he did not think proper to cast off from the ancients the charge of a *puerile idolatry*, on the account of their worship of *bulls, calves, alligators, snakes, beetles*, and *bugs*, for they must have entertained a somewhat similar notion. But the doctor goes further, and says, that as the lower grades of the animal world have this *quality*, in which "the Divine energy seems to act with most unimpeded power," so the holiest of men has it also, but consciously and willingly, and it then becomes his ruling principle, "Divine counsellor, his never-failing help, a light to his feet, and a lantern to his path." (Page 513.) It is quite evident that the doctor's instinct is the same with the "unerring conscience," "the innate principle of light," "the moral sense," "the spiritual power, "the Divine reason," "the internal teaching," "the perfect light of nature," and "the Divine afflatus" of the theologico-abolition speakers and writers of the present day, which, they say, is the gift of God to every man. This strange error of some of these writers we have already had occasion to notice. But it is to be regretted, for the good credit of *religious profession*, that they did not acknowledge from whom they borrowed the idea; or, will they at this late day, excuse themselves, and frankly acknowledge they took it, not from Dr. Hancock, or any other modern, but as a deduction from the practices of ancient idolatry?

Since we have ventured an opinion on the subject of instinct, we trust forgiveness for the introduction of that of others.

Our desire is to present such considerations as lead to the conclusion that men are born into the world with different physical and mental aptitudes: in short, that their corporeal and intellectual organizations are not of equal power; or, if some prefer the term, that their *instincts* are not of equal extent and activity.

For substantially, upon a contrary hypothesis, are founded all those beautiful arguments in favour of the entire equality of man. Some whole systems of political justice are founded upon the proposition that there is no innate principle; and one class of philosophers argue that, as there is no innate principle, therefore all men are ushered into the world under the circumstance of perfect equality; consequently, all the inequality afterwards found is the result of usurpation and injustice.

Do they forget that organization itself is innate, and that different organizations must direct the way through different paths? But these philosophers still persist that there is no such disparity among the human race whereby the inferiority of one man shall necessarily place him in subjection to another. This doctrine is perhaps confuted by practice better than by argument. Counsellor Quibble saw his client Stultus in the stocks, on which he cries out, "It is contrary to law. The court has no such power. They cannot do it." Nevertheless, Stultus is still in the stocks! But what would it avail, even if all men were born equals? Could they all stand in the same footsteps, do the same things, think the same thoughts, and be resolved into a unit? Who does not perceive the contrary?—but that from their birth they must stand in different footsteps, walk in different paths, think different things, and, in the journey of life, arrive at different degrees of wealth, honour, knowledge, and power?

Men organized into some form of government cannot be equal; because the very thing, government, proves the contrary: among perfect equals, government is an impossibility. If laws were prescribed, they could never be executed until some of these equals shall have greater power than those who infringe them. Man is never found so holy as to punish himself for his own impulses. Thus the idea of government among equals is a silly fiction.

Men without government cannot be equal, because the *strong* will have power over the *weak.*

The inequality of men is the progenitor of all civil compact. One man is strong, another weak; one wise, another foolish: one virtuous, another vicious: each one yielding himself to a place in the compact, all acquire additional protection, especially so long as all shall adhere to the terms of the compact. But the compact itself is the result of the proposition that the majority shall have more power than the minority, because they are supposed to have more animal force, and that they hold the evidence of a more lofty mental development. Here has sprung forth the doctrine that *the good of the greater part is the good of the whole:* hence, under this system, an opposing fraction is often sacrificed to the ruling power. We must here remark that this doctrine was changed at an early day into, "The good of the ruling power is the good of the whole."

Although not a part of our study, we may turn aside here to remark that, from this *monad* in the composition of the doctrines of government, did emanate the idea of all those strange sacrifices that now deform the pages of ancient idolatry. In its aid the idol divinity vouched its influence, and the daughters of Ham yielded her new-born to the flaming embraces of her god. Even now the ancient sources of the Ganges still pour down their holy waters, are still drinking in an excessive population from the arms of the Hindoo mother. Nor is this idea only an ancient thought; it is not half a century since it was broached in one of the European parliaments to so hedge around the institution of marriage with thorny impediments, that none excessively poor could legally propagate. But to our minds these things strangely show forth the facts that prove "men are not equal."

But even the lowest grades yield their obedience, and are protected from greater evils. Even though they may have been so low as to have not been able to take any part in the formation of the compact, yet they are as certainly benefited as the most elevated.

Such has been the condition of the race through all time, while falsehood has often mingled in her ingredients, adding misery to the degradation of man;—for it is truly observable that falsehood has for ever led to deeper degradation, to an increased departure from the laws of civil rule. So far as human intellect has threaded its way along the path of truth and through the mazes of human depravity, so far has man improved his condition by increasing his knowledge and power,—while a reversed condition has ever attended a retrograde movement. May not the conclusion then be had, such is the ordinance of God! But equality among men is a chimera, not possible to be reduced to practice, nor desirable if it could be. They never were so, nor was it intended they ever should be. Cain and Abel were not equal: God told Cain that if he behaved well, he should have rule over Abel; but if he did not, he should suffer the consequences of sin. "Who art thou that repliest against God? Shall the thing formed say unto him that formed it, Why hast thou made me thus? Hath not the potter power over the clay, of the same lump to make one vessel to honour and another to dishonour?" *Rom.* ix. 20, 21. "Who hath made thee to differ one from another?" 1 *Cor.* iv. 7. "And the Lord said unto her, Two nations are in thy womb; and two manner of people shall be separated from thy bowels; and the one people shall be stronger than the other people, and the older shall *serve* (יַעֲבֹד *ya avod, be a slave to*) the younger." *Gen.* xxv. 23. See also *Rom.* ix. 12. Can the inequality of man be more strongly inculcated? And St. Paul seems to suggest that such inequality will exist hereafter. "There is one glory of the sun, another glory of the moon, and another glory of the stars; for as one star differeth from another star in glory, so also is the resurrection of the dead." 1 *Cor.* xv. 41, 42.

The idea that the souls of men are unequal in a future state of existence seems to be consonant with the faith of most of the Christian churches. "And his lord said unto him, Well done, thou good and faithful servant: thou hast been faithful over a few things, I will make thee ruler over many things: enter thou into the joy of thy lord. For unto every one that hath shall be given, and he shall have abundance; but from him that hath not, shall be taken away even that he hath; and cast ye the unprofitable servant into outer darkness: there shall be weeping and gnashing of teeth." *Matt.* xxv. 21, 29, 30.

Some politicians say, government is founded on opinion. Be it so; yet opinion is predicated upon the very incidents of men's conduct, which, when analyzed, are found to prove their inequality. So also, when, by the aid of the compact formed, one individual holds a part of the community in subjection, such extended rule is dependent on the same principles as the elementary case. The truth is, human society never recedes far from elementary influences, notwithstanding all the artificials in government that ever have or ever can be brought into use. The conditions to govern and to be in subjection necessarily imply superiority and inferiority: change these relative qualities, and the condition of the parties is changed also. But, upon the organization of society, in all countries and at all times, we find inequality in the conditions of men, growing out of their social state; distinctions between them, affecting their personal considerations, and often disposing of them for life. Thus, in one country a man is born a monarch, in another a priest of the Lord, a prince, a peer, a noble, a commoner, a freeman, a serf, a slave. This arrangement of the conditions of social and civil life, from long habit, may well be said to become constitutional, and necessary to the happiness of that society, although thereby one may seem forced to be a tinker and another a tailor. Hence we infer, inequality among men is the necessary result of the rules of civil life.

LESSON V.

JUSTICE, as a general term, means all moral duty. One of its rules is, that we should "love our neighbours as ourselves." Some men have construed this to include each individual of the human family. Such construction we deem to be error. The word "neighbour," as here used, includes those virtues which render one good man acceptable to another and to God. "And who is my neighbour?" "And Jesus answered and said, A certain man went down from Jerusalem to Jericho, and fell among thieves, which stripped him, and departed, leaving him half dead. And by chance there came down a certain priest that way, and when he saw him, he passed by on the other side. And likewise a Levite, when he was at the place, came and looked on him, and passed by on the other side. But a certain Samaritan, as he journeyed, came where he was: and when he saw him, he had compassion on him, and went to him and bound up his wounds, pouring in oil and wine, and set him on his own beast, and brought him to an inn, and took care of him. And on the morrow, when he departed, he took out two pence, and gave them to the host, and said unto him, Take care of him, and whatsoever thou spendest more, when I come again I will repay thee." *Luke* x. 30–36.

Who has given a better definition of the word neighbour? And how shall we esteem him, who, instead of loving such an one as himself, shall treat him with ingratitude, fraud, and cruelty? "God is angry with the wicked every day." *Ps.* vii. 2. If to "love our neighbour as ourselves" implies that we should love all men equally alike, it also necessarily will imply a subversion of order, and consequently lead to acts of injustice, because all men are not equal. "For if any provide not for his own, and especially for those of his own house, he hath denied the faith, and is worse than an infidel." 1 *Tim.* v. 8.

It would be ungrateful and unjust to not save a parent from death in preference to a stranger—the life of him on whom the life and happiness of thousands depended, in preference to an obscure individual.

One man may be of more value to me, and to the public, than another, because he is further removed from being a mere animal. He has more knowledge, more power, and does dispense more happiness to his fellow-man.

A very evil man and a good one may be in the vicinity or elsewhere; but to regard them equally alike is a contradiction of Christian duty. When we love our neighbour as ourselves, we love the man, his acts, his character; but when we are taught to love our enemies, the mind reaches him as a creature of God, our erring fellow-mortal, our brother steeped in sin—and we look upon him with pity, forgiveness; and yet hate his qualities and conduct. The cases are quite dissimilar. "Love not the world, neither the things that are in the world. If any man love the world, the love of the Father is not in him." 1 *John* ii. 15.

LESSON VI.

VIRTUE is always an appellant to justice. It is manifested by the acts of an intelligent being of correct and benevolent motives, contributing to the general good. Consequently an act, however benevolent may have been the motive of the actor, cannot be a virtuous act if it have an evil tendency. Ignorance can never be virtue: so, no man can be virtuous who acts from a wicked motive, however beneficial may be the result. The motive must be pure, and the effect good, before the act or the actor is virtuous. A man may be virtuous, but in so low a degree as to not merit the appellation: we must compare what he does, with what he has the power of doing. The widow's mite may be an example.

We submit the inquiry—Is not the deduction clear, that men are not equal—neither physically, religiously, mentally, or morally? Can they then be so politically? Will not the proposition be correct, that political equality can never exist with an inequality in these previous terms?

Raynal has said, we think correctly, "that equality will always be an unintelligible fiction, so long as the capacities of men are unequal, and their claims have neither guarantee nor sanction by which they can be enforced." "On a dit que nous avions tous les mêmes droits. J'ignore ce que c'est que les mêmes droits, où il y a inégalitè de talens ou de force, et nulle garantie, nulle sanction." *Raynal, Revolution d'Amerique*, p. 34.

LESSON VII.

THE rules of Christianity are always coadjuvant to those of justice. The least deviation from justice begins to mark the unchristian character. "Just balances, just weights, a just *epha* and a just *hin* shall ye have." *Lev.* xix. 36. "But thou shalt have a perfect and just weight, a perfect and just measure shalt thou have; that thy days may be lengthened in the land which the Lord thy God giveth thee." *Deut.* xxv. 15. "Ye shall have a just balance and a just epha, and a just bath." *Ezek.* xlv. 10.

"Justice and judgment are the habitation of thy throne; mercy and truth shall go before thy face." *Ps.* lxxxix. 14.

"As I hear I judge, and my judgment is just."

"Finally, brethren, whatsoever things are true, whatsoever things are honest, whatsoever things are just, whatsoever things are pure, whatsoever things are lovely, whatsoever things are of good report, if there be any virtue, if there be any praise, think on those things." *Phil.* iv. 8.

But justice, as an act emanating from the rules of right, is wholly dependent on the law: with the abolition of all law, justice or its opposite would cease to exist.

We are aware there are a class who say that Christians have nothing to do with the law of God; that they believe in Christ, and are excused from obedience to the law; that they are not under the law, but the gospel; that the law to them is of none effect; that the laws of God as revealed to Moses have been repealed;—or rather they seem to have but a confused idea of what they do believe touching the matter, while they fashion a theory of Divine providence to suit their own fancies, and substantially, by their own hands, fashion Jehovah into an idol, although not of wood or stone, yet as much in conformity to their own notions; perhaps but little thinking that their notions may have arisen from pride or ignorance. We cannot promise any benefit by addressing such. He who dares take the character of Jehovah into keeping, selecting from among the manifestations of his providence, and decide this law to be repealed, or this only in force, would seem to be as far beyond the reach of human reason as his position is beyond the bounds of moral sense.

But let us, who claim not so high prerogative, who are able only to notice some faint emanations of the Divine mind, as He has seen fit to reveal himself to our feeble perceptions,—who have been taught by the exercise of faith to perceive them in the holy books of his record of what is past, and the present display of his power and rule in the government of the world,—take counsel together, and examine and compare the teachings they may give of the unchangeableness of, and our relation with, the laws of God.

The Creator of things may be deemed able to impose such relations between the things created as he may judge suitable to effect the object had in their creation. Such relations we call law; because, as we notice things, they are the rules by which they act or are acted upon. So far as human reason has been able to examine, such laws are as unchangeable as the Deity who imposed them. To such certainty and unchangeableness we give the name of truth, and hence we say God is truth, having reference to the unchangeableness of his nature and of his laws.

With the idea of the changeability of his laws, of necessity must be associated the idea of the changeability of God himself. The wickedness of such argument is announced in its tendency to the dethronement of Jehovah. It was the very argument used by the serpent in Eden.

The conclusion is, it is inconsistent with the Deity that his laws should be repealed; the same circumstance, under which his law has been noticed to manifest itself, reappearing, and it is again developed. They are the laws of eternity. They are the voice of God. The doctrine of the gospel is bold and plain upon this subject.

"Wherefore the law is holy, and the commandment holy and just and good." *Rom.* vii. 12.

"Now we know that what things soever the law saith, it saith to them who are under the law, that every mouth may be stopped, and all the world may become guilty before God. Therefore by the deeds of the law, there shall no flesh be justified in his sight, for the law is the knowledge of sin." "Do we then make void the law through faith? God forbid; yea, we establish the law." *Rom.* iii. 19, 20, 31.

"Whosoever committeth sin transgresseth also the law, for sin is the transgression of the law." 1 *John* iii. 4.

"Think not that I am come to destroy the law or the prophets; I am not come to destroy, but to fulfil. Whosoever therefore shall break one of these least commandments, and shall teach so to do, he shall be called the least in the kingdom of heaven; but whosoever shall do and teach them, the same shall be called great in the kingdom of heaven." *Matt.* v. 17, 19.

LESSON VIII.

Another of the rules of Christian justice which will be found applicable to our subject, is, "Therefore all things whatsoever ye would that men should do unto you, do ye even so unto them: for this is the law and the prophets." *Matt.* vii. 12.

The remarks made upon the first rule are in some measure applicable to this.

The desire of something to be done must be founded on good reason and conformable to justice. Folly ever marks an unreasonable desire; and that desire is always unjust which merely reaches to the taking from another without the corresponding desire to reciprocate. Such desires are changed instantly into the action of the mind called "*coveting*," and are most strictly forbidden, for this good reason, that very action of the mind is a mental theft; and the moral wickedness in the individual "coveting" is the same as though he were practically a thief. But, further, the desire must be predicated upon a presumable condition; for, by the rule, it would be unjust to desire that which it would not be possible to have done to us; so it would be to desire any other impossibility. Suppose A. should desire that you would make him rich, does it follow that he must make you rich when he has no ability to do so? The case is not founded upon a presumable condition, nor, on good reason, upon a desire to reciprocate, consequently unjust.

But suppose A. feels anxious for your warm regard for his prosperity in his lawful understandings, here the desire reaches to nothing unjust, to no disorder in society, or beyond your power, and clearly within his power to reciprocate; he is then bound by the rule to feel a warm desire for your prosperity in all your lawful undertakings. And who does not perceive that if one desires your good wishes, he must of necessity feel good wishes for you. Whether the desire imply merely a mental or physical action, similar examples will illustrate. The rule is truly a golden one, and, so far as acted upon, binds society together in peace and good-will.

It is quite analogous to the twenty-fourth maxim of Confucius, which reads thus: "Do unto another as thou would be dealt with thyself; thou only needest this law alone: it is the foundation and principle of all the rest." And is in spirit with the fifty-third maxim of the same philosopher: "Acknowledge the benefits by the return of other benefits; but never revenge injuries." We trust the rule is none the less sacred because it was revealed to man at an early period.

Let us illustrate the correctness of these views by the inconsistency of those opposite. Others say that if we were in slavery we should wish to be made free, therefore we are bound by this rule to set free all who are in slavery now.

If this be true, in order that the whole circle of action may be consistent, there must be another link added to the chain; hence we find that the advocates of this interpretation say, also, "that same inward principle which teaches a man what he is bound to do for others, teaches equally, and at the same instant, what others are bound to do to him." *Channing*, vol. ii. p. 33. This proposition inevitably follows the preceding; for who is he that can say among men that that is a good rule which is not reciprocal.

This imaginary rule would perhaps be less obnoxious in case of universal equality. For, in that case, we may suppose an universal equality of desire, without which one wishes one thing and another its opposite. But so long as God rules, universal equality can only happen in case of universal perfection, in which case neither sin nor slavery can exist, and in which case the argument will not be wanted. But the rule as left by Jesus Christ was made for man in his fallen state.

But again, if the interpretation of our opponents be true, then the proposition may be resolved into this state:—A. is as much bound by the desire of B. as by his own, and the whole world is fully bound by both. But the whole world individually desire adversely to each other, yet each desire is to be harmoniously gratified. Let each one make out the examples; we think they will find them extremely ridiculous in the result. The doctrine involves plainly the most gross contradictions, and is therefore a naked nullity.

Again, if it be the law of God, that because we desire a thing, therefore we are bound to give that thing to another, it implies that the desire was the manifestation of God's will; in short, that the desire was a portion of his revealed law; consequently, whatever any man desires is a portion of inspiration. Hence Channing says, (page as above,) "his conscience, in revealing the moral law, does not reveal a law for himself only, but speaks as a universal legislator." Now it follows, that, as each man desires an opposite, therefore there are as many opposite systems of the laws of God as there are individuals who desire them; in other words, it would be making God's law just what each one desired it to be. Thus making the law of God a perfect nullity.

But again, if the interpretation of the golden rule, as employed by them who use it to inculcate immediate emancipation, be true, then it contradicts the spirit of the command, "Thou shalt not covet thy neighbour's house. Thou shalt not covet thy neighbour's wife; nor his *man-servant*, (וְעַבְדּוֹ *ve abeddo, male slave*,) nor his *maid-servant*, (וַאֲמָתוֹ *va amatho, female slave*,) nor his ox, nor his ass, nor any thing that is thy neighbour's." *Exod.* xx. 17. Here the word "covet" is used to mean a strong desire without the wish or ability to reciprocate; therefore without good reason—consequently unjust. It is the same exercise of the mind that leads a man to acts of theft that is here forbidden: an exercise of the mind that leads to many disorders in society, and hence this command. The command does not extend to him who desires his neighbour's house, man-servant, maid-servant, ox, or ass, upon the condition that the desire is founded upon good reason. The neighbour having the will and power to part with, and he who desires the power and will to reciprocate, these qualifications bring the desire within the purview of the golden rule, and remove all tendency to disorders in society. To buy and sell with the view to reciprocate gain, has a very strong tendency to bind society together in peace and good-will.

In the lesson of the golden rule, the Saviour gave a check to impetuous and improper desires,—to the wicked and improper hankering after the substance or condition of others,—by bringing to view the propriety of performing themselves such acts as they demanded of others: that they should prove themselves worthy of the solicited favour by a reciprocity of feeling and action.

This we think evident from what precedes: "If then ye, being evil, know how to give good gifts unto your children, how much more shall your Father that is in heaven give good things unto them that ask him."

The doctrine of the golden rule seems to be often misunderstood. We quote from the great Selden: "Guided by justice and mercy, do unto all men as you would have them do to you, were your circumstances and theirs reversed. If the prisoner should ask the judge whether he would be content to be hanged were he in his case, he would answer, No! Then says the prisoner, Do as you would be done to. Neither of them must do as private men; but the judge must do by him as they have publicly agreed: that is, both judge and prisoner have consented to the law, that if either of them steal, he shall be hanged." *Selden.*

"If the wickedest wretches among yourselves, the most peevish, weak, and ill-natured of you all, will readily give good gifts to their children when they cry for them, how much rather will the great God, infinite in goodness, bestow blessings on his children who endeavour to resemble him in his perfections, and for that ask his grace and other spiritual and heavenly blessings;" but God grants these blessings alone upon this condition, that, "animated by his goodness, you study to express your gratitude for it by your integrity and kindness to your fellow-creatures, treating them in every instance as you would think it reasonable to be treated by them, if you were in their circumstances, and they in yours; for this is, in effect, a summary and abstract of all the human and social virtues recommended in the moral precepts of the *law* and the *prophets*, and it was one of the greatest ends of both to bring men to this equitable and amiable temper." *Doddridge.*

Such are the comments of these men upon this subject.

But permit us to remark that the word *man-servant*, in the command just quoted, is translated from the Hebrew עֶבֶד *ebed*, and means what we mean by the word *slave*. And let it be remembered that, in the decalogue, in one of the original laws of God the Father, delivered to Moses from Sinai, the slave is classed with the ox, the ass, in short, with all other property, as an article of possession; and that we are commanded not to have a desire to change the possession unjustly. And that, by a fair interpretation of the golden rule issued by the living lips of Jesus Christ, if we reasonably and justly desire to change the possession, we must honestly reciprocate the full value thereof.

Let the candid world, the truth-searching philosopher, and the humble Christian examine, and say whether these conclusions are not founded on reason, justice, and the laws of God.

LESSON IX.

We suppose all Christians will agree that God is a Spirit eternal and infinite, unchangeable and unaccountable, omnipotent, omnipresent, and omniscient, most wise, most true, most holy, and most good, without beginning or without end. Such from eternity were his qualities, and such to eternity they will remain.

In contemplation of these characteristics of Jehovah, we are led to deduce that God must originally and essentially within himself be eternally happy. "My counsel shall stand, and I will do all my pleasure." *Isa.* xlvi. 10. If it is proper to say that God has desires, then it must be his desire that his "counsel shall stand," because it is inconsistent with happiness to be unable to gratify desire or fail in counsel; besides, it would prove some deficiency of power. Before God created some other being or thing, he existed alone. Can it be said he had wants? For what purpose then did he create other things? What object had he in view? The object must have been worthy of calling forth his action. What other object could have been worthy of his action than himself? Because his work must in all its parts reflect his power, his every quality, we must therefore conclude God is the sole and ultimate end of every thing he does. If all the labours of Deity were not solely for himself, then of the greatness and rectitude of many of his providences and acts, perhaps none could ever be comprehended or even perceived by mortals. For God legislates not merely for a city, a tribe or nation, but for the universe: not for an hour, a day or a thousand years, but for eternity. "I know that whatsoever God doeth it shall be for ever: nothing can be put to it, nor any thing taken from it; and God doeth it, that men shall fear before him." *Eccl.* iii. 14.

If God himself is the ultimate end of all things, then that moral philosopher, a poor, ignorant man, a worm of but momentary existence, mistakes, who teaches in substance that true religion, that is, worship of God, consists in an advantageous, successful, and well-directed selfishness in favour of himself; for, upon that principle the vilest enemy may take shelter under the cloak of his adversary,—but will he be the more worthy? If God is the supreme object of creation, then this righteous selfishness must be in extreme opposition to God. There are important deductions emanating from these reflections, which we are unwilling to deprive others the pleasure of drawing out for themselves. The use God makes of his creations proves the end for which he made them. We might rest here; but we have heard some say that God's object in creation was the happiness of all his sentient creatures. If so, then they all would be happy; which is not the fact. Human misery is the first object we behold everywhere. True, man can never have a very competent idea of God. His powers of thought are too low; his associations too trivial. But if the object God had in creation was the development of his own glory, then there can be no greater conformity unto God than there is knowledge of his character. Hence, where we see, hear, and learn the most of God, we become the most pure and holy. Holiness depends on a knowledge of God. The reason is obvious: a holy man is a more perfect exhibition of the Divine character. If so, then the happiness of man depends upon his perception of God. Therefore man can ever be happy only in proportion as he is holy. But if the glory of God is the ultimate end of creation, and if the happiness of his rational creatures depends upon their perception of him, then the ultimate end secures in the highest possible degree their happiness.

The great cause of human misery will be found to proceed from the unquenchable desire in the unregenerate man to rebel against God—to set up a government of his own, more wise than he conceives the government of God to be; in fact, he does not perceive his government, for he has no perception of him.

We might deduce an argument in proof that a perception of God is happiness to man, from the formation of his mental powers. To whom does it not give deep distress to behold what we call talent and virtue hid in obscurity and bowed down beneath oppression and want? To whom does it not give great delight to perceive a lucid manifestation of these qualities? The great object in the individual creation of man is his improvement; his advance towards an approximation of being able to see God as he is. The business of angels and saints in heaven is to intensely seek after a more full knowledge of God.

If the happiness of man is thus dependent upon his perception of the greatness and power of God, then we may conclude that a continued manifestation of it is essential to him in producing before his mind an increasing brilliancy of view of the great Jehovah.

The order and gradation in the power bestowed on the different objects his hand has made, displaying his foresight in the work of creation, from the seraph down to the veriest mite, would seem an arrangement that might furnish the mind of man or an angel with never-ending study, with a never-ending employment to find out God.

If the wide and permanent diversity of character and condition in the present world, and in that which is to come,—if the relations we find between man and man,—if the great sacrifice for sin and the redemption wrought therefrom,—if the eternal wrath of Jehovah against the incorrigible sinner, all in combination manifest the greatest display of the power and perfections of God; —in short, if the providences of God collectively, as we see them manifested in the world, are the true developments of his character, then it will follow that they all, in combination, terminate in the greatest good, and, in their external consequences, subserve to the greatest extent of happiness to which the human mind, in the pursuit of its only legitimate employment, is now or ever will be susceptible.

The first deduction is that sin must always be accompanied with misery, but that holiness is as surely accompanied with happiness, no matter what may be the physical condition. It may not be improper here to advert to one of the characteristics of our intellectual constitution, which is this: whatever is presented to the mind calling on its energy and our physical action can never be approached by us with any tolerable degree of perfectedness unless by constant and long-continued repetitions; whence we say, "practice makes perfect." Whereas, whatever is presented wherein we are wholly passive, repetition and familiarity are in constant action to diminish, weaken, and wash out the impressions first made. Examples in proof of the first position are found in the necessary and long-continued exertions before we become adepts in the arts and practices of civilized life. In the African savage, often, many generations of constant exertion in the same direction are required before that race is found to have attained such a state of perfectibility in these things as is required to sustain a position in civilized life; and it is to this they owe their state of pupilage among the civilized races.

Examples of the second position are found in the ready and

quick adaptation of ourselves to the condition in which we are placed: even our senses, from constant repetition and familiarity, often cease to loathe that which was obnoxious. The mind to which the starry firmament is first unfolded will be filled with astonishment and wonder; but the familiarity of a constant gaze does not even excite an emotion.

This characteristic of the human intellect gives strong proof of the power and wisdom of God. For through its means, all in civilized and Christian life and practice, from the king upon the throne down to the slave, are rendered equally happy and contented with their condition. Therefore he is not a correct philosopher who measures the happiness of a lower grade in life by his own feelings.

LESSON X.

From consideration of our previous lesson, we should make the deduction that Christianity is incompatible with savage life. The Christian can no longer be a savage, notwithstanding the habits of civilization may be yet too weakly established to guaranty against lapses to former habits. The habits of the savage must be changed so as to approximate civilized life before Christianity can be successfully taught him. Hence one error into which the missionary and the teacher of the Negro sometimes fall. They confine their labours to instructions concerning the more abstruse doctrines of Christianity; but the savage has no capability to comprehend them: his mind has never been prepared for their reception.

The child can never comprehend the laws of astronomy till he has first learned mathematics. The savage must first be made to comprehend the necessity that individual wants must be supplied by individual labour, and all the consequent attendants of such a state of things, before the possibility can exist that he will comprehend the higher moral duties. Because, without that, he remains passive under such teachings; and in such case, the more familiar such lessons are made to him the less they affect him. Instances are not wanting where such a state of facts exists in circles of society where it would seem they should be the least expected! and from whence the great truth is deducible, that mental and physical idleness is a most deadly poison to good morals and intellectual improvement, and the conduct of such men is always found searching the way back to a deteriorated condition.

The animal propensities require to be forced into habits contributive to the relations and duties of civilized and Christian life. The mind must be made to comprehend what our relative duties are, both experimentally and habitually, and also the impossibility of their being dispensed with, before it will be able to perceive the laws which bind our action to their performance. And it may be here remarked, that a perception of these laws sufficiently strong to influence the conduct of a man will at least place him in the position of Agrippa before Paul. The history of man does not point to an instance where an individual has regenerated himself from the depth of human degradation, except under the pupilage and control of a superior wisdom.

Upon this state of facts was founded the necessity of a Saviour for the children of men.

LESSON XI.

THE lowness of individual condition, in relation to our fellow men, or to human society generally, is not incompatible with the humility of the Christian in the performance of our duty to man or God, because the Christian is not required to display intellectual powers which he does not possess, nor possessions not his own. If he has but one talent, its occupation alone is required,—the desire to bestow one mite marks his character. It is therefore a very great error which some of the abolitionists seem to suppose, that, because a man is a slave, he is thereby prevented from being a Christian or hindered from the worship of God. On the contrary, so essential is humility to the Christian character, that Jesus Christ, in a lesson to his disciples, says, "Whosoever will be chief among you, let him be your servant," δοῦλος, *doulos, slave;* a figure, a sentence, which the Divine Being could never have pronounced, if slavery was inconsistent with his doctrine, either as to the condition of the slave or that of the master. With great similarity of figure and sameness of the humility in the worshipper of God, David addresses Jehovah: "O Lord, truly I am thy servant," (עַבְדְּךָ *abedeka, thy slave,*) "I am thy servant (עַבְדְּךָ *abedeka, thy slave*) and the son of thy *hand-maid,*" (בֶּן־אֲמָתֶךָ *amatheka, thy female slave,*) "thou hast loosed my bonds." Compare with *John* viii. 36, also 1 *Cor*. vii. 22.

LESSON XII.

The institutions of slavery and Christianity can never be antagonistic. Slavery enforces obedience in the inferior to a superior power, for the reciprocal benefit of both. Any deviation from the law of God pertinent to the case, to some extent lessens the benefit and diminishes what should have been the quotient of the general good. Slavery is therefore, however rude in its obedience or commands, an attempt at civilized life; and we may therefore judge of the amount of its abuses by its greater or less success in the cultivation of those virtues incident to that condition. True, this result is scarcely perceptible where the most elevated are still deeply degraded, as is for ever the case in all those regions where the light of Christianity has never been diffused. And it is from these facts we find the providence of God to be that slavery, in such regions, is always seeking abroad for a more enlightened master.

LESSON XIII.

The path of the Christian is described as strait and narrow; in it there are no broad provisions for licentiousness, immorality, crime, or sin of any kind, nor, at suitable distances, are there private apartments prepared, wherein cunning expediency may change her apparel; nor will the poor traveller be perplexed with ambiguous directions, whereby any thing is to be performed contrary to the plain understanding of the law. But each step therein must be in conformity to the directions of him who made known and governs all.

How feeble then shall prove the man, swelled with the pride of his own supposed holiness, who shall attempt to straighten, alter, and make better this highway to heaven! "For who hath known the mind of the Lord? or who hath been his counsellor? or who hath first given to him, and it shall be recompensed unto him again? For of him, and through him, and to him are all things!" *Rom.* xi. 34–36. On every step of this footway to heaven, made for poor sinners to walk in, for the slave as well as for the crowned head, are engraven, in letters of the light of God himself, directions for the poor traveller, so that "the wayfaring men, though fools, shall not err therein." *Isa.* xxxv. 8. And let us now read some of these records, and see how they comport with the doctrine of universal equality as involved in the labours before us:

"Let every soul be subject unto the higher powers; for there is no power but of God: the powers that be are ordained of God.

"Whosoever therefore resisteth the power resisteth the ordinance of God; and they that resist shall receive to themselves damnation.

"For rulers are not a terror to good works but to the evil. Wilt thou then not be afraid of the power, do that which is good, and thou shalt have praise of the same.

"But if thou do that which is evil, be afraid; for he beareth not the sword in vain; for he is the minister of God, a revenger to execute wrath upon him that doeth evil.

"Wherefore ye must needs be subject, not only for wrath, but also for conscience sake.

"For, for this cause pay ye tribute also; for they are God's ministers, attending continually upon this very thing.

"Render therefore to all their dues: tribute to whom tribute is due; custom to whom custom; fear to whom fear; honour to whom honour." *Rom.* xiii. 1–8.

LESSON XIV.

Before we close our present Study, let us survey for a moment the position of the truly Christian character. Let us see and examine a position, whether filled by *lord*, *subject*, or *slave*, that seems so surrounded with hope, so particularly the focus of all the irradiations of heaven, that the distinctions and miseries of human life, even wrongs done us. are blotted out by the brilliancy of their illumination.

But let us view it in connection with man in an unchristianized state, under the control of the appetites, passions, and influences of an unredeemed world; and it may be we shall behold with wonder the operation of that redemption by which his felicity is made steadfast.

The uncertainty and vanity of human pursuits have for ever been a subject of remark.

And, if we examine the motives of human conduct and see the fallacious objects of human hope, we always perceive the constant attendance of pain, misery, and woe.

As the visions of early life are relinquished, we transfer to the future that confidence which has been for ever betrayed by the past, and as these illusions are successively dispelled, new objects continue to fill the imagination, till the very moment when all our prospects are involved in the darkness of the tomb. Nor think ye that the miseries that flow from ambition, avarice, voluptuousness, and open crime, are the only ones that attend us. Each refinement of life is accompanied with its own peculiar symptom. Besides, there are sufferings that no foresight can foresee, which no excellence can elude.

The imperfection of a master, or of him placed in power, may bring to his slave or other dependant unutterable wo!

The lassitude of sickness, the agony of its pain, the distresses, the imperfections of our friends, their alienation from us, and our final separation from the objects of our tenderest regard, would transform paradise itself into a wilderness of wo, did not the light of God keep it for ever illumined.

Even could we escape from all the external causes of wo, yet the waters of bitterness would continue to flow from the never-ceasing sources of sorrow that lie deep in our own bosoms buried.

We are therefore constrained, forced to conclude, that the balance of our moral constitution has been destroyed; and by the derangement of a system once harmoniously attuned, our principles of action, no longer in unison, are thrown into perpetual collision: maintaining no longer their original or their relative strength, they lead us into perpetual error, and by their conflicts produce a moral discord incompatible with the happiness of man. "For the creature was made subject to vanity, not willingly, but by reason of him who hath subjected the same in hope." "Because the creature itself shall be delivered from the bondage (δουλειας, *slavery*) of corruption into the glorious liberty of the children of God." *Rom.* viii. 20.

Had we been made acquainted merely with the fall of man and its effect upon his moral constitution, we should have still been bewildered in the perplexities of our condition. A consciousness of guilt would have filled our minds with apprehension, and the fear of the Divine displeasure would have mingled its bitterness with every gratification, would have seized upon every hope. Like Cain, we should have cried out, "Our punishment is greater than we can bear," and solicited the black mark of slavery as an antidote to threatened and instant death.

But the mercy of God, which always tempers even the natural events to the delicate sensibilities of our physical perceptions, concealed from our view the desolation of our condition, till, in the maturity of his counsels, he saw fit to blend with the discovery the bright visions "of the glory about to be revealed." *Rom.* viii. 18.

The heathen nations, although painfully alive to the brevity of human life, and deeply impressed with the vanity of our hopes, were equally ignorant of our fallen nature, and of the holiness of that God before whom we are to be adjudged. Their conception of an existence after death was cheerless and indistinct, although, even at this late day, among the most lofty intellects of their time, we can now perceive a longing desire after something to them unknown, a hankering for the proof of a spiritual immortality. Thus, while there was but little in their anticipations of a future state to excite their apprehension or alarm, there was but little to stimulate their hope.

The vulgar were sometimes alarmed by the majestic terrors of the Thunderer, and the philosopher was sometimes penetrated by those perfections which he was led to ascribe to the mighty Mind.

Yet the wisest sages of antiquity do not seem to have perceived in human guilt an internal malignity, which no penitence can expiate, nor blood of dying victims wash away.

If some glimpses of the miseries and dangers in which sin had involved us were disclosed to the favoured few, yet visions of prophecy dispelled the gloom; for, "where there is no vision the people perish." *Prov.* xxix. 18.

It was not till our Saviour had sealed the charter of our hope, that our condition, with a full view of its desolation, was proclaimed to a fallen world. A knowledge of the disease and the remedy has in mercy kept pace with each other. If we learn that the "creature was made subject to vanity," we also learn that he was made so in hope.

Now, when we behold our condition, although we see evidences of our fallen state, of the degradation of our intellectual and moral faculties, yet we see also a provision of mercy by which the creature may be delivered from "the bondage (*δουλειας*, *slavery*) of corruption into the glorious liberty of the children of God."

Viewed in connection with this sublime truth, the value of human interests, the pain of human sufferings, and the grief of human wrongs disappear; yea, vanish from the eye of the true believer. The grandeur of his future prospects dignifies his present state, however humble. His present evils, which might overwhelm him if attached to his ultimate condition, lose all their bitterness when converted by redeeming love into mere lessons of moral discipline. The pain is softened by the endearment of paternal tenderness, and he feels and knows that they will only accompany the mere infancy of his being.

The poor, humble, but Christian slave, hears constantly the les sons of Titus, and is happy in his obedience to his own master, that he may please him well in all things, watchful to not contradict, nor purloin from any one, and careful to show all good fidelity, that he may adorn the doctrine of God. He feels that no one has a deeper interest in that grace; for it hath equally appeared to all men.

He remembers his fellow-slaves of Colosse, and while with singleness of eye he heartily serves his earthly master, he feels that the act is ennobled, and is transferred to be an act of devotion and obedience to the great Jehovah.

Sympathy carries him back to his Corinthian brethren, in common with whom he feels no anxious care to change the condition in which he was called, for while he is content to abide where God has placed him, he knows that he has been purchased by the blood of Christ, and promoted to the rank of a freeman of the Lord.

With his fellow-slaves of Ephesus, he may tremble with fear lest his obedience to his master shall not be performed with good-will and singleness of heart, as unto Christ himself, for he knows that God has not required of him merely eye-service; yet he also knows that Christians, whether bond or free in this world, will hereafter be remembered of God for whatever good they do. Yea, he yields himself to the exhortations of Timothy, and accounts his own master worthy of all honour and obedience, that the name of God and his doctrine should not be blasphemed; nor does he feel the less reverence for his believing master, but rather does his service with alacrity as to a brother, and with heart-felt joy, because he is a faithful and beloved partaker of the benefits of his labour.

And when he hears men, whose ignorance of God has caused them to be puffed up with the idea of their own importance and purity, evidently filled with pride, as though they could teach God a more holy government, attempting to exhort and teach them a different doctrine, he feels, he knows that such are not only evil and bad men, but ignorant ones, such as dote about questions, and strifes of words, which have no other tendency than to fill the mind with envy, strife, railing, and evil surmises, such as are among men of corrupt minds, among men who are destitute of the truth, and among men who suppose that gain is godliness. He will view such men, however thoughtless they may be of their true position or sincere in their belief, as standing in the position of the serpent in Eden. Their lessons to him are disobedience to God. From such he will withdraw himself; yea, he will fly from them as from a deadly poison, because disobedience to God for ever ends in ruin and death. But from Timothy he learns contentment, for, as he brought nothing into the world with him, and as he can most certainly carry nothing out, so, having food and raiment, he will be content, and especially so as contentment and godliness are great gain.

And finally he hears as it were a trumpet sounding from the very gates of heaven, and looking, he beholds Peter standing there; he hears a still small voice, the voice of Jesus Christ, saying, "Thou art Peter, and on this rock I will build my church, and the gates of hell shall not prevail against it, and I will give unto thee the keys of the kingdom of heaven, and whatsoever thou shalt bind on earth shall be bound in heaven." *Matt.* xvi. 18, 19. And then Peter, raising his arm in the direction of the Gentile nations, says to the slaves: "Be subject to your masters with all fear; not only to the good and gentle, but also to the froward: for this is thank-worthy, if a man for conscience towards God endure grief, suffering wrongfully. For what glory is it, if, when ye be buffeted for your faults, ye take it patiently? But if, when ye do well, and suffer for it, ye take it patiently, this is acceptable to God. For even hereunto were ye called; because Christ also suffered for us, leaving us an example, that ye should follow his steps, who did no sin, neither was guile found in his mouth; who when he was reviled, reviled not again; when he suffered he threatened not, but committed himself to him that judgeth righteously; who his own self bare our sins in his own body on the tree, that we, being dead to sins, should live unto righteousness: by whose stripes ye were healed. For ye were as sheep gone astray, but are now returned unto the Shepherd and Bishop of your souls."

LESSON XV.

From the immense disproportion between our finite minds and the infinite objects of future hope, our conceptions of the disimbodied spirit must necessarily be feeble. But while we anticipate the promised freedom of the celestial world, the disenthralment of our intellectual faculties, and the deliverance of our moral powers from all corruption, the mind becomes more and more habituated to the scenes thus disclosed, and even reaches to prospects of resplendent beauty; to visions of unclouded truth; to the solution of the little difficulties of our own earthly trials; to the evolutions of the Divine character in connection with our little planet, and even to that infinitude that mocks the bounds of time and space.

Thus the pious Christian, who meditates upon God and the heavens, the work of his hand, feels a divine influence spread over his soul, while the active and the retired, the ardent and the timid, the philosopher whose mind is illumined by the varied lights of science, and the pious *slave*, whose researches are confined to the sayings of some unlettered expositor, will each cherish anticipations congenial to his peculiar state of mind. Yet all will grow in grace; all will rise above the level of temporal delights; and all will embrace in their expanding conceptions the mighty import of that glorious promise, that "eye hath not seen, nor ear heard, neither hath it entered into the heart of man, the things that God hath prepared for them that love him," 1*Cor.* ii. 9, till elevated so far above earthly associations, that each can say, "I shall be satisfied when I awake in thy likeness." *Ps.* xvii. 15.

What degree of moral likeness will gradually be produced by a near contemplation of unveiled perfection is reserved for eternity to disclose. But the time will at length come when to every sincere Christian and true disciple, dazzled by the refulgence that will break upon his astonished sight, Jesus Christ will address the language of affection, as he did to Martha: "Said I not unto thee that if thou wouldst believe thou shouldst see the glory of God?" *John* xi. 40.

"Then we all, with open face, beholding, as in a glass, the glory of God, are changed into the same image, from glory to glory." 2 *Cor.* iii. 18.

Such, then, is the picture and such the prospect of the Christian character; and well may Christians, even the slave, "Reckon that the sufferings of this present time are not worthy to be compared with the glory which shall be revealed." *Rom.* viii. 18.

From the monarch down, viewed from the distance of eternity, man occupies but a point. All earthly distinctions become so small that nothing short of the eye of omnipotence can see them. The same language describes, and the same God will prepare their rest.

The Christian slave feels exalted even while on earth, for he is well persuaded "that neither death, nor life, nor angels, nor principalities, nor power, nor things present, nor things to come, nor height, nor depth, nor any creature, shall be able to separate us from the love of God." *Rom.* viii. 38.

If for a few days the afflicted Christian and *slave* "wander in the wilderness in a solitary way;" if, "hungry and thirsty, their souls faint in them," he is yet "hastening to a city of habitations." *Ps.* cvii. 4, 5, 7.

If even the sun of his earthly hopes be set, yet he is hastening to a country where "thy sun shall no more go down; neither shall thy noon withdraw itself; for the Lord shall be thine everlasting light, and the days of thy mourning shall be ended." *Isa.* lx. 20.

With such views the heart is elevated above the pains and miseries of this transitory world to the contemplation of hope celestial.

The mere philosopher, who views the mutilated structure of the moral world, sees no renovating principle to reorganize its scattered fragments. He mourns with unavailing sorrow over the ruins of his race, and chills with horror at the prospect of his own decay. But the Christian sees a fairer earth and a more radiant heaven. And should the poor slave, forgetful of this high destiny of his Christian character, and of his ultimate home, feeling, like Hagar, the slave of Sarah, the hand of his mistress dealing hardly by him, and, like her, attempt a remedy by flight; like her, he will hear the voice of God, saying, "Return to thy mistress, and submit thyself under her hand." *Gen.* xvi. 9.

Like her, in humble submission, he obeys the command, and prays, "O Lord, correct me," for "I know that the way of man is not in himself; it is not in man that walketh to direct his steps." *Jer.* x. 23.

In the miseries and vanities with which he is surrounded, the Christian only sees proofs of a fallen, not of a hopeless state. He, like old Æneas, is seeking and looking for a home in a foreign land, and, like him, constantly requires the interposition of some friendly providence to warn him that he is still distant from the destined shores.

> Mutandæ sedes; non hæc tibi littora suasit,
> Delius, aut Cretæ jussit considere Apollo.—*2d Ænead.*

Like the Israelites, he has pitched his tent in a wilderness of sin, and feels grateful for those afflictions that reiterate the admonition: "Arise and depart, for this is not your rest." *Micah* ii. 10.

He knows that "this corruptible will put on incorruption, that this mortal will put on immortality, and that as he has borne the image of the earthly, he shall also bear the image of the heavenly." See 1 *Cor.* xv. 49, 53.

Why then should our hearts sink in sadness, because, as we have seen, sin has destroyed the balance of moral power among men,—even the foundation on which their universal equality could exist, whence some races of men have gone deep down in the pit of human degradation, until the man and the brute are found in the same animal tenement.

Such is the poisonous nature of sin, that the heart that deviseth wicked imaginations always finds "feet running swiftly to ruin." See *Prov.* vi. 18.

But God hath promised that the remnant of Israel shall not speak lies: "Neither shall a deceitful tongue be found in their mouth, for they shall feed and lie down, and none shall make them afraid." *Zeph.* iii. 12, 13.

But the ways of God are not as the ways of man; he makes his enemies build his throne.

Therefore, be ye not deceived, for "there shall be false teachers among you, who privily shall bring in damnable heresies, even denying the Lord that bought them, and bring upon themselves swift destruction." 2 *Pet.* ii. 1.

Study and pray to improve the powers that God hath given, while you compare the things that be with the causes and designs of Providence; and while you note that "the evil bow before the good, and the wicked at the gates of the righteous," note also that "the way of the ungodly shall perish." They shall be "like the chaff which the wind driveth away." For "the hand of the diligent shall bear rule; but the slothful shall be under tribute." "He that hath not sells himself to him that hath." Therefore, "the borrower is *servant* to the lender," and wherefore, "*wisdom* is better than rubies;" for "by me princes rule, and nobles, even all the judges of the earth. I love them that love me, and those that seek me early shall find me. Riches and honour are with me: yea, durable riches and righteousness."

But God hath promised that "the whole earth shall be full of the knowledge of the Lord, as the waters cover the sea." *Isa.* xi. 9. Therefore, so long as the tares and the wheat shall grow together, "Wait ye upon me, saith the Lord, until the day that I will rise up to the prey: for my determination is to gather the nations, that I may assemble the kingdoms to pour out upon them mine indignation, even all my fierce anger; for all the earth shall be devoured with the fire of my jealousy. For then will I turn to the people a pure language that they may all call on the name of the Lord, to serve him with one consent. From beyond the rivers of Ethiopia my suppliants, even the daughter of my *dispersed*, (בַּת־פּוּצַי *Bath Putsi, the daughter of Phut, the most degraded of the African tribes,*) shall bring mine offering." *Zeph.* iii. 8–10.

The slavery of the African tribes to those of the true faith is here clearly announced, and the great benefit of their conversion to the worship of the true God proclaimed as an abundant reason.

Thus Isaiah, speaking of the house of Israel, the prototype of the church of God, says—"Thus saith the Lord, The labour of Egypt, and the merchandise of Ethiopia and the Sabeans, men of stature, shall come over unto thee, and they shall be thine; they shall come after thee; in chains they shall come over, they shall fall down unto thee; they shall make supplication unto thee, saying, Verily, God is in thee, and there is no God" *beside*. *Isa.* xlv. 14.

And these people, in a state of pupilage, are thus referred to by

---

Zephaniah: "I will also leave in the midst of thee an afflicted and poor people, and they shall trust in the name of the Lord."

God ever requires of the powerful the protection of the weak, of the more learned the instruction of the ignorant, and of the more wise the government of those who cannot govern themselves.

"For so hath the Lord commanded us, saying, I have set thee to be a light to the Gentiles, that thou shouldest be for salvation unto the ends of the earth." *Acts* xiii. 47.

Study VI

LESSON I.

SIN IS any want of a conformity to the law of God. Man was created free from sin. He was placed under the government of laws adapted to his condition. But a want of conformity to any item of such law necessarily disorganized and deranged some portion of his original condition. Let us cast a hasty view at the operation of these laws. It is contrary to the law of God that a man should put his hand in the fire; when he does so, his condition is somewhat physically changed, and he is in trouble.

It is contrary to the law of God that a man should bear false testimony; he having done so, his condition is changed mentally, and his troubles increase.

It is contrary to the law of God that a man should remain ignorant; he doing so, is not in the condition of him who has multiplied and replenished his mental and physical capabilities: he is less capable, he has less power.

The law of God is all powerful, and will be executed. The punishment of its breach is certain. It is effect following cause. The whole of God's creation is planned by this principle.

A want of conformity to the law operates as a poison, that spreads through the moral and physical man, sinking, forcing him down to trouble, pain, misery, ruin, and death.

The boy, intending to appropriate to himself, takes a pin. If there is naught that checks him, petty thefts push him on to deeper crimes, that end in death. The young gentleman drinks the social glass, nor thinks harm to himself; he feels strong, he fears nothing: but habit becomes excess; his physical appearance becomes sickly; his mind obtuse, his pleasures gross; his condition is changed; he is evidently tending downwards to the grave. And such are the course and progress of every other sin; for, whatever has a tendency to injure the character, health, mind, and body, is sin.

Speculators upon the holy writ may say what they will; yet it is certain, that act, called the eating the apple, was an act, whatever it may have been, that necessarily injured the character. health, mind, and body of man. It is certain, because it did so. It was the very birth of death itself. The wages of sin are death—the Lord God Almighty hath spoken it!! Another law of God, till then unknown to man, was brought instantly into operation. His wants were changed; the earth no longer produced spontaneously to them. In the emphatic language of that day, it was cursed, that he might have less leisure time and opportunity to continue in the downward course of sin to sudden destruction and death. He was in great mercy condemned to labour for the supply of his daily wants; he was made the slave to the necessities of animal life. Is it necessary to quote Scripture to show that it abounds with the doctrine that idleness is a wonderful promoter of sin? God in great mercy contrived that his hungry body and naked back should in some measure keep him from it.

"Therefore, the Lord sent him forth from the garden of Eden *to till* the ground from which he was taken." *Gen.* iii. 23, "To till" is transferred from לַעֲבֹד *la avod, to slave.* It is the very word that means a slave; but is here used as a verb, and literally means *to slave the ground.* In this early instance of its use in holy writ, in relation to man, it is used as a verb, to show us, not that he had become the property of any other person, but a slave to his own necessities, and that the labour required was the labour of a slave.

Until man had become poisoned by sin there was no want of a law, of an institution to interpose between him and his sudden destruction and death.

This is the first degree of slavery among poor, fallen men, and upon which now depend their health, happiness, and continuance of life.

LESSON II.

"But Cain was a tiller of the ground." The word *tiller* is translated from the same word used as a noun, *a slave of the ground*, having reference to its cultivation for his support and sustenance. And here we see the peculiar propriety of the language of the Psalmist: "He causeth the grass to grow for the cattle, and herb for the *service* of man, that he may bring forth food out of the earth." *Ps.* civ. 14. In this instance, "service" means slavery, and is translated from the same word, לַעֲבֹדַת *la avodath.* "He causeth the grass to grow for the cattle, and herb for the slavery of man, that he may bring forth food out of the earth."

But we are directly informed that the Lord had no respect for the offering of Cain; that Cain was very wroth, and his countenance fell; and the Lord reasoned with him and said, "If thou doest well, shalt thou not be accepted? and if thou doest not well, sin lieth at the door;" also promising him, if he would do well, he should have rule over his younger brother! All this shows that Cain's progress in sin had become very considerable, notwithstanding the mild yet unavoidable slavery already imposed. But, like many other sinners, he ran his race rapidly, until his hands were dyed in his brother's blood.

"When thou tillest the ground, it shall not henceforth yield unto thee her strength: a fugitive and a vagabond shalt thou be in the earth." *Gen.* iv. 12. Here *tillest* is also translated from the same word, and means "when *thou slavest the ground*," showing most clearly that the slavery imposed on Adam was attached to Cain, with the additions, that the earth should not yield unto him her strength,—that he should be a fugitive and a vagabond,—and a mark was placed upon him. The expression that the ground should not yield unto him its strength, may be understood to mean that it should not be as productive, or, that some other person should enjoy a portion of the benefit of his labour, or in fact both: his labours were to be in some measure fruitless. And let us notice how this portion of his sentence compares with other announcements of Jehovah:

"Treasures of wickedness profit nothing, but righteousness delivereth from death."

"The Lord will not suffer the soul of the righteous to famish, but he casteth away the substance of the wicked."

"The hand of the diligent shall bear rule, but the slothful shall be under tribute."

"Poverty and shame shall be to him that refuses instruction, but he that regardeth reproof shall be honoured."

"A good man leaveth an inheritance to his children's children, but the wealth of the sinner is laid up for the just."

"The righteous eateth to the satisfying of his soul, but the belly of the wicked shall want." *Proverbs.*

"He should be a fugitive and a vagabond.

"The wicked flee when no man pursueth; but the righteous are bold as a lion." *Prov.* xxviii. 1.

"Blessed is the man that walketh not in the counsel of the ungodly, nor standeth in the way of sinners, nor sitteth in the seat of the scornful. But his delight is in the law of the Lord; and his law doth he meditate day and night. And he shall be like a tree planted by the rivers of water, that bringeth forth his fruit in his season; his leaf also shall not wither; and whatsoever he doeth shall prosper. The ungodly are not so, but are like the chaff which the wind driveth away. Therefore the ungodly shall not stand in the judgment, nor sinners in the congregation of the righteous. For the Lord knoweth the way of the righteous; but the way of the ungodly shall perish." *Ps.* i.

And again: "Set thou a wicked man over him; and let Satan stand at his right hand. When he shall be judged, let him be condemned; and let his prayer become sin. Let his days be few, and let another take his office. Let his children be fatherless, and his wife a widow. Let his children be continually vagabonds and beg; let them seek their bread also out of their desolate places. Let the extortioner catch all that he hath; and let the strangers spoil his labour. Let there be none to extend mercy unto him: neither let there be any to favour his fatherless children. Let his posterity be cut off; and in the generation following let their name be blotted out. Let the iniquities of his fathers be remembered with the Lord, and let not the sin of his mother be blotted out." *Ps.* cix. 6–14.

Such is the prospect of the desperately wicked: "The curse of the Lord is in the house of the wicked: but he blesseth the habitation of the just." *Prov.* iii. 33.

LESSON III.

BUT Cain had a mark set upon him. The word translated *mark* is אוֹת *oth:* it means a mark of a miraculous nature, whereby some future thing is of a certainty known, and may be something done or only said. Whatever it may have been, the object was to prevent him from being slain by any one meeting him, by its proclamation of the burden of the curses under which he laboured. It was, therefore, absolutely the mark of sin, sealing upon him and his race this secondary degree of slavery. The mark distinguished them as low and servile as well as wicked, and hence its protective influence.

But what was the mark of sin? What is it now? and what has it ever been? If one is accused of some vile offence, a little presumptive evidence will make us say, It is a very dark crime; it makes him look very black. This figure, if it be one, now so often applied, is so strongly used in Scripture, and in fact by all in every age, that the idea seems well warranted that the downward, humiliating course of sin has a direct tendency, by the Divine law, to even physically degrade, perhaps blacken and disbeautify, the animal man.

A similar doctrine was well known to the Greeks. Demosthenes says to the Athenians, "It is impossible for him who commits low, dishonourable, and wicked acts, not to possess a low, dirty intellect; for, as the person of a man receives, as it were, a colouring from his conduct, so does the mind take upon itself a clothing from the same acts." See Second Olynthiac. So the Arabians: "God invited unto the dwelling of peace, and directed whom he pleaseth into the right way. They who do right shall receive a most excellent reward, and a superabundant addition; neither blackness nor shame shall cover their faces." *Koran*, chap. x.

"On the day of the resurrection, thou shalt see the faces of those who have uttered lies concerning God, become black.' *Koran*, chap. xxxix.

So, the Mohammedan belief is that a man who has some good qualities may die; but, on the account of his wickedness, he will be sent to hell, and there tormented until his skin is black; but that if he shall ever be taken thence, by the mercy of God, he will be immersed in the river of life, and his skin become whiter than pearls; see *Pocock, notis in part. Moris*, p. 289 and 292; but that the faces of the wicked will ever remain black. See *Yalkut Shemuni*, part ii. fol. 86; also *Sale, Prelim. Disc.* p. 104, 105.

So the Mohammedan tradition, that the bad spirits, Monker and Nakir, who, upon the death of a man, come to examine him, are awful and black. See *Prelim. Disc.* p. 90. And hence the belief is that the wicked, even before judgment, will stand looking up to God with their faces obscured by blackness and disfigured by all the marks of sorrow and deformity. *Idem*, p. 99.

So also the fable, that a precious stone of paradise fell down to the earth to Adam, whiter than milk, but turned black by the touch of a wicked woman, or, as others say, by wickedness of mankind generally; but the story is that its blackness is only skin-deep, and hence the Arabians carefully preserved it in the Caaba at Mecca. *Idem*, p. 125. Also, *Al Zamakh*, &c. *in Koran;* and *Ahmed Ebĕn Yusef;* and *Pocock, Spec.* p. 117.

Similar traditions and quotations may be gathered from all quarters of the world, and from all portions of time; but let us turn to the book that never lies nor misleads. "Behold, I am against thee, saith the Lord of hosts; and I will discover thy skirts upon thy face, and I will show the nations thy nakedness, and the kingdoms thy shame." *Nahum*, iii. 5.

The word here translated skirts, is שׁוּלַיִךְ *shulaik*. We believe that all scholars agree the Hebrew root of this word is borrowed from the Arabic شُبُلٌ, of which the meaning is *postremum cujusque rei;* and, hence the idea *skirt*, the extreme of something hanging down, tending downward.

And from the same source we have the Hebrew word שׁוֹלָל *sholal*, a captive, a thing captured, &c., because the captive is in an extreme condition; and thus שׁוּל *shūl* is made to mean a hem or skirt, from its cognate and Arabic root, the extreme of something tending downwards. Thus شَأَلَ *shaal, to be loose, to hang down.* From these considerations, the word was often used to mean a prisoner, a captive. Thus, *Job* xii. 19: "He leadeth princes away spoiled," שׁוֹלָל *sholal, captive, reduced to the lowest extremity*, &c.

Therefore, although perhaps not as literal, the idea of the prophet would have been more exactly conveyed had it been translated, "*And I will discover the low extremity of your condition upon your face;*" and in this same sense the word is used in *Jer.* xiii. 22: "If thou say in thine heart, Wherefore come these things upon me? For the greatness of thine iniquity are thy skirts (שׁוּלַיִךְ *shulaik*) discovered, and thy heels made bare." Evidently proclaiming the doctrine, that a course of sin, through the Divine providence, will leave its mark.

"She is empty, and void, and waste, and the heart melteth, and the knees smite together, and much pain is in all loins, and the faces of them all gather blackness. Behold, I am against thee, saith the Lord." *Nah.* ii. 10, 13.

"At Tehaphnehes also the day shall be darkened, when I shall break there the yokes of Egypt; and the pomp of her strength shall cease in her: as for her, a cloud shall cover her, and her daughters shall go into captivity. Thus will I execute judgments in Egypt: and they shall know that I am the Lord." *Ezek.* xxx. 18, 19.

"Our necks are under persecution: we labour and have no rest. We have given the hand to the Egyptains, and to the Assyrians, to be satisfied with bread. Our fathers have sinned, and are not; and we have borne their iniquities. *Servants* (עֲבָדִים *abadim, slaves*) have ruled over us: there is none that doth deliver us out of their hand. We get our bread with the peril of our lives, because of the sword of the wilderness. Our skin is black like an oven, because of the terrible famine." *Lam.* v. 5–10.

"For the hurt of the daughter of my people I am hurt; I am black; astonishment hath taken hold on me." *Jer.* viii. 21.

"Judah mourneth, and the gates thereof languish; they are black unto the ground; and the cry of Jerusalem is gone up." *Jer.* xiv. 2.

"Her Nazarites were purer than snow; they were whiter than milk; they were more ruddy in body than rubies; their polishing was of sapphire. Their visage is blacker than a coal; they are not known in the streets." *Lam.* iv. 7, 8.

"For ye are not come unto the mount that might be touched,

and that burned with fire; nor unto blackness, and darkness, and tempest." *Heb.* xii. 18.

"Raging waves of the sea, foaming out their own shame; wandering stars, to whom is reserved the blackness of darkness for ever." *Jude* 13.

"For though thou wash thee with nitre, and take thee much soap, yet thine iniquity is marked before me, saith the Lord God." *Jer.* ii. 22.

"The show of their countenance doth witness against them." *Isa.* iii. 9.

LESSON IV.

BUT experience proved that even this second degree of slavery was not a sufficient preventive of sin to preserve man upon the earth. "That the sons of God saw the daughters of men, that they were fair; and they took them wives of all which they chose. And the Lord said, My spirit shall not always strive with man." *Gen.* vi. 2, 3. The word translated "fair," and applied to the daughters of men, is טֹבֹת *to voth;* it is in the feminine plural, and comes from טָב *tav*, and cognate with the Syriac word ܛܒܐ *tov* or *tob;* it merely means *good*, *excellent*, as the quality may exist in the mind of the person taking cognisance.

It implies no quality of virtue or complexion, but in its use is reflective back to the nominative. It is one of those words which we find in all languages, of which rather a loose use is made. We find it in *Dan.* ii. 32, (the 31st of the English text,) "*excellent;*" also *Ezra* v. 17, "*good.*" When it is said of Sarah, in *Gen.* xii. 11, that she was "fair," meaning that she was of a light complexion, the word יְפַת *yĕphath* is used, and is the same with our Japheth, the son of Noah, and comes from יָפַע *yapha*, and means to *shine*, *to give light*, and, as an adjective, well means lightness of complexion, fairness, and brilliancy of beauty. So in *Esth.* ii. 7, "and the maid was fair and beautiful," יְפַת *yephath.* 1 *Sam.* xvi. 12, "Now he was ruddy and of a fair countenance," יְפֵה *yepha.* 1 *Kings* i. 4, "and the damsel was fair," יָפָה *yaphah.*

It is true that in *Solomon's Song*, i. 16, "Behold, thou art fair, my beloved,"—ii. 10, "My beloved spake and said unto me, Rise up my love, my fair one, and come away,"—iv. 1, "Behold, thou art fair, my love; behold, thou art fair; thou hast doves' eyes,"—iv. 7, "Thou art fair, my love; there is no spot in thee," and also v. 9, "O thou fairest among women," the word יָפָע *yapha*, in grammatical form, is used in the original, and that the term is applied to a black woman. But this whole song is written in hyperbole. In the description of Solomon's person, it says, v. 11, "His head is as the most fine gold;" in the original, "His head is the most fine gold." 14: "His hands are as gold rings set with the beryl: his belly as bright ivory overlaid with sapphires. 15: His legs are as pillars of marble, set upon sockets of gold: his countenance is as Lebanon, excellent as the cedars."

Asiatic poetry always abounded in hyperbole. Thus an Arabian poet, speaking of his mistress, says—

"I behold in thine eyes, angels looking at me.
Deformity in another, in thee is excellent beauty;
The garments of the shepherd, upon thee, are the finest tissue,
And brass ornaments become fine gold.
Thy excellence, so great among men, the god beholds,
And is astonished at thy beauty."

It is not from such productions that we are to look for the simple, original, and radical meaning of terms; and probably even in the case of Canticles, the word יָפָע *yapha* would not have been allowed by the rules of composition, had it not been first announced in a calm, initiatory manner, that she was a black woman, in order that no misconception might arise from such hyperbole.

Let us suppose ourselves in Arabia, and some poet announces that, for our evening entertainment and diversion, he will deliver a panegyric upon some black woman, and, among other things, says—

Thy neck is as a tower of ivory.
Thy teeth are like a flock of sheep.
Thy lips are like a thread of scarlet.
Thy nose like the tower of Lebanon,
That looketh towards Damascus;
And the smell of thy nose like apples;
And the smell of the roof of thy mouth like the best wine
Thy stature is like the palm-tree.
Thy skin is fairer than snow,
And thy breasts like two clusters of grapes.

Thy head is as Mount Carmel,
And the hair of thy head like purple,
And the curls of thy hair like a flock of goats.
Behold, thou art fair, my love; thou hast doves' eyes.

True, amid such hyperbole, we might have mistaken her colour, if he had not previously informed us on that subject. But, as it stands, there is no falsehood asserted; there is no liability to mistake. The poet merely means that, at least in his conception, she is as lovely, beautiful, and desirable as all those hyperboles would make her. And we think we have reason to contend, that the hyperbolic use of the word יָפֶע *yapha*, in Canticles, does not alter in any sense its real meaning, or, in any ordinary use of language, make it a term applicable to people of colour, or in any sense whatever a synonyme of the טָב *tav*, or טֹבֹת *to voth*, as used in Genesis. This explanation is thought necessary, since it is seen that we shall hereafter contend that the descendants of Cain were black.

LESSON V.

If we take the passage, *Gen.* vi. 2, 3, as it stands in connection, it seems to us an obvious deduction that the commingling of the races of Seth and Cain was obnoxious to the Lord.

It is placed in position as the cause why his Spirit should not always strive. He saw that such amalgamation would, did deteriorate and destroy the more holy race of Seth; and therefore determined, with grief in his heart, to destroy man from the earth. All were swept away, except Noah, his three sons, and their four wives. Yet sin found a residence among the sons of Noah, and Canaan was doomed to perpetual bondage, as it now exists upon the earth. "And he said, Cursed be Canaan: a servant of servants shall he be unto his brethren. And he said, Blessed be the Lord God of Shem, and Canaan shall be his servant. God shall enlarge Japheth, and he shall dwell in the tents of Shem, and Canaan shall be his servant." *Gen.* ix. 25–27.

The expression "*servant of servants*" is translated from the words עֶבֶד עֲבָדִים *ebed abadim, slave of slaves.* The expression is idiomatic, and means *the most abject slave.*

In the passage quoted, the word servant, in all cases, is translated from *ebed*, and means slave. There was no master placed over Adam,—it is not certain there was over Cain,—but here the master is named and blessed; and the slave is named, and his slavery pronounced to be of the most abject kind. If we mistake not, it is an article of the Christian creed of most churches, that Adam was the federal head and representative of his race; that the covenant was made, not only with Adam, but also with his posterity; that the guilt of his sin was imputed to them; that each and every one of his posterity are depraved through his sin; that this, their original sin, is properly sin, and deserves God's wrath and curse. If so, can we say less in the case of Cain? or that a new relation did intervene in the case of Ham?

LESSON VI.

Having traced the institution of slavery down to its third and final degree, and finding it firmly lodged in the family of Ham, let us now inquire what proof there may be that his descendants are also the descendants and race of Cain. This evidence is to be found in the fact, 1st. That the descendants of Ham were black, inheriting the mark of Cain. 2d. That the traditions and memorials of the family of Ham are also traditions and memorials of the family of Cain. 3d. That Naamah, of the family of Cain, is found to be kept in memory by the earlier descendants of Ham. 4th. That the characteristics of these families are the same, and that no facts are found to exist discordant to the proposition of their being one and the same race; but on the contrary, every vestige of them is in unison with such proposition.

In presenting the evidence touching the several facts of the inquiry, we cannot claim the most lucid or logical arrangement, nor that our remarks will be classed in the best methodical order for the subjects of consideration. But we present the proposition that aboriginal names are always significant terms: thus, Abram, the high father; Abraham, the father of a multitude; Jacob, holding by the heel, supplanting; Israel, one who wrestles with God; and Cain, one that has been purchased or bought: "And she bare Cain, and said, I have *gotten* a man from the Lord." *Gen.* iv. 1. The word Cain is from קָנָה *Cana*, and means to buy, to purchase, and, as a noun, a thing bought; and the word "gotten," קָנִיתִי *canithi*, terminating with its verbal formation, means, *I have bought* or *purchased*—his name signified *one purchased.*

There is an allusion to Cain in the Koran; and, although we do not present it as or for authority, yet it may not be out of place to notice what the ancient Arabians have said on the subject: "Verily, I (the prophet) am no other than a denouncer of threats, and a messenger of good tidings unto the people who believed. It is he who hath created you from one person and out of him produced his wife, that he might dwell with her; and when he had known her, she carried a light burden for a time, wherefore she walked easily therewith: but when it became more heavy, they called upon God their Lord, saying, If thou give us a child rightly shaped, we will surely be thankful. Yet when he had given them a child rightly shaped, they attributed companions unto him, for that which he had given them. But far be that from God, which they associated with him! Will they associate with him false gods, which create nothing, but are themselves created, and can neither give them assistance nor help themselves?" *Koran*, chap. vii.

The Arabian commentators, in explanation of this passage, relate a tradition among them. They say, when Eve was big with her first child, the devil came to frighten and fill her mind with apprehension. But he pretended to her that by his prayers to God he could persuade him to cause her to have a well-shaped child, a son, the likeness of Adam, and that she should be safely delivered of it, upon the condition that she should dedicate or name the child *abed al hareth, the slave of the devil*, instead of the name that Adam would give it, *abed Allah, the slave of God;* that Eve accepted the terms, and the child was born, &c. The legend is varied by the commentators, some saying the child died as soon as born, or that the devil applied to Adam instead of Eve, &c.; but they all agree that *al hareth* was the name the devil went by among the angels.

It is a little remarkable that the passage in *Gen.* iv. 2, "But Cain was a tiller of the ground," Heb. *obed adamah, the slave of the ground*, would be, in Arabic, this phrase, *abed al hareth*, the cognate of the Hebrew word ארץ *erets*, the earth. And therefore the Arabic, *abed al hareth*, will be a translation of the Hebrew in Genesis. This legend will be found in *Al Bederoi, Jallado' adim, Zamakhshari, et al.* See *Sale's Koran*, vol. i. p. 360.

The discovery of the western continent by Columbus was the great and absorbing event of the age in which it happened. It was an event which, in consideration of the characteristics of men, would be held in commemoration: in all parts of the world it would be a matter of such record as literature made convenient, or the relative influence of the event rendered constant to the mind. And hence we find it referred to not only in books, but in the continent discovered; it is commemorated by the application of the name of the discoverer to its seas, lakes, rivers, mountains, districts of country, cities, towns, &c. Now, if at the time of the event, the world had not advanced to the achievement of literary records, it is evident that the latter mode of commemoration could have been the only one practicable; and history shows us that this mode of commemoration was adopted at the earliest ages, nor laid aside even at this day. This disposition to commemorate is one of the characteristics of the whole human family. Thus Eve commemorated some event, described as the purchase of her first-born of the Lord, by giving said first-born the name of "*one purchased.*"

"And the sons of Noah that went forth of the ark were Shem, and Ham, and Japheth: and Ham is the father of Canaan." "And Ham, the father of Canaan, saw the nakedness of his father, and told his two brethren without." "And Noah awoke from his wine, and knew what his younger son had done unto him. And he said, Cursed be Canaan." *Gen.* ix. 18, 22, 24, 25. The things here recorded took place in quick succession from the removal of Noah's family from the ark. Ham ultimately had four sons, the youngest of whom he named Canaan. Is there any evidence, at the time of these records, that any of the children of Ham were born, and especially his youngest?

It does appear to us that the word Canaan, as here used, does not mean any particular son of Ham. It is evidently used at a time before he had any sons. From the manner of the relation it seems probable the planting of the vineyard was among the first things Noah did after the flood. Two or three years was all the time required for the consummation of this event. In case Ham had married a female of the race of Cain, he had also identified himself with that race, and might well be called by his father, especially at a moment of displeasure, by a term emphatically showing, yea announcing prophetically, his degradation through all future time,—the degradation to which that connection had reduced him.

The ill-manners of Ham towards his father were not the great cause of the curse. The cause must have previously existed. The ill-manners only influence the time of its announcement. Even had it never been announced, the consequences would have been the same. The sentence of the law is only declaratory of the relation in which one has placed himself. The cause of the curse or degradation here pronounced must have been something adequate, to have produced it. The ill-manners could have no so great effect. And let us inquire, where are we to find an adequate cause for the immediate degradation of an unborn race, unless we find it in intermarriage. His intermarriage, then, could have been with no other than the race of Cain? When Noah spoke to Ham, and said, "Cursed be Canaan," he had no reference to any particular descendant of Ham, but included them all, as the race of Cain, and, in reproof and disparagement to his son, reproaching the connection. Suppose, even at this day, a descendant of Japheth should choose to amalgamate with the Negro, could not his father readily foretell the future destiny of the offspring,—their standing among the rest of his family? The term *Canaan*, thus spoken and applied to Ham, was significant of the character his conduct had created, by identifying himself with the race of Cain. It was a new name, deeply and degradingly distinguishing him from the rest of his father's family. Jacob was called Israel, after having wrestled with God; but an honourable cognomen would be made known and used, whereas one of reverse character might or might not.

It cannot be expected, at this late day, to account for the anomalies of the ancient Hebrew. Terms applied as proper names, whether significant or not, are in all languages, and in all ages, subject sometimes to strange and even oblique alterations. Thus, in the family of Benjamin, "*Ard*," of Genesis and Numbers, is changed into *Addar* in Chronicles; and thus *Colon* of Genoa was converted into *Columbus* in the western continent.

Thus, *Muppim* and *Huppim*, in Genesis, are changed into *Shupham* and *Hupham* in Numbers, and into *Shephupham* and *Huram* in Chronicles. See *Gen.* xlvi. 21, *Num.* xxvi. 39, and 1 *Chron.* viii. 5. The Kenites, Kennizites, and Canaanites of *Gen.* xv. 19; the Kenaz, xxxvi. 11 and 42; the Kenite and Kenites of *Num.* xxiv. 21; the *Kenites* of 1 *Sam.* xxvii. 10, xv. 5, 6; *Judges* iv. 11–17; and the city called "*Cain*," הַקַּיִן *ha Kain*, *Josh.* xv. 57, also *Kinah*, קִינָה, *idem* 22,—are all legitimately derived and descended from the name given to the first-born of mankind. Doubtless a critical search would find many more; but in all these instances the derivative is used for and by the descendants of Ham. But no instance is found where any such derivative is in use by the unmixed posterity of Shem or Japheth. We surely need not point in the direction of the cause of these facts.

In *Judges* iv. 11, we have, "Now, Heber the Kenite, (הַקֵּינִי *ha Keni*,) which was of the children of Hobab, (the Jethro of Genesis,) the father-in-law of Moses." We shall hereafter have occasion to show that the father-in-law of Moses was a descendant of Misraim, the second son of Ham; that he dwelt in the mountains of Midian, and, when spoken of in regard to his country, was called a Midianite; but his daughter, when spoken of in regard to her colour, was called an Ethiopian; but now, when he is spoken of in regard to his race, he is called a Cainite, *Kenite.*

In *Josh.* xv. 17, we have a derivative in common origin of the foregoing, in "Kenaz," the brother of Caleb; but upon examining 1 *Chron.* ii., we shall find a sufficient reason in the blood of that family; and in all instances where such derivative is found, we shall find the same cause to warrant its use.

LESSON VII.

Such evidence as there may be that Ham did take to wife some particular female of the race of Cain, will also be the most positive evidence that their descendants are one and the same.

Let it be noticed that, immediately preceding the account of the flood, and the causes which led to that judgment upon the earth, we are presented with the genealogical tables of the families of Cain and Seth, down to that period; and that these tables terminate with Ham, in that of Seth, and in the female Naamah, the daughter of Lamech, in the genealogy of Cain. Ham and Naamah are thus placed upon a parallel, so far as it regards these tables.

It surely is not difficult to perceive the cause why, in the table of Seth, the genealogical line ending in the family of Noah was selected; but, if the entire race of Cain were to be destroyed by the flood, why was the particular line ending in Naamah chosen?

Why was any such table of his race required? Beside Eve, the two wives of Lamech and this Naamah are the only females whose names are given before the flood? If the entire race of Cain was destroyed, how was the name of Naamah of more importance for us to know than that of thousands of the same race? Why has God sent these facts down to us? Has he ever revealed to us any thing unnecessary for us to know? Is it consistent with his character to do so? There have been, through all time since the deluge, traditions and legends among the Arabians, and many other Asiatic tribes, that this Naamah and her posterity continued upon the earth subsequent to that period. We give in substance a tale of traditionary lore among the Eastern nations, found in the Book Zohar, and referred to by Sale, page 87. They believe that at an extremely ancient time, there was an inferior race of beings, whom they call "jin," (query, a cognate of ינה *yana* or *jana*, to cast down, destroyed, used in a bad sense, to cast away;) that this race was created from, by, or someway connected with fire, heat, &c., either in their original state or in an acquired condition; that they eat, drink, propagate, and die, and are subjects of salvation or reprobation, like men; that they inhabited the world for ages before Adam was created; that they fell at length into general corruption; that, therefore, Eblis (one of the names of the devil) drove them into a remote part of the earth, and confined them there; but, however, some of their race remained; and that Tahmunah, (the Noah of the Hebrew Scriptures,) one of the ancient kings of Persia, drove them into the mountains of *Kâf.*

Another version of the same legend is, that this race of beings was begotten by Aza with Naamah, the daughter of Lamech. (Let us here note, אזא *aza* is a Chaldaic word, meaning *heat, to grow hot*, &c., and as such is used in *Dan.* iii. 22,—therefore a synonyme with Ham, as applied to the son of Noah.) But some have it that the race is the joint offspring, or from the double paternity, of Aza and Azael. (Let us also notice, that this monstrosity of paternity is reduced to a single personage by the fact, that the Hebrew suffix *el* merely gives quality, even by repetition, as thus,—Aza the mighty Aza.) But this version of the legend denominates the race "*Shedim*," the plural of *shed*, a word sometimes used to express idols, but more often used to mean desolation, distraction, &c.; and because the nursing breast is often exhausted, or from the notion that such exhaustion is akin to a thing destroyed, this word is applied to the female breast; and hence a posterity strongly marked by natural peculiarities would very readily take some name expressive of such fact. Even at this day, in reference to such peculiarities, we say, they took it from the "breast."

We deem it unnecessary to enter into a critical history of the word *shed* or *shedim*, as used by the Arabians, the "*sed*" of the Hebrews; but we may be permitted to remark that, from its conveying the idea of destruction, desolation, so strongly, the Hebrews applied it also to mean a "field," or country, in a destroyed or desolate or uncultivated condition; and it is thus used in many places. See *Genesis* iii. 1.; and is thus the word we call *Sodom*. It always carries with it the idea opposite to improvement; and, governed by the same leading idea, writers have applied it, perhaps rather figuratively, to any living existence found wandering over waste and solitary districts. We might pursue the subject of this tradition, and from the analogy of language, as well as from ancient associations, at least find some evidence that *Zahmurah* was no other than Noah; that the affix "*el*" with *Aza* arose from the acknowledged superiority of the race of Seth to that of Cain, in consequence of which they were sometimes described as "the sons of God," *Gen.* vi. 4; and that the tradition points to the race of Ham, and their humble condition in the world.

Traces of this legend will not only be found as above, but also in Gemara, in Hagiga, and Igrat Baale Hayyin, c. 15.

If it be a fact that the Negro race are the descendants of Ham and Naamah, the daughter of Lamech, of the race of Cain, it might be thought there would still be existing some traditions of such an extraordinary fact. As such we present the legend: not that we attach to it any undue importance, and especially not to be received as evidence at all, in contradiction of one word found in the holy books. But if a legend of ancient time shall be found, when sifted from the ignorance of fable or the fraud of design, to coincide with facts as related in the holy books, we may be permitted to consider the same as a circumstance not altogether unworthy of consideration.

But, we repeat, unless Naamah was to survive the destruction of the deluge, why was her name, why was her genealogy recorded and sent down to future time?

We think it certain that if she did survive the flood, she must have done so as the wife of one of Noah's sons. Now, as it is evident that the intermixture of the two races was regarded by Jehovah as a sin, it is not probable that either Shem or Japheth took her to wife, since they were both most honourably distinguished by a public blessing immediately after the flood.

But again: Noah had been preaching the then impending ruin near a hundred years. Lamech might well have had some glimpses of the subdiluvian world, and certainly saw the consequential ruin to young Ham, of the holy family of Noah, from such a connection with his daughter, Naamah. It could not otherwise than operate as a moral death to all the high hopes of him and his posterity. In case such connection was formed, and Lamech was forward in aiding or influencing it, then well might his troubled soul exclaim to his two wives as related.

But in case Ham did take to wife this daughter of Lamech, we might expect her name also to be held in remembrance by her posterity, as we have seen to some extent was that of Cain; and if we find such fact to exist in regard to her, it will be to our mind strong additional proof, that the descendants of Ham were in common the descendants of Cain. We notice here the fact, which we may hereafter deem necessary to prove, that, of the children of Ham, Cush originally settled in Arabia and the southwestern parts of Asia generally, Misraim in Egypt, Phut in the northern parts of Africa and southward indefinitely, and Canaan in Palestine.

When this latter country came to be conquered by Joshua, he found a city by the name of "Naamah," situated in that portion which was given to the tribe of Judah. See *Josh.* xv. 41. But we shall directly see that there must have also been another city by the name of "Naamah," situated probably in the region originally occupied by Cush. The book of Job is supposed to have been written as early as the days of Abraham. One of the men named in it is Zophar the "Naamathite." See *Job* ii. 11; also xi. 1.; also xlii. 9. He was an inhabitant of "Naamah," at a much more ancient period than the time of Joshua. Job is represented as of the land of "Uz," far distant from the land of Canaan, in the eastern parts of Arabia. His intimate friends and acquaintances cannot be expected to have been of so distant a country as was the land of Judea. The evidence is then that there must have been a city in the land of Cush by the same name. But in *Gen.* x. 7, one of the sons of Cush is called *Raamah:* we think those who will examine the subject will find this term a mere narration or adulteration of *Naamah*, as there are many others, a tedious explanation of which might not be excused at our hand. Suffice it then to say that among the Cushites at a very early period one whole tribe were called "*Naamathites,*" dictinct from the *Naamathites* that lived in the city of *Naamah* conquered by Joshua. Another variation of this word will be found in the word "*Hamathites,*" *Gen.* xvi. 18. This word is used, differently varied, in *Num.* xiii. 21, xxvi. 40; *Judges* iii. 3; 1 *Kings* x. 65, xiv. 21–31; 2 *Kings* v. 1–27; 2 *Sam.* viii. 9; 1 *Chron.* viii. 4, 7; 2 *Chron.* viii. 3, xii. 13; *Isa.* x. 9, also xi. 11, also xvii. 10; *Ezek.* xlvii. 16, 20, also xlviii. 1, and perhaps many other places; and in all cases in reference to individuals, the people and country of the Canaanites, and no doubt in memory of their great female progenitor, Naamah, the daughter of Lamech, of the race of Cain.

LESSON VIII.

Before we close this branch of our inquiry, let us examine into the significancy and composition of the name "Naamah," as applied to the daughter of Lamech: and we take occasion here to say how deeply we are indebted to the labours of the Rev. Dr. Lee, the regius professor of Hebrew in the University of Cambridge, England, and whom we have no question in believing to be among the most penetrating oriental scholars of the age. By an intimate knowledge of the Asiatic languages, he discovered that in many instances where, in a cognate case, the Heemanti would be used in Hebrew, in them the word was supplied with a particle, changing or influencing the sense. Upon full research, he determined that the Heemanti, in Hebrew, were the fragments of ancient or obsolete particles, still influencing the significance as would have done the particles themselves. Let us take an example in our own language: *able* implies fulness of power; add to it the prefix *un*, and you reverse the sense wholly. Yet we do not perceive, without reflection, that the prefix really is a contraction of something similar to "*I am not,*" &c.

With this door open to a constitutional knowledge of the language, let us take the word עם *am.* The terminating aspirate of the word Naamah will be readily formed from this by the usual feminine, as a fragment of the בות *buth*, later בַּת *bath.* And for the prefix *nun*, we beg leave to quote from Lee's Lectures, pages 123 and 124:

"We come now to propose a conjecture on the prefix *nun*, and on the modification of sense which primitive words undergo in consequence of its influence. If then we take this (נ) as the defective form of some primitive word, appearing sometimes in the form of הנ, at other times as נ only, we may suppose it to have been derived from the (Arabic) root, which, had it been preserved in Hebrew, might have been written הָנָה *hanah*, אָנָה *anah*, or אָנָא *ana*. The senses attributed to it by Castell (in his Arabic Lexicon) are, among others, 'ad extremum perfectionis terminum pervenit—assecutus fuit, seu percepit—retinuit, detinuit, coercuit, —lenitate, modestia et patientia usus fuit,' &c. Supposing this word, or some defective form of it, to be construed with any other, the sense of both taken together would, in general, give the force of the forms thus compounded. And as this form of compound is often in the leading word of one of the conjugations, it becomes the more important to ascertain its properties. Primitive words receiving this particle will have a sort of passive sense, or will exhibit subjection to the action implied by the primitive accidentally, but not habitually. Words receiving this augment, subjecting them to the action implied by the primitive word, may, when the context requires it, also be construed as having a reciprocal sense, or as implying possibility," &c.

Now then, let us present examples of the influence of this particular Heemanti:—שָׂכוּר *sakur*, *a hireling*, one whose habit is to be hired, one whose occupation is that of being hired by others. Add נ *nun*, and we have נִשְׂכָּרוּ *niskkaru*, as in 1 *Sam.* ii. 5, and translated thus: "They that were full have hired out themselves for bread." The idea in Hebrew is: They who were habitually full, from the force of the circumstances influencing the case, have been compelled to hire themselves to others for bread. The *sakur* is a hireling from habit, from constitution, from custom, &c., and which idea enters into the meaning of the word. But the prefix of the proposed Heemanti at once destroys all idea of habit, fitness, constitution, or custom; but yet the individual is a "hireling," but only as the force of circumstances influencing the case compelled him to be so. Thus this Heemanti gives a reflective quality, reflecting back upon the agent or actor, as thus: שָׁמַר *shamar*, *he guards*, נִשְׁמַר *nishmar*, *he guards himself;* that is, under the force of circumstances affecting the case, he was compelled to guard himself. Thus כמר *chemar* is sometimes used to express the idea *black*, as a constant, habitual quality. In *Lam.* v. 10, we find it with this Heemanti, thus, נִכְמָרוּ *nichemari*, "our skin was black;" not that their skin was naturally and habitually black, but made so by the facts of the case: and this same word, with this Heemanti, is used in *Gen.* xliii. 30, and translated, by attempting to express a Hebrew cognate idea, into "*yearn.*" The idea is, his bowels did not habitually "yearn," but the action was forced upon him by the facts of the case; and the same again in 1 *Kings* iii. 26. In *Hosea* xi. 8, we find it again translated "my repentings are kindled:" because his people were bent on backsliding, which would cause the Assyrian to be their king, and war to be in their cities continually, and their bad counsels themselves to be destroyed, his repentings were forced to be "kindled." See the passage.

This particle then prefixed to the word עם *am*, with its feminine termination, makes the word נעמה *Naamah*, with the meaning, under the condition of things, she was to become a people distinct to herself; not that she would be a people absolutely, by the habitual action of constituent ability, but she would be a people distinct to herself, only as the peculiar influencing causes made her so,—showing also that these causes gave distinction and character to her posterity. Thus her very name shadowed forth the condition of her race. A Frenchman goes to England, or *vice versa:* a generation passes and nationality is lost. Not so with the Ethiopian. For "though thou wash thee with nitre and take thee much soap, yet thine iniquity is marked before me, saith the Lord God." *Jer.* ii. 22.

A form of the word "Naamah" is used in character of a masculine plural, in *Isa.* xvii. 10, and translated "pleasant," as if from נעם *nam*. Forced to differ from this translation, we beg leave to place the whole passage before the scholars of the day:

כִּי שָׁכַחַתְּ אֱלֹהֵי יִשְׁעֵךְ וְצוּר מָעֻזֵּךְ לֹא זָכָרְתְּ עַל־כֵּן תִּטְּעִי נִטְעֵי נַעֲמָנִים וּזְמֹרַת זָר תִּזְרָעֶנּוּ׃

It is translated thus: "Because thou hast forgotten the God of thy salvation, and hast not been mindful of the rock of thy strength, therefore shalt thou plant pleasant plants and shalt set it with strange slips."

We beg to inquire whether there is not a material defect in the latter clause of this translation? The verb "to plant," in Hebrew, governs two accusatives, to wit, the plantation and the thing planted. In English, we are compelled to render one of the names as governed by a preposition. Thus, he planted a field with corn, or he planted corn in a field. The word זִמְרָת *zemorath*, is often translated a song, as "The Lord Jehovah is my strength and song." See *Ps.* cxviii. 14 and *Isa.* xii. 2. But the idea is more comprehensive than is our idea expressed by the term "song." It includes the result of a course of conduct. Thus the result of a devout worship of God is that Jehovah becomes the "*Zemorath*" of the worshipper; and we doubt not our term *result*, although imperfect, will give a better view of the prophet's idea in this place than the *song*. In this sense this word is used in *Gen.* xliii. 11, and translated "fruits:" thus, "take of the best fruits of the land," that is, the best results of our cultivation. The prophet informs his people that they intermix and amalgamate with the Naamathites because they have forgot God, and that the result is the two last words in the passage, to wit, the "*zar*" and "*tizera-ennu*," that is, a "stranger." See *Exod.* xxx. 33; *Levit.* xxii. 10, 12, 13, where "*zar*" is translated "stranger;" also, *Job* xix. 15, 17; also, *Prov.* v. 10, 17, and 20; and many other places, surely enough to determine its meaning here. The original sense of the last word in the passage was to *sow seed*, hence to *scatter* and *destroy*. The result of such amalgamation then is, their posterity will be a deteriorated race, and the pure Hebrew stock sown to the winds, scattered, wasted away and destroyed.

In these highly excited and poetic effusions of the prophet, we are to notice the chain of thought and mode of expression by which he reaches the object in view. This chapter commences with the information that Damascus shall cease to be a city; that Arver shall be forsaken, and Ephraim be without a fortress to protect her; and finally that Jacob shall be made thin, like a few scattering grapes found by the gleaner, or a few berries of the olive left in the top of the bough, and the house of Jacob become desolate. In the passage under consideration the causes of this condition of Jacob are announced. If our view of the word "Naamah" be correct, in the masculine plural, as here used, it will be quite analogous to Ethiopians. But we have no one word of its meaning; perhaps the idea will be more correctly expressed by Naamathites. Evidently the idea intended to be conveyed by the prophet by the word נַעֲמָנִים *Naamanim*, is, a people whose cultivation would be abortive as to them and injurious to the cultivator; that is, a people with whom intermarriage will produce nothing but injury and destruction to the house of Jacob.

By the use of some such paraphrasis the idea of the prophet will be brought to mind: "Because thou hast forgotten the God of thy salvation, and hast not been mindful of the rock of thy strength, therefore shalt thou (or therefore dost thou) plant *Naamathites*," (that is, amalgamate with the descendants of Ham and Naamah,) "and the fruits of the land shall be a stranger" (that is, their adulterated posterity will be heathen) "scattering thee away;" that is, wasting away not only the purity of the Hebrew blood, but their worship also.

Repeat: "Because thou hast forgotten the God of thy salvation, and hast not been mindful of the rock of thy strength." Therefore dost thou cohabit with the heathen, and thy posterity, O Jacob, shall be an enemy, and thou scattered away and destroyed! Such is the announcement of the prophet.

One of the most bitter specimens of irony contained in the Scriptures is the answer of Job to the Naamathite: "No doubt but ye are the people, and wisdom shall die with you." The passage needs no comment.

The view we take of the word "*Naamanim*," as used by Isaiah, we think warranted by the succeeding sentence, which we ask the scholar to notice.

"For a day thou shalt make thy plant to grow, for a morning thou shalt make thy seed to flourish, but the harvest shall be a heap" (a burden unbearable) "in the days of grief and desperate sorrow." And such has ever been the lot of the white parent who has amalgamated with the negro; as to posterity, it is ruin.

The prophet borrowed his figure from agriculture. His intention was to present to the mind the abortiveness of such a course of sin, by presenting a bold and distinct view of the mental and moral character of the descendants of Naamah; and is on a par with—"Are ye not as the children of the Ethiopians unto me, O children of Israel? saith the Lord." *Amos* ix. 7.

LESSON IX.

By referring to the instances where we allege are to be found variations of the names *Cain* and *Naamah*, it will be at once noticed that some of them are quite remarkable. Shall we be excused for a few remarks in explanation, by way of example, of other lingual changes? Queen Elizabeth lived but yesterday; and her history has not advanced through a very great variety of languages, yet we find, in commemoration of her, one place named Elizabeth, Elizabeth City, Elizabethtown, Elizabethville, Elizabethburg, and another, even Betsey's Wash-tub, and because she was never married, one is called Virgin Queen, and another Virginia.

Now, we all know that at a very ancient period, the worship of the sun and of fire was introduced into the British Isles. Is there nothing left at this day in commemoration of that fact? The sun became an object of great and absorbing consideration. The ancient Celtic word *grian* meant the sun; from the application of this word and its variations, we have a proof, not only of how words are made to change, but also of the fact that the people of that country were once addicted to the worship of the sun or fire. Hence Apollo, who was the sun personified, was called Grynæus. At once we find a singular change in the name of the Druidical idol *Crom-Cruach*, often called *Cean Groith*, the head of the sun. This was the image or idol god to whom the ancient inhabitants of Ireland offered infants and young children a sacrifice. It was in fact the same as the Moloch of the ancient Hamitic occupants of Palestine, and was so firmly established in the superstitions of the world, that whatever race had the ascendency in Ireland, it continued to be thus worshipped, giving the name of the "Plains of slaughter" to the place of its location, until St. Patrick had the success to destroy the image and its worship; and hence also the names *Knoc-greine* and *Zuam-greine*, hills where the sun was worshipped, and other places in Ireland, even now keep in memory that worship: *Cairn-Grainey*, the sun's heap, Granniss' bed, corrupted from *Grian-Beacht*, the sun's circle. A point of land near Wexford is called *Grenor*, the sun's fire, and the town of *Granaid*, because the sun was worshipped there. And we may notice a still greater variation in *Carig-Croith*, the rock of the sun—and even our present word *grange*, from the almost obsolete idea, a place enclosed, separate and distinct, but open to the sun, now used as a synonyme of *farm*.

Let us take our word *fire*, and we shall perceive remarkable changes through all the languages from the Chaldaic down. *Gen.* xi. 28, " *Ur*" is translated from אור which means fire. Abraham was a native of Chaldea, and from a place where they worshipped fire, or the sun. It was used to mean the sun, *Job* xxxviii. 12; also, in the plural, *Isa.* xxiv. 15: " Wherefore glorify ye the Lord in the fires?" It is here אֻרִים *urim*. Because fire emitted light, it became used to mean light. The words *urim* and *thummim* meant lights or fires, and truth: among the fire-worshippers the same term meant *fire* and *sun*. The Copts called their kings *suns*. Hence from this term they took the word *ouro*, to mean the idea of royalty; their article *pi*, made *pianro*, the sun or the *king*, which being carried back to the Hebrews, they made it *Pharaoh;* but the sun was regarded as a god, and hence the Egyptian kings came to be called gods; but the Chaldaic and Hebrew אור, when applied to fire or the sun by the Copts, as an object of worship, was distinguished from the idea of royalty by the term *ra* and *re*, with the particle *pira* and *pire*, generally written *phra* and *phre*. Hence the Greek πυρ, *pur*, to mean fire, and hence pyrites, which means a fire-stone, a stone well burned, or a stone containing fire, &c.

And hence also the Hebrew word ראי *rai*, a mirror, vision, the god of vision, and by figure a conspicuous or illustrious person. But according to Butman, the Sanscrit root *Raja* is the original of the obsolete Greek word, *'Ra*, *'Raia*, *'Rawn*, and if so, possibly of the Chaldaic word under view. But however that may be, it is evident that the Greek *radios* is at least derived through the channel indicated; and we now use the term *ray* to mean an emanation from great power. Our word *regent* is also from the same source, through the Latin *rex*, and may be found, slightly modified, through all the European dialects. And it may be remarked that, cognate therewith, we have the Arabic word *raiheh*, or *raygeh*, to mean fragrancy; the poetic minds of the Arabians uniformly applying this image to legitimate rule and government.

And if we take a view of the filiations of languages, even as they are now found, such changes cannot be deemed unusual, especially if we take into consideration the inevitable variation words are found to undergo in their progress through different countries and ages of time; and more especially, if we notice the precise manner in which lingual variations are found to operate.

Changes of language sometimes take place upon a single word apparently by caprice, among different tribes of people,—sometimes by the transposition of the consonant or vowel sound; by the insertion of a letter or letters for the sake of euphony; by the contraction or abbreviation of letters for the sake of despatch; by the reduplication of a letter or syllable on the account of some real or fancied importance or emphasis attached to it; and by the deletion or addition of a letter or syllable at the commencement or end of a word, for a real or supposed more felicitous enunciation of certain sounds in succession; and hence alterations, slight at first, are liable to become quite remarkable.

Thus μορφη in Greek, becomes *formæ* in Latin; *regnum* becomes *reign; cœlum, ciel; ultra jectum, Utrecht;* and עבד *ebed*, *eved*, as variously pronounced, meaning a *slave*, becomes *obediens*, *obedienter*, *obedio*, *obedientia*, in Latin, and *obey*, *obedient*, &c., in English. The Celtic *ros* becomes *herse*, and the English *grass* becomes *garse*. Consonants of the same order are interchanged; p becomes *b*, and b *v*, d *t*, g *k* and sometimes *n*,—φ becomes *ph* or *f*, d or t becomes *th*, and g or c *gh*. It is therefore impossible that such changes should not have taken place, and therefore they give proof of the genuineness of the history they may develop.

LESSON X.

We have heretofore remarked that such names as are derived from *Cain* or *Naamah* are never found in the holy books, except among and applied to the descendants of Ham. But there are some few instances of the application of these terms in the family of the Benjamites. It is therefore our design now to prove, so far as may be, that such instances, in the family of Benjamin, are wholly confined to those cases where the Benjamite was a mixed-blooded person, and a descendant of Ham, as well as of the youngest son of Jacob. The holy books do give evidence that individuals of the race of Shem did sometimes commingle with the descendants of Ham.

From the proximity of the Israelite tribes to those of Ham; from their co-habitation of Palestine itself, it was natural to expect among the low and vulgar, as well as among those whose morals hung loosely about them, that such intermixture should take place. "Now Sheshan had no sons, but daughters. And Sheshan had a servant, (עֶבֶד *ebed*, a *slave*,) an Egyptian, (מִצְרִי *Mitsri*, a *Misraimite*, a descendant of the second son of Ham,) whose name was Jarha. And Sheshan gave his daughter to Jarha his servant, (עֶבֶד *ebed*, *slave*) to wife." 1 *Chron.* ii. 34, 35. Proving the wisdom and truth of the saying of Solomon, "He that delicately bringeth up his servant (עֶבֶד *ebed*, *slave*) from a child, shall have him become his son at length." *Prov.* xxix. 21.

"Rehoboam was forty-one years old when he began to reign; and he reigned seventeen years in Jerusalem, the city which the Lord did choose out of all the tribes of Israel to put his name there: and his mother's name was Naamah, an Ammonitess. And Rehoboam slept with his fathers, and was buried with his fathers in the city of David. And his mother's name was *Naamah*, an *Ammonitess*." 1 *Kings* xiv. 21, 31.

"For Rehoboam was one-and-forty years old when he began to reign, and he reigned seventeen years in Jerusalem, the city which the Lord had chosen out of all the tribes of Israel, to put his name there, and his mother's name was *Naamah*, an *Ammonitess*." 2 *Chron.* xii. 13.

"But King Solomon loved many strange women, together with the daughter of Pharaoh; women of the Moabites, *Ammonites*, Edomites, Zidonians, and Hittites; of the nations concerning which the Lord said unto the children of Israel, Ye shall not go in to them, neither shall they come in unto you." 1 *Kings* xi. 1, 2.

By thus personally amalgamating with the various nations over whom he ruled, Solomon, no doubt, expected more firmly to establish his throne. This led to the selection of the son of this woman for his successor.

A vast majority of the tribes over whom his reign extended were the descendants of Ham.

But this very act, which he thought to be political wisdom, although contrary to the laws of God, brought ruin to the permanency of his dynasty. The great majority of his Jewish subjects, hunting up, as was natural, plausible excuses, rejected with scorn the contamination of the royal house.

And we see such manifestation of Divine providence even at the present day: even among ourselves, men whose talents and patriotism might authorize them to look to any station, are forced back by public sentiment, degraded by a notorious amalgamation with the descendants of Ham.

We shall hereafter see some proof that this "*Naamàh*," the mother of Rehoboam, was the individual whose praises are celebrated in the book of Canticles: at any rate, she was an Ammonitess, a descendant of Ham, and the prophet Hanani includes the Ammonites among those whom he calls Ethiopians. See 2 *Chron.* xvi. 8.

If then it be true that Naamah, the daughter of Lamech, was the great female progenitor of the race of Ham, we should expect to find some testimony of her remembrance even among her mingled offspring. And since the unmixed race of Ham have generally, at all times of the world, been too degraded to even leave behind them any written memorials, it is to the mixed race, and their connection with the races of Shem and Japheth, that we are principally to look for any particular fact concerning them; and it is reasonable to conclude, as we find this kind of memorial among the mixed race, that the same kind of memorial existed much more frequently among the unmixed races of Ham.

"And the sons of Benjamin were Belah, and Becher, and Ashbel, Gera, and *Naaman*, Ehi, and Rosh, Muppim, and Huppim, and Ard." *Gen.* xlvi. 21.

"The sons of Benjamin after their families of Bela, the family of the Belaites; of Ashbel, the family of the Ashbelites; of Ahiram, the family of the Ahiramites; of Shupham, the family of the Shuphamites; of Hupham, the family of the Huphamites. And the sons of Bela were Ard and Naaman; of Ard, the family of Ardites, and of Naamàn, the family of Naamanites." *Num.* xxvi. 38–40.

"Now Benjamin begat Bela his first-born, Ashbel the second, and Ahirah the third, Nohah the fourth, and Rapha the fifth. And the sons of Bela were Addar, and Gera, and Abihud, and Abishua, and *Naaman*, and Ahoah, and Gera, and Shephuphan, and Huram. And these are the sons of Ehud: these are the heads of the fathers of the inhabitants of Geba, and they removed them to Manahath. And *Naaman*, and Ahiah, and Gera, he removed them, and begat Uzra and Ahihud. And *Shaharaim* begat children in the country of Moab, after he had sent them away." 1 *Chron.* viii. 1–8.

The hurried reader might well apprehend these three different accounts of the same matter to be somewhat contradictory. We think otherwise. We had, in fact, prepared several sheets, elucidating these genealogies of Benjamin, but upon a review we found much irrelevant to the subject of our present inquiry: we deem only a few remarks necessary.

Our object is to show that these genealogies prove that some portion of the family named were coloured people, descended from Ham, and that *Naaman* is distinguished most clearly to be of that class.

It will be readily perceived that *Muppim* מֻפִּים, in Genesis, is formed from מֹף *Moph*, and thus used in *Hos.* ix. 6: "*Memphis* (מֹף *Moph*) shall bury them." Our word is a Hebraism of the Coptic word נֹף *Noph*, the *Nod* of Genesis, the *No* of the prophets Ezekiel and Nahum, and finally confounded with *Memphis*.

It is here used after the form of a Hebrew masculine plural, and as a caput, to aid in the classification of the descendants of Benjamin; and clearly designates, whatever may have been their blood, that one class were *Memphites*.

So the word *huppim* חֻפִּים is formed from the quite ancient word חַף *haph*, which means innocence, purity; whence also the word חָפָה *haphah*, covered, shielded, protected; and hence, חֻפָּה *hupah*, *bride-chamber*, *the marriage-bed*, and *marriage* itself. In this sense the word is used in *Joel* ii. 16, and in several other places, where the translator has so paraphrased the idea as to make it imperceptible to the English reader.

Nor is it an unworthy consideration in the etymology of this word, that from the idea *purity*, the Arabians borrowed from it their word حَارِى *hhar*, to mean *white*, which was quickly introduced into Hebrew in the word חוּר *hur*, and חוֹר *hor*, to mean *white* also. Hence, Mount חָר *Hor*, "the white mountain;" and from which branch of the derivation the corresponding words in Numbers and Chronicles have taken their origin. Here, then, we have another word used in the same manner, to designate another class of the descendants of Benjamin, as of the *pure stock*, *legitimate* and *white*.

The word וְאָרְדְּ *va ard* or *ared* in Genesis, and אַרְדְּ *ard* or *ared* in Numbers, is changed by *dagesh* and transposition into

אֲדָר *addar* in Chronicles. It is unnecessary to go into an explanation of Hebrew peculiarities. It is probable that we never have had the true pronunciation of any of these words. But however that may be, the analogy of language seems to show that this word is a cognate of the Arabic غُرض *gharadh*, and the Syrian ܥܪܕ *dharadh*, and from whence עֲרָד *harad* or *arad;* yet there is nothing more common than for *aleph* and *ghain* to interchange in one and the same word. They are ever regarded as cognates. But again, the word is not of Hebrew origin, and with the latter spelling, we find it in *Num.* xxi. 1, xxxiii. 40, *Josh.* xii. 14, and *Judges* i. 16, as the name of a Canaanitish city. The Arabic is more guttural than Hebrew, and it has two *ghains*, one more guttural than the other, distinguished by רְבִיעַ *rĕviă*, a *resting upon;* thus, in translating Arabic into Hebrew, the one will take the Hebrew *ghain*, but the Arabic *ghain* with which this word is spelled is at once converted into the Hebrew *aleph;* so that while we thus find the very word, we find it with the evidence of a Canaanitish admixture.

Its application in Hebrew seems to be mostly confined to the *wild ass*, (see *Dan.* v. 21;) but the Syriac gives it *effrænatus*, *effrænis fuit*, and the Arabic, *durus fuit*, *fugit*. Such, then, being its signification in these languages, we may well perceive its adaptedness to the *wild ass.* We all know that the wild Arabs are the descendants of Ishmael; now a true synonyme in Hebrew of this word was applied to him: "He shall be a *wild man;*" he was illegitimate, mixed-blooded. The term can apply to no other than such a race as that of Ishmael,—*wild*, *illegitimate*, and of *impure blood.*

In Numbers we find *Shupham*, and in Chronicles *Shephuphan*, substituted for the *Muppim* in Genesis; both being the same word in different forms. The root is שְׁפִי *shephi*, a high situation; hence שָׁפָט *shaphat*, a judge, and its derivatives are applied to the person or thing adjudged. Hence שִׁפְחָה *shiphehhahh*, a *female slave;* (See *Gen.* xvi. 16; i. 2, 3; also xx. 14; also xxxii. 22;) and hence, also the Syrian ܫܦܦܐ *shafefa*, a *serpent*, because the serpent had been adjudged, condemned. Whence the Hebrew *shephiphim*, poetically used to mean a serpent, as, "Dan shall judge his people; Dan shall be a serpent by the way." *Gen.*

xlix. 16. In this passage in Hebrew, there is a beautiful *paronomasia* in the word *Dan*, which also means a judge, *judge* and the *serpent*. But the serpent is called שְׁפִיפֹן *shephiphon*, only as it had been adjudged; and it is to be noticed, as here used, it has the same points and accents as in Chronicles, and is substantially the same word,—not, as here, borrowed from the Syriac, to mean a serpent, but used to mean the adjudged, condemned to some condition or degradation. "And they removed them to *Manahath*." *Manahath* was a district of country near the Dead Sea, near the ancient city Zoar; and it is a little remarkable that Zoar was by the Canaanites called *Bela*, the very name of the son of Benjamin. The whole country was called by the general term Moab. The fact that it was a custom to send persons of a certain description there, seems to be alluded to by the prophet: "Let mine outcasts dwell with thee, O Moab!" *Isa.* xvi. 4.

But, who were sent there? "*Naaman*, *Ahia*, and *Gera*, he removed them. * * * And *Shaharaim* begat children in the land of Moab after he had sent them away." This explains the whole matter. *Shaharaim* is a plural formation of *Shihor*, and means *black*. "*And these blacks begat children in the land of Moab after he had sent them away*,"—that is, *Naaman*, *Ahia*, and *Gera*; further establishing the fact that the word *Naamah* is kept in remembrance only by the descendants of Ham. One class of the race of Benjamin is described in Genesis as *Memphites;* in fact, that whole genealogy substantially divides them into those who were white, and of pure descent, and into those who were not white, and of impure descent. Numbers and Chronicles confirm and warrant the same distinction.

The seventh Psalm commences thus:—"Shiggaion of David, which he sang unto the Lord, concerning the words of Cush, the Benjamite." It would have been more readily understood, and more decidedly a translation thus: *A song of lamentation of David, which he sang unto the Lord, concerning the words of an Ethiopian, a Benjamite.*

The word "Cush," as often elsewhere, is here used to designate a descendant of Ham by his colour. But it clearly proves an amalgamation, to some extent, of the race of Ham, in the family of Benjamin.

Indeed, the race of Benjamin had become deeply intermixed with the descendants of Ham; and this fact well accounts why they did, upon an occasion, behave like as the Sodomites to Lot; and why the other tribes of Israel so readily joined in league to utterly destroy and annihilate this tribe, and did put to death fifty thousand warriors in one day, and every man, woman, and child of the whole tribe, except a few hundred men, who hid in the rock Rimmon. See *Judges* xix. xx.

LESSON XI.

It remains now to examine what proof there exists that the descendants of Ham were black. We wish to impress upon the mind the fact, that among all aboriginal nations, and in all primitive languages, proper names are always significant terms. Such is the fact among the Indian tongues of America at this day. The holy books give ample proof that such was eminently the case among the ancient Hebrews. Every name that Adam bestowed was the consequence of some cause that operated on his mind. And if we examine minutely into the influences operating even among ourselves, in such cases, we shall be unable to deny that such is the universal law. There is a cause for every thing.

"And the sons of Ham (*were*) Cush and Misraim, and Phut and Canaan." *Gen.* x. 6.

It will not be denied that the word Ethiopian, as used in Scripture, means a black man. "Can the Ethiopian change his skin, or the leopard his spots." *Jer.* xiii. 23. The word "Ethiopian," in this passage from Jeremiah, is translated from כּוּשִׁי *Cushi*, the very name of the oldest son of Ham. And we shall find in every instance where in the Old Testament the word Ethiopia or Ethiopian is used, that it is translated from the same word, varied in termination according to the position in which it is used, and as applied to country or people. "Are ye not as the children of the Ethiopians (כֻּשִׁיִּים *Cushiim*) unto me?" *Amos* ix. 7. It became and was used as a general term, by which all descendants of Ham were designated by their colour, in the same manner as we now use the Latin word *negro* to designate the same thing. "And Miriam and Aaron spake against Moses because of the Ethiopian woman whom he had married: for he had married an *Ethiopian* woman." *Num.* xii. 1. And we deem these facts alone sufficient to establish the truth of the proposition that that branch of Ham's family were black.

In the examination of what evidence may now be found that the family of Misraim were black, we beg to notice a fact which we suppose no scholar will dispute—that he settled in Egypt, and, in fact, gave his name to that country. As Cush gave his name to all Ethiopia and its inhabitants, as Canaan gave his name to the land of Canaan, and Canaanites to its inhabitants, so Misraim gave his name to Egypt and its inhabitants. Whenever we find the word Egypt or Egyptian in our English version, we never fail to find מִצְרַיִם *Mitsraim* in the Hebrew text. His descendants took upon them the particular appellation *Misraimites*, as in *Gen.* xvi. 1: "And she had a handmaid, (שִׁפְחָה *shiphehhah, a female slave,*) an Egyptian, (מִצְרִית *Mitsrith*) a descendant of Misraim,) whose name was Hagar." She was a *Misraim*, a descendant from the second son of Ham. The word is translated "Egyptian." A family feud growing up upon the occasion of her having a son by her master Abraham, she and her son were sent away to the wilderness of Paran; where, when the son was grown, she took him a wife of her own *race*, from the land of Egypt. See *Gen.* xxi. 21. The descendants of Ishmael, therefore, were three-fourths of Misraimitish blood, and are known and distinguished as of his *race*, by the particular name of Ishmaelites.

Midian was a district of country lying near to and including Mount Sinai. The people, in reference to the country, were called Midianites, but without any reference to their descent or race. From the position of the district of country called Midian, it would be reasonable to suppose the inhabitants in after times to be descended from Ishmael; and in fact, whenever we find any allusion made to the whole country of the Ishmaelites, we shall find it to include Midian. But it may be proper to remark, that from a notable mountain called *Gilead*, situated in this region, the whole country was sometimes called by that name, and one of the cities in it also called Gilead.

We are all acquainted with that most beautiful and pathetic history of Joseph; but let us read a passage—and we pray you to notice with distinctness the language:

"And they lifted up their eyes and looked, and behold a company of Ishmaelites came from Gilead, with their camels bearing spicery and balm and myrrh, going to carry it down to Egypt. * * * And Judah said, * * * Come, let us sell him to the

Ishmaelites, and let not our hand be upon him. * * * And his brethren were content. Then there passed by Midianites, merchantmen, and they drew and lifted up Joseph out of the pit, and sold Joseph to the *Ishmaelites;* and the Midianites sold him into Egypt unto Potiphar. And Joseph was brought down to Egypt, and Potiphar, an officer of Pharaoh, captain of the guard, an Egyptian, bought him of the hands of the Ishmaelites which had brought him down thither." *Gen.* xxxvii. 25–36, and xxxix. 1. Is it not positive and clear that the Ishmaelites and the Midianites were one and the same people ?

But again, there was, during the days of the judges, a destructive war between the Israelites and the Midianites. "And the Midianites and the Amalekites, and all the children of the east, lay along in the valley, like grasshoppers for multitude. * * * And when Gideon was come, behold, there was a man that told a dream. * * * And when Zeba and Zalmunna fled, he pursued after them, and took the two kings of Midian, Zeba and Zalmunna, and discomfited all the host.

"And Gideon the son of Joash returned from the battle before the sun was up. * * * Then the men of Israel said unto Gideon, Rule thou over us, both thou and thy son, and thy son's son also, for thou hast delivered us from the hand of Midian. And Gideon said unto them, I would desire a request of you, that you would give me every man the ear-rings of his prey. (For they had golden ear-rings, because they were Ishmaelites.)" See *Judg.* vii. 12–14, also viii. 12–24.

Here then is another instance where the Midianites and the Ishmaelites are announced to be the same people. "At the mouth of two witnesses shall the matter be established." See *Deut.* xix. 15; also 2 *Cor.* xiii. 1. "Now Moses kept the flock of Jethro his father-in-law, the priest of Midian." *Exod.* iii. 1.

"When Jethro, the priest of Midian, Moses' father-in-law, heard of all that God had done for Moses, and for Israel his people, and that the Lord had brought Israel out of Egypt, then Jethro, Moses' father-in-law, took Zipporah, Moses' wife, (after he had sent her back,) and her two sons." *Exod.* xviii. 1, 2, 3.

"And Miriam and Aaron spake against Moses, because of the Ethiopian woman whom he had married, for he had married an Ethiopian woman." *Num.* xii. 1.

Even in the poetic strain of the prophet, there is a vestige that goes to prove the sameness between the *Midianites* and the *Ethio pians.* "I saw the tents of *Cushan* (כּוּשָׁן *Ethiopians*) in affliction, and the curtains of the land of Midian did tremble." *Hab.* iii. 7.

Are these facts no proof that the descendants of Misraim were black?

Let us then proceed to the same inquiry concerning the descendants of Phut.

In the Antiquities of Josephus, book i. 6, we find the following: "The children of Ham possessed the land from Syria and Amanus and the mountains of Lybanus; seizing upon all that was upon the seacoasts and as far as the ocean, and keeping it as their own. Some, indeed, of its names are utterly vanished away; others of them being changed, and another sound given, hardly to be discovered; yet a few there are, which kept their denominations entire. For of the four sons of Ham, time has not at all hurt the name of *Chus;* for the Ethiopians, over whom he reigned, are even at this day, both by themselves and by all men of Asia, called *Chusites.*" "The memory also of the Mesraites is preserved in their name, for we who inhabit this country (Judea) call Egypt *Mestra,* and the Egyptians *Mestreans.* Phut also was the founder of Lybia, and called the inhabitants Phutites, from himself. There is also a river in the country of the Moors which bears that name, whence it is that we may see the greatest part of the Grecian historiographers mention that river, and the adjoining country, by the appellation of Phut. But the name it has now has been by change given it from one of the sons of Mestraim, who was called Lybios." His name, in the English version of Genesis, is *Ludim.* From him the Lybian desert has taken its name, and the country now called Lybia. Thus we discover from Josephus that the memorials of the nephew had obliterated those of Phut, his uncle. As Phut was the founder of Lybia, which was at one time called by his name, it may be well to inquire as to the extent of that region, that we may know where the descendants of Phut have resided from the time of their progenitor till now.

In order to form a tolerably correct idea of what was the country once called Phut, we have to examine how far the son of Misraim extended his name in superseding him. We quote from the Melpomene of Herodotus, where he compares the extent of Lybia, Asia, and Europe. Concerning Lybia, he says—

"Except in that particular part which is contiguous to Asia, the whole of Lybia is surrounded by the sea. The first person who has proved this was, as far as we are able to judge, Necho, king of Egypt: when he had desisted from his attempt to join, by a canal, the Nile with the Arabian Gulf, he despatched some vessels, under the conduct of Phœnicians, with directions to pass the columns of Hercules, and, after penetrating the Northern Ocean, to return to Egypt.

"These Phœnicians, taking their course from the Red Sea, entered into the Southern Ocean. On the approach of autumn they landed in Lybia, and planted some corn in the place where they happened to find themselves. When this was ripe, and they had cut it down, they again departed.

"Having thus consumed two years, they in the third doubled the columns of Hercules and returned to Egypt. Their relation may obtain attention from others, but to me it seems incredible; for they affirm that, having sailed round Lybia, they had the sun on their right hand. Thus was Lybia for the first time known."

Hanno, a Carthaginian, was sent, about 600 years before our era, with 30,000 of his countrymen, to found colonies on what is now the western coast of Africa. His account commences—"The voyage of Hanno, commander of the Carthaginians, round the parts of *Lybia*, which lie beyond the pillars of Hercules."

In the body of the work he says—"When we had passed the pillars on our voyage, and sailed beyond them two days, we founded the first city, which we named Thurmiaterium. Below it lay an extensive plain. Proceeding thence towards the west, we came to Solous, a promontory of Lybia."

Having proceeded on with his voyage, he says—"We came to the great *Lixus*, which flows from Lybia; on its banks the Lixitæ, a shepherd tribe, were feeding their flocks, among whom we continued several days, on friendly terms. Beyond the Lixitæ dwell the inhospitable *Ethiopians*."

Herodotus, immediately preceding our quotation of him, says—"Lybia commences where Egypt ends; about Egypt the country is narrow; one hundred thousand orgiæ, or one thousand stadia, comprehend the space between this and the *Red Sea*. Here the country expands and takes the name of Lybia."

Africa, to an indefinite extent, was the country of Phut.

The result of the inquiry thus far is, that the tribes of Phut amalgamated with the descendants of Misraim, until all family memorials of them became extinct. But let us examine what memorials of Phut are to be found in the holy books. "Ethiopia and Egypt were thy strength, *Put* and *Lubim* were thy helpers." *Nahum* iii. 9.

Put is the same Phut; in the text the *letter* is *dagheshed*, which takes away the aspirate sound. We here notice that *Put* and *Lubim* are associated together.

"They of Persia, and of Lud, and of Phut, were in thine army, thy men of war." *Ezek.* xxvii. 10.

"Persia, Ethiopia, and Lybia with them: all of them with shield and helmet." *Ezek.* xxxviii. 5.

In this instance the word *Lybia* is translated from *Phut.* We take this as proof that the country of the son of Misraim and Phut was the same, and the two families amalgamated.

"Come up, ye horses, and rage, ye chariots: and let the mighty men come forth, the Ethiopians and the Lybians that handle the shield." *Jer.* xlvi. 9. *Lybians* is also here translated from *Phut.*

"Were not the Ethiopians and the Lubims a huge host?" 2 *Chron.* xvi. 8. There Phut is lost in that of Lubim, as accounted for by Josephus. The families were wholly amalgamated, the nephew carrying off the trophy of remembrance.

The proof that the family of Phut were black is rather inferential than positive; but can the mind fail to determine that it is certain?

But again, Phut, as an appellative, signifies *scattered.* Thus Num. x. 30. "Let thine enemies be scattered," (פֻּצוּ *phutsu.*) In Genesis x. 18, it is used with the same Heemanti, and with the same effect, which we have noticed in the word *Naamah*, thus: "And afterwards were the families of the Canaanites *spread abroad*," נָפֹצוּ *naphotsu.* The idea is, by the influence of the circumstances attending them, *they were scattered.* The condition is involuntary, the action implied is reflective. A similar use of the word occurs in 2 Samuel xviii. 8: "The battle was scattered," נָפֹצוֹת *naphotseth;* that is, it was scattered only as it was forced to be by the circumstances attending it. The distinctive appellation thus of the family of Phut, means a scattered people. The phonetic synonyme of Phut means scattered, in all the Shemitic tongues.

Thus in Arabic, فَلْطَس *phats*, and its variations, put down, *abiit, peregrinatus fuit* in terra, &c. In Coptic, ⲫⲏⲧ *phet* has the same meaning; but in the hieroglyphical writings of the Copts, found in Egypt, the idea *scattered* is represented by an arrow. But an arrow is called *phet*, because it is shot away, scattered. And the country or people of the *Phutites* is represented by a *bow*, *segment* of a *globe*, *nine arrows*, and an *undulating surface*. Those who have made researches in such matters say, the phonetic power of this is *nephaiat*. It will be perceived to be quite analogous to the *Heemanti* prefixed to the root. *The people who have been compelled to be exceedingly scattered.*

When Jonathan wished in an emphatic manner to signify to his friend David that he should depart, go off from his family, &c., he shot an arrow beyond him. Was not the arrow emblematical of what was supposed his only safe condition?

These explanations as to the significance of the word Phut will enable us better to understand *Zephaniah* iii. 10. "From beyond the rivers of Ethiopia, my suppliants, *even the daughter of my dispersed*, (בַּת־פּוּצַי *bath Putsa*, the descendants of Phut,) shall bring mine offering." Unknown and scattered as they are over the trackless wastes of Africa, yet even to them shall come the knowledge of the true God. They shall, at one day, come to the knowledge of the truth.

The hieroglyphical record relating to the Phutites is considered, by those versed in such matters, to point to a period of at least 2000 years anterior to our era. The inference, to our mind, is clear, that the family of Phut at an exceedingly ancient period was wholly absorbed and lost sight of among the other families of Ham, especially in that of Ludim, the oldest son of Mitsraim: that they were of the same colour and other family distinctions, unless it may be they differed in a deeper degradation: that for numberless ages the mass of the descent are alone to be found in the most barbarous portions of Africa.

LESSON XII.

In the inquiry, What evidence have we that the Canaanites were black? we may find it necessary to refer to various facts which have come down to us, connecting their history with that of the Israelitish people.

Perhaps no fact could be better established than that Abraham lived on the most friendly terms with the Canaanites. He was a confederate with their kings. When they lost a battle, he retrieved it. They treated him with the utmost regard, and he them with a generous liberality. Could he not have wedded his son among them, to whom he chose?

"And Abraham said unto the eldest servant of his house, that ruled over all that he had, Put, I pray thee, thy hand under my thigh: and I will make thee swear by the Lord, the God of heaven, and the God of the earth, that thou shalt not take a wife unto my son of the daughters of the Canaanites among whom I dwell." *Gen.* xxiv. 2, 3.

Under the circumstances of the case, what could have influenced such a determination?

"And Rebecca said unto Isaac, I am weary of my life, because of the daughters of Heth: if Jacob take a wife of the daughters of Heth, such as those which are the daughters of the land, what good shall my life do me? And Isaac called Jacob, and blessed him, and charged him, Thou shalt not take a wife of the daughters of Canaan." *Gen.* xxvii. 46, xxviii. 1.

On what rational ground are we to account for this extraordinary repugnance?

The conduct of the sons of Jacob does not determine them to have been very sincerely religious. The soul of Shechem, a prince of the country, clave unto Dinah their sister; he was rich, and offered ever so much dowry for an honourable marriage with her; and to show his sincerity, even abandoned his old, and adopted their religion. There must have been some other deep and unalterable cause for their unchangeable aversion to that proposed marriage of their sister.

"When the Lord thy God shall bring thee into the land whither thou goest to possess it, and hath cast out many nations before thee, the Hittites, and the Girgashites, and the Amorites, and the Canaanites, and the Perizzites, and the Hivites, and the Jebusites, seven nations greater and mightier than thou;

"And when the Lord thy God shall deliver them before thee, thou shalt smite them and utterly destroy them; thou shalt make no covenant with them, nor show mercy unto them:

"Neither shalt thou make marriages with them; thy daughter thou shalt not give unto his son, nor his daughter shalt thou take unto thy son." *Deut.* vii. 1, 2, 3.

The laws of God are always predicated upon some sufficient cause: in such cases we may ever notice a tendency towards the prevention of deterioration.

"Whosoever lieth with a beast shall surely be put to death." *Ex.* xxii. 19.

The terms Japhet, Laban, Hor, and their derivatives in significancy ever include the idea white, of a light colour. These terms are applied among the descendants of Japheth and Shem, as the appellatives of their races and individual names, and as adjectives in description of their personal appearance, too frequently to permit a doubt of these families belonging to the white race.

There is but a single case in all the holy books, where any of these terms is applied to a person of colour, and which we trust we have explained; and if our view be correct, how came the poet to require its use there, unless to elevate the character he celebrates! Do we use any term to signify that a person is white in a country where there are none but white people? Whatever evidence then there may be that the families of Abraham, Isaac, and Jacob were white people, is also just as positive testimony that the Canaanites were black. See *Gen.* xxvi. 34, 35.

But in Judges i. 16, we find that the family of the race of Ishmael out of which Moses took his wife are denominated Kenites. We think that we have abundantly proved that they were black. From this connection of Moses, the Israelites seem to have felt some regard for that race. Now it appears that some of that descent were afterwards residing in the cities of Amalek; for we find in 1 Samuel xv. 6, that "Saul said unto the Kenites, Go, depart, get ye down from among the Amalekites, lest I destroy you with them, for ye showed kindness to all the children of Israel when they came out of Egypt. So the Kenites departed." How should it be a fact, since they were black, that he could not distinguish them from the Amalekites, unless the Amalekites were black also?

The Amalekites were Canaanites, notwithstanding they claimed Esau in their ancestry. "Esau took his wives of the daughters of Canaan. Adah the daughter of Ebon the Hittite; * * * and Adah bore to Esau, Eliphaz; * * * and Timna was concubine to Eliphaz, Esau's son; and she bore to Eliphaz, Amalek." *Gen.* xxxvi. 2, 4, 12.

The Amalekites were one of those tribes, that the Israelites were particularly commanded to destroy from off the earth; and in them, he who amalgamates with the daughters of Ham may see his own prospect as to posterity.

LESSON XIII.

THERE are circumstances in evidence that the descendants of Ham were black, more properly referable to the whole family than to either particular branch.

Among this class of circumstances, we might mention the tradition so universal through the world, that we know no age of time or portion of the globe that can be named in exception, that the descendants of Ham were black; and that the fact announced by that tradition is made exceedingly more probable by the corresponding tradition, that the descendants of Japheth and Shem were white.

The holy books provide proof that Abraham and Sarah, Isaac and Rebecca, Jacob, Leah, and Rachel, were white. Their descendants sojourned in Egypt in a state of bondage about four hundred years, in the course of which time there was a law that all the male Hebrew children should be put to death at their birth. When the mother of Moses put him in the ark of bulrushes, she would have disguised his birth as much as possible, for the safety of his life. Yet no sooner had the daughter of Pharaoh beheld the infant than she proclaimed it to be a Hebrew child. If there was no difference of colour, from whence this quick decision as to the nationality of an infant three months old?

But during the residence of the Israelites in Egypt, it is to be apprehended there was more or less commixture between the two races; and, if the two races were of different colour, that there would have been left us some allusion to such offspring; and so we find the fact.

"And the children of Israel journeyed from Rameses to Succoth, about six hundred thousand on foot, that were men, besides children. And a mixed multitude went up also with them." *Exod.* xii. 37, 38. The word "*mixed*" is translated from עָרָב *ereb*, *arab*. The word means *of mixed-blood*, that is, the mixture of the white man with the black; and in consequence thereof is often used to mean black itself, and is universally applied as the appellative, and has become the established name of the mixed-blooded people of Arabia, the *Arabs;* and because it became a common term to express the idea black, a dark colour, &c., it was applied to the raven; and even at this day, who can tell whether Elijah was fed by the *ravens* or the *Arabs*, because the one word was used to mean both or either. *And a multitude of persons of colour, of Hebrew and black parentage, went up also with them.*

This word is used to express the idea of a mulatto race, in *Num.* xi. 4, and the "*mixed multitude;*" also *Neh.* xiii. 3, "They separated from Israel all the *mixed multitude;*" also *Jer.* xxv. 20,24, thus: "And all the mingled people," *mixed-blooded*, "and all the kings of Arabia, and all the kings of the *mingled people*," *mixed-blooded people*. By the expression *mixed multitude*, it is clear Moses included the offspring of the Hebrew with the race of Ham. But would there have been such distinction if there was no difference of colour? It will be recollected that the children of Ishmael were three-fourths of Misraimitish blood, consequently quite dark. It will also be recollected that when Esau perceived how extremely offensive to his father and mother was his connection with the Canaanitish women, that he took wives of the house of Ishmael. It should also be recollected that Ishmael named one of his sons *Kedar*. As we shall hereafter refer to this word, we propose to examine its meaning and formation. It is of Arabic derivation, *Arab.* دُر, Hebrew דַּר *dar*, and in this form is used *Esth.* i. 6, and translated *black marble*. With the prefix of the Hebrew koph it becomes קֵדָר *Kedar*, and is equivalent to "*the black.*" It is used in Hebrew to mean black, in 1 *Kings* xviii. 45; *Job* vi. 16, 30, 28; *Isa.* lx. 3; *Jer.* iv. 28; *Ezek.* xxxii. 7, 8, and many other places.

The very name of the son of Ishmael was tantamount to "*the black.*"

In the poem called Solomon's Song, the female whose praises are therein celebrated, says, "I am *black*, but comely, O ye daughters of Jerusalem, as the tents of *Kedar*, as the curtains of Solomon. Look not upon me because I am *black;* because the sun hath looked upon me: my mother's children were angry with me, they made me the keeper of the vineyards, but mine own vineyards have I not kept." *Cant.* i. 5, 6.

The word *black*, which twice occurred in the text, is translated from שָׁחַר *shahar*, with many variations. The words mean abstractly the idea *black*. Examples of its use will be found in *Lev.* xiii. 31, 37, thus: "And there is no *black* hair in it." "And there is *black* hair grown up therein." *Job* xxx. 30: "My skin is *black* upon me." *Zech.* vi. 2, 6: "And in the second chariots *black* horses. The *black* horses that are therein." *Lam.* iv. 8: "Their visage is *blacker* than a coal." *Cant.* v. 11: "His locks are bushy and *black* as a raven." There is no mistake about the meaning of this word; she was surely *black*, and she says that she is as *black* as the tents of *Kedar*.

The inquiry, then, now is, who was she? When we take into consideration the Asiatic mode of expression, from the term "because the sun hath looked upon me," we are forced to understand that she was from a more southern region. That she was not a native of Palestine, or especially of Jerusalem. Figures of somewhat analogous import are occasionally found among the Roman poets. But we suppose, no one will undertake the argument that she was black, merely because she had been exposed to the sun!

In vii. 1 of the Hebrew text, she is called *Shulamite*. Some suppose this is a formation of the Gentile term שׁוּנֵם *Shunem*, because they say the *lamda* was sometimes introduced. In that case it would be the synonyme of *Shunamite*, and would locate her in the tribe of Issacar. But we see no necessity of a forced construction, when a very easy and natural one is more obvious. We omit the *dagesh*. שׁוּלַמִּית *Shulammith* is readily formed as the feminine of שְׁלֹמֹה *Shelomoh*, *Solomon*, after the Arabic form سُلَيْمَان *Suleiman*, and, so used, would be quite analogous to what is now quite common—to apply the husband's name as an appellative of the wife. Upon the occasion of her consecration into Solomon's household, she well might, even at that age, be called by a term that would imply such consecration, especially in the poem celebrating her nuptials. And we may remark that the use of this word is in strict conformity to the usage of the Hebrew and Arabic poets, because it creates an implied *paronomasia*, derived from שׁוֹל, signifying that she was a captive by her love to Solomon, and if she stood in any such relation to him politically, the beauty of the figure would at that age have been considered very greatly increased. The poets, at that age of time, in compositions of the character of this poem, appear to have been ever on the search for an occasion to introduce figures of this class; and the more fanciful and extreme, the more highly relished. We fail therefore to derive any knowledge of her origin from this term. We have dwelt upon this particular thus long, merely because commentators have been so desirous to find out a clue to the history of the poem. Some commentators of elevated character, suppose this subject of their epithalamium to have been the daughter of Pharaoh, simply because she was *black*, and is addressed: "O prince's daughter!" Undoubtedly she was the daughter of some prince or king. But the question now, is of what one? There is no probability that the kings of Egypt, nor even the nobility of that kingdom, had been of the race of Ham for many ages. Egypt had been conquered by the Shemites as early as the days of Abraham, and there is no proof that the descendants of Ham ever again ascended the throne; although, perhaps, their religion had been adopted by their successors from motives of policy, the great mass of the population being of the old stock.

In fact, the mixed-blooded races, and indeed the Shemites of pure blood, have, from time immemorial, shown a disposition to settle in Egypt. The Persians and the Greeks have also, for a very long time, aided in the amalgamation of the Egypt of the middle ages of the world.

But she is made to say that she is "the rose of Sharon;" as much as to say, *the most excellent of her country*. This district of country will be found to embrace the Ammonites, and perhaps some other of the ancient tribes of the family of Ham, at that time under the government of Solomon. And, iv. 8, we find Sharon called by its Ammonitish name, amid a cluster of figures having relation to the locality and productions of that country.

In short, the whole body of this extraordinary poem points to the region of the Ammonites for her native place of abode. Now, since Solomon had an Ammonitess by the name of Naamah for a wife, and since he selected her son to succeed him on the throne, it seems at least quite probable she was the person it commemorates; and that fact will make quite intelligible the allusion to her having been elevated from a servile condition. But, nevertheless, if it shall be thought not sufficiently proved that she was the mother of Rehoboam, yet she surely was of some one of the Canaanitish or Hamitic tribes, and was as surely black; and so far is in direct proof that the descendants of Ham generally were black also.

There are incidents of this poem which it would seem cannot be explained on other ground than that this marriage was one of state policy on the part of Solomon; and the queen upon this occasion selected was from some one of the heathen nations of the descendants of Ham, whom he had subjected to his government. It will be recollected that these nations, whom the Israelites had failed to destroy, had omitted no occasion to make war on the Hebrews, from the time of Joshua down to that of David; and that they occasionally had them in subjection.

Solomon had no guarantee how long his rule over them would prove quiet, or how far they would yield obedience to his successor. What could induce him to marry an Ammonite princess, and place her son upon his throne, if not to effect this purpose? Even at the time of the nuptials a reference to this political union might well find a place in the songs to which it gave birth. We introduce one of the incidents to which we allude: we select the close of the sixth strain. This poem is written in the form of a dialogue, mostly between the bride and groom.

Solomon. Return, return, O Shulamite; return, return, that we may look upon thee.

Naamah. What will ye see in the Shulamite?

Solomon. As it were the company of two armies.

This surely needs no comment. The poem had already recited every mental and personal quality; was it then unnatural delicately to allude to her political importance? The art of the poet, however, to cover the allusion, recommences a view of her personal charms, changes his order, and commences with her feet.

Much learning has come to many untenable conclusions concerning this poem, among which, that of the Targum may be placed in the lead.

LESSON XIV.

We have heretofore noticed how, in 2 *Chron.* xvi. 8, the name Phut is lost in that of Lubim, as accounted for by Josephus. But it should be recollected that the prophet Hanani most distinctly refers to one of the wars between the black tribes and the Jewish people, of which there had been a long series from the exodus down.

We propose to adduce an argument from the language used in the description of these wars.

In the time of King Ora, the invading army is described thus: "And there came out against them Zerah, the Ethiopian, with a host of a thousand thousand and three hundred chariots. And Asa cried unto the Lord his God; so the Lord smote the Ethiopians before Ora, and before Judah, and the Ethiopians fled: and Asa, and the people that were with him, pursued them unto Gerar, and the Ethiopians were overthrown." These people the prophet calls Ethiopians and Lubims. This term proves that many of them were from Lybia. Now is it to be presumed that so vast an army, one million of men and three hundred chariots, was not composed of all the tribes between the remotest location of any named and the place of attack?

But this battle was commenced in the valley of Zephathah, in Philistia, and pursued to Gerar, a city of the same country. "And they smote all the cities round about Gerar. For the fear of the Lord came upon them, and they spoiled all the cities, for there was exceeding much spoil in them. They smote all the tents of cattle, and carried away sheep and camels in abundance, and returned to Jerusalem." See 2 *Chron.* xiv. 14, 15.

These facts could not have existed had not the Philistines composed a part of the army.

Yet they are all Ethiopians. Is this no evidence that the tribes of Ham generally were black?

But again, with the view to arrive at a greater certainty as to what races did compose these armies, we propose to examine that which invaded Jerusalem during the reign of Rehoboam.

"And it came to pass when Rehoboam had established the kingdom, and had strengthened himself, he forsook the law of the Lord, and all Israel with him; and it came to pass in the fifth year of King Rehoboam, Shishak, king of Egypt, came up against Jerusalem, because they had transgressed against the Lord, with twelve hundred chariots and threescore thousand horsemen; and the people were without number that came with him out of Egypt, the Lubims, the Sukkims, and the Ethiopians; and he took the fenced cities, which pertain to Judah, and came to Jerusalem." 2 *Chron.* xii. 1–10. "And the people were without number that came with him out of Egypt, *the Lubims, the Sukkims, and the Ethiopians.*" The Hebrew construction of the latter clause of this is thus: מִמִּצְרַיִם לוּבִים סֻכִּיִּים וְכוּשִׁים׃ *Mim-mits-raim, Lubim, Sukkiyyim ve Cushim.* We suggest a slight error in the translation of these words. The prefix מ *mem* preceding *Mitsraim*, we read a preposition, *out of, from*, &c., influencing and governing the two following words also; as, *from Egypt, from Lybia, from Succoth.* It will be noticed that *Cushim* is preceded by the prefix ו *vav.* Grammarians have written much upon this particle: we cannot enter into an argument on Hebrew grammar, but, with all the learning that has been expended on this particle, the Hebrew scholar must find the fact to be, that it is sometimes used to designate a *result;* and we take occasion here to say that, in our opinion, Professor Gibbs has given a more definite and philosophical description of the Hebrew use of this particle, than any lexicographer of modern research.

Suppose an ancient Hebrew physician wished to teach that certain diseases were incurable, that they ended in death, might he not have said, מִשַּׁחֶפֶת קַדַּחַת אָנוּשׁ וָמוּת׃ *mish shahhepheth kaddahhath amish vemuth,—from consumption, burning fever, the mortal sickness, termination is death?* Or, allow our Hebrew not to be so classical, could he not have expressed the idea after this form? "The army was without number, from Egypt, from Lybia, from the Nomads, all Ethiopians." And we here suggest the query, whether this is not the true reading? We do not propose that this prefixed ו *vav* has the power of an adjective or a verb, although it might require the one or the other to give the idea in English. What we say is, that it is the sign of the thing which is the result of the preceding nouns. If it had been used here as a connective particle, then the two preceding nouns would also have had it for a prefix. Such was the Hebrew idiom. It would then have read,

"And the people were," &c., from Egypt, and from Lybia, and from the Nomads, and from Ethiopia, as the translator seems to have supposed. But, as it is, it determines them all to have been Ethiopians. This will be in strict conformity with the description of the army at the time of Asa. The invading army, at that time, was denominated Ethiopian, although it is evident that many of the Hamitic tribes composed it.

The real cause of all these wars was the contest whether Palestine should be held by the Hamitic race, or by the Shemitic, who were bearing rule. Keeping this in mind, let us note how perfectly natural is this description of those who composed the army under Shishak. The troops first collected would be from among his own immediate people, the Egyptians. The next, those who lived beyond him from the point of attack, to wit, the Lubims, who lived to the west of Egypt. These being collected together, they would commence their march, and the Nomads be added to the list of the army after they joined it; but none other than those governed by the same impulses would attach themselves to it. Suffer us to illustrate this description of Shishak's army by supposing a somewhat analogous case, in much more modern times:—That during the reign of Elizabeth, King Philip of Spain had made war on England, upon the issue of whether the Protestant or Catholic faith should prevail in that country. Philip would have first collected troops in Spain. He may be supposed to collect large numbers in Portugal. These Spanish and Portuguese troops may be supposed to march through France, and his army vastly increased there; and, when upon the coast of England, some Froissart would have said, that the people who came with Philip were without number, Spaniards, Portuguese, French, all Catholics. The manner of such description would be in exact similitude with this description of Shishak's army. Any one who is acquainted with the history of the Crusades will readily see how a similar description would have in truth fitted the army of the Cross. We think it proof conclusive that the descendants of Ham were black. But we might add some proof from sketches of profane history. In the 22d section of Euterpe, Herodotus says that the natives on the Nile are universally black. In the 32d section, giving an account of a party of Neesamonians, who in Africa were out upon an excursion, he says—"While they were thus employed, seven men, of dwarfish stature, came where they were, seized their persons, and carried them away. They were mutually ignorant of each others' language. But the Neesamonians were conducted over marshy grounds to a city, in which all the inhabitants were of diminutive appearance and of a black colour."

In the 57th section, he gives an account of an Egyptian priestess who was brought among the Threspoti. He says that "the circumstance of her being black explains to us her Egyptian origin."

In the 104th section, he says—"The Cholchians certainly appear to be of Egyptian origin, which indeed, before I had conversed with any one on the subject, I had always believed. But as I was desirous of being satisfied, I interrogated the people of both countries. The result was, that the Cholchians seemed to have a better remembrance of the Egyptians, than the Egyptians of the Cholchians. The Egyptians were of the opinion that the Cholchians were descended of a part of the troops of Sesostris: to this I myself was also inclined, because they are black, and have their hair short and curling."

Cambyses fought the black tribes of Egypt and Africa under Amasis, in the western parts of Arabia. Herodotus says, (Thalia, section 12th,) "The bones of those who fell in the engagement were soon afterwards collected, and separated into two distinct heaps. It was observed of the Persians, that their heads were so extremely soft as to yield to the slight impression even of a pebble. Those of the Egyptians, on the contrary, were so firm that the blow of a large stone could hardly break them. * * * I saw the very same fact at Papremis, after examining the bones of those who, under the conduct of Achæmenes, son of Darius, were defeated by Inaius the African."

Herodotus notices the distinction between the Arabs and the Negroes, but calls them all Ethiopians. In the 70th section of Polymnia, he says—"Those Ethiopians who came from the most eastern part of their country, served with the Indians. These differed from the former in nothing but their language and their hair. The Oriental Ethiopians have their hair straight: those of Africa have their hair more crisp and curling than other men."

Herodotus lived and wrote about five hundred years before our era. We have quoted him through a translation, but not without examining the original.

We shall close our evidence on this point with a single quotation from *Judg.* iii. 8 and 10. The children of Israel intermarried with the Canaanites: the writer says, "Therefore the anger of the Lord was hot against Israel, and he sold them into the hand of

Chusan rishathaim," *the wicked Ethiopians.* Whereas it is as well known as any other fact of biblical history, that these "*wicked Ethiopians*" were none other than the Philistines and other aboriginal tribes of the land of Canaan.

Upon the conquest of Palestine by the Israelites, portions of the Canaanites overspread the approachable parts of Africa, where numerous hordes of their race were already in possession. For ages, there is said to have stood near Tangier, a monument with inscriptions signifying that it was built in commemoration of the people who fled from the face of *Joshua* the robber. From the presumption of this being a fact, and from a collection of other facts connected with early commerce, Moore, in the first volume of his History of Ireland, has strongly suggested that the ancient Irish are partially indebted to the ancient Canaanites for their origin; whereas we think we have sufficiently proved that they were black. We hope the impulsive sons of the Emerald Isle will repel the insult. But, if what Moore says be true, it only proves another portion of our theory; for, as sin sinks to all moral and physical degradation and slavery, so virtue and holiness elevate to freedom and all animal and mental perfections; and since *Jern* was for ages regarded as an island of saints, Moore may have the benefit of the argument, if he chooses, whereby to account for the high-toned feeling and personal perfections of the modern Irish.

In conclusion, from the history of the family of man, we may all know that the descendants of Japheth and Shem, when free from amalgamation with the black tribes, are white people. Unless then the descendants of Ham were black, how are we to account for the phenomena of the existence of that colour among men? Philosophy has been in search, and history has been on the watch; facts upon facts have been recorded touching every matter; but have you ever heard of the uncontaminated descendants of Japheth, living in the extreme, or in the central zone, exhibiting the woolly crown of the sons of Ham?

LESSON XV.

We suggest some origin, some complexion of thought, from whence may have emanated the word "Ham," and its derivatives, as found to have existed in the days of the prophets; and we may here state that the Shemitic languages seem to exist all in a cluster, like so many grapes; nor are we able to say which stands nearest the vine. Doubts may be raised as to the priority of any one named; yet we might adduce some proof that the Coptic is younger, as we could that the Greek is younger still.

The Arabic word مَا *ma* corresponds with the Syriac ܡܳܢ *ma*, and the Hebrew מָה *mah*, and has been translated into the Latin *quid*, as an interrogatory, used in all languages very elliptically. Thus, *Gen.* iv. 10: מֶה עָשִׂיתָ "*What have you done?*" If the עָשִׂיתָ had been omitted, the מֶה would have expressed the whole idea.

It was an interrogatory expression of exclamation and astonishment, to one who had committed a heinous offence. So when Laban pursued, Jacob said, מָה *mah*, *What is my trespass?* &c., as if in derision,—*What is my horrid crime?* Ever since the days of Cain some have manifested wicked acts, as though they were operated on by some strong desire, some coveting overwhelming to reason,—as if the action was in total disregard of the consequences that must follow it. This state of mind seems to have been expressed, in some measure, by the particular use of this particle. Let us conceive that such a state of mind must be a heated, a disturbed state of mind, as was that of Cain, and as must have been that of Jacob, had he stolen the goods of Laban. The word thus incidentally expressive of such an idea, by being preceded or influenced by a particle implying particularity, giving it definiteness and boundary, must necessarily be converted into an action or actor, implying some portion of the primitive idea; and hence we find הָמָה and هَمّ and هَمِّيّ *ham* and *hami* in Arabic, ܚܡܳ *ham* in Syriac, to mean a cognate idea, i. e. *to grow hot*, &c., *to boil*, *rage*, &c., sometimes *tumult*, &c., &c. And we now ask, these being facts, is it difficult to point in the direction of the origin of the word Ham? Nor is it a matter of any importance, if the relationship exists, whether the noun and verb have descended from such exclamatory particle, or the reverse; yet we can easily imagine, in the early condition of things, that the mind, taking congnisance of some horrid act, would impel some such exclamation, and that it would become the progenitor of the name of the act or actor.

However this may be, each Hebrew scholar will inform us that the word הָם is an irregular Hebrew word. Grammarians have usually arranged words of this peculiar class among the Heemanti and augmented words, and they have accurately noticed that the punctuatists have always preceded the ם *mem* by a (ָ) *Kamets*, or a (ֹ) *Kholem*. This circumstance has induced Hiller to suppose that the מ *mem*, as a *Heemanti*, was a particle, while the adjunct was either הֵם or אוֹם; but all agree that the form of these nouns shows that they are intensive in their signification.

If then הָם *ham* is a particle of הָמָה *hamah*, which carries with it the ideas before named, it may be less difficult to conceive how the particle, when added to other nouns, will make them intensive also, while the particle itself would be used alone to express some intensity in an emphatic manner, more particularly of its root.

But we find the word חָם *ham*, as applied to the son of Noah, from the root חָמָה *hammah*, or חֵמָה *hhma*, of cognate meaning, and used in Hebrew thus: In *Josh.* ix. 12, "This our bread we took hot חָם for our provision," &c. *Job* xxxvii. 17, and vi. 17: "How thy garments *warm* (חַמִּים *hammin, hot*) when he quieteth the earth by the south wind." "What time they wax warm, they vanish when it is *hot*," בְּחֻמּוֹ *behummo, in the heat.* So *Gen.* viii. 22: "While the earth remaineth, seed-time and harvest, cold and heat וָחֹם, and summer and winter, and day and night, shall not cease." *Gen.* xviii. 1: "And he sat in the tent door in the heat כְּחֹם of the day." 1 *Sam.* xi. 9–11: "To-morrow, by the time the sun is hot, (בְּחֹם *be hom, in heat.*) And slew the Ammonites until the heat of the day," עַד־חֹם *ad hom, until the hot.* xxi. 7 (the 6th of the English text): "To put *hot*, חֹם *hot* in the day," &c. 2 *Sam.* iv. 5: "And came about the *heat* of the day," כְּחֹם *ke hom, at the hot.* *Isa.* xviii. 4: "Like a clear *heat* כְּחֹם upon herbs, and like a cloud of dew in the heat בְּחֹם of harvest." *Hag.* i. 6: "Ye clothe you, but there is none warm," לְחֹם *be hom, not hot.* *Jer.* li. 39: "In their heats," כְּחֻמָּם *be hummon, in their heats,* &c.

But in Hebrew, as in some other languages, the phonetic power expressing the idea *hot, heat,* &c. was cognate with rage, stubbornness, anger, wickedness, &c. &c., and hence we say *hell is hot,* and hence, in *Dan.* iii. 13, 19: "Then Nebuchadnezzar in his rage," חֱמָא *hama, heat, hot.* "Therefore shall he go forth with great fury," בִּחְמָא *be hama, heat, rage, fury,* &c.

Should it be said, the words in their declination, or rather the affixed and suffixed particles, differ, and are marked with different vowel points, we answer by quoting *Lee's Heb. Lex.* p. 205: "This variety in the vowels may be ascribed either to the punctuatists or the copyists, and is of no moment. But as the word חָם *ham* was thus applied in Hebrew to the original idea of active caloric, as emanating from the sun, so it will agree with its homophone in Arabic and Syriac; for let it be noticed, that the Arabic word حم *ham* or *haman,* means to be *hot,* as of the sun. So the Syriac ܚܡܐ *hama* means *castus, calor,* &c. But in *Deut.* xxxii. 24, 33, it is translated *poison;* thus, poison of serpents, and 'the poison of dragons,' from the notion that great heat, rage, anger, &c. are cognate with poison."

This word occurs in *Zeph.* ii. 12. The received version is, "Ye Ethiopians also, ye shall *be* slain by my sword." The original is, גַּם־אַתֶּם כּוּשִׁים חַלְלֵי חַרְבִּי הֵמָּה, and has been subject to much investigation. Gesenius considers the word הֵמָּה a pronoun in the second person, and Lee seems to side with him, but says, "the truth is, the place is inverted and abrupt, and should read thus: גַּם־אַתֶּם חַלְלֵי חַרְבִּי כּוּשִׁים הֵמָּה," and which he translates thus—"*Even ye (are) (the) wounded of my sword,*—they are *Cushites.*" We do not perceive how he has made the passage more plain. Let us, for a moment, examine how the Hebrews used this form הֵמָּה or הֵם, that we may the better comprehend its sense in the present instance. *Jer.* v. 22: "Though they *roar,*" וְהָמוּ *ve hamu, rage,* &c., "yet can they not pass over it!" vi. 23:

"Their voice roareth like the sea," יֶהֱמֶה rageth, &c. xxxi. 35: "Which divideth the sea, when the waves thereof *roar*," וַיֶּהֱמוּ *say ye*, *hemen*, *rage*, &c. li. 15: "When her waves do roar (וְהָמוּ *ve hamu se*, *rage*, &c.) like great waters." *Isa.* li. 13: "But I am the Lord thy God that divided the sea, whose waves roared," *raged*. li. 13: "Because of the *fury* (חֲמַת *rage*, &c.) of the oppressor," "and where is the fury (חֲמַת *hamath*, *rage*, &c.) of the oppressor?" li. 15: "whose waves *roared*," וַיֶּהֱמוּ *raged*, &c. *Ps.* xlvi. 4 (the 3d of the English text): "*Though* the waters thereof *roar* (יֶהֱמוּ *rage*, &c.) and be troubled," יֶחְמְרוּ *great agitation*, *rage*, &c.

But let us take a more particular view of this word, as used in the passage from *Zephaniah*. The Septuagint has translated this passage in Καὶ ὑμεῖς Αἰθίοπες τραυματίαι ῥομφαίας μοῦ ἐστέ, which is very much like our received version.

But it should be noticed that it has translated the Hebrew word חַלְלֵי into τραυματίαι; τραῦμα would imply the injury, wounds, carnage, or slaughter of a whole nation, army, or body of people; but τραυματίαι implies individuality, and reaches no farther than the person or persons named. The prophet had been uttering denunciations against many nations, but in this passage emphatically selects the Ethiopians as individuals; and the Greek translator evidently discovered there was in this denunciation something peculiarly personal as applied to the Ethiopians.

The Hebrew conveys the idea of reducing, subjecting, or bringing low, as by force, to cause to sink in character; as in *Ps.* lxxxix. 40 (39th of the English text): "Thou hast made void the covenant of thy servant: thou hast חִלַּלְתָּ *wounded*, *subjected*, or *reduced* his crown to the earth." *Ezek.* xxii. 26: "Her priests have violated my law, and have חִלְּלוּ (*wounded*, *subjected*, *lowered the character of*) my holy things."

But the word חַלְלֵי is here used in the construct state, showing that the idea imposed by this word was brought about by the following term, חַרְבִּי, which the Septuagint translates ῥομφαίας, which properly means the Thracian spear; but חַרְבִּי means any weapon, a good harpoon as well as a sword. The fact is, neither of these words were the usual Hebrew or Greek term to mean a sword. The Greeks would have called a sword μάχαιρα, and the Hebrews חֲנִית or רֹמַח or כִּידוֹן, or perhaps שֵׂכָה; and Dr. Lee has given Ἄρπη as the Greek translation of חַרְבִּי, which means a sickle, a goad for driving elephants, &c. It was a thing to inflict wounds by which to enforce subjection, and the idea is that the Ethiopians are covered by wounds by their being reduced by it, or that they shall be. When Jeremiah announced captivity and slavery to the Egyptians and the adjacent tribes, he used this word as the instrument of its execution. Thus *Jer.* xliv. 14: "Declare ye in Egypt, and publish in Migdol, and publish in Noph, and in Taphanhes; say ye, Stand fast, and prepare thee, for the *sword* חֶרֶב shall devour round about thee." 16: "Arise and let us go again to our own people, and to the land of our nativity, from the oppressing *sword*," חֶרֶב. Many such instances might be cited, showing the fact that, in poetic strain, this was the instrument usually named, as in the hand of him subjecting others to bondage; and much in the same manner, even at this day, we use the term "whip," in the hand of the master, in reference to the enforcement of his authority over his slave.

In a further view of the word הֵמָּה, as used in this passage, we deem it proper to state that Gibbs considers it a pronoun of the third person plural, masculine, *they*, and adds, "sometimes" (probably an incorrectness drawn from the language of common life) "used in reference to women," and quotes *Zech.* v. 10; *Cant.* vi. 8; *Ruth* i. 22. And he further adds, "It is used for the substantive verb in the third person plural, 1 *Kings* viii. 40, ix. 20; *Gen.* xxv. 16; also for the substantive verb in the second person, *Zeph.* ii. 12: 'Also, ye Cushites חַלְלֵי חַרְבִּי הֵמָּה *shall be slain by my sword.*'" *Gibbs's Lex.* p. 175. In Stuart's Grammar, p. 193, he says, "*Personal pronouns of the third person sometimes stand simply in the place of the verb of existence;*" e. g. he cites *Gen.* ix. 3, *Zech.* i. 9, and says, "Plainer still is the principle in such cases, as follows: *Zeph.* ii. 12, 'Ye Cushites, victims of my sword אַתֶּם הֵמָּה are ye.'"

The fact is, the verb of existence, called the verb "to be," and the verb substantive, in Hebrew, as in all other languages, is often not expressed, but understood. This circumstance is well explained in Gessenius' Hebrew Grammar, revised by Rodiger, and translated by Conant, p. 225, thus, "When a personal pronoun is the subject of a sentence, like a noun in the same position, it does not require for its union with the predicate a distinct word for the copula, when this consists simply in the verb 'to be,' אָנֹכִי הָרֹאֶה '*I* (*am*) *the seer*,' 1 *Sam.* ix. 19." And again: "The pronoun of the third person frequently serves to convert the subject and predicate, and is then a sort of substitute for the copula of the verb *to be*, e. g. *Gen.* xli. 26: '*The seven good cows*, שֶׁבַע שָׁנִים הֵנָּה *seven years* (are) *they*.'" To say in English, "The seven good cows, seven years they," would be thought too elliptical; but we do not perceive how the expression converts "*they*" into the verb "to be."

But again, the same author says, p. 261: "The union of the substantive or pronoun, which forms the subject of the sentence, with another substantive or adjective, as its predicate, is most commonly expressed by simply writing them together without any copula. 1 *Kings* xviii. 21: יְהוָה הָאֱלֹהִים '*Jehovah* (is) *the true God*.'" The idiom of the language then does not necessarily convert הֵמָּה in the passage before us into the verb "to be." And here let us repeat the sentence, גַּם־אַתֶּם כּוּשִׁים חַלְלֵי חַרְבִּי הֵמָּה *Zeph.* ii. 12. It will be perceived that גַּם־אַתֶּם are connected *by Makkaph*. Hebrew scholars do not agree as to how far this character is effective as an accent. But the rules for its use are—"Makkaph is inserted in the following cases: 1. Particles, which, from their nature, can never have any *distinctive* accent, are mostly connected with other words by the mark *Makkaph*: גַּם־לְאִישָׁהּ *even to her husband*; בְּתָם־לְבָבִי *in the integrity of my heart*. *Gen.* xx. 5, &c. 2. When words are to be construed together, &c., as זַרְעוֹ־בוֹ *its seed* (is) within itself. *Gen.* i. 11," &c. —*Lee's Lectures*, p. 61.

But Stuart, seeing no way to translate the sentence without making הֵמָּה the verb "*to be*," 3d person plural, "*are*," takes אַתֶּם the personal pronoun, 2d person plural, equivalent to *ye* or *you*, away from גַּם, to which it is attached by *Makkaph*, and carries it down to precede הֵמָּה in the sentence, and thus reads "*are ye*," while he supplies another אַתֶּם as understood to precede כּוּשִׁים, and reads, "ye Cushites, victims of my sword are ye." We consider this as quite as objectionable as Dr. Lee's—"*Even ye* (are) (the) *wounded of my sword*,—*they are Cushites*."

But permit us now to inquire into the probability of הֵמָּה being even a pronoun. אָנֹכִי *a-no-khi* is not believed to be a Hebrew word. It is a homophone of the Coptic word ϫⲛⲟⲕ, and used by the Egyptians, who spoke Coptic, as the personal pronoun *I.* This word is believed to have been borrowed by the Hebrews at the time they were in bondage in Egypt, and the habit of it so strongly established during their four hundred years of servitude, that neither the literature of the age of Moses nor the genius of the people could ever eradicate it. Their original personal pronoun was probably totally lost; nothing analogous to this Coptic term can be found in any other of the Shemitic tongues. But Lee says that Gessenius has found it in Punic, and quotes Lehregebaude, note, p. 200. In Chaldaic, *the personal pronoun, first person singular,* is אֲנָה *a-nah,* and its phonetic cognates are found in all the other sister dialects. We may then well suggest that *the last* Hebrew term was אֲנָא *a-na,* or quite analogous thereto.

Such then being the facts, let us inquire into the origin, composition, and signification of this Coptic pronoun. It will be agreed that some language must have had precedence in the world, and it is usually yielded to the Hebrew. That such precedence was the property of some one of the Asiatic dialects all agree; and the nearer the subsequent language exists to its precedent, the more plainly will its descent be manifest. If the Hebrew was such precedent, or any other of its immediate sisters, the Coptic, existing in their immediate neighbourhood, must have been originally very analogous to them.

It is immaterial whether our suggestion be right or wrong as to what particularly was the lost Hebrew pronoun; let us take the Chaldaic, which, of all these dialects, was the most nearly like the Hebrew—the personal pronoun אֲנָה *I, I am,* and the word כִּי *ki,* which means a *mark as a stigma,* indelibly fixed, as burned in, a mark intended pointedly to indicate something; and hence it became a particle attached to a word often by Makkaph, whence the attention was to be particularly called, as, *mark me, mark ye,* are *just,* &c. &c. *Isa.* iii. 14: כִּי תַחַת יֹפִי *a burned mark of stigma,* instead of beauty. Some have doubted the accuracy of the Hebrew in this instance, and the fact is, no doubt, that it is rather an Arabicism; but that in no way affects our deduction; it matters not whether the Coptic borrowed from Chaldean, Hebrew, or Arabic. These two words are beyond question the origin, the compound of the Coptic pronoun, meaning and including the individuality of the first person singular, and originally expressing also the fact, that such person was *marked* as a stigma indelibly, *as burned in,* &c. *Anoki, I, a marked one; I, one deformed as if branded*, &c.; *I*, *one that carry the mark of*, &c. &c., was the original idea expressed by this Coptic term of individuality. Thus it expressed the fact that the person was a successor in the curses of Ham and Cain, and in no other manner can the extraordinary appearance of הֵם and sometimes הֵמָּה in the third person of the pronoun be accounted for. It is evidently from a new and other source, the same or cognate with the term applied to the son of Noah.

These adjective associations of the pronoun, through the losses of ages, would naturally be forgotten by the Copts themselves, and were probably unknown to the Hebrews; just as we ourselves have forgotten that our word *obedient* still expresses some of the qualities of the Hebrew word עֶבֶד *ebed* and *abed*, from which it has been derived through the Latin.

This pronoun אָנֹכִי *I*, &c. was often contracted by the Hebrews into אֲנִי *ani*, and in its declination stood thus:

1st person singular, common gender:

אָנֹכִי sometimes אֲנִי .... *I.*

Plural:

אֲנַחְנוּ .... *We.*

2d person singular masculine:

אַתָּה .... *Thou.*

Plural:

אַתֶּם .... *You.*

Singular feminine:

אַתְּ .... *Thou, fem.*

Plural:

אַתֵּן .... *You, fem.*

3d person singular, masculine:

הוּא .... *He.*

Plural:

הֵם *hem*—occasionally הֵמָּה.................. *They.*

Here we find the word in question, if a pronoun. The feminine of the third person is הִיא, and plural נָה, and yet הֵמָּה is used in *Canticles* in a condition evidently feminine; and yet in *Zeph.* ii. 12, it is said it must be in the *second person plural.* But can any one believe that these words, thus arranged in the declination of this pronoun, could ever have had a common origin? The fact is, no original language was ever formed from rules; the rules are merely its description after it is formed. Language, in the infancy of its formation, resents a restraint and all laws, except such as apply to its incipient state. Suppose a soldier for life should persist in calling his infant son *soldier*, either playfully or mournfully; the child would associate the term "soldier" with his individuality, and say *soldier am sleepy*, &c. In case the soldier's family was isolated from the rest of the world, in the land of Nod, or elsewhere, then the family of languages would be quite apt to have a new term as a personal pronoun.

More pertinent examples would explain our idea perhaps more fully. There never was a language upon this earth, of which any thing is known, that does not show an extraordinary irregularity in the formation of its personal pronouns,—often giving proof that the different cases and persons have been formed from different roots. Webster says—"*I*, the pronoun of the first person, the word which expresses one's self, or that by which a speaker or writer denotes himself." "In *the plural*, we use *we* and *us*, which appear to be words radically distinct from *I*." Under *we*, he says, "From plural of *I*, or rather a different word, denoting," &c. Does any one imagine that *I*, you, me, and *us* are from the same root? Webster noticed the discrepancy; we could have hoped that he would have given the world a history of the personal pronoun of all languages: we know of no intellect more capable. Such a history would develop many curious things in the history of man, but would be attended with great labour; and human life has too few days for such a man.

Thus we may, hypothetically at least, point out the class of operating causes whereby the Copts introduced הֵם or occasionally הֵמָּה as a person of the pronoun, with the signification that the person to whom it was applied was a descendant of the son of Noah; and the pronoun so introduced derived from the noun חָם *Ham*. For, can we suppose the *first person singular* אָנֹכִי *a-no-ki*, and its third person plural הֵם *hem*, occasionally הֵמָּה *hemmah*, have the same root, or are of the same origin? This הֵם and the word חָם *the son of Noah*, are identical, except the son of Noah is generally written with a *heth*, instead of a *he;* but all know, who have studied the matter, these characters very often interchange, and that copyists have often inadvertently placed the one for the other. That which would seem the pronoun is used in *Gen.* xiv. 5, and the Septuagint has translated it as a *pronoun;* but our received version has no doubt restored the true reading. The passage בְּהָם is translated "in *Ham,*" *i. e.* the land occupied by the descendants of Ham, the son of Noah. The change of *Kamets* into *Tsere*, is really of no moment. These characters were never invented until after the language ceased to be spoken, and was long since dead. The points, in reality, are no part of the language. The word in Genesis is indisputably a noun, preceded and governed by the *preposition* בְּ.

Perhaps no one has ever yet succeeded to satisfy himself and others in the translation of this passage of Zephaniah; all, or others for them, find it full of difficulty: but let us consider הֵמָּה a noun of the same order as the הָם of xiv. 5 of *Genesis,*—in some respect in opposition to כּוּשִׁים, but more emphatic, as the affix of ה would seem to indicate, by its increase of the intensity, as well as its accounting for the *dagesh* of the מ *mem*, or its duplication. Let us consider it to mean the descendants of Ham,—to express the idea, with great intensity, that the *Cushites* were *Hamites.* True, it is not in the usual form of a patronymic. But we know not who will account, by grammatical rules, for all the anomalies found in Hebrew, a language so full of ellipses that some have thought it a mere skeleton language. With this view of the subject it will read elliptically, thus: *So ye Ethiopians wounded of the sword, Hamites*—with the meaning, that the Ethiopians were subject to bondage, and at the same time putting them in mind that the curse of slavery, as to the posterity of Ham, was unalterable.

The meaning of the prophet is—So ye Ethiopians, reduced to a condition of bondage, remember ye are the inheritors of the curse of Ham!

The arrangement of the language to us clearly indicates that sense. Besides, we must take into consideration the peculiar meaning of the words חַלְלֵי and חַרְבִּי,—that the prophet is writing in a highly figurative and poetic strain; and we would also compare what this prophet says to the Ethiopians with what the other prophets have said of the same people. כּוּשִׁים is here applicable to all the tribes of Ham, as in *Amos* ix. 7: "Are ye not as children of the Ethiopians unto me? O children of Israel, saith the Lord." It may be well here to notice also that the word

"Ethiopian" is of Greek origin, and associates with the idea blackness, like that of Ham. Thus, Αιθιοψ, *Aithiops, sun-burnt, swarthy as Ethiopians;* αιθος, *warmth, heat, fire, ardent, blazing like fire, blackened by fire, black, dark;* αιθοψ, *burning, fiery, blazing, burned, darkened by fire, dark-coloured, consuming, destroying. Donnegan* p. 34. But Isaiah speaks of the descendants of Ham perhaps in a more figurative language, and in a more elevated and poetical strain:

1. Wo to the land shadowing with wings,
Which *is* beyond the rivers of Ethiopia:

2. That sendeth ambassadors by the sea,
Even in vessels of bulrushes upon the waters,
Saying, Go, ye swift messengers, to a nation scattered and peeled;
To a people terrible from the beginning hitherto;
A nation meted out and trodden down,

3. Whose land the rivers have spoiled!
All ye inhabitants of the world, and dwellers on the earth,
See ye, when he lifteth up an ensign on the mountains,
And when he bloweth a trumpet, hear ye!

4. For so the Lord said unto me, I will take my rest,
And I will consider in my dwelling-place,
Like a clear heat upon herbs,
And like a cloud of dew in the heat of harvest.

5. For afore the harvest, when the bud is perfect,
And the sour grape is ripening in the flower,
He shall both cut off the sprigs with pruning-hooks,
And take away and cut down the branches.

6. They shall be left together unto the fowls of the mountains,
And to the beasts of the earth;
And the fowls shall summer upon them,
And the beasts of the earth shall winter upon them.

7. In that time shall a present be brought unto the Lord of hosts,
Of a people scattered and peeled,
And from a people terrible from the beginning hitherto;
A nation meted out and trodden under foot,
Whose land the rivers have spoiled,
To the place of the name of the Lord of hosts, the Mount Zion.

Isa. 18.

The denouncements of Jehovah against the children of Ham are more plainly expressed in the promises of God to these of the true worship, his peculiar people:

Thus saith the Lord,
The labour of Egypt, and merchandise of Ethiopia,
And of the Sabeans, men of stature,
Shall come over unto thee, and they shall be thine:
They shall come after thee;
In chains they shall come over;
And they shall fall down unto thee.
They shall make supplication unto thee,
Saying, Surely God *is* in thee;
And there is none else,
There is no God (*beside*),—(*or, there is no other God.*)

Isa. xlv. 14.

So *Jeremiah*: "Declare ye in Egypt, and publish it in Migdol, and publish in Noph and in Taphanhes; say ye, Stand fast, and prepare thee; for the sword shall devour round about thee.

"O thou daughter dwelling in Egypt, furnish thyself to go into captivity: for Noph shall be waste and desolate, without an inhabitant.

"The daughter of Egypt shall be confounded; she shall be delivered into the hands of the people of the north." *Jer.* xlvi. 1, 19, 24.

"And the sword shall come upon Egypt, and great pain shall be in Ethiopia, when the slain shall fall in Egypt, and they shall take away her multitudes, and her foundations shall be broken down.

"Ethiopia, and Lybia, and Lydia, and all the mingled (*mixed-blooded*) people, *Chub* and the men of the land that is in league, shall fall with them by the sword.

"In that day shall messengers go forth from me in ships to make the careless Ethiopians afraid, and great pain shall come upon them, as in the day of Egypt: for, lo, it cometh.

"The young men of Aven and of Pibeseth shall fall by the sword: and these cities shall go into captivity.

"At Taphanhes also the day shall be darkened, when I shall break there the yokes of Egypt: and the pomp of her strength shall cease in her: as for her, a cloud shall cover her; and her daughters shall go into captivity.

"And I will scatter the Egyptians among the nations and disperse them among the countries, and they shall know that I am the Lord." *Ezek.* xxx. 4, 5, 9, 17, 18, 26.

"And I will sell your sons and your daughters into the hands of the children of Judah, and they shall sell them to the Sabeans, to a people afar off: for the Lord hath spoken it." *Joel* iii. 8.

It may be we have occupied too much time, in remarks too obscure and indistinct for biblical criticism, upon this passage of *Zephaniah;* and it may be that, in the judgment of some, we have thus made ourselves obnoxious to the satire of the reverend and witty commentator upon the words:

> "Strange such difference there should be
> 'Twixt tweedle-dum and tweedle-dee."

But we were sure the passage had been greatly misunderstood, and were, perhaps, too much emboldened by the hope, that the providence of the All-wise might yet again issue forth the truth from the tongue of the feeble.

LESSON XVI.

From the root חמה has also been derived the Arabic word حَمَّن *aaman,* and the Syriac ܚܡܢܐ *hamania,* and adopted by the Hebrews in the word חַמָן *haman,* which Castell translates "*images,*" dedicated to the worship of the sun, the worship of fire, heat, &c.

The Hebrew use of this word will be found in a plural form in *Lev.* xxvi. 30, thus: "And I will destroy your high places, and cut down your *images,*" *hammanekem.* 2 *Chron.* xiv. 3 (the fourth of the Hebrew text:) "And brake down the *images,*" חַמָּנִים *hammanim;* also xxxiv. 4, 7: "And the *images,* (חַמָּנִים *hammanim*) that were on high above them, he cut down," "and had beaten the graven images (חַמָּנִים *hammanim*) into powder." *Isa.* xvii. 8: "Either the groves or the *images,*" חַמָּנִים *hammanim;* also xxvii. 9: "The groves and *images* (חַמָּנִים *hammanim*) shall not stand up." *Ezek.* vi. 4, 6: "Your altars shall be desolate, and your *images* (חַמָּנֵיכֶם *hammanekem*) shall be broken," "and your *images* (חַמָּנֵיכֶם *hammanekem*) may be cut down." We have no possible word to express literally this term, but the *hammanekens,* or little hams, or fire-houses, the objects of religious adoration, were conical towers, from fifty to one hundred feet high, and fifteen to twenty feet in diameter at the base, and gradually decreasing upward, with a small door or opening fifteen or twenty feet above the base, and four smaller ones near the apex, looking towards the cardinal points.

The moderns have no certain knowledge of their particular use, yet all believe that in them was attempted to be kept the perpetual or holy fire, and perhaps into them was thrust the infant sacrificed to the god. May we not suppose that Daniel and his brethren would have informed us, had it been necessary for us to know more? Spencer, Heb. Laws, lib. ii. cap. 25, § 3, says of these edifices: "*They were of a conical form and of a black colour.*" It seems to us this identifies these edifices with the round towers of Persia and elsewhere, remains of many of which were anciently found in Ireland. The curious about this matter are referred to Gessenius's Thesaurus, p. 489; also Lee's Lex. p. 297, where he quotes Henrici Arentii Hamaker Miscellanea Phœnicia, pp. 49, 54; also Diatribe Philologico-Critica aliquot monumentorum Punicorum; Selden, de Diis Syris, ii. cap. 8, and the authors severally cited by them. Upon a full consideration of the subject, Dr. Lee says—"Upon the whole, I am disposed to believe that the term חָם (*haman*) is rather derived from חָם *Ham*, the father of Canaan, of Mitsraim, &c., *Gen.* x. 6–20; and hence by the latter worshipped as presiding angel of the sun, under the title of Ἄμουν, *Greek* Ἄμμων (*Ammon*), which is probably our very word." If so, then his very name became significant of the worship of fire, and even expressive of the fire-temples themselves.

By some fanciful relation, not relevant to our subject, between the fire or sun worshippers and astronomy, when the sun was in aries (the ram), the god Ham, *Ammon*, *Hammon*, or *Jupiter Hammon*, was represented with a ram's head for his crest; with this crest became associated the idea of the god, and hence chonchologists, even to this day, call certain shells, that are fancied to resemble the ram's horn, *Ammonites*, giving further evidence, even now, of how deeply seated was the association between the earlier descendants of Ham and the fire worship of their day.

The long and fanciful story of *Io*, changed by Jupiter into a white cow; of her flight from the fifty sons of Egyptus; of her becoming the progenitor of the *Ionians;* the Egyptians claiming her under the name of *Isis;* of her marriage with *Osiris*, who became at length *Apis* and *Serapis*, worshipped in the image of a black bull with a white spot in his forehead, and many such tales, are all legitimately descended from his family peculiarities, their relative condition in the world, and the fact that Ham became the imaginary *deity* of his descendants.

Much evidence may be had proving that Ham became inseparably associated with, and in fact the very father of, idolatry, and of all those enormities growing out of it; enormities with which idolatry has ever been attended, and which time and the history of man for ever give proof to be a total preventive of all physical and moral elevation and improvement; and which, like other breaches against the laws of God, have, at all times, among all men, for ever been accompanied by both physical and moral degradation. But the descendants of Ham gave his name to their country. ⲬⲎⲘⲒ *Chemi* was the Coptic name for Egypt, which the Septuagint translates into Χαμ *Cham.* Plutarch styles Egypt Χημία *Chemia*, from the Coptic ⲬⲎⲘⲒ *Chemi*, and, as if he wished to give some account of its origin, adds, *θερμή γάρ ἐστὶν καὶ ὕγρα*, "for it is *hot and humid;*" showing that the ⲬⲎⲘⲒ *Chemi* of the Copts signified the same as the Ham of the Hebrews. But the Coptic word ⲬⲎⲘⲒ *Chemi*, Χημι and Χημε of Plutarch, also signified the adjective *black.* See Gibbs's Hebrew Lexicon, under the word חָם *Ham;* and with this signification the word *Ham* is used in *Ps.* lxxviii. 51: "The chief of their strength in the tabernacles of *Ham:*" Septuagint, Χαμ, *Cham*, from the Coptic ⲬⲎⲘⲒ *chemi*, black. cv. 23: "And Jacob sojourned in the land of *Ham*," חָם *Ham:* Septuagint, Χαμ, *Cham*, from the Coptic ⲬⲎⲘⲒ *chemi*, black. 27: "And wonders in the land of *Ham:*" Septuagint, Χαμ, *Cham*, from the Coptic ⲬⲎⲘⲒ *chemi*, black. cvi. 22: "Wondrous works in the land of *Ham:*" Septuagint, Χαμ, *Cham*, from the Coptic ⲬⲎⲘⲒ *chemi*, black. The idea is, the land of the black people.

In this sense also the word is used in *Gen.* xiv. 5: "And smote the Rephaims in Ashteroth Karnaim, and the Zuzims in *Ham.*" The Septuagint translates this passage into Καὶ ἔθνη ἰσχυρὰ ἅμα αὐτοῖς, as though the בְּהָם *be Ham* was a pronoun, and which seems to have been the view of several ancient translators. But such certainly was not the view of the translators of the received version; nor of Martindale, and others from whom he compiled. He says of this passage—"2. *Ham*, crafty, or heat; the country of the Zuzims, the situation of which is not known:" p. 326. We certainly agree with the Septuagint that זוּזִים *Zuzim* was a significant term, and perhaps well enough explained by *ἔθνη ἰσχυρά*, for which a suitable translation would seem to be *wicked, perverse, strong, numerous*, or *stubborn heathen.* They were probably the זַמְזֻמִּים Zamzummims of *Deut.* ii. 20.

The word בְּהָם *be Ham*, unless a pronoun as above, against which much can be said, is evidently used as in the *Psalms* quoted. In all these cases *Ham* is used somewhat as a synonyme of כּוּשׁ *Cush;* and when applied to a country generally, meant whatever country was occupied by the descendants of *Ham.* The sense of the sentence, *and Zuzims in Ham*, will then be, *and the stubborn heathen in Ethiopia*, or, *the perverse tribes of Cush*, or *the wicked nations of Ham;* all meaning the black tribes, descendants of Ham, or some one of them, when particularity is intended, as probably in this case; and let it be noticed, that Martindale, p. 241, gives "blackness" as his first definition of *Cush.* The descendants of Ham applying his name to themselves and country, they being black, it necessarily became significant of that colour. We have Germans, Swedes, English; but if we say "Negroes," or if we say Africans, we mean black men, because those words, as now used, mean men of colour; and in a sense analogous, the word *Ham* seems to have been used in the passages quoted.

This view of the word *Ham* we think elucidates the history of Esther and that of Haman הָמָן, the son of Hamadatha—*Agagite, ha Agagi.* The word is a patronymic of אֲגָג *Agag*,—hence he was an Amalekite: "Agag, the king of Amalek"—"Agag, the king of the Amalekites." 1 *Sam.* xv. 20, 32. "Now there was one Haman, the son of Amadatha, by birth an Amalekite." *Josephus*, book ii. cap. vi. 5. This shows the cause of the extraordinary hatred that existed between her people and his. His very name shows that he was a descendant of *Ham*, and we think also proves that the Amalekites were black; and which fact is confirmed by 1 *Sam.* xv. 6: "And Saul said unto the Kenites, Go, depart; get ye down from among the Amalekites, lest I destroy you with them,"—evincing the fact that by mere inspection he could not distinguish the one from the other. We have before shown that the Kenites were black. The argument follows, that the Amalekites were also.

The word *Ham* is also used in 1 *Chron.* iv. 40, in the same manner as it is in *Psalms* and *Genesis*, thus: "For they of *Ham* חָם had dwelt there of old." This is said of Gedar, "*even unto the east* side of the valley." Now Gedar was in the mountains of Judea, (see *Josh.* xv. 48–60,) or in the valley, (see *Josh.* xv. 36;) and as that account of the country of Judea closes (see *idem,* 63) by informing us whom the inhabitants of Judah could not drive out, and as the inhabitants of Gedar are not included in such list, it is to be presumed that the inhabitants of Gedar were so driven out at the time of Joshua; and leaves us nothing else to conclude than that, whoever they were, they who are spoken of in this passage, as having dwelt there of old, were the people driven out by him. But *Josh.* xii. 7, 8 informs us who the people were on the west side of Jordan, both in the mountains and valleys, and names them as Hittites, Amorites, Canaanites, Perizzites, and Hivites, and Jebusites; and from the 9th to the 24th gives us an account of their kings, among whom is named the king of Gedar, who was smitten and driven out. It is immaterial which of the tribes they were. They were inhabitants of Palestine, (see 2 *Chron.* xxviii. 18 and 1 *Chron.* xxvii. 28,) of the land of Canaan, not of south, east, nor of northern Arabia, nor of Egypt or any part of Africa; yet they are emphatically spoken of as of *Ham,* clearly having reference to their descent and colour. Here we have an additional key whereby to unlock the meaning of this word as used in *Psalms* and *Genesis.* There can be no doubt these primitive inhabitants of Gedar were the descendants of Canaan. Yet they are described by the same term which in other places is used to describe the descendants of Cush and Mitsraim; a term which most unquestionably determines them to have been black.

But the Coptic word *chemi,* which we have seen had the same significancy as חָם *ham* in Hebrew, opens to the view the real meaning of a few Hebrio-Coptic words that grew into common use among the Hebrews subsequent to their bondage in Egypt. We allude solely to the derivatives of ⲭⲏⲙⲓ *Chemi.* כָּמַר *Chemar* is thus derived, and occasionally used by the holy writers to signify black; thus, *Lam.* v. 10: "Our skin was *black*" נִכְמָרוּ *ni chemaru.* True, some have disputed the accuracy of this translation. They take a cognate meaning, and say *our skin was not,* &c. We hope to be excused for adopting the received version. But either meaning proves the origin of the word from the Coptic ⲭⲏⲙⲓ *chemi,* the same as the *ham* of the Hebrews. The fact is, the cognate meaning, sometimes, necessarily forces itself into an English translation, as in *Gen.* xliii. 30: "For his bowels did yearn," נִכְמְרוּ

grew hot, warmed, became agitated, &c. 1 *Kings* iii. 26: "Her bowels *yearned*," נִכְמְרוּ *grew hot, troubled*, &c.; and also *Hosea* xi. 8: "My repentings are kindled," נִכְמְרוּ *became hot*, &c.

But in all these instances the figure of speech is more particularly Asiatic, and more obscure than is well suited to our modern dialect, as we think will be seen by comparing them with *Job* iii. 5, "Let the blackness of day terrify it."

From this Coptic name of HAM has *also* been derived the appellative term of the Moabitish and Ammonitish god כְּמוֹשׁ *Chemosh*. The Syrians applied this term to the fancied being who oppresses mankind during the dark hours of their sleeping, and hence *distressing dreams, incubus*, &c. *Chemosh* is ranked with the god of destruction among the Hindoos, *Muha Dēvā*. The worshippers of this god are in Scripture called עַם־כְּמוֹשׁ *am Chemosh*, the people of Chemosh, particularly the Moabites and Ammonites. The image of this god was a *black stone*.

The term applied to the priesthood in this worship among the black tribes is also derivative from the same Coptic word to which we have often added in translation the word "idolatrous." Thus, 2 *Kings* xxiii. 5, "and he put down the *idolatrous* priests הַכְּמָרִים *ha chemarim*." *Hosea* x. 5, "And the *priests* thereof" כְּמָרָיו. *Zeph.* i. 4, "And the name of the *Chemarims*," הַכְּמָרִים *ha Chemarim*, i. e. the *priests* of the Hamitic fire-worshippers, &c. Some commentators, not connecting these words with the Coptic, and the *priest*, as the term applies, with the black families of Ham, have conceived that the idea *blackness*, as associated with these idolatrous priests, had reference to their apparel. Hence they conceive that these priests always wore black apparel; whereas the fact is they were *black men*, and, as such, are described by a term indicating that fact, as well as that of their idolatry and descent; and here we find the foundation of that modern and common prejudice, that the appropriate dress of the clergy is *black*.

But we find another derivative from the word *Ham*, *Gen.* xxxviii. 13: "And it was told Tamar, saying, Behold thy *father-in-law* חָמִיךְ goeth up." 25: "She sent to her *father-in-law*," חָמִיהָ. So also 1 *Sam*. iv. 19: "And that her *father-in-law was dead*." 21. "And because of her father-in-law," חָמִיהָ. This word is used in the feminine in *Micah*, vii. 6, thus: "Against her *mother-in-law*," בַּחֲמֹתָהּ *la hamtha*. We notice the word is preceded by the word כַּלָּה, which word, in *Gen.* xxxviii. 11, is applied to *Tamar*, and in *Jer.* ii. 32, evidently to a "bride" taken from the heathen, which was forbid; and is also used in *Cant.* iv. 8, for the "spouse," who is made to declare herself a *black woman*, giving evidence that the word in *Micah* is used in character.

This word is also used in the feminine in *Ruth* i. 14: "And Orpah kissed her *mother-in-law*," לַחֲמוֹתָהּ *la hamotha.* ii. 11: "All that thou hast done unto thy *mother-in-law*," חֲמוֹתֵךְ *hamothek.* 18: "And her *mother-in-law* saw what she had done," *hamotha.* 19: "And her *mother-in-law* (*hamotha*) said unto her;" "and she showed her *mother-in-law*," *la hamotha.* 23: "And dwelt with her *mother-in-law*," *hamotha.* iii. 1: "Then Naomi her *mother-in-law*," *hamotha.* 6: "All her *mother-in-law* bade her," *hamotha.* 16: "And when she came to her *mother-in-law*," *hamotha.* This is certainly not the most usual word in Hebrew to express the idea of *parent-in-law*.

But these instances of its use are too frequent, its declination too varied, and in both genders, to admit the idea that they are the result of error or casualty, although some lexicographers seem to reject it. It may be noticed that the individual holding the junior position was a female—that in each case the *parent-in-law* was most unquestionably of pure Shemitic race.

But suspicion may at least be allowed to such purity in these young females. Tamar's husbands were half of Canaanitish blood. It would be expected that she was of that race, but if not, her intermarriage with those sons of Judah placed her in that rank. The sons of Eli were notoriously wicked and licentious, and although the widow of Phinehas appears to have been of a devout cast, yet God had determined to destroy the house of Eli on their account, and to wrest the priesthood from the family. The suspicion as to her race grows out of these facts and the character of her husband. Ruth was declaredly a Moabitess, and Orpah was of that country.

Much might be said in favour of the position that in these cases the parents-in-law on the husband's side were of pure Shemitic blood, and the reverse as to the daughters-in-law. Now as this peculiar term is nowhere else used in the holy books, are we not to suppose that this peculiar state of facts is nowhere else thus described? In *Gen.* xviii., when the *father-in-law* of Moses is named, this term is not used, but the more usual one; and the reason is because the position of the parties is changed. Had the father or mother of Moses been spoken of as the *parent-in-law* of Zippora, then we may presume this peculiar term would have been used and expressed the fact as to the distinction of races; that he would have been called חָמִיהָ, and she her חֲמוֹתָהּ. And we now present the inquiry, how came the name of Ham to be thus compounded and used to express this particular position of relationship and distinction of race, unless from the fact that he had placed his parents in a similar position, liable to have been called by these peculiar terms?

LESSON XVII.

HAVING thus, at some length, passed these subjects in review, we present our reflections to the impartial mind.

But there are grown up upon this earth some men who would seem to be so holy and pure that even the providences of God are defective in their sight, and by their conduct seem to evince their opinion to be that Jehovah could not well manage the government of the world without their especial counsel and aid. And do such really mean to condemn God, unless his government shall comport with their views? In kindness of heart, and for the benefit of such poor fallen ones, we propose to close this our present Study by reading to them the thirty-third chapter of Ecclesiasticus, omitting the five verses irrelevant to the subject.

"There shall no evil happen unto him that feareth the Lord, but in temptation even again he will deliver him. A wise man hateth not the law; but he that is a hypocrite therein is as a ship in the storm. A man of understanding trusteth in the law; and the law is faithful unto him as an oracle. Prepare what to say, and so thou shalt be heard; and bind up instruction, and then make answer." "Why doth one day excel another, where as all the light of every day in the year is of the sun? By the knowledge of the Lord they were distinguished: and he altered seasons and feasts. Some of them hath he made high days, and hallowed them, and some of them hath he made ordinary days. And all men are from the ground, and Adam was created of earth. In much knowledge the Lord hath divided them, and made their ways diverse. Some of them hath he blessed and exalted, and some of them hath he sanctified, and set near himself: but some of them hath he cursed and brought low, and turned them out of their places. As the clay is in the potter's hand, to fashion it at his pleasure, so is man in the hand of him that made him, to render to them as liketh him best. Good is set against evil, and life against death: so is the godly against the sinner, and the sinner against the godly. So look upon all the works of the Most High; and there are two and two, one against another. I awaked up last of all, as one that gathereth after the grape-gatherers; by the blessing of God I profited, and filled my wine-press, like a gatherer of grapes. Consider that I laboured not for myself only, but for all them that seek learning. Hear me, O ye great men of the people, and hearken with your ears, ye rulers of the congregation." "In all thy works keep to thyself the pre-eminence; leave not a stain on thy honour. At the time when thou shalt end thy days, and finish thy life, distribute thine inheritance. Fodder, a wand and burdens, are for the ass; and bread, correction, and work, for a servant. If thou set thy servant to labour, thou shalt find rest, but if thou let him go idle, he shall seek liberty. A yoke and a collar do bow the neck, so are tortures and torments for an evil servant. Send him to labour, that he be not idle; for idleness teacheth much evil. Set him to work, as is fit for him; if he be not obedient, put on more fetters. But be not excessive toward any, and without discretion do nothing. If thou have a servant, let him be unto thee as thyself, because thou hast bought him with a price. If thou have a servant, entreat him as a brother: for thou hast need of him as thine own soul: if thou entreat him evil, and he run from thee, which way wilt thou go to seek him."

The doctrine is, that man is not exempt from the general law, that governs the animal world; that among all the animated races upon this earth, certain causes produce deterioration; and that it may take a longer course of time for the restoration of a degenerate race, under the controlling influences of opposite causes, than even that occupied in a downward direction. "Quickly is the descent made to hell; but to recover from the fall, and regain our former standing, is a labour, a task indeed." *Virgil.* In short, that sin has a tendency forcing downward to moral and physical ruin; to deteriorate the mental powers, to rot, tc blast, as with a mildew, all animal perfections; to fill life with disease and pain, and its hours with misery and wo, and that it never willingly ceases its iron hold until it can shake hands with death.

That God, in mercy, by the wisdom of his providence, has contrived as it were a shield, sheltering poor fallen man from the action of such portion of this deadly poison as would have destroyed every hope of intercession, and for ever excluded from our view, perhaps, even the advent of a *Saviour*. When the patient is dead, the physician is not called. The law which produced the deluge and destruction of the antediluvian world was a law established from all eternity, meet for just such a case as the moral and physical condition of man then was. For the sake of ten, Sodom would not have been destroyed; but it was less than ten for whom the Ark was provided; and we are to remember that quick upon the promise that all flesh were not again to be cast off, the lowest grade of slavery was promulgated, and its subjects ordered into the protection of the master; and may we not hence infer that slavery is intended, to some extent, as a preventive, as a shield against sin? And do we not notice that this shield is more or less weighty, more or less heavy to be borne, as the safety of the individual bearing it may require; and that it is so cunningly contrived, that its weight and burden are diminished in proportion as the danger abates?

"He poureth contempt upon princes, and causeth them to wander in the wilderness where there is no way; yet setteth he the poor on high from affliction, and maketh him families like a flock. The righteous shall see it and rejoice, and all iniquity shall stop her mouth. Whoso is wise, and will observe these things, even they shall understand the loving-kindness of the Lord." *Ps.* cvii. 40–43.

In close, we may everywhere notice that some among the family of man have become so poisoned with sin, so destroyed, that they are no longer safe guardians to themselves, even under the general interdict, that animal wants enslave us all. That for such God provides, as the general safety may seem to require. That, in the history of man, some races have become so deteriorated by a continued action in opposition to the laws of God, that he has seen fit to care for them, by placing them under the control of others; or by placing them, in mercy, under the guidance of a less deteriorated race, whom, no doubt, he holds responsible for the good he intends them. And may we be permitted of the humble Christian to inquire, if this position presents any thing contrary to the general law of benevolence of the Deity,—contrary to the welfare of man on earth, or his hopes of heaven?

Will you reject the doctrine, saying the biblical proofs are too scattered, too deeply buried under the dust of time? or, because the prophet has not appeared, or one arisen from the dead? The geologist, from a few fragments of bone, now dug from the deep bowels of the earth, is able to set up the osseous frame, to clothe with muscle and sinew, and give character to the animals of ancient time. And shall it not be recollected by you, who are striving to make your descendants the very princes of intellect and talent, that similar researches may be made in the moral history of man?

We submit the foregoing, confident, although there may be obscurity and darkness yet surrounding the subject, which we have not the ability to dispel, that the time will come, when it will be made plain to the understanding of all. We therefore resign the subject, touching the colour of the descendants of Ham, of their relationship with the family of Cain, and the ordinances of God influencing their condition in the world, to those more learned, more critical, and of more mental power, and in the hands of those whose lips have been touched by a more living coal from the altar of the prophet.

Study VII.

LESSON I.

In the inquiry into the scriptural views of slavery, by Albert Barnes, Philadelphia, 1846, page 322, we find the following assertion: "No man has a right to assume that when the word δοῦλος, *doulos*, occurs in the New Testament, it means a slave, or that he to whom it was applied was a slave."

Our object in our present study is to prove that this assertion is not true; and our object further is to prove that when the word δοῦλος, *doulos*, occurs in the New Testament, it means a slave, and that he to whom it was applied, as an appropriate distinctive quality, was a slave.

Suppose some infidel, a monomaniac in the study of infidelity, should put forth the proposition that when the words Jesus Christ occur in the New Testament, no one had the right to assume that they meant the Messiah, the Son of God, the Saviour of the world. We should feel it a needless labour to refute it; a foolish, false assertion often does not merit or require refutation, but the falsity of propositions may not be equally obvious to all, as in the present case.

The premises include the observance of the constitution, idioms, and use of the Greek language.

To him whose mind can flash upon the volume of Greek literature, like the well-read schoolboy upon the pages of Dilworth,—our present study and argument will be unnecessary and useless; but, as unsavoury as it may seem, from the evidence that reaches us, we doubt whether the great mass of those called learned, do not remember and practise their Greek only as the old veterans in sin do the evening and morning prayers of their childhood.

But, however that may be, a great proportion of us know no

language but our own, and take on trust what any Magnus Apollo may choose to assume concerning others. The assertions of one man, unaccompanied by evidence, may excite little or no attention; but we have seen the substance of this assertion put forth by the abolition clergy in various small publications, no doubt having great weight in their immediate vicinage.

We fear those who sit under such teaching may grope in deep darkness; and may we humbly pray, that, like the stroke of Jove, the light of the Almighty may reach them from afar.

LESSON II.

WHEN the untruthfulness of the lesson taught involves a misconception of the character and laws of God, its direct tendency is to create in the mind an idea of, we may say, an image of God and his laws, as decidedly different from him and his law as is the lesson taught from the truth; and here, perhaps, through all time, has been the commencement of idolatry.

Is it not as much idolatry to worship a false image of the mind, as it would be an image of wood or stone?

You teach that δοῦλος, *doulos*, does not mean *slave* in the word of God; you consequently teach that God disapproves of it, and that his laws forbid it. We say the exact contrary. It is therefore evident that the idea, the image we form in the mind of our God, is quite different from the idea you form in your mind of your God. But God cannot possess a contradiction in quality; therefore the God we worship must be a different God from the God you worship. But there can be but one God; therefore your God is a false God, or our God is a false God. You are an idolater, or we are one.

And shall it be said that our language is too strong?—unnecessarily extreme in its denunciation?—unwarranted by the views, by the language held by the advocates of abolition and the friends of the anti-slavery movements now in action in the Northern sections of our country? Hear the proclamation of Mr. Wright, an eloquent speaker, before the Anti-Slavery Society, as reported in the Boston papers, May 30th, 1850:

"Down with your Bible!—down with your political parties!—

down with your God that sanctions slavery! The God of Moses Stuart, the Andover God, the God of William H. Rogers, which is worshipped in the Winter-street Church, is a monster, composed of oppression, fraud, injustice, pollution, and every crime, in the shape of slavery. To such a God I am an atheist."

Thus the enemies of Jehovah give rapid proof of their idolatry.

It may be well here to remark, that the doctrine thus strange and astray from truth, may be expected to engraft itself upon such intellects as are led to the conclusion that man possesses within himself an unerring guide between right and wrong,—a doctrine which to us appears deeply fraught with ruin to the individual, and degradation to public morals.

We therefore condemn, most decidedly, the doctrine that man possesses a mental power called "moral sense," "conscience," or the "light within us," which enables him unerringly to decide on right and wrong. You may as well say it will always enable him to discern the truth. Nor do we comprehend how the mind can entertain such a notion, unless the intellect is thus impressible that the mind can believe in the existence of what would be a sister faculty, clairvoyance, or a thousand other such fantasies.

Man possesses no power by which he can know God, only as he has revealed himself by inspiration and by the daily manifestations of his law. We prefer to worship the God of Abraham and Moses, who gave them directions how slaves should be governed, and of whom they should be purchased:—the God of the Bible, in which he has plainly revealed the reason why they are slaves. The history of the human intellect gives proof that among its strong characteristics is a desire, a fondness to search into mystery. While this quality stimulates to inquiry after truth, in well organized minds, it is an important means of man's improvement and progression. But in the absence of all guides which can direct the path to successful inquiry, or by the substitution of false lights, man has ever gone astray. Here idolatry commences her reign.

The condition of man, from the most exalted instance of mental power, down to the most abject degradation of the African savage, is for ever marked and located by the fact, whether the guides to truth in their influence on him and his race have been universal, or only occasional; whether their influence has been obeyed only at distant periods, or at all times rejected. It is the law of God, man shall not progress to greatness only under the guidance of truth; under the guidance of falsehood, man degenerates to insignificance, crime, slavery, or to inglorious death.

We do not propose that any man or any race has, without exception, been under the constant influence of those axioms that guide the mind along the thread of truth; but that some men and some races have deviated far more than others, and that the effect of such difference is quite perceptible. Some races have become highly improved, while others only give evidence that they belong to the animal race of men.

Distinctions from this source arose between Cain and Abel; between the sons of Noah, Abraham, and the fire-worshippers of his day; between Jacob and Esau; and between the Israelites and the idolaters of the surrounding Hamitic tribes. This love of searching into mystery without using the aids to find truth, has at all times of the world, when supreme power was the object of contemplation, led men to idolatry, sometimes of the grossest kind; to the belief in mysterious influences, supernatural agencies, of spirits and demons, magic, witchcraft, &c.

To the same order of causes we are to attribute the sentiment entertained by some, that certain portions of Scripture and certain words sometimes contain unknown, hidden, secret, or mysterious meanings or instructions. Such views involve the proposition that such words, when used in the Scripture, have a different meaning than when otherwise used by men, and are to be translated into another language by substituting different ideas than those expressed by such words when used by man in his own oral or written language.

Do they forget that the language of man is the language of God? That revelation is always adapted to the understanding of men? They forget to know this first, that no prophecy of the Scripture is of any private interpretation. It happens that men take their own circumscribed view of the providence of God, as God's ordinance touching a matter, and if Scripture is in contradiction, then they search for mysterious or unusual meaning, and give it such interpretation as they imagine suits the case.

Hence theologians who deny that slavery is of Divine authority, are led to the necessity of also denying that the Greek word δοῦλος, *doulos*, means slave; or that, in its verbal formation, it expresses a cognate action.

The frequency of the use of this word in the copies of the ancient Greek Testament, as left us in the evangelical writings of the apostles; the varied manner in which they have applied the term, in figurative illustration, in comparison, in the most simple explanations, as well as in the expression of the primitive idea which they intended to convey by it, would seem to be sufficient proof that whatever such primitive idea may have been, yet that it surely was in exact conformity to the common and received opinion of its signification among those who wrote in and used the Greek language. This is very clear, since it is often used and addressed to the Greeks themselves, insomuch that no temerity has ever yet asserted that this word is of different import when found in the writings of the apostles than when found in the Greek authors generally.

LESSON III.

THE Greek noun δοῦλος, *doulos*, which we say means a slave unconditionally, so far as we have been able to examine, took its origin, both phonetically and literally, among the Greeks. Let us take δοῶ, as theme for διδῶμι, and λούω, or from the radical λοῶ, *lŏō:* both phonetically and significantly the word is complete. At the most ancient period of the Greeks, it is said they had no slaves, and it is a little remarkable that the word "*doulos*" is very seldom found in the most ancient of the Greek writers: but other nations more advanced had slaves. The idea, slave, was then expressed by them by the term δμώς, *dmos*, evidently of foreign origin. This latter term was nearly or quite obsolete as early as the days of Alexander, when the word *doulos* is found to have taken its place.

The ancient and Eastern nations were particular in their custom of bathing their bodies and washing their feet, &c. One of the first and most important uses to which the early Greeks seem to have applied slaves, was in these personal purifications; and hence the peculiar name δοῦλος originated; δου-λοίω, one whose office it was to bathe and wash them, a bondman for that particular use.

There is no instance in which Homer has used the word incompatible with such an association. The most affecting, we may say afflicting, circumstance in which he has introduced the word is the parting of Hector and Andromache; when Hector, anticipating his own death, and the probability of her being made a slave to the Greeks, emphatically laments her being compelled to carry water for her master, as if that was a particular employment in which the *doulos* was engaged.

But it does not affect the force of our argument, even if it shall be thought that the origin we give the word is doubtful. All we at the present moment propose is, that it is an original Greek term, all of which terms, either remotely or immediately, spring from particles having a significant and phonetic relation with the derivative. Such has been the doctrine of all who have written upon the philology and origin of the Greek language. Valckenaerus (the edition of Venice, published by Coletos) says, p. 8—

"Verba simplicia apud Græcos sunt vel 'primitiva,' vel a primitivis per varios flexus 'derivata.'

"Primitiva verba admodum sunt 'pauca:' 'derivatorum' numerus est infinitus.

"'Binæ' literarum syllabæ verbum primitivum constituunt.

"Verba primitiva, secundum observationem tertiam, dissyllaba sunt vel 'bilittera,' vel trilittera, vel quadrilittera.

"Primitiva 'bilittera,' per rei naturam, dari possunt in universum (si vel totam linguam perscrutemur) tantum quinque, nempe ἄω, ἔω, ὄω, ἴω, ὔω. Primitiva 'trilittera' sunt, quæ a 'vocali,' 'quadrilittera' (pleraque saltem) quæ a 'consonante,' incipiunt. Hoc certum est: sed de eo etiamnum addubito, an nonnulla verba 'quinque' litteris constantia pro 'primitivis' debeant haberi?" &c.

And Lennepius, de Anologia Linguæ Græcæ, (eadem editio,) p. 38:

"Cognita literarum potestate, earumque antiquitate, ad primas linguæ Græcæ origines indagandas progrediendum est. Videndum itaque primo loco, quænam voces pro 'simplicissimis originibus' haberi possint, quænam minus? Hoc autem ut rite peragatur, quædam de 'partibus orationis' ante sunt monenda.

"Ex viii. partibus quas vulgo statuunt grammatici, 'Verbum et Nomen' principem obtinent locum: quum reliquæ omnes facillime ad harum partium alterutram referi possint. Quapropter etiam 'Aristoteles,' aliique de veteribus, revera 'duas' tantum esse 'partes orationis' voluerunt.

"Addunt quidem alii tertiam partem, utriusque, nempe et 'verbi et nominis, ligamentum,' sive particulas, quod, nempe, particulæ orationem in unum corpus veluti connectant et devinciant. Sed, qui attentius 'particularum' naturam inspexerit, facile animadvertat, omnia fere, quæ 'particularum' nomine insigniuntur, si 'exteriorem formam' eorumque naturam grammaticam inspiciamus, referenda esse vel ad 'nomen' vel ad 'verbum.'

"Ita verbi gr.: particula ὂν, Lat. igitur, revera participium est, contracta pro ἐὸν, quod neutrum a masculo ἐὼν est, quo modo participium verbi ἔω, vel εἰμὶ, pronuntiarunt Iones, quum Attici ἐὸν contraxerint in ὂν. Apparet itaque, Græcum ὂν revera pertinere ad nomina participialia. Eadem ratio cernitur quoque in particulis ποὶ, πῆ, πῶ, quæ 'adverbia loci' dicuntur, quorum duo priora proprie 'dativa antiqua' sunt, postremum vero genitivus est; quemadmodum similis ratio cernitur in adverbiis quæ dicuntur 'Loci' apud Latinos, *quò*, *quà*, et similibus.

"Ad 'verba' porro referenda sunt ἄγε, φέρε, ἰδῶ, ἴθι, εἶα vel ἕα, et plura alia similia, id quod in aliis clarius, in aliis minus manifesto, apparet. Horum tamen omnium rationem eandem fuisse in prima linguæ Græcæ infantia, non est quod dubitemus.

"Hæc igitur quum revera sic sese habeant, jam porro inquirendum est, utrum verba, an vero nomina, 'primas' linguæ Græcæ stirpes nobis subministrent.

"Docet autem ipsa rei natura, si de 'simplicissimis' verbis sermo fiat, 'nomina' a 'verbis,' non verba a nominibus, primum esse formata.

"Quum enim omnes res vocabulis, tanquam nominibus, signatæ, ab usu qui singulis adest, vel quacumque etiam actione, nomina sua acceperint: clare apparet, sicut ipsam actionem unde res denominata sit, ita etiam verbum, quo actio designetur, præcedere nomini, quod ab actione aliqua rei sit inditum. Atque hoc adeo certum est, non solum in lingua Græca, sed etiam omnibus omnino linguis, ut extra omnem controversiam positum esse videatur: nisi quis delabatur illuc, ut linguas integras, qua late patent, nullo artificio humano accedente, uno temporis articulo hominibus divinitus datas esse, eosque statim caluisse tot myriadas quot in singulis linguis sunt vocabulorum; tametsi res ipsas vocabulis istis designandas plerosque primos homines ignorasse certum est.

"Hoc autem quam sit rationi contrarium, atque ipsi experientiæ, facile apparet, si modo consideremus, ea ratione multa vocabula existere jam debuisse priusquam eorum utilitas inter homines ulla esset, quæque proinde, non nisi vani et inutiles soni, facile et sine ulla jactura dediscenda fuissent.

"Quin imo experientia abunde docet, primum res ipsas inveniri hominum industria, deinde autem inventis nomina imponi, sive ab utilitate sive alia qualitate ducta. Ex quo porro apparet, quo plures res ab aliquo populo inveniantur, eo ditiorem et uberiorem eorum linguam fieri, ut adeo mirandum non sit tantam esse linguæ Græcæ copiam et ubertatem, quum exculta ea fuerit a populo ingeniosissimo, cui omnes artes et disciplinæ non tantum primordia sua, sed etiam omnem fere splendorem, debent. Linguas itaque diligenter consideranti, idem quod in artibus, in iis quoque usu venire apparebit: eas nimirum a paucis simplicissimisque initiis profectas, non nisi sensim et progressu temporis ad eam qua postea patuerunt amplitudinem pervenisse. Quum autem hominum natura ita sit comparata, ut primum eas res circumspiciat, quæ necessario ad vitam sustentandam, et cum aliis quibuscum homo societatis vinculo conjunctus est secure agendam, requirantur, dein vero ea excogitat quæ vitam jucundiorem possint reddere, valde verisimile fit vocabula ea in linguis antiquissima esse quibus res designantur ad vitam degendam necessariæ, si recesseris ab iis vocabulis, quæ in antiquissimorum vocabulorum locum deinceps substituta sunt, ut revera hujus generis multæ vocabulorum formæ inveniantur, quæ verborum obsoletorum locum occupaverunt.

"Porro non alienum erit hic observasse non tantum ejusmodi vocabula antiquissima existimari debere, sed etiam 'ipsas' significationes verbis subjectas tanto antiquioris usus esse, tantoque magis proprias esse habendas, quanto sunt propiores iis rebus quas corporis sensibus percipimus. Ab iis enim semper servata quadam similitudine ad reliquas quascumque verborum significationes progrediendum est: ut adeo appareat, paucissimas revera esse proprias verborum 'significationes,' nec alias esse nisi corporeas, sive eas quibus res sensibus externis expositæ designantur.

"E contrario autem, translatarum significationum copiam immensam, quæ ex propria notione, tanquam ex trunco arboris rami, quaquaversum pateant; manente similitudine inter eas omnes et propriam seu primam stirpis significationem, similiter atque rami, utcumque dispersi, et communem et communis trunci naturam retinent.

"Ex his præterea intelligitur ea verba, quæ *ὀνοματα πεποιημενα* a Græcis vocantur, sic dicta quia a 'nomine' vel 'sono' formentur, 'propriam' eam significationem quæ soni, unde facta sunt, naturam referat. Quorum verborum numerus ingens revera in linguis est, et longe major quam vulgo credi solet. Sed, ut ad propositum redeamus, ex iis quæ supra dicta sunt, clare apparet, simplicissimas origines non posse repeti nisi ab ejusmodi verbis, quibus actiones ipsæ significentur; adeoque a verbis sic proprie dictis.

"Quumque actiones infinitæ, sive nulli certæ personæ adsignatæ, per rei naturam antecedere debeant iis quæ certæ personæ attribuuntur, verba 'infinitiva' simplicissima proprie primas linguæ Græcæ origines continere certum est.

"Harum autem plurimæ, quum jam a longissimis temporibus, una cum plerisque notionibus propriis, ex usu ceciderint, ac difficillimæ sæpe indagatu sint, quo certiores progredi possimus, id semper tenendum est, ne quidquam admittamus quod constanti analogiæ linguæ repugnet; dein etiam, ut ex ipsis linguæ reliquiis, rite inter se comparatis, inquiramus a quo verbo originali vocabulum quodque oriatur: etiam tum, quum minus ipsum verbum originale superstes sit.

"Ubi enim in sequentibus agetur de 'simplicissimis' verbis 'primitivis,' id non ita accipiendum est quasi ea omnia, sicut etiam multa derivata simpliciora, florente lingua Græca, in sermone Græcorum adhuc exstitisse vellem; sed tantum, in primo linguæ Græcæ ortu, aut exstitisse revera aut saltem existere potuisse. Neque enim, in hoc linguæ Græcæ defectu, æque certo sciri potest, an tanta copia, quantam fingere verborum per linguæ naturam constanti analogiæ ductu liceat, prima linguæ Græcæ ætate reipsa viguerit."

Our object is here to present the Greek scholar, who may not have reflected on the subject, such suggestions as will lead him to perceive that δοῦλος, *doulos*, is an original Greek word, not borrowed; and although he may not agree with us in the derivation of the term, yet that he may readily satisfy himself what is the true derivation. It is true, Scheidius, in his "Animadversiones ad analogiam linguæ Græcæ," has criticized the views of Lennepius, and has devoted near thirty pages to that which is our quotation from him; and we did fancy, upon its examination, that he had rather established than weakened the argument of Lennepius: in fact we did propose to quote him as authority; but to the most of us long quotations, in a language to us unknown, are quite objectionable. We therefore refer to his work, pp. 246 to 275, apud Paddenburg et filium, 1790, "Traiecti ad Rhenum." It has been said by some of those who contend that δοῦλος, when found in the Greek Testament, does not mean slave, that the Greek, like all other languages of modern date, is a compilation from the more ancient ones; and since the Greeks at an early day had no slaves, it is evident, it is good proof that the more ancient tribes, from whom they and their language descended, had none; and in all such early periods of the world men never had words in their language to express things which did not exist among them, of which they could have no idea.

Therefore δοῦλος could not have meant slave,—"an idea of which they had no notion." Even if this statement were true, we do not perceive how it proves their proposition. To show the futility of such argument, we consent, for the moment, that δοῦλος is not an original Greek word, but was borrowed from some other language, in which it meant something distinct from the idea of slave: say, a freeman, if you choose. Language, and all its parts, has ever been found to conform itself to the habits and wants of those who use it. Wherefore we often find a term, which some centuries ago expressed a certain distinct idea, now to express quite a different one. We therefore cannot say, with any propriety, that, because the word δοῦλος meant a "freeman," at the age of Noah, that it also meant the same thing at the age of Alexander. If it meant a "freeman" at the age of Noah, we are to determine that fact by its use at that period; if otherwise, we should be able to prove that our word *slave* does not mean a slave now, but a proud and lofty distinction.

It is a term borrowed from the Schlavonic, where its significance was *fame*, *renown*, &c.; but the Schlavonians going into bondage to other nations, upon their inroads on Europe, the term implying *fame* in their ancient national distinctions came to signify in succeeding ages the condition of bondage. But although, as we have seen, a language is modified by the habits of those who apply it, yet this liability to change ceases when the language ceases to be the common vehicle of thought. Such substantially has been the case with the ancient Hebrew, since the era of the prophets; and such has, emphatically, been the case with the ancient Greek since the breaking down of the Roman Empire.

And even at the age of the apostles, the Greek had already arrived at the very highest point of its cultivation. No history, no writer gives proof of any subsequent improvement. If, then, we desire with seriousness and truth to determine the significance of any term then in use, the same is alone to be found by an investigation of the Greek literature of that age.

There are two modes by which an idea expressed in one language is explained in another. Where both languages contain words of synonymous meaning, then the expressing the idea through the medium of the words in another language, is properly what we mean by "translation." But in many instances, the second language contains no word or words which are synonymes of the term by which the idea is expressed in the language which we wish to translate. In that case we can accomplish the object only by transferring the term expressing the idea from the one language to the other. Example:—When the French exhibited to the natives here a padlock, the natives associated the thing with their idea of the tortoise, from the fancied mechanical resemblance, and with them the name of the one became the name of the other also. But when we exhibited to them a steamboat, they found their language destitute of any word to express their idea of the thing exhibited; consequently, they transferred into their own language the word steamboat, to express the new idea.

With a view to be enabled to come to a truthful decision as to the definiteness of the idea intended to be conveyed by the word *doulos*, when used in the writings of the apostles, let us make a suitable inquiry among the Greek authors read and studied at their time, regardless of what may be the result as to the establishment of any peculiar theory or favourite notion. Let a development of the truth be the sole object of the research, careless of what else may stand or fall thereby. And since all have not chosen to burden themselves with the toilsome lesson necessary in a preparation for such examination, we consent that such may pass it by with the same indifference with which they regard the study.

LESSON IV.

We commence our quotations from the Greek authors with the Cebetis Tabula, from the Gronovius edition, Glasgow, 1747:

P. 17. ——*διὸ καὶ ὅταν ἀναλώσῃ πανθ' ὅσα ἔλαβε παρά τῆς τύχης, ἀναγκάζεται ταύταις ταῖς γυναιξὶ δουλεύειν, καὶ πάνθ' ὑπομένειν, καὶ ἀσχημονεῖν, καὶ ποιεῖν ἕνεκεν τούτων ὅσα ἐστὶ βλαβερά.*

P. 34. *Τοὺς μεγίστους, ἔφη, καὶ τὰ μέγιστα θηρία, ἃ πρότερον αὐτὸν κατήσθιε, καὶ ἐκόλαζε, καὶ ἐποίει δοῦλον. Ταῦτα πάντα νενίκηκε, καὶ ἀπέῤῥιψεν ἀφ' ἑαυτοῦ, καὶ κεκράτηκεν ἑαυτοῦ, ὥστε ἐκεῖνα νῦν τούτῳ δουλεύουσι, καθάπερ οὗτος ἐκείνοις πρότερον.*

Æschylus, Prometheus Chained. Line 463:

κἄζευξα πρῶτος ἐν ζυγοῖς κνώδαλα
ζεύγλαισι δουλεύοντα.

In his Chœphoroi line 75:

ἐκ γαρ οἴκων
πατρῴων δούλιον ἐσᾶγον αἶσαν,
δίκαια καὶ μὴ δίκαια,
πρέποντ' ἀρχαῖς βίου,
βίᾳ φερομένων αἰνέσαι πικρόν φρενῶν
στύγος κρατούσῃ.

Burney translates this passage thus:
Etenim e domo paterna servilem induxeram sortem, *stat* juste et injuste, convenienter origini meæ, eorum qui vi agunt laudare acerbum mentis odium coërcenti.

Line 133. *κἄγω μὲν ἀντίδουλος* —which the same author translates, Et ego quidem pro serva habeor.

Anacreon, *Sur l'Amour Esclave:*

Αἱ Μοῦσαι τὸν Ἔρωτα
Δήσασαι στεφάνοισι,
Τῷ Κάλλει παρέδωκαν.
Καὶ νῦν ἡ Κυθέρεια
Ζητεῖ, λύτρα φέρουσα,
Λύσασθαι τόν Ἔρωτα.
Κἂν λύσῃ δέ τις αὐτόν,
Οὐκ ἔξεισι, μενεῖ δέ·
Δουλεύειν δεδίδακται.

Lucian, Dialogues of the Gods—Jove, Æsculapius, and Hercules:

ἐγὼ δε, εἰ καὶ μηδέν ἄλλο, οὔτε ἐδούλευσα ὥσπερ σύ.

Translation: Ego vero, si nihil aliud, neque servivi quemadmodum tu, &c.

Mercury and Maia:

——*ὥσπερ οἱ ἐν γῇ κακῶς δουλεύοντες,*

Ut in terris solent, qui malam servitutem serviunt.

Charon sive Contemplantes. Mercury:

Οὐ γὰρ οἶσθα ὅσοι πόλεμοι διὰ τοῦτο, καὶ ἐπίβουλαι, καὶ λῃστήρια, καὶ ἐπιορκίαι, καὶ φόνοι, καὶ δεσμὰ, καὶ πλοῦς μακρὸς, καὶ ἐμπορίαι, καὶ δουλεῖαι;

Nescis enim quot propterea bella existant, et insidiæ, latrocinia, perjuria, cædes, vincula, navigatio longinqua, mercaturæ, servitutes denique?

Cataplus sive Tyrannus:

Clotho.—Ἄκουε· μᾶλλον γὰρ ἀνιάσῃ μαθών. Τὴν μὲν γυναῖκά σοι Μίδας ὁ δοῦλος ἕξει, καὶ πάλαι δὲ αὐτὴν ἐμοίχευεν.

Audi, magis enim iis auditis lugebis: uxorem tuam Midas habebit, servus qui olim adulterio illi cognitus est.

Megapenthes.—Κἂν ἰδιώτην με ποίησον, ὦ Μοῖρα, τῶν πενήτων ἕνα, κἂν δοῦλον, ἀντί τοῦ πάλαι βασιλέως.

Vel privatum me facito, Parca, pauperum unum, vel servum, pro eo, qui rex nuper fui.

Necyomantia, Menippus:

* * * ἐκολάζοντό τε ἅμα πάντες, βασιλεῖς, δοῦλοι, σατράπαι, πένητες, πλούσιοι· καὶ μετέμελε πᾶσι τῶν τετολμημένων. ἐνίους δὲ αὐτῶν καὶ ἐγνώρισαμεν ἰδόντες, ὁπόσοι ἦσαν τῶν ἔναγχος τετελευτηκότων. οἱ δε ἐνεκαλύπτοντο καὶ ἀπεστρέφοντο· εἰ δὲ καὶ προσβλέποιεν, μάλα δουλόπρεπές τι, καὶ κολακεύτικον· καὶ ταῦτα, πῶς οιει, βαρεῖς ὄντες καὶ ὑπερόπται παρὰ τὸν βίον;

Unà autem omnes puniebantur, reges, servi, satrapæ, pauperes, divites, mendici; cunctosque pœnitebat patratorum; nonnullos agnovimus etiam conspicati, eorum de numero scilicet qui nuper vitam finierant; illi vero præ pudore vultus tegebant seseque avertebant; quod si forte respicerent, valde quidem *servilem* in modum, atque adulatorie, illi ipsi, qui fuerant quàm putas graves et superbi aliorum contemtores in hac vita.

Deorum Comitia:

Momus: * * * τοιγαροῦν οἱ Σκύθαι καὶ οἱ Γέται ταῦτα ὁρῶντες αὐτῶν, μακρὰ ἡμῖν χαίρειν εἰπόντες, αὐτοὶ ἀπαθανατίζουσι, καὶ θεοὺς χειροτονοῦσιν, οὓς ἂν ἐθελήσωσι, τὸν αὐτὸν τρόπον ὅνπερ καὶ Ζάμολξις, δουλος ὤν, παρενεγράφη, οὐκ οἶδ' ὅπως διαλαθών.

Proinde Scythæ ac Getæ hæc illorum videntes, longum nobis valere jussis, immortalitati se donant, et deos quoscunque voluerint feris suffragiis consalutant, eodem modo quo Zamolxis etiam, servus cum esset, in album nescio quomodo delitescens, irrepsit.

Demosthenes. Leipsic Ed. 1829, in 4 vols. Vol. i.

Olynthiac 2d. * * * ἢ ὡς οἱ παρά τὴν αὐτῶν ἀξίαν δεδουλωμένοι Θετταλοὶ νῦν οὐκ ἂν ἐλεύθεροι γένοιντο ἄσμενοι— which Leland translates thus: * * * "or that the Thessalians, who have been so basely, so undeservedly *enslaved*, would not gladly embrace their freedom."

P. 70. ——ὅτι Λακεδαιμονίοις καταδουλουμένοις, &c.

Philippic 4th, p. 142. ——μήτε δουλεύειν ἄλλῳ.

P. 148. ——εἰς δούλειαν, &c.

Idem. ——τήν δε τῶν δούλων ἀπέχεσθαι δήπου μη γένεσθαι δεῖ.

Idem, p. 149. ——δούλῳ δὲ, πληγαὶ, καὶ ὁ τοῦ σώματος αἴκυσμος· &c.

Idem, p. 158. * * * ὑπόλοιπον δουλεύειν.

Idem. ——οἶδε γὰρ ἀκριβῶς ὅτι δουλεύειν μεν ὑμεῖς οὔτ᾽ ἐθελησετε.

Idem, p. 159. ——ὑπηγάγετο εἰς τὴν νῦν παροῦσαν δουλεὶαν.

On the Treaty with Alexander, p. 227. * * * ἢ πείσθεντας γε δουλεύειν ἀντὶ τῶν ἀργυρωνήτων.

Idem, p. 229. ——τόν δ᾽ εἰς δουλείαν ἄγοντά με, &c.

De Corona, p. 208. ——πότερ᾽ ὡς ὁ πατήρ σου, Τρόμης, ἐδούλευε παρ᾽ Ἐλπίᾳ τῷ πρός τῷ Θησείῳ διδάσκοντι γράμματα, &c.

Idem. ——ἀλλ᾽ ὡς ὁ τριηραύλης Φορμίων, ὁ Δίωνος τοῦ φρεαῤῥίου δοῦλος, &c.

Idem, p. 289. ——ὥστ᾽ ἐλεύθερος ἐκ δούλου, καὶ, &c.

Idem, p. 309. ——τοὺς Ἑλλήνας καταδουλουμένους.

Idem, p. 315. ——προσθεμένην ἀσφαλῶς δουλεύειν.

Idem, p. 316. ——δι᾽ ὅτου δουλεύσουσιν εὐτυχῶς.

Idem. ——ὁ δὲ καὶ τῇ πατρίδι ὑπέρ τοῦ μὴ ταύτην ἐπιδεῖν δουλεύουσαν ἀποθνήσκειν ἐθελήσει, καὶ φοβερωτέρας ἡγήσεται τάς ὕβρεις καὶ τας αἰτίμιας, ἅς ἐν δουλευούσῃ τῇ πόλει φέρειν ἀνάγκη τοῦ θανάτου.

Idem, p. 343, (*in the Epitaph.*) ——ὡς μὴ ζυγὸν αὐχένι θέντες δουλοσύνης, &c.

Idem, p. 345. ——ἕως δούλους ἐποίησαν.

Oratio de Falsa Legatione, vol. ii. p. 37. ——ἀλλὰ δουλεύειν, καὶ τεθνᾶναι τῷ φόβῳ, καὶ τοὺς Θηβαίους, καὶ τοὺς Φιλίππου ξένους, [οὓς] ἀναγκάζονται τρέφειν, διῳκισμένοι κατὰ κώμας, καὶ παρῃρημένοι τὰ ὅπλα.

Idem, p. 54. ——καὶ γάρ τοι, πρῶτον μὲν Ἀμφίπολιν, πόλιν ὑμετέραν, δούλην κατέστησεν, ἥν τότε σύμμαχον αὐτοῦ καὶ φίλην ἔγραψεν.

Idem, p. 60. ——ὥστ' ἐκεῖνος ὁ δουλεύσων ἔμελλεν ἔσεσθαι τοῖς ἀπὸ τῆς εἰρήνης λυσιτελοῦσιν, οὐχ ὑμεῖς.

Idem, p. 78. ——ὅτι ταῦτα μὲν αὐτῷ συνῄδει πεπραγμένα, καὶ δοῦλος ἦν τῶν ῥημάτων τούτων.

Idem, p. 95. Ἐλεγεῖα Σολωνος.

Εἰς δὲ κακὴν ταχέως ἤλυθε δουλοσύνην,
Ἣ στάσιν ἔμφυλον, πόλεμόν θ' εὕδοντ' ἐπεγείρει,
Ὃς πολλῶν ἐρατὴν ὤλεσεν ἡλικίην.

Idem, p. 97. ——οἱ γὰρ ἐν ταῖς πόλεσι γνωριμώτατοι, καὶ προεστάναι τῶν κοινῶν ἀξιούμενοι, τὴν αὑτῶν προδιδόντες ἐλευθερίαν, οἱ δυστυχεῖς, αὐθαίρετον αὑτοις ἐπάγονται δουλείαν, Φιλίππου φιλίαν, καὶ ξενίαν, καὶ ἑταιρίαν, καὶ τὰ τοιαῦθ' ὑποκοριζόμενοι.

Oratio adversus Leptinem, p. 174. ——πῶς γὰρ οὐχὶ καὶ κατὰ τοῦτο δεινότατ' ἂν πεπονθὼς ὁ Χαβρίας φανείη, εἰ μὴ μόνον ἐξαρκέσειε τοῖς τὰ τοιαῦτα πολιτευομένοις τὸν ἐκείνου δοῦλον Λυκίδαν πρόξενον ὑμετερον πεποιηκέναι, ἀλλ' εἰ καὶ δια τοῦτον πάλιν τῶν ἐκείνῳ τι δοθέντων ἀφελοιντο, καὶ ταῦτ' αἰτίαν λέγοντες ψευδῆ;

Oratio contra Midiam, p. 207. ——καὶ τοσαύτῃ γ' ἐχρήσατο ὑπερβολῇ, ὥστε, κἂν εἰς δοῦλον ὑβρίζῃ τις, ὁμοίως ἔδωκεν ὑπὲρ τούτου γραφήν. * * * ἐπειδὴ δὲ εὗρεν οὐκ ἐπιτήδειον, μητε πρὸς δοῦλον, μηθ' ὅλως ἐξεῖναι πραττεῖν ἐπέταξεν.

P. 208. Νομος.—Ἐὰν τις ὑβρίσῃ εἴς τινα, ἢ παῖδα, ἢ γύναικα, ἢ ἄνδρα, τῶν ἐλευθέρων, ἢ τῶν δούλων, ἢ παράνομόν τι ποιήσῃ εἴς τούτων τινὰ, γραφέσθω πρός τοὺς θεσμοθέτας ὁ βουλόμενος Ἀθηναίων, οἷς ἔξεστιν. * * * ἀκούετε, ὦ ἄνδρες Ἀθηναῖοι, τοῦ νόμου τῆς φιλανθρωπίας, ὃς οὐδὲ τούς δούλους ὑβρίζεσθαι ἀξιοῖ.

P. 209. ——ὅμως οὐδ᾽ ὅσων ἂν τιμὴν καταθέντες δούλους κτήσωνται.

P. 210. ——Ἀπόλλωνι ἀποτροπαίῳ βοῦν θῦσαι, καὶ στεφανηφορεῖν ἐλευθέρους καὶ δούλους, καὶ ἐλινύειν μίαν ἡμέραν.

Idem, p. 253. ——τύπτειν, ἀλλὰ τὴν ἐπὶ τῆς πομπῆς καὶ τοῦ μεθύειν πρόφασιν λαβὼν, ἀδικεῖν, ὡς δούλοις χρώμενος τοῖς ἐλευθέροις.

Oratio adversus Androtionem, p. 293. ——ὑπέρ τοῦ μή τό σῶμα ἁλούς εἰς τό δεσμωτήριον ἕλκεσθαι, ἢ ἄλλα ἀσχημονοίη, ἃ δούλων, οὐκ ἐλευθέρων, ἐστὶν ἔργα, &c.

Idem. ——καὶ μὴν, εἰ θέλοιτε σκέψασθαι, τί δοῦλον, ἢ ἐλεύθερον εἶναι, διαφέρει, τοῦτο μέγιστον ἂν εὕροιτε, ὅτι τοῖς μὲν δούλοις τὸ σῶμα τῶν ἀδικημάτων ἁπάντων ὑπεύθυνόν ἐστι.

Idem, p. 295. ——πότερ᾽ οὖν οἴεσθε τούτων ἕκαστον μισεῖν, καὶ πολεμεῖν αὐτῷ, διὰ τὴν εἰσφορὰν ταύτην, ἢ τὸν μὲν αὐτῶν, ὅτι, πάντων ἀκουόντων ὑμῶν, ἐν τῷ δήμῳ δοῦλον ἔφη, καὶ ἐκ δούλων εἶναι, καὶ προσήκειν αὐτῷ τὸ ἕκτον μέρος εἰσφέρειν μετὰ τῶν μετοίκων.

Idem, p. 298. ——εἰ γὰρ ἀνδραπόδων πόλις, ἀλλὰ μὴ τῶν ἄρχειν ἑτέρων ἀξιούντων, ὡμολογεῖτε εἶναι, ὀυκ ἂν, ὦ ἄνδρες Ἀθηναῖοι, τὰς ὕβρεις ἠνέσχεσθε τὰς τούτου, ἃς κατὰ τὴν ἀγοραν ὕβριζεν, ὁμοῦ μετοίκους, Ἀθηναίους, δέων, ἀπάγων, βοῶν ἐν ταῖς ἐκκλησίαις, ἐπὶ τοῦ βήματος, δούλους καὶ ἐκ δούλων καλῶν, ἑαυτοῦ βελτίους, καὶ ἐκ βελτίονων, ἐρωτῶν.

Idem, p. 299. ——νῦν δ᾽ ἐπὶ ταῖς εἰσφοραῖς, ὃ δίκαιον ἐσθ᾽ ὁρίσας, μὴ σοὶ πιστεύειν, ἀλλὰ τοῖς αὐτῆς δούλοις, τὴν πόλιν, ὁπότ᾽ ἄλλο τι πράττων, &c.

Oratio adversus Timocratem, vol. iii. p. 128. ——καὶ γὰρ ἐκείνων, ὦ ἄνδρες δικασταὶ, ὅσοι ἂν ἐλεῦθεροι γένωνται, οὐ τῆς ἐλευθερίας χάριν ἔχουσι τοῖς δεσπόταις, ἀλλὰ μισοῦσι μάλιστα ἀνθρώπων ἁπάντων, ὅτι συνίσασιν αὐτοῖς δουλοῦσασιν.

Idem, p. 133. ——εἰ οὖν μὴ τιμωρήσησθε τούτους, οὐκ ἂν φθάνοι τὸ πλῆθος τούτοις τοῖς θηρίοις δουλεῦον.

Idem, p. 141. ——καὶ μὴν εἰ θέλοιτε σκέψασθαι παρ' ὑμῖν αὐτοῖς, ὦ ἄνδρες δικασταὶ, τι δοῦλον, ἢ ἐλεύθερον εἶναι διαφέρει, τοῦτο μεγίστον ἂν εὕροιτε, ὅτι τοῖς μὲν δούλοις τὸ σῶμα τῶν ἀδικημάτων ἁπάντων ὑπεύθυνόν ἐστι, τοῖς δ' ἐλευθέροις ὕστατον τοῦτο προσήκει κολάζειν.

Oratio III. adversus Aphobum, p. 242. ——καίτοι εἴγ' ἦν δοῦλος ἄνθρωπος, καὶ μὴ προωμολόγητο πρὸς τοῦδ' ἐλεύθερος εἶναι, &c.

Idem, p. 243. ——ἀλλά καὶ δοῦλον εἶναι τὸν ἄνθρωπον τῷ ὄντι.

Idem, p. 247. ——διόπερ τοὺς ὁμολογουμένως δούλους παραβὰς, τὸν ἐλεύθερον ἠξίου βασανίζειν, ὃν οὐδ' ὅσιον παραδοῦναι, &c.

Oratio I. adversus Onetorem, p. 266. ——καὶ ὁπόταν δοῦλοι, καὶ ἐλεύθεροι παραγένωνται, δεῄ δ' εὑρεθῆναι τὸ ζητούμενον, οὐ χρῆσθε ταῖς τῶν ἐλευθέρων μαρτυρίαις, ἀλλὰ τοὺς δούλους βασανίζοντες οὕτω ζητεῖτε τὴν ἀλήθειαν εὑρεῖν τῶν πεπραγμένων. * * * δούλων δὲ βασανισθέντων, οὐδένες πώποτ' ἐξηλέγχθησαν, ὡς οὐκ ἀληθῆ τὰ ἐκ τῆς βασάνου εἶπον.

Oratio in Phormionem, vol. iv. p. 13. ——νῦν δ' οὐκ ἐμοὶ, * * * ἀλλ' ἐν Βοσπόρῳ, καὶ τῆς συγγραφῆς σοι κειμένης Ἀθήνησι καὶ πρὸς ἐμὲ, καὶ, ᾧ τὸ χρυσίον ἀπεδίδους, ὄντος θνητοῦ, καὶ πέλαγος τοσοῦτον μέλλοντος πλεῖν, μάρτυρα οὐδέν' ἐποιήσω, οὔτε δοῦλον, οὔτ' ἐλεύθερον.

Oratio in Pantænetum, p. 80. ——τίς γὰρ πώποτε τῷ δεσπότῃ λαχὼν, τοῦ δούλου τὰ πράγματα, ὥσπερ κυρίου, κατηγόρησεν;

Oratio in Macartatum, p. 173. ——ἐπαγγέλλειν δὲ, περὶ μὲν τῶν δούλων τῷ δεσπότῃ περὶ δὲ τῶν ἐλευθέρων τοῖς τὰ χρήματ' ἔχουσιν.

Oratio in Stephanum, I. p. 217. ——φανήσεται γὰρ οὐ πατρὸς, ὑπὲρ υἱέων γράφοντος, ἐοικυῖα διαθήκῃ, ἀλλὰ δούλου λελυμασμένου τὰ τῶν δεσποτῶν, ὅπως μὴ δώσει δίκην σκοποῦντος.

Idem, p. 231. ——καὶ εἰ μὲν πένης οὗτος ἦν, ἡμεῖς δ' εὔποροῦντες ἐτυγχάνομεν, καὶ συνέβη τι παθεῖν, οἷα πολλὰ, ἐμοὶ, οἱ παῖδες ἂν οἱ τούτου τῶν ἐμῶν θυγατέρων ἐδικάζοντο, οἱ τοῦ δούλου τῶν τοῦ δεσπότου· * * * οὗτος δ' αὖ τοὐναντίον τόν δεσπότην ὁ δοῦλος ἐξετάζει, ὡς δῆτα πονηρὸν καὶ ἄσωτον ἐκ τούτων ἐπιδείξων.

Idem, p. 234. ——ὄντων γὰρ ἡμῶν τοιούτων, ὁποίους τινὰς ἂν καὶ σὺ κατασκευάσῃς τῷ λόγῳ, σὺ δοῦλος ἦσθα.

Idem, p. 235. ——καὶ δέομαι καὶ ἀντιβολῶ καὶ ἱκετεύω, μὴ ὑπερίδητέ με καὶ τὰς θυγατέρας, δι' ἔνδειαν τοῖς ἐμαυτοῦ δούλοις, καὶ τοῖς τούτου κόλαξιν ἐπιχάρτους γενομένους. * * * δοῦλοι μεν ἐκεῖνοι, δοῦλος δ' οὗτος ἦν, δεσπόται δ' ὑμεῖς. δεσπότης δ' ἦν ἐγώ.

Oratio in Timotheum, p. 312. ——ὁ δέ οὔτε μαρτυρίαν παρέσχετο, οὐδ' ὡς δοῦλον τον Αἰσχρίωνα παραδοὺς, ἐκ τοῦ σώματος τὸν ἔλεγχον ἠξίου γενέσθαι, φοβούμενος, ἂν μὲν μαρτυρίαν παράσχηται, ὡς ἐλευθέρου ὄντος, &c.

Sophocles, Electra, line 814:

ἤδη δεῖ με δουλεύειν πάλιν
ἐν τοῖσιν ἐχθίστοισιν ἀνθρώπων ἐμοί,
φονεῦσι πατρός.

This Francklin translates thus: "Left at last, a slave to those whom most on earth I hate."

Antigone, line 202. ——τοὺς δὲ δουλώσας ἄγειν.

Francklin thus—"And made you slaves."

Idem, line 478.

οὐ γαρ ἐκπέλει
φρονεῖν μέ γ' ὅστις δοῦλός ἐστι τῶν πέλας·

Thus—"'Tis not for slaves to be so haughty."

Idem, line 517. ——οὐ γάρ τι δοῦλος, ἀλλ' ἀδελφὸς ὤλετο.

Thus—"He was a brother, not a slave."

Idem, line 756. ——γυναικὸς ὢν δούλευμα, μὴ κώτιλλέ με.

Thus—"Think not to make me thus thy scorn and laughter, thou woman's slave."

Ajax, line 489. ——νῦν δ' εἰμὶ δούλη.

Thus—"Though now a wretched slave."

499. ——ξὺν παιδὶ τῷ σῷ δουλίαν ἕξειν τροφήν.

Thus—"And thy loved son shall eat the bread of slavery."

1020. ——δοῦλος λόγοισιν ἀντ' ἐλευθέρου φανείς.

Francklin thus—"And to slavery doomed."

1235. ——ταῦτ' οὐκ ἀκούειν μεγάλα πρὸς δούλων κακά;

Thus—"Shall we be thus insulted by our slaves?"

1289. ——ὁ δοῦλος, ὁ ἐκ τῆς βαρβάρου μητρὸς γεγώς.

Thus—"I am a slave, born of a barbarian mother."

Oedipus Tyrannus, line 1062—

σύ μὲν γάρ, οὐδ' ἂν ἐκ τρίτης ἐγὼ
μητρός φανῶ τρίδουλος, ἐκφανεῖ κακή.

Thus—"Were I descended from a race of slaves, 'twould not dishonour thee."

1123. ——ἦ δοῦλος, οὐκ ὠνητός, ἀλλ' οἴκοι τραφείς.

Thus—"Although I am a slave, yet I was not purchased, but born and reared up in his house."

1168. ——ἦν δοῦλος, ἤ κείνου τις ἐγγενὴς γεγώς;

Thus—"Was he the son of a slave; if not, of whom?"

Oedipus Coloneus, line 917—

καί μοι πόλιν κένανδρον ἢ δούλην τινὰ
ἔδοξας εἶναι.

Francklin thus—"Or didst thou think I valued a desert land, or that my people were a race of slaves?"

Trachiniæ, line 53. ——δούλαις, *female slaves.*

Line 63—

ἥδε γὰρ γυνή
δούλη μέν, εἴρηκεν δ' ἐλεύθερον λόγον.

Francklin thus—"This woman, though a slave, hath spoken what would have well become the mouth of freedom's self to utter."

257. ——ξὺν παισὶ καὶ γυναικὶ δουλώσειν ἔτι.

Thus—"And bind in slavery his wife and all his race."

267. ——φωνεῖ δέ, δοῦλος ἀνδρὸς ὡς ἐλευθέρου
ῥαίοιτο.

Francklin thus—"And said a slave like him should bend beneath a freeman's power."

283. ——πόλις δέ δούλη.

302. ——τανῦν δε δοῦλον ἴσχουσιν βίον.

367. ——οὐδ' ὥς τε δούλην.

467. ——ἔπερσέ κᾳ δουλωσεν.

Philoctetes, line 995—

οἴ μοι τάλας. ἡμᾶς μὲν ὡς δούλους σαφῶς
πατὴρ ἄρ' ἐξέφυσεν, οὐδ' ἐλευθέρους.

Aristophanes, Ranæ (Batrachoi), line 191—

δοῦλον οὐκ ἄγω,
εἰ μὴ νεναυμάχηκε τὴν περὶ τῶν κρεῶν.

531. —ὡς δοῦλος ὢν καὶ θνητός.

541. —εἰ Ξανθίας μὲν δοῦλος ὤν.

584. —δοῦλος ἅμα καὶ θνητὸς ὤν;

632. —ἀθάνατος εἶναί φημι Διόνυσος Διὸς,
τοῦτον δὲ δοῦλον.

694. —κᾀντὶ δούλων δεσπότας.

742. —ὅτι, δοῦλος ὢν, ἔφασκες εἶναι δεσπότης.

743. —τοῦτο μέντοι δουλικὸν
εὐθὺς πεποίηκας.

949. —ἀλλ' ἔλεγεν ἡ γυνή τ' ἐμοὶ χῶ δοῦλος οὐδὲν ἧττον.

Aves (Ornithes), line 69. —ὄρνις ἔγωγε δοῦλος.

Line 763—

τοῦ Φιλήμονος γένους
εἰ δὲ δοῦλός ἐστι Κὰρ, &c.

911. —ἔπειτα δῆτα δοῦλος ὢν κόμην ἔχεις.

Equites (Hyppes), line 44—

οὗτος τῇ προτέρᾳ νουμηνίᾳ
ἐπρίατο δοῦλον.

Lysistrate, line 330. —δούλησιν ὠστιζομένη.

Acharnenses, 401—

ὅδ' ὁ δοῦλος οὑτωσὶ σαφῶς ἀπεκρίνατο.

Vespæ (Sphekes), 517—

ἀλλά δουλεύων λέληθας.
παῦε δουλείαν λέγων,
ὅστις ἄρχω τῶν ἁπάντων.

Line 602—

ἣν δουλείαν οὖσαν ἔφασκες χὐπηρεσίαν ἀποδείξειν.

Line 681—

ἀλλ' αὐτήν μοι τὴν δουλείαν οὐκ ἀποφαίνων ἀποκναίεις.
οὐ γὰρ μεγάλη δουλεία 'στὶν, τούτους μὲν ἅπαντας ἐν ἀρχαῖς.

Thesmophoriazusæ, line 537—

αὗται γε καὶ τα δουλάρια, &c.

564. ——*οὐδ' ὡς σὺ, τῆς δούλης τεκούσης ἄρρεν'.*

Ecclesiazusæ, line 651. ——*οἱ δοῦλοι.*

Line 721—

καὶ τάς γε δούλας οὐχὶ δεῖ κοσμουμένας
τὴν τῶν ἐλευθέρων ὑφαρπάζειν Κύπριν,
ἀλλὰ παρὰ τοῖς δούλοισι κοιμᾶσθαι μόνον,
κατωνάκῃ τὸν χοῖρον ἀποτετιλμένας.

Homer, Iliad iii. 407—

Μηδ' ἔτι σοῖσι πόδεσσιν ὑποστρέψειας Ὄλυμπον,
Ἀλλ' αἰεὶ περὶ κεῖνον ὀΐζυε, καί ἑ φύλασσε,
Εἰσόκε σ' ἢ ἄλοχον ποιήσεται, ἢ ὅγε δούλην.

Which Pope has paraphrased thus—

"A handmaid goddess at his side to wait,
Remove the glories of thy heavenly state,
Be fix'd for ever to the Trojan slave,
His spouse, or slave, and mount the skies no more."

Iliad vi. 460—

Ἕκτορος ἥδε γυνή, ὃς ἀριστεύεσκε μάχεσθαι
Τρώων ἱπποδάμων, ὅτε Ἴλιον ἀμφεμαχοντο.
Ὥς ποτέ τις ἐρέει· σοὶ δ' αὖ νέον ἔσσεται ἄλγος
Χήτεϊ τοιοῦδ' ἀνδρός, ἀμύνειν δούλιον ἦμαρ.

We should be happy to see the exquisite tenderness of the original transferred into English. We offer:—"This is the wife of Hector, the bravest of the horse-taming Trojans, when our people fought about Ilion. Thus perchance some one will say: and this will be to thee a fresh sorrow, to feel the want of thy husband to ward off the day of slavery."

Odyssey xiv. 339—

Ἀλλ' ὅτε γαίης πολλὸν ἀπέπλω ποντοπόρος νηῦς,
Αὐτίκα δούλιον ἦμαρ ἐμοὶ περιμηχανόωντο.

Pope thus—

"Soon as remote from shore they plough the wave,
With ready hands they rush to seize the slave."

Odyssey xxii. 421—

Πεντηκοντά τοί εἴσιν ἐνί μεγάροισι γυναῖκες
Δμωαί, τάς μεν τ' ἔργα διδάξαμεν ἐργάζεσθαι,
Εἰριά τε ξαίνειν, καὶ δουλοσύνης ἀνέχεσθαι.

Pope thus—

"Then she: In these thy kingly walls remain
(My son) full fifty of the handmaid train;
Taught by my care to cull the fleece or weave,
And servitude with pleasing tasks deceive."

Euripides, Iphigenia in Tauris, line 130—

πόδα παρθένιον
ὅσιον ὁσίας
κληδούχου δούλα (*a slave*) πέμπω.

Line 451. ——δουλείας ἐμέθεν δειλαίας πανσίπονος.
Potter thus—"And bid the toils of slavery cease."

Troades (Trojan Dames), line 140—

δούλα δ' ἄγομαι γραῦς ἐξ οἴκων.

"I, an old woman, am led from my home a slave."

Idem, 159. ——δουλείαν αἰάζουσιν.
"Bemoan their slavery."

186. ——τῷ πρόσκειμαι δούλα τλάμων.
"Assigned a slave," &c.

197. ——δουλεύσω γραῦς.
"An old woman enslaved."

214. ——ἔνθ' ἀντάσω Μενέλᾳ δούλα.
"Exposed me a slave to Menelaus."

Idem, 235—

δοῦλαί γαρ δὴ
Δωρίδος ἐσμέν χθονὸς ἤδη.

"We are slaves of the Dorian land, even now."

284. ——φωτὶ δουλεύειν.
"I am enslaved," &c.

599. ——ζυγά δ' ἤνυσε δούλια Τροία.
"Troy yields to the yoke of slavery."

615. ——εἰς δοῦλον ἥκει.
"Is sunk in slavery."

661 ——δουλεύσω δ', &c.

Idem, 678—

ναυσθλοῦμαι δ' ἐγὼ
πρὸς Ἑλλάδ' αἰχμάλωτος εἰς δοῦλον ζυγόν.

"I go by sea to Greece, a prisoner of war, to a yoke of *slavery.*"

957. ——κείνης δὲ δοῦλός ἐστι.
"But is her slave."

971. ——πικρῶς ἐδούλευσ'.
"Harshly *enslaved.*"

1341. ——ἴτ' ἐπὶ τάλαιναν
δούλειον ἁμέραν βίου.

Bacchæ, 366. ——γὰρ τῷ Διὸς δουλευτέον.

803. ——τί δρῶντα; δουλεύοντα δουλείαις ἐμαῖς;
Potter thus—"What should I do? be to my slaves a slave?"

1028. ——ὥς σε στενάζω, δοῦλος ὢν μέν, ἀλλ' ὅμως
χρηστοῖσι δούλοις συμφορὰ τὰ δεσποτῶν.

Potter thus—

"How I lament thee, though a slave; yet slaves,
If faithful, mourn the ruin of their lords."

Cyclops, 76—

ἐγὼ δ', ὁ σος πρόσπολος,
θητεύω Κύκλωπι
τῷ μονοδέρκτᾳ,
δοῦλος ἀλαίνων σὺν τᾷδε
τράγου χλαίνᾳ μελέᾳ
σᾶς χωρὶς φιλίας.

Helena, 283—

καὶ φίλων τητωμένη,
δούλη καθέστηκ', οὖσ' ἐλευθέρων ἄπο.
τὰ βαρβάρων γὰρ δοῦλα πάντα, πλὴν ἑνός.

Potter thus—

"Of friends deprived,
I, from the free who draw my generous blood,
Am made a *slave;* for 'mong barbarians all
Are slaves, save one."

299. ——ἀσχήμονες μὲν ἀγχόναι μετάρσιοι,
κᾀν τοῖσι δούλοις δυσπρεπὲς νομίζεται.

Potter thus—

"The pendent cord
Disgraces; even in *slaves* it is deemed base."

Line 728—

ἐγὼ μὲν εἴην, κεἰ πέφυχ' ὅμως λάτρις,
ἐν τοῖσι γενναίοισιν ἠριθμημένος
δούλοισι, τοὔνομ' οὐκ ἔχων ἐλεύθερον,
τόν νοῦν δε· κρεῖσσον γὰρ τόδ' ἢ δυοῖν κακοῖν
ἕν' ὄντα χρῆσθαι, τὰς φρένας τ' ἔχειν κακὰς,
ἄλλων τ' ἀκούειν δοῦλον ὄντα τῶν πέλας.

Potter thus—

"It is my wish,
Though born a slave, among the generous slaves
To be accounted, bearing a free mind,
If not the name; for better this I deem,
Than two bad things, to harbour a base mind,
And hear from those avowed the name of slave."

We deem this translation defective, because it makes no distinction between the ideas conveyed by the words λάτρις and δουλος. True, at this late day, the passage is somewhat obscure. But the speaker was not a slave: he says he was born a λάτρις—a character far less elevated than the δοῦλος, yet a freeman, but possessing a greater servility of mind than even the *doulos*, and his condition often far more abject. The slave possessed the protection of his master; but the *latris*, with all the destitution and degradation incident to the lowest conditions of the freeman, often coveted the happier condition of the *doulos*. The idea conveyed by this messenger is literally this: "Although born a *latris*, I had rather be considered among the home-born slaves, not having the name of freedom, than to have merely the name; for I consider this a good choice between the two evils—the being supposed to have the base mind of the *latris*, and the being truly called a slave by those near us." The substance is, he had rather be a *doulos* than a *latris*.

That he was not a slave is evident from what follows in the 797th line, where Menelaus calls him emphatically his *prospolon*, merely an attendant.

1630. ——ἀλλὰ δεσποτῶν κρατήσεις, δοῦλος ὤν;
Potter—"Slave as thou art, wilt thou control thy lord?"

Idem, 1640.

πρὸ δεσποτῶν
τοῖσι γενναίοισι δούλοις εὐκλεέστατον θανεῖν.

"To home-born slaves, it is glory to die for their masters."

Ion, line 132. ——θεοῖσι δούλαν χέρ' ἔχειν.

"To be a slave to the gods."

182. ——Φοίβῳ δουλεύσω, &c.

327. ——τοῖς τοῦ θεοῦ κοσμούμεθ', ᾧ δουλεύομεν.

556. ——ἐκπεφεύγαμεν τὸ δοῦλον.

761. ——δούλευμα πιστόν, &c.

837. ——ἐκ δούλης τινός, &c.

854. ——ἕν γάρ τι τοῖς δούλοισιν, &c.

855. ——τοὔνομα· τὰ δ' ἄλλα πάντα τῶν ἐλευθέρων
οὐδεὶς κακίων δοῦλος, ὅστις ἐσθλὸς ᾖ.

Potter—

"It is the name; in all else than the free
The slave is nothing worse, if he be virtuous."

983. ——ἐπίσημον ὁ φόνος, καὶ τὸ δοῦλον ἀσθενές.

Potter—"An open murder, and with coward *slaves*."

1109. ——τί δ' ἔστιν, ὦ ξύνδουλε;

"What is the matter, my fellow-slave?"

Hercules, 190. ——ἀνὴρ ὁπλίτης δοῦλός ἐστι τῶν ὅπλων.

Potter—

"—— the man array'd in arms
Is to his arms a *slave*."

Electra, 110. ——δούλης γυναικός, *female slave.*

633. ——δούλων γὰρ ἴδιον τοῦτο, σοὶ δὲ σύμφορον.

Potter—"Such the slave's nature, but this favours thee.'

Line 898—

σὸς γάρ ἐστι νῦν
δοῦλος.

"He is thy *slave* now."

Medea, line 54—

χρηστοῖσι δούλοις ξυμφορὰ τὰ δεσποτῶν
κακῶς πίτνοντα·καὶ φρενῶν ἀνθάπτεται.

"Slaves who are faithful, suffer in the afflictions of their masters."

Line 65. ——μή, πρὸς γενείου, κρύπτε σύνδουλον σέθεν.
"Now by this beard, deceive not by secrecy thy fellow-slave."

Hecuba, line 234—

εἰ δ' ἔστι τοῖς δούλοισι τοὺς ἐλευθέρους
μὴ λυπρὰ μηδὲ καρδίας δηκτήρια
ἐξιστορῆσαι, σοὶ μὲν εἰρῆσθαι χρεών,
ἡμᾶς δ' ἀκοῦσαι τοὺς ἐρωτῶντας τάδε.

Potter thus—

"But may *slaves* be permitted of the free
To ask—I mean no rudeness, no reproach—
But may we ask? And wilt thou answer us?"

247. ——τί δῆτ' ἔλεξας, δοῦλος ὢν ἐμὸς τότε;
Potter—"What didst thou say, when thou wast then my *slave?*"

Idem, 291—

νόμος δ' ἐν ὑμῖν τοῖς τ' ἐλευθέροις ἴσος
καὶ τοῖσι δούλοις αἵματος κεῖται πέρι.

Potter thus—

"The laws of blood
Are equal to us *slaves*, and you our lords."

331. ——αἰαῖ· τὸ δοῦλον ὡς κακὸν πεφυκέναι.
"Ah well, how great the evil to have become a *slave!*"

356. ——νῦν δ' εἰμὶ δούλη.
"But I am now a slave."

Idem, 365—

λέχη δε τἀμὰ δοῦλος ὠνητός πόθεν
χρανεῖ.

"And then, a female stewardess, a slave purchased somewhere, shall defile my bed."

Idem, 444—

αὔρα, ποντιὰς αὔρα,
ἅτε ποντοπόρους κομίζεις
θοὰς ἀκάτους ἐπ' οἶδμα λίμνας,
ποῖ με τὰν μελέαν πορεύσεις;
τῷ δουλόσυνος πρὸς οἶκον
κτηθεῖσ' ἀφίξομαι;
ἢ Δωρίδος ὅρμον αἴας,
ἢ Φθιάδος.

Potter—
"Tell me, ye gales, ye rising gales,
That lightly sweep along the azure plain,
Whose soft breath fills the swelling sails,
And wafts the vessel dancing o'er the main;
Whither, ah! whither will ye bear
This sickening daughter of despair?
What proud lord's rigour shall the *slave* deplore,
On Doric or on Phthian shore?"

495. ——*αὕτη δὲ δούλη, γραῦς, ἄπαις, ἐπὶ χθονὶ*
κεῖται, κόνει φύρουσα δύστηνον κάρα.

Potter—
"Herself a *slave*, old, childless, on the ground
She lies, and soils her hoar head in the dust."

741. ——*ἀλλ' εἴ με δούλην πολεμίαν θ' ἡγούμενος*
γονάτων ἀπώσαιτ', ἄλγος αὖ προσθείμεθ' ἄν

Potter—
"But should he treat me as a *slave*, a foe,
And spurn me, I should add to my afflictions."

757. ——*οὐ δῆτα· τοὺς κακοὺς δὲ τιμωρουμένη,*
αἰῶνα τὸν ξύμπαντα δουλεῦσαι θέλω.

Potter—
"Not freedom, but revenge; revenge on baseness:
Grant me revenge, and let me die a *slave*."

798. ——*ἡμεῖς μὲν οὖν δοῦλοί τε κἀσθενεῖς ἴσως.*

Potter—"But we are *slaves*, but we perchance are weak

809. ——*τύραννος ἦν ποτ', ἀλλὰ νῦν δούλη σέθεν.*

Potter—"Erewhile I was a queen, but now a slave."

Idem, 864—

οὐκ ἔστι θνητῶν ὅστις ἔστ' ἐλεύθερος·
ἢ χρημάτων γὰρ δοῦλός ἐστιν ἢ τύχης,
ἢ πλῆθος αὐτὸν πόλεος ἢ νόμων γραφαὶ
εἴργουσι χρῆσθαι μὴ κατὰ γνώμην τρόποις.

Potter—
"Vain is the boast of liberty in man:
A slave to fortune or a slave to wealth,
Or by the people or the laws restrained,
He dares not act the dictates of his will."

1252. ——οἴμοι, γυναικός, ὡς ἔοιχ᾽, ἡσσώμενος
δούλης, ὑφέξω τοῖς κακίοσιν δίκην.

Potter—

"What! from these wretches shall I suffer thus,
Defeated by a woman and a *slave?*"

Phœnissæ, line 94. ——ὡς δούλῳ, *as a slave.*

189. ——δουλείαν περιβαλών.
"To lead in *slavery.*"

192. ——δουλοσύναν τλαίην.
"To suffer slavery."

205. ——Φοίβῳ δούλα. "Slave to Phœbus."

1606. ——ἀλλὰ δουλεῦσαι τέ με—Πολύβον, &c.
"Slave to Polybus," &c.

Orestes, line 221. ——ἰδοὺ τὸ δούλευμ᾽ ἡδύ, κοὐκ ἀναίνομαι.

Idem, 715—

——νῦν δ᾽ ἀναγκαίως ἔχει
δούλοισιν εἶναι τοῖς σοφοῖσι τῆς τύχης.

937. ——ἢ γυναιξὶ δουλεύειν χρεών.
Potter—"Vile *slaves* to your wives."

1115. ——οὐδὲν τὸ δοῦλον πρὸς τὸ μὴ δοῦλον γένος.

Such was the reply of Pylades to his friend Orestes, in reference to the Phrygian slave; and we shall close our quotations from this remarkable tragic poet, with an interview between Orestes and one of these Phrygian slaves.

Line 1522—

Orestes. Δοῦλος ὢν φοβεῖ τὸν ῞Αιδην, ὅς σ᾽ ἀπαλλάξει κακῶν;
Slave. Πᾶς ἀνήρ, κἂν δοῦλος ᾖ τις, ἥδεται τὸ φῶς ὁρῶν.

Potter—

Orestes. "Fears a *slave* death, the end of all his ills?
Slave. "To slave or free, sweet is the light of heaven."

Alcestes, line 638—

δουλίου δ᾽ ἀφ᾽ αἵματος
μαστῷ γυναικὸς σῆς ὑπεβλήθην λάθρα.

Potter—"But, the base offspring of some *slave*, thy wife stole me, and put me to her breast."

We find the following in a short notice of the life of Isocrates, by Dionysius of Halicarnassus.

Page 23. ——διδάσκει δ᾽ ὡς οὐ Μεσσηνίοις τοῖς οὐκετ᾽ οὖσιν, ἀλλὰ δούλοις καὶ εἵλωσιν ὁρμητήριον καὶ καταφυγὴν παρέξουσι τὴν πόλιν.

Also, page 26. ——δουλεύει γὰρ ἡ διάνοια πόλλακις τῷ ῥυθμῷ τε λέξεως, καὶ τῶν κομψοῦ λείπεται τὸ ἀληθινὸν.

Idem, 35. ——ἡμεῖς δε καταδούλευμενοι, καὶ τἀναντία τοῖς τότε πράττοντες.

Idem, 36. ——καὶ τότε μὲν εἰ τριήρεις πληροῖεν, τοὺς μὲν ξένους καὶ τούς δούλους ναύτας εἰσεβίβαζον, τούς δε πολίτας μεθ᾽ ὅπλων ἐξέπεμπον.

Isocrates, (Cantabrigiæ, 1686,) Orat. ad Demonicum, page 52—ἐν δὲ τοῖς τερπνοῖς, ἂν αἰσχρὸν ὑπολάβῃς, τῶν μὲν οἰκετῶν ἄρχειν, ταῖς δι᾽ ἡδοναῖς δουλεύειν.

Ad Nicoclem, p. 74. ——καὶ τοῦτο ἡγοῦ βασιλικώτατον ἐὰν μηδεμίᾳ δουλεύῃς τῶν ἡδονῶν, ἀλλὰ κρατῇς τῶν ἐπιθυμιῶν μᾶλλον ἢ τῶν πολιτῶν.

Panegyricus, p. 121. ——τῶν δὲ βαρβάρων οἵ βουλομένοι καταδουλώσασθαι τοὺς Ἑλλήνας, ἐφ᾽ ἡμᾶς πρώτους ἰόντες.

Idem, 133. ——ἡροῦντο δὲ τῶν εἱλώτων ἐνίοις δουλεύειν, ὥστε εἰς τὰς ἑαυτῶν πατρίδας ὑβρίζειν.

Idem, 137. ——νῦν δὲ εἰς τοσαύτην δουλείαν καθεστώτων.

Idem. ——μέγιστόν δε τῶν κακῶν, ὅταν ὑπὲρ αὐτῆς τε δουλείας ἀναγκάζωνται συστρατεύεσθαι.

Idem. ——κατορθώσαντες δὲ μᾶλλον εἰς τὸν ἐπίλοιπον χρόνον δουλεύσουσιν.

Idem, 144. ——πρός μὲν τὸν πόλεμον ἐκλελύμενος, πρὸς δὲ τὴν δουλείαν ἄμεινον τῶν παρ᾽ ἡμῖν οἰκετῶν πεπαιδευμένος.

Idem. ——ἅπαντα δὲ τὸν χρόνον διάγουσιν, ὡς μέν τοὺς ὑβρίζοντες, τοῖς δὲ δουλεύοντες.

Idem, 150. ——Σικελία δὲ καταδεδούλωται.

Idem, 151. ——ὡς ὑπὲρ τούτων δουλεύειν ἠναγκασμέναι.

Idem, 153. ——δημοσίᾳ δε τοσούτους τῶν συμμάχων περιορᾶν αὐτοῖς δουλεύοντας.

Orat. ad Philippum, p. 161. ——ζητεῖν δὲ ἐκείνους τοὺς τόπους τοὺς πόῤῥω μὲν κειμένους τῶν ἄρχειν δυναμένων, ἐγγὺς δε τῶν δουλεύειν εἰθισμένων.

Archidamus, p. 235. ——νῦν καὶ τὴν τῶν δούλων παῤῥησίαν ὑπομένοντας φαίνεσθαι.

De Pace, sive Socialis, page 281. ——καὶ τότε μὲν εἴ τριήρεις πληροῖεν, τοὺς μὲν ξένους καὶ τοὺς δούλους ναύτας εἰσεβίβαζον.

Idem, p. 280. ——ὑμεῖς δὲ καταδουλούμενοι.

Idem, p. 306. ——μὴ δουλείας ἀλλά σωτηρίας αὐτοῖς αἰτίαν γενέσθαι.

Evagoras, p. 310. ——οὐ μὴν δουλεύτεον.

Idem, p. 320. ——τοὺς μὲν φίλους ταῖς εὐεργεσίαις ὑπ' αὐτῷ ποιούμενος τοὺς δέ ἄλλους τῇ μεγαλοψυχίᾳ καταδουλούμενος.

Idem, p. 326. ——οἱ δέ Ἕλληνες ἀντί δουλείας αὐτονομίαν ἔσχον Ἀθηναῖοι δὲ τοσαῦτον ἐπέδοσαν.

Panathenaicus, p. 396. ——οὓς μὲν ἐλευθερώσειν ὡμολόγησαν κατεδουλώσαντο μᾶλλον ἢ τοὺς εἵλωτας.

Idem, p. 400. ——καὶ τὸ μη δικαίως τῶν ἄλλων ἄρχειν μᾶλλον ἢ φεύγοντας τὴν αἰτίαν ταύτην, ἀδίκως Λακεδαιμονίοις δουλεύειν.

Idem, p. 412. ——τοὺς δὲ ἄλλους Ἑλλήνας καταδουλώσασθαι πρὸς μὲν τοιοῦτον κρατίσασαι ῥαδίως ἂν αὐτοῦ.

Idem, p. 418. ——καταδουλωσαμένους.

Plataicus, p. 459. ——οἱ μὲν οὐδὲν ἧττον τῶν ἀργυρωνήτων δουλεύουσιν.

Idem. ——τε δὲ τῶν ἄλλων δουλείας αὐτοὺς κυρίους καθιστᾶσι.

Idem, p. 463. ——δουλεύειν.

Idem, p. 465. ——δουλευουσῶν.

Idem, p. 466. ——ἀλλὰ πολλοὺς μὲν μικρῶν ἕνεκα συμβουλαίων δουλεύοντας, ἄλλους δὲ ἐπὶ θητείαν ἴοντας.

Orat. de Permutatione, p. 493. ——τὴν δε τῷ γένει τῆς σωτηρίας αἰτίαν οὖσαν, δουλεύειν αὐτοῖς ἀξιοῦν.

Idem, p. 494. ——τῶν δέ βαρβάρων οἱ βουλόμενοι καταδουλοῦσθαι τοὺς Ἑλλήνας.

Idem, p. 502. ——τοῖς δ' ἄλλοις τὴν δουλείαν αἱρουμένοις.

Idem. ——οὕτω καὶ τῶν πόλεων ταῖς ὑπερεχούσαις λυσιτελεῖν ἐξ ἀνθρώπων ἀφανισθῆναι μᾶλλον ἢ δούλας ὀφθῆναι γενομένας.

Idem. ——ὥστε μὴ τοῖς Ἕλλησιν αἴτιον γενήσθαι τί δουλείας.

Idem, p. 510. ——ἡμεῖς δὲ καταδουλούμενοι.

Idem, p. 511. ——τοὺς μὲν ξένους καὶ τοὺς δούλους.

De Bigis, p. 530. ——τοὺς πολίτας ἰδεῖν δουλεύοντας.

Epistolæ: to Philip, p. 611. ——ἃ Ξέρξῃ τε τῷ καταδουλώσασθαι τοὺς Ἕλληνας βουληθέντι.

To Jason, a freedman, p. 629. ——καὶ τὰς τιμὰς ἡδίους νομίζω τὰς παρὰ τῶν μέγα φρονούντων, ἢ τὰς παρὰ τῶν δουλευόντων.

LESSON V.

But if it shall be objected, that by these writers the word δουλος, *doulos*, and its derivatives are used in a figurative sense, since these writers all exhibit minds deeply excited, or used all language with poetic license; we think such objection unfounded, so far as it alleges that they have used this word in an unusual manner, or have attributed to it any other sense than was attributed to it by all the Greeks.

Nevertheless, we propose now to present this word as it was used by Thucydides, Herodotus, and Zenophon, against whose use no cavil can be made; and we now fear not to assert that their use of this word will be in the most strict accordance with the authors already examined.

Plutarch, who was somewhat disposed to criticize other authors, speaking of Thucydides, expresses the idea that he wrote in such a manner that the reader saw the picture of what he represented. (See his *De Gloria Atheniensium.*) Plutarch was then clearly of opinion that the language of Thucydides was most appropriately accurate.

We here premise, that we shall not presume to offer our own translation to the extract we propose to make from Thucydides. From the many that have been made, we have selected that of the Rev. Dr. William Smith, of the cathedral of Chester, England,

and concerning whom it may be proper to say a word. He translated Longinus with great accuracy and beauty. The Weekly Miscellany of Dec. 8th, 1739, says of this translation, "It justly deserves the notice and thanks of the public." Father Phillips says, 1756, "A late English translation of the Greek critic, by Mr. Smith, is a credit to the author, and reflects lustre on Longinus himself." Laudits of this work will fill a volume. In 1753 he translated Thucydides, and was directly created a doctor of divinity,—and we find in his epitaph now in the cathedral of Chester, "as a scholar his reputation is perpetuated by his valuable publications, particularly his correct and eloquent translations of Longinus, Thucydides, and Xenophon." We have been thus minute that it may be known with what spirit we prepare this work.

THE PELOPONNESIAN WAR, *by Thucydides.*

Book i. chap. 8. *Οἵ τε ἥσσους ὑπέμενον τὴν τῶν κρεισσόνων δουλείαν.*

"And the great, who had all needful supplies at hand, reduced less powerful cities into their own *subjection.*"

At that age of the world, when one city was conquered by another, all were reduced to slavery, unless by the especial favour of the conqueror. In this instance it would have been more literal to our present idiom to have used the term *slavery*, instead of *subjection;* because now there has grown up a wide distinction between the mere subjugating and enslaving.

Chap. 16. *Κῦρος καὶ ἡ Περσικὴ βασιλεία, Κροῖσον καθελοῦσα, καὶ ὅσα ἐντὸς Ἅλυος ποταμοῦ πρὸς θάλασσαν, ἐπεστράτευσε, καὶ τὰς ἐν τῇ ἠπείρῳ πόλεις ἐδούλωσε.*

"For Cyrus, after he had completed the conquest of Crœsus, and all the country which lieth between the river Halys and the sea, invaded them, and enslaved their towns upon the continent."

Chap. 18. *Δεκάτῳ δὲ ἔτει μετ' αὐτὴν αὖθις ὁ βάρβαρος τῷ μεγάλῳ στόλῳ ἐπὶ τὴν Ἑλλάδα δουλωσόμενος ἦλθε.*

"And in the tenth year after that, the barbarian, with a vast armament, invaded Greece in order to *enslave* it."

Chap. 34. *Οὐ γὰρ ἐπὶ τῷ δοῦλοι, ἀλλ' ἐπὶ τῷ ὅμοιοι τοῖς λειπομένοις εἶναι, ἐκπέμπονται.*

"They are not sent out to be the *slaves*, but to be the equals of those who remain behind."

Chap. 55. Καὶ τῶν Κερκυραίων ὀκτακοσίους μὲν, οἳ ἦσαν δοῦλοι, ἀπέδοντο.

"Eight hundred of their Corcyrean prisoners, who were *slaves*, they sold at public sale."

Chap. 68. Νῦν δὲ τί δεῖ μακρηγορεῖν, ὧν τοὺς μὲν δεδουλωμένους ὁρᾶτε.

"But now, what need can there be of multiplying words, when some you already see *enslaved*."

Chap. 69. Ἐς τόδε τε ἀεὶ ἀποστεροῦντες οὐ μόνον τοὺς ὑπ' ἐκείνων δεδουλωμένους ἐλευθερίας, ἀλλὰ καὶ τοὺς ὑμετέρους ἤδη ξυμμάχους. οὐ γὰρ ὁ δουλωσάμενος ἀλλ' ὁ δυνάμενος μὲν παῦσαι, περιορῶν δὲ, ἀληθέστερον αὐτὸ δρᾷ.

"Ever since you have connived at liberty overthrown, not only in whatever communities they have proceeded to enslave, but now where even your own confederates are concerned. For not to the men who rivet on the chains of *slavery*, but to such as, though able, yet neglect to prevent it, ought the sad event with truth to be imputed."

Chap. 74. Τῶν ἄλλων ἤδη μέχρι ἡμῶν δουλευόντων, &c.

"And every state already *enslaved*," &c.

Chap. 81. Οὕτως εἰκὸς, Ἀθηναίους φρονήματι, μήτε τῇ γῇ δουλεῦσαι, μήτε ὥσπερ ἀπείρους καταπλαγῆναι τῷ πολέμῳ.

"It is by no means consistent with the spirit of Athenians to be *slaves* to their soil, or, like unpractised soldiers, to shudder at war."

Chap. 98. Πρώτη τε αὕτη πόλις ξυμμαχὶς παρὰ τὸ καθεστηκὸς ἐδουλώθη.

"This was the first confederate state which was *enslaved* to gratify their aspiring ambition."

Chap. 101. Πλεῖστοι δὲ τῶν Εἱλώτων ἐγένοντο οἱ τῶν παλαιῶν Μεσσηνίων τότε δουλωθέντων ἀπόγονοι· ᾗ καὶ Μεσσήνιοι ἐκλήθησαν οἱ πάντες.

"Most of the Helots were descendants of the ancient Messenians, then reduced to *slavery*, and on this account all of them in general were called Messenians."

Chap. 103. Ἢν δέ τις ἁλίσκηται, τοῦ λαβόντος εἶναι *δοῦλον*.

"What if any one of them be ever found there, he should be made the *slave* of whoever apprehended him."

Chap. 121. Εἰ οἱ μὲν ἐκείνων ξύμμαχοι ἐπὶ *δουλείᾳ* τῇ αὐτῶν φέροντες οὐκ ἀπεροῦσιν.

"Which rivet *slavery* on themselves," &c.

Chap. 122. Καὶ τὴν ἧσσαν, εἰ καὶ δεινόν τῷ ἀκοῦσαι, ἴστω οὐκ ἄλλο τι φέρουσαν ἢ ἄντικρυς *δουλείαν*.

"Such a triumph, how grating soever the bare mention of it may be to any of your ears, yet be it known, can and is nothing else but plain and open *slavery*."

Chap. 124. Καὶ τοὺς νῦν *δεδουλωμένους* Ἕλληνας, ἐλευθερώσωμεν.

"And shall immediately recover liberty for those Grecians who are already *enslaved*."

Chap. 138. Καὶ τοῦ Ἑλληνικοῦ ἐλπίδα, ἣν ὑπετίθει αὐτῷ *δουλώσειν*.

"As the hope be suggested to him of *enslaving* Greece."

Chap. 141. Τὴν γὰρ αὐτὴν δύναται *δούλωσιν*.

"The very same tendency to make them *slaves*."

Book ii. chap. 61. *Δουλοῖ* γὰρ φρόνημα τὸ αἰφνίδιον καὶ ἀπροσδόκητον, καὶ τὸ πλείστῳ παραλόγῳ ξυμβαῖνον.

"Accidents sudden and unforeseen, and so opposite to that event you might reasonably have expected, *enslave* the mind."

Chap. 63. Μηδὲ νομίσαι περὶ ἑνὸς μόνου, *δουλείας* ἀντ' ἐλευθερίας.

"Think not you have only one point at stake, the alternative of *slavery* instead of freedom."

Idem. Οὐδὲ ἐν ἀρχούσῃ πόλει ξυμφέρει, ἀλλ' ἐν ὑπηκόῳ ἀσφαλῶς *δουλεύειν*.

"Slavery is never to be endured by a state that once hath governed. Such a situation can be tolerable only to that which has ever been dependent."

Chap. 71. Στρατεῦσαί τε μηδένα ποτὲ ἀδίκως ἐπ' αὐτοὺς, μηδ' ἐπὶ *δουλείᾳ*.

"That no one should unjustly make war on them, or endeavour to *enslave* them."

Idem. Ἐπὶ δουλείᾳ τῇ ἡμετέρᾳ ἥκετε.

"Are come hither to *enslave* us," &c.

Chap. 78. Καὶ ἄλλος οὐδεὶς ἦν ἐν τῷ τείχει, οὔτε δοῦλος, οὔτε ἐλεύθερος.

"Nor was there any other portion within the wall, either *slave* or free."

Book iii. chap. 10. Ξύμμαχοι μέντοι ἐγενόμεθα οὐκ ἐπὶ καταδουλώσει τῶν Ἑλλήνων Ἀθηναίοις.

"We made an alliance with the Athenians—not to *enslave* the rest of Greece to the Athenians."

Idem. Ἐπειδὴ δὲ ἑωρῶμεν αὐτοὺς τὴν μὲν τοῦ Μήδου ἔχθραν ἀνιέντας, τὴν δὲ τῶν ξυμμάχων δούλωσιν ἐπαγομένους, οὐκ ἀδεεῖς ἔτι ἦμεν. ἀδύνατοι δὲ ὄντες καθ' ἓν γενόμενοι, διὰ πολυψηφίαν ἀμύνασθαι, οἱ ξύμμαχοι ἐδουλώθησαν, πλὴν ἡμῶν καὶ Χίων.

"But when we perceived that they relaxed in their zeal against the Mede, and were grown earnest in riveting *slavery* upon allies, we then began to be alarmed. It was impossible, where so many parties were to be consulted, to unite together in one body of defence; and thus all the allies fell into *slavery* except ourselves and the Chians."

Chap. 38. Δοῦλοι ὄντες τῶν ἀεὶ ἀτόπων, ὑπερόπται δὲ τῶν εἰωθότων.

"Slaves as you are to whatever trifles happen always to be in vogue, and looking down with contempt on tried and experienced methods."

Chap. 56. Ἐν ἐκείνῳ δὲ τῷ καιρῷ, ὅτε πᾶσι δουλείαν ἐπέφερεν ὁ βάρβαρος, οἵδε μετ' αὐτοῦ ἦσαν.

"But at that season, when the barbarians struck at *enslaving* us all, these Thebans were then the barbarians' coadjutors."

Chap. 58. Πρὸς δέ, καὶ γῆν, ἐν ᾗ ἠλευθερώθησαν οἱ Ἕλληνες, δουλώσετε;

"Will you further *enslave* the spot on which the Grecians earned their liberty?"

Chap. 63. Τοὺς μέν, καταδουλουμένους τὴν Ἑλλάδα, τοὺς δέ, ἐλευθεροῦντας.

"The Athenians truly have *enslaved* your country; and the others would regain its freedom."

Chap. 64. Ἀπελείπετε γὰρ αὐτὴν, καὶ παραβάντες, ξυγκατεδουλοῦσθε μᾶλλον Αἰγινήτας, καὶ ἄλλους τινὰς τῶν ξυνομοσάντων, ἢ διεκωλύετε.

"You renounced, you violated first the oaths, which rather concurred to *enslave* the Æginetæ and some other people of the same association, than endeavoured to prevent it."

Chap. 70. Ὑπάγουσιν αὐτὸν οὗτοι οἱ ἄνδρες εἰς δίκην, λέγοντες Ἀθηναίοις τὴν Κέρκυραν καταδουλοῦν.

"And therefore against him the accomplices prefer an accusation, as plotting how to subject Corcyra to Athenian *slavery*."

Chap. 71. Δράσαντες δὲ τοῦτο, καὶ ξυγκαλέσαντες Κερκυραίους, εἶπον ὅτι ταῦτα καὶ βέλτιστα εἴη, καὶ ἥκιστ' ἂν δουλωθεῖεν ὑπ' Ἀθηναίων.

"After this bold assassination, they summoned the Corcyreans to assemble immediately, where they justified their proceedings as most highly for the public good, and the only expedient of preventing Athenian *slavery*."

Chap. 73. Τῇ δ' ὑστεραίᾳ ἠκροβολίσαντό τε ὀλίγα, καὶ ἐς τοὺς ἀγροὺς περιέπεμπον ἀμφότεροι, τοὺς δούλους παρακαλοῦντές τε, καὶ ἐλευθερίαν ὑπισχνούμενοι. καὶ τῷ μὲν δήμῳ τῶν οἰκετῶν τὸ πλῆθος παρεγένετο ξύμμαχον, τοῖς δ' ἑτέροις ἐκ τῆς ἠπείρου ἐπίκουροι ὀκτακόσιοι.

"The day following they skirmished a little with their missive weapons, and both parties sent out detachments into the field to invite concurrence of the slaves, upon a promise of their freedom. A majority of the slaves came in to the assistance of the people, and the other party got eight hundred auxiliaries from the continent."

It will be noticed that οἰκετῶν in this passage is also translated *slave;* but the οἰκετος was a slave whose condition was above the mere δοῦλος. In English the word will imply a *house-slave.* The οἰκετος enjoyed a greater portion of his master's confidence, and consequently was under a less rigorous government. The truth of what Thucydides states is evident to those acquainted with the character: the higher class of slaves ever take sides with their masters in such cases. It is this word St. Paul uses, by which he describes the character of Onesimus in his letter to Philemon. He had acted as Paul's house-slave at Rome.

Book iv. chap. 86. Ἀλλὰ τοὐναντίον, ὑμῖν δεδουλωμένοις ὑπὸ Ἀθηναίων ξυμμαχήσοντες.

"But, on the contrary, are to act in support of you, who are oppressed with Athenian *bondage.*"

Idem. Οὐδὲ ἀσαφῆ, τὴν ἐλευθερίαν νομίζω ἐπιφέρειν, εἰ, τὸ πάτριον παρεὶς, τὸ πλέον τοῖς ὀλίγοις, ἢ τὸ ἔλασσον τοῖς πᾶσι δουλώσαιμι.

"I am convinced that liberty can never be re-established by me, if, disregarding ancient constitutions, I *enslave* the multitude to the few, or the few to the crowd."

Chap. 87. Οἱ δὲ Ἕλληνες ἵνα μὴ κωλύωνται ὑφ' ὑμῶν δουλείας ἀπαλλαγῆναι.

"For the sake of the Grecians, that they may not be obstructed by you in their deliverance from *bondage.*"

Chap. 92. Καὶ πρὸς τούτοις γε δὴ, οἳ καὶ μὴ τοὺς ἐγγὺς, ἀλλὰ καὶ τοὺς ἄπωθεν πειρῶνται δουλοῦσθαι, πῶς οὐ χρὴ καὶ ἐπὶ τὸ ἔσχατον ἀγῶνος ἐλθεῖν;

"Let me add further, that when men are bent on *enslaving*, not neighbours only, but such people as are more remote, how can it be judged improper to encounter such, so long as we can find ground whereon to stand?"

Idem. Οἷς δὲ γενναῖον, τήν τε αὑτῶν αἰεὶ ἐλευθεροῦν μάχῃ, καὶ τὴν ἄλλων μὴ δουλοῦσθαι ἀδίκως, ἀναγώνιστοι ἀπ' αὐτῶν οὐκ ἀπίασι.

"But from men who were born to vindicate their own country for ever by the *dint* of arms, and never unjustly to *enslave* another, that from such men they shall not get away without that struggle which honour enjoins."

Chap. 114. Οὐδὲ γὰρ ἐπὶ δουλείᾳ.

"They had no *enslaving* views."

Chap. 118. Μήτε ἐλεύθερον, μήτε δοῦλον.

"Whether they be free men or *slaves.*"

Book v. chap. 9. Καὶ τῇδε ὑμῖν τῇ ἡμέρᾳ, ἢ ἀγαθοῖς γενομένοις ελευθερίαν τε ὑπάρχειν, καὶ Λακεδαιμονίων ξυμμάχοις κεκλῆσθαι, ἢ Ἀθηναίων τε δούλοις, ἢ τὰ ἄριστα ἄνευ ἀνδραποδισμοῦ ἢ θανατώσεως πράξητε, καὶ δουλείαν χαλεπωτέραν, ἢ πρὶν εἴχετε.

"That this very day, if you behave with valour, you are henceforth free, and will gain the honourable title of Lacedæmonian allies; otherwise you must continue to be the *slaves* of Athenians, where the best that can befall you, if neither sold for *slaves* nor put to death as rebels, will be a heavier yoke of tyranny than you ever yet have felt, while the liberty of Greece must by you for ever be obstructed."

Chap. 23. Ἢν δὲ ἡ δουλεία ἐπανίστηται, ἐπικουρεῖν Ἀθηναίους Λακεδαιμονίοις παντὶ σθένει, κατὰ τὸ δυνατόν.

"That if there happen any insurrection among the *Helots*, the Athenians march to the succour of the Lacedæmonians with their whole strength, to the full extent of their power."

In this instance the translator has substituted "*Helots*" for *slaves*, because the Helots were the slaves at Sparta, and the usual term by which slaves were designated in Lacedæmonia, *Helot* and δοῦλος, were synonymous terms there.

Chap. 27. Ὡς χρὴ, ἐπειδὴ Λακεδαιμόνιοι οὐκ ἐπ' ἀγαθῷ, ἀλλ' ἐπὶ καταδουλώσει τῆς Πελοποννήσου.

"That since the Lacedæmonians, not in order to serve, but to *enslave* Peloponnesus," &c.

Chap. 29. Μὴ μετὰ Ἀθηναίων σφᾶς βούλωνται Λακεδαιμόνιοι δουλώσασθαι.

"That the Lacedæmonians might strike up a bargain with the Athenians to *enslave* other states."

Chap. 69. Καὶ ὑπὲρ ἀρχῆς ἅμα καὶ δουλείας.

"Either such on *slavery*."

Chap. 86. Περιγιγνομένοις μὲν τῷ δικαίῳ, καὶ δι' αὐτὸ μὴ ἐνδοῦσι, πόλεμον ἡμῖν φέρουσαν, πεισθεῖσι δὲ, δουλείαν.

"Since if, superior in debate, we for that reason refuse submission, our portion must be war; and if we allow your plea, from that moment we become your *slaves*."

Chap. 92. Καὶ πῶς χρήσιμον ἂν ξυμβαίη ἡμῖν δουλεῦσαι, ὥσπερ καὶ ὑμῖν ἄρξαι;

"And how can it turn as beneficial for us to become your *slaves* as it will be for you to be our masters?"

Chap. 100. Ἤπου ἄρα, εἰ τοσαύτην γε ὑμεῖς τε, μὴ πανσθῆναι ἀρχῆς, καὶ οἱ δουλεύοντες ἤδη, ἀπαλλαγῆναι, τὴν παρακινδύνευσιν ποιοῦνται, ἡμῖν γε, τοῖς ἔτι ἐλευθέροις, πολλὴ κακότης καὶ δειλία, μὴ πᾶν πρὸ τοῦ δουλεῦσαι ἐπεξελθεῖν.

"If this be, and if you, ye Athenians, can readily embark in so many perils to prevent the desolation of your empire; if states, by you *enslaved*, can do as much to throw off your yoke, must it not be wretchedly base and cowardly in us, who yet are free, to leave any method, even to the last extremity, untried of averting *slavery*."

Book vi. chap. 20. Ἐπὶ δὲ τῷ παρόντι ἃ γιγνώσκω σημανῶ. ἐπὶ γὰρ πόλεις, ὡς ἐγὼ ἀκοῇ αἰσθάνομαι, μέλλομεν ἰέναι μεγάλας, καὶ οὔθ' ὑπηκόους ἀλλήλων, οὔτε δεομένας μεταβολῆς, ἣ ἂν ἐκ βιαίου τὶς δουλείας ἄσμενος ἐς ῥᾴω μετάστασιν χωροίη.

"According to the last information I have been able to procure, we are now going to invade a number of powerful cities; cities independent of one another, nor standing in need of public revolutions; which people, who cringe under the yoke of *slavery*, might easily embrace, in order to render their condition more supportable."

Chap. 27. Μηνύειν ἀδεῶς τὸν βουλόμενον καὶ ἀστῶν καὶ ξένων καὶ δούλων.

"He should boldly inform the public of it, whether he were a citizen, or a foreigner, or a *slave*."

Chap. 76. Δουλωσαμένους ἔχειν.

"They hold fast riveted the yoke of *slavery*."

Idem. Καταδουλώσεως. "By *enslaving*," &c.

Chap. 77. Ὡς ἐδουλώθησαν. "Who will be *slaves*," &c.

Chap. 80. Δουλείαν. "*Slave*," &c.

Chap. 82. Οὓς ξυγγενεῖς φασὶν ὄντας ἡμᾶς Συρακούσιοι δεδουλῶσθαι.

"Whom the Syracusans say we thought proper to *enslave*, though connected with us by ties of blood."

Idem. Δουλείαν δὲ αὐτοί τε ἐβούλοντο ὑμῖν τὸ αὐτὸ ἐπενεγκεῖν.

"They made *slavery* their choice, and in the same miserable fate would have been glad to envelop us."

Chap. 83. Καὶ οὐ δουλωσόμενοι, μὴ παθεῖν δὲ μᾶλλον τοῦτο κωλύσοντες.

"So far from the view of *enslaving* them to ourselves, that we are solely intent on preserving them from being enslaved by others."

Chap. 84. Ὃν ἀλόγως ἡμᾶς φησὶ δουλωσαμένους.

"Whom, after unjustly *enslaving*," &c.

Chap. 88. Πλὴν καθόσον εἰ τὴν Σικελίαν ᾤοντο αὐτοὺς δουλώσεσθαι.

"Save only the ambition they showed of *enslaving* Sicily."

Book vii. chap. 75. Μέγιστον γὰρ δὴ τὸ διάφορον τοῦτο τῷ Ἑλληνικῷ στρατεύματι ἐγένετο, οἷς ἀντὶ μὲν τοῦ ἄλλους δουλωσομένους ἥκειν.

"For a most cruel turn of fortune this really proved to a Grecian army; who, coming hither to *enslave* others, were departing now with the sad alternative of fearing to be made slaves themselves."

Book viii. chap. 15. Τάς τε τῶν Χίων ἑπτὰ ναῦς, αἳ αὐτοῖς ξυνεπολιόρκουν τὰς ἐν τῷ Πειραιῷ, ἀπαγαγόντες, τοὺς μὲν δούλους ἐξ αὐτῶν ἠλευθέρωσαν, τοὺς δ' ἐλευθέρους κατέδησαν.

"Having, moreover, fetched off the seven vessels belonging to the Chians, which assisted in forming the blockade at Piræus, they set at liberty the *slaves* who were on board them, and threw all the freemen into prison."

Chap. 43. Ἐνῆν γὰρ καὶ νήσους ἁπάσας πάλιν δουλεύειν.

"For thus he might be enabled once more to *enslave* all the islands."

Chap. 48. Δουλεύειν μᾶλλον, &c.

LESSON VI.

XENOPHON, *Memorabilia, &c.*

Book i. chap. 3, § 11. *Ὦ τλῆμον, ἔφη ὁ Σωκράτης, καὶ τί ἂν οἴει παθεῖν, καλὸν φιλήσας; ἆρ' οὐκ ἂν αὐτίκα μάλα δοῦλος μὲν εἶναι ἀντ' ἐλευθέρου;*

"Miserum te, ait Socrates, quid eventurum tibi existimas, si formosum osculeris? annon subitò pro libero *servus* esses?" *Leunclavius.*

Chap. 5. § 2. *Δούλῳ δ' ἀκρατεῖ ἐπιτρέψαιμεν ἂν ἢ βοσκήματα ἢ ταμιεῖα ἢ ἔργων ἐπιστασίαν;*

"Et servo intemperanti num vel pecora, vel penum, vel ut operi præesset, committeremus?" *Leunc.*

§ 3. *Ἀλλὰ μὴν εἴ γε μηδὲ δοῦλον ἀκρατῆ δεξαίμεθ' ἄν, πῶς οὐκ ἄξιον αὐτόν γε φυλάξασθαι τοιοῦτον γενέσθαι;*

"Enimvero si ne *servum* quidem intemperantem accepturi simus, quî non operæ pretium sit cavere ne quis ipse talis fiat?" *Leunc.*

§ 5. *Ἦ τίς οὐκ ἄν, ταῖς ἡδοναῖς δουλεύων, αἰσχρῶς διατεθείη καὶ τὸ σῶμα καὶ τὴν ψυχήν;*

"Quis voluptatibus *serviens* non turpiter tum corpore tum animo affectus sit?" *Leunc.*

Ibid. *Ἐμοὶ μὲν δοκεῖ, νὴ τὴν Ἥραν, ἐλευθέρῳ μὲν ἀνδρὶ εὐκτέον εἶναι, μὴ τυχεῖν δούλου τοιούτου, δουλεύοντα δὲ ταῖς τοιαύταις ἡδοναῖς, ἱκετεύειν τοὺς θεούς, δεσποτῶν ἀγαθῶν τυχεῖν.*

"Equidem ita profectò statuo, homini libero optandum esse, ut hujusmodi *servum* non consequatur, atque illi qui voluptatibus ejusmodi servit deos esse obsecrandos ut dominos bonos nanciscatur." *Leunc.*

Book ii. chap. 1. § 11. *Ἀλλ' ἐγώ τοι, ἔφη ὁ Ἀρίστιππος, οὐδὲ εἰς τὴν δουλείαν αὖ ἐμαυτὸν τάττω· ἀλλ' εἶναί τις μοὶ δοκεῖ μέση τούτων ὁδός, ἣν πειρῶμαι βαδίζειν, οὔτε δι' ἀρχῆς, οὔτε διὰ δουλείας, ἀλλὰ δι' ἐλευθερίας, ἥπερ μάλιστα πρὸς εὐδαι-*

μονίαν ἄγει. (12.) Ἀλλ', εἰ μέντοι, ἔφη ὁ Σωκράτης, ὥσπερ οὔτε δι' ἀρχῆς οὔτε διὰ δουλείας ἡ ὁδὸς αὕτη φέρει, οὕτω μηδὲ δι' ἀνθρώπων, ἴσως ἄν τι λέγοις.

"I surely, says Aristippus, do not place myself in slavery; but my doctrine is, that the condition equally free from the objections of those who govern and of those who are in *slavery*, is true liberty. But, says Socrates, the condition of which you speak, beyond the influences affecting those who bear rule or those in *slavery*, can never exist among men; for," &c. § 12. ὡς δούλοις χρῆσθαι—"for safety they desire *slavery*."

§ 13. Ἕως ἂν πείσωσιν ἑλέσθαι δουλεύειν ἀντὶ τοῦ πολεμεῖν τοῖς κρείττοσι;

"Donec persuaserint eis *servire* potiùs quàm bellum cum potioribus gerere?"

§ 15. Ἦ διότι καὶ δοῦλος ἂν οἴει τοιοῦτος εἶναι, οἷος μηδενὶ δεσπότῃ λυσιτελεῖν;

"An quòd talem te *servum* esse putas, qui nulli domino prosit?"

Chap. 6. § 9. Χαλεπὸν δὲ καὶ δήσαντα κατέχειν, ὥσπερ δοῦλον.

"Neque minùs difficile vinctum retinere tanquam *servum*." *Leunc.*

Chap. 7. § 3 and 4. Ὅτι νὴ Δί', ἔφη, ὁ μὲν δούλους τρέφει, ἐγὼ δὲ ἐλευθέρους. (4.) Καὶ πότερον, ἔφη, τοὺς παρὰ σοὶ ἐλευθέρους οἴει βελτίους εἶναι ἢ τοὺς παρὰ Κεράμωνι δούλους;

"By Jupiter, (says Aristarchus,) *the reason is obvious.* He (Ceramon) rears up *slaves*, while I only employ freemen. Well, then, truly, says (Socrates), which do you esteem the most valuable, your freemen or Ceramon's *slaves?*"

Chap. 8. § 4. Χαλεπῶς ἄν, ἔφη, ἐγώ, ὦ Σώκρατες, δουλείαν ὑπομείναιμι. Καὶ μὴν οἵ γε ἐν ταῖς πόλεσι προστατεύοντες καὶ τῶν δημοσίων ἐπιμελόμενοι οὐ δουλοπρεπέστεροι ἕνεκα τούτου, ἀλλ' ἐλευθεριώτεροι νομίζονται.

"But it is difficult, O Socrates, for me to submit to *slavery*. But (says Socrates) high political officers, and all those who have charge of public affairs, are not esteemed to be in a *slavish* employment, but in that which is the most appropriate to the most elevated of freemen."

Book iii. chap. 12. § 2. Πολλοὶ δὲ δι' αὐτὸ τοῦτο ζῶντες ἁλίσκονται, καὶ ἁλόντες ἤτοι *δουλεύουσι* τὸν λοιπὸν βίον, ἐὰν οὕτω τύχωσι, τὴν χαλεπωτάτην *δουλείαν*.

"Many endure the most burdensome *slavery*, produced by their having been taken captives in war, and as captives, *slaves* themselves through the remainder of life."

Book iv. chap. 2. § 33. Τί δέ; τὸν Δαίδαλον, ἔφη, οὐκ ἀκήκοας, ὅτι ληφθεὶς ὑπὸ Μίνω διὰ τὴν σοφίαν, ἠναγκάζετο ἐκείνῳ *δουλεύειν*, καὶ τῆς τε πατρίδος ἅμα καὶ τῆς ἐλευθερίας ἐστερήθη, καὶ ἐπιχειρῶν ἀποδιδράσκειν μετὰ τοῦ υἱοῦ τόν τε παῖδα ἀπώλεσε καὶ αὐτὸς οὐκ ἠδυνήθη σωθῆναι, ἀλλ' ἀπενεχθεὶς εἰς τοὺς βαρβάρους πάλιν ἐκεῖ *ἐδούλευε*;

"Is it truly so? You have not heard (says Socrates) that Dædalus, captured, deprived of his liberty, and torn from his country and forced into *slavery*, on account of his knowledge and wisdom was detained by Minos; and, when afterwards attempting to make his escape with his son, who was slain in the attempt, was not able to save himself, but was seized by the barbarians and again forced into *slavery*."

Ibid. Ἄλλους δὲ πόσους οἴει διὰ σοφίαν ἀναρπάστους πρὸς βασιλέα γεγονέναι, καὶ ἐκεῖ *δουλεύειν*;

"How many others are born and remain creeping, fawning about the king (of Persia); and because he deems them his, he there *enslaves* them."

Chap 5. § 5. *Δουλείαν* δὲ ποίαν κακίστην νομίζεις εἶναι; Ἐγὼ μὲν, ἔφη, τὴν παρὰ τοῖς κακίστοις δεσπόταις. Τὴν κακίστην ἄρα *δουλείαν* οἱ ἀκρατεῖς δουλεύουσιν;

Of which Leunclavius gives the following: "Pessimam *servitutem*. Et quam esse arbitraris? Eam ait, quæ apud pessimos dominos *serviatur*. Ergone intemperantes *servitutem* pessimam *serviunt?*"

For the benefit of the mere English scholar, we give it thus: "Now, where do you esteem the most degraded slavery? Why, to be sure, says he, when the master is most degraded. It follows then, (says Socrates,) that the slaves of intemperance are the most degraded of *slaves*."

In the 30th section of the defence of Socrates before his judges, by Xenophon, we find thus:—

῞Ωστε φημὶ, αὐτὸν ἐπὶ τῇ δουλοπρεπεῖ διατριβῇ, ἣν ὁ πατὴρ αὐτῷ παρεσκεύακεν, οὐ διαμενεῖν.

By Leunclavius: "Itaque aio, non permansurum in illo *servili* vitæ genere, quod pater ei præscripsit."

We offer: "So that, I said, it is not becoming that his son should remain in an occupation only proper for a *slave*, in which alone his father educated him."

LESSON VII.

At the close of the 23d chapter of the first book of Xenophon's Cyropædia, we find:

Πολλοὶ δὲ, οἷς ἐξῆν φίλοις χρῆσθαι, καὶ ἣν ποιεῖν καὶ ἣν πάσχειν, τούτοις δούλοις μᾶλλον βουληθέντες ἢ φίλοις χρῆσθαι, ὑπ' αὐτῶν τούτων δίκην ἔδοσαν.

"There are instances of many, who, when they might have used others as their friends in a mutual intercourse of good offices, and who, choosing to hold them rather as *slaves* than as friends, have met with revenge and punishment at their hands." *Ashley.*

Book iii. § 2. Καὶ γάρ ἐστιν, ἔφη ὁ Κῦρος, καλὸν μάχεσθαι, ὅπως μὴ ποτέ τις δοῦλος μέλλοι γενήσεσθαι· ἢν δὲ δὴ ἢ πολέμῳ κρατηθεὶς, ἢ καὶ ἄλλον τινὰ τρόπον δουλωθεὶς, ἐπιχειρῶν τις φαίνηται τοὺς δεσπότας ἀποστερεῖν ἑαυτοῦ, τοῦτον σὺ, πρῶτος εἰπὲ, πότερον ὡς ἀγαθὸν ἄνδρα καὶ καλὰ πράττοντα τιμᾷς, ἢ ὡς ἀδικοῦντα, ἢν λάβῃς, κολάζεις; κολάζω, ἔφη, &c.

"It is indeed noble, said Cyrus, to fight, in order not to be made a slave! But if a man be conquered in war, or by other means be reduced to *slavery*, and be found attempting to throw off his masters, do you yourself first pronounce whether you reward and honour such a one as an honest man, and as one that does noble things, or, if you take him, do you punish him as one that acts unjustly? I punish him, said he." *Ashley.*

Ibid. Ἦν ἤ, νὴ Δί', ἑαυτῷ σύνοιδεν ἐλευθερίας μὲν ἐπιθυμήσας, δοῦλος δ' ὡς οὐδεπώποτε γενόμενος.

"Why, by Jupiter, being conscious of himself that, affecting his liberty, he has become by far much more of a slave than ever."

Ibid. Οἴει οὖν τι, ἔφη ὁ Τιγράνης, μᾶλλον καταδουλοῦσθαι ἀνθρώπους τοῦ ἰσχυροῦ φόβου;

"Can you, said Tigranes, imagine what brings men into yielding to *slavery* more effectually than very great fear?"

Ibid. Καὶ οἱ πλέοντες, μὴ ναυαγήσωσι, καὶ οἱ δουλείαν καὶ δεσμὸν φοβούμενοι, οὗτοι μὲν οὔτε σίτου οὔθ' ὕπνου δύνανται τυγχάνειν διὰ τὸν φόβον· οἱ δὲ ἤδη μὲν φυγάδες, ἤδη δ' ἡττημένοι, ἤδη δὲ δουλεύοντες, ἔστιν ὅτε δύνανται καὶ μᾶλλον τῶν εὐδαιμόνων ἐσθίειν τε καὶ καθεύδειν.

"They that are at sea, and dread shipwreck, and they that fear servitude and chains, are neither able to eat nor sleep for fear: but they who are already under banishment, who are already conquered, and already *slaves*, are often in a condition to eat and sleep better than the fortunate themselves." *Ashley.*

Ibid. Τὸν δ' ἐμὸν πατέρα, ἔφη, νῦν πῶς δοκεῖς διακεῖσθαι τὴν ψυχὴν, ὃς οὐ μόνον περὶ ἑαυτοῦ, ἀλλὰ καὶ περὶ ἐμοῦ, καὶ περὶ γυναικὸς, καὶ περὶ πάντων τῶν τέκνων δουλείας φοβεῖται;

"In what state of mind then, said he, do you take my father to be, he who fears not only for his own life, but that his wife, myself, and all his children will be plunged into *slavery?*"

Ibid. § 4. Ἀλλὰ μὰ Δί', ἔφη, οὐκ ἐκεῖνον ἐθεώμην. Ἀλλὰ τίνα μήν; ἔφη ὁ Τιγράνης. Τὸν εἰπόντα, νὴ Δία, ὡς τῆς αὐτοῦ ψυχῆς ἂν πρίαιτο ὥστε μή με δουλεύειν.

"Truly, said she, I did not look at him. At whom then did you look? said Tigranes. At him who said, that to save me from *servitude* he would ransom me at the expense of his own life." *Ashley.*

Ibid. § 9. Ὡς ὀλίγα δυνάμενοι προορᾷν ἄνθρωποι περὶ τοῦ μέλλοντος, πολλὰ ἐπιχειροῦμεν πράττειν. Νῦν γὰρ δὴ καὶ ἐγὼ, ἐλευθερίαν μὲν μηχανᾶσθαι ἐπιχειρήσας, δοῦλος ὡς οὐδεπώποτε ἐγενόμην· ἐπεὶ δ' ἑάλωμεν, σαφῶς ἀπολωλέναι νομίσαντες, νῦν ἀναφαινόμεθα σεσωσμένοι ὡς οὐδεπώποτε.

"How few things in futurity are we men able to foresee! and how many projects do we undertake! I have endeavoured upon this occasion to obtain liberty, and I have become more a *slave* than ever: and, after having been made a captive, and thinking our destruction certain, we now again appear to be in a condition of greater safety and security than ever." *Ashley.*

Book iv. chap. 8. *Αὐτίκα μάλα ὄψεσθε, ὥσπερ δούλων ἀποδιδρασκοντων καὶ εὑρημένων, τοὺς μὲν ἱκετεύοντας αὐτῶν, τοὺς δὲ φεύγοντας, τοὺς δ' οὐδὲ ταῦτα φρονεῖν δυναμένους.*

"You will see them, like *slaves* that have run away and are discovered, some supplicating for mercy, some flying, and some without presence of mind enough to do either." *Ashley.*

Chap. 18. *Ἐὰν δέ τις ὑμῶν, καὶ ἰὼν ὡς ἡμᾶς εὐνοϊκῶς καὶ πράττων τι καὶ διδάσκων φαίνηται, τοῦτον ἡμεῖς ὡς εὐεργέτην καὶ φίλον, οὐχ ὡς δοῦλον, περιέψομεν.*

"But, then, if you shall come to us, and shall appear to do any action, or give any information, in friendship and good-will to us, him will we treat as a benefactor and a friend, not as a *slave.*"

Chap. 23. *Αὐτὸς δὲ ὁ Κῦρος ἀνειπεῖν ἐκέλευσεν, εἴ τις εἴη ἐν τῷ Ἀσσυρίων ἢ Σύρων ἢ Ἀραβίων στρατεύματι ἀνὴρ δοῦλος, ἢ Μήδων, ἢ Περσῶν, ἢ Βακτριανῶν, ἢ Καρῶν, ἢ Κιλίκων, ἢ Ἑλλήνων, ἢ ἀλλοθέν ποθεν βεβιασμένος, ἐκφαίνεσθαι.*

"Cyrus himself ordered them to make proclamation, that whatever *slave* there might be, either in the Assyrian, Syrian, or Arabian armies, whether he were Mede, Persian, Bactrian, Carian, Cilician, or Greek, or of any other country, forced to serve, that he should appear." *Ashley.*

Chap. 24. *Ἔχθιστος ὢν ἐμοί, ἥκω πρὸς σέ, καὶ ἱκέτης προσπίπτω, καὶ δίδωμί σοι ἐμαυτὸν δοῦλον καὶ σύμμαχον, σὲ δὲ τιμωρὸν αἰτοῦμαι ἐμοὶ γενέσθαι.*

"I bow myself at your feet, a suppliant, and give myself a *slave* to you, and a confederate in the war."

Book v. chap. 1. *Καὶ τοίνυν ὁμοίαν ταῖς δούλαις εἶχε τὴν ἐσθῆτα.*

"And was clothed in the same manner as were her *female slaves.*"

Ibid. *Ἀλλ' ἐγώ, ἔφη, ἑώρακα καὶ κλαίοντας ὑπὸ λύπης δι' ἔρωτα, καὶ δουλεύοντάς γε τοῖς ἐρωμένοις· καὶ μάλα κακὸν νομίζοντας, πρίν γε ἐρᾷν, τὸ δουλεύειν.*

"But I have seen, says he, people in grief and tears when in love, *slaves* to those with whom they were in love, yet they deemed *slavery* a very great evil when not in love."

Chap. 32. *Οὐ γάρ ἀγνοῶ τοῦτ', ἔφη, ὅτι οὐ σύ μου μόνον μείζων εἶ, ἀλλὰ καὶ οἱ ἐμοὶ δοῦλοι ἰσχυρότεροι ἐμοῦ ὑπαντιάζουσί μοι, καὶ*, &c.

"I am not ignorant, says he, that you are above me, but that my own *slaves* are above me in power," &c.

Book vi. chap. 26. *Καὶ Κύρῳ δὲ δοκῶ μεγάλην τινὰ ἡμᾶς χάριν ὀφείλειν, ὅτι με, αἰχμάλωτον γενομένην καὶ ἐξαιρεθεῖσαν ἑαυτῷ, οὔτε με ὡς δούλην ἠξίωσε κεκτῆσθαι, οὔτε ὡς ἐλευθέραν ἐν ἀτίμῳ ὀνόματι· διεφύλαξε δέ σοι ὥσπερ ἀδελφοῦ γυναῖκα λαβών.*

"Then I think we are both under great obligation to Cyrus, who, when I was captured, and chosen and selected particularly for him, thought proper not to receive me as a *slave*, nor even as a free woman of low standing, but detained me under such restraint as if I had been his brother's wife."

Book vii. chap. 20. *Καὶ πάντας δὲ τοὺς ἀόπλους τῶν ὑποχειρίων γενομένων σφενδονᾷν ἠνάγκαζε μελετᾷν, νομίζων τοῦτο τὸ ὅπλον δουλικώτερον εἶναι.*

"All those whom he conquered, he compelled to practise with the sling, which he deemed more suitable for *slaves*."

Chap. 30. *Νόμος γαρ ἐν πᾶσιν ἀνθρώποις ἀΐδιός ἐστιν, ὅταν πολεμούντων πόλις ἁλῷ, τῶν ἑλόντων εἶναι καὶ τὰ σώματα τῶν ἐν τῇ πόλει καὶ τὰ χρήματα.*

"For it is a perpetual law among all men, that when a city is taken from an enemy, both the persons and treasures of the inhabitants belong to the captors." *Ashley.*

Ibid. *Θάλπους μὲν οὖν καὶ ψύχους, καὶ σίτων καὶ ποτῶν, καὶ πόνων καὶ ὕπνου ἀνάγκη καὶ τοῖς δούλοις μεταδιδόναι.*

"In heat, and in cold, in meat and drink, in work and rest, we necessarily allow our *slaves* a portion."

Ibid. *Ὅτι, ἐπεὶ κεκτήμεθα δούλους, τούτους κολάσομεν, ἢν πονηροὶ ὦσι; καὶ τί προσήκει αὐτὸν ὄντα πονηρὸν πονηρίας ἕνεκα ἢ βλακείας ἄλλους κολάζειν;*

"When we acquire *slaves*, we punish them if they are slothful and vicious. But does it become him who is slothful and vicious himself, to punish others for vice and sloth?"

Book viii. chap. 1. *Τοσοῦτον δὲ διαφέρειν ἡμᾶς δεῖ τῶν δού-*

λων, ὅσον οἱ μὲν δοῦλοι, ἄκοντες τοῖς δεσπόταις ὑπηρετοῦσιν· ἡμᾶς δὲ, εἴπερ ἀξιοῦμεν ἐλεύθεροι εἶναι, ἑκόντας δεῖ ποιεῖν, ὅ τι πλείστου ἄξιον φαίνεται εἶναι.

"We ought to distinguish ourselves so far from *slaves*, as that *slaves* do service to their masters against their wills; and if we desire to be free, we ought willingly to perform what appears to be most excellent and worthy." *Ashley.*

Chap. 14. Οὓς δ' αὖ κατεσκεύαζεν εἰς τὸ δουλεύειν, τούτους οὔτε μελετᾷν τῶν ἐλευθερίων πόνων οὐδένα παρώρμα, οὔτε ὅπλα κεκτῆσθαι ἐπέτρεπεν.

"But in the management of *slaves*," &c.

Chap. 41. Βουλοίμην δ' ἂν ὑμᾶς καὶ τοῦτο κατανοῆσαι, ὅτι τούτων, ὧν νῦν ὑμῖν παρακελεύομαι, οὐδὲν τοῖς δούλοις προστάττω.

"And I desire likewise that you should observe, that of all these orders that I now give you, I give none to those that are of *servile* condition."

Chap. 47. Καὶ τοὺς μὲν φίλους ἐπεῖδον δι' ἐμοῦ εὐδαίμονας γενομένους, τοὺς δὲ πολεμίους ὑπ' ἐμοῦ δουλωθέντας.

"By my means my friends have been made happy, and my enemies *enslaved.*"

In Xenophon's Expedition of Cyrus, usually termed the *Anabasis*, book i. chap. 9, we find—

Ὥστε φαίνεσθαι τοὺς μὲν ἀγαθοὺς, εὐδαιμονεστάτος, τοὺς δὲ κακοὺς δούλους τούτων ἀξιοῦν εἶναι.

"So that brave men were looked upon as most fortunate, and cowards as deserving to be their *slaves.*" *Spelman.*

Ibid. Παρὰ μὲν Κύρου, δούλου ὄντος, οὐδεὶς ἀπῄει πρὸς βασιλέα.

"No one, not even a *slave*, ever deserted Cyrus to go to the king."

Book ii. chap. 3. Δοῦλοι δὲ πολλοὶ εἵποντο.

"They were attended by a great many *slaves.*"

Chap. 5. Μετὰ δὲ ταῦτα τῶν βαρβάρων τινὲς ἱππέων, διὰ τοῦ πεδίου ἐλαύνοντες, ᾧτινι ἐντυγχάνοιεν Ἕλληνι ἢ δούλῳ ἢ ἐλευθέρῳ, πάντας ἔκτεινον.

"After this, some of the barbarian horse, scouring the plains, killed all the Greeks they met with, both freemen and *slaves*." *Spelman.*

Ibid. Ἑαυτοῦ γὰρ εἶναι φησὶν, ἐπείπερ Κύρου ἦσαν τοῦ ἐκείνου δούλου.

"For, he says, they are his, having belonged to his *slave* Cyrus."

Book iii. chap. 1. Ἡμᾶς δὲ, οἷς κηδεμὼν μὲν οὐδεὶς πάρεστιν, ἐστρατεύσαμεν δ' ἐπ' αὐτὸν ὡς δοῦλον ἀντὶ βασιλέως ποιήσοντες καὶ ἀποκτενοῦντες, εἰ δυναίμεθα, τί ἂν οἰόμεθα παθεῖν;

"How then will he treat us, who have no support, and who have made war on him, with the design to reduce him from the condition of a king to that of a *slave*, and, if in our power, to put him to death?"

Book vii. chap. 4. Ὁ δ' εἶπεν· Ἀλλ' ἔγωγε ἱκανὴν νομίζω νῦν δίκην ἔχειν, εἰ οὗτοι δοῦλοι ἔσονται ἀντ' ἐλευθέρων.

"And then he said, but I think myself sufficiently revenged, if these people, instead of *freemen*, are to be made *slaves*."

Chap. 7. Σοῦ μὲν γὰρ κρατοῦντος, δουλεία ὑπάρχει αὐτοῖς· κρατουμένου δὲ σοῦ, ἐλευθερία.

"For if you conquer, they are *slaves*,—but if you are conquered, they are free."

LESSON VIII.

Herodotus *of Halicarnassus.*

We often find the word δοῦλος, and its various derivatives, in the plain, the simple narrative of this author. His use of the term is as follows:

Book i. chap. 7. Παρὰ τούτων δὲ Ἡρακλεῖδαι ἐπιτραφθέντες ἔσχον τὴν ἀρχὴν ἐκ θεοπροπίου, ἐκ δούλης τε τῆς Ἰαρδάνου γεγονότες καὶ Ἡρακλέος.

"The Heraclidæ are descended from Hercules and a *female slave* of Jardanus."

Chap. 27. Λαβεῖν ἀρώμενοι Λυδοὺς ἐν θαλάσσῃ, ἵνα ὑπὲρ

τῶν ἐν τῇ ἠπείρῳ οικημένων Ἑλλήνων τίσωνταί σε, τοὺς σὺ δουλώσας ἔχεις;

"Can they wish for a better opportunity than to meet the Lydians on the Ocean, to revenge those of the Greeks reduced by you to *slavery* on the continent?"

Chap. 94. *Λυδοὶ μὲν δὴ ὑπὸ Πέρσῃσι δεδούλωντο.*

"Thus the Lydians were *enslaved* by the Persians."

Chap. 95. *Καὶ ἀπωσάμενοι τὴν δουλοσύνην ἠλευθερώθησαν.*

"And rejecting *slavery*, they became *free.*"

Chap. 114. *Ὦ βασιλεῦ, ὑπὸ τοῦ σοῦ δούλου.*

"O king! by your *slave.*"

Chap. 126. *Οὐδένα πόνον δουλοπρεπέα ἔχουσι.*

"*Slavish* employment," &c.

Chap. 129. *Καὶ ἄλλα λέγων ἐς αὐτὸν θυμαλγέα ἔπεα, καὶ δὴ καὶ εἴρετό μιν πρὸς τὸ ἑωυτοῦ δεῖπνον, τό μιν ἐκεῖνος σαρξὶ τοῦ παιδὸς ἐθοίνισε, ὅ τι εἴη ἡ ἐκείνου δουλοσύνη ἀντὶ τῆς βασιληΐης.*

"Among other things, he asked him what was his opinion of that supper, in which he had compelled a father to feed on the flesh of his child; a supper which had reduced him from a monarch to a *slave.*" *Beloe.*

Ibid. *Ἀδικώτατον δέ, ὅτι τοῦ δείπνου εἵνεκεν Μήδους κατεδούλωσε.*

"(He said that he was) most wicked, on the account of the supper, to *enslave* the Medes."

Ibid. *Νῦν δὲ Μήδους μὲν ἀναιτίους τούτου ἐόντας δούλους ἀντὶ δεσποτέων γεγονέναι, Πέρσας δὲ δούλους ἐόντας τὸ πρὶν Μήδων νῦν γεγονέναι δεσπότας.*

"The Medes, who were certainly not accessary to the provocation given, had exchanged situations with their *slaves.* The Persians, who were formerly the *slaves*, were now the masters."

Chap. 170. *Καὶ οὕτω ἀπαλλαχθέντας σφέας δουλοσύνης εὐδαιμονήσειν.*

"And thus, freed from *slavery*, deem themselves happy."

Chap. 173. *Καὶ ἢν μέν γε γυνὴ ἀστὴ δούλῳ συνοικήσῃ, γενναῖα τὰ τέκνα νενόμισται.*

"If any free woman marries a *slave*, the children of such marriage are reputed free." *Beloe.*

Chap. 174. Οἱ μὲν νῦν Κᾶρες οὐδὲν λαμπρὸν ἔργον ἀποδεξάμενοι ἐδουλώθησαν.

"The Carians made little or no exertion, and were easily *enslaved.*"

Chap. 210. Ὃς ἀντὶ μὲν δούλων ἐποίησας ἐλευθέρους Πέρσας εἶναι.

"You have raised the Persians from *slavery* to freedom." *Beloe.*

Book ii. chap. 1. Ὡς δούλους πατρωΐους ἐόντας ἐνόμιζε.

"He considered them as *slaves* by right of inheritance."

Chap. 56. Ἔπειτα δουλεύουσα αὐτόθι ἱδρύσασθαι ὑπὸ φηγῷ πεφυκυίῃ Διὸς ἱρόν.

"Although in a state of *slavery*, she there constructed, under a green spreading beech, a natural little temple to her god."

Book iii. chap. 125. Ὅσοι δὲ ἦσαν ξεῖνοί τε καὶ δοῦλοι τῶν ἑπομένων, ἐν ἀνδραπόδων λόγῳ ποιεύμενος εἶχε.

"All the strangers, and their *slaves* accompanying them, were detained in *bondage.*" See 1 *Tim.* i. 10.

Chap. 138. Καί σφεας δουλεύοντας ἐνθαῦτα Γίλλος.

"And they being *enslaved*, Gillus immediately *ransomed them,*" &c.

Chap. 140. Ἐμοὶ μήτε χρυσὸν, ὦ βασιλεῦ, μήτε ἄργυρον δίδου, ἀλλ' ἀνασωσάμενός μοι δὸς τὴν πατρίδα Σάμον, τὴν νῦν ἀδελφεοῦ τοῦ ἐμοῦ Πολυκράτεος ἀποθανόντος ὑπὸ Ὀροίτεω ἔχει δοῦλος ἡμέτερος, ταύτην μοι δὸς ἄνευ τε φόνου καὶ ἐξανδραποδίσιος.

"I would have neither gold nor silver; give me Samos, my country, and deliver it from *servitude.* Since the death of Polycrates, my brother, whom Orœtes slew, it hath been in the hands of one of our *slaves.* Give me this, without any effusion of blood, or reducing my countrymen to servitude." (*Beloe.*) See 1 *Tim.* i. 10.

Chap. 153. Ἀπείπας τοῖσι δούλοισι μηδενὶ φράζειν τὸ γεγονὸς ἐβουλεύετο.

"He counselled *with himself about that* which was foretold, that *Babylon* should not be reduced to *slavery* until this *prodigy* should be brought forth."

Book iv. chap. 1. Αἱ γὰρ τῶν Σκυθέων γυναῖκες, ὥς σφι οἱ ἄνδρες ἀπῆσαν χρόνον πολλὸν, ἐφοίτεον παρὰ τοὺς δούλους.

"For the women, deprived so long of their husbands, had associated with their *slaves*." *Beloe.*

Chap. 2. Τοὺς δὲ δούλους οἱ Σκύθαι πάντας τυφλοῦσι τοῦ γάλακτος εἵνεκεν τοῦ πίνουσι ποιεῦντες ὧδε.

"It is a custom with the Scythians, to deprive all the *slaves* of sight, on the account of the milk, which is their customary drink." *Beloe.*

Chap. 3. Ἐκ τούτων δὴ ὦν σφι τῶν δούλων καὶ τῶν γυναικῶν ἐπετράφη νεότης.

"From the union of these *slaves* with the Scythian women, a numerous progeny was born." *Beloe.*

Ibid. Δούλοισι τοῖσι ἡμετέροισι μαχόμενοι αὐτοί τε ἐλάσσονες κτεινόμενοι γινόμεθα.

"In this contest with our *slaves*, every action diminishes our number." *Beloe.*

Ibid. Μαθόντες ὥς εἰσι ἡμέτεροι δοῦλοι.

"They will be impressed with a sense of their *servile* condition." *Beloe.*

Book v. chap. 35. Ὁ δὲ τῶν δούλων τὸν πιστότατον ἀποξυρήσας τὴν κεφαλὴν ἔστιξε καὶ ἀνέμεινε ἀναφῦναι τὰς τρίχας.

"He therefore took one of the most faithful of his *slaves*, and inscribed what we have mentioned on his skull, being first shaved." *Beloe.*

Chap. 49. Ἰώνων παῖδας δούλους εἶναι ἀντ' ἐλευθέρων ὄνειδος καὶ ἄλγος μέγιστον μὲν αὐτοῖσι ἡμῖν, ἔτι δὲ τῶν λοιπῶν ὑμῖν, ὅσῳ προέστατε τῆς Ἑλλάδος. νῦν ὦν πρὸς θεῶν τῶν Ἑλληνίων ῥύσασθε Ἴωνας ἐκ δουλοσύνης, ἄνδρας ὁμαίμονας.

"The Ionians, who ought to be free, are in a state of *servitude;* which is not only disgraceful, but also a source of the extremest sorrow to us, as it must be to you, who are so pre-eminent in Greece. I entreat you therefore, by the gods of Greece, to *relieve* the Ionians from *slavery*, who are connected with you by the ties of consanguinity." *Beloe.*

Book vi. chap. 83. Ἄργος δὲ ἀνδρῶν ἐχηρώθη οὕτω ὥστε οἱ δοῦλοι αὐτῶν ἔσχον πάντα τὰ πρήγματα ἄρχοντές τε καὶ διέποντες, ἐς ὃ ἐπήβησαν οἱ τῶν ἀπολομένων παῖδες, ἔπειτά σφεας οὗτοι ἀνακτώμενοι ὀπίσω ἐς ἑωυτοὺς τὸ Ἄργος ἐξέβαλον· ἐξωθεύμενοι δὲ οἱ δοῦλοι μάχῃ ἔσχον Τίρυνθα. τέως μὲν δή σφι ἦν ἄρθμια ἐς ἀλλήλους, ἔπειτα δὲ ἐς τοὺς δούλους ἦλθε ἀνὴρ μάντις Κλέανδρος, γένος ἐὼν Φιγαλεὺς ἀπ' Ἀρκαδίης· οὗτος τοὺς δούλους ἀνέγνωσε ἐπιθέσθαι τοῖσι δεσπότῃσι.

"Argos, however, was deprived of so many of its citizens, that the *slaves* usurped the management of affairs, and executed the offices of government; but when the sons of those who had been slain grew up, they obtained possession of the city, and after some contest expelled the *slaves*, who retired to Tyrinthe, which they seized. They for a time forebore to molest each other, till Cleander, a soothsayer, and an Arcadian of the district of Phigalis, came among the *slaves*, when he persuaded the slaves to attack their masters."

Book ix. chap. 48. Ἐν Ἀθηναίοισί τε τὴν πρόπειραν ποιευμένους αὐτούς τε ἀντία δούλων τῶν ἡμετέρων τασσομένους.

"We see you delegating to the Athenians the more dangerous attempt of opposing us, and placing yourselves against our *slaves*." *Beloe.*

In the "Libellus de Vitâ Homeri," attributed to Herodotus, in the 23d section we find the word συνδούλῳ, used to mean a *fellow-slave.*

LESSON IX.

WE now propose to notice the scriptural use of the word δουλος, *doulos*, and its derivatives, not only that its use may be compared with the Greek writers, but that it may be seen, as we believe is true, that its use in these carries with it abundant proof, even in the absence of all other, that "it means a slave," and "that he to whom it was applied was a slave."

Whenever a thing is made any part of discourse, it is necessarily placed in a position of commendation, reprehension, or of perfect indifference. One of these conditions must unavoidably attend its mention. A little reflection will enable us to perceive these distinctive positions. For instance, in the sentence, "Lay up treasures in heaven, where moth and rust doth not corrupt, nor thieves break through nor steal," who does not feel the commendable position of the things, treasure and heaven, and the reverse of moth, rust, and thieves? Let us apply this view to the word *servant*, selecting only those instances in the Christian Scriptures, where the word is translated from the Greek word δουλος, *doulos*, and means nothing except what we mean by the word *slave*.

St. Paul commences his epistle to the Romans, to the Philippians, and to Titus, with the appellation of servant. In the two first cases he calls himself the servant and apostle of Christ. In the last instance, he terms himself the servant of God and apostle of Jesus Christ. Peter, in his second epistle, styles himself a *servant* and apostle: Jude, the servant of Christ. In all these instances the word means *slave*, and is used commendatively, but figuratively, to signify their entire devotedness to the cause in which they are engaged,—devoted to the cause wholly, as a good slave is to his master. And it may be here remarked, that the professing Christian is indebted to the institution for the lesson of humility and devotedness here plainly taught him, and without which, perhaps, he never could have been taught his duty in these particulars so pertinently and clearly. The humility and devotedness of the Christian are illustrated by this ordinance in *John* xv. 20: "Remember the words that I said unto you, the servant is not greater than his Lord."

In the parable of the vineyard, *Luke* 20 and *Matt.* 21, the *servant* (δοῦλος, *doulos*, slave) is presented in a position evincing the trustworthiness, devotion, and obedience implied in that character, clearly indicating the idea that these qualities inspire the mind of the proprietor with a confidence surpassed only by that in his son and heir. And it may be well remarked, that the position of the slave is one of great facility for the generating of such confidence in the mind of the master. Between the good slave and the good master there can be no dissimilarity of interest; but not so with the *hired man*, see *Matt.* 20; for the very moment those hired in the morning for a penny a day perceived that those who had not laboured the whole day received the same amount of wages, they commenced a quarrel with the proprietor.

This distinctive use of language we think also perceptible in the parable of the prodigal son, *Luke* xv. 17: "*How many hired servants* (πόσοι μίσθιοι, *posoi misthioi*) of my father have bread enough and to spare," περισσεύουσιν ἄρτων, *perisseuousin arton*, *an overflowing of bread.*

He is not made to say that his father's slaves had bread enough, but that even his hired men had enough. "Make me as one of thy *hired servants*," μισθίων, *misthion*. He does not ask to be received as a son, not even to be accounted as a slave,—he feels unworthy of either. "But the father said to his servants," δούλους, *doulous*, slaves, "Bring forth the best robe." Having slaves, it would have been quite out of place to have called one of his μίσθους, *misthous*, hired men. But the elder son "called one of the servants;" nor would it have been natural for him to have called a *hired-man*, nor yet one of the *common slaves*, but a confidential servant, whose position in the family would enable him to possess the information required; and so we find the fact by the expression τῶν παίδων αὐτοῦ, *ton paidon autou*, his young confidential, favourite slave.

But the elder brother said to his father, "Lo, these many years do I serve thee;" the verb used is δουλεύω, *douleuo*, and expresses the faithful and devoted service of a good slave, not of a *hired man*, who would feel no real interest beyond his own personal benefit. And this word is put in the mouth of the angered son, whereby to show more forcibly his sense of his own merits.

While we cast reflection back upon the incidents of this parable, let us suppose the owner of slaves also to employ hired labourers: if from famine or other cause he finds himself unable to supply them all with bread, which would he turn away, his slaves, or hired men? or, if they refused to go, which would he feel disposed to put on small allowance?

Jesus Christ seems to have understood that if there was to be any deficiency of bread, the hired-men might be expected first to feel it. Our Lord and Saviour, in pronouncing this parable, has given us the most explicit assurance that he intimately understood the domestic relations of the *slave*, and has taught us the lesson by placing him side by side with the *hired servant*.

From the fact that the good slave was wholly devoted and faithful to his master, the idea was not only applied to Paul, Peter, and Jude, but also to Noah, Abraham, Isaac, Jacob, Moses, Joshua, and David, and others, to express these qualities in them towards Jehovah; and we find it so used in the Christian Scriptures: "He hath holpen his servant Israel," Ἰσραὴλ παιδὸς αὐτοῦ, *Israel paidos autou*, *Luke* i. 54. It is noticed that with the word "*Israel*" is associated the same term to mean *slave* which was applied to the slave called by the elder brother; and the reason seems to be because the name *Israel* is supposed to be in higher regard than the word Jacob,—the word in apposition should also be expressive of such elevated regard. Therefore, if the word Jacob had been used, the word δοῦλος would have followed it. This word παῖς, *pais*, when applied to a *slave*, was a word of endearment, and hence was used in the case of the centurion's servant. And we may here well remark that the case of the centurion is one in point, presenting an instance where slave-holding was brought to the immediate and particular notice of the Saviour, and the record shows his conduct and language upon the occasion.

"For I am a man under authority, having soldiers under me, and I say to this man, Go, and he goeth; and to another Come, and he cometh; and to my servant, (δούλῳ, *doulo, slave,*) Do this, and he doeth it.

"When Jesus heard it, he marvelled, and said to them that followed, Verily I say unto you, I have not found so great faith, no, not in Israel." *Matt.* viii. 9, 10.

"And as he was now going down, his servants (δοῦλοι, *douloi, slaves*) met him, and told him, saying, Thy son liveth." *John* iv. 51.

LESSON X.

THE Christian Scriptures use the institution of slavery figuratively, in illustration of the Christian character and duty, and also in happy illustration of the providences of God to man.

"Who is that faithful and wise servant, (δοῦλος, *doulos*, *slave*,) whom his lord hath made ruler over his household, to give them meat in due season? Blessed is that servant (δοῦλος, *doulos*, *slave*,) whom his lord, when he cometh, shall find so doing. But if that evil *servant* (δοῦλος, *doulos*, *slave*) shall say in his heart, My lord delayeth his coming; and shall begin to smite his fellow-servants, (συνδούλους, *sundoulous*, *fellow-slaves*,) and to eat and drink with the drunken, the lord of that servant (δούλου, *doulou*, *slave*) shall come in a day when he looketh not for him, and in an hour that he is not aware of." "For the kingdom of heaven is as a man travelling into a far country, who called his own servants, (δούλους, *doulous*, *slaves*,) and delivered unto them his goods." "His Lord said unto him, Well done, thou good and faithful *servant*, (δοῦλε, *doule*, *slave*,) thou hast been faithful over a few things, I will make thee ruler over many things: enter thou into the joy of thy Lord." "His lord answered and said unto him, Thou wicked and slothful servant, (δοῦλε, *doule*, *slave*,) thou knewest that I reap where I sowed not, and gather where I have not strewed," &c. "And cast ye the unprofitable servant (δοῦλον, *doulon*, *slave*) into outer darkness: there shall be weeping and gnashing of teeth." *Matt.* xxiv. 45–50; xxv. 14, 30.

"And he called his servants (δούλους, *doulous*, *slaves*), and delivered them ten pounds, and said unto them, Occupy till I come. And it came to pass, that when he was returned, having received the kingdom, then he commanded these servants (δούλους, *doulous*, *slaves*) to be called unto him, to whom he had given money, that he might know how much every man had gained by trading." "And he said unto him, Well, thou good servant (δοῦλε, *doule*, *slave*), because thou hast been faithful in a very little, have thou authority over ten cities." "And he saith unto him, Out of thine own mouth will I judge thee, thou wicked servant, (δοῦλε, *doule*, *slave*.) Thou knewest that I was an austere man, taking up that I laid not down, and reaping that I did not sow." *Luke* xix. 13–28.

"Blessed is that servant, (δοῦλος, *doulos, slave*) whom his lord, when he cometh, shall find so doing. But if that servant (δοῦλος, *doulos, slave*) say in his heart, My lord delayeth his coming; and shall begin to beat the men-servants (τοὺς παῖδας, *male-slaves*) and maidens, (τὰς παιδίσκας, *female slaves,*) and to eat and drink and be drunken; the lord of that servant (δούλου, *doulou, slave,*) will come in a day when he looketh not for him, and in an hour when he is not aware, and will cut him in sunder." "And that servant (δοῦλος, *slave*) which knew his lord's will, and prepared not himself, neither did according to his will, shall be beaten with many stripes." *Luke* xii. 43–48.

Here is an instance when the most favourite slave, called by the term expressing such favouritism, when supposed to be disobedient, is immediately designated by the term δοῦλος, *doulos.*

"Blessed are those servants (δοῦλοι, *douloi, slaves*) whom the lord when he cometh shall find watching; and if he shall come in the second watch, or come in the third watch, and find them so, blessed are those servants," (δοῦλοι, *douloi, slaves.*) *Luke* xii. 37, 38.

"And sent his servant (δοῦλος, *doulos, slave*) at supper-time," &c. * * * "So that servant (δοῦλος, *doulos, slave*) came and showed his lord these things. Then the master of the house being angry, said to his servant," (δούλῳ, *doulo, slave.*) "And the servant (δοῦλος, *doulos, slave*) said, Lord, it is done. And the lord said unto the servant, (δοῦλον, *doulon, slave,*) Go out into the highway," &c. *Luke* xiv. 17–23.

"And ye shall know the truth, and the truth shall make you free, (ἐλευθερώσει *eleutherosei, free.*) They answered him, We be Abraham's seed, we were never in bondage (δεδουλεύκαμεν, *dedouleukamen, slavery*) to any man: how sayest thou, Ye shall be made free? Jesus answered them, Verily, verily, I say unto you, whosoever committeth sin, is the *servant* of sin, (δοῦλος, *doulos, slave.*) And the *servant* (δοῦλος, *doulos, slave*) abideth not in the house for ever. If the Son therefore shall make you free, ye shall be free indeed." *John* viii. 32–35.

"But which of you, having a servant (δοῦλον, *doulon, slave*) ploughing or feeding cattle, will say unto him by and by, when he is come from the field, Go and sit down to meat? And will not rather say unto him, Make ready wherewith I may sup, and gird thyself, and serve me, till I have eaten and drunken; and afterward thou shall eat and drink? Doth he thank that servant (δούλῳ, *slave*) because he did the things that were commanded him? I trow not. So likewise ye, when ye shall have done all those things which are commanded you, say, We are unprofitable servants (δοῦλοι, *slaves*): we have done that which was our duty to do." *Luke* xvii. 7–10.

In all these instances slavery is made a lesson of instruction, and always in the position commendable.

LESSON XI.

THE Christian Scriptures recognise the force and application of the command, "Thou shalt not covet thy neighbour's man-servant, nor his maid-servant," as applicable to slaves at the time of the apostles; and that the act of "coveting," extended into action, becomes "stealing," the property named in the command. "Now the end of the command is charity out of a pure heart, and of a good conscience, and of faith unfeigned: from which some having swerved, have turned aside unto vain jangling; desiring to be teachers of the law; understanding neither what they say, nor whereof they affirm. But we know that the law is good, if a man use it lawfully, knowing this, that the law is not made for a righteous man, but for the lawless and disobedient, the ungodly, and for sinners, for unholy and profane, for murderers of fathers, and murderers of mothers, for manslayers, for whoremongers, for them that defile themselves with mankind, for *men-stealers*, (ἀνδραποδισταῖς *andrapodistais*, *slave-stealers*,) for liars, for perjured persons, and if there be any other thing that is contrary to sound doctrine, according to the glorious gospel of the blessed God, which was committed to my trust." 1 *Tim.* i. 5–11.

It may be well remembered that the preceding third verse of this chapter beseeches Timothy to still abide at Ephesus, that he may charge some that they teach no other doctrine, &c.

The word *andrapodistais*, of the original Greek text, here translated *men-stealers*, means the stealing, or enticing away from the possession and ownership of their masters, their slaves. St. Paul speaks of it as a part of the law,—speaks of the offence as one well known, and as too well known to be a part of the law to require any explanation. When we come to know that that act of the mind called *coveting*, indulged to action, becomes stealing,—that the crime in action includes the crime in mind,—we may readily perceive what particular law is referred to. Is it difficult to decide that property, which the law forbids us to covet, it also forbids us to steal, even if "thou shalt not steal" had not preceded?

The idea stealing was expressed by the Greeks by the word *κλέπτω*, *klepto*, but the idea *stealing slaves* was expressed by the word in the text. The formation is ἀνήρ, *a man*, πούς, *a foot*, and signifies the condition of slavery, as a man bound by the foot. A whole class of words of this formation, all including the idea of slavery, were in use by the Greeks, and found in their authors. When used to express the substantive, the idea of slavery is associated with the idea of some change of position or ownership; hence its use in this instance. The thing stolen involves the idea of a change of position, possession, &c. Yet in many instances it may be difficult to perceive this distinction, it rather appearing to have been often used as a synonyme of *doulos*, both as a verb and substantive.

In the 8th section of the 4th book of the Cyropædia, Xenophon uses this word to mean a slave, the quality growing out of the imputed change in the condition of the soldier, thus: *Ὡς ὁ τοῦτο ποιῶν οὐκέτι ἀνήρ ἐστιν, ἀλλὰ σκευοφόρος, καὶ ἔξεστι τῷ βουλομένῳ ἤδη χρῆσθαι τούτῳ ὡς ἀνδραπόδῳ.* Which Ashley translates, "And as he that does this can no longer be reckoned a man, but a mere bearer of baggage, so any one that will is free to use him as a slave." The Romans so understood this word. In the translation of Xenophon into Latin by Amelburnus, we find this passage: "Nam qui hoc facit non miles et vir est, sed sarcinarius calo; quem uti mancipium tractare cuivis licet;" nor can it be said that this learned man misunderstood his Greek, for we have before us the critical translations of Oxford and Cambridge, in which the sentence reads, "Nam qui hoc facit, non amplius vir est et miles, sed sarcinarius calo, atque hoc adeò uti mancipium licet." They have made no change as to this word, nor as to the sense of the sentence.

Xenophon uses this word also in the 14th section of the 8th

book, to mean slaves, and in the same passage with δοῦλος, the adjective sense existing in the presumed unwillingness in the slaves to seek freedom, on the account of their happiness being probably better secured in a state of *slavery* to Cyrus than it would be in a state of freedom. We give it entire:

Ὅυς δ' αὖ κατεσκεύαζεν εἰς τὸ δουλεύειν, τούτους οὔτε μελετᾷν τῶν ἐλευθερίων πόνων οὐδένα παρώρμα, οὔτε ὅπλα κεκτῆσθαι ἐπέτρεπεν· ἐπεμελεῖτο δ' ὅπως μήποτε ἄσιτοι μήτε ἄποτοι ποτὲ ἔσοιντο, ἐλευθερίων ἕνεκα μελετημάτων. Καὶ γὰρ ὁπόταν ἐλαύνοιεν τὰ θηρία τοῖς ἱππεῦσιν εἰς τὰ πεδία, φέρεσθαι σῖτον εἰς θήραν τούτοις ἐπέτρεπε, τῶν δὲ ἐλευθέρων οὐδενί. Καὶ ὁπότε πορεία εἴη, ἦγεν αὐτοὺς πρὸς τὰ ὕδατα ὥσπερ τὰ ὑποζύγια. Καὶ ὁπότε δὲ ὥρα εἴη ἀρίστου, ἀνέμενεν αὐτοὺς ἔστ' ἂν φάγοιέν τι, ὡς μὴ βουλιμιῷεν· ὥστε καὶ οὗτοι αὐτὸν ὥσπερ οἱ ἄριστοι, πατέρα ἐκάλουν, ὅτι ἐπεμέλετο αὐτῶν ὅπως ἀναμφιλόγως ἀεὶ ἀνδράποδα διατελοῖεν.

Which may be translated thus: "But in rearing up his *slaves*, he never permitted them to practise the employment of the free, nor allowed them the possession of arms, but took care that they would never be without their meat and drink for the sake of the practices of the free; for when with their horses they drove out the wild beasts into the plains, he allowed meat and drink to be carried for the use of these people during the hunt, but not for the free; and when he was upon a march, he led them to water, as he did the beasts of burden; and when the time for dinner came, he waited till they had eaten something, that they might not be distressed with hunger; so that these people, as likewise the more elevated, called him their father; so he was careful, beyond a doubt, that they would always remain his *slaves*," ἀνδράποδα, *slaves*, *i. e.* they would have no desire to change their situation.

Amelburnus translates it thus: "Quos autem ad serviendum instruebat, eos nec ad labores ullos liberales excitabat, nec habere arma sinebat: studiosèque dabat operam, ne unquam liberalium exercitationum causa vel cibo vel potu carerent. Permittebat enim *servis*, quoties equitibus feras in campos adigerent, ut cibum ad venationem secum sumerent; ingenuorum verò nemini. Quando item faciundum erat iter, ad aquas eos, perinde ac jumenta, ducebat. Quum prandii tempus erat, expectabat eos donec aliquid comedissent, ne furcilla sive fames acrior eos affligeret. Quo fiebat ut, non aliter ac optimates, etiam hi Cyrum *patrem* appellarent, qui curam ipsorum gereret ut semper sine dubio *mancipia* manerent."

The Oxford translation, which was published in 1737, has perhaps made the Latin more classical, but has strictly adhered to the same meaning of the words *δουλεύειν* and *ἀνδράποδα*. We give their version also, that the curious may compare, and have no doubt about this matter. It reads thus:

"Quos autem ad serviendum instruebat, eos nec ad se in laboribus ullis liberalibus exercendos excitabat, nec habere arma sinebat. Studiosèque dabat operam, ne unquam liberalium exercitationum causa vel cibo vel potu carerent. Etenim his permittebat, ut cibum ad venationem secum sumerent, ingenuorum verò nemini: quando item faciendum erat iter, ad aquas eos, perinde ac jumenta, ducebat. Et cùm prandii tempus erat, expectabat eos donec aliquid comedissent ne fames ingens eos invaderet; quo fiebat ut etiam hi, non aliter ac optimates, Cyrum patrem appellarent, qui curam ipsorum gereret ut semper sine dubio *mancipia* manerent."

We deem it proper to add a word concerning the use of this term, especially as some, who claim to be learned divines, also claim that Paul by its use totally forbid slavery. See *Barnes, on Slavery*, p. 355. He says—"'The law is made for *manstealers*,' ἀνδραποδισταῖς, 1 *Tim.* i. 9, 10. The meaning of this word has been before considered. It needs only to be remarked here, that the *essential* idea of the term is *that of converting a freeman into a slave*. Thus Passon defines the word ἀνδραπόδισμος, *andrapodismos:* Verwandlung eines freyen Mannes in einen Sklaven, besonders durch Varkauf, Unterjochung, U. S. W.: a changing of a freeman into a slave, especially by traffic, subjection, &c. Now, somehow this 'conversion of a freeman into a slave,' the sin forbidden in the passage before us, occurs essentially in the case of every one who ever becomes a slave."

We know not why Mr. Barnes chose to go to a Dutch dictionary for his quotation, since he might have found the true signification in that of any schoolboy.

But we think it a singular argument that, because *andrapodismos* means the making or selling a slave, *andrapodistais* means the exact same thing. The truth is, the essential idea conveyed by this word is *slave*, *slavery*, &c. If I wish to say "stealing a slave," I use one form of it; if "selling a slave," another, and so on; but the stealing a *freeman* with the view to make *him a slave* was not expressed by this word, or any form of it. The Greeks used the term *anthropokleptais*, but the legal reduction of a man to slavery was quite a different matter. St. Paul's animadversion comprehended the idea of slavery and stealing,—what? a freeman, or a slave? Had it been a freeman that occupied the objective case, it is presumable that his language would have had some analogy to that used in the Septuagint, *Deut.* xxiv. 7.

This word, or some form of it, is of most frequent occurrence in the Greek authors. We need quote but a few passages to show their use of the term, whether it included the idea of a freeman, or only that of a slave. Thucydides, Leipsic edition, 1829:

Οἱ δ' Ἀθηναῖοι οὔτε τἆλλα ὑπήκουον, οὔτε τὸ ψήφισμα καθῄρουν, ἐπικαλοῦντες ἐπ' ἐργασίαν Μεγαρεῦσι τῆς γῆς τῆς ἱερᾶς, καὶ τῆς ἀορίστου, καὶ ἀνδραπόδων ὑποδοχὴν τῶν ἀφισταμένων.

"But the Athenians listened to none of these demands, nor would revoke the decree, but reproached the Megarians for tilling land that was sacred, land not marked out for culture, and for giving shelter to runaway slaves."

Vol. ii. p. 138. *Αἱ δὲ νῆες περίεπλευσαν, τα ἀνδράποδα ἀγοῦσαι.*

"But the vessels came back along the coast, on board of which were the *slaves*."

Idem. *Καὶ τὰ ἀνδράποδα ἀπεδόσαν.*

"And here they offered the *slaves* for sale."

P. 118. *Ἀνδράποδα Ὑκκαρικά*—"Hyccarian *slaves*."

P. 201. *Καὶ ἀνδραπόδων πλέον ἢ δύο μυριαδες ηὐτομολησαν.*

"And more than twenty thousand slaves had deserted."

P. 314. *Καὶ σκεύη μὲν καὶ ἀνδράποδα ἁρπαγὴν ποιησάμενος, τοὺς δὲ ἐλευθέρους πάλιν κατοικίσας, ἐπ' Ἄβυδον ἦλθε.*

"He gave up all the effects and slaves to pillage, and after establishing such as were free people in their old habitations, he went against Abydos."

The instances of the use of this word are so frequent that we know not whether more of them should not be given; but may we not presume that those who read the language have some knowledge of the matter? and we therefore ask them to relieve us from that burden. We think it no hazard to maintain the fact that *ἀνδραποδίζω*, its *cognates* and *derivatives*, both *nouns* and *adjec-*

tives, are never used in the Greek language unassociated with the idea of slavery. If so, then it follows that the idea *stealing*, as it existed in the mind of St. Paul, was not associated with the idea "*man*," but "*slave*," and that he used the term ἀνδραποδισταῖς, *andrapodistais*, to express the idea "slave-stealers."

LESSON XII.

But as the verb ἀνδραποδίζω, *andrapodizo*, and its conjugates, are sometimes used to express the action of subjecting to slavery, it is asked, how are we to know whether Paul did not mean such subjugation? It was surely in the compass of the Greek language for Paul so to have used the proper mood and tense of this verb, with other suitable words, and effectually forbid the subjecting of others to slavery. But is it probable he could have consistently done so? Such forbidding would have been forbidding what the law prescribed. It would have been a rebellious teaching against the laws of the land, as well as against the laws delivered to Moses for the civil government of the Israelites. "When thou comest nigh unto a city to fight against it, thou shalt proclaim peace unto it; and it shall be, if it make answer of peace, and open unto thee, then it shall be, that all the people that are found therein shall be tributaries unto thee, and they shall serve thee," (וַעֲבָדוּךָ *va abaduka, be slaves to thee—and they shall be slaves to thee.)* "But if it will make no peace with thee, but will make war against thee, then thou shalt besiege it: and when the Lord thy God hath delivered it into thy hands, thou shalt smite every male thereof with the edge of the sword. But the women, and the little ones, and the cattle, and all that is in the city, even all the spoil thereof, shalt thou take to thyself." *Deut.* xx. 10–14.

Such, substantially, was the law of all nations at the very time Paul wrote to Timothy. The verb proposed the making of a *slave* in a legal manner, reducing to the condition alluded to by the prophet. "Shall the prey be taken from the mighty, or the lawful captive restored?" *Isa.* xlix. 24. The verb *andrapodizo* expressed a lawful act. If individuals, without law, had seized upon the others with the view to make them slaves, such act would have been called by a different name. It would not have been a name formed from ἀνὴρ and πούς, (*aner* and *pous*,) unaccompanied by explanations. We have an example before us in *Deut.* xxiv. 7: "If any man be found stealing any of his brethren of the children of Israel, and maketh merchandise of him, or selleth him, then that thief shall die." Here the individual stolen was not a slave, either by the laws of God or man: and hence we find that the Septuagint uses no word to signify slave. The passage reads thus:

Ἐὰν δὲ ἁλῷ ἄνθρωπος κλέπτων ψυχὴν ἐκ τῶν ἀδελφῶν αὐτοῦ τῶν υἱῶν Ἰσραὴλ, καὶ καταδυναστεύσας αὐτὸν ἀποδῶται, ἀποθανεῖται ὁ κλέπτης ἐκεῖνος.

And had St. Paul merely in his mind the idea *man-stealing*, unconnected with slavery, he would have used analogous language. In the passage in Timothy, he might well have used the term ἀνθρώποκλεπταις, *anthropokleptais*, which would have expressed the same thing,—an unlawful act, an act forbidden in the passage just quoted,—the act of stealing a freeman, with an intention of making him a slave, contrary to law; and Paul would have probably added this offence, if the Ephesians had been guilty of the crime. But Paul did not use a word even conjugated from ἀνδραποδίζω, *andrapodizo*, but a cognate substantive, used almost technically to mean those who stole slaves, not *freemen*.

The word used by Paul is translated into Latin, in the Vulgate, by the word *plagiariis*, which also means those who stole slaves. It is formed from *plagiger*, *one born to be whipped*, (the Romans were cruel to their slaves,) and *areo*, *to be parched up, to be thirsty*, and hence *plagiarius*, from the notion that he who stole slaves *coveted* the slave with such intensity that he thirsted for the slave, and appropriated *him* to himself as a thirsty man does water. It originally was a mere cant word. But it expressed the contempt the Romans entertained for the act of slave-stealing. Hence has come our word *plagiary;* only used now to mean the act of appropriating the literary property of another, but still retaining, to some extent, the expression of contempt. The learned men who translated the New Testament into Latin well knew that Paul told Timothy that the law was made against those who stole slaves: and so we find it, *Thou shalt not steal.* Thou shalt not even *covet* thy neighbour's *slave.* (See *Exod.* xx. 15, 17; also *Deut.* v. 19, 20.) Had Paul used the word *andrapodizo*, or some form of it, and had he really intended to have told Timothy that he or others should no longer, under any circumstances, subject others to slavery, or under the Christian dispensation he should not; that Christianity forbid it; yet he could not have been so shallow as to have added the sentiment that it was against the law, for such addition, such part of his instruction, Timothy would have at once known to be not true; and we trust but few will entertain a position so full of gross consequences. This discourse to Timothy was founded upon the fact that "some had swerved" from the end of the law, and turned to vain jangling, desiring to be teachers of the law, understanding neither what they say nor whereof they affirm,—probably teaching doctrines that led essentially to the crimes here exposed. Paul's object, in part, was to expose their ignorance and wickedness, to sustain the supremacy of the law, and by his counsel to warn him against a shipwreck of faith, as in the case of Hymeneus and Alexander.

Can it be supposed that under such circumstances he would have undertaken to have repealed a law, or to have asserted that the law prohibited what it sustained? In such case, he would have done the very act himself for which he condemned Hymeneus and Alexander, and have proved himself one of the lawless and disobedient, for whom the law was made.

There is another consideration, which to our mind is of moment in the review of this subject. The religion of Jesus Christ never undertook to meddle with the civil institutions of the law. Its object was to make its devotees happy under and resigned to its adjudications, whatever they may have been, by reason of the greater considerations of a hereafter; nor do we recollect an instance where either Christ or his apostles even suggested any repeal. His kingdom was not of this world, and therefore his followers could not act in reference to the things of this world. Peter in his zeal smote off the ear of the slave of the high-priest, but Christ immediately rebuked the act and restored the injury done. Had Paul intended to have suggested that the subjecting to slavery, as that subject then existed and ever had from the time of Moses, was no longer to be countenanced, then, it seems to us, he would have travelled beyond the mission of an apostle, the precepts of his Master, and out of his kingdom into the problematical questions of civil government.

Paul, in the passage before us, enumerates a class of the breaches of the law which came within the view of Timothy, which breaches of the law he pronounces to be "contrary to sound doctrine," and "to the glorious gospel of the blessed God, which was committed to my trust," having previously notified him "that the law was good if a man use it lawfully." Now, one of the plain and well-known laws on the subject of slavery was, "Both thy bond-men and thy bond-maids which thou shalt have, shall be of the heathen that are around about you; of them shall you buy bond-men and bond-maids. Moreover, of the children of the strangers that do sojourn among you, of them shall ye buy, and their families that are with you, which they beget in your land, and they shall be your possession. And ye shall take them as an inheritance for your children after you, to inherit them for a possession. They shall be your bond-men for ever."

Under such a state of facts can any thing be conceived more inconsistent, than that Paul should, under such circumstances, design to slip in a word repealing in fact this law, and directly producing all the other ill effects which he so pointedly complained of in others. Whoever can believe such a thing, surely, whatever he may pretend, can have no respect for the character of Paul, nor for his religion.

But the character of Paul remains consistent, his religion unblemished and spotless, and the preaching of Jesus Christ in relation to the matter vindicated and supported, by giving to the word *andrapodistais*, as here used by Paul, its plain, legitimate, and usual meaning, *slave-stealers*, persons who steal, or entice away from the possession of their masters, individuals who according to the law are slaves.

LESSON XIII.

THE inquiry naturally occurs, how happened it that St. Paul found it necessary to instruct and inform Timothy that the law forbid the stealing or enticing away other men's slaves. By an examination of his writings and letters to the Gentile churches, the fact is plainly proven that there had grown up among them some new doctrines, which his office as apostle made it his duty to reprehend. What these doctrines were we are enabled in some measure to discover, by examining the 7th of the 1*st Corinthians*, which commences thus: "Now concerning the things whereof ye wrote unto me," disclosing the fact that the Corinthians had written to him for advice and counsel, whom he now answers with instructions against the abolition of marriage, and against the abolition of slavery, &c.

Some of the Gentile churches advocated the doctrine that if a man or a woman of the faith were married to one not of the faith, that such marriage should be abolished; so also, that a slave of the faith should be set free, and especially from his believing master; so also, the believing child should be discharged from the authority of the unbelieving parents. The promulgation of these doctrines filled society with disorder there, and the church with confusion.

In his lesson to *Timothy*, he complains of the doctrines taught by Hymeneus and Alexander, as *blasphemous*. Now, in this same lesson, he applies this epithet to these new abolition doctrines, leaving us plainly to infer that these doctrines were also taught by them, and for which he "delivered" them "unto Satan." And here we have a connecting link between this lesson to Timothy and his whole instruction to the Gentile churches on this subject. But these doctrines, as taught by Hymeneus and Alexander, or others analogous, have found advocates ever since; for folly has never been so foolish nor wickedness so wicked as not to find followers. These new doctrines Paul reprehended in many other places, and touching the subject of our present inquiry, let us examine how he treated the matter during the time of his apostleship.

"Let every man abide in the same calling wherein he was called. Art thou called being a servant, (δοῦλος, *doulos*, *slave*,) care not for it; but if thou mayest be *made free*, use it rather. For he that is called in the Lord, being a servant, (δοῦλος, *doulos*, *slave*,) is the Lord's *freeman;* likewise, also, he that is called, being free, is Christ's *servant*, (δοῦλος, *doulos*, *slave*.) Ye are bought with a price; be ye not the servant (δοῦλος, *doulos*, *slave*) of men. Brethren, let every man, wherein he is called, therein abide with God." 1 *Cor.* vii. 20–24. And this is consistent with his introduction to the subject in the 17th verse: "But as God hath distributed to every man, as the Lord hath called every one, so let him walk, and so ordain I in all churches." Compare this with his instruction to *Titus:* "Exhort servants (δούλους, *doulous*, *slaves*,) to be obedient unto their own masters, and to please them well in all things. Not answering again, not purloining, but showing all good fidelity; that they may adorn the doctrine of God our Saviour in all things.

For the grace of God that bringeth salvation hath appeared to all men, teaching us that, denying ungodliness and worldly lusts, we should live soberly, righteously, and godly in this present world; looking for that blessed hope, and the glorious appearing of the great God, and our Saviour Jesus Christ; who gave himself for us, that he might redeem us from all iniquity, and purify unto himself a peculiar people, zealous of good works. These things speak, and exhort, and rebuke with all authority. Let no man despise thee." *Titus* ii. 9–15.

And to the *Colossians:* "Servants, (*δοῦλοι, douloi, slaves,*) obey in all things your masters according to the flesh; not with eye-service, as men-pleasers; but in singleness of heart, fearing God: and whatsoever ye do, do it heartily, as to the Lord, and not unto men; knowing that of the Lord ye shall receive the reward of the inheritance: for ye serve (*δουλεύετε, douleuete, ye slave yourselves to*) the Lord Christ. But he that doeth wrong shall receive for the wrong which he hath done: and there is no respect of persons. Masters, give unto your servants (*δούλοις, doulois, slaves*) that which is just and equal; knowing that ye also have a Master in heaven." *Col.* iii. 22, 25; iv. 1.

And to the Ephesians: "Servants, (*δοῦλοι, douloi, slaves,*) be obedient to them that are your masters according to the flesh, with fear and trembling, in singleness of your heart, as unto Christ; not with eye-*service* (*ὀφθαλμοδουλείαν, ophthalmodouleian, slavery to the eye*) as men-pleasers; but as the servants (*δοῦλοι, douloi, slaves*) of Christ, doing the will of God from the heart; with good-will doing service (*δουλεύοντες, douleuontes, slaving yourselves*) as to the Lord, and not to men; knowing that whatsoever good thing any man doeth, the same shall he receive of the Lord, whether he be *bond* (*δοῦλος, doulos, slave*) or *free* (*ἐλεύθερος, eleutheros, a freeman*). And ye masters, do the same things unto them, forbearing threatening: knowing that your Master is also in heaven, neither is there respect of persons with him." *Eph.* vi. 5–9.

And, finally, to Timothy: "Let as many servants (*δοῦλοι, douloi, slaves*) as are under the yoke count their own masters worthy of all honour, that the name of God and his doctrine be not *blasphemed.* And they that have believing masters, let them not despise them because they are brethren; but rather do them service, (*δουλευέτωσαν, do them slave-labour,*) because they are faithful and beloved, partakers of the benefit. These things teach and exhort. If any man teach otherwise, and consent not to wholesome words, even the words of our Lord Jesus Christ, and to the doctrine which is according to godliness, he is proud, knowing nothing, but doting about questions and strifes of words, whereof cometh envy, strife, railings, evil surmisings, perverse disputings of men of corrupt minds, and destitute of the truth, supposing that gain is godliness: from such withdraw thyself. But godliness with contentment is great gain. For we brought nothing into this world, and it is certain we can carry nothing out. And having food and raiment, let us be therewith content. But they that will be rich fall into temptation and a snare, and into many foolish and hurtful lusts, which drown men in destruction and perdition. For the love of money is the root of all evil: which while some coveted after, they have erred from the faith, and pierced themselves through with many sorrows. But thou, O man of God, flee these things; and follow after righteousness, godliness, faith, love, patience, meekness. Fight the good fight of faith, lay hold on eternal life, whereunto thou art also called, and hast professed a good profession before many witnesses. I give thee charge in the sight of God, who quickeneth all things, and before Christ Jesus, who before Pontius Pilate witnessed a good confession, that thou keep this commandment without spot, unrebukable, until the appearing of our Lord Jesus Christ." 1 *Tim.* vi. 1–14.

From the arguments here presented to Timothy in support of the doctrine which Paul invariably taught in relation to slavery, we may well suppose he felt a deep interest, even anxiety, to prevent these new doctrines from affecting Timothy's mind in their favour; and we cannot but notice, that while, with the dignified authority of an apostolic teacher, his instructions are full, distinct, and certain, yet they are accompanied with a courteousness of explanation consolatory even to the slave, the subject of them, and with a solemnity of attestation that fathoms the very foundation of the Christian faith.

LESSON XIV.

Jesus Christ announced to the Jews that whosoever committeth sin is the servant (δοῦλος, *doulos, slave*) of sin; that the servant (δοῦλος, *doulos, slave*) abideth not in the house for ever, but the son abideth ever, &c.; therefore, if the son make them free, they shall be free indeed, &c. Of the doctrine here inculcated by the Saviour himself, it seems to us St. Paul has given a full and happy illustration; and, by his using the institution of slavery as a principal medium of his illustration, and by referring to facts well-known in the history of the institution of slavery, has not only recognised its existence, but also that it existed in conformity with the ordinances of God: and we deem his illustration not the less valuable, because it explains what is meant by, and how we are to understand, the Christian equality of all in that church. In addition to what we have already read from his writings, we may also notice, "Is the law then against the promises of God? God forbid; for if there had been a law given which could have given life, verily righteousness should have come by the law. But the scripture hath concluded all under sin, that the promise by faith of Jesus Christ might be given to them that believe. But before faith came, we were kept under the law, shut up unto the faith which should afterwards be revealed. Wherefore the law was our schoolmaster to bring us unto Christ, that we might be justified by faith. But after that faith is come, we are no longer under a schoolmaster. For ye are all the children of God by faith in Christ Jesus. For as many of you as have been baptized into Christ, have put on Christ. There is neither Jew nor Greek, there is neither bond (δοῦλος, *doulos, slave*) nor free, there is neither male nor female: for ye are all one in Christ Jesus. And if ye be Christ's, then are ye Abraham's seed, and heirs according to the promise." *Gal.* iii. 21–29.

"Now I say, that the heir, as long as he is a child, differeth nothing from a servant, (δοῦλος, *doulos, slave*) though he be lord of all; but is under tutors and governors until the time appointed of the father. Even so we, when we were children, were in bondage (δεδουλωμένοι, *dedoulomenoi, a state of slavery*) under the elements of the world. But when the fulness of the *time* was come, God sent forth his Son, made of a woman, made under the law, to redeem them that were under the law, that we might receive the adoption of sons. And because ye are sons, God hath sent forth the Spirit of his Son into your hearts, crying, Abba, Father. Wherefore thou art no more a servant, (*δοῦλος, doulos, slave,*) but a son; and if a son, then an heir of God through Christ. Howbeit then, when ye knew not God, ye did service (*ἐδουλεύσατε, edouleusate, did slave yourselves*) unto them which by nature are no gods. But now, after that ye have known God, or rather are known of God, how turn ye again to the weak and beggarly elements, whereunto ye desire again to be in bondage?" (*δουλεύειν, douleuein, to be in slavery.*) *Gal.* iv. 1–9.

"Tell me, ye that desire to be under the law, do ye not hear the law? For it is written, that Abraham had two sons; the one by a bond-maid, (*παιδίσκης, paidiskes, a favourite female slave,*) and the other by a free-woman. But he who was of the bond-woman (*παιδίσκης, paidiskes, a favourite female slave*) was born after the flesh, but he of the free-woman was by promise. Which things are an allegory: for these are the two covenants; the one from the mount Sinai in Arabia, which gendereth to bondage, (*δουλείαν, douleian, slavery,*) which is Agar. For this Agar is mount Sinai in Arabia, and answereth to Jerusalem which now is, and is in bondage (*δουλεύει, douleuei, slavery*) with her children. But Jerusalem which is above is free, which is the mother of us all." *Gal.* iv. 21–26.

"Now we, brethren, as Isaac was, are the children of promise. But as then he that was born after the flesh persecuted him that was born after the Spirit, even so it is now. Nevertheless, what saith the scripture? Cast out the bond-woman (*παιδίσκην, paidisken, favourite female slave*) and her son: for the son of the bond-woman (*παιδίσκης, paidiskes, favourite female slave*) shall not be heir with the son of the free-woman. So then, brethren, we are not children of the bond-woman, (*παιδίσκης, paidiskes, favourite female slave,*) but of the free. Stand fast therefore in the liberty wherewith Christ hath made us free, and be not entangled again with the yoke of bondage," (*δουλείας, douleias, slavery.*) *Gal.* iv. 29–31, v. 1.

In these lessons of Paul we not only find the Greek use of the word "doulos," but we find also the doctrine that slavery is the quotient of sin. It is true he often uses the word figuratively to illustrate the devotion and obedience of the humble followers of Jesus Christ; but in him who spurns obedience to the laws of God, and rejects the faith of the gospel, the character is fixed and permanent, as is the course of conduct that gives it.

While in this portion of our present Study, we desire to bring to mind the word *doulos* and its cognates, as used in the ancient Greek Scriptures, with the design that it may be easily compared with its use by the classical authors in that language. We shall be happy if successful in the attempt to present it in such form that the mind may acknowledge the doctrine inculcated to be consistent with the justice of Divine providence and the mercy of a redeeming love; that the deduction shall be evident; that slavery is a creation of Divine justice upon the model of mercy, every way adapted to benefit the most degenerate and wicked races of mankind; and that its whole action manifests the principle, that he whom the Father loveth, him he chasteneth;—and such, indeed, is the object of our entire study.

LESSON XV.

From the writings of St. Paul, we deem the deduction clear, that he considered slavery to be a consequent of sin, and plainly set it forth in his address to the Romans. "Wherefore as by one man sin entered into the world, and death by sin, and so death passed upon all men, for that all have sinned. For until (ἄχρι, *achri*, *as far as*—see Iliad, xvii. 599) the law, sin was in the world: but sin is not imputed where there is no law. Nevertheless, death reigned from Adam to Moses, even over them that had not sinned after the similitude of Adam's transgression, who is the figure of him that was to come." *Rom.* v. 12–24.

"Know ye not, that to whom ye yield yourselves servants (δούλους, *doulous*, slaves) to obey, his servants (δοῦλοι, *douloi*, slaves) ye are to whom ye obey; whether of sin unto death, or of obedience unto righteousness? But God be thanked, that ye were the servants (δοῦλοι, *douloi*, slaves) of sin, but ye have obeyed from the heart that form of doctrine which was delivered you. Being then made free from sin, ye became the servants (ἐδουλώθητε, *edoulothete*, ye enslaved yourselves) to righteousness unto holiness. For when ye were the servants (δοῦλοι, *douloi*, slaves) of sin, ye were free from righteousness. What fruit had ye then, in those things whereof ye are now ashamed? for the end of those things is death. But now, being free from sin, and become servants (δουλωθέντες, *doulothentes*, slaving yourselves) to God, ye have fruit unto holiness, and in the end everlasting life. For the wages of sin is death: but the gift of God is eternal life, through Jesus Christ our Lord." *Rom.* vi. 16–23.

"For as many as are led by the Spirit of God, they are the sons of God. For ye have not received the spirit of bondage (δουλείας, *douleias*, slavery) again to fear, but ye have received the spirit of adoption, whereby we cry, Abba, Father. The Spirit itself beareth witness with our spirit, that we are the children of God; and if children, then heirs: heirs of God, and joint heirs with Christ: if so be that we suffer with him, that we may be also glorified together. For I reckon, that the sufferings of this present time are not worthy to be compared with the glory which shall be revealed in us. For the earnest expectation of the creature waiteth for the manifestation of the sons of God. For the creature was made subject to vanity, not willingly, but by reason of him who hath subjected the same in hope. Because the creature itself also shall be delivered from the bondage (δουλείας, *douleias*, slavery) of corruption, into the glorious liberty of the children of God. For we know that the whole creation groaneth and travaileth in pain together until now: and not only they, but ourselves also, which have the firstfruits of the Spirit, even we ourselves groan within ourselves, waiting for the adoption, to wit, the redemption of our body." *Rom.* viii. 14–23. "So then, with the mind I myself serve (δουλεύω, *douleuo*, slave myself to) the law of God, but with the flesh the law of sin." *Rom.* vii. 25. "For they that are such serve (δουλεύουσιν, *douleuousin*, slave themselves to) not our Lord Jesus Christ, but their own belly." *Rom.* xvi. 18.

The word "doulos" is used by Peter in a similar manner: "For so is the will of God, that with well-doing ye may put to silence the ignorance of foolish men: as free, not using your liberty for a cloak of maliciousness, but as the servants of God," (δοῦλοι, *douloi*, slaves.) Idem: "While they promise them liberty, they themselves are the servants, (δοῦλοι, *douloi*, slaves) of corruption: for of whom a man is overcome, of the same is he brought in bondage," (δεδούλωται, *dedoulotai*, is he enslaved.)

Further instances of the use of the word "doulos" in the original Greek Scriptures will be found as follows:—"But I keep under my body and bring it into subjection, (δουλαγωγῶ, *doulagogo*, and guide it as in slavery,) lest that by any means when I have preached to others, I myself should be a castaway." 1 *Cor.* ix. 27. "For by one Spirit we are all baptized into one body, whether we are Jews or Gentiles, whether we are bond (δοῦλοι, *douloi*, slaves) or free, and have been all made to drink into one spirit." 1 *Cor.* xii. 13. "Where there is neither Greek nor Jew, circumcision nor uncircumcision, barbarian, Scythian, bond (δοῦλος, *doulos*, slave) nor free." *Col.* iii. 11. "As ye also learned of Epaphras, our dear fellow-servant" (συνδούλου, *sundoulou*, fellow-slave.) *Col.* i. 7. "But if the unbelieving depart, let him depart; a brother or a sister is not under bondage (δεδούλωται, *dedoulotai*, is enslaved) in such cases." 1 *Cor.* vii. 15. "For ye suffer if a man bring you into bondage," (καταδουλοῖ, *katadouloi*, reduce you to slavery,) &c. 2 *Cor.* xi. 20. "For he that in these things serveth (δουλεύσει, *douleusei*, shall slave himself to) Christ is acceptable to God and approved of men." *Rom.* xiv. 18. "It was said unto her, the elder shall serve (δουλεύσει, shall *slave* himself to) the younger; for it is written, Jacob have I loved, but Esau have I hated." *Rom.* ix. 12, 13. "And behold, one of them which were with Jesus, stretched out his hand, and drew his sword, and struck a servant (δοῦλον, *doulon*, slave) of the high-priest, and smote off his ear." *Matt.* xxvi. 51. "And one of them that stood by drew his sword, and smote a servant (δοῦλον, *doulon*, slave,) of the high-priest, and cut off his ear." *Mark* xiv. 47. "And one of them smote a servant (δοῦλον, *doulon*, slave) of the high-priest, and cut off his right ear." *Luke* xxii. 50. "Then Simon Peter, having a sword, drew it, and smote the high-priest's servant (δοῦλον, *doulon*, slave,) and cut off his right ear. The servant's (δούλῳ, *doulo*, slave) name was Malchus." "One of the servants (δούλων, *doulon*, slaves) of the high-priest (being his kinsman whose ear Peter cut off) saith, Did not I see thee in the garden with him?" *John* xviii. 10, 26. "And the servants (δοῦλοι, *douloi*, slaves) and officers stood there, who had made a fire of coals, (for it was cold,) and they warmed themselves: and Peter stood with them and warmed himself." *John* xviii. 18.

There are several instances where the word is used figuratively, as a submissive epithet, as an example of which we cite *Acts* iv. 29: "And now, Lord, behold their threatenings, and grant unto thy servants (δούλοις, *doulois*, slaves) that with all boldness they may speak thy word." "And God spake on this wise, That his seed should sojourn in a strange land; and that they should bring them into bondage, (δουλώσουσιν, *doulosousin*, should enslave them,) and entreat them evil four hundred years. And the nation to whom they shall be in bondage (δουλεύσωσι, *douleusosi*, to whom they shall be enslaved) will I judge, said God." *Acts* vii. 6, 7. "Not now as a servant (δοῦλον, *doulon*, slave,) but above a servant, (δοῦλον, *doulon*, slave,) a brother beloved," &c. *Philem.* 16. "Lord, now lettest thou thy servant (δοῦλον, *doulon*, slave) depart in peace." *Luke* ii. 29.

LESSON XVI.

The English words *servant, to serve, service, servile, servilely, serving*, &c. have descended into the language from the Latin word *servus*, a slave, and these words, when first introduced into the language, as distinctly carried with them the idea of slavery as does now our present term, and will continue to do so wherever the English language and slavery prevail. In no slave-holding country will the word servant be applied to a freeman as a legitimate term of description, but in non-slaveholding communities these words are sometimes used in a somewhat different sense, yet erroneously, because they are then used without adherence to their derivation and analogy. These words, when found in the received translation of the Christian Scriptures, are in the most of instances translated from some Greek word that signified or included the idea slavery. But notwithstanding the obvious error in giving the word *servant*, &c. as the translation of a word that did not carry with it the idea which was in unison with the original of these words, yet we find some few instances of such error. We give a few examples.

"Jesus answered, My kingdom is not of this world: if my kingdom were of this world, then would my *servants* fight." *John* xviii. 36.

Here *servants* is translated from ὑπηρέται, *huperetai*, and signifies a subordinate. In English it sometimes requires attendants, assistants, inferior officers, &c., but never associates with the idea of slavery.

"Peter followed him afar off unto the high-priest's palace, and he sat with the *servants*, (ὑπηρετῶν, *attendants*, &c.,) and warmed himself at the fire." *Mark* xiv. 54. "And the servants (δοῦλοι, *douloi*, *slaves*) and officers (ὑπηρέται, *huperetai*, *attendants*, *inferior officers*, &c.) stood there, who had made a fire of coals, (for it was cold,) and they warmed themselves." *John* xviii. 18.

That the word here used never conjugates with the idea slavery, we quote it as used in *Luke* iv. 20, in proof: "And he closed the book, and he gave it again to the minister," (ὑπηρέτῃ *huperete*, *attendant*, *inferior officer*, &c.) Also, *Acts* xxvi. 16: "But rise and stand upon thy feet: for I have appeared unto thee for this purpose, to make thee a *minister* (ὑπηρέτην, *hupereten*, *attendant*, *assistant*, *minister*, &c.) and a *witness* both of those things which thou hast seen and of those things in the which I will appear unto thee."

Here the requisites of the character required are totally incompatible with the character of the *doulos*, proving with the greatest certainty that these two words have no analogy whatever. For we may well here remark, that human learning has never arrived at a more nicely distinct and definite perfection in the use of language than is even now manifest in the sayings of Him "who spoke as never man spake."

Besides, in the case of *John* xviii. 18, servants, *douloi*, and officers ὑπηρέται, *huperetai*, being used consecutively and coupled together by a conjunction, is a strong proof that the idea appropriated here severally to these terms could not be expressed by either term alternately by substitution, and that these terms were by no analogy synonymous.

The word *servant* has also in error been rendered from other terms: see Hebrews iii. 5: "And Moses verily was faithful in all his house as a *servant*," (θεράπων, *therapon*.) We have not in English any single term that fully expresses the idea conveyed by this. It means an associate or companion who is voluntarily under the direction of one whom he takes and acknowledges to be his superior. The old Roman *umbra*, when applied to an attendant, conveyed the idea more exactly than any one term of ours. Thus, the warrior was called the *therapon* of Mars, and of the muses and kings of the gods generally. Thus, Menelaus is called the *therapon* of his chief, &c. &c. (See *Iliad*, viii. 113, xviii. 244, xix. 143.)

A similar error is occasionally found in the use of the terms *to serve, served, service*, &c., as if they were legitimately derived from some form of *doulos*. Thus, Luke ii. 37 : "But *served* God with fasting and prayers night and day,"—"served," λατρεύουσα, *latreuousa*, from *latreuo*. The more appropriate term is "to worship," &c.

The term was used by the Greeks, "to worship" the gods by sacrifices and offerings. (See *Euripides, Electra*, 131; *Iphagenia in Tauris*, 1115.) So in *Acts* vii. 7 : "And after that shall they come forth and *serve* me in this place,"—"serve," λατρεύσουσι, *latreusousi*. It should have been, "and worship me in this place." *Rom.* ix. 4 : "And the *service* of God, and the promises," λατρεία, *latreia*, worship, &c. So also *Heb.* ix. 1 : "Then verily the first covenant had also ordinances of divine service," λατρείας, *latreias*, worship. So also *Heb.* xiii. 10 : "We have an altar whereof they have no right to eat which *serve* the tabernacle,"—"serve," λατρεύοντες, *latreuontes*, who are worshipping in the, &c. &c.

Διάκονος, *diakonos*, is also sometimes erroneously translated *servant, service, to serve*, &c. An instance occurs, *John* ii. 5 : "And his mother saith unto the *servants*," διακόνοις, *diakonois*, from *diakonos:* as a verb, it means to minister unto, to wait upon, to manage affairs, to perform some function to another ; and hence, in English, we may occasionally require some other term of cognate meaning. From this term our word "deacon" has been legitimately derived. The word is of less elevated import in Greek than *therapon* (see Aristophanes, *Ornithes*, line 1322, ὡς βλαχικῶς διακονεῖς,) but never consorts in the least degree with the idea slavery. "Saith unto" them who ministered, who waited upon the guests, &c. So also *John* ii. 9 : "But the *servants* which drew the water knew,"—servants, διάκονοι, *diakonoi*, "they who ministered unto." See also *Rom.* xvi. 1 : "I commend unto you Phebe our sister, which is a *servant* of the church," &c., διάκονον, *diakonon*, *one who ministers unto*, &c. So also *John* xii. 26 : "If any man *serve*," διακονῇ, *diakone*, wait upon, minister unto me. "And where I am there shall my *servant* be," διάκονος, *diakonos*, one who waits upon, who ministers unto ; "him will my Father honour." It is not always in English easy to select a phrase distinctly the best adapted to express the precise difference between the words *diakonos* and *huperetes*, but it may be remarked that the *huperetes* was of an employment more of public character: hence those who in the ships held certain banks of oars were called by that name; also those of a particular rank in the army, or in civil government; but the word *diakonos* was used as a term more applicable to domestic, personal, or private life. Keeping this distinction in mind, the same word may often, in English, give the sense of either; yet *huperetes* will often appear in Greek where *diakonos* would be ill used. A more correct use of this word than the preceding will be found in *Matt.* iv. 11: "Then the devil leaveth him, and behold, angels came and *ministered* unto him," *διηκόνουν, diekonoun*, ministered unto, attended to.

Matt. xx. 26: "But whosoever will be great among you, let him be your *minister*," *διάκονος, diakonos*, minister, &c. And here is shown the distinction between this word and *doulos*, a slave; for he proceeds, "And whosoever will be chief among you, let him be your *servant*," *δοῦλος, doulos*, slave. Also, *Luke* viii. 3: "And Joanna the wife of Chuza, Herod's steward, and Susanna, and many others which ministered unto him of their substance," *διηκόνουν, diekonoun*, ministered, &c. We have deemed it proper to notice these inaccuracies in our translation, to prevent the word *servant*, &c., when used to mean *slave*, &c., being confounded with its use when given in translation as above; and it may be proper also to notice that the *hired* labourer, a freeman *hired* into the employ of another, is never described by any term implying *slavery*, or even having any analogy with it, as examples will show:

"For the kingdom of heaven is like a man that is a householder, which went out early in the morning to *hire labourers* (*μισθώσασθαι ἐργάτας, misthosasthai ergatas*, to hire labourers) into his vineyard." "They say unto him, Because no man hath hired us," (*ἐμισθώσατο, emisthosato*, hath hired.) "So when the evening was come, the Lord of the vineyard saith unto his steward, call the labourers and give them *their hire*," *μισθὸν, misthon*, wages, &c. "And when they had received it, they murmured against the good man of the house." *Matt.* xx. 1, 7, 8, 11. "And when he came to himself, he said, How many *hired servants* (*μίσθιοι, misthioi*, hired persons) of my father's have bread," &c. *Luke* xv. 17. "But he that is a hireling, (*μισθωτὸς, misthotos*, a person hired,) and not the shepherd, whose own the sheep are not, seeth the wolf, &c. and the wolf catcheth them and scattereth the sheep. The *hireling* (μισθωτὸς, *misthotos*, a person hired) fleeth because he is a *hireling* (μισθωτὸς, *misthotos*, a person hired,) and careth not for the sheep." *John* x. 12, 13. "For the labourer is worthy of his *hire*," τοῦ μισθοῦ, hire, wages, payment, &c. *Luke* x. 7. "Behold, the hire (ὁ μισθὸς, payment for being hired) of the labourers (τῶν ἐργατῶν, *ton ergaton*, the labourers, not slaves) who have reaped down your fields." *James* v. 4.

He who is seeking to obtain a correct view of the truth will perceive the propriety of keeping in mind the distinction between the different characters thus in our version called by the same name, "*servants*," and not suffer his mind to be governed, or even influenced, by any bias which has been produced by an incomplete examination of the whole gospel of God.

Study VIII.

LESSON I.

THE Hebrew letters ע ain, ב beth, and ד daleth, compose the words by which the Hebrews meant what we mean by the word slave. There is some variation among men of letters, even among the Jews themselves, as to the pronunciation of this word, some following the Asiatic, some the Portuguese, and some the Polish method.

Out of respect and in deference to King James's translators of the Old Testament, of the learned and critical Dr. Blany, and of that indefatigable biblical scholar, Dr. Bagster, we have adopted their pronunciation of this word, and call it *ebed.*

This word, as left untranslated by them, will be found in *Jer.* xxxviii. 7–12; also xxxix. 16, 17, thus:—"Now, when Ebed-melech the Ethiopian, one of the eunuchs which was in the king's house." "Ebed-melech went forth out the king's house." "When the king commanded Ebed-melech the Ethiopian." "So Ebed-melech took the man with him." "And Ebed-melech the Ethiopian said to Jeremiah." "Go, speak to Ebed-melech the Ethiopian." The words Ebed-melech are here left untranslated, because we have not, in English, words to express the idea conveyed by them, except by paraphrasis, as, for instance, they would have had to have said, his majesty's private, or principal, and confidential body-servant: and this is the exact meaning implied by the words Ebed-melech, as here used: the word servant, meaning a slave. In *Judges* ix. 26, 28, 30, 31, 35, the word Ebed is also left untranslated. Also in *Ezra* viii. 6: "Ebed, the son of Jonathan." And in some other places.

We trust that our authority for the pronunciation of the word עֶבֶד *ebed*, will be deemed sufficient: yet, we admit that, in Hebrew pronunciation, it will be varied by suffix, affix, and points, as has been found by the learned rabbis long since to but agree with their rules of cantation and the idiomatic construction of the language.

This word *ebed* is used as a *noun*, *verb*, *adjective*, participle, and adverb; but we make the proposition, that, however used, and in whatever form, it is never used disconnected from the idea of slavery. Philological history will develop to us, at least, one human weakness:—pride to be thought learned, has more or less, among the European nations and languages, had its effect in the compilation of dictionaries.

In some instances, men of learning have undertaken their compilation without using their ability to fathom the depths of language, or to discover the sources of its streams, or describe the qualities of their combinations. And the world is full of servile imitations of former and old errors; and each one seems to think that the authority of a book warrants their perpetuation.

But there will occasionally arise, in the walks of knowledge, some Moses, some Confucius, some Homer, some Euclid, some Socrates, some Bacon, some Newton, some Franklin, some Champollion, before the fire of whose genius and mental power, all imitations of error wither away.

Touching the subject of the Asiatic languages generally, and the darkness that has for ages overspread them, may we not fondly hope that such a luminary is now culminating in the region of the universities of England. Permit us, at least, to have some hope for the Regius Professor of Cambridge.

But to our subject:—We sometimes find the philologist yield his sceptre and borrow his definitions from a bad translation. And we often find the translator sacrificing his original upon the altar of his own imperfections. Now, it is not uncommon that a word in one language may be in such peculiar use, that, consistently with the constitution of some other language, it cannot be translated therein by any one single term; and even if so, not always by the same word. Should all the different terms and words that might thus be legitimately used in translation, be collected together, and put down as the descriptive meaning of some foreign or ancient term, our lexicons would, of necessity, contain some portions of error. For example, suppose we take the Arabic word عَبْدٌ *abed*, which means absolutely a slave in that language: we all know that an Arabian, speaking or writing to one far his superior, would someway call himself by this term. He uses it to express great devotedness, honesty, and integrity of intentions to the one addressed. If we were composing an Arabic lexicon, what would the scholar have good reason to say, if we should put as the definition of this word,—honesty, integrity of intention, &c.? This Arabic word is the same as in Hebrew, and the word is used in both languages with great similarity: also in Chaldee, Syriac, and other Shimetic dialects.

While we premise that the Koran is taken as the standard of Arabic literature, we present this word, as used in that language, as a sample of its use in the other Shimetic dialects.

This word, as above, in Arabic, is composed of the letters *gain*, or *ain*, under point *jesm*, which is equivalent to the Hebrew *quiescent sheoa*, but really having the shortest possible trace of the sound of our short *ĕ*, and terminated by the letter *dhal*, or *dal*, under the diacritical sign of nunnation.

Mr. Sale, who had great experience in Arabic literature, has left this word frequently untranslated in his notes, quoting Beidawi and Iolalo'ddin, to his version of the Koran, and in Roman letters expressed it thus, *abda*, and, without annunation thus, *abd*. We confine ourselves to this particular *form* of the word. If, by long experience we supply the shortest possible trace of our vowel *ĕ* between the *b* and *d*, and in *annunation* cause the terminating vowel to coalesce in some trace of our consonant *n*, we should perhaps arrive at as correct a pronunciation as could be attained by mere rules and it will be seen that the *ebĕd* of Jerusalem became *abĕd* at Mecca.

We copy from Sale's translation, without burthening our page with a repetition of the original; our object is to show the precise idea for the expression of which the Arabians appropriated this word.

"God causeth some of you to excel in worldly possessions: yet, they who are caused to excel do not give their wealth unto the *slaves* whom their right hands possess, that they may become equal sharers therein." *Koran*, chap. 16.

Al Beidoive, an Arabian commentator on the Koran, upon this passage says—

"A reproof to the idolatrous Meccans, who could admit created beings to a share of the divine honour, though they suffered not their slaves to share with themselves in what God had bestowed on them."

The expression of a thing done, held, or "possessed by the right hand," in Arabic, is a full concession that the doing, holding, or possessing, is just, rightful, and righteous.

"God propoundeth, as a parable, a *possessed slave*, who hath power over nothing, and him on whom we have bestowed a good provision from us, and who giveth alms thereout, both secretly and openly; shall these two be esteemed equal? God forbid." *Koran*, chap. 16.

Of this, the above commentator says, "The idols, we have likened to a *slave*, who is so far from having any thing of his own, that he is himself in the possession of another." *Idem.*

"And this is the favour which thou hast bestowed on me, that thou hast enslaved the children of Israel." *Koran*, chap. 26.

"O prophet, we have allowed thee thy wives, unto whom thou hast given their dower, and also the *slaves* which thy right hand possesseth, of the booty which God hath granted to thee." *Koran*, chap. 33.

Yet, so it is, we find in our Hebrew lexicons, among the significations of this word עבד *ebed*, not only its true signification,—slave, slavery, &c.,—but also, *to labour*, *cultivate*, *labour generally*, *worship*, *to make*, *to do*, or *deal with any one*, *to take place* or *happen*, *work*, *business*, *tillage*, *cultivation of land*, *agriculture*, *implements*, *utensils*, *appurtenances*, *a worship of God* or *of idols*, *wearied*, *to be wearied with labour*, *complied with*, *assented to*, *performed*, *religious service*, *a submissive epithet*, *a minister*, *to minister unto*, *any one employed in the service of a king*, *any one who worships*, *adores God*, *one who is commissioned by him for any purpose*, *benefit*, *employment of any kind*.

But we will desist from increasing this catalogue of definitions, for fear of being charged with slander on the Hebrew lexicons. Must not that be a very strange language in which one little word of only three letters has so many varied and adverse meanings? Yet, in all sobriety, we might double the number. If each and every Hebrew word were like this, thus loaded with lexicographical learning, we beg to know who would undertake and what would be the use of its study; for surely, from the same page, there might be a very great number of adverse and contradictory translations, all equally correct. But, if such catalogue is not legitimate, to what cause are we to look for its existence? to some abiding influence, secret but persevering, in the minds of the lexicographers for the last thousand years? Or shall we rather confine our views to the casualities of hurried translations and bad readings, to the facility of the copyist in book-making, instead of the laborious study of the investigator?

This circumstance, from whatever cause it may have sprung, will impose on us some labour to show the correctness of our proposition, to wit, the word עֶבֶד *ebed*, however used, and in whatever form, is never used in Hebrew disconnected from the idea of slavery.

We first propose to show that the Hebrew is abundantly supplied with words to express all these other meanings, *disconnected* with the idea of slavery.

Aware that such examination may be extremely uninteresting to the most of us, yet, deeming it of great importance to our subject, we humbly ask indulgence, while we examine a few of the most leading *terms* as examples, whose significations have been appropriated to the word עֶבֶד *ebed.*

LESSON II.

But, before we enter into such examination, it may be proper to remark that the Hebrew, in common with all the Shemitic languages, makes abundant use of what we call rhetorical figures. The word בֵּן *ben* means a son; but by *prosopopœia* it is made to mean an *arrow*. Thus, *Lam.* iii. 13, "He hath caused the *arrows of his quiver*," בְּנֵי אַשְׁפָּתוֹ *beney, ashpatho*—literally, the *sons of his quiver*, from the notion that the arrow is the produce, issue, adjunct, &c. of the quiver. We might quote a great number of instances where the word בֵּן *ben*, by the same figure, is used to express some other idea than *son*, yet never unassociated with the primitive idea; but, what would be the value of the lexicographical assertion that this word in Hebrew meant an arrow? The following fifteen verses are wholly of the same character: "He hath filled me with bitterness, he hath made me drunk with wormwood."

The Arabians have a common way of expressing "*one of great affliction*," by saying that he is a "*wormwood beater*." Yet the Arabic word that means *affliction*, by no means is synonymous of *wormwood.*

The figure of Lamentations is also used in *Ps.* cxxvii. 4, 5: "As awards are in the hand of a mighty man, so are children of the youth. Happy *is* the *man* that hath his quiver full of them." Yet, the word אֶת־אַשְׁפָּתוֹ is in no sense a synonyme of whatever word for which it is here figuratively used. A singular instance of this figure is found in *Lam.* ii. 18: "Let not *the apple of thine eye* cease;" בַּת־עֵינֵךְ *bath eynek*, the *daughter of the eye.* The translators have understood this to mean the "*pupil*," otherwise called the apple of the eye; but, the word *bath*, *daughter*, shows that the thing meant is a *produce* of the eye; hence, it cannot mean the *apple* or *pupil* of the eye, but *tears*. But how stupid the page that shall put down as a signification of the word בַּת *bath*, an apple, or the apple of the eye, or the pupil, or yet, what it here means, a tear?

These two words *ben*, a *son*, and *bath*, a *daughter*, sometimes *beth*, are associated in so many different forms of figure and in connection or compound with other Hebrew words, to express some complex idea, that, if each different idea thus conveyed was to be considered a legitimate signification of these words, their description would be quite lengthy, and contradictory; for instance, *Gen.* xxiv. 16, בְּתוּלָה is used to mean a *virgin*. But, 1 *Sam.* i. 16, בַּת־בְּלִיַּעַל is used to mean quite a different character, as if of different origin. In *Eccl.* xii. 4, בְּנוֹת הַשִּׁיר is generally understood to mean the voice of an old man. But in *Dan.* xi. 17, בַּת הַנָּשִׁים is understood to mean a princess. We might multiply examples without number; yet, in all instances, the leading idea, a daughter, is ever present: other primitive words, whose signification was an idea of great and leading interest, will be found in similar use. And it may be remarked, that, at one age of the world, when a large proportion of the children of men were slaves, that the word signifying that condition would be naturally and exceedingly often used in a figurative manner. Even among us, our word *servant*, which, from use, has become merely a milder term to express the same idea, is in the mouth of every devout man, while *slave* is in constant use among the moral and political agitators of the day.

One among the causes of our finding in the lexicons so many and adverse significations of the word *ebed*, is the fact, that the Hebrew often expressed an adjective quality, by placing the substantive expressing the quality as if in apposition with the substantive qualified, thus, עֲבָדֶיךָ מְרַגְּלִים *they*, slaves (not) spies;

עֲבָדֶיךָ אַחִים *they slaves,* brethren, *Gen.* xlii. 11–13, לְעַבְדְּךָ לְאָבִינוּ *thy slave our father, Gen.* xliii. 28.

In an analagous sense the word אִישׁ is used in 2 *Kings* i. 9, 10, 11, 12, 13. Also iv. 25 and 27, preceding הָאֱלֹהִים a *man of God,* meaning one so wholly devoted to God as to partake of the divine nature. But such use in no manner changes the meaning of the word אִישׁ or אֱלֹהִים. This mode of expressing quality, by placing one of the substantives in the genitive, is quite common even in the modern languages. Grammarians will also inform us that substantives are often used adverbially, designating the time, place, and quality of the action of the verb.

But again, the Hebrew adjectives are in disproportional scarcity to the substantives, which the language remedies by a kind of circumlocution; this, אִישׁ דְּבָרִים *a man* (of) *words, i. e.* an eloquent man, as in *Ex.* iv. 10; *the son of strength* בֶּן־חַיִל *valiant* or *worthy man,* 1 *Kings* i. 52; בְּנֵי־קֶדֶם the sons of the East, *i. e.* the orientals, *Gen.* xxix. 1; בֶּן מָוֶת the son of death, *i. e.* doomed to death, 1 *Sam.* xx. 31; בַּתבְּלִי־עַל the daughter of baseness, *i. e.* a base woman, 1 *Sam.* i. 16.

This use of language is common to our word, *ebed, slave;* עֲבַד אֱלָהָא slaves of God, *i. e.* a man devoted to God, as a slave to a master, *i. e.* a man who most devotedly worships God, *Dan.* iii. 26; עֲבַד אֱלָהָא *slave of God, i. e.* devoted worshipper of God, &c., *Dan.* vi. 21, the 20th of the English text; and to express this adjective quality, is thus compounded in *Ezra* v. 11, עַבְדוֹהִי slaves of God, *i. e.*, devoted to God as slaves are to their masters, &c., to express the adjective qualities of devotion and obedience. This word is used and compounded with many other words in a great variety of instances.

But, doubtless, another cause which has led the lexicographers into the alleged error, is the peculiar disposition of the Hebrew, (common to all the Shemitic tongues) to express the idea intended, by expressing another to which it has a real or supposed analogy, either in primitive relation or in ultimate result. For example, let us take the word *ben,* a son, thus: *Isa.* v. 1, *keren,* have used to mean the top of a mountain, because they fancied an analogy between the top of a mountain and a *horn. Ben,* a son, *shamen,* fat, son of fatness, is here used to mean a fruitful mountain. But, do these words acquire new significations from this figurative use of them? The sons of the quiver, *i. e.* arrows. *Lem.* iii. 13. Shall we say that *ben*, means an arrow? *Ben kasheth*, the son of the bow, (*cannot make him flee*,) *i. e.* the arrow, *Job* xli. 20, (the 28th of the English text.) Shall we indeed then say that *ben* means an arrow? *Ben shahor*, the son of *blackness*, here used to express night,—*son of the night*,—used to convey our idea, the *morning star*. Shall we say that *ben* means a star? or, that *blackness* means the morning? *Isa.* xiv., 12 בֶּן יוֹנָה *ben yonah*, the *son of a dove*, *i. e.* a young dove, a squab? *Lev.* xii. 6. Shall we say that בֵּן *ben* means a squab? *Lev.* xii. 8, *beni yonah*, sons of a dove, *i. e.* two young doves or squabs. Shall we then, surely say that *beni* means two squabs? But, in *Lev.* xiv. 22, we have the same words used in the same sense: must we say that this word means squabs? בְּנֵי עֹרֵב *bene oreb*, *the sons of the raven*, *i. e.* young ravens, *Ps.* cxlvii. 9: does *beni* then mean young ravens also? בֶּן בָּקָר, *ben baker*, the son of an ox, *i. e.* a calf, *Ex.* xxix. 1. What, does *ben* mean a calf? *Num.* xxix. 2–8, *son* of an *ox*, also; *ben* the son of an ox—meaning a calf, does *ben* most surely mean a calf? *Job* xxxix. 16, speaking of ostrich-eggs, calls them, בָּנֶיהָ, the plural: what! does this word also mean ostrich-eggs? But, *Eccl.* ii. 7, *canithi*, I purchased, *ebadim*, male slaves, *shepaphath*, and female slaves, and *sons*, *bayith*, of my house, *haya*, there were, *li*, to me:—here בְּנֵי *bené* is used to express the idea "*home-born slaves.*" But, shall we say that this word means such young slaves? Would such a catalogue of significations placed to the word *ben*, a son, be legitimate or truthful?

But, in *Jer.* ii. 14, we again find this word *bayith*, preceded by *yelid*, *born of the house*, meaning a house-born slave. The same words are used to mean the same thing in *Gen.* xiv. 14, meaning *house-born slaves;* and again, *Gen.* xvii. 12, meaning a *house-born slave;* also, *idem.* 13, meaning a slave born in thy house—thy *house-born slave.*

God did not speak to Abraham in an unintelligible language: every one knew what the idea was, even down to this day. Yet, are either of these words a synonyme of *ebed*, a slave?

But we will close this portion of our remarks by stating that the lexicographers might, in the manner here pointed out, (which they have pursued to great extent,) have still increased their catalogue of significations to the word *ebed*.

Let us show an instance. It is well known that the ancient eastern nations punished great offenders by *cutting them in pieces*. The term expressing and threatening this punishment was used somewhat technically, as is now the term *to guillotine*, meaning *to cut off a man's head*. The term used by the ancients to express this *cutting in pieces*, as introduced in Hebrew, was, עֲבַד הַדָּמִין *abad haddamin*, which literally was "*to enslave in pieces*." The term is expressed thus in *Dan*. ii. 5: הַדָּמִין תִּתְעַבְדוּן *in pieces ye shall be enslaved*, *i. e.* "Ye shall be cut in pieces."

The lexicographers might have continued their catalogue with the same truthfulness with which they have extended it to such length, and have said that עבד *ebed* also meant to hew, to cut, &c., and have cited this instance in proof.

But in *Dan*. iii. 29, the term is used again thus הַדָּמִין יִתְעֲבֵד *in pieces shall be enslaved*, *i. e.* "shall be cut in pieces." Surely, they should have added, that *ebed* means *to cut*. It is true that the literal meaning of this term cannot always be given in English so as to be in pleasant accordance with our use of language.

But the same is true as to many other phrases and terms, and perhaps applicable to every other language. This form and use of this word as here used by Daniel, is rather a Persian adulteration than pure Hebrew, of which several instances may be found in some of the later books. The Babylonian and Persian kings considered even *all their* subjects as slaves to them, and this word was evidently used with greater latitude among them than it appears to have been among the Hebrews at the time of Moses.

LESSON III.

The lexicons seem tenacious that a very usual signification of the word עבד *ebed* is labour, both as a *noun* and *verb;* and inasmuch as to many there may seem some relation between the ideas *slavery* and *labour*, we wish to be particular in examining the Hebrew use of the terms expressive of these ideas. It appears to us that the Hebrew word יָגַע *yaga*, and its derivations, carries with it simply our idea of labour, more closely than any other word. Yet this word is never disconnected with the idea *fatigue* and *weariness*, and perhaps something of the same character will be perceived to be attached to our word *labour*. In *Gen.* xxxi. 42, it is used and translated, "the יְגִיעַ *labour* of my hands." *Deut.* xxv. 18, "and when thou wast faint and וְיָגֵעַ weary." *Josh.* vii. 3: "And make not all the people to תְּיַגַּע *labour* thither." xxiv. 13: "And I gave you a land for which you did not יָגַעְתָּ *labour*." 2 *Sam.* xvii. 2: "And I will come upon him while he is יָגֵעַ weary." *Neh.* v. 13: "So shall God shake out every man from his house and from his וּמִיגִיעוֹ labour." *Job* iii. 17: "And the יְגִיעֵי weary be at rest." ix. 29: "If I be wicked, why then אִיגָע labour I in vain." x. 13: * * "despised the יְגִיעַ work of thy hands * *." xxviii. 18: "That which he יָגָע laboured for shall he restore." xxxix. 11: * * "Wilt thou leave thy יְגִיעֶךָ labour to him." 16: * * * "her יְגִיעָהּ labour is in vain without fear?" *Ps.* lxix. 4: "They that *hate* me without a cause;" the idea is, they that labour to injure, &c. "And their וִיגִיעָם labour unto the locust." cix. 11: "let the stranger spoil his יְגִיעוֹ labour." cxxviii. 2: "For thou shalt eat the יְגִיעַ labour of thy hands." *Prov.* xxiii. 4: "תִּיגַע *labour* not to be rich." *Eccl.* xii. 12: "Much study is יְגִעַת weariness to the flesh." *Isa.* xliii. 22, 23, 24: "But thou hast been יָגַעְתָּ weary of me—nor הוֹגַעְתִּיךָ wearied thee with incense." "Thou hast הוֹגַעְתַּנִי wearied me with thine iniquities." xlv. 14: "The יְגִיעַ labour of Egypt." xlvii. 15:

"with whom thou hast יָגַעַתְּ *laboured.*" lv. 2: "And your וִיגִיעֲכֶם *labour* for that which satisfieth not." lxv. 23: "They shall not יִגְעוּ labour in vain." *Jer.* iii. 24: "For shame hath devoured the יְגִיעַ labour." xx. 5: "And all the יְגִיעָה labours thereof." xlv. 3: "I יָגַעְתִּי *fainted* in my sighing." The idea is, my sighing was a labour of great weariness, &c. *Ezek.* xxiii. 29: "And shall take away all thy יְגִיעֵךְ *labour.*" *Hag.* i. 11: "And upon all the יְגִיעַ labour of thy hands." *Mal.* ii. 17: "Ye have הוֹגַעְתֶּם wearied the Lord with your words, yet ye say, Wherein have we הוֹגַעֲנוּ wearied him?" *Eccl.* i. 8: "All things are full of יְגֵעִים labour." x. 15: "The (עָמָל *amal*) *labour* of the foolish (תְּיַגְּעֶנּוּ) *wearieth* every one of them." The word *labour* in this sentence is translated from *amal*, another Hebrew word, which signifies *labour*, but in its signification is implied the association of the idea *grief*, *sorrow*, &c. The adjective quality of this word is mental—in *yaga*, it is physical. This word *amal* seems to be derived from the Arabic عَمِلَ *amelan*, and from thence the Syriac ܥܡܠ, having nearly the same signification. In Arabic the signification is put down by Castell, *operator*, *mercenarius;* and in Syriac, *labore defessus.* It is used in Hebrew as follows: *Gen.* xli. 51: "And Joseph called the name of his first-born Manessa; for God, said he, hath made me forget all my עֲמָלִי toil," (*labour*, *sorrow.*) The word *manessa* means to forget, to cause to forget, &c. *Num.* xxiii. 21: "He hath not beheld עָמָל *iniquity* in Jacob," *i. e.* labour designed to give trouble, perplexity, or sorrow. *Deut.* xxvi. 7: "The Lord heard our voice and looked upon our affliction, and our עֲמָלֵנוּ labour and our oppression." *Judg.* v. 26: "And her right hand to the workman's (עֲמֵלִים *labourer's*) hammer." *Job* iii. 10: "Nor hid עָמָל sorrow from mine eyes." 20: "Wherefore is light given unto him that is in לְעָמֵל *misery.*" iv. 8: "They that plough iniquity and sow עָמָל *wickedness* shall reap the same." v. 7: "Yet man is born to לְעָמָל trouble." vii. 3: "So I am made to possess months of vanity, and עָמָל wearisome nights are appointed to me." xv. 35: "They conceive עָמָל mischief and bring forth vanity." xvi. 2: עָמָל "Miserable comforters are ye all." xx. 22: "In the fulness of his sufficiency he shall be in עָמֵל *straits.*" But it should be remembered that the Hebrew copy of Job is itself a translation. *Ps.* vii. 15: "He made a pit and digged it, and has fallen into the עָמָל *ditch* (sorrow bringing labour) which he made." 16: "His עֲמָלוֹ *mischiefs* shall return upon his own head." x. 7: "Under his tongue is עָמָל mischief and vanity." 14: "Thou beholdest עָמָל *mischief* and spite." xxv. 18: "Look upon mine affliction and my וַעֲמָלִי pain, and forgive my sin." "Yet is their strength עָמָל *labour* and *sorrow.*" cv. 44: "And they inherit the וַעֲמַל *labour* of the people." cxxvii. 1: "Except the Lord build the house, they *labour* in vain." *Prov.* xvi. 26: "He that עָמֵלוֹ *laboureth* עָמֵל עָמְלָה *laboureth* for himself." *Isa.* liii. 11: "He shall see of the מֵעֲמַל *travail* of his soul," (labour producing sorrow, &c.) "And that write עָמָל grievousness which they have prescribed," (a labour producing sorrow, &c.) *Jonah* iv. 10: "Thou hast had pity on the gourd for which thou hast not עָמַלְתָּ *laboured.*" *Eccl.* i. 3: "What profit hath a man of all his עֲמָלוֹ *labour* which he taketh under the sun?" ii. 10: "For my heart rejoiced in all my עֲמָלִי *labour.*" 11: "And then I looked on all the work that my hands had wrought, and on all the וּבֶעָמָל *labour* that I had שֶׁעָמַלְתִּי *laboured.*" 18: "Yea, I hated all my עֲמָלִי *labour* which I had עָמֵל *taken* (laboured) under the sun." 19: "Yet shall he have rule over all my עֲמָלִי *labour* wherein I have שֶׁעָמַלְתִּי *laboured.*" 20: "Therefore I went about to cause my heart to despair of all the הֶעָמָל *labour* which I שֶׁעָמַלְתִּי took (laboured) under the sun." 21: "For there is a man whose שֶׁעֲמָלוֹ *labour* is in wisdom, and in knowledge, and in equity—yet to a man that hath not עָמַל *laboured* herein shall he leave it for his portion." 22: "For what hath man of all his עֲמָלוֹ *labour* and of the vexation of his heart, wherein he hath עָמֵל *laboured* under the sun?" iv. 4: "Again I considered all עָמָל *travail*," (labour and sorrow.) 8: "Yet there is no end to all his עֲמָלוֹ *labour*, neither saith he, For whom do I עָמֵל *labour*." iii. 9: "What profit hath he that worketh in that wherein he עָמֵל *laboureth?*" v. 18: "And to enjoy the good of all his בַּעֲמָלוֹ *labour*." vi. 7: "All the עֲמַל *labour* of a man is for his mouth." ix. 9: "For that is thy portion in this life and in thy וּבַעֲמָלְךָ *labour*." x. 15: "The עֲמַל *labour* (*amal*) of the foolish תְּיַגְּעֶנּוּ *wearieth* every one of them."

מְלָאכָה *melahkah* is also quite analogous in its signification to our word *labour*, insomuch that our word *labour* may be often used in translation without impairing the sense. *Gen.* ii. 2: "On the seventh day God ended his work," מְלַאכְתּוֹ *labour*. xxxix. 11: "Joseph went into the house to do his *business*," (labour.) *Exod.* xx. 9: "And do all thy *work*," מְלַאכְתֶּךָ. 10: "In it thou shalt not do any *work*," (labour, מְלָאכָה.) xxxi. 3: "All manner of *workmanship*," מְלָאכָה. 14: "For whosoever doeth any *work*," מְלָאכָה. 15: "Six days may *work* מְלָאכָה be done." *Lev.* xiii. 48: "Of any thing *made* מְלֶאכֶת of skin," (done, laboured, manufactured.) *Ezra* iii. 8: "To set forward the *work* of the house." 9: "To set forward the workman," הַמְּלָאכָה. *Esther* iii. 9: "And those that have charge of the king's *business*," הַמְּלָאכָה. ix. 3: "And officers הַמְּלָאכָה of the king."

Without multiplying examples, it may suffice to say, that this word, as expressive of *labour*, is ever associated with the idea of particularity, or class of *labour*, *business*, *employment* or *job*, without reference to any other adjective quality; and hence it came to mean a message, or one charged with a message, and is therefore sometimes used to mean an angel, because they were supposed to be messengers, charged to do a particular labour; hence, also, applied to a prophet; and hence, also, the prophet Malachi's name.

עָשָׂה *Asa* properly means work or labour, as the result of *making*, *procreating*, *producing*, *doing*, *acting*, or *performing*, without any regard to the condition of the agent or actor. *Gen.* i. 7: "God *made* וַיַּעַשׂ the firmament." 16: "God *made* וַיַּעַשׂ two great lights." ii. 2: "God ended his *work* מְלַאכְתּוֹ which he had *made*," עָשָׂה. This word is also used to express the *result* of labour in acquiring slaves and other property generally, as in *Gen.* xii. 5: "All their substance that they had gathered, and the souls they had gotten in Haran," *i. e.* all the property and slaves that they had *laboured* for, &c. עָשׂוּ. *Exod.* xxxi. 4: "To work in gold and silver." 5: It is used with *malabkah*, thus: "to *work* לַעֲשׂוֹת in all manner of workmanship," (מְלָאכָה malakah.) These two words occur together again in *Neh.* iv. 15, the iv. 21 of the English text: "So *we laboured* עֹשִׂים *in the work*," בַּמְּלָאכָה. *Ezek.* xxix. 20: "I have given him the land of Egypt for his *labour*," עָשׂוּ. *Exod.* xxx. 25: "And thou shalt make it (וְעָשִׂיתָ labour it) an oil of holy ointment, an ointment composed after the art of the apothecary." Art is here translated from מַעֲשֵׂה *maase*, which is another word of very similar import, and is derived from עָשָׂה, and expresses the idea of labour, as of a *thing done*, or *wrought*, a *work*, *deed*, *action*, *concern*, *business*, *i. e.* a labour emanating from a habit, or an occupation of business. *Gen.* xliv. 15: "*What deed* הַמַּעֲשֶׂה is this that ye have done?" xlvii. 3: "What is your *occupation?*" מַּעֲשֵׂיכֶם. *Exod.*

xxiii. 16: "And the feast of the harvest, the firstfruits of thy *labours* מַעֲשֶׂיךָ, which thou hast sown in the field, and the first of the ingathering, which is the end of the year, when thou hast gathered in thy *labours*," מַעֲשֶׂיךָ. *Hag.* ii. 17: "And I smote you with blasting and with hail in all the *labours* מַעֲשֵׂה of your hands." *Hab.* iii. 17: "Although the fig-tree shall not blossom, neither shall fruit be in the vine, the *labour* מַעֲשֵׂה of the olive shall fail."

סֵבֶל *sebel* is sometimes translated *labour*, but it more often means something consequent to labour, as the burthen of *labour* is consequent to the labour: it is sometimes used to mean the produce of labour, and hence the Syrian Ephraimitish word סִבֹּלֶת *siboleth*, which is said to mean an ear of corn, because an ear of corn was the produce of labour. Hence, it is sometimes used to mean prolific and fruitful, because the produce of labour is *prolific and fruitful;* and because to sustain a burthen, as of labour, carries with it the idea of physical ability and strength, it is used in the sense of bearing up, to elevate, to deliver from, &c. A few instances of its use will suffice. *Exod.* i. 11: "To afflict them with their *burthens*," בְּסִבְלֹתָם. *Ps.* lxxxi. 70: "I delivered מִסֵּבֶל thee." cxliv. 14: "That our oxen may be strong to *labour*," מְסֻבָּלִים. The Hebrews had thus several ways by which they could express the idea *labour* accompanied with different adjective qualities. So the word עֶבֶד *ebed* may express the idea *labour;* but when so, it is always *slave-labour*, the labour peculiar to, or performed by a slave; as in *Isa.* xix. 9: "They that *work* עֹבְדֵי in fine flax." The meaning is, they that *labour* or slave themselves in fine flax. The working in fine flax was *slave-labour*. If it were good English for us to say, *they that slave in fine flax*, it would be exactly what the prophet did say in this passage. So in *Exod.* xx. 9: "Six days shalt thou *labour* and *do all thy work*." Here labour is translated from *ebed* תַּעֲבֹד, as a verb "*do*" is from וְעָשִׂיתָ and "*work*" from מְלַאכְתֶּךָ. The literal meaning of this is—Six days shalt thou slave and labour all thy work;—or, more plainly—Six days shalt thou slave thyself (*i. e.* do slave labour) and וְעָשִׂיתָ *labour*, or make all thy מְלַאכְתֶּךָ particular, accustomed, professional or usual work or labour. This command is addressed to all mankind, and the propriety of it, as here explained, will be seen in the succeeding verse. "But the seventh day is the Sabbath of the Lord thy God; in it thou shalt not do תַעֲשֶׂה *any work* כָל־מְלָאכָה thou nor thy son, nor thy daughter, nor thy man-servant, (עַבְדְּךָ *ebeddeka, slave.*)" So, then, if this particular word had not been used, we could not have said that the command applied to slaves.

But the Hebrews had a way of expressing the idea of labour alone, associated with the idea of industry as its adjective quality: Should I say, By your hands you shall be sustained, the idea would be that you shall be sustained by your labour; that is, your personal industry. So the Hebrews used the words עַל־יָד *el yod*, which means "*by hand*," and is used to mean labour. Thus, *Prov.* xiii. 11: "He that gathereth by vanity shall be diminished, but he that gathereth by *labour* (עַל־יָד *by hand, i. e.* by his own industry) shall increase." Is it not clear, then, that the Hebrews stood in no need of the word *ebed* to mean labour generally. They did use it to mean slave-labour, and slave-labour alone, as we shall more fully see hereafter.

This language enabled its writers to express the distinctive shades of meaning—those adjective qualities associated with the idea *labour*. These facts may appear to the mere English scholar as matters of no importance—not worth investigation. But, touching the Hebrew use of this word עבד *ebed* and its compounds, as it affects and expresses the institution of slavery, amid the eras of Divine inspiration, we hope to be sustained in the consideration of its very great importance.

LESSON IV.

Some of the lexicons say that this root עֶבֶד *ebed* means also *worship*, to *worship* God, or idols, &c., without any connection with the idea of slavery. In *Gen.* xxii. 5: "And I and the lad will go yonder and *worship;*" here, worship is from וְנִשְׁתַּחֲוֶה, from the root שחה *shahah*, which means to bow down. xxiii. 12: "*And* Abraham *bowed down himself* before the people of the Lord," *bowed down himself* וַיִּשְׁתַּחוּ. xlvii. 31: "*And* Israel bowed himself upon the bed's head," וַיִּשְׁתַּחוּ. *Exod.* iv. 31: "Then they bowed their heads and worshipped," וַיִּשְׁתַּחֲווּ. This root, like all others, takes upon itself a change of shape, according to the condition in which it is used. We will present a few instances of its application in Hebrew. *Exod.* xi. 8: "And bow down themselves unto me," וְהִשְׁתַּחֲווּ. xx. 5: "*Thou shalt not bow down thyself* תִשְׁתַּחֲוֶה *unto them.*" xxxiii. 10: "And the people rose up and *worshipped,*" וְהִשְׁתַּחֲווּ. *Deut.* xxvi. 10: "And *worship* וְִּשְׁתַּחֲוִיתָ before the Lord thy God." *Josh.* v. 14: "And Joshua fell on his face to the earth and did *worship,*" וַיִּשְׁתָּחוּ. 1 *Sam.* xv. 30: "That I may *worship* וְהִשְׁתַּחֲוֵיתִי the Lord thy God." 31: "And Saul worshipped וַיִּשְׁתַּחוּ the Lord." 2 *Sam.* i. 2: "That he fell to the earth and did *obeisance,*" וַיִּשְׁתָּחוּ. xiv. 33: "And *bowed himself* וַיִּשְׁתַּחוּ on his face to the ground before the king." 1 *Kings* i. 23: "He *bowed himself* וַיִּשְׁתַּחוּ before the king with his face to the ground." 2 *Kings* v. 18: "When my *master* goeth into the house of Rimmon to *worship* לְהִשְׁתַּחֲוֹת there, * * * and I bow myself וְהִשְׁתַּחֲוֵיתִי in the house of Rimmon, * * * *when I bow myself down* בְּהִשְׁתַּחֲוָיָתִי in the house of Rimmon." xviii. 22: "Ye shall worship תִשְׁתַּחֲווּ before the altar of Jerusalem." xix. 37: "And it came to pass as he was *worshipping* מִשְׁתַּחֲוֶה in the house of Nishrosh, his God." *Job* i. 20: "Then Job arose and fell down upon the ground and *worshipped*," וַיִּשְׁתַּחוּ. *Ezek.* viii. 16: "And they *worshipped* מִשְׁתַּחֲוִיתֶם the sun towards the east."

Before we close our examples, let us notice how the Hebrews applied this word in poetry. *Ps.* xlv. 12 (11 of the English text): "Worship וְהִשְׁתַּחֲוִי thou him." xcix. 5: "Exalt ye the Lord our God, and *worship* וְהִשְׁתַּחֲווּ at his footstool." cvi. 19: "They made a calf in Horeb and worshipped הִשְׁתַּחֲווּ the molten image." xcvii. 7: "Confounded be all they that *serve* (עֹבְדֵי slave themselves to) graven images; that boast themselves of idols: *worship* הִשְׁתַּחֲווּ him, all ye gods." In this instance, the word *serve* associates with the idea of slavery, as does the original; but the *worship* with that of reverence. Both words occurring in the same sentence, will give us some idea of their different uses; yet some think this word in such instances synonymous with the word worship, notwithstanding the Hebrew writers thought differently; yet true it is, this word is sometimes used (as it were by figure) to express humility, subserviency, and devotedness of the true *worshipper*. In the same manner, St. Paul expresses the idea, when he says, that he is the *doulos* (δοῦλος, slave) of Jesus Christ. In an analogous sense, the Arabic words هَلّ *hel* and هَلَّلَ *hallel*, Hebrew הִלֵּל *hallal*, are used to mean worship, &c. *Ps.* cl.: "Praise ye the Lord, praise God in his sanctuary," &c., where this word is in frequent use, and from which our word *hallelujah* has arisen. Also the Arabic word هُود *hōd*, Hebrew הוֹד *hōd*, is in somewhat similar use: *Ps.* cxxxvi. 1, 2, 3, all commencing, "O give thanks to the Lord," meaning glory, majesty, or dignity to the Lord, as the worship of the Almighty. We trust no one has ever found the word *ebed* used in such a sense.

But it is said that עֲבֹדָה *avoda* means implements, utensils, appurtenances, (see *Gessenius*,) and *Num.* iii. 26, 31, and 36, is quoted in proof: "And the hangings of the court and the curtains for the door of the court, which is by the tabernacle, and by the altar round about, and the cords of it, for all the *service* thereof." *Service* is translated from עֲבֹדָתוֹ *avodatho*. The word, as here used, means *slave-labour*, and might well have been translated, "For all the slave-labour thereof," *i. e.* of the tabernacle. We cannot perceive that it means the hanging of the court, or the curtains, or cords. The other instances quoted are of the same character, and we dismiss their consideration, asking the passages to be read.

But it is said, to *minister*, to *minister unto*, is sometimes translated to the word *ebed*. 1 *Kings* xix. 21: "Then he arose and went unto Elijah, and *ministered* וַיְשָׁרְתֵהוּ unto him." The word is from the root שֵׁרֵת *shereth*, and means to wait upon, to attend to, &c., distinct from the idea of slavery. In *Matt.* iv. 11: "Then the devil leaveth him, and, behold, angels came and *ministered* (διηκονουν, *diekonoun*) unto him." This Greek word, we deem, would be a good translation of this word from Hebrew into Greek. This word is used in *Num.* iii. 6: "That they may *minister* unto him." 31: "Wherewith they may *minister* יְשָׁרְתוּ unto it." iv. 12: "And they shall take all the instruments of ministry יְשָׁרְתוּ wherewith they *minister*." 14: "Wherewith they *minister* about it." xviii. 2: "That they may be joined unto thee and *minister* וִישָׁרְתוּךָ unto thee." 1 *Kings* i. 4: "And the damsel was very fair, and cherished the king and *ministered* וַתְּשָׁרְתֵהוּ to him." 15: "The Shunammite *ministered* מְשָׁרַת unto the king." If the word *ebed* had been used, it would have shown that she was a *slave*. The same word is continued to be used to mean *minister*. In 1 *Sam.* ii. 11: "And the child did *minister* unto the Lord before Eli." 18: "But Samuel *ministered* מְשָׁרֵת before the Lord, being a child." iii. 1: "And the child Samuel *ministered* מְשָׁרֵת unto the Lord before Eli." 2 *Sam.* xiii. 17: "Then he called his servant (נַעֲרוֹ *his young man*) that *ministered* מְשָׁרְתוֹ unto him." Now, had the *ebed* been here used instead of this word, as a verb, in the required mood and tense, &c., it would have been proof that the young man was a slave. But, in case the word *ebed*, as a noun, had been used, instead of נער *nar*, then this word might have been used as it is, without affecting the slave character of the servant. 1 *Kings* x. 5: "And the sitting of his servants, (עֲבָדָיו *slaves*,) and the attendance of his ministers," מְשָׁרְתָיו.

This passage shows with great distinctness the different use and meaning of the words *ebed* and *shereth*, between those who *minis-*

tered unto him, and those who did slave-labour, between the minister and the slave; and so we ever find the distinct uses and meanings of these words. See *Exod.* xxviii. 43: "Or when they come near unto the altar to *minister* לְשָׁרֵת in the holy place." *Deut.* x. 8: "To stand before the Lord to *minister* לְשָׁרְתוֹ unto him." xviii. 5: "For the Lord thy God hath chosen him out of all thy tribes to stand to *minister* לְשָׁרֵת in the name of the Lord, him and his sons for ever." 1 *Kings* viii. 11: "So that the priests could not stand to *minister* לְשָׁרֵת because of the cloud." 2 *Kings* xxv. 14: "And all the vessels of brass wherewith they *ministered*, יְשָׁרְתוּ, took they away." 2 *Chron.* xxiv. 14: "Even vessels to *minister*," שָׁרֵת. *Neh.* x. 36 (the 27th of the Hebrew text): "Unto the priests that *minister* in the house of God." 39 (the 40th of the Hebrew text): "And the priests that *minister*," הַמְשָׁרְתִים. *Isa.* lx. 7: "The rams of Nebaioth shall *minister* יְשָׁרְתוּנֶךָ unto thee." Let it be noticed that the word *strangers* is translated from the word נֵכָר *nechar*. The word is of Arabic derivation from *eker*, and has a privative sense, as *nescivit*, *abrogavit*, *improbavit*. Hence, the Hebrews used it to mean *strange*, *foreign*, and sometimes *false*, as in *Deut.* xxxii. 12: "No strange (*false*) God with him." *Mal.* ii. 11: "The daughter of a *strange* (*false*) God." And this word was used to mean the *strangers*, idolaters, and rejected people, out of whom the Hebrews were allowed to make slaves, and therefore it was used in *Gen.* xvii. 12: "Or bought with thy money of any stranger (נֵכָר *neker*) which is not of thy seed." And therefore the propriety of the use of this word in the description of those who should be their drudges and slaves, is beautifully expressed by the idea of building up their walls, as here expressed by the prophet. But the idea of the kings *ministering*, is as before, from the root, *shereth*. Many more examples of the use of this word might be quoted; but we trust the foregoing are sufficient to establish its meaning to be altogether different and distinct from any use of the word *ebed*. Yet, there are in the received translation of the holy books, a few instances where this word is translated erroneously, as though it were a synonyme of the word *ebed*.

In *Num.* xi. 28, "And Joshua the son of Nun, the *servant* of Moses," the word servant is translated from מְשָׁרֵת, and should have been the *minister* of Moses. In *Exod.* xxiv. 13: "Moses rose up and Joshua his *minister*" מְשָׁרְתוֹ. In this last quotation, *minister* is correctly translated from the word as above, proving the error in Numbers. A similar error occurs also in *Ezek.* xx. 32; it reads thus: "And that which cometh into your mind shall not be at all that ye say, We will be as the heathen, as the families of the country to *serve* לְשָׁרֵת wood and stone." Serve is translated from as above, and should have been *to minister unto wood and stone.* A like error occurs in *Exod.* xxxiii. 11: "But his *servant* וּמְשָׁרְתוֹ Joshua," should have been rendered, "his *minister* Joshua." So, also, in *Num.* iv. 47, the word *ebed* is translated as a synonyme of *sherath.* The passage reads thus: "*From thirty years old and upward, even unto fifty years old,* every one that comes to do the service of the ministry, and the service of the burden in the tabernacle of the congregation." In this passage, the word *ebed*, with affixes, is used four times consecutively, and immediately followed by the word *massa*, which we have before seen means *labour*, with the idea of the burden of labour altogether predominating.

In the translation, it is plain to see that one of these words is totally left out, which, we suppose, no one will pretend is not an error. The translation made of these five words at the Theological College at Andover, is far more correct than the received version. It is thus: "*to perform the business of the service and the business of the burden,*" &c. Yet this is not the language of the original, which reads thus: לַעֲבֹד עֲבֹדַת עֲבֹדָה וַעֲבֹדַת מַשָּׂא.

If our proposition is correct, that the word *ebed* is never used in Hebrew expression unassociated with the idea of slavery, then this passage from Numbers should read: "From thirty years old and upwards, even to fifty years old, every one that comes to slave in the slavery of the slave labour, and in the *slavery* of the burdens of the tabernacle of the congregation." We agree that the passage is somewhat difficult to render into English; but because we may find some difficulty in making good English, we are not to translate from other words of different meaning from the ones used. The holy penmen said what they meant, and surely meant what they said: there was no double dealing in the spirit of Jehovah, who dictated to them. But that translators should have, in some few instances, mistaken or confounded the use of the word, is not to be thought strange. Taking into view the volume of the holy books, it is truly wonderful that greater errors were not committed. And we take occasion here to remark, that, of all the ideas, qualities, and actions, given in definition of the word *ebed*, unassociated with the idea of slavery, upon examination of the language, we shall find graphic symbols representing their phonetic signs, distinct from the idea of *slavery*, as we have these already examined.

LESSON V.

To show more clearly that the word עֶבֶד *ebed* is never used in Hebrew expression unassociated with the idea of slavery, we now propose to examine that word as used by the Hebrew writers in the holy books. Our words SERVANT, servitude, service, &c. are all derived from the Roman word SERVUS, which meant a SLAVE; and our word *servant*, when first introduced into our language, as absolutely meant a slave as now does that term itself, and even now fully retains that meaning, where the English language and slavery coexist. The oriental scholar (and let him be invited to examine) will perceive that the word עֶבֶד *ebed* was common to all the Shemitic tribes, and almost with the same phonetic particulars; but as their figures representing the same phonetic power were quite dissimilar, we think it a proof, almost demonstration, that the word עֶבֶד *ebed* was used as a phonetic symbol by them long before any of those languages were written. This circumstance shows the extreme antiquity of the word; and if we succeed to establish the fact, that this word meant nothing but what is now meant by the word *slave*, we shall also have established the extreme antiquity of the thing itself. A *word* means nothing, until it is by some means agreed what it shall represent, what idea, or association of ideas it shall excite in the mind. Hence, it not unfrequently occurs that a thing may be better described by paraphrasis than by the expression of a single term. In *Gen.* xii. 5: "And Abram took Sarai his wife, and Lot his brother's son, and their substance that they had gathered, and the *souls that they had gotten in Haran.*" The latter clause of this sentence is from this Hebrew expression, וְאֶת־הַנֶּפֶשׁ אֲשֶׁר־עָשׂוּ בְחָרָן,

which is correctly translated in the Andover lexicon, "The souls they had acquired in Haran." Every one knows that the things here meant are *slaves*. But, when the scholar comes to examine the power of the language of this Hebrew paraphrasis, he will discover three incident attendants. הַנֶּפֶשׁ *hannephesh*, translated souls, also carries with it the idea a living soul, to have life, the life itself, the living principle, and is so translated in many places. A slave, therefore, must have life: when dead, the condition ceases. In the same way, the sentence expresses the idea of acquiring property by purchase, or any other way in which property may be acquired so as to be property. The three incidents then are life, a capacity of being acquired, and, when so acquired, property. All this could not have been expressed by the single term עֶבֶד *ebed*, only as it is made the representative of this complex idea: and God has no doubt caused this passage to be on record at this early period, that these incidents should finally come to the knowledge of all men. A somewhat similar expression is used in *Rev.* xviii. 13. Every one knows that Babylon had been a great slave-market. St. John, after naming the various articles of her merchandise, adds *και των σωματων, και την ψυχην*, *kai ton sōmatōn, kai tēn psuchēn*, which is translated, "*slaves and souls of men*:" *σωματων* does not mean slaves, but a dead body, and is so used by Homer, Xenophon, and by the New Testament itself; but, when united with *και την ψυχην*, means slaves alone. The phrase "souls of men," therefore, in the translation, is surplusage. But the xii. 16 of *Genesis* is more particular in giving the different kinds of property and their appropriate names. "And he had sheep and oxen, and he-asses, and men-servants (עֲבָדִים *abadim*), and maid-servants, and she-asses, and camels." The word *men-servants* is translated from the plural of עֶבֶד *ebed*. Here we find the conventional term expressing the complex idea, previously expressed by the phrase "souls gotten," persons in life, subject to be purchased, and when purchased, property, as were sheep and oxen, and he-asses and she-asses, and camels. In *Gen.* xvii. 9–13, we begin to find the law influencing the conduct of Abraham in the management of this property: "And God said unto Abram, thou shalt," &c. 12: "And he that is eight days old shall be circumcised," &c.: "He that is born in thy house, or *bought with money* of any stranger which is not of thy seed." 13: "He that is born in thy house, and he that is *bought with thy money*, must needs be circumcised." And let it here be remembered that God recognises the possession of this property, by giving directions with his own voice concerning its government. And in *Gen.* xx. 14, we have some account of the origin of Abraham's title to some portion of this property: "And Abimelech took sheep and oxen and *men-servants* (עבדים *ebedim*, the plural of *ebed*), and gave them to Abraham." xxiv. 35: "And the Lord hath blessed my master greatly, and he is become great; and he hath given him flocks and herds, and silver and gold, and *men-servants* and maid-servants, and camels and asses." Here the plural of *ebed* is also used. *Such* is the title by which he possessed this property, described as given to him by the Lord. But God had promised that he would bless Abraham, *Gen.* xvii. 1: "The Lord appeared unto Abraham, and said unto him, *I am the Almighty God.*" 2: "And I will make my covenant between me and thee." 7: "And I will establish my covenant between me and thee, and thy seed after thee in their generations, for an everlasting covenant." 10: "This is my covenant." (This covenant extends from the beginning of the 10th to the end of the 14th verse.) One part of this covenant was, that these *ebeds*, translated *men-servants*, whether born in his house or bought with his money of any stranger, should be circumcised. Wherefore, the possession of these *ebeds* as property became agreeable to the terms of the covenant, a part of the covenant itself—a covenant first proposed and promulgated by the great Jehovah; as he styles himself in the covenant, the Almighty God! *Gen.* xxvi. 2: "And the Lord appeared unto him (Isaac), and said, Go not down into Egypt: dwell in the land which I shall tell thee of: sojourn in this land, and I will be with thee, and will bless thee." 4: "And I will make thy seed to multiply as the stars of heaven, and I will give unto thy seed all these countries; and in thy seed shall all the nations of the earth be blessed." 13: "And the man (Isaac) waxed great, and went forward and grew until he became very great." 14: "For he had possession of flocks, and possession of herds, and great store of *servants* (עֲבֻדָּה *abuddah*, *slaves*, a plural formation of *ebed*), and the Philistines envied him."!!!

LESSON VI.

Gen. xxvii. 29: "Let people serve thee (יַעַבְדוּךָ *be slaves to thee*), be lord over thy brethren, and let thy mother's sons bow down to thee; cursed be every one that curseth thee, and blessed be he that blesseth thee." Let us notice the conformity of this passage with *Gen.* xxv. 23: "And the Lord said unto her, two nations are in thy womb, and two manner of people shall be separated from thy bowels, and the one people shall be stronger than the other people, and the elder shall serve (יַעֲבֹד *be a slave to*) the younger." *Gen.* xxx. 43: "And the man (Jacob) increased exceedingly, and had much cattle, and maid-servants, and *men-servants* (וַעֲבָדִים the plural of *ebed*), and camels and asses." *Exod.* xx. 1, 2, 9, 10, 17: "And God spake all these words, saying," 2: "I am the Lord thy God, which have brought thee out of the land of Egypt, out of the house of bondage" (עֲבָדִים out of *slavery*): 5: "Thou shalt not *bow down* (תִשְׁתַּחֲוֶה *worship them*) thyself to them, nor *serve* (תָעָבְדֵם *be a slave to them*) them." 9: "Six days shalt thou *labour* (תַּעֲבֹד *slave thyself*, or do SLAVE-LABOUR) and do (*oso, labour or do work*) all thy work," (וְעָשִׂיתָ all thy accustomed labours.) This command embraces all classes, the slave as well as the most elevated. All men, by the fall of Adam, had become subject to slave-labour. 10: "But the seventh day is the sabbath of the Lord thy God, in it thou shalt not do any work, thou, nor thy son, nor thy daughter, thy *man-servant* (עַבְדְּךָ thy *slave*), nor thy maid-servant." 17: In this commandment we are directed not to covet any thing that is our neighbour's, including his man-servant and maid-servant. Here the same word עַבְדּוֹ is also used. *Exod.* xxi. 1: "Now these are the judgments which thou shalt set before them." 2: "If thou buy a Hebrew *servant* (עֶבֶד *ebed*), six years shall he *serve* (יַעֲבֹד *shall slave himself*)," 5: "And if the *servant* (הָעֶבֶד *ha ebed, slave*) shall plainly say, I love," &c. *Exod.* xxi. 7: "She shall not go out as the *men-servants* do." (הָעֲבָדִים the plural is here used.) 20: "If a man smite his *servant* עַבְדּוֹ or his maid with a rod, and he die under his hand, he shall be surely punished: for he is his money." 26: "If a man smite the eye of his *servant*," עַבְדּוֹ. 27: "If he smite out his *man-servant's* tooth," עַבְדּוֹ. 32: "If the ox shall push the *man-servant* עֶבֶד or *maid-servant*, he shall give unto their master thirty shekels of silver, and the ox shall be stoned."

Lev. xxv. 44: "Both thy *bond-men* וְעַבְדְּךָ and thy bond-maids which thou shalt have, shall be of the heathen that are round about you, of them shall ye buy *bond-men*," (עֶבֶד *ebed.*) 45: "Moreover, of the children of the strangers that do sojourn among you, of them shall ye buy, and of their families that are with you, which they beget in your land, and they shall be your possession." 46: "And ye shall take them as an inheritance for your children after you, to inherit them for a possession; they shall be your *bond-men* תַּעֲבֹדוּ for ever."

Deut. v. 14: "But the seventh day is the sabbath of the Lord thy God; in it thou shalt not do any work, thou, nor thy son, nor thy daughter, nor thy *man-servant* וְעַבְדְּךָ, nor thy maid-servant, that thy *man-servant* and thy maid-servant may rest as well as thou." 15: "And remember that thou wast a *servant* (עֶבֶד *ebed*) in the land of Egypt." 21 (18th of Hebrew text): "Neither shalt thou covet thy neighbour's house, his field, or his *man-servant* וְעַבְדּוֹ, or his maid-servant." *Deut.* xii. 12: "And ye shall rejoice before the Lord your God, ye, and your sons, and your daughters, and your *men-servants* (וְעַבְדֵיכֶם a plural form of *ebed*), and your maid-servants, and the Levite," &c. 18: "And thy son, and thy daughter, and *thy man-servant*," וְעַבְדְּךָ. *Deut.* xv. 12: "If thy brother, a Hebrew man, or a Hebrew woman, be sold unto thee, and *serve* וַעֲבָדְךָ thee six years." 15: "And thou shalt remember that thou wast a *bond-man* (עֶבֶד *ebed*) in the land of Egypt." 17: "And he shall be thy servant (עֶבֶד *ebed*) for ever." *Deut.* xvi. 11: "And thou shalt rejoice before the Lord thy God, thou, and thy son, and thy daughter, and thy *man-servant* וְעַבְדְּךָ, and thy maid-servant, and the Levite that is within thy gates, and the stranger, and the fatherless, and the widow, that are among you." 12: "And thou shalt remember that thou wast a *bond-man* (עֶבֶד *ebed*) in Egypt." 14: "And thou shalt rejoice in thy feast, thou, and thy son, and thy daughter, and thy *man-servant* וְעַבְדְּךָ, and thy *maid-servant*, and the Levite, the stranger, and the fatherless, and the widow." *Deut.* xx. 10: "When thou comest nigh unto a city to fight against it, then proclaim peace unto it." 11: "And it shall be if it make thee an answer of peace and open unto thee, then it shall be, that all the people found therein shall be *tributaries* (לָמַס *lamas*, afflicted, cast down, to pay tribute, &c.), and they shall *serve* (וַעֲבָדוּךָ *be thy slaves*) thee." *Deut.* xxiii. 9–17 contains certain laws to be observed in time of war with their enemies, &c., one of which is, that a slave escaped to them from the enemy should not be restored, &c. *Deut.* xxiii. 16 (15th of the English text): "Thou shalt not deliver unto his master the *servant*," (עֶבֶד *ebed, slave.*) xxiv. 18: "But thou shalt remember that thou wast a *bond-man*," (עֶבֶד *ebed, slave.*) 22: "And thou shalt remember that thou wast a bond-man," עֶבֶד. *Gen.* ix. 25: "And he said, Cursed be Canaan, a *servant* of *servants* (*ebed-ebedim*) shall he be unto his brethren." 26: "And he said, Blessed be the Lord God of Shem, and Canaan shall be his *servant*," (עֶבֶד *ebed.*) Many more instances of a similar use of this word might be selected from the holy books; some of which we hope to notice in the progress of our study. Such, then, was the Hebrew use of the word, to mean slave, a person purchased or otherwise acquired, and the unquestionable *property* of the master. Such then being the condition of the *ebed*, slave, it is evident that he could not be contented and happy, in case he had ambition to gratify, with hopes and prospects before him adverse from those of his master; his whole earthly felicities are bound up in his master's welfare and prosperity; like an individual of an army, he feels that the elevation, the brilliancy of the commander is reflected upon him; and with a Christian spirit, he obeys his master in all things, "not with eye-service, but with singleness of heart, fearing God." See *Col.* iii. 22. In such a state of mind, the slave finds no unhappiness in his condition, but joy and gladness; and with the slave of Abraham, he implores Jehovah: "*O Lord God of my master Abraham! I pray thee send me good speed this day, and show kindness unto my master Abraham*: Blessed be the Lord God of my master Abraham, who hath not left destitute my master of his mercy and truth." *Gen.* xxiv. 12 and 27. Expressive of a character of perfect devotedness, humility, and obedience. The term *ebed* might well be borrowed to express the earnest devotion of a worshipper of Jehovah, and is so often used in connection with the patriarchs, Moses, David, and the prophets. The term thus used expresses the quality of their devotedness and obedience, and not necessarily the quality of the individual. In this sense, the apostles style themselves the (*δουλοι*, *douloi*) slaves of Jesus Christ; not that they were personally *douloi*, but in their devotion and obedience to him, they were what the *doulos* was or should be to his master. It is probable that, in some sense, all men feel that in the hand of God they are as clay in the hands of the potter; that the great Jehovah overrules and governs all things; that, as existences, they are from and dependent on him: under such a sense, we sometimes find the term *ebed* applied, as in the name *Obadiah*, *Obadyahu*, the slave of God, and used as a proper noun. But such compound words are dependent for their meaning upon the complex ideas of what their primitives signified; and, in a somewhat analogous sense, the term *ebed* is applied to Nebuchadnezzar, he being in the hands of the Almighty, as clay in the hands of the potter, the mere instrument, the fabrication of his hand. There is, however, in the books of Ezra, Nehemiah, and Daniel, a use of this word peculiar to them; but we should recollect that they were educated in the Persian capital and employed in high stations by the Persian monarch. We may therefore well expect some variation in their dialect.

LESSON VII.

And we may well bring to mind the fact that there are two distinctly marked eras in the Hebrew language. The first ends at the Babylonish captivity. The Pentateuch and older prophets, Ruth, Samuel, Kings, Psalms, and Proverbs, come within this era. The second commences with the return of the Israelites from that captivity, and extends to the introduction of Greek into Palestine, subsequent to the conquests of Alexander. The first period may be emphatically called ancient Hebrew; and the latter, more modern. The Hebrew of this period is strongly marked by an approximation to the Chaldee and Persian. To this period of the language belong the books of Nehemiah, Ezra, Daniel, Esther, Jonah, Haggai, Malachi, Ecclesiastes, and a part of the Psalms;

and these works will ever be regarded by the oriental scholar as inferior in classical literature to those of earlier date, notwithstanding their other merits of high excellence. But some of the peculiarities of the writings of the second period are not to be regarded as recent alterations, but as the phonetic, unwritten Hebrew of the more remote districts of Palestine itself. The variations of this more modern from the ancient Hebrew are extremely numerous, both as to the substitution of one word for another, but also as to a change of meaning of the same word; as, for instance, the more ancient would have used the word מָלַךְ *malak* to signify a king, to rule, &c.; but the more modern have used a word, which, from its strong phonetic relation, has evidently been derived from it, שָׁלַט *shalat*, to mean *to rule*, &c., and so used *Ps.* cxix. 133, *Eccl.* ii. 19, *Esther* ix. 1, *Neh.* v. 15, *Dan.* ii. 39, and in many other places. So also the ancient would use the word אָמַר *amar*, to signify *to speak*, *to say;* but the more modern uses the same word to signify *to command.* What we say is, that we cannot always learn the original meaning of a word from the more modern use of it. We will now notice the use of the ancient word *ebed* in this more modern dialect of the Hebrews. In *Ezra* iv. 19, we find, "And that rebellion and sedition *have been made* therein" is translated from מִתְעֲבֵד *mithabed.* Let us examine the circumstances under which this sentence was written. Rehum had written to the monarch Artaxerxes in opposition to the building of the walls of Jerusalem, informing him that it had ever been a rebellious city, hurtful to kings, &c.; in answer to which, the king writes, " that the records have been examined, and it is found that this city of old time hath made insurrection against kings, and that rebellion and sedition *hath been made therein.*" The Persian monarchs were all absolute; they regarded those whom they conquered as slaves; and when they rebelled, they used this word to signify that it was slaves who rebelled. Our word *servile* is somewhat analogous, and might very properly be substituted for it in the foregoing text, thus: "And it is found, this city of old time hath made insurrection against kings, and that there hath been servile rebellion and sedition therein." When we speak of insurrection, sedition, rebellion, or war with slaves, we call it *servile*, as Artaxerxes did in this case, to show the fact that the war was with slaves. *Ezra* iv. 24, this word עֲבִידַת is translated *work.* So in v. 8, עֲבִידְתָּא *work*, vi. 7, עֲבוֹדַת *work*, to show that the labour was done by *slaves*, or, figuratively, that the *labour* was intense, devoted, and obedient, as of slaves. vi. 8: תַּעַבְדוּן "*Ye shall do.*" 12: יִתְעֲבֵד "Let it be done with speed." 13: עֲבַדוּ "*So they did speedily.*"

vii. 18: תַּעַבְדוּן } "*That do* after the will of your God."
and לְמֶעְבַּד } "*To do* with the rest of the silver and gold."

21: יִתְעֲבֵד "It be done speedily." 23: יִתְעֲבֵד "Let it be diligently *done.*" 26: עָבֵד "Will not *do.*" מִתְעֲבֵד "Let judgment *be executed* speedily." These instances of the use of this word seem somewhat peculiar; but we must recollect that the monarch of Persia is speaking, who regarded not only the Jews, but all his subjects, as slaves. It was the court manner of the eastern monarchs in such decrees to throw in occasionally an exclamation of the nature of an imperative interjection, such as, *Slave, attend! Pay attention, slaves! Listen, slaves!* &c., all in substance meaning that those to whom the decree is issued should perform it quickly and without further notice. And we find the same custom existing among them even at this day, and such is the true sense in which the term is here used. Let us exemplify it. *Ezra* vi. 12: "I, Darius, have made a decree;" then follows the Persian adverb אָסְפַּרְנָא *asepporna*, which means quickly, speedily, diligently, &c.; then the word in question, as before noticed: "*quickly, slaves,*" is therefore the literal meaning, *i. e.* what he had decreed they should instantly perform. We do not pretend to say that translating it *to do*, &c. gives a substantially wrong sense; but it seems it may have led lexicographers to an erroneous conception of the meaning of the word. *Jer.* x. 11: "The gods that have not made the heavens and the earth:" *made* is translated from עֲבַדוּ. If this word is the correct reading, the idea of the prophet had regard to the *power*, not to the *act* of a creator,—the gods that have not *subjected*, have not placed in *subjection*, as if in slavery to, whose laws do not govern the heavens and the earth. The gods who could not do these things are *not* gods, and they shall perish. This was the idea of the prophet. But this word is marked in all the best copies with a keri, showing that this reading was suspected by the Jewish scholars to be bad; and they supply in the margin the words פתח באתנח, which is at least some proof that they thought its use in this instance unusual; and Kennecott and De Rossi found these words used instead of עבדו in some copies.

LESSON VIII.

But we have a sure method by which we may discover what meaning Ezra did affix to this word—by examining his use of it in those cases where its meaning cannot be doubtful. See *Ezra* iv. 11: "Thy servants," עַבְדָיךְ. v. 11: "We are the servants," עַבְדוֹהִי, having relevance to their devotedness to God. vi. 16 commences with the word יַעַבְדוּ, which is omitted in our translation. The sentence should commence thus: "*And the slaves*, the children of Israel, the priests," &c. ix. 9: "For we were *bondmen* עֲבָדִים, yet our God hath not forsaken *us in our bondage*," וּבְעַבְדֻתֵנוּ. These instances clearly show how Ezra understood this word: notwithstanding his writings were touched with the Persian and Chaldee idioms. A similar result will be found upon the examination of Nehemiah and Daniel. *Neh.* ii. 10 and 19: "And Tobiah the *servant* הָעֶבֶד, the Ammonite heard of it"—"And Tobiah the *servant* הָעֶבֶד, the Ammonite." v. 5: "Yet now our flesh is as the flesh of our brethren, our children as their children: and lo, we bring into *bondage* (כֹּבְשִׁים *kovshim*) our sons and our daughters to be *servants* (לַעֲבָדִים *slaves*), and some of our daughters are brought into *bondage* (נִכְבָּשׁוֹת *subjections*, not necessarily slavery) already," (כָּבַשׁ *kovash*.) The root from which these two words are formed in no sense means slavery, but to reduce, to subdue, to humble; and in this sense is used in *Esther* vii. 8, and translated "*force*." But this word aids very much in showing what idea was affixed to the word *ebed;* and we ask to compare this passage of Nehemiah with *Jer.* xxxiv. 8–16: "This is the word that came unto Jeremiah from the Lord, after that king Zedekiah had made a covenant with all the people which were at Jerusalem, to proclaim liberty unto them; * * * that every man should let his *man-servant*, (עַבְדּוֹ *male slave*,) and every man his maid-servant שִׁפְחָתוֹ, being a Hebrew or Hebrewess, go free; that none should *serve* (עֲבָד־ *slave*) himself of them, to wit, of a Jew his brother. Now, when all the princes, and all the people which had entered into the covenant, heard that every one should let his *man-servant* (עַבְדּוֹ *male slave*), and every one his maid-servant, go free, that none *serve themselves* (עֲבָד־ *slave themselves*), of them any more, then they obeyed and let them go. But afterwards they turned and caused the *servants* (הָעֲבָדִים *ha abadim, slaves*), and the *hand-maids*, whom they had let go free, to return. Therefore the word of the Lord came to Jeremiah, from the Lord, saying, Thus saith the Lord, the God of Israel, I made a covenant with your fathers in the day that I brought them forth out of the land of Egypt, out of the house of bond-men (עֲבָדִים *ebedim, slaves*), saying, At the end of seven years, let go every man his brother a Hebrew, which hath been sold unto thee; and when he hath *served* thee (וַעֲבָדְךָ *slaved for thee*) six years, thou shalt let him go free from thee; but your fathers hearkened not unto me, neither inclined their ear. And ye were now turned, and had done right in my sight, in proclaiming liberty every man to his neighbour; and ye had made a covenant before me in the house which is called by my name. But ye turned and polluted my name, and caused every man his *servant*, (עַבְדּוֹ *ebeddo, slave*,) and every man his *hand-maid*, whom he had set at liberty at their pleasure, to return, and brought them into *subjection* (וַתִּכְבְּשׁוּ) to be unto you for *servants* (לַעֲבָדִים *for slaves*), and for *hand-maids*." The comparison of these passages proves the fact that Nehemiah and Jeremiah used the word *ebed* to mean a slave, without any variation of meaning. Nor will we hold Nehemiah responsible for his word כָּבַשׁ *kavash, subjection*, being translated *bondage*. *Neh.* vii. 66, 67, gives an account of the captive Israelites that returned from Susa and Babylon to Jerusalem. "And the whole congregation together was forty and two thousand three hundred and threescore. Besides their *man-servants* (עַבְדֵיהֶם *male slaves*), and their maid-servants, of whom there were seven thousand three hundred and thirty score." We trust that so varied, particular, and descriptive are the records left in the holy books through which we may search out what the Hebrews meant by their use of the word *ebed* (עבד), that its certainty and definiteness must place the inquiry beyond doubt.

But as in this instance the word כָּבַשׁ *kavash* has been translated *bondage*, it may be well to give a few examples of its use in the holy books, that all may see and know that its meaning is totally distinct from that of slavery. *Gen.* i. 28: "Multiply and replenish the earth and subdue it," וְכִבְשֻׁהָ. *Num.* xxxii. 22: "And the land *be subdued* וְנִכְבְּשָׁה before the Lord." 29: "And the land *shall be subdued* וְנִכְבְּשָׁה before you." *Josh.* xviii. 1: "And the land *was subdued* נִכְבְּשָׁה before them." 2 *Sam.* viii. 1: "Which he *subdued*," כִּבֵּשׁ. 2 *Chron.* ix. 18: "With a footstool," וְכֶבֶשׁ, because a footstool was in the place of subjection. *Zech.* ix. 15: "And *subdue* וְכָבְשׁוּ with sling-stones." *Micah* vii. 19: "He will *subdue* יִכְבּוֹשׁ our iniquities." The foregoing examples, we trust, are sufficient to disabuse the mind of the idea of any synonyme of meaning of these two words.

LESSON IX.

WE propose to examine the Hebrew use of the word *ebed* in the 5th and 15th of the second chapter of Genesis: "In that day the Lord God made the earth, and the heavens, and every plant of the field before it grew; for the Lord God had not caused it to rain upon the earth, and there was not a man *to till* לַעֲבֹד the ground." *To till* is here translated from this word *ebed*, with the affix of the preposition לְ. This is the first instance in which the word is used in the holy book; and it may seem extremely strange that the writers of these books found its use necessary in their description of events even before the creation of man. It is not our business to draw out theological doctrine unconnected with the subject of our present inquiry; but we suppose it will not be disputed that the great Jehovah as well knew, before he created the heavens and the earth, and man upon the earth, all and every particular of what would happen, as at any subsequent time: with him, a day is as a thousand years, and a thousand years as one day. *We* may behold the birth, maturity, and death of some animalcula, in a day or in an hour. But, with him the succession of generations, of the animal life of a thousand years, pass in instantaneous and present view. *Time* appertains alone to mortals. *He* saw the most ultimate condition of man; and the earth and the herb were made to suit it. But from the manner of the expression of the text, may we not conclude that the herb, although made, would not grow until man was created, and in the condition *to till* (לַעֲבֹד *to slave*) the ground? The support of the animal world, independent of man, is spontaneously presented before them: not so with man in his fallen state. "He sendeth the springs into the valley, which run among the hills. They give drink to every beast of the field: the wild asses quench their thirst. By them shall the fowls of heaven have their habitation, which sing among the branches. He watereth the hills from his chambers; the earth is satisfied with the fruit of thy works. He causeth the grass to grow for the cattle, and herb *for the service* (לַעֲבֹדַת *for the slavery*) of man: that he may bring forth food out of the earth," *Ps.* civ. 10–14. The second instance in which this word is used is in *Gen.* ii. 15: "And the Lord God took the man and put him into the garden of *Eden to dress it*, and to keep it." *To dress it* is translated from this word לְעָבְדָהּ. There is certainly much obscurity in the use of the word in this instance. Professor Stuart, of Andover, supposes that it inculcates the doctrine that *labour* was imposed on man in the paradisiacal state; consequently, that labour was no part of the curse which followed the apostacy. (See his Chreestomathy, page 105.) This view excludes the idea that the word, as here used, is associated with the idea of slavery, and that, if, in the interchange of language, although the idea of labour may predominate, nevertheless, it must be *slave* labour. Our mind does not yield its assent to his position. We had associated with our idea of this paradise the most perfect heaven, the dwelling-place of Jehovah!! and that the generations of man, when guided and governed by Divine mercy in such a manner that we could be happy therein, that it would yet become our ultimate home,—("He that hath an ear, let him hear what the Spirit saith unto the churches; To him that overcometh will I give to eat of the tree of life, which is in the midst of the paradise of God," *Rev.* ii. 7,)—and that the humble worshipper of Jehovah while in a state of progressive preparedness, would therefore cry out with the Psalmist, "Unto thee I lift mine eyes, O thou that dwellest in the heavens! Behold, as the eyes of *servants* (עֲבָדִים *male slaves*) look unto the hand of their master; and as the eyes of a *maiden* (שִׁפְחָה *shiphhah, female slave*) unto the hand of her mistress, so our eyes wait upon the Lord our God until he have mercy upon us." *Ps.* cxxiii. 1, 2. If then the paradise of old was the type of the paradise eternal, it would seem that the labour of the *ebed* was excluded therefrom: "Because the creature itself also shall be delivered from the *bondage* (*δουλείας, slavery*) of corruption into the glorious liberty of the children of God." *Rom.* viii. 21. And for this very good reason, that slavery, the consequent of sin, could never find entrance there: regeneration is therefore indispensable.

"It strikes me that the use of the verb (עָבַד .*abad, Gen.* ii. 5) presents no difficulty that calls for explanation. The language of inspiration is man's language, though employed by God. The events, facts, things, acts, that preceded man's creation, must still be described by language and terms that *had come into use after man's creation.* Man must first exist before there could be *words* to be used in conveying knowledge to man. A word implying *slavery* might therefore most reasonably be found in a *description* of things *prior* to the existence of man, or of slavery, which description was written long afterwards by Moses, and in language which was in use amongst the men for whom he wrote. When Moses wrote, when God inspired him, עֶבֶד *ebed* was a familiar word." *Extract from manuscript letter of the Rev. J. B. Stratton to the author.*

But in the pursuance of the chain of thought that first was impressed on our mind, we have to remark that the word *Eden* meant pleasure, happiness. It seems to have been derived from or cognate with the Arabic word غَطَن *aden*, and means softness, gentleness, mildness, tenderness, and daintiness, in that language. The Hebrews had also another word from this same root, עֲדִי *adi*, to mean ornaments, &c., and עֲדָיִן *adain*, to mean luxuriousness and delicate. The word, as used in the text before, is applied to a district of country, and confers the adjective qualities to said district, *i. e.* a district of country of great pleasure and delight. The general boundaries are given and described by the naming of its rivers. It was of considerable extent, embracing, perhaps, more than the whole of the ancient Armenia.

"And a garden was planted eastward in Eden." Garden is translated from גַּן *gan.* The word is derived from גנן *ganan.* The word means, to protect, protection, a thing protected. The idea expressed by it is not confined to a single walled area; but the two words are often used together, as if it was intended to convey the idea of the fact that the protection extended to the whole of Eden. And it may be well conceived that *innocency* was its protection. Here cunning art never wove its web for the entanglement of its victim. Here no crocodile tears enticed sympathy within the reach of harm. Here no vile wretch ever betrayed a brother's confidence. Here the lion and the lamb might have couched together, and the infant have played with the tiger's paw. We are aware that some modern scholars consider the description of the garden of Eden by Moses a mere picture of the mind. Rosenmaeler says that it is on a par with Virgil's description of the Elysian fields. This class of philosophers consider the whole as a fiction: but man had his commencement somewhere, and it is a fact that four large rivers, answering to the outlines of the general description of Moses, do flow from fountain-heads not more than thirty or forty miles apart, in the central and most elevated region of Armenia. These streams meander through the same countries described by him, and exhibit the same mineral productions: nor would it be any thing remarkable, if investigation should yet prove that they were all indebted to one and the same source. Let us consider then, whether it was not a fact that the garden of Eden was not confined to a little plat of ground, but included a whole district of country, embracing the visible sources of the rivers named: a district of country, from the mildness of its climate, fruitfulness, and other causes of pleasure and delight, exceedingly well adapted to the early residence of man. We have therefore no well founded reason to believe that the account given by Moses of the garden of Eden was a fiction, independent of Divine authority. But his account must be understood so as to be consistent with itself, and with the facts now existing of which it speaks. We are not under the necessity of supposing that the felicity of our first parents was confined to the locality named: a paradise was to them anywhere. It was their innocence, not the location, that made it so; and thus they were driven out of paradise, perhaps, without a change of location. The use of the word *ebed* עבד, in ii. 15 of *Genesis*, might then well be of the same foreshadowing import as in the first instance of its use, even before the creation of man. For, who must not conclude, when man was first placed in paradise, that God did not as clearly see his apostasy then, as now? By his wisdom, power, and mercy, all nature was ready-prepared for the change, and poor fallen man, without change of habitation, found that habitation no longer heaven, and commenced his first act of slavery by the vain attempt to hide himself from God and his own contempt. And here, let us remark, *we find the true commencement of slavery.* "And Jesus answered them, Verily, verily, I say unto you, whosoever committeth sin is the *servant* (*δουλος, slave*) of sin." *John* viii. 34. *Force, disease, ruin,* and *death* were now introduced to man. For, "A *servant* (עֶבֶד *slave*) will not be corrected by words." *Prov.* xxix. 19. God had mercifully contrived that he should be forced to action. "He that *tilleth* (עֹבֵד *slaveth*) his land shall have plenty of bread; but he that followeth after vain persons shall have poverty enough." *Prov.* xxviii. 19. When God made "every plant of the field before it was in the earth, and every herb of the field before it grew," foreseeing the apostasy of man—its poisonous effect upon his moral and physical condition—its direct influence to produce immediate ruin and death, he also provided, ordained, and decreed a relation, a law between man and his mental and physical wants, which must cleave unto him, upon his apostasy, and be of the utmost value and efficacy in alleviating, removing, and preventing the final evils incident to his poisoned condition. This relation, law, institution, was the *ebeduth*, the *institution of slavery*, as expressed in *Ezra* ix. 8, 9: "And give us a little reviving *in our bondage* (עַבְדֻתֵנוּ *ebeduthenu, slavery*). For we were *bond-men* (עֲבָדִים *abedim, slaves*), and yet our God hath not forsaken us in our bondage," עבדתנו. So in 2 *Chron.* xii. 8: "Nevertheless, ye shall be his *servants* (לעבדים *le-obedim,* his *slaves*), that they may know my *service* (עֲבוֹדָתִי *slavery*), and the *service* (וַעֲבוֹדַת *and the slavery*) of the kingdoms of the countries." So in *Esther* vii. 4: "For we are sold, I and my people, to be destroyed, to be slain, and to perish. But if we had been sold for *bond-men* (לַעֲבָדִים וְלִשְׁפָחוֹת) and bond-women, I had held my tongue."

LESSON X.

Towards the close of the book of Deuteronomy, Moses, having delivered to the children of Israel such of the laws of the Almighty as were then deemed necessary for their government and guidance, proceeds to inform them of the consequences of disobedience; and boldly informs them, xxviii. 15, "But, if it shall come to pass if thou wilt not hearken unto the voice of the Lord thy God, to observe and to do all his commandments, and his statutes which I command thee this day, that all these curses shall come upon thee and overtake thee. 16: Cursed shalt thou be in the city, and cursed shalt thou be in the field. 17: Cursed shall be thy basket and thy store. 18: Cursed shall be the fruit of thy body and the fruit of thy land, the increase of thy kine, and the flocks of thy sheep. 19: Cursed shalt thou be when thou comest in, and cursed shalt thou be when thou goest out. 20: The Lord shall send upon thee cursing, vexation, and rebuke, in all thou settest thy hand unto for to do, until thou be destroyed, and until thou perish quickly, because of the wickedness of thy doings whereby thou hast forsaken me." "And the Lord shall bring thee into Egypt again with ships, by the way whereof I spake unto thee. Thou shalt see it no more again, and there ye shall be sold unto your enemies for *bond-men* (לַעֲבָדִים *la obedim*, for *slaves*), and bond-women, and no man shall buy you." They should be so trifling and worthless that no one would wish to buy them. *Josh.* ix. 23–27: "Now, therefore, ye are cursed, and there shall none of you be freed from being bond-men (עֶבֶד *slaves*), and hewers of wood and drawers of water," &c. "And Joshua made them that day hewers of wood and drawers of water, for the congregation, and for the altar of the Lord, even unto this day."

LESSON XI.

Before closing this subject we offer a few more examples of the Hebrew use of this word. "Who is David? and who is the son of Jesse? There be many *servants* (עֲבָדִים *slaves*) now-a-days that break away every man from his master." 1 *Sam.* xxv. 10. Nabal pretended in his drunkenness, that he might be a runaway *slave.* 1 *Kings* ii. 29, 40: "And it came to pass at the end of three years, that two of the *servants* (עֲבָדִים *ebedim*, *slaves*) of Shimei ran away unto Achish, son of Maachah king of Gath; and they told Shimei, saying, Behold thy *servants* (עֲבָדֶךָ *slaves*) be in Gath. And Shimei arose and saddled his ass, and went to Gath to Achish to seek his *servants* (עֲבָדָיו *slaves*), and Shimei went and brought his *servants* (עֲבָדָיו *slaves*) from Gath." 1 *Kings* ix. 20, 21, and 22: "And all the people that were left of the Amorites, Hittites, Perizzites, Hivites, and Jebuzites, which were not of the children of Israel, their children that were left after them in the land, whom the children of Israel also were not able utterly to destroy, upon these did Solomon levy a tribute of *bond-service* (עֹבֵד *obed*, *slavery*) unto this day. But of the children of Israel did Solomon make no *bond-men*," (עֶבֶד *ebed*, *slaves.*) 2 *Chron.* viii. 9: "But of the children of Israel did Solomon make no *servants* (לַעֲבָדִים *la ebedim*, no *slaves*) for his work, (לִמְלַאכְתּוֹ *his works*, *labours.*) But they were men of war, and chief of his captains, and captains of his chariots and horsemen." 2 *Kings* iv. 1: "Now there cried a certain woman of the wives of the sons of the prophets unto Elisha, saying, Thy servant, my husband, is dead, and thou knowest that thy servant did fear the Lord, and the creditor is come to take unto him my two sons to be *bond-men*," (לַעֲבָדִים *la ebedim*, for *slaves.*) In 1 *Chron.* xxvii. 26, this word is used in a sense quite analogous to slave-labour, thus: "And over them that did the *work* (*melekheth*, *i. e.* the particular work or labour) of the field for *tillage* (לַעֲבֹדַת *slave-labour*) of the ground, was Ezra, the son of Chelub." *Job* i. 2, 3: "And there were born unto him seven sons and three daughters. His substance also was seven thousand sheep, and three thousand camels, and five thousand yoke of oxen, and five hundred she-asses, and a very great *household*." The word "household" is here translated from וַעֲבֻדָּה *va ebudda*, a body of slaves, *i. e.* a large family of slaves. *Job* iii. 19: "The small and the great are there, and the *servant* (וְעֶבֶד *ve ebed*, the *slave*), is free from his master." *Job* xxxi. 13: "If I did *despise* (מִשְׁפַּט *misjudge*) the cause of my *man-servant*," (עַבְדִּי my *slave*.) *Job* xxxix. 9: "Will the unicorn be willing to *serve* thee?" (עָבְדֶךָ be a *slave* to thee.) *Ps.* cxvi. 16: "O Lord, truly I am thy *servant* (עַבְדֶּךָ *obedeka*, *slave*); I am thy *servant* (עַבְדְּךָ *slave*), and the son of thy *hand-maid* (אֲמָתֶךָ *amatheka*, *female slave*): thou hast loosed my bonds." It is a little remarkable how similar is this sentiment of David to one expressed by St. Paul. *Prov.* xii. 9: "He that is despised and hath a *servant* (עֶבֶד *ebed*, *slave*) is better than he that honoureth himself and lacketh bread." *Prov.* xvii. 2: "A wise *servant* (עֶבֶד *ebed*, *slave*), shall rule over a son that causeth shame, and shall have part of the inheritance among the brethren." *Prov.* xxx. 21, 22, 23: "For three things is the earth disquieted, and for four which it cannot bear: For a *servant* (עֶבֶד *ebed*, *slave*) when he *reigneth* (יִמְלוֹךְ *imlok*), and a fool when he is filled with meat. For an odious woman when she is married, and a *hand-maid* (וְשִׁפְחָה *female slave*) that is heir to her mistress." *Eccl.* ii. 7. "*I got me* (קָנִיתִי *kanithi*, *I purchased*) *servants* (עֲבָדִים *male slaves*) and *maidens* (וּשְׁפָחוֹת *female slaves*), and had servants born in my house." *Eccl.* vii. 21: "Also take no heed unto all words that are spoken, lest thou hear thy *servant* (עַבְדְּךָ *slave*) curse thee." *Jer.* ii. 14: "Is Israel a *servant* (הַעֶבֶד a *slave*)? is he a home-born *slave?* why is he spoiled?" In the latter part of this quotation, the word עבד *ebed* is not expressed in Hebrew, but *understood*, as is often the case in English: yet King James's translators did not hesitate to supply it in English with the word *slave*, giving indisputable proof of what they understood the word *ebed* to mean, and also, that they used the English word *servant* as a synonyme of the word *slave.* The omission to express the word עֶבֶד *ebed* in Hebrew, in this instance, has the effect to make the idea conveyed by the prophet more emphatic; and hence the translators seem to have felt the necessity of using the most forcible synonyme, in order that they might truly and beyond doubt convey the full import of the prophet's meaning. *Mal.* i. 6: "A son honoureth his father, and a *servant* (וְעֶבֶד *slave*) his master." This passage is a connecting link in a chain of reasoning, and the prophet continues thus: "If then I be a father, where is my honour? If I be a *master*, where is my fear? saith the Lord of hosts unto you, O priests that despise my name. And ye say, Wherein have we despised thy name?" As though they were astonished at the accusation! And this is the answer—7: "Ye offer polluted bread upon mine altar." A figure, to show that they had become wholly disobedient, and held in disregard the law of God. By their disobedience, they were degenerating from the condition of the son to that of the *ebed.* Instead of being influenced by love, they were about to be operated upon by fear, and hence the prophet continues, ii. 1: "And now, O ye priests, this commandment is for you. If ye will not hear, and if ye will not lay it to heart, to give glory unto my name, saith the Lord of hosts, I will even send a curse upon you, and I will curse your blessings, yea, I have cursed them already, because ye do not lay it to heart. 3: Behold, I will corrupt your seed, and spread dung upon your faces." He would curse them with the hateful curse of Cain. And we beg to notice this scriptural glancing at the doctrine that a course of sin does produce some change upon the physical man,—some change of countenance, which is continued, degenerating and deteriorating the succeeding generations,—and ask, is not such a doctrine alluded to in *Ezek.* xviii. 2, "The fathers have eaten sour grapes, and the children's teeth are set on edge." And, again, in *Ps.* lviii. 2, 3: "The wicked are estranged from the womb: they go astray as soon as they are born, speaking lies. Their poison is like the poison of a serpent." Again, in *Jer.* vii. 19: "Do they provoke me to anger? saith the Lord. Do they not provoke themselves to the confusion of their own faces?" And, in *Isa.* iii. 9: "The show of their countenance doth witness against them, and they declare their sin as Sodom. They hide it not. Wo unto their soul! for they have rewarded evil unto themselves." *Jer.* xiii. 22: "If thou say in thy heart, wherefore have these things come upon me? for the greatness of thine iniquities are thy skirts discovered and thy heels made bare." And ii. 22: "For though thou wash thee with nitre, and take thee much soap, yet thine iniquity is marked before me, saith the Lord God." We will not enter into the examination of this doctrine at present, but hasten to close our view of the Hebrew use of the word עֶבֶד *ebed.* In *Joel* iii. 2 (ii. 29th of the English text) is this remarkable passage: "And also upon the *servants* (הָעֲבָדִים *ha ebedim,* the *male slaves*) and upon the *hand-maids* (הַשְּׁפָחוֹת *hashshephahoth,* the *female slaves*) in those days will I pour out my Spirit." This passage was translated at Jerusalem by St. Peter, into Greek. See *Acts* ii. 18: "And on my *servants,* and *on my hand-maids* (δουλους και επι τας δουλας), will I pour out in those days my Spirit,"—using those Greek words that most unconditionally mean a *slave,* and showing as effectually as language can show, and proving as distinctly as language can prove, that St. Peter well understood these words of Joel to mean *male* and *female slaves.* He translates the passage, referring to it, and quoting it. There can have been no mistake. Besides, the passage is rendered definite by its particularity; for the preceding sentence avers that his Spirit should be poured out "upon all flesh," and goes on to particularize, "your sons" and "daughters," "your old men," "your young men," and then in this passage includes the *slaves,* thus explaining whom he means by "all flesh." It was on the day of Pentecost, when the disciples of Jesus Christ "were all with one accord in one place, and suddenly there came a sound from heaven as of a rushing mighty wind, and it filled all the house where they were sitting; and there appeared upon them cloven tongues like as of fire, and it sat upon each of them, and they were all filled with the Holy Ghost." *Acts* ii. 1, 2, 3.

Such were the circumstances under which this translation was made—just after the death of Jesus Christ. Circumstances more solemn, more imposing, more awful to the human mind cannot well be conceived. In the immediate presence of God the Father, and the Holy Ghost operating upon the mind of St. Peter!! Should any one, timorous, decline to believe men, or mortals, permit us, in the name of that Jehovah whose work we all are, to call their reflection on what may be the nature of that sin which contemns, denies, or treats as untruth the very language of the Holy Ghost.

LESSON XII.

The Hebrew noun *ebed* belongs to the declension of *factitious, euphonic segholate* nouns of two syllables, with the tone on the penult and a furtive vowel on the final:

Singular absolute.	*Construct state.*
עֶבֶד or עָבֶד	עֶבֶד
With light suffix.	*Grave suffix.*
עַבְדִּי	עַבְדְּכֶם
Plural absolute.	*Construct state.*
עֲבָדִים	עַבְדֵי
With light suffix.	*Grave suffix.**
עֲבָדַי	עַבְדֵיכֶם

Declined with the personal pronoun, thus:

Absolute singular,	עֶבֶד	*a slave.*
Suff. 1.	עַבְדִּי	*my slave.*
2. m.	עַבְדְּךָ	*thy slave.*
2. f.	עַבְדֵּךְ	*thy slave.*
3. m.	עַבְדוֹ	*his slave.*
3. f.	עַבְדָּהּ	*her slave.*
1. (plur.)	עַבְדֵּנוּ	*our slave.*
2. m.	עַבְדְּכֶם	*your slave.*
2. f.	עַבְדְּכֶן	*your slave.*
3. m.	עַבְדָּם	*their slave.*
3. f.	עַבְדָּן	*their slave.*

* Termed grave, because they always have the tone accent.

Absolute plural, עֲבָדִים *slaves.*

Suff. 1. עֲבָדַי *my slaves.*

2. m. עֲבָדֶיךָ *thy slaves.*

2. f. עֲבָדַיִךְ *thy slaves.*

3. m. עֲבָדָיו *his slaves.*

3. f. עֲבָדֶיהָ *her slaves.*

1. (plur.) עֲבָדֵינוּ *our slaves.*

2. m. עַבְדֵיכֶם *your slaves.*

2. f. עַבְדֵיכֶן *your slaves.*

3. m. עַבְדֵיהֶם *their slaves.*

3. f. עַבְדֵיהֶן *their slaves.*

Prefixed by a preposition, it will stand thus: בְּעבד *in, at, with,* &c. a slave; or with ל thus, לְעבד *to, at, in, towards, till, until,* &c. a slave; or, when the word עבד is used as a verb, it will stand in place of our infinitive mood, thus, לַעֲבֹד *to slave,* as in *Num.* iv. 47. So this word עבד or any form of it may be prefixed by מ as a contraction of מן, a preposition of various meanings or applications, as *from, apart from, of, out of, by,* &c. &c.; and so it may be prefixed by any of the letters הָאֶמַנְתִּי forming the word *heemanti,* each prefixed letter giving to the *root word* some shade of meaning, emphasis, or adjective quality. So, also, it may be prefixed by כ, used both as a preposition, and as a conjunction, thus, כְּעָבֶד *as, so, according to, after, about, nearly, almost,* &c. &c. *a slave.* Hebrew nouns may also be prefixed by particles of old obsolete words, varying their form, and exceedingly so their phonetic representation; as for example, שְׁלֹמֹה *Shelomah* was the son and successor of King David. Now שׁ, as the particle of some ancient word, and followed by ל, becomes the sign of the possessive case; but when the word begins with these two letters, they then will be duplicated, as in *Canticles* iii. 7, מִטָּתוֹ שֶׁלִּשְׁלֹמֹה *mittatho shellishlomoh, Solomon's bed,* &c.

Prepositions, sometimes two or more, are, or seem to be, compounded, yet used in the sense of the last in the compound, thus: מִן and עַל used thus, מֵעַל for עַל, or לְמִן for מִן, &c. &c.

The noun עֶבֶד *ebed* may also be prefixed by a conjunction, thus, וְעֶבֶד *and a slave*, &c. &c.

It may also often be compounded with other nouns. Thus, עֹבַדְיָהוּ *the slave of God.* In this manner the composition of significant terms, and their conversion into proper names, is unlimited: thus, עַבְדוֹן *the judgment*, or *government of a slave*, and made the name of a city. See *Josh.* ii. 30; also 1 *Chron.* i. 59, the 74th of the English text; and hence the word *abaddon* has been used by some to signify a place of punishment. We can give but a mere sketch of the grammatical formations and variations of the word *ebed;* aware that even such sketch, can be considered of value only by a few, we refrain from even a glimpse of its phonetic variations and peculiarities, deeming them only interesting to the advanced and more critical of the proficients in the language; but we cannot refrain from giving a sketch of its declension as a verb, for the benefit of the Greek and Roman scholar.

Conjugation of the word עָבַד as a verb, *to slave*, &c.

In Kal.

Praet. 3. p. m.	עָבַד
3. f.	עָבְדָה
2. m.	עָבַדְתָּ
3. (plur.)	עָבְדוּ
2. m.	עֲבַדְתֶּם
Infinitive absolute,	עָבוֹד
Construct state,	עֲבֹד
Future, 3. m.	יַעֲבֹד
2. m.	תַּעֲבֹד
3. (plur.)	יַעַבְדוּ
3. f.	תַּעֲבֹדְנָה
Imperative, 2. p. m.	עֲבֹד
2. f.	עִבְדִי
Participle, act.	עוֹבֵד
pass.	עָבוּד

NIPHAL.

Praet. 3. m.	נֶעֱבַד
2. m.	נֶעֱבַדְתָּ
Infinitive,	הֵעָבֵד
Future,	יֵעָבֵד
Imperative,	הֵעָבֵד
Participle,	נֶעֱבָד

PIEL, (*poel, polel.*)

Praet.	עִבֵּד
Infinitive,	עַבֵּד
Future,	יְעַבֵּד
Participle,	מְעַבֵּד

PUAL, (*poal, polal.*)

Praet.	עֻבַּד
Infinitive,	עֻבַּד
Future,	יְעֻבַּד
Participle,	מְעֻבָּד

HIPHIL.

Praet.	הֶעֱבִיד
2. m.	הֶעֱבַדְתָּ
Infinitive,	הַעֲבִיד
Future,	יַעֲבִיד
Participle,	מַעֲבִיד

HOPHAL.

Praet.	הָעֳבַד
Infinitive,	הָעֳבַד
Future,	יָעֳבַד
Participle,	מָעֳבָד

HITHPAEL.

Praet.	הִתְעַבֵּד
Infinitive,	הִתְעַבֵּד
Future,	יִתְעַבֵּד
Participle,	מִתְעַבֵּד

The unusual conjugations sometimes found in the form of some Hebrew words, *hothpaal*, *pilel*, *pulal*, *hithpalel*, and the Arabic *iq-talla*, *pealal*, *pilpel*, and the Aramaen *tiphel*, and the Syriac *shaphel*, are not known to the writer to have an example in the Hebrew Scriptures in the word עבד, and are therefore not exemplified.

Paradigm of the verb עָבַד *to slave*, as a 1. guttural in KAL.

Praeter, *singular*,	3. m.	עָבַד
	3. f.	עָבְדָה
	2. m.	עָבַדְתָּ
	2. f.	עָבַדְתְּ
	1. com.	עָבַדְתִּי
Plural,	3. com.	עָבְדוּ
	2. m.	עֲבַדְתֶּם
	2. f.	עֲבַדְתֶּן
	1. com.	עָבַדְנוּ
Infinitive absolute,		עָבוֹד
Infinitive construct,		עֲבֹד
Imperative, *singular*,	m.	עֲבֹד
	f.	עִבְדִי
Plural,	m.	עִבְדוּ
	f.	עֲבֹדְנָה
Present, *singular*,	3. m.	יַעֲבֹד
	3. f.	תַּעֲבֹד
	2. m.	תַּעֲבֹד
	2. f.	תַּעַבְדִי
	1. com.	אֶעֱבֹד
Plural,	3. m.	יַעַבְדוּ
	3. f.	תַּעֲבֹדְנָה
	2. m.	תַּעַבְדוּ
	2. f.	תַּעֲבֹדְנָה
	1. com.	נַעֲבֹד
Pres. apocope,		יַעֲבֹד
Participle, *active*,		עֹבֵד
passive,		עָבוּד

Paradigm of the verb עבד *to slave*, as a 1. guttural in NIPHAL.

Praeter, singular,	3. m.	נֶעֱבַד
	3. f.	נֶעֶבְדָה
	2. m.	נֶעֱבַדְתָּ
	2. f.	נֶעֱבַדְתְּ
	1. com.	נֶעֱבַדְתִּי
Plural,	3. com.	נֶעֶבְדוּ
	2. m.	נֶעֱבַדְתֶּם
	2. f.	נֶעֱבַדְתֶּן
	1. com.	נֶעֱבַדְנוּ
Infinitive,		הֵעָבֵד
Imperative, singular,	m.	הֵעָבֵד
	f.	הֵעָבְדִי
Plural,	m.	הֵעָבְדוּ
	f.	הֵעָבַדְנָה
Present, singular,	3. m.	יֵעָבֵד
	3. f.	תֵּעָבֵד
	2. m.	תֵּעָבֵד
	2. f.	תֵּעָבְדִי
	1. com.	אֵעָבֵד
Plural,	3. m.	יֵעָבְדוּ
	3. f.	תֵּעָבַדְנָה
	2. m.	תֵּעָבְדוּ
	2. f.	תֵּעָבַדְנָה
	1. com.	נֵעָבֵד
Participle,		נֶעֱבָד

Paradigm of the verb עבד *to slave*, as a 1. guttural in PIHEL or *piel*, (*poel, polel.*)

Praeter, singular,	3. m.	עִבֵּד
	3. f.	עִבְּדָה
	2. m.	עִבַּדְתָּ
	2. f.	עִבַּדְתְּ
	1. com.	עִבַּדְתִּי
Plural,	3. com.	עִבְּדוּ
	2. m.	עִבַּדְתֶּם
	2. f.	עִבַּדְתֶּן
	1. com.	עִבַּדְנוּ
Infinitive,		עַבֵּד

Imperative, singular, m.	עבד
f.	עבדי
Plural, m.	עבדו
f.	עבדנה
Present, singular, 3. m.	יעבד
3. f.	תעבד
2. m.	תעבד
2. f.	תעבדי
1. com.	אעבד
Plural, 3. m.	יעבדו
3. f.	תעבדנה
2. m.	תעבדו
2. f.	תעבדנה
1. com.	נעבד
Participle,	מעבד

Paradigm of the verb עבד *to slave,* as a 1. guttural in PUHAL, (*pual, poal, polal.*)

Praeter, singular, 3. m.	עבד
3. f.	עבדה
2. m.	עבדת
2. f.	עבדת
1. com.	עבדתי
Plural, 3. com.	עבדו
2. m.	עבדתם
2. f.	עבדתן
1. com.	עבדנו
Infinitive,	עבד
Present, singular, 3. m.	יעבד
3. f.	תעבד
2. m.	תעבד
2. f.	תעבדי
1. com.	אעבד
Plural, 3. m.	יעבדו
3. f.	תעבדנה
2. m.	תעבדו
2. f.	תעבדנה
1. com.	נעבד
Participle,	מעבד

Paradigm of the verb עבד *to slave*, as a 1. guttural in Hiphil.

Praeter, singular,	3. m.	הֶעֱבִיד
	3. f.	הֶעֱבִידָה
	2. m.	הֶעֱבַדְתָּ
	2. f.	הֶעֱבַדְתְּ
	1. com.	הֶעֱבַדְתִּי
Plural,	3. com.	הֶעֱבִידוּ
	2. m.	הֶעֱבַדְתֶּם
	2. f.	הֶעֱבַדְתֶּן
	1. com.	הֶעֱבַדְנוּ
Infinitive,		הַעֲבִיד
Imperative, singular,	m.	הַעֲבֵד
	f.	הַעֲבִידִי
Plural,	m.	הַעֲבִידוּ
	f.	הַעֲבֵדְנָה
Present, singular,	3. m.	יַעֲבִיד
	3. f.	תַּעֲבִיד
	2. m.	תַּעֲבִיד
	2. f.	תַּעֲבִידִי
	1. com.	אַעֲבִיד
Plural,	3. m.	יַעֲבִידוּ
	3. f.	תַּעֲבֵדְנָה
	2. m.	תַּעֲבִידוּ
	2. f.	תַּעֲבֵדְנָה
	1. com.	נַעֲבִיד
Pres. apocope,		יַעֲבֵד
Participle,		מַעֲבִיד

Paradigm of the verb עבד *to slave*, as a 1. guttural in Hophal.

Praeter, singular,	3. m.	הָעֳבַד
	3. f.	הָעָבְדָה
	2. m.	הָעֳבַדְתָּ
	2. f.	הָעֳבַדְתְּ
	1. com.	הָעֳבַדְתִּי
Plural,	3. com.	הָעָבְדוּ
	2. m.	הָעֳבַדְתֶּם
	2. f.	הָעֳבַדְתֶּן
	1. com.	הָעֳבַדְנוּ
Infinitive,		הָעֳבֵד

Present, singular, 3. m.	יָעֳבַד
3. f.	תָּעֳבַד
2. m.	תָּעֳבַד
2. f.	תָּעָבְדִי
1. com.	אָעֳבַד
Plural, 3. m.	יָעָבְדוּ
3. f.	תָּעֳבַדְנָה
2. m.	תָּעָבְדוּ
2. f.	תָּעֳבַדְנָה
1. com.	נָעֳבַד
Participle,	מָעֳבָד

Paradigm of the verb עבד *to slave,* as a 1. guttural in HITHPAEL.

Praeter, singular, 3. m.	הִתְעַבַּד
3. f.	הִתְעַבְּדָה
2. m.	הִתְעַבַּדְתָּ
2. f.	הִתְעַבַּדְתְּ
1. com.	הִתְעַבַּדְתִּי
Plural, 3. com.	הִתְעַבְּדוּ
2. m.	הִתְעַבַּדְתֶּם
2. f.	הִתְעַבַּדְתֶּן
1. com.	הִתְעַבַּדְנוּ
Infinitive,	הִתְעַבֵּד
Imperative, singular, m.	הִתְעַבֵּד
f.	הִתְעַבְּדִי
Plural, m.	הִתְעַבְּדוּ
f.	הִתְעַבֵּדְנָה
Present, singular, 3. m.	הִתְעַבֵּד
3. f.	תִּתְעַבֵּד
2. m.	תִּתְעַבֵּד
2. f.	תִּתְעַבְּדִי
1. com.	אֶתְעַבֵּד

Present, plural,	3. m.	יִתְעַבְּדוּ
	3. f.	תִּתְעַבֵּדְנָה
	2. m.	תִּתְעַבְּדוּ
	2. f.	תִּתְעַבֵּדְנָה
	1. com.	נִתְעַבֵּד
Participle,		מִתְעַבֵּד

In close, it may be remarked that there is perhaps no Hebrew verb found in all the forms of conjugation in the Holy Books.

THE END.

www.ingramcontent.com/pod-product-compliance
Lightning Source LLC
LaVergne TN
LVHW021059110826
845150LV00001B/116
* 9 7 8 1 4 2 5 5 6 6 2 6 5 *